Modern American Drama, 1945–2000

In this new edition of the widely acclaimed *Modern American Drama* Christopher Bigsby completes his survey of post-war and contemporary theatre and brings the reader up to 2000. While retaining the key elements of the first edition, including surveys of those major figures who have shaped post-war American drama, such as Eugene O'Neill, Tennessee Williams, Arthur Miller, Edward Albee, David Mamet and Sam Shepard, Bigsby also explores the most recent works and performances: these include plays by established dramatists such as Miller's *The Ride down Mount Morgan* and Albee's *Three Tall Women*, as well as works by relatively newer playwrights Paula Vogel, Tony Kushner and Terrence McNally among others. Bigsby also provides a new chapter, 'Beyond Broadway', and offers an analysis of how theatre has formed and influenced the millennial culture of America.

CHRISTOPHER BIGSBY is Professor of American Studies at the University of East Anglia and has published more than twenty-five books covering American theatre, popular culture and British drama, including *A Critical Introduction to Twentieth-Century American Drama* and *Contemporary American Playwrights*. He is co-editor, with Don Wilmeth, of *The Cambridge History of American Theatre*. He is also an award-winning novelist and regular radio and television broadcaster.

MODERN AMERICAN DRAMA, 1945–2000

MODERN AMERICAN DRAMA, 1945–2000

C.W.E. BIGSBY

CAMBRIDGE
UNIVERSITY PRESS

PUBLISHED BY THE PRESS SYNDICATE OF THE UNIVERSITY OF CAMBRIDGE
The Pitt Building, Trumpington Street, Cambridge, United Kingdom

CAMBRIDGE UNIVERSITY PRESS
The Edinburgh Building, Cambridge CB2 2RU, UK   www.cup.cam.ac.uk
40 West 20th Street, New York, NY 10011-4211, USA   www.cup.org
10 Stamford Road, Oakleigh, Melbourne 3166, Australia
Ruiz de Alarcón 13, 28014 Madrid, Spain

Modern American Drama, 1945–2000 succeeds and replaces *Modern American Drama, 1945–1990*,
published by Cambridge University Press, 1992 (hardback: 0 521 41649 3;
paperback: 0 521 42667 7)

Transferred to digital printing 2001

Printed in Great Britain by Biddles Short Run Books, King's Lynn

Typeface Monotype Baskerville 11/12½ pt   *System* QuarkXPress™   [SE]

A catalogue record for this book is available from the British Library

Library of Congress cataloguing in publication data

Bigsby, C. W. E.
Modern American drama, 1945–2000 / C. W. E. Bigsby.
p.   cm.
Includes bibliographical references and index.
ISBN 0 521 79089 1 (hardback) – ISBN 0 521 79410 2 (paperback)
1.   American drama – 20th century – History and criticism.   I. Title.

PS350.B54   2000
812′.5409 – DC21   00-028931

ISBN 0 521 79089 1 hardback
ISBN 0 521 79410 2 paperback

Contents

Preface to First Edition

Ten years ago I wrote a study of twentieth-century American drama. It quickly outgrew its proposed length, expanding from one brief volume to three extensive ones. Eight years later I was asked to write a 30,000 word section of the Cambridge History of American Theatre. I had reached 170,000 words before I realised I had inadvertently written another book. Discipline has never been my strong suit. I did then complete the original commission but what follows is that accidental study. It covers territory I have charted before and there are bound to be a few echoes, but it is surprising how a familiar country can change over time. The book is offered as a series of reflections on American drama in the second half of the twentieth century. It does not aim to be comprehensive. What I hope it does is reflect my fascination with writers who in staging their plays have also staged the anxieties, the tensions and the myths of a nation en route from a world war to the end of a millennium.

Preface to Second Edition

Eight years after the first edition, I return to bring the story up to the year 2000. In 45,000 additional words I have tried to expand on the careers of those in the original edition and add something on those who should have been given greater space the first time around or whose careers blossomed in the 1990s.

All organising principles are suspect. No taxonomy without misrepresentation. Nonetheless, necessity rules and I have chosen to gather a number of writers in a chapter called 'Beyond Broadway'. It is, heaven knows, a vague enough term, and indicates a structural change in the American theatre that goes back several decades. It is, however, probably as good as any, provided one remembers that those gathered together in this way are heterogeneous talents united by nothing, necessarily, beyond a belief that Broadway was to be neither natural home nor validating agency.

When Henry Luce declared that his was to be the 'American Century', he was hardly making a high-risk prophecy. Financial and military power were already accruing in the face of collapsing empires. I doubt, however, that he gave much thought to culture. That his prophecy should also have proved true, in large degree, of the novel, poetry, art, music and dance would no doubt have surprised him. That it should also have proved true of the theatre would surely have been more of a shock. After centuries of laments at the lack of native playwrights (a lament not entirely justified), America produced a series of dramatists who not only engaged with the realities, the illusions and values of their own society but proved to be powerful and defining presences on the international stage.

The process, of course, was already underway when this book begins, O'Neill receiving the Nobel Prize in 1936, still, astonishingly, the only American playwright to be so honoured. The second half of the century, however, saw the emergence of writers (and also actors, directors, designers) who helped shape the way we see the world and whose impress is clear on the work of their contemporaries around the world.

Again, I must underscore what I said in the preface to the first edition. This is not an encyclopedia. Even expanded space precludes addressing the work of all those writers whose achievement I would wish to acknowledge. Nonetheless, I trust that at the very least it provides evidence of the continuing power and significance of American playwrights as we passed through that artificial barrier which separates one disordered century from another.

Perhaps in the future we shall no longer speak of American drama but of an English language drama. Perhaps even that will begin to seem unnecessarily parochial and limiting. Is difference, after all, not being sandblasted away by a homogeneity claimed as evidence of the modern, or postmodern? National cultures, competing ideologies, it is argued, may be nothing more than quotations, so many stories within a master story which speaks of a planetary consciousness, to be welcomed as evidence of a new understanding and deplored as a consequence of transnational corporations imposing their own models of the desirable. I rather doubt it.

As we passed through the invisible barrier of the millennium, filling the sky with fireworks, from Beijing to Boston, as if to light our way and cast out demons, nationalism, religious fundamentalism, cultural and gender difference seemed to many to contain the essence of their being, to define, in effect, who they were.

On the other hand, writers, like all of us, inhabit a world not defined by national, or, indeed, other borders. *King Lear*, as Peter Brook has said, is the story of a family and that is the door through which we can all enter that annihilating play. There is a shared world of experience, of symbols, of knowledge. Then, again, writers reach out to other writers as their source and inspiration, and feel happier, often, in their own company than in that of their fellow citizens, who care less for striking through the pasteboard mask. Yet, even so, we are in part shaped, in our acquiescence and our rebellion, by the proximate world. We are contained (if not absolutely) not only within a language but a set of presumptions, values, myths which speak of the particular as well as the general. And though America remains a contested space, in which identity must, immigrant country that it is, constantly be making and remaking itself, the theatre remains a place where that identity continues to be explored.

By the same token, the triumphs and failures of a country born out of a utopian impulse are still, it seems, to be examined and tested, and where else but on a stage which brings together the private and the public, which presents us simultaneously with appearance and the real, the dream and the actuality. Perhaps, indeed, in some ways it is that tension between a utopian rhetoric and a diminished and flawed experience which not only connects the various writers in this book but defines the very nature of the American writer.

CHAPTER ONE

The absent voice: American drama and the critic

In recent years attempts have been made to fill some of the more obvious absences in the literary canon. The battle for the future, as ever, begins with the past. First blacks and then women chose to define present reality in terms of a redefined tradition. The project was an implicit critique of a critical practice that had filtered out experiences not felt to be normative, that had denied a voice to those marginalised by the social or economic system – hence the significance of the title of Tillie Olsen's book *Silences* and the potency of Richard Wright's image of laboratory dogs, their vocal chords cut, silently baying to the moon, in *American Hunger*. Language is power, the shaping of language into art is power and the codification of that literature in the form of literary history is also a source of power.

It is, however, not merely the literary expression of the experiences of particular sections of American society that have fallen below the threshold of critical attention. There is also another surprising absence, another silence, another example of critical reticence. Whatever happened to American drama? Why is it that literary critics, cultural historians, literary theorists, those interested in the evolution of genre, in discourse and ideology, find so little to say about the theatre in general and the American theatre in particular? Can it really be that an entire genre has evaded the critic who was once drawn to the poem and then the novel and who, more recently, has chosen to concentrate on literary theory? There are, of course, honourable exceptions, but on the whole the silence has been remarkable.

Any account of American drama must begin by noting the casual disregard with which it has been treated by the critical establishment. There is no single history of its development, no truly comprehensive analysis of its achievement. In the standard histories of American literature it is accorded at best a marginal position. Why should this be? Is it perhaps the nature of drama which takes it outside the parameters of critical discourse, unless, like Shakespeare, its canonical status as scholarly text has been established by time? After all, is drama, and the theatre in which it takes place, not inherently ideological? Does the transformation of the word on the page into the mobility of performance not raise questions about discourse and text? Is the stage, the most public of the arts, not a place to see dramatised the tensions and concerns of a society? Is a concern with the reception of a work, with the way in which it is 'read', not of special significance to an art in which that reception may profoundly modify the work in question? May questions of authorship not have special bearing on an art which might be thought to be collaborative? Is the very nature and status of criticism not challenged by work which to a large degree incorporates a critical reading in the very processes of its transmission? These might be thought to be rhetorical questions, but the history of literary criticism and cultural studies suggests otherwise.

It was Umberto Eco who reminded us that though the intervention of the actor complicates the act of reception, the process remains the same in that every 'reading', 'contemplation' or 'enjoyment' of a work of art represents a tacit form of 'performance': and every performance a reading. That reader may, of course, be in the theatre. He or she may be on their own, confronted with the printed word. It could even be argued that the latter may, in a perverse way, be in a more privileged if exposed position in that the individual imagination is not coerced by the interpretative strategy of director and actor. As David Mamet has said, 'the best production takes place in the mind of the beholder'.[1] But of course the theatre's attraction lies in its power to transcend the written word. That is the key. It is physical, three-dimensional, immediate, and perhaps that very fact has itself intimidated the critic. It should instead have challenged him. Too often, we are offered reductive versions, even by those who acknowledge drama as an aspect of literature. Thus, in his diatribe against the American playwright, Robert Brustein, as a young critic, had denounced Eugene O'Neill as a 'charter member of a cult of inarticulacy' who perversely suggested that the meaning of one of his plays might lie in its silences, and Tennessee Williams for emphasising 'the incontinent blaze of live theatre, a theatre meant for seeing and feeling', a plastic theatre which did not reward the literary critic. This view, expressed in *Harper's* magazine in 1959, has been echoed sufficiently widely since then to merit consideration.

Roland Barthes describes the author as a man

who radically absorbs the world's *why* in a *how to write* . . . by enclosing himself in the *how to write*, the author ultimately discovers the open question, par excellence! Why the world? What is the ultimate meaning of things? In short, it is precisely when the author's work becomes its own end that it regains a mediating character: the author conceives of literature as an end, the world restores it to him as a means: and it is in this perpetual inclusiveness that the author rediscovers the world, an alien world, since literature represents it as a question – never finally as an answer.[2]

But who more than Eugene O'Neill was engaged in this restless search? No other playwright has committed himself so completely to the 'how' of literature, restlessly testing every style, strategy, concept of character, linguistic mode, theatrical device. And the 'how' does indeed lead him towards the 'why'.

The process of O'Neill's *The Emperor Jones* is one in which style is substance, in which the theatricalised self is left disabled by its own imaginative projections. It is like the film of a life run backwards, from sophistication and power to innocence and total vulnerability; the portrait of a social world unmaking itself, of a language dislocated and in retreat from coherence, of a civilisation reverting to origins, of an individual stripping off the accretions of logic and civility, of a society tracing its roots back to myth.

In so far as language is power, the absence of language is an index of relative powerlessness. So it is that Brutus Jones's language slips away with his loss of social control as the lowly night porter, in O'Neill's *Hughie*, barely contributes a coherent sentence. On the other hand a steady flow of language does not of itself imply a confident control of experience. Indeed in this latter case the hotel guest's articulate accounts of personal triumph merely serve to underline the social silence which is his life. What is spoken betrays the centrality of what is not. The truth of his life is what can never make its way into language. He keeps alive by the stories he tells. He is a down-market Scheherazade. The dramas he invents are his defence against the world and his own insignificance. They are also all that stands between him and despair.

The theatre is unique in its silences. In the literary text such spaces close. Even the blank page of a Laurence Sterne can be turned in a second. In the theatre silence is not merely kinetic potential. It may teem with meaning. We are used to the notation 'silence' in a Beckett or Pinter play, but Susan Glaspell and Eugene O'Neill were fully alive to the possibilities of reticence forty years earlier. In *The Outside* Susan Glaspell created a character stunned into silence by experience; but the aphasia of Anna Christie and the inarticulateness of Yank in O'Neill's *The Hairy Ape* equally compacted meaning into those moments when language is inadequate to feeling.

If the word, spoken or withheld, is a central and potent fact of theatre, so, too, is space and the occupation of that space by the body. Nor is it simply a matter of proxemics, of the meaning generated by gesture or appearance; it is that the word is made flesh. The theatre is by its nature sensuous. Even didactic drama alchemises its arguments through the mind made body. The severity of words on the page is corrupted by the mouth which articulates them. The minimalism of the printed word gives way to plenitude. That seduction, implicit in the text, becomes explicit in production. It cannot be extirpated. The Puritans were right to close the theatres. However irreproachable the sentiments, their theatricalising required a waywardness the elect were bound to suspect. For Tennessee Williams, for example, that sensuousness was crucial, since theatre is not merely the condition of his art but also his subject.

Thus *A Streetcar Named Desire* is pre-eminently aware of its own constitutive conventions; that is to say it is concerned, in the Russian formalist Viktor Schlovsky's terms, with the generation of plot from story. It foregrounds the processes of theatre, the elaboration of a structure of meaning out of mere events. It defamiliarises the real by dramatising the extent to which, and the manner in which, that reality is constituted. Blanche is self-consciously her own playwright, costume designer, lighting engineer, scenic designer and performer. You could say of her world what Roland Barthes says of the actor – it is artificial but not factitious. The dramas which she enacts – southern belle, sensitive virgin, sensuous temptress, martyred daughter, wronged wife – are all carefully presented performances embedded in their own narrative contexts. In Fredric Jameson's terms, it is a play that speaks of its own coming into being, of its own construction. If, to Jameson, all literary works emit a kind of lateral message about their own process of formation, in *Streetcar* it seems more central and more deliberate. And not here alone. Laura, in *The Glass Menagerie*, enters the theatre of her glass animals, making mobile in her imagination what is immobile in a world of mere facticity, just as Tennessee Williams himself enters his own drama, charging the words on the page with a kind of static potential which gives them the energy to be discharged in performance. There is, indeed, a real sense in which Williams is a product of his work. When he began to write he was plain

Tom, poor Tom. The invention of 'Tennessee' was not merely coterminous with the elaboration of theatrical fictions, it was of a piece with it.
In that sense it is not entirely fanciful to suggest that he was the product
of the discourse of his plays. Indeed he created female alter egos, such
as Blanche in *Streetcar* and Alma in *Summer and Smoke*, before he began, as
he did in later life, to dress up as a woman. Later he even turned performer, stepping into one of his own plays as actor in a work called *Small
Craft Warning* where the part he played, that of a failed doctor who had
lost his licence to practise, was in effect itself an expression of his sense
of his own disintegrating powers. Where did the work end and the life
begin? The man who consigns Blanche to insanity later found himself in
a straitjacket. Later still he wrote a play set in an empty theatre in which
two characters fill the emptiness of their lives by speaking lines from a
play generated out of those lives, a metadrama of fascinating intellectual and ontological complexity. And if by that stage of his career there
was a terrible appositeness in a play in which characters address an
empty auditorium, is there not another significance to it, for though
America's playwrights have found huge and appreciative audiences
around the world and though their plays are reviewed and widely published and read, the academic critic, the cultural historian, the literary
theorist for the most part has turned his or her head away.

Tennessee Williams saw himself as a poet. Why, then, turn to the
stage? I think because the body had a significance to him beyond the
homosexual reveries which recur in his *Memoirs*. It – the body – was
everything the world was not. It was warm; it was animate; it was three-
dimensional. It inscribed its own meaning; it generated its own discourse,
independent of and at a tangent to a verbal language which threatens to
pull the self into history. It was its own act of resistance in a world in
which the mechanical dominated. And how could that body's violations,
its temporary alliances, its vulnerabilities, its resistances be better communicated than on the stage? So much of the tension of his work (as of
O'Neill's) comes from placing the body in a situation essentially oppressive to and at odds with its needs. The immobility towards which he
presses his characters, the catatonia which awaits them, derives its
impact precisely from their earlier manifest motility – a motility most
easily invested with immediacy and meaning in the theatre. Then again
the protean gesture of pluralising the self and, indeed, meaning itself –
not as in a novel where a narrator controls and contains the multiple self
– offers a protection against being too completely known and hence vulnerable. For a man for whom the concealment of his true sexual identity

was for long a literal necessity, the fragmentation of the self into multiple roles offered a possible refuge.

A novel is more fixed, more stolid, more resistant to subversion by its own form (though of course we have the evidence of *Tristram Shandy* that such subversion is perfectly possible). Since Williams is the poet of the unauthorised, the unsanctioned, the outlawed, it seems logical that he should choose a form which more easily releases its pluralism of meanings – under the pressure of actors, director, audience – than does the poem or the novel. It is not that novels have restrictive meanings but that the incompletions of the theatrical text are readily apparent, indeed implicit in the form. If Roland Barthes is right in saying 'Who *speaks* is not who *writes*, and who *writes* is not who *is*',[3] it is equally true to say of the theatrical text that what is *written* is not what is *spoken*, and what is *spoken* is not what *is*. In the theatre language is deliberately played against gesture, *mise en scène*, appearance; the mouth which shapes the word also subverts the word, as facial expression, tone, inflection, volume offer a counter-current. It is uttered in a social context, the silent receiver of language on the stage communicating with no less force than its transmitter. Meaning is communicated proxemically, annihilated by its own expressive gestures. In the novel, speech is sequential, part of a serial logic in which one word replaces or supersedes another; actions which may be simultaneous have to be recreated in a way which denies their simultaneity and simultaneity is a crucial virtue of the theatre. Theatre is the only genre which habitually operates in the present tense and which makes that presentness an acknowledged part of its own methodology. It is the only genre which unavoidably foregrounds its processes. The lighting scaffold, the conscious frame of the proscenium arch – abandoned in the sixties and resurrected in the eighties – the co-presence of other members of the audience underlines one's own status as 'reader' of the text of the performance. The curtain separating the performance on stage from that off, the ticket you hold in your hand (the sign of your entry into otherness and itself a text inscribed with meaning), the whole paraphernalia involved in visiting the theatre, is part of the process of defamiliarising, which is what theatre is about. The novel can be put down, picked up, interleaved with other experiences; the theatre makes its demands. The price of entry in terms of energy and commitment and sometimes financial cost is high. We go to the theatre as ourselves part of a ceremony knowing that our own involvement will be central to the meanings which proliferate.

Mikhail Bakhtin argues for the primacy of the novel on the grounds that its generic skeleton 'is still far from having hardened, and we cannot foresee all its plastic possibilities'. While the other genres are older than written literature, 'it has no canon of its own . . . it alone is . . . receptive to . . . reading'.[4] This sounds to me a little like special pleading. In Tennessee Williams's *Camino Real* there is a gypsy girl whose virginity is restored by every full moon. It's a good trick if you can pull it off, but the theatre is a little like that. It is surely the most sensuous, the most alluring, the most unformed of the genres. Each production restores a kind of innocence only to take pleasure in violating it. When Bakhtin argues that in drama 'there is no all encompassing language that addresses itself dialogically to separate languages, there is no second all encompassing plotless (non-dramatic) dialogue outside of the (non-dramatic) plot',[5] this, too, seems to me a virtue. In the theatre I am in fact more free from the author's discourse, which in the novel invites me to align my imagination with his. For Bakhtin, 'The fundamental condition, that which makes a novel a novel, that which is responsible for its stylistic uniqueness, is the *speaking person and his discourse* . . . [*which*] is an object of *verbal* artistic representation.' In contrast to drama it is represented by means of 'authorial discourse'.[6] Since there is clearly such a thing as an implied author as well as an implied reader, the distinction he draws is perhaps rather too sharp but in so far as he is correct to suggest an instability in drama, a plurality of possibilities, this is surely one of its strengths. Indeed in some ways it is the author's loss of control which constitutes something of the attraction of theatre. For the playwright, at any rate, it may offer a means of breaking with an aestheticism that has overtones of inauthenticity. And that leads us in the direction of ideology.

In 'Authors and Writers' Roland Barthes insists that

for the author, *to write* is an intransitive verb; hence it can never explain the world, or at least, when it claims to explain the world, it does so only the better to conceal its ambiguity: once the explanation is fixed in a work, it immediately becomes an ambiguous product of the real, to which it is linked by perspective.[7]

Barthes distinguishes between the author and the writer, for the latter the verb 'to write' being transitive. Thus, the notion of a committed author is a contradiction in terms. As he says, it is

absurd to ask an author for 'commitment': a 'committed' author claims simultaneous participation in two structures, inevitably a source of deception . . . whether or not an author is responsible for his opinions is unimportant; whether or not an author assumes, more or less intelligently, the ideological implications of his work is also secondary; the author's true responsibility is to support literature as a failed commitment, as a Mosaic glance into the Promised Land of the real.[8]

But frequently, of course, those impulses are indeed contained in the same sensibility. There *is* an ambiguity about the committed author/writer whose commitment is necessarily a double one – to the word and to the word's transparency. Commitment requires that the word should dissolve into its own social fulfilment, declare its own ultimate irrelevance, its second-order status, as the writer serves a cause whose demands go beyond his own imagining. But the author also wants to refashion language, ease it away from its history, separate it from the social world which exercises its restraints.

　James Baldwin was all too aware of this ambivalence and seized on the theatre as a way of resolving the tension. Drama offered a way to loosen his grip on aestheticism. The balanced sentences, the carefully sculpted prose that had distinguished his essays, and which many blacks in America felt were distancing him from his own and their experience and aligning him with an alien literary tradition rather than a social cause, were broken open by the glossalalia, the profusion of voices which is the essence of theatre. He turned to the theatre precisely because he needed to deny himself a controlling voice, because he wished to subvert his own authority. It was almost as though the surrender of total responsibility implicit in theatre was in some way a guarantee that subject had primacy over style, that he was not allowing aesthetic issues to dominate experiences whose authenticity could only be diminished by the transformations of art. LeRoi Jones plainly felt much the same, his change of name coinciding with a retreat from metaphor into a literalism which intensified as black nationalism gave way to Marxism–Leninism and the dense and profoundly ambiguous images of *Dutchman* and *The Slave* led first to the crude melodrama of his black revolutionary plays and then to works such as *S1* and *The Motions of History*, in which social reality was allowed primacy. Ultimately, he followed his own logic and abandoned the stage for the factory gate and the dramatic text for the political leaflet. It was a logic followed, too, by a number of politically motivated theatre groups whose distrust of the ideology implicit in the fact of the theatre building took them onto the streets, and whose distrust of what Barthes called 'fine writing' led them to the communal creation of texts which were an assault on the authority of the writer and whose openness to audience participation was another antidote to a self-referring art.

As Baraka has his black protagonist confess in *Dutchman*, there is a seductive quality in language. Words have a detachment from experience. They are not the thing itself. They stand in the place of action. They have a coherent structure which may be at odds with the unregulated passion which generates them. To that extent they are a betrayal, representing a kind of sanity when a holy madness is required. In the case of Clay, in *Dutchman*, the safety that he seeks in words is finally only securable in action. He dies because he cannot relinquish his grasp on the detachment that language brings – the detachment of the writer. It is a debate that Baraka continued in *The Slave* in which the intellectual leader of a black revolt remains enslaved to his own articulateness no less than his emotions. So the battle rages outside the window while he engages in debate with a white professor, husband to the white wife he had abandoned. Since Baraka, university educated, separated from his white wife and drawn to the literary world which showed every sign of responding to his talent, was himself caught in just such a dilemma, it is hard not to see the play as a debate in which he engages himself, a debate whose power derives, at least in part, from the honesty with which he confesses to and dramatises his own ambivalence. What the theatre offers is a social context for language, a language now energised as it becomes the action it invokes.

Literature requires and is an act of renunciation. The condition of its creation is withdrawal. Its nature implies abstinence. But the theatre offers a special grace. Drama may be privately conceived but it is publicly created. It is a re-entry into the world. The word becomes action, albeit action drained of true risk. It gives back to the writer what he has sacrificed in order to write. It restores in the public action of the play the power to act, to offer the body as a sign of authenticity. What is conceived in a denial of community ends with a restoration of community. A word silently inscribed sounds forth in confident expectation of communication. The act of distributing that language between characters and the actors who articulate them is itself a confident sign of shared experience and of the possibility of sharing language.

The actor who speaks another's words and endeavours to mould them to his own shape, to bend the language to his own reality and accommodate himself to the language (a compromise without which he would lack all conviction) mirrors our own relationship to the words that we speak, words we do not devise but which we struggle to make our own. His attempt to negotiate the terms on which necessity and freedom, the given and the created, can co-exist is a model of those other such negotiations in which we participate daily. For the black writer there is a special irony in deploying a language which was the instrument and sign of slavery. To distrust the words you speak, words which have a history, is to place yourself at odds with your own articulateness, and the theatre, which never carries the voice of the writer, only his or her characters, offers a release from that paradox which can then become subject rather than means.

Roland Barthes has suggested that 'literature is always unrealistic' since language 'can never explain the world, or at least, when it claims to explain the world, it does so only the better to conceal its ambiguity; once the explanation is fixed in a work, it immediately becomes an ambiguous product of the real, to which it is linked by perspective'.[9] And there is, indeed, a revealing suspicion of language not merely on the part of the avant-gardist, disassembling his art in a radical gesture of defamiliarisation, but also on the part of the committed playwright for whom that language is a barrier between the urgencies of a tangible world and those he would make aware of those realities. More than that, the gap between act and word is a reproach, that between fact and word an irony; the disproportion between need and its expression is a constant reminder of the impossible project in which the writer chooses to engage. In becoming itself a 'product of the real' the play simultaneously submits to the condition it would resist and becomes a rival for attention with the circumstance which inspired its creation but to which it is only analogically connected. Those who left Clifford Odets's *Waiting for Lefty* shouting out the need to 'Strike! Strike! Strike!' re-entered a world whose social structure and political arrangements lacked the ordered logic and casual resolutions of the play, a world in which character and action were more profoundly ambiguous, a world, indeed, in which theatre itself is regarded as marginal and as implicated in the values of the system it purports to challenge. At base it was its lack of realism that was its most noticeable characteristic and perhaps its redemption. The same logic would apply with equal force to the committed writing of the fifties, sixties, seventies and eighties. The most striking aspect of this theatre is its naivety, a willed innocence that conceives of character, language and action as elements in a dialectic, as compressed images of oppression or revolt. Amira Baraka's *Four Black Revolutionary Plays* offered a catechism of revolutionary faith which divided the world not so much into contending racial forces as into platonic models of rebel or collaborator. These were agit-prop gestures, a theatre of praxis designed to intervene in the political system at the level of personal epiphany, to be achieved through group experience. But it was always an uneasy theatre, acutely aware of the inadequacy of its own gestures, expressive and direct, preferable to an inert prose contained and constrained by the page, but still disproportionate to the fact.

There is a poem by the Czechoslovak poet Miroslav Holub which explains something of this desire to *show* in theatre rather than *tell* in the novel. The poem is called 'Brief Reflection on the Word Pain':

> Wittgenstein says the words 'It hurts' have replaced
> tears and cries of pain. The word 'Pain'
> does not describe the expression of pain but replaces it.
> Replaces and displaces it.
> Thus it creates a new behaviour pattern
> in the case of pain.
>
> The word comes between us and the pain
> like a pretence of silence.
> It is a silencing. It is a needle
> unpicking the stitch
> between blood and clay.[10]

It is not that the theatre can wholly close this gap but that it can remind us of its existence by pitching word against dramatised experience. Perhaps that is one reason why the committed writer has been drawn to the theatre. It is out of a desire to replace that stitch which will reconnect blood and clay. Either way the aesthetic and literary implications of committed theatre, particularly in the American context, have barely even been registered let alone addressed with any sophistication or theoretical concern.

And what of those critics attracted by theory in recent years? After all, Derrida takes a brief look at the theatre of cruelty and Roland Barthes at Brecht and Bunraku theatre. On the whole, theatre has commanded very little interest from the major theorists or those who have taken up their theories. Not even the question of authorship seems to have stirred much interest, except among those most immediately involved.

Antonin Artaud believed that no one had the right to call himself author, that is to say creator, except the person who controls the direct handling of the stage. In the 1960s even this claim on behalf of the director was challenged in the name of the group. Texts were deliberately broken open and invaded by actors who chose thereby to imprint themselves more directly on the performance. In one of the Open Theatre's productions the actors literally spelt out words with their bodies, in revolt against the canonical text. When the Wooster Group chose to do this to Arthur Miller's *The Crucible* in their work, *LSD*, he threatened to go to law, as did Samuel Beckett, over the American Repertory Theatre's version, in that same year, of *Endgame*, and Harold Pinter, over an Italian version of *Old Times*, which presented that play as a lesbian tryst. In an earlier production the Wooster Group stirred up the Thornton Wilder Estate by playing selections from *Our Town* on video monitors juxtaposed with pornographic images. What was at stake was copyright. What was at stake was ownership. It was in effect a debate about authority and authorship. The authors were in effect asserting the significance of the printed text. Granted that in order to move from page to stage a series of transformations, of interpretations, were necessary but the authors wished, as a bare minimum, to insist on the retention of the words as written, on the right to define the limits of an interpretive range. And that of course raises questions entirely familiar in other genres but scarcely addressed at all in theatre criticism. What constitutes the text, who could be said to write it, how do we describe it or define its reception? It may make legal sense to demand that a play be performed 'without changes or alterations' – a phrase from legal contracts – but it scarcely makes theatrical let alone epistemological sense. Beckett's own response was to suggest that the best possible play was one in which there are no actors, only text, adding, perhaps only partly ironically, that he was trying to write one. It is hard to resist the thought that he almost made it. Can critics, though, afford to be equally cavalier? Can they, moreover, continue to regard the American theatre as socially and culturally marginal, peripheral to the concerns of the critic, whether that critic be committed to an exploration of the structure of language, the generation of character, the elaboration of plot, the nature of readership or the aesthetic response to ideological fact.

After all, could Barthes's description of a text of bliss, of jouissance – the text that imposes a state of loss, the text that discomforts, unsettles the reader's historical, cultural, psychological assumptions, the consistency of his tastes, values, memories, brings to a crisis his relations with language – not be said to apply to O'Neill's *The Emperor Jones*, Williams's *Outcry* and even *Streetcar*, Miller's *The Archbishop's Ceiling*, Albee's *Listening*, Mamet's *American Buffalo*, or Shepard's *Icarus's Mother*.

The conditions of theatre do radically disrupt accustomed readings. It may be indeed that this insecurity over the object of study is the real reason for critical withdrawal. Should it not, however, rather be a reason for critical engagement? The aim is not to arrest that mobility, to deny drama's protean quality by generating normative versions, critical models which are stable because inert, but to acknowledge the legitimacy of analysis, of readings of a text which is in truth only a pretext for a performance that will in turn constitute a new text.

CHAPTER TWO

Eugene O'Neill's Endgame

The bridge between the pre-war and post-war world in the American theatre is provided by a single man, albeit a man who, by 1945, had been silent for more than a decade. If any one writer can lay claim to having invented that theatre it was he. From a disregarded and parochial entertainment he had raised it to a central cultural activity, making it thereby a focus of world attention. His name was Eugene O'Neill and throughout his career and subsequently he has created a sense of unease in literary and dramatic circles. There is something altogether too uncontrolled, too eclectic, too unformed about his talent to inspire respect. He paints with a broad brush. His characters are pressed to social and psychological extremes by experience. He shared with his father, whose own theatre he so despised, a taste for the melodramatic and overstated. His characters lurch between self-conscious lyricism and aphasia. He is, in short, something of an embarrassment. And yet there is no way around him. For thirty years his work constituted America's claim to have created a powerful modern dramatic literature. However, by 1936, when he was awarded the Nobel Prize for literature, his reputation was already in decline and hardly recovered in the immediate post-war years. For twelve years, between 1934 and 1946, no new O'Neill play was produced; and after a poor production of *The Iceman Cometh*, in 1946, no further play was produced before his death in 1953 – *A Moon for the Misbegotten* dying on the road. Critics know they cannot do without O'Neill; their problem is to know what to do with him.

Whatever his eclecticism, O'Neill's rough talent – because sometimes it is a rough talent – is firmly in the American grain. Fine feelings and expression were all very well but the characters and experiences that elbowed their way into his plays often lacked both. There is a democratic urge in O'Neill that is reminiscent of a Twain or a Steinbeck. He reveals something of the inclusiveness of Walt Whitman, Theodore Dreiser or Thomas Wolfe. There are few of his plays that would not benefit from a blue pencil, but he was constitutionally drawn to excess. He had a life-long argument with America and such arguments are hardly likely to be small-scale. So, his plays grew from the early sea sketches, and from such a finely controlled work as *The Emperor Jones*, to great juggernauts where theatres had to allow for dinner breaks so that audiences would not expire of sheer hunger and fatigue.

Nothing inhibited him: modern versions of Greek tragedy, the reno-vation of the soliloquy or the mask, the use of film on the stage, plays about miscegenation or incest. He planned multi-play cycles, wrote works that in certain respects are all but unstageable and stands as the great incontrovertible fact of the American theatre he once set out so single-mindedly to invent. He pulled into the orbit of that theatre and domesticated Greek classical tragedy, Strindbergian domestic drama, Ibsenesque social plays, Irish dramatic tone poems, expressionist melo-dramas. The church of his drama was constantly being reconsecrated to different faiths, faiths which he served with total commitment, only to abandon them for others.

In a very American way he was, he confessed, 'always trying to do the big thing'.[1] He wanted to create 'big work' by tackling a 'big subject'. He admitted to 'dreaming of championship belts', almost as though he were Hemingway. It was not success that he sought, dismissing the Theatre Guild as 'success ridden'. What he was after was a theatre that could expand to incorporate all aspects of experience within a vision that was poetical 'in the broadest and deepest sense'. For post-war America he seemed at first a remnant of another world – reclusive, a writer whose career had effectively ended (like that of so many others) with the award of the Nobel Prize. A weak production of *The Iceman Cometh* seemed to confirm this model of a man whose plays had a remorseless, demanding and unforgiving quality seemingly at odds with contemporary theatre and audiences. He was a ghost haunting an American theatre that had discovered new enthusiasms and new authors. Yet, in a paradoxical way, it was precisely these late plays that constitute a great part of his claim on our attention while his discontent with the American theatre was life-long.

In 1926 he had written to his friend and colleague Kenneth Macgowan, lamenting the inadequacy of that American theatre as a vehicle for his needs and dreams:

What's the use of my trying to get ahead with new stuff until some theatre can give that stuff the care and opportunity it must have in order to register its new significance outside of the written page in a theatre. I've had exactly ten years of it as a playwright . . . and my ambition to see my stuff performed on any stage I know (never very avid!) is beginning almost to cease, and this at a time when I *know* I have most to give to a theatre.[2]

Fourteen years later, in 1940, he wrote a further letter. It was by then already six years since his last play had been staged on Broadway, though only four since his Nobel Prize. Ahead lay only one further full production during his lifetime and a declining reputation. 'I dread', he explained,

the idea of a production because I know it will be done by people who have really only one standard left, that of Broadway success. I know beforehand that I will be constantly asked, as I have been before, to make stupid compromises for that end . . . The fact that I will again refuse to make them is no consolation. There are just groups, or individuals, who put on plays in New York commercial theatres. The idea of an Art Theatre is more remote now, I think, than it was way back in the first decade of this century, before the Washington Square Players or the P.P. [Provincetown Players] were ever dreamed of . . . To have an ideal now, except as a slogan in which neither you nor anyone else believes but which you use out of old habit to conceal a sordid aim, is to confess oneself a fool who cannot face the High Destiny of Man![3]

Now the plays that he despaired of finding adequate theatrical expression for were those in which he tried to come to terms both with his own life and with the processes and implications of theatre itself.

The Iceman Cometh, which alone of these last works secured production in his lifetime, was a crucial play for O'Neill. As he explained in a letter to Macgowan, it was 'something I want to make life reveal about itself, fully and deeply and roundly'. It takes place, he insists, 'in a life not in a theatre' while the fact that 'it is a play which can be produced with actors is secondary and incidental to me and even, quite unimportant – and so it would be a loss to me to sacrifice anything of the complete life for the sake of stage and audience'. Urged by Macgowan to make cuts he explained why he could not do so:

what I've tried to write is a play where at the end you feel you know the souls of the seventeen men and women who appear – and women who don't appear – as well as if you'd read a play about each of them. I couldn't condense much without taking a lot of life from some of those people and reducing them to lay figures. You would find if I did not build up the complete picture of the group as it now is in the first part – the atmosphere of the place, the humour and friendship and human warmth and *deep inner contentment* of the bottom – you would not be interested in these people and you would find the impact of what follows a lot less profoundly disturbing.[4]

His comment about refusing to make any sacrifice 'for the sake of stage and audience' seems a curious one. The fact is that in his work acting, performing, theatre, are frequently invoked as images of betrayal, falsehood and inauthenticity as well as the only resource for man as actor, as performing being, as story-teller. And so it proves here as he explains the scene in which each character offers his 'face-saving version of his experience when he went out to confront his pipe dreams' by asserting,

I don't write this as a piece of playwrighting. *They do it. They have to.* Each of them! In just that way! It is tragically, pitifully important to them to do this! They *must* tell these lies as a first step in taking up life again . . . If our American acting and directing cannot hold this scene up without skimping it, then to hell with our theatre!

It was not theatre itself – he felt sure that the Moscow Art Theatre or the Kamerny Theatre of Moscow could 'sustain the horrible contrast and tension of this episode and make it one of the most terrible scenes in the play, as it is to me now'.[5] It was the falsity, the betrayal of the ideal, the substitution of artificial for real values which he felt characterised the American theatre.

O'Neill's characters in his last plays are caught in decline. This is a theatre of entropy. When he says of Jamie Tyrone that 'the signs of premature disintegration are on him'[6] he could be referring to virtually any of his characters. Something has ended. They are, to use another of his favourite expressions, only a ghost of their former selves. Decisions have been irrevocably made, postures struck, betrayals committed.

Process has stopped or must be arrested. To live is to stare in the face of the Gorgons and be turned to stone, or the face of Pan: 'You see him and you die – that is, inside you – and have to go on living as a ghost.' For how many of O'Neill's characters is that an accurate description. In a situation, therefore, in which the logical question becomes, 'Who would want to see life as it is, if they can help it?' the only hope lies in unreality, 'another world where truth is untrue and life can hide from itself', a place where it is, 'As if I had drowned long ago. As if I was a ghost belonging to the fog, and the fog was the ghost of the sea' and salvation lies in being 'nothing more than a ghost within a ghost'.[7] That place where salvation lies and where ghosts walk was perhaps the theatre, as Mary Tyrone becomes detached from her surroundings, offering a parodic performance of her youthful self, the convent girl who surrendered her innocence to a man whose own inner self was so at odds with the persona he projected on stage.

Con Melody, in *A Touch of the Poet*, scarcely exists outside of his role-playing. He has, we are told, 'been visibly crumbling . . . until he appears to have no character left in which to hide and defend himself'.[8] It is a description which could apply to many of O'Neill's characters who perform lives largely evacuated of purpose and content. What is left to them is the mutual support of fellow performers. As Nora says of her response to Melody, 'I'll play any game he likes and give him love in it.'[9] Con Melody, dressed in his uniform, is the quintessential actor reminiscent of the costumed figure with whom O'Neill's mother had fallen in love, a moment recalled, in effect, by Mary Tyrone in *Long Day's Journey into Night*, for she remembers a man 'handsomer than my wildest dream, in his make-up and his nobleman's costume that was so becoming to him', a man 'different from all ordinary men, like someone from another world'.[10] Indeed, O'Neill specifically tells us in a stage note that the actor 'shows in all his unconscious habits of speech, movements and gestures'.[11] Jamie's comment on the beauty of a dawn sky in *A Moon for the Misbegotten* is, 'I like Belasco better. Rise of curtain. Act-Four stuff.'[12]

Rather than speak their own lives they hide in the language of others. When Tyrone is accused by his wife of a bias in favour of the second-hand, that accusation could be addressed with equal validity to the words he deploys. The abstracted Mary is cynically described as playing the mad Ophelia while all the male Tyrones appropriate the language of poets. *Long Day's Journey into Night* is a play full of texts. The opening stage direction lists the authors and titles of the books which frame the scene while the characters themselves frequently converse by means of quotations, sometimes extensive quotations, from Kipling, Wilde, Baudelaire, Swinburne, Rossetti, Dowson. To speak as another is for the moment to evade the self which can be vulnerable to pain. The theatre has dominated their lives; it continues to do so. It is, ultimately, their protection. They carefully detach themselves from the language they speak, in an effort to relieve themselves of responsibility.

The spill of language with which Mary Tyrone struggles to conceal her collapsing world is no less appalling than the autism towards which she is pulled and which, largely self-directed as it is, it paradoxically mimics. Her language becomes echoic. Phrases are repeated in a linguistic circularity which is not only an accurate reflection of her drug-induced state but also her protection against the dangers of real communication. Just as she welcomes the fog because 'it hides you from the world and the world from you',[13] so language, a language of mirrors, does much the same. It constitutes the 'blank wall' she builds around herself; it is the fog in which 'she hides and loses herself'.[14]

The apparently rambling nature of the plays – the way in which language is layered, slabs of soliloquy are placed one upon the other, characters make speeches rather than engage in dialogue – is evidence not of an inadequate grasp of dramatic structure but of this sense of a space between the self and its expression. O'Neill presents a critique of language, a profound suspicion of utterance. Again and again he offers not only a dramatisation of the inadequacy of words to feelings but enacted evidence of the betrayal of truth by words. 'How we poor monkeys hide from ourselves behind the sounds called words',[15] declares Nina in *Strange Interlude*, a woman whose mental instability hardly detracts from her awareness of 'the lies in the sounds called words . . . those sounds our lips make and our hands write'.[16] O'Neill's work abounds with liars, deceivers, fantasisers, actors, those who push language forward as though it could offer them some protection or distraction. The rhetorical flourish of his father's theatre stood as an image of a falsity that was more profound. He was always concerned to get behind language. His fascination with sailors lay in part in their inarticulateness, in what he identified as their 'silence'. His concern, likewise, for those who existed at the bottom of a social order that placed a value on a facility with words lay in the fact that their experiences were nonetheless sharp for all their failure to make their way fully into language. Indeed language may be figuratively what it is literally for the professor in *Strange Interlude* – dead.

The pace in these last plays is almost as languid as in his first, his sea plays. There is little physical movement. We rarely escape a single room. Time very nearly obeys the natural laws. The O'Neill who had restlessly experimented with form, deconstructed character, vocalised the subconscious, splintered the sensibility, energised the *mise en scène*, now settled for a drama which, *Hughie* excepted, seemed conventional. But in an essential way that conventionality becomes subject, as theatre itself is invoked as image and fact, as a defence mobilised by characters in recoil from the real. To enter these plays is to be pulled into a world of actors, deserted by their audience, who perform their lives with diminishing confidence. Once, the characters in *The Iceman Cometh* performed on centre stage, acknowledged in a public arena; now they speak their lines only to themselves or their fellow actors. These are characters trapped in a theatre of their own devising. They are adrift in a world in which to live is to perform and the performances they give are akin to those against which O'Neill had once rebelled. When Tyrone, in *Long Day's Journey into Night*, embraces his drug-addict wife and implores her 'for the love of God, for my sake and the baby's sake and your own, won't you

stop now?"[17] the line could have come out of any of the nineteenth-
century melodramas O'Neill had so despised. What redeems it is
O'Neill's consciousness of its rhetorical falsity, of the extent to which, at
a moment of genuine emotional power, his characters turn to a conventionalised and denatured language.

There is no doubting the melodramatic nature of O'Neill's imagination, but the melodramatic lies at the heart of drama from Sophocles to
Shakespeare in that the common theme is disproportion: event to
response, feeling to utterance, cause to effect. The imagination leads the
self to its own betrayal. The nineteenth-century theatre of James
O'Neill Sr may have chosen to stage a debased version of this theme,
recasting it as crude morality play, but to O'Neill himself it touched on
the tragic which was itself concerned with transgression, with over-
reaching. 'The people who succeed and do not push on to a greater
failure' he insisted in 1921, 'are the spiritual middle-classers. Their stopping at success is the proof of their compromising insignificance. How
petty their dreams must have been!'[18] That exclamation mark is implicit
in much of his drama.

In a letter to George Jean Nathan, in 1921, O'Neill had voiced his conviction that 'in moments of great stress life copies melodrama'. He was
writing in the context of his own play *Anna Christie*, in which 'Anna forced
herself on me . . . at her most theatric'. The problem was to convey this
sense of the 'sincerity of life pent up in the trappings of theatre',[19] a
project which he then thought virtually impossible. It was a problem to
which he returned in his last plays, in which his characters are all self-
conscious performers seeking protection in the artifice of theatre,
playing roles which will deflect the pain of the real.

The word 'belong' echoes throughout his work, from *The Hairy Ape* to
A Moon for the Misbegotten. It hints at a disharmony that his characters
struggle to resolve, at a space in experience and language that can never
be closed. Few gestures are ever completed, few statements allowed to
stand uncontradicted. The word 'dream' likewise provides a kind of
pivot round which the lives of his characters revolve. Such dreams represent simultaneously the possibilities which sustain them and the unattainable that mocks them. They exist in a no man's land, terrified alike
of past and future, yet unable to seize the moment to inhabit a present
whose commitments would pull them into time.

In the late plays his characters seek oblivion through alcohol, through
memory or through narrative, repeating the story of their lives as though
thereby to create those lives. They hold the real at bay. Their capacity

for self-deceit is matched only by their need to be believed, to be taken for what they present themselves as being. To perform is to be.

The characters in these last plays are all self-conscious performers, jumping from one role to another. Deborah, in *A Touch of the Poet*, accuses Melody of an 'absurd performance', but is nonetheless fascinated and seduced by it. He is described by one of his drinking cronies as being 'like a play-actor'. Tyrone, in *A Moon for the Misbegotten*, is an actor, alive to the factitious nature of his role-playing with the woman he loves but afraid to remove his mask. In *The Iceman Cometh* and *Hughie* play-acting is a desperate strategy for survival as, in the theatrical and theatricalised household of *Long Day's Journey into Night*, it is the essence of lives played on the edge of despair. And, of course, O'Neill, in dramatising himself as Edmund, in *Long Day's Journey into Night*, in effect turned himself into an actor.

There is a special effect that comes from the writer incorporating himself in his own work. A certain boundary is breached. An act of inversion occurs. As Luis Borges pointed out, speaking of different narrative levels in a work, 'Such inversions suggest that if the characters in a story can be readers or spectators then we, their readers or spectators, can be fictitious.' The conclusion that Gerard Genette draws from such devices is what he calls the 'unacceptable and insistent hypothesis' that story-teller and listener 'perhaps belong to some narrative'.[20] But that is precisely the conceit with which O'Neill flirts in the late plays. Thus, if O'Neill can enter his own play as Edmund in *Long Day's Journey into Night*, where he speaks not only lines generated by his other self but also those created by the poets from whom Edmund recites, we who listen may become aware of our own performances. For the characters in the play, it is their inability to break away from such roles that is their fate. The freedom of the audience is similarly constrained, but eased by their awareness of that fact.

One of the curiosities of human physiognomy, or perhaps pathology, is that the older the individual becomes the sharper and more complete are the memories from a distant past and the less secure those from the immediate past.

Such memories are, of course, the root of a profound irony, as youth and age are thereby forced together. They are also perhaps part of a recoil from the implications of a radically foreshortened future, a means of slowing down and if possible freezing process into a series of tableaux, of memories aesthetically reshaped. Thought and imagination, formerly projected confidently forward, now bounce against an implacable ending, once literally unimaginable and unimagined. The mirror of the future reflects only the past.

O'Neill was aware of the way in which irony had darkened his vision, in which a certain reflexiveness had entered his work. The mirror into which Con Melody looks in *A Touch of the Poet*, seeking a reflection from another time, is the mirror into which O'Neill also stares, a ghost haunting himself. In the words of a poem, written in 1942:

> Through indolence,
> Irony,
> Helplessness, too, perhaps,
> He let the legends go,
> The lying legends grow;
> Then watched the mirror darken.
> Indolently,
> Ironically,
> Helplessly, too, perhaps
> Until one final day
> Only a ghost remained
> To haunt the shallow depths –
> Himself,
> Bewildered apparition,
> Seeking a lost identity.[21]

There is an atavistic element in O'Neill. The past had always exerted a gravitational pull. At first this was the past of primitivism (*The Hairy Ape*, *All God's Chillun Got Wings*) and paganism (*The Emperor Jones*), then that of classicism wedded to the historical (*Mourning Becomes Electra*). Even an engagement with contemporary capitalism was displaced into the world of Marco Polo. It is not simply that the past has the virtue of completion, nor even, as is the case with Arthur Miller, that it establishes that moral and social continuity that ties individual and society to responsibility, event to consequence, action to result. It is that the past is a kind of nether world. It exists somewhere beneath the civilities of the present. It is a place where truths bubble relentlessly and uncensored to the surface. The past is the key to a world whose coherences only become fully apparent with distance and with time. Towards the end of his career, of course, the past to which he increasingly returned was his own and the truths he travelled so far back to confront precisely those he had otherwise been so steadfast in resisting. So, in 1946, he observed that 'I do not think you can write anything of value or understanding about the present. You can only write about life if it is far enough in the past. The present is too mixed up with superficial values; you can't know what is important and what is not. The past which I have chosen is one I know.'[22]

The last plays, then, all looked backward – to 1926 in *Hughie*, 1912 in the case of *The Iceman Cometh* and *Long Day's Journey into Night*, 1828 in *A Touch of the Poet*, 1923 in *A Moon for the Misbegotten*, the 1830s in *More Stately Mansions* – as though time had hit some ultimate limit and rebounded. Writing in 1939 he looks back to 1926 or 1912 only to encounter characters who themselves look further back. Meaning, once presumed to lie ahead, is now assurned to lie in the past. The possible has become the irrevocable, until, that is, it is transformed into narrative where it can be recast as possibility. Yet in a curious way these plays also looked forward in that this was an O'Neill who seemed natural kin to Samuel Beckett, a man aware of the vortex of absurdity. His characters pile up words against the silence they fear, create a barricade of language. It is a world lit occasionally by lyricism, by the desperate cameraderie of the doomed, a humour, a faith in performance, a belief in the possibility of renewal, albeit a renewal denied again and again by thought and action in such a way that the rhythm of that denial becomes the source of an irony that is definitional. The American theatre, in all other ways resistant to the absurd (to the point where Arthur Miller, like Saul Bellow, denounced it as an abnegation of human responsibility) finds its poet of the absurd in these last plays, though even he is tempted to offer a benediction, not least because the grace he offers is extended retrospectively not only to his father, whom he imagined himself to hate, to the brother of whom he was so clearly jealous and the mother who had sent him spinning into an early despair, but also to himself.

As his own ability to inscribe meaning slipped away from him and he edged towards the silence his art was designed to deny, O'Neill became a ghost haunting his own past as his past haunted him, an image that he himself used in another sense when describing his attempts to overcome his increasing physical incapacity. Sent a dictation machine he read into it his favourite part of the third act of *The Iceman Cometh* in which Larry Slade delivers what he calls his 'let me live' speech:

When I played the record back and listened to the voice that was my voice and yet not my voice saying: 'I'm afraid to live, am I? – and even more afraid to die! So I sit here, my pride drowned on the bottom of a bottle, keeping drunk so I won't see myself shaking in my britches with fright, or hear myself whining and praying, O Blessed Christ, let me live a little longer *at any price!*' well it sure did something to me. It wasn't Larry, it was my ghost talking to me, or I to my ghost.[23]

Such a conversation lies at the heart of a play which was to be part of a cycle pointedly called 'By Way of Obit.'.

Hughie was written at the beginning of the war. But certain works have a prophetic power – witness Kafka, who created in the labyrinthine absurdities of *The Trial* and *The Castle* a portrait which matched Hitler's nightmare reality more precisely than the Austro-Hungarian bureaucracy which it seemed to mirror (even, according to George Steiner, anticipating the denatured language of the camps). *Hughie*, so different, so much a part of O'Neill's own development, has that power. One element that recurs in accounts of the Holocaust is the persistence, to the very doors of the gas chambers, of hope. As George Steiner has remarked, speaking of the Warsaw uprising, but also of those who stared chaos in the face and refused to see it for what it was, 'The memory of hope cries out' from those times. That hopeless hope equally energises the characters in O'Neill's final plays, plays he forebore to release on an American public confronted with the reality of war.

Of course the gap between *Hughie* and those events is enormous. But it is a play that sees in the persistence of hope a final and bewildering irony, the root of an absurdity bred by the space between it and the life it is designed to redeem.

The action of *Hughie* takes place in the lobby of a hotel 'forced to deteriorate in order to survive'. It is a setting whose ironic description could apply to a number of O'Neill's characters in these last plays, and, on the eve of the Depression, to a society for which the Great Hollow Boom of the twenties, the 'Everlasting Opulence of the New Economic Law', is about to end.

Like so many of Susan Glaspell's plays, or indeed Beckett's *Godot*, *Hughie* works on a principle of absence. Its central character never appears. Of the two we do see, one is for the most part silent. There is little or no movement. There is little or no plot. The ruling principle seems to be negativity.

The night clerk has eyes that are described as being 'without character'. So, too, are his mouth and ears. His eyes, moreover, are 'blank' and, the stage directions tell us, 'contain no discernible expression'. He is 'not thinking', as later he can only 'think about nothing'. He is 'not sleepy'. He stares 'at nothing'. Indeed there are indications that O'Neill toyed with the idea of using a puppet to represent the role of what is in effect a listener, an audience, for the theatre is in some sense a subject and a metaphor in this play.

Roland Barthes observed of theatre that 'the written text is from the first carried along by the externality of bodies, of objects, of situations, the utterance immediately explodes into substances'.[24] *Hughie* seems to resist that fact, to eschew its own theatrical possibilities. Indeed O'Neill gave serious thought to publishing it as a book rather than stage it.

The set looks like an Edward Hopper painting and it is almost as though O'Neill, like Hopper, is trying to deny himself a third dimension, to offer a fixed and unyielding surface, its implied narrative locked securely away from the possibility of animation. Hopper's *The Nighthawk*, painted in the same year that O'Neill finished *Hughie*, implies a narrative contained within and by the tableau which represents it. It is eternally night, as it is in *Hughie* which, like Edward Albee's *Who's Afraid of Virginia Woolf?*, might justifiably be called *Long Night's Journey into Day*, except that the day never dawns. And Hopper offers a useful parallel. His paintings, which include an alienated view of a hotel lobby, a portrait of a solitary figure in a hotel bedroom and a number of bleak portraits of the theatre world, reveal a favourite trope. Time and again his pictures show two figures in a run-down setting who share space but nothing else. They are contained within the same frame but not within the same experience. They stare ahead of themselves, apparently oblivious to those seated or standing beside them. The space between them is not only psychological. The listener in O'Neill's play is almost as static as Hopper's figures and almost as anonymous. He has 'half forgotten' his own name which is, anyway, virtually identical with that of the dead man he has replaced, a fact which is suitable enough for a man whose 'mind is blank'.

In the course of the play he is actually referred to in the stage directions or the text as 'a dummy', 'a corpse', and a 'drooping waxwork'. He envies the blind. Conversations become at best competing monologues, as they are, perhaps, in *Long Day's Journey into Night* and *The Iceman Cometh*.

The stage directions refer obsessively not to the man who speaks, who wears bright clothes, who moves around, who narrates the story, but to the listener. He is an almost Beckett-like character who longs to be blind and deaf as the only way to defeat the absurdity of his life. When he hears the El-train approach it stirs a memory of hope, even as its noise annihilates that memory. The only hope that remains is that each train that passes leaves fewer still to pass. Death, in other words, becomes perversely the source of hope: 'so the night recedes, too, until at last it must die and join all those other long nights in Nirvana, the Big Night of Nights. And that's life.'[25] The absence of the trains is a harbinger of another absence which will finally destroy absurdity by succumbing to it. Hope, unjustifiable, unrealisable, is the essence of absurdity – hence the names of Harry Hope and Jimmy Tomorrow in *The Iceman Cometh*, the play he had barely completed when he turned his hand to *Hughie*.

Erie's 'Better beat it up to my cell and grab some shut-eye', followed by a stage direction that indicates '*He makes a move to detach himself from the desk, but fails, and remains wearily glued to it*',[26] is an equivalent of Beckett's 'Let's go (*they do not move*)' from *Waiting for Godot*. And this is the rhythm of these last plays: assertion is instantly followed by denial, affection by revulsion. Language is denied by action. The *non sequitur* becomes normative. Language is seldom transitive. The night clerk conducts conversations in his mind which frustrate the possibility of communicating with the man who faces him.

When Kristin Morrison, in her book on Beckett and Pinter (*Cantors and Chronicles*), suggests that narrative has in some senses replaced the soliloquy in drama, characterising O'Neill's attempts to deploy the latter as a late and none too successful effort, she forgets just how important narrative was to O'Neill. 'Never', she says, have narrative elements in drama been used, as they are in the work of Beckett and Pinter, to 'reveal deep and difficult thoughts and feelings while at the same time concealing them as fiction', in such a way that 'in the telling of a story, the conflict between facing issues and fleeing them is actually dramatized', a conflict which is itself 'the real action of the play'. But what else is *The Iceman Cometh*? What else is *Hughie*? For surely, in these plays, too, by choosing 'to *perform*, to focus on a narrated past rather than an actual present, characters betray their deepest, most incompatible feelings'.[27] Narrative compulsion conceals literal and spiritual inertia for O'Neill's characters no less than for Beckett's or Pinter's. In O'Neill, too, the tension between a narrated past and a narrative present is the root of irony no less than of temporary consolation. In the persons of Erie and Hughes we have the two irreducible aspects of story or, indeed, of theatre: a speaker and a listener. They meet, if at all, only in the fictions which they momentarily agree to give the force of reality. Otherwise their only consolation lies in habit or the stasis of boredom. And Proust's remark, quoted by Beckett in his study of that writer – 'Of all human plants . . . Habit requires the least fostering, and is the first to appear on the seeming desolation of the most barren rock'[28] – describes the world of *The Iceman Cometh* and *Hughie* no less precisely than that of *Waiting for Godot* or *Endgame*. The night clerk in *Hughie*, we are told, had 'even forgotten how it feels to be bored', boredom, Beckett remarking, being one pole of human experience of which the other is suffering.

O'Neill's characters are story-tellers as well as the victims of story, as narrative logic pulls them towards annihilation. In *The Iceman Cometh* they extend their lives along the path of their narratives, but since those stories project a future defined entirely in terms of an imagined past they are trapped in the future historic, a reflexive tense which accurately reflects their circumstances. As Con Melody confesses to his wife in *A Touch of the Poet*: 'no future but the past'. For Tyrone, likewise, in *A Moon for the Misbegotten*, 'There is no present or future – only the past happening over and over again – now. You can't get away from it.'[29] The characters in *Long Day's Journey into Night* are 'trapped within each other by the past'.[30] The figures in *Iceman* are stranded in a timeless world, caught in the pure irony that is bred out of a tension between an irrecoverable past and a future that involves nothing more than infinite repetition. So, in *A Touch of the Poet*, not merely is Con Melody reflected in a mirror but the scene is itself repeated. As O'Neill observes in the second act, 'What follows is an exact repetition of his scene before the mirror in Act one.' Similarly, Con Melody's habit of dressing up in a uniform is a reflection, a repetition, of Simon Hartford's grandfather's habit of dressing up in the uniform of the French Republic National Guard. When asked to cut the repetitions in *The Iceman Cometh* O'Neill refused, insisting that 'they are absolutely necessary to what I'm trying to get over'.[31] His characters are caught in their own dramas and, as Ingmar Bergman has reminded us, the essence of theatre is 'Repetition, living, throbbing repetition. The same performance every night, the same performance and yet reborn.'[32] These last plays seem to me quintessentially about performance as the characters enact the roles in which they have cast themselves.

Erie Smith is described as 'a teller of tales', an honourable profession you might think, not least because it happens to be O'Neill's as well. Yet Hemingway's remark that 'all true stories, if continued long enough, end in death', is not without its relevance. For narrative logic carries its own death threat. The distance between a narrated past and a narrative present – the present in which the story is told – is a measure of time, the very time against which the narrative is offered as talisman. This is the world in which the night clerk knows and O'Neill tells us, 'It would be discouraging to look at the clock.'[33]

Michel Foucault has observed that 'speaking so as not to die is a task . . . as old as the word'. Discourse, he insists, has the power to arrest the flight of an arrow and 'it is quite likely that the approach of death . . . hollows out in the present and in existence the void towards which and from which we speak'.[34] So Erie's stories are uttered in the presence and the face of death as, in a series called 'By Way of Obit.' and in a play

that recounts the life of a dead character, thereby, paradoxically, infus-
ing him with life, we see death held at arm's length by language.

Erie is not so much *caught* in what Foucault calls the 'labyrinth of repetition' – in which language divides itself and becomes its own mirror;
he aspires to it. Not only does the name of the desk clerk Hughes mirror
that of his predecessor Hughie, he must be made to be a pure reflection
of him. Old stories are repeated, actions re-enacted, fantasies replayed
in a closed system designed to resist transcendence and to deny process.
Erie tells stories not simply to force a listener to acknowledge his existence but to prevent him climbing the stairs of the hotel and turning his
key in the lock of a solitary room whose silence appals him by its power
to mimic the death he both resists and welcomes. It is habit that shores
him up against suffering.

The pipe dreams of those in Harry Hope's bar are stories that have
to be told alike each time. Just as a child will detect the slightest variation in a bed-time story, stories usually designed to be incomplete at the
moment of sleep as a subtle guarantee of reawakening, so the essence of
their stories is that they should not be organic, because the organic
carries the logic of death at its heart. They are objects, aesthetically complete, unchanging, habitual, boring in the redemptive way in which
boredom redeems us alike from thought and feeling. The stasis of the
characters in *The Iceman Cometh* is that of the boy in Beckett's *Endgame*. It
is their protection against the absurd where the absurd is born out of the
conviction that things could be other. The phrase 'pipe dreams' recurs
not merely *like* an echo. It is an echo. It is language reassuringly bounc-
ing back off itself – resisting its own capacity for transcendence. And
memory, too, is an echo, a repeated sound or image that comes back to
us, whether from a world of reality or from the echo chamber of the
imagination, from the refracting mirror of the past.

In drama, the privilege of narrative is surrendered to characters who,
though plainly themselves the product of narrative, have the function of
speaking themselves (a privilege that, in some degree, O'Neill fought to
resist through stage directions which threatened to expand in the direction of the novel). But in *The Iceman Cometh*, in *Long Day's Journey into Night*
and in *Hughie* the narratives generated by O'Neill's characters as their
defence against entrapment in the plot of time are also the essence and
mechanism of that entrapment. Nonetheless, Erie's stories are what
keep him alive. The clerk, too, is aware that 'He is awake and alive. I
should use him to help me live through the night.' O'Neill perhaps used
his stories to perform much the same function. Life, according to the

night clerk, is 'a goddamned racket . . . But we might as well make the best of it, because – Well, you can't burn it all down, can you? There's too much steel and stone. There'd always be something left to start it going again.'[35] It is hard not to relate such a statement to the situation in Beckett's *Waiting for Godot* or *Endgame*, and there is something both in structure and style that pulls the two writers together. O'Neill became increasingly conscious of what he called 'a sort of unfair *non sequitur*' in experience as he also increasingly became aware of a comedy that 'doesn't stay funny very long'. It is a humour that in part depends on the *non sequitur*, the space between intent and action, a humour very like Beckett's. That space exists, too, in language. O'Neill's concern with the radical incompletions of language is rooted in his sense of a world whose inner coherences have attenuated to the point of collapse. The grammar, the syntax of experience have dissolved. He acknowledged being drawn to 'the clotted, clogged and inarticulate', feeling that 'great language' was no longer possible for anyone living in the 'discordant, broken, faithless rhythm of our time'. The best one can do, he suggested, was to 'be pathetically eloquent by one's moving dramatic inarticulations'.[36]

There is a sense of exhaustion, of depleted energy, of entropy about the characters in these last plays, and certainly in *Hughie*, and exhaustion, excess, limit and transgression are, as Foucault observed, related categories. Erie's stories exhaust themselves in the telling; they leach energy until they collapse into silence. He tries to find meaning not in his experience but in the retelling of that experience as story. He is the playwright confronting his audience and deriving his meaning from that audience, an audience only momentarily distracted. And if Erie is in a sense a portrait of Jamie O'Neill, Hughes is perhaps a version of himself – certainly Virginia Floyd has pointed out that in an early version of *Long Day's Journey into Night* he had called a character, modelled on himself, Hugh, a name that he deployed, too, in *Mourning Becomes Electra*.[37] Perhaps O'Neill was both – the animated story-teller and the man immobile behind a desk, trapped in a decaying setting and drawn more and more to silence – the man who speaks in the night-time to the puppet he summons into existence to annihilate his solitariness. In the words of Hamm in *Endgame*, 'babble, babble, words, like the solitary child who turns himself into children two, three, so as to be together, in the dark'.[38]

Or again – doesn't this come close to describing the world, the tone, the essence of *Hughie*?

How long before our masquerade will end its noise . . . and we shall find it was a solitary performance? . . . Our relations to each other are oblique and casual . . . Nothing is left us now but death. We look to that with a grim satisfaction, saying, there at least is reality that will not dodge us . . . It is very unhappy but too late to be helped, the discovery we have made, that we exist.[39]

But that, as it happens, was not Beckett, not somebody steeped in the absurd, but a writer O'Neill turned to at the time he was writing *Hughie*. The author, perhaps surprisingly, was Ralph Waldo Emerson. For all his eclecticism O'Neill was very much a writer in the American grain.

Hughie begins in silence; it ends in a tumble of language that is no more than another version of that silence. To O'Neill, writing in the same year that he completed *Hughie*, silence was a temptation and a fate:

> . . . I have tried to scream!
> Give pain a voice!
> Make it a street singer
> Acting a pantomime of tragic song . . .
>
> But something was born wrong.
> The voice strains towards a sob.
> Begins and ends in silence . . .
>
> All this,
> As I have said before,
> Happens where silence is;
> Where I,
> A quiet man,
> In love with quiet,
> Live quietly
> Among the visions of my drowned,
> Deep in my silent sea.[40]

Hughie is a kind of ghost, an echo, a memory, a reflection, an image replayed so many times his outline begins to blur. Mythicised by Eric, he becomes the usable past to which O'Neill himself now turned. And as Eric works desperately to hold the attention of his indifferent audience, without whom his identity is threatened, so O'Neill could feel a gulf begin to open between himself and those he would address. And his own increasing disability reminded him, too, that the time must eventually come when he, no less than Erie, would be left without his audience to climb those hotel stairs alone to a solitary room where death awaited. 'Born in a hotel room and, goddamn it, died in a hotel room.'

CHAPTER THREE

Tennessee Williams: the theatricalising self

The pre-war world was another country. From the distance of the mid-to late forties and early fifties it seemed secure, reassuring, but in fact the Depression had destroyed one version of America and the Hitler–Stalin pact another. Wartime rhetoric had reinvented smalltown America, an amalgam of Thornton Wilder's *Our Town* and *Saturday Evening Post* covers, where old values were preserved and celebrated, a world worth fighting for; now that was already fading into history. William Inge, Carson McCullers and Robert Anderson might continue to place it at the centre of their work, but in doing so showed how bleak it could be until redeemed by an ambiguous love.

And of course, something radical had happened. In Europe 6 million Jews had been systematically put to death. In Japan, the heat of the sun had been replicated by man over two major cities. If Virginia Woolf had suggested that human nature changed in 1910 there were now other dates with greater claim to mark a shift in human affairs. Certainly American notions of the autonomous self, secure and morally inviolable, seemed suddenly more difficult to sustain. The enemy was no longer simple modernity, the inhuman scale, the mechanical rhythms against which Eugene O'Neill and Elmer Rice, Sidney Kingsley and the young Miller and Williams had railed. It was a flaw in the sensibility that made betrayal seem a natural impulse and the self complicit in its own annihilation. It was no longer a case of pitching an integral self against anonymity and social despair for now that self is presented as fragmented and insecure.

Death of a Salesman and *The Crucible*, *The Glass Menagerie* and *A Streetcar Named Desire*, seemed to suggest the end of a particular model of America and of individual character. Time seemed to be gathering pace. Basic myths having to do with family and community, civility and responsibility, style and grace had dissolved. The future seemed to offer little more than a bland materialism or a drugged conformity.

The choice was between Happy Loman and Stanley Kowalski. In such circumstances the past had a seductive attraction. So, Willy Loman, in *Death of a Salesman*, is pulled ever more back into the past of his own imagining, before the city encroached on his freedom, before the wire recorder cut across a simple act of human communication, before the automobile threatened his life and the world became such a mystery to him. So, John Proctor, in *The Crucible*, struggles to accommodate himself to a language which no longer speaks his life and to a system which denies him reality. Laura's glass menagerie is frozen. Time is suspended as it will continue to be suspended for her, as it has been suspended for the woman on whom she was based and who has spent a lifetime in a mental hospital in recoil from the real. Like so many of William Faulkner's characters Laura Wingfield in *The Glass Menagerie* stands as a paradigm of the culture of which she is a part. The world of modernity, the dance hall and the typewriter, is outside of her experience. Vulnerable, she chooses instead a world of myth, symbolised by the glass unicorn. It is a factitious security broken as easily as the unicorn's glass horn. Blanche, too, in *A Streetcar Named Desire*, resists the pull of time, terrified of the first signs of age, aware that something has ended and that it can only be recovered at the level of story, only through the roles that she so desperately performs and which finally offer her no immunity. Insanity, literal or metaphoric, seems to threaten. Williams acknowledges the impossibility of recovering the past. Indeed he accepts the equivocal nature of that past, stained, as it is, by cruelty and corruption. But the future is worse: power without charity, passion without tenderness.

Williams had the romantic's fascination with extreme situations, with the imagination's power to challenge facticity, with the capacity of language to reshape experience, with the self's ability to people the world with visions of itself. He deployed the iconography of the romantic: fading beauty, the death of the young, a dark violence, a redeeming love. Like the romantic he was inclined to blur the edge of the divide between his life and his art. It would be tempting to see his fondness for drink and drugs as yet another aspect of the romantic's twin quest for vision and self-destruction except that in his case it had more to do with terror and despair. It was certainly as a romantic in an unromantic world that he wished to present himself, transfiguring the failed enterprise that is life with nothing more than language and the imagination.

Tennessee Williams's explanation for his career as a dramatist was that he was 'creating imaginary worlds into which I can retreat from the real world because . . . I've never made any kind of adjustment to the real world'.[1] It was an honest remark and one that could be applied with equal force to his characters. In one direction such a failure of adjustment may generate neurosis and psychosis; in another, art. And if his characters are indeed pulled towards mental instability they also tend to be artists, literal and symbolic. Blanche turns her life into an art work. Her trunk is full of clothes for the various roles she plays while she transforms the Kowalski apartment with the eye of a theatre director. Laura arranges her menagerie with an artist's touch. Val Xavier is a musician, Chance Wayne an actor. Sebastian, in *Suddenly Last Summer*, and Nonno, in *The Night of the Iguana*, are both poets. But this sense of failed adjustment is not entirely a pose of romantic alienation nor the imagination simply an agent of the self in retreat from the real. The social and political seldom disappear entirely from Williams's work. As he himself remarked,

I'm not sure I would want to be well-adjusted to things as they are. I would prefer to be racked by desire for things better than they are, even for things which are unattainable, than to be satisfied with things as they are . . . I am not satisfied with the present state of things in this country and I'm afraid of complacency about it.[2]

At the beginning of his career he had insisted that 'My interest in social problems is as great as my interest in the theatre . . . I try to write all my plays so that they carry some social message along with the story.' He had favoured the one-act form because he 'found it easier to get across a message and with more impact if I made it brief'.[3] Later in his career, and sometimes to the surprise of critics, he was prone to draw political significance from plays which seemed precisely to evade the political. So, while insisting that he had thought *Camino Real* 'a sort of fairy tale or masque' set originally in Mexico and containing elements of Fez, Tangiers and Casablanca, he felt constrained to add that 'Each time I return here [the United States] I sense a further reduction in human liberties, which I guess is reflected in the revisions of the play.'[4] And it is worth recalling that the play was indeed a product of the same year as *The Crucible*. The crushing of the wayward spirit, the artist, the man whose sympathies extend to the dispossessed, the poor, those not dedicated to a material world of acquisition and conformity, had its correlative in an American society wilfully submitting to the corrupt power of Senator Joseph McCarthy.

Williams was aware of his tendency to 'poetize', explaining that that was why he had created so many southern heroines: 'They have a tendency to gild the lily and they speak in a rather florid style which seems to suit no one because I write out of emotion.'[5] Such language, however, is less poetic than effusive. It is a style of speech designed to draw attention to itself, to distort, to deceive. Detached from the reality of experience, it is a mask which conceals a truth which the characters cannot articulate. It is that, doubtless, that contradiction, that irony which is heightened by theatre in which appearance and reality co-exist in the same instant, in which language and action are in conflict and words are placed under a tension which may be felt rather than heard.

His observation that 'poetry doesn't have to be words . . . In the theatre it can be situations, it can be silences',[6] is a critical one and in part explains why he was drawn to the theatre. His sets have a meta- phoric force, sometimes too literally so. His characters expose their lives through the smallest gesture. Blanche and Stanley, personally confront- ing one another across a space charged with sexual energy, generate a meaning which does not lie in their words. There is a rhythm to their relationship which creates its own inevitability, its own crescendos and diminuendos.

Williams has said that:

everything is in flux, everything is in a process of creation. The world is incom- plete, it's like an unfinished poem. Maybe the poem will turn into a limerick and maybe it will turn into an epic poem. But it's for all of us to try to complete this poem and the way to complete it is through understanding and patience and tolerance among ourselves.[7]

This sense of incompletion applies equally to his characters who resist being too fully known. As he has suggested, 'Some mystery should be left in the revelation of character in a play, just as a great deal of mystery is always left in the revelation of character in life, even in one's own char- acter to himself.' To define too closely is to accept 'facile definitions which make a play just a play, not a snare for the truth of human expe- rience'.[8] That incompletion is vital to his work. At its best it moves him away from metaphor and towards the symbolic whose essence lies in its inexhaustible significations. And the truth of human experience he sets himself to capture? That has to do with a particular kind of desperate dignity in defeat. His subject, he has said, is human valour and endu- rance, even arguing that Amanda's courage constitutes the core of *The Glass Menagerie:* 'She's confused, pathetic, even stupid, but everything has got to be all right. She fights to make it that way in the only way she knows how.'[9]

Williams was never interested in realism. Like O'Neill before him he was hostile to an art of surfaces. So he set his face against 'the straight realist play with its genuine frigidaire and authentic ice cubes, its characters that speak exactly as the audience speaks'. This has 'the same virtue of a photographic likeness' and 'Everyone should know nowadays the unimportance of the photographic in art.'[10] There are no sets in a Williams play which merely provide the context for action. They are, without exception, charged with a symbolic function, from the enclosing space of *The Glass Menagerie* and *Streetcar* through to the primal garden of *Suddenly Last Summer*, the collapsing house of *The Kingdom of Earth*, the urban wasteland of *The Red Devil Battery Sign* and the empty theatre of *Outcry*. There is no prop that does not function in terms of character and theme, whether it be a glass animal, a covering over a lamp, an anatomical chart, a liquor glass or a hammock. Williams himself cited the dropping out of the window, by the hotel proprietor, of Casanova's shabby portmanteau of fragile memories in *Camino Real*. This, he suggested, was 'a clearer expression of an idea than you might be able to do with a thousand words'.[11] He might equally have invoked the phonograph-cum-liquor-cabinet in *Cat on a Hot Tin Roof* or the urn of ashes in *The Rose Tattoo*. The fact is that if there was more than a touch of the poet in Tennessee Williams, there was also something of the artist. Certainly he had a strong visual imagination which translated poetic images into practical correlatives in terms of staging.

At the beginning of his career Tennessee Williams saw himself as a radical, creating a series of protest plays for a political theatre group in St Louis. It was a radicalism that at first was precisely directed. The villains were industrialists, war profiteers, prison officials, those who presided over public squalor. Behind these lay a political and economic system that encouraged corruption and broke the individual on the rack of private profit. Such power as the plays had was generated less by their dramatic force than by the melodrama of daily life which appeared to validate such a Manichaean vision. Despite these origins and a persistent regard for those who lived lives at a tangent to capitalist enterprise, audiences and critics preferred to respond to him as southern gothicist or the mordant poet of dissolution and despair, as an aesthetic bohemian offering a vicarious sexuality. He was certainly all of those things and his vote for the socialist candidate for the presidency (the only vote he ever cast) should not deceive us into the belief that his was an ideological drama, any more than should his appearance on a public platform, thirty years later, to protest the Vietnam war. His radicalism was neither

Marxist nor liberal. In a way, indeed, it was profoundly conservative. What he wanted above all was for the individual to be left alone, insulated from the pressure of public event. But he never forgot the cruelties which he dramatised in those early days, cruelties which left the individual a victim of a system resistant to human needs.

It is tempting to suppose that his response to the repressiveness of the public world, his patent alienation, perhaps stemmed from another source. As Arthur Miller suggested,

If only because he came up at a time when homosexuality was absolutely unacknowledged in a public figure, Williams had to belong to a minority culture and understood in his bones what a brutal menace the majority could be if aroused against him . . . Certainly I never regarded him as the sealed-off aesthete he was thought to be. There is a radical politics of the soul as well as of the ballot box and the picket line. If he was not an activist, it was not for lack of a desire for justice, nor did he consider a theatre profoundly involved in society and politics . . . somehow unaesthetic or beyond his interest.[12]

But even if his radicalism is better viewed as a celebration of the outcast or the deprived, a sympathy for those discarded by a society for which he anyway had little sympathy, his work reveals a consistent distrust of the wealthy and the powerful, a suspicion of materialism. Although, in stark contrast to Faulkner, scarcely a black face is to be seen in Williams's South, in *Orpheus Descending* and *Sweet Bird of Youth* he made clear his contempt for the racist, his association of bigotry with sterility and death. If, after the 1930s, Williams rarely chose to formulate his sense of oppression in overtly political ways, his portraits of individuals pressed to the margins of social concern, trapped in a diminishing social and psychological space, are not without ideological significance, for, as Michel Foucault has reminded us, there is a link between space and power.

Many of his early plays – the largely unknown plays of the 1930s – tend to be set in claustrophobic and constrictive spaces (a prison in *Not About Nightingales*, the lobby of a flophouse in *Fugitive Kind*, a coal mine and its surroundings in *Candles to the Sun*, a tenement building in *Stairway to the Sky*). In *Fugitive Kind* the city itself becomes both naturalistic trope and coercive presence ('a great implacable force, pressing in upon the shabby room and crowding its fugitive inhabitants back against their last wall').[13] Already, though, he was bending naturalism in the direction of symbolism and there were to be few of his characters who would not find themselves similarly trapped in the suffocating constraints of a small back room, in an asylum, real or metaphorical, or, as one of his characters remarks, inside their own skins, for life. Shannon, the defrocked priest, tied in his hammock in *The Night of the Iguana*, can stand as an image of many of Williams's protagonists.

It would be a mistake, therefore, to regard Williams's radicalism as not only a product of but also contained by the 1930s. His insistence that art is a 'criticism of things as they exist',[14] should be taken entirely seriously. Indeed there is a surprising consistency in the comments that he made about his society from the beginning of his career to its end. In 1945 he commented on the weight of reactionary opinion that descended 'on the head of any artist who speaks out against the current of prescribed ideas', likening investigating committees to Buchenwald. Two years later he insisted that it was no longer safe to enunciate American revolutionary ideals. In 1950 he objected that 'Our contemporary American society seems no longer inclined to hold itself open to very explicit criticism from within.' Faced with the 'all but complete suppression of any dissident voices' the artist was forced to withdraw into 'his own isolated being'.[15] Seven years later (and a year after writing to the State Department to protest the withdrawing of Arthur Miller's passport) he attacked the simplistic dualism of cold war politics, insisting that 'no man has a monopoly of right or virtue any more than a man has a corner on duplicity and evil and so forth',[16] suggesting that failure to acknowledge this fact had bred 'the sort of corruption' which he had 'involuntarily chosen as the basic, allegorical theme' of his plays.

In 1975, speaking in the context of his apocalyptic *The Red Devil Battery Sign*, he placed the moment of corruption in the 1950s: 'The moral decay of America', he insisted, 'really began with the Korean War, way before the Kennedy assassination.' Vietnam, which he described as an 'incomprehensible evil' merely proved that 'this once great and beautiful democracy' had become 'the death merchant of the world'.[17]

By 1978 he had backdated the corruption, seeing Hiroshima and Nagasaki as marking the effective end of civilisation, and while suggesting that 'No rational, grown up artist deludes himself with the notion that his inherent, instinctive rejection of the ideologies of failed governments, or power-combines that mask themselves as governments, will in the least divert these monoliths from a fixed course toward the slag-heap remnants of once towering cities', still insisted that 'there must be somewhere truth to be pursued each day with words that are misunderstood and feared because they are the words of an Artist, which must always remain a word most compatible with the word Revolutionary'.[18] Thus it was that he later insisted that the title of his play *A House Not Meant to Stand* was 'a metaphor for our society in our times' and denounced the

'Me Generation' for its apathy with respect to American involvement in
El Salvador and Guatemala and the 'plutocracy' whose power was reinforced under President Nixon. So it is that he asserted, with some
justification, that all of his plays 'have a social conscience'. So they do.
But the very implacability of history as he presents it suggests the extent
to which the artist becomes less a social rebel than a Quixote transforming the real at the level of the imagination. Instead of corruption being
a product of recent history it becomes the given against which the artist
must rebel. Thus it is that the decay of American idealism is seen as
beginning when 'it ceased to be able to exist within its frontiers'.[19] And
that, of course, pushed the date back beyond the twentieth century,
beyond his own appearance. America's fallen state thus becomes the
implacable fact against which the artist must protest and rebel.

Tennessee Williams's plays are not naturalistic. The determinisms
which his characters resist are not primarily the produce of physical
environment or heredity. They are built into the structure of existence.
When, in the 1970s, he wrote *Gnädiges Fräulein* it seemed a belated gesture
in the direction of European absurdism. In fact, the absurd was deeply
rooted in his sensibility. The irony which governs the lives of his protagonists, whose needs are so patently at odds with their situation, is less a
social fact than a metaphysical reality. His characters, too, give birth
astride the grave and try to make sense of their abandonment (*Camino
Real*, perhaps his most obviously absurdist work, was actually produced
in the same year that Beckett's *Waiting for Godot* opened in Paris). But
Williams, unlike Beckett, is enough of a romantic to feel heat even in the
cold flame of such ironies. Beckett's figures are the uncomprehending
products of their situation, drained of substance, alienated even from
the language they speak. Williams's characters resist with the only
weapons they possess – their imaginations and, on occasion, a vivifying
sexuality which sometimes transcends the irony in which it is rooted –
the illusion of connectiveness dissolving even as it is proposed, time
asserting its hegemony even as it is denied. His is the romantic's sense of
doom. That was why he was drawn to F. Scott Fitzgerald, to Hart Crane
and to Byron. Jay Gatsby and Dick Diver both tried to remake the world
in their own image; both were destroyed by the hard-edged realities of
American power, as they were, more profoundly, by the ultimate futility
of their attempts to resist natural process and the pull of time. Much the
same could be said of Blanche in *A Streetcar Named Desire*, of Laura in *The
Glass Menagerie*, of Alma in *Summer and Smoke*, or of Shannon in *The Night
of the Iguana*.

Theatrically, he set himself to dissolve the surface of a naturalism whose propositions he denied. What he was after, he insisted, was a plastic theatre, fluid, evanescent, undefined and undefining. His was to be an attempt to find in the style of his theatre an equivalent to that resistance to the given which characterised his protagonists. Thus the set of *The Glass Menagerie*, his first Broadway success which premiered in 1945, was to indicate those 'vast hive-like conglomerations of cellular living units that flower as warty growths in overcrowded urban centres' and which deny a 'fundamentally enslaved section of American society . . . fluidity and differentiation'.[20] That set was not created to suggest a social reality that could be modified by political action or radical reform. It was the context for a play having to do with the desperate strategies developed by those whose options have run out. Tom, a writer, returns in memory to a family he had deserted in order to claim his freedom to write. The family consists of his mother, Amanda – voluble, neurotic, surviving on memories and will – and his sister, Laura, whose crippled foot is an image of a damaged spirit in recoil from the real. Tom, as narrator, stands outside this world, literally and figuratively. He is the one who has found an avenue of escape through his art. By summoning the scene into existence he asserts his power over it. And yet what he has achieved is what Jerry, in Edward Albee's *The Zoo Story*, was to call 'solitary free passage'. Indeed, the very fact of his summoning this world into existence demonstrates its continued power over him and the guilt which was later to send Blanche Dubois to her appointment in another tenement in New Orleans. Such solitude, though, is perhaps the price to be paid by the artist, and *The Glass Menagerie*, like others of his plays, is in part a contemplation of the role of the artist. In this case it is a very personal account of his relationship with his own family. Not for nothing is the narrator given the author's own name. Like his character, Williams was all too aware that he had claimed his own freedom at the expense of his mother and sister, Rose, the lobotomy which destroyed her life being performed while he was away at university beginning his career as writer. Even in the context of the play Tom's escape seems too much like his father's desertion of the family to seem like anything but abandonment. As he was to show in *Suddenly Last Summer*, Williams was acutely aware of the degree to which art could be said to serve the self, the extent to which the artist moved himself outside the normal processes of social life.

Williams came to distrust the framing device of the narrator in *The Glass Menagerie* but it is that which, by introducing another time scale, creates the ironies on which the play depends. It is, indeed, a play in which time becomes a central concern. So, Amanda's present, in which she exists on the margins of society, surviving by pandering to those whose support she needs, is contrasted to a past in which, at least on the level of memory and imagination, she was at the centre of attention. Laura's wilful withdrawal into the child-like world of her menagerie derives its sad irony precisely from the fact that it is a denial of her own maturity, of time. Even her 'gentleman caller' is momentarily forced to confront the discrepancy between the promise of his high school years (recalled by the photograph in a school year book) and the reality of his present life. Time has already begun to break these people as their fantasies and dreams are denied by the prosaic facts of economic necessity and natural process alike. Laura seeks immunity by withdrawing into the timeless world of the imagined, Amanda by retreating into a past refashioned to offer consolation. Tom alone seems to have escaped these ironies, at the price of abandoning those whose lives he had shared. But the play itself is the evidence that he has no more escaped that past than have his family. For why else does he summon this world into existence but for the fact that the past continues to exert its power, as the guilt engendered by his abandonment pulls him back to those whose sacrifice he had believed to be the necessary price of his freedom. The play, in other words, is purely reflexive as Williams creates a play about a writer, named after himself, who dramatises his own life in order to exorcise the guilt which is the price he has paid for his freedom.

The metatheatrical element in Williams's work is central. The theatre was not only Williams's avocation, it was his fundamental metaphor. His characters tend to be writers and actors, literal or symbolic, who theatricalise their world in order to be able to survive in it. The theatre is their protection as it was Williams's. What it chiefly protects them from is time:

It is this continual rush of time . . . that deprives our actual lives of so much dignity and meaning, and it is, perhaps more than anything else, the *arrest of time* which has taken place in a completed work of art that gives to certain plays their feeling of depth and significance . . . In a play, time is arrested in the sense of being confined . . . The audience can sit back in a comforting dusk to watch a world which is flooded with light and in which emotion and action have a dimension and dignity that they would likewise have in real existence, if only the shattering intrusion of time could be locked out. The great and only possible dignity of man lies in his power deliberately to choose certain moral values by which to live as steadfastly as if he, too, like a character in a play, were immured against the corrupting rush of time.[21]

Williams's characters inhabit a linguistic universe which privileges the prosaic, the literal, the unambiguous; but they themselves speak another language. They claim the right to detach words from their literal meanings. They deal in ambivalence, the poetic, the allusive, the metaphorical. If at times they spill words recklessly, as Blanche does, in *Streetcar*, this is liable to be a defence against the real. More often they prefer silence, like Val in *Orpheus Descending*, Brick in *Cat on a Hot Tin Roof*, Shannon in *The Night of the Iguana* and Chris in *The Milk Train Doesn't Stop Here Any More*.

In *The Glass Menagerie* Williams is careful to distinguish between the constant flow of chatter from Amanda, a neurotic flood of language with which she seeks to still her fears, and the reticence and finally the silence of her daughter. In some ways speech is suspect. The gentleman caller, who disappoints Laura's hope of another life, is learning the art of public speaking, hoping that this will open up a clear path to power. He believes that language will give him control over a life that otherwise seems to be slipping away from him. There is little to suggest that it will. The only true moment of contact comes at the end of the play when the final scene between mother and daughter is played out as 'through soundproof glass'. Her speech stilled, Amanda suddenly has a 'dignity and tragic beauty'. Her daughter smiles a reply, her stuttering uncertainties calmed. Only the narrator, the poet (in effect the playwright) who summons up this scene, retains access to words, all too aware of their falsity and cruelty. Perhaps that is one reason why the dramatic symbol acquires the significance it does in his work.

For most of his life Tennessee Williams chose to dramatise himself as alienated romantic. A homosexual, at a time when this was illegal and in some states attracted severe penalties, he felt threatened and marginalised. A writer, in a culture which valued art merely as material product, he regarded himself as the victim of other people's ambition. His characters find themselves pressed to the very edge of the social world, face to face with their own desperation and with no resources beyond their powers of self-invention. In a world 'sick with neon', whose basis is identified by the young gentleman caller in *The Glass Menagerie* as 'Knowledge! . . . Money! . . . Power!', they struggle to survive.

Williams pictures a society on the turn. Not for nothing was Chekhov his favourite playwright. The southern setting of most of his plays suggests a culture whose past is no longer recoverable, except as myth, and whose future represents the threat of dissolution. Language has been evacuated of meaning, ironised by time. History has swept on by. Private illusions and public values are shattered by the quickening pace of a modernity that implies the corruption alike of style and morality. Art alone, it seems, has the power to halt, however momentarily, the rush towards extinction. And for Williams, writing was, indeed, a way of freezing time, of abstracting himself from process. It was a defence equally deployed by his characters who are all compulsive fictionalisers. Having run out of time and space they seek to shore up their lives with fragments of the past, invented or recalled, and elaborate fictions which confer on them a significance they could otherwise never aspire to.

The problem is that unless they can persuade others to join them in their illusions they are thereby condemning themselves to isolation. Safety seems to lie in flight. To rest for a moment is to risk definition, to risk being fully known, to become vulnerable. And yet flight is solitary and as such denies the only other consolation offered to his characters, love; but such relationships carry with them the potential for further pain, as virtually all of his figures discover.

For the most part his characters are without jobs or have simply fled them. Laura, in *The Glass Menagerie*, runs away from her secretarial course, Blanche, in *Streetcar*, is dismissed from her post as teacher, as Shannon, in *The Night of the Iguana*, is from his role first as a priest and then as tour guide. These are not people who work to play their part in the great commercial enterprise of America. They are not mesmerised, as is Miller's Willy Loman, by its dreams of wealth and success, though Maggie in *Cat on a Hot Tin Roof* and Brick in *Sweet Bird of Youth* feel its pull. They are damaged, emotionally, sexually. They are hyper-sensitive to their surroundings. They frequently tread the boundary of insanity, driven towards this territory partly by the callousness of others (as in *Streetcar*, *Suddenly Last Summer*, *The Night of the Iguana*) and partly by their own preference for the fictive, the imaginary, the unreal.

Tennessee Williams's characters resist being incorporated into other people's plots. They distrust alike the causal implications and the temporal logic of narratives which can have only one conclusion for them. They reject the characters offered to them – Blanche, the tramp, Val Xavier, the bum, Brick, the homosexual – and seek to neutralise the plots that threaten to encase them by elaborating their own. Theatrically, his plays reflect this process. Sets dissolve, time is made to reverse itself, lighting softens the hard edges of naturalism. The transforming imaginations of his characters find a correlative in a theatrical style which makes its own assertions about the relative values of the real and the fictive. Sometimes the imagination can be bizarrely destructive – as in *Suddenly*

Last Summer – more often it is offered as a transfiguring grace to those discarded by the plot of history and displaced from a narrative of national aggrandisement but still subject to its destructive drive. The structure of his plays reflects this resistance to a national plot which now included investigating committees and a distrust of the deviant. As he asked, somewhat plaintively, 'What choices has the artist, now, but withdrawal into the caverns of isolation?'[22]

Williams's plays are in effect elaborations of the metaphors they enclose: the glass menagerie, the anatomical chart (*Summer and Smoke*), the dried-up fountain (*Camino Real*), the burning rose garden (*Orpheus Descending*), the exotic garden and cannibalism of *Suddenly Last Summer*, the bound priest of *The Night of the Iguana*, the wasteland of *The Red Devil Battery Sign*, the house built over a cavern in *The Rose Tattoo*, or over a flooding river in *Kingdom of Earth*. In a note written in 1943 he had warned himself against an over-reliance on dialogue and committed himself to thinking in more directly visual terms, developing each play through a series of pictures. The note related to a forerunner of *A Streetcar Named Desire* but the commitment to images which crystalised the dramatic essence of a play remained, sometimes debased into crude and obvious metaphors, sometimes elevated into symbols which extended the thematic core of his plays.

The success of his first Broadway play, *The Glass Menagerie*, was considerable. It ran for 561 performances, but the new young playwright was in fact thirty-four years old and very conscious of the pressure of time. As he was later to imply, loss became a central theme. It was certainly a concern of the protagonist of his second great success, *A Streetcar Named Desire*. With an epigraph from Hart Crane which identified the fragility of love, it placed at its centre a woman herself acutely aware of loss and the passage of time, a woman, it seems, in her early thirties. Certainly she spends much of her time trying to conceal what she assumes to be the depredations of time and experience. She (and the world from which she comes) has lost something of her natural grace; her original vivacity has given way to artifice. Her marriage to a homosexual husband had in effect been a logical extension of her desire to aestheticise experience, her preference for style over function. Her entirely natural but cruel exposure of him, besides being the origin of a sense of guilt to be expiated by her own sexual immolation, is itself evidence of that neurotic recoil from the real which is the essence of her life. Indeed, in some sense her choice of this fey young man and of the adolescents with whom she subsequently conducts her empty relationships represents her desire to resist the implications of maturity. She does not want to be part of a world in which actions have consequences and in which the logic of relationship (in her sister Stella's case, courtship, marriage, pregnancy) pulls her into the narrative of history. She wishes to freeze time. It is not hard to see how her life mirrors that of the South, whose myths she in part embraces.

Desire may, as she believes, neutralise death but desire allowed to follow its course leads to death. Blanche needs the sanctuary implied by a relationship but she fears the trap which it represents. Perhaps that is why she is now drawn to another man whose sexuality seems in some way suspect, a mother's boy weak enough, she supposes, to be made to enact the essentially adolescent fantasies which she stage-manages with such care. Meanwhile, the relationship between her sister Stella and her Promethean husband, Stanley, must be destroyed not simply because he threatens to eject her from her last refuge (this he only does when she reveals herself as a threat) but because then the clock will be turned back. The two sisters will become as once they were, inhabiting a world that yields nothing to time, in which, like the South itself, the intrusion of the real can be denied. For the South is no less a conscious fiction, a deliberate construct, than is the life which Blanche attempts to play with true conviction. Blanche's life and the South alike become art objects, admirable for their style, compelling in their artifice but surviving only because they are no longer animate. Blanche enters the play, an actress creating her entrance. Her 'character' consists of a series of performed roles, constructions. 'You should have seen Blanche when she was young', says Stella. She is young no longer. Whatever was natural, whatever was spontaneous, whatever was true seems to have given way to performance. To be is to act; to act is to be. But her audience withdraws its belief – first Stanley, then Mitch, then Stella – and she is left, finally, an actress alone, her performance drained of meaning, inhabiting a world which is now unreal because unsanctioned.

At the other extreme, it seems, stands Stella, pregnant with life, generous in her affections and ready to acknowledge a natural process which pulls her even further from her origins and, by implication, ever closer to her end. Yet she, too, is forced to a refusal of the real at the end of the play, to a denial of the brute destructiveness of Stanley, a man who represents the forces which have thrust aside the myths of the past. Indeed that denial becomes as essential to her continued survival as Blanche's had to her. As the play's first director, Elia Kazan, recognised, she is doomed, too. Even Stanley now has to live a life hollowed out, attacked at its core.

When Blanche Dubois faces Stanley Kowalski, class and gender are in ambiguous confrontation. For Blanche is powerfully attracted by the social crudity and masculine directness which she simultaneously despises, as Stanley is fascinated by those very qualities of aristocratic arrogance and neurotic sexuality which he affects to hold in contempt. With echoes of Strindberg's *Miss Julie*, a play Williams had admired as a student, *Streetcar* explores the energy created across the gender and class divide. Like Chekhov's *The Cherry Orchard*, which he similarly admired, it focuses on a culture on the turn, an old world, elegant but reflexive, inward turned and inward turning, in process of surrendering to a new order, lacking the civility of a passing world but lacking, too, its neurotic, enervated products. There is an ambivalence, a doubleness which here, and throughout his career, takes him to the edge of androgyny. It is not merely that male and female are locked in a relationship that breeds cruelty and consolation, meaning and absurdity, in equal parts but that each represents part of a divided sensibility. Though in interview he was prone to celebrate Blanche for her courage in the face of the implacable, her own destructiveness makes her a deeply suspect source of values.

The androgynous had a powerful appeal to Williams. As he remarked, 'the androgynous is a myth . . . an ideal. You can seek it but never find it. However, the androgynous is the truest human being.'[23] Its power lies in its denial of definition, its functional ambivalence, its fusion of opposites, its transcendence of barriers. It was partly what drew him to Hart Crane. Gilbert Debusscher has commented on Williams's gloss on Crane's lines (from 'For the Marriage of Faustus and Helen'): 'There is the world dimensional for those untwisted by the love of things irreconcilable.' Acknowledging that it is open to multiple readings, Debusscher asks, 'Could he have meant that his vocation as a poet of extraordinary purity, as well as intensity, was hopelessly at odds with his nighttime search for love in waterfront bars',[24] a contradiction which precisely mirrored Williams's own. The yoking of a gentle, lyrical self to predatory sexual aggression was one he experienced as well as dramatised. His homosexuality, like Crane's, came to stand for him as an image of a revelationary contradiction. When Jessica Tandy, the original Blanche Dubois, objected to the use, for advertising purposes, of Thomas Hart Benton's oil painting of the poker night scene (the cast were to be posed in the same positions as those in the painting, for a *Look Magazine* photograph), a work that stressed the sexuality of Blanche and Stanley, Williams replied:

I have such a divided nature! Irreconcilably divided. I look at Benton's picture and I see the strong things in it, its immediate appeal to the senses, raw, sensual, dynamic, and I forget the play was really about those things that are opposed to that, the delicate half-approaches to something much finer. Yes, the painting is only one side of the play, and the Stanley side of it. Perhaps from the painter's point of view that was inevitable. A canvas cannot depict two worlds very easily, or the tragic division of the human spirit, at least not a painter of Benton's realistic type.[25]

But that division equally affects the individual characters. So it was that Kazan said of Brando, 'he is bisexual in the way an artist should be: he sees things both as a man and a woman'. It was that, too, that the critic Eric Bentley detected in his performance: 'Brando has muscular arms, but his eyes give them the lie . . . a rather feminine actor overinterpreting a masculine role.'[26] Later in his career Williams was to express satisfaction with the title of his play, *Something Cloudy, Something Clear*, precisely because it expressed 'the two sides of my nature. The side that was obsessively homosexual, compulsively interested in sexuality, and the side that in those days was gentle and understanding and contemplative.'[27]

Blanche may be the representative of a world of elegance and style corrupted by brute materialism but she is also the source of a cruelty which associates her most clearly with the death she seeks to neutralise through desire. Stanley may set his strength against Blanche's desperation but he has what Blanche does not, the ability to survive and dominate. Nor is he without tenderness, as Blanche is capable of a cold callousness. She is history as artifact; he is history as dynamic force.

In *Lady Chatterley's Lover* (originally entitled *Tenderness*) D.H. Lawrence distinguishes between a soulless sexuality, obsessive and self-destructive, and a sexuality which vivifies and regenerates the self through its surrender. Connie Chatterley knows both kinds. In *Streetcar*, Blanche and Stella represent those two opposing interpretations, two poles of experience. But such contradictions are, to Williams, the essence of human existence. As he explained, 'We love and betray each other in not quite the same breath but in two breaths that occur in fairly close sequence.'[28]

Williams's comment about the realism of Thomas Hart Benton, and still more his sense of the inadequacy of the two-dimensional nature of art, is a revealing one. It stands as an implicit claim for the potential of the theatre and for his belief in a drama that pressed beyond realism. *Streetcar* seems to replicate the world of 1920s and 1930s realism. The set appears to make a social statement, as the characters are hemmed in by surrounding tenements, while in the background we glimpse the flow of social life (emphasised still more in the London production). But Williams was not writing *Street Scene* or *Dead End*. His aim was to create a lyric theatre, a poetic theatre in which, as with a poetic image, opposites could be yoked together.

The virtue of the South, for Williams, as also the source of its particular pathos, lay in the fact that it had jumped the rails of history. Its psychological investment was in the past. As the twentieth century rushed away from it, the South became an aesthetic rather than a social fact. This had certain advantages. Taste and style could be retained as primary virtues; the vertiginous dangers that accompany maturity denied as time is frozen and reality transposed into myth. So it is that Faulkner's Quentin, in *The Sound and the Fury*, smashes his watch and seeks to isolate his sister and himself in such a way as to deny her organic need for change. But there is a price to be paid for such a refusal of life. Stasis slides into decay. Time, it appears, can only be denied at the level of the imagination, only sustained by a violence of thought or action rooted in a fear of natural process. So it is that Tennessee Williams's characters are in part the victims of modernity – inviting our sympathy and concern – and in part the enemies of all that is vital and unpredictable. Terrified of death, they become its collaborators imagining, as they do, that the world can be made to align itself to their demands for perfect order. The southern racist insists that the world conform to his will, accommodate itself to a model whose authority lies in its history; Blanche Dubois insists that it respond to her need for a life carefully shaped into art.

The gothic tinge to a number of his plays is an expression of this violence that seeps out of the culture like the juice from a windfall apple. This is a society which has lost its connection with the living tree. Its dissolution is only a matter of time. Blanche, in *Streetcar*, and Laura, in *The Glass Menagerie*, are perfect images of the world that they in part represent. Trapped in psychosis or stranded in an imagined world, they win immunity from time only by stepping into an existence where there is no love as there is no ageing. As Williams remarked, after writing these two plays, 'It appears to me, sometimes, that there are only two kinds of people who live outside what E E Cummings has defined as this "so-called world of ours" – the artist and the insane.'[29] In Williams's world the two are not always separable. They both exist within the shadow of artifice.

What Richard Gray says of Faulkner's language could be said with

equal force of Tennessee Williams's. It 'never ceases calling attention to
its artificiality. His prose is insistently figurative, intricately playful, as if
he were trying to remind us all the time that what he is presenting us with
is, finally, a verbal construct.'[30] Language is, indeed, the central device
with which his characters seek to shape their worlds. Blanche's mannered prose, her self-conscious archaisms, her strained lyricism is at the
heart of her attempt to generate a space which she can inhabit without
fear. Like Williams himself she uses language to pull her out of the
prosaic, the direct, the implacable. Her allusiveness, her irony, her
playful use of French to a man who understands nothing but his own
baffled need is an expression of her desire to evade too precise a
definition. What she seeks to accomplish in covering the lamp light for
fear that it will reveal the truth of her fast-fading youth, she also tries to
achieve linguistically. She recasts experience through the words with
which she chooses to engage it. She spins images and fantasies linguistically, hoping that these filaments will harden into a cocoon. Inside: the
butterfly. Outside: threat. The long series of disasters she has suffered
can be denied so long as they have not found their way into her language.

There is no denying Faulkner's love affair with words. His sentences
perform arabesques, words tumble out, pile up and finally exhaust themselves in the telling. Working with drama Williams is more constrained.
Only his characters can speak and their language is contained and
shaped by individual experience. But even so it is those who radically
recast language, force it to bear the imprint of their own needs and fantasies, who most clearly carry his sympathy. The poet, not the salesman;
the bohemian, not the businessman; the actor, not the politician.

Stanley Kowalski has no past. He comes into existence ready-made
and fully known. Directness is his keynote and his virtue. Blanche is quite
other. She is the end result of process. She resists the given and denies
all definition. An observation from Faulkner's *Requiem for a Nun* applies
with equal force to her: 'The past is never dead. It's not even past.' So,
the music playing when she forced her young husband to confront his
suspect sexuality still plays in her ears as the family history of debauch-
ery seems to be enacted in her own life.

Blanche is deeply narcissistic in a narcissistic culture. She transforms
her life into myth, demanding acquiescence in her own mythic inventions. The South itself scarcely does less. Her affairs with young boys and
a homosexual husband leave her if not inviolate at least untroubled by
consequences. Sex is emptied of its provocative implications. It becomes
reflexive.

The myth encloses Blanche. Stella could purge whatever inheritance of guilt she might have received. Blanche cannot. Denying herself or being denied the vivifying effect of marriage to the future, she is trapped in the past. The barren woman condemned to an asylum becomes a perfect image of the South. Why does she seek to transform experience with myth? Because she thereby removes its sting – the sting of death. As Frank Kermode observed, discussing Eliade's theory of myth: 'Myths take place in a quite different order of time – in *illo tempore* . . . *Then* occurred the events decisive as to the way things are; and the only way to get at *illud tempus* is by ritual re-enactment. But here and now, in *hoc tempore*, we are certain only of the dismal linearity of time.'[31]

Williams has said that:

I write out of love for the South . . . But I can't expect Southerners to realize that my writing about them is an expression of love. It is out of regret for a South that no longer exists that I write of the forces that have destroyed it . . . the South had a way of life that I am just old enough to remember – a culture that had grace, elegance . . . an inbred culture . . . not a society based on money, as in the North. I write out of regret for that . . . I write about the South because I think the war between romanticism and the hostility to it is very sharp there.[32]

Inadvertently, in the original production the play became more of a clash between North and South than Williams had intended. In his notebook for the production, Elia Kazan saw Stanley as representing 'the crude forces of violence, insensibility and vulgarity which exist in our South',[33] but because Marlon Brando's accent was incorrigibly northern it became necessary to adjust the slant of the play and even individual lines to make it clear that Stanley came from outside the South. In essence, though, what matters is less his origin than his force as a cold, pragmatic and powerful, if spiritually maimed, future.

The shock of *Streetcar* when it was first staged lay in the fact that, outside of O'Neill's work, this was the first American play in which sexuality was patently at the core of the lives of all its principal characters, a sexuality with the power to redeem or destroy, to compound or negate the forces which bore on those caught in a moment of social change. Familiar enough from *Lady Chatterley's Lover*, then still a banned book and indeed clearly a none too distant inspiration for Williams, it brought a dangerous *frisson* to the public stage. It was, of course, in his sexuality that Williams was most directly menaced by the public world. It is scarcely surprising, therefore, that, besides his faith in a Lawrentian revolutionising of a decadent culture, he should choose to make this the arena in which his plays had their being. With surprising consistency

Miller associated sexuality with betrayal and guilt. For Tennessee Williams it was otherwise: betrayal and redemption, torment and consolation. It provided the grammar of his drama.

These ironies intensified in his next play, *Summer and Smoke* (1948), though now they were spelled out with a clarity which obscured their real force. The tension in his work between the physical and the spiritual, in *Streetcar* and elsewhere contained within the sensibility of individual characters, is here flung off in pure form. The gap between the two parts of a riven sensibility is now crudely externalised and the ironic commentary which each constitutes of the other emphasised by a reversal too mechanical to be taken seriously. Although written at the same time as *Streetcar* (opening at Margo Jones's Dallas Theatre in the same year), it lacks its subtlety. There is an echo of Lawrence's image of the mind redeemed by the body but there is too much of the autodidact and the pedagogue to make it theatrically compelling.

John Buchanan is Stanley Kowalski with intellect, a Lawrentian Promethean 'brilliantly and restlessly alive in a stagnant society'. A doctor, he understands the physical basis of experience but is aware, too, of a sense of incompletion, being drawn to Alma Winemiller, whose first name, we are pointedly reminded, is Spanish for soul. She has a distaste for sexuality, which she keeps at a distance by an obscuring language no less than by her evasion of the relationship which might release her from her isolation. In the course of the play she seems to undergo a moral education, realising that the spiritual focus of her life has denied her the vivifying consolation of human relationships. What she fails to understand, however, is the need for a self in which the physical and spiritual combine. As a result the pendulum swings too far and she shows signs of embracing that empty sexuality which had characterised Blanche Dubois's relationship with strangers and the brittle relationship in which Lawrence's Connie Chatterley had engaged before the fulfilment offered by Mellors, a man and a force associated with the natural world. Meanwhile, Buchanan has moved the other way, embracing precisely that arid spirituality which he had once urged Alma to abandon. This simplistic irony is typical of a play in which character is subordinated to symbolic function and the stage is divided into discrete areas representing body, soul and eternity and dominated by a stone angel and an anatomical chart – a naive symbolism which offers a redundant correlative to the play's thematic concerns.

The essence of Laura and Blanche was that they had been simultaneously drawn in two different directions – out into the public world of relationship, of time, of process, and back into a private world where time is suspended and the self must substitute its own imaginings for the causalities and pain of an engagement with the other. In *Summer and Smoke*, *The Rose Tattoo* and *Camino Real* (1953), such tension is relaxed and externalised and as a result immobilised into pure image, *The Rose Tattoo* (1950), in particular, setting out simply to celebrate the Dionysian. One of his few comedies, it was inspired by his relationship with Frank Merlo, whose later death of cancer was to play its part in precipitating Williams's personal and artistic collapse. As a result it has an element of the carnivalesque, the ludic, the celebratory, as passion becomes an unambiguous value. Its energy, though, is too easily dissipated as character is pressed in the direction of comic grotesque.

The central character in *The Rose Tattoo* is a kind of Stanley Kowalski, lacking his cunning and presented with a rival more easily challenged and overcome, since all that stands between him and Serafina, the woman he loves, is the memory of her dead husband, a memory kept alive by an urn containing his ashes. The play, in other words, is a celebration of the life principle. But since the resolution is clear from the very beginning – the characters being wholly unambiguous – when it comes it carries little interest or conviction. In a way he was deliberately working against the assumption and the methods of his earlier success. Aware that *The Glass Menagerie*, *A Streetcar Named Desire* and *Summer and Smoke* had all drawn on the same experiences, he was afraid of falling into a predictable pattern. *The Rose Tattoo* and *Camino Real* in particular were his attempts to break this rhythm. But the generosity and openness of the former, in which all ambiguity is resolved in a sexuality and harmony that are untested and unquestioned, carry far less conviction than do the tensions and ironies of plays in which that ambiguity is definitional and, for their characters, in the end, disabling.

Camino Real was a far more radical effort on his part to challenge his own methods and assumptions. Indeed he liked to think that it was an open challenge to the realistic conventions of the American theatre that would liberate that theatre from its conservatism. As a play it owes something to the comic strip. Locating the action in a kind of spacial and temporal void, he fills the stage with characters from other works by other writers – Camille, Casanova, Don Quixote. These are mostly romantics brought face to face with the fact of death as they find themselves abandoned in a dusty town from which there appears to be no escape. Beyond lies only Terra Incognita, while in the town they are constantly menaced by the street cleaners, the agents of death who patrol the streets in search of victims. The central character is also a fiction, though one defined normally by his absence. Kilroy owed his identity to the name scrawled up by soldiers during the Second World War. 'Kilroy Was Here' was a joke difficult to decode. He was in a sense a gesture of resistance, both heroic and anti-heroic at the same time. The essence of Kilroy was that he could never be seen because he was always in the vanguard, always ahead of the game. He could never be caught.

But in *Camino Real*, as in so many other of Williams's plays, the free spirit is caged. Past tense changes to present. Now Kilroy is here. He has waited too long. He is trapped. From ironic hero he has been turned into eternal clown, a naive victim of experience. Denied the assumption that truth lies in movement, which is to say time, he has to plunder the moment for meaning. But he always learns too slowly to save himself from abuse and degradation. Meanwhile the romantic waifs who inhabit this world sustain their hope in the face of evidence of its fatuity, the absurd victims of their own romantic expectations. They are not without their consolation. The virtue of being trapped in the continuous present (which is the condition and precondition of theatre) is the possibility of connection with others who share the same moment, if not the same apprehension of the moment. But the vice of being trapped in that moment is that there can be no change, no growth. Life becomes aestheticised, theatricalised. So they become, like Vladimir and Estragon in *Waiting for Godot*, clown-like performers, absurd products of their own hopes.

Camino Real reveals a baroque impulse on Williams's part to allow his art to overspill its frame. In the 1960s it became commonplace for actors to invade the audience, thereby potentially, if not actually, redefining the nature of the relationship between audience and performer, underlining the degree to which the audience is implicated in the processes of theatre and the gestures and assumptions of performance. Tennessee Williams was doing this in 1953. It was, he insisted, a play in which he laid claim to a freedom which was equally a central object of his characters and an expression of his own need, as he saw it, to break out of a dramatic style and a thematic concern that had brought him such success but which was threatening to suffocate him. So he stepped not just outside the South but into nowhere.

Not only did he lay aside the figure of the fragile southern woman assailed by the real, he laid aside also the concept of character as a stable function of plot or a single governing imagination. And so characters from other plots settle down for a moment in his house of fiction while Kilroy proves no more substantial or resistant than did Nathanael West's

Balso Snell. West, however, felt no inclination to celebrate Balso Snell. Kilroy was too close to Williams's own image of himself as a butt of the gods for him not to feel a certain solidarity and compassion (lapsing into sentimentality). After all, this was to be his portrait of a non-conformist in modern society, an assurance of the bohemian's power to resist his degradation. But there was a paradox nestling at the heart of the play as characters seek a freedom denied by their status as objects of the writer's imagination. If some of them successfully escape the texts which entrap them, but which give them their significance, they do not escape the manipulative power of Williams who releases them from one fictional context only to place them in another. That absurdity works to neutralise the liberating power of carnival. Faced with the terror of Terra Incognita and with the ominous threat of the street cleaners (harbingers and celebrants of death), they cling together seeking in relationship that momentary annulment of absurdity that Williams liked to claim he knew so well in his life and purported to recommend in his work. As Marguerite Gautier (Camille) observes, 'although we've wounded each other time and time again – we stretch out hands to each other in the dark that we can't escape from – we huddle together for some dim communal comfort. But this "love" is "unreal bloodless" like a violet growing in a crevice in the mountain "fertilized by the droppings of carrion birds".'[34] Though such self-conscious rhetoric is not free from the romantic posturing for which she is known it seems to have more conviction than Jacques' reply that 'the violets in the mountains can break the rocks if you believe in them and let them grow'.[35] In Blanche's words, 'It's a Barnum and Bailey world.'

Camino Real was not a success. Critics regretted his abandonment of the poetic realism which they saw as his strength and were largely baffled by characters whose two-dimensionality was celebrated. The tightly controlled dramatic structure of the earlier plays here gave way to a series of loosely related scenes, images and gestures. The critical response left Williams embittered. Believing the play to have freed the American theatre of its commitment to realism, he was depressed by the failure of critics and audiences to respond to what he regarded as its openness of form and thought. Indeed so depressed was he by the failure of both this play and *Summer and Smoke* that he felt himself under pressure and reportedly even considered abandoning his career. Instead he completed his most successful work of the 1950s, *Cat on a Hot Tin Roof* (1955), a play which, apart from anything else, came close to moving his own sexual ambivalence to the centre of attention.

Margaret (Maggie the cat) is married to a former football star, Brick Pollitt, the son of Big Daddy. Big Daddy himself is dying of cancer and the future of his huge estate lies between Brick and his other son, Gooper. Though Brick is the favourite he has produced no sons and seems unlikely to do so, since his relationship with his wife has been seemingly destroyed by doubts about his own sexuality. Suspecting the nature of the relationship between her husband and his friend Skipper, Maggie provokes a sexual confrontation with that friend. His failure to perform leads directly to his death as Blanche's similar exposure of her husband's homosexuality had provoked his suicide. The logic of this situation leaves Brick suspended in self-guilt and doubt. Maggie, therefore, sets out to restore their relationship and thereby, as she sees it, secure the property rightly his; but Brick, now intent on blotting out the memory of his pain through alcohol, refuses the physical relationship she offers, unwilling to face his own ambivalence or the person who had forced affairs to a crisis.

On one level *Cat on a Hot Tin Roof* seems to offer a caustic account of a corrupting capitalism as Big Daddy and his wife plunder Europe of cultural artifacts which mean nothing to them and Gooper and his wife lay plans to seize the assets of a dying man. There is an irony, however, which the play scarcely begins to address. For the logic of the play proposes Brick's redemption through heterosexual intercourse, despite the fact that this is deeply implicated in the processes of capitalist succession. But, then, this represents only one of the paradoxes of a play in which a fiercely acquisitive greed is defeated by a yet more tenacious materialism, social deceit is challenged by a convenient lie, and accommodation to coercive social norms is presented as a value. It is a play in which Williams's social instincts are in evidence as he creates a portrait of a society whose corruption is reflected in the cancer eating away at the man who epitomises its pointless acquisitiveness and fierce egotism – Big Daddy. It is a world in which relationships are deeply implicated in the processes of exchange and transaction. Only that between Brick and Skipper seems to have an idealism which distinguishes it from all others. It is the more surprising, therefore, that the play is resolved by the reestablishment of a relationship re-forged by Maggie into an agent of capitalist greed. Brick must live with the person who 'raped' his friend as Stella has had to live with Stanley who had raped her sister. Her bold lie – that she is pregnant by a man who in fact shuns physical contact with her – must be transformed into truth if Maggie is to survive and Gooper be defeated.

The social logic of heterosexuality is clear; its moral logic, in the context of this play, less so. The estate had originally been accumulated by two homosexuals whose relationship, Williams pointedly tells us, must have involved 'a tenderness which was uncommon'. Brick's relationship with Skipper seems to have been characterised by a similar quality. To Arthur Miller, Brick has implicitly thrown down a challenge to the values of his society, a challenge which that society, through its representatives, refuses to acknowledge. More seriously, it is a challenge which he implicitly withdraws. In the version offered to director Elia Kazan there was no such accommodation. The play ended with Brick's response to Maggie's declaration of love: 'Wouldn't it be funny if that was true?', an echo of the irony which had concluded Hemingway's novel of mismatched sexuality, *The Sun Also Rises*. In the revised Broadway version the final speech is cut, Brick expresses his admiration for Maggie and her concluding speech is expanded, emphasising her strength and thus the likelihood of reconciliation. Kazan believed that there should be some evidence of a transformation in Brick's attitude in the face of his father's verbal assault. Williams objected that, 'I felt that the moral paralysis of Brick was a root thing in this tragedy, and to show a dramatic progression would obscure the meaning of that tragedy in him.' Nonetheless, he agreed to the changes that Kazan required, thus blurring the moral perspective of the play.

On the other hand, Brick's idealism is not untinged with an adolescent resistance to process. He wants to cling on to the world of college sports and male relationships and when that fails him he turns to alcohol. The crutches on which he hobbles (having injured himself trying to hurdle) are a patent symbol and literal demonstration of his inability to stand on his own two feet. We are offered, in other words, a choice between arrested development and commitment to a corrosive materialism. What Brick is converted to is the need to survive. Maggie the cat has clawed her way up to the point at which she dominates her circumstances. She refuses the role of victim. It is that lesson she passes on to Brick, won back to life or at least to the compromise which is apparently the precondition for life. But that saddles Williams with an ambiguity he is not disposed to examine.

The great strength of *Cat on a Hot Tin Roof* lies in Williams's ability to fuse the psychological, the social and the metaphysical in a play whose realistic set belies its symbolic force. This mansion, like Faulkner's, betokens power made simultaneously substantial and abstract, as religion – in the form of a grasping minister in pursuit of a large bequest –

represents a spiritual world corrupted by material values. This is a world in which the denial of reality is a primary concern. The clink of ice in a liquor glass, a record on a phonograph, are means to blot out other sounds, other thoughts. Words are designed to deceive, appearances to mislead. The bed which dominates the opening and closing scenes has been rendered ironic as its literal and symbolic functions have been denied by a man who fears the future it may engender. If Williams was wrong to accede to Kazan's request for changes (though his insistence that Big Daddy should reappear in the second act was doubtless correct) it remains a play whose subtleties go considerably beyond the sexual ambivalence which first attracted concern. For the *New York Times* reviewer, commenting on a 1975 revival, the political corruptions of Watergate had restored its concern with mendacity to its central role in the drama. Beyond the social lie, though, there are other deceits, more profound, more disturbing, which required no Watergate to validate them and which make *Cat on a Hot Tin Roof* the achievement that it is.

The disease from which Big Daddy suffers is uremia, defined as a 'poisoning of the whole system due to the failure of the body to eliminate poisons'. The disease from which his society suffers is essentially the same. Its governing principles are greed and mendacity and Brick, in common with Laura in *The Glass Menagerie*, is illequipped to survive. As she is drawn to the child-like mythic world of her glass animals he is attracted to the unproblematic mythic world of his former sporting successes on the football field and the track. When he tries to re-experience that world, however, he breaks his leg, tripped by a high hurdle as he has been immobilised by experience. In the same way the relationship with Skipper had been an attempt to deny process – a process which Big Mama identifies all too clearly: 'Time goes by so fast. Nothin' can outrun it. Death commences too early – almost before you're half acquainted with life – you meet with the other.'[36] The fundamental theme is thus Williams's perennial one, the losing game which we play with time, and the necessity, in Big Mama's words, 'to love each other an' stay together, all of us, just as close as we can'.[37] The irony is that none of the characters has succeeded in negotiating even this limited grace. If truth is in short supply then so too is love untainted by power. In revising the ending of the play Williams deflected irony in the direction of sentimentality, thus losing something of the force of a work whose achievement lay precisely in its refusal to capitulate to such a simple resolution. The incomplete sentences and tentative statements of hope subverted by cynicism now make way, in the revised version, to an overly explicit and over-written speech in which

Maggie spells out her redemptive role as Brick expresses his open admiration for her.

In the persons of Maggie and Big Daddy Tennessee Williams created two of the most powerful and original characters in American drama – one seemingly on the edge of death, the other on the edge of life. But the play's epigraph – Dylan Thomas's 'Do not go gentle into that good night . . . / Rage, rage against the dying of the light' – should not be seen as applying simply to the man whose roar of pain and terror sounds out with an energy rendered ironic by his circumstances. It applies with equal force to Maggie whose whole being is a resistance movement, a denial, a refusal. If she does not exactly pronounce Melville's 'No, in thunder!' she does pitch her whole self into a battle with the given. What Williams does not explore is the extent of her complicity with the forces she derides – as she exchanges truth for power – or the meaning of the life she is intent on creating by the force of her will and imagination.

Cat on a Hot Tin Roof has more than a little in common with two later works, both of which he was working on when *Cat* was still running on Broadway. *Orpheus Descending*, a reworking of his earlier disastrous *Battle of Angels*, dramatises a society in which corruption seems endemic and in which a brutal materialism has its sexual correlative. It is a corruption rooted in and exemplified by racism. Essentially the same point is made in *Sweet Bird of Youth* (1959) in which a southern racist takes his vengeance on those who would break out of a hermetic world of greed and power, a world in which sexuality is warped and deformed by those who acknowledge nothing but the authority of their own material needs.

In *Orpheus Descending* Williams dramatises the immolation of a Lawrentian fox set loose in a South dying of its own narcissism. Val Xavier has an animal vitality – a fact redundantly underlined by his snakeskin jacket. Lady, having lost her father to the violence of a group of racists, and her lover, David Cutrere, to a society hostess, marries Jabe Torrence, the owner of a dry goods store. Unbeknown to her, he had been one of her father's killers and now destroys her spirit. Then Val Xavier comes into town. He brings her back to life, a recovery symbolised by her pregnancy. When Jabe Torrence discovers this, however, he murders his wife and frames her lover, who is tortured to death. The only survivor is Carol Cutrere, sister to David, whose resolute bohemianism is a deliberate affront to the southern mores which condemn her.

Written before the Civil Rights movement made such a resolute condemnation of southern bigotry and racism fashionable, the play is as sharply political as anything Williams had written since his days with the

Mummers in St Louis. Indeed, there is an echo of that period in the fact
that Carol Cutrere had once protested over the Scottsboro case in which
nine black youths had been charged with the rape of two white prostitutes in Scottsboro, Alabama. Bessie Smith's death, purportedly as a consequence of the institutional racism of southern hospitals, is invoked
while Lady's father, we are told, was murdered because of his willingness
to serve alcohol to Negroes. In terms of the play, only his women resist –
Lady, the Sheriff's wife, Vee (an artist), and Carol Cutrere – and they have
no social power, any more than does Val. Nor can this Orpheus redeem
his Eurydice. The life which he offers her is instantly destroyed. Williams's
ironic invocation of one myth is designed to expose another. The South,
with its corrupt medievalism, its denial of history, its suspicion of a sexuality which may prove subversive, is dying of its own denials. Its darkness
is lit only by the glare of vengeful flames. Death, decay and disease
provide the imagery for a play in which refusal becomes a fundamental
trope. It is an intransitive society in a double sense. It refuses to abandon
its destructive myths and it fears a sexuality which may unite individuals
across barriers sustained by prejudice, a sexuality which stands as an
image of that natural process and development which is to be evaded not
least because it pulls the isolated individual into history. In a perverse way
the South inhabits its own destructive metaphor.

Writing in the context of a new production of the play in 1988,
Vanessa Redgrave remarked that

It's about dispossession – of Lady's people from the old country, of negroes, of
people like Val who have nothing and no place. It's about racism and intolerance, which leads to a society trying to destroy everything which doesn't fit in
with what it says it wants life to be about – leads it to kill Negroes, to kill Jews,
and if you're Sicilian and Roman Catholic, you're a wop, and wop comes from
guappo which in Neapolitan means thief. The character I play – known as a
wop bootlegger's daughter – is automatically therefore a thief.

But to her mind it was a play that had 'long ago stopped being a play
about a Southern problem, it's about an American problem, and now a
world problem'.

Williams saw his own fictions as challenging the fictions of the state,
the myths which had seemingly generated the energy on which America
had thrived. Those fictions were to do with authority, power, money, the
utility rather than the value of relationships. They had no place for the
loser, the bohemian, the artist. But though Val is destroyed, something
survives. As Vanessa Redgrave observed of the passing on of the protagonist's snakeskin jacket: 'to the generation that follows, on the shoul-

ders of those who've been destroyed, there are things passed on in the form of scripts, historical documents . . . the dead records of living history, that living people need. That's what Tennessee is saying.'[38]

The Negro conjure man is bedecked with talismans; Val's guitar is covered with the inscriptions of black musicians. These texts tell another story, identify another plot not delineated or dramatised here but running like a counter-current to the narrative of a dying civilisation. The Negro conjure man does not speak but utters a Choctaw cry. His magic is from another era, from a time before the world became 'sick with neon'. Then, the country was animated by wildness, now by a systematic cruelty designed to freeze the unpredictable and the vital into an unyielding and unchanging object, an icon to be worshipped. That history of animal vitality is inscribed in Val's snakeskin jacket, handed on at the end of the play to Carol Cutrere who walks out of the play as the Negro conjure man smiles his appreciation. It is hard, though, to take the gesture seriously, as Carol's resistance seems to offer little more than another desperate flight as another legless bird momentarily takes to the air. A girl 'not built for childbearing', she can do nothing to engender change, only to sustain the irony.

Orpheus Descending is not offered as a realistic portrait of the South, for all the anger which crackles through the text. Indeed, the stage directions repeatedly steer director and actors away from realism. We are in a gothic landscape. The images we are offered – darkness, cobwebs, dust, emptiness, dusk, skeleton – all suggest an unreal world, void of life.

On the one hand it is a play in which the gothic politics of the South – with its spectral white-sheeted bigots and dark-skinned unvoiced mystics – move to centre stage; on the other, this is a work in which absurdity is not only a social construct. The southern love affair with sanctioned violence, its desire to wrench experience into line with myth, is a losing game with death, but in that respect it merely reflects a fundamental condition. *Orpheus Descending* is Williams's version of the myth of Sisyphus, his *Waiting for Godot*. Those of his characters who have not chosen to embrace absurdity by enacting its ironies as social policy, killing life wherever it threatens to burst through the arid soil, are its victims through the persistent and self-mocking hope which they embrace. They try to outlive their fate, cling to notions of justice denied by the circumstances of their existence and look for a freedom which is merely another name for solitariness. They wait with no less resolution than Beckett's Vladimir and Estragon and with no more likelihood of a resolution to their questions. As Val observes,

What does anyone wait for? For something to happen, for anything to happen, to make things make sense . . . I was waiting for something like if you ask a question you wait for someone to answer, but you ask the wrong question or you ask the wrong person and the answer don't come. Does everything stop because you don't get the answer? No, it goes right on as if the answer was given, day comes after day and night comes after night, and you're still waiting for someone to answer the question and going on as if the question was answered.

For Val, the true state of the human predicament lies in a sentence of 'solitary confinement inside our own skins, for life!'[39] Only two consolations are offered: love and flight. But the commitments of the one conflict with the necessities of the other. When Val speaks of the legless bird that must die if it ever alights he describes himself destroyed by his love for Lady as by his implicit challenge to those trapped by their own past.

Lady seeks to defeat this absurdity by simple resistance – 'not to be defeated'. Defeat, though, is woven into the fabric of life in this play. Finally we are left with nothing but the paradox whereby the contingent power of art is pitched against the contingency it attempts to neutralise. So it is, within the play, that the Sheriff's wife, Vee, struggles to come to terms with the anarchic violence which she witnesses by turning it into art: 'Before you started to paint it didn't make sense . . . existence didn't make sense.'[40]

The absurd has never been wholly detached from the romantic impulse to pitch art against decay, but where the romantic leaves art its triumph and finds the gulf between experience and representation the source of sentimental regret, the absurdist finds only irony. A distrust of art is built into its central strategies. Indeed, in *Suddenly Last Summer* (called, by Williams, a fable of our times), which followed the relative disaster of *Orpheus Descending*, the writer is purely destructive while sexuality – specifically homosexuality – is seen as compounding the cruelty at large in the world.

Sebastian is a poet who produces only one poem a year, but there is something familiar in Williams's portrait of a writer for whom art is a means of resisting the chaos that menaces him, a chaos partly external and partly at the heart of his own imaginings. If we are back in the familiar morality play in which the rich are corrupt and corrupting, however, this time the principal corrupter is a writer. Sebastian is a homosexual who is eventually destroyed and consumed by those whose company he seeks. His literary talent is faltering. *Suddenly Last Summer* is a play that seems to express a number of private fears having to do with both

Williams's sexual identity and his avocation as a writer, and he later admitted that if the play had its roots in a 'developing tension and anger and violence' in the world, it also reflected his 'own steadily increasing tension as a writer and person'.[41] There is, as he admitted, an atmosphere of hysteria in his work. He is drawn to violence, often of the most extreme kind. It is as though he wants to put his characters under maximum stress, not, as in Miller's work, in order to test their authenticity, but to rupture the self, break open an identity exposed as a series of desperate performances. His own explanation for this obsession is his sense of contingency, his morbid fear of death. In a curious way the vivid deaths to which he consigns a number of his characters carry their own grace, not merely because such characters are the victims of a corrupt society but because they thereby refuse the definitional power of that society. *Suddenly Last Summer* is set in part in a mock jungle. Exotic plants frame the action. There is something elemental about this world in which physical need deploys its camouflages and develops its subtle strategies. Sebastian is a homosexual, but to set the stage for his seductions he peoples it with the help of Catherine, the lure who, in her semi-transparent swimsuit, must transform the beach into a place fit for sexual drama.

It is a play in which Williams turns metaphor into reality. Sebastian's need is all-consuming and he is himself duly consumed, literally fed upon by those he would attract. The god he worships is a cruel one and that cruelty is not deflected by his pretences to refinement. The poetry he produces is merely the brittle surface, the patina of culture that conceals the depth of his need and cruelty. It is hard not to see a personal dimension to this play. Certainly Williams's art co-existed with crude appetites which set him cruising the streets for sexual partners. He was acutely aware of a potentially destructive dualism to his sensibility. And there are other personal elements in a play in which Catherine is threatened with the lobotomy actually inflicted on his sister Rose, but then here, and elsewhere, the sensibility of his characters seems always on the point of dissolution. So, too, does the world they inhabit where for the most part power is in the hands of those who represent moral anarchy and whose sexual impotence stands for an apocalyptic potential. In *Sweet Bird of Youth* the southern racist Boss Finley desires his own daughter, an incestuous motif which reflects Freud's association of incest with anarchy. Himself impotent, or so it seems, he urges his daughter into relationships which will serve his political purposes. She, meanwhile, has contracted venereal disease from her lover and is incapable of bearing children while that lover is himself emasculated, at Boss Finley's command, on Easter Sunday.

Sweet Bird of Youth is a bitter play, touched by sentimentality. Chance Wayne, the protagonist, has already sold his soul for the success he equates with fulfilment while the fading movie star, through whom he hopes to advance his career in Hollywood, is also at the end of a personal road. The title of Princess Kosmonopolis is one she invents to console herself for her dwindling public significance. Having invested her whole being in such fictions, in the artificial performances which are the substance of her life no less than her career, she stands cruelly exposed when those performances are no longer observed (a theme which recurs in Williams's work). For a brief moment she finds consolation in her relationship with Chance Wayne, the consolation, Williams remarks, of those who face the firing squad together. When she is unexpectedly reprieved by Hollywood, however, she reinvests her role with energy and conviction, abandoning her lover to his fate. Williams toyed with the idea of allowing Wayne to escape, driving off with the Princess towards Hollywood. It is hard to believe that this would have been anything other than ironic, though, since we have already seen the consequences of inhabiting unreality in the person of the Princess herself.

Sweet Bird of Youth is another indictment of southern bigotry, another portrait of a terminal society trapped in its own myths and blind to the hermetic and incestuous implications of its denial of history. It is also yet another account of the corrupting power of time. So many of Williams's plays take as their protagonists those whose youth has slipped away from them, whose options have run out, whose lives bear the marks of disillusionment, that it becomes more a mannerism than a motif. His characters, no less than Beckett's, give birth astride the grave. As Chance Wayne observes, time 'Gnaws away, like a rat gnaws at its own foot caught in a trap, and then, with the foot gnawed offand the rat set free, couldn't run, couldn't go, bled and died.'[42] The cruel god of *Suddenly Last Summer* prevails.

This image was one he picked up again in his next work, *The Night of the Iguana* (1961), a play in which a group of individuals, whose lives have run down, come together 'like . . . actors in a play which is about to fold on the road, preparing gravely for a performance which may be the last one'.[43] Again the image of a failing theatre and the desperate performances it witnesses becomes a correlative for Williams's sense of a life emptied alike of function and purpose. Here, however, the desperation of his characters, symbolised by an iguana tied to a veranda by its foot

– as the play's central character, a defrocked priest and failed tour guide called Shannon, is tied to a hammock in his delirium – is banished by a simple gesture. The artist who creates the symbol dissolves it. The iguana is released, as is Shannon. The severity of Williams's vision is neutralised by a sentimentality which is always a presence in his plays. It is almost as if they reflect a mood swing – the ironies of his early plays being balanced by the comedy of *The Rose Tattoo*, the defeats of *Camino Real* by the victory of *Cat on a Hot Tin Roof*, the murderous traps of *Orpheus Descending* and *Sweet Bird of Youth* by the grace of *The Night of the Iguana*.

But such benign gestures were about to disappear from his work. The 1960s were to prove a personal and artistic debacle. His dependence on drink and drugs led him to the mental hospital and to the violent ward. Committed by his brother, as his sister Rose had once been committed by his mother, he came close to dying. The plays that he produced (*The Milk Train Doesn't Stop Here Any More*, *Kingdom of Earth*, *In the Bar of a Tokyo Hotel*, *The Mutilated*, *The Frosted Glass Coffin*) were often brutal, apocalyptic and death-centred. He frequently came close to self-parody, a kind of narcissism which reflected his paranoia and self-concern. His talent fed off itself and the effect was a series of shrill, neurotic appeals having to do with the intolerable pressures which threaten to destroy the sensitive, the poetic, the betrayed. Character is represented by little more than idiosyncratic speech patterns and mannered behaviour. Urging the centrality of human contact he created a series of grotesques, animated symbols, whose fate carries neither interest nor conviction. High-camp figures, they spell out their significance with an explicitness which squanders whatever expressive power might lie in action. Self-pitying, these plays moved his own condition to centre stage. Simplistic allegories about the compromises forced by experience and the depredations worked on body and spirit by mortality, they offer little more than attenuated reveries. Gestures at a wider social significance are perfunctory and unconvincing. Occasional lyricism collapses of its own weight, his language hollowed out, rooted in neither character nor situation.

Small Craft Warning (1972), originally, and significantly, called *Confessional*, represented a desperate attempt to recover lost ground but, in certain respects, it, too, proved ill judged. Once again we are in the presence of a group of people whose luck has run out, desperate, lonely, maimed individuals in search of momentary relief. But where once this had proved the substance of powerful drama, now it seemed an ironic echo. There is only a single voice, and that too thin and undifferentiated to command attention. Also, at a time when the mood of the American theatre tended to be confident and celebratory, when sexuality was deployed as an image of freedom and liberation, Williams's bleak dramas of defeat, of sexual depletion and spiritual collapse, seemed largely irrelevant. At a time when community was announced as a social virtue and adapted as a theatrical tactic and theme he chose to stress the collapse of relationship. At a time when the young took centre stage, celebrating the body and asserting their power over history, he focused on the dying, the wounded and the destroyed. The power which he had once been able to draw on from the public suppression of sexuality was now lost to him as its open and joyous expression undermined its subversive power.

The principal exception to this history of decline was the play that he worried away at throughout the sixties and early seventies – the play that most completely expressed his sense of the ambivalent nature of his own resort to theatre. Called *Two Character Play* when it was first produced in 1967, it became, significantly, *Outcry* in the early seventies. It is a play in which he squarely faces the metaphor which underlies so much of his work – the self as actor, society as a series of coercive fictions. The two characters, apparently ex-patients from a mental hospital and now ostensibly actors, play out their lives before an empty auditorium, literally trying to neutralise their fear through performance. The mask is the only reality; nothing is certain. We are, indeed, dealing with the ostensible, the apparent, the seeming. This is Beckett's world. It is governed by an irony which can only be acted out and not transcended. The tension no longer comes, as once it did, from the space which opens up between illusion and the real. Now it is generated by the language itself, brittle, incapable of sustaining communication. The self threatens to dissolve. Even gender roles are unclear, both characters having names which are ambivalent. The blurred identity of androgyny merely underlines the equivocal nature of experience. It is no longer a case of resisting the real with the strategies of the theatre, offering the performed life as a subversion of the real. Now the theatre becomes a governing trope. For Williams, who was trapped in the echo chamber of his own emotions, the play expressed his sense of imprisonment but equally his fear of abandoning familiar structures and beliefs. When one of his characters cries out against the anarchy of improvisation she reflects a fear likewise felt by Williams himself, just as the figure of an old painter huddled in rigor mortis before a blank canvas 'tea kettle boiled dry' reflects the fear of silence which kept him writing and rewriting until the last. At least to act is to convince yourself that you are still alive; to write is to resist a blankness which is no longer that of possibility, but that of nullity. But Williams's characters have a grace or suffer a pain denied to Beckett's. For the most part they know their predicament.

His characters had always been self-conscious actors (sometimes literally, as in *Sweet Bird of Youth*, sometimes figuratively, as in *Streetcar*), playing out their roles in the desperate hope of finding a sympathetic audience, proposing their own theatricalising imagination as a valid opposition to a world which otherwise seemed so prosaic and unyielding; but with *Outcry* this process became central. In this play a brother and sister find themselves in an underground theatre in an unspecified country. The doors are locked so that there is no escape. Apparently abandoned by their company, there is nothing for them to do but speak their lines with diminishing confidence, perform their lives even if that performance has been drained of meaning. The audience, if it ever existed, disappears, leaving them to enact a play, apparently based on their own lives, in an empty theatre. They have no alternative but to continue their performance though, denied an audience, they are denied equally the significance which that audience might have been prepared to grant to that performance. These are no longer figures with a choice. The theatre is the condition of their existence; acting the only verification of their being.

In the late seventies Williams wrote a series of plays in which he revisited his youth: *Vieux Carré* (1977), *A Lovely Sunday for Crève Cœur* (1979) and *Something Cloudy, Something Clear* (1981). A sense of doom seems to hang over them, projected backwards to the 1930s and 1940s. Young hopes and young friends are recalled, though now the irony that surrounds them seems to glow. Nothing lasts, nothing, that is, except perhaps the work of art which thereby falsifies the world it offers to portray. His plays had always borne directly on his life, but with the years the degree of refraction lessened until he began to write more and more directly about himself as blighted young poet or debilitated artist for whom writing was a way of denying his mortality. His subject, indeed, had in some essential way always been the artist, and at the end of his life it was to that that he returned with *Clothes for a Summer Hotel* (1980), a play about Scott Fitzgerald, whose own self-image was in many respects so close to Williams's. For Fitzgerald, no less than his creation Gatsby, was his own Platonic creation. It is hard to imagine anyone more dependent on performance than Fitzgerald and Zelda – a fact acknowledged by Williams in a stage direction which insists that, though at times the dialogue which he writes for Zelda might be tentative and though her words might fail to communicate, her 'presentation – performance – must'. Much the same could be said of Williams himself.

Williams was afraid that insanity and creativity derived from the same source. In *Clothes for a Summer Hotel* Zelda Fitzgerald talks of escaping 'into madness or into acts of creation'. The real is unendurable but the alternative carries the threat of dissolution. Towards the end of his career Williams seems to have become increasingly alive to the limits of language. Here Zelda's words blow away in the wind. In a late screenplay, *Secret Places of the Heart*, Janet is a speech therapist who rescued her husband-to-be, Sven, by pulling him into a linguistic world. Her commitment ends his aphasia. But she herself ends up in a mental hospital, separated from her husband, and when he visits her to explain that he will not be returning, making his life with another woman, she becomes catatonic, while he virtually loses the power of speech. Her final reconciliation to her fate is signified by her uttering a single word. In the face of real need, of the limits of experience, language fails. It is, perhaps, what made the theatre such an expressive form for Williams. It is what lies beyond a purely verbal language.

For Tennessee Williams, the social world – the world of power, authority, history, time – is perceived only indefinitely. It is a sense of menace, a corruption, a pressure which bears on the self but is not implicated in that self. That public world is seen only through a peripheral vision; its existence can be presumed to the extent that we see its consequences. Instead, by a trick of perspective, the marginal moves to the centre of our attention. The dispossessed are reinstated, as the artist redresses the balance in their favour. The problem is that the imagination thereby becomes complicit in the absurd. For its gestures imply the possibility of suspending process, of shaping order out of chaos, of winning a reprieve from the very forces whose authority had created the necessity for such imaginings. It is the absurdity which holds his characters in thrall; it is equally the absurdity which his work exemplifies even as it offers to resist it. The desperate fictions of his characters, whose lives have reached their apogee and who can look forward only to a decline whose reality they choose not to confront, are purely contingent. They try to live with compromise, to soften the edges of a reality which they see as threatening. What others may see as lies they cling to as strategies of survival, but when the real exerts its authority they have only two real choices: submission, a kind of martyrdom, as Williams permits them a ritual death; or insanity, as they let go of the world which torments them, and myth, illusion or the lie subsume them completely. They have staged a rearguard action against the implications of their own humanity, and lost. They have struggled to live on the other side of despair. They have aestheticised their lives, becoming themselves fictional constructs. But if that buys them a limited and temporary immunity it does so at the cost of that physical contact which is their only other antidote to the absurd – an antidote, however, which pulls them back into the world which torments them.

In 1960, on the very verge of his vertiginous plunge into the drink and drugs which came close to annihilating his personality, Williams remarked that 'When the work of any kind of creative worker becomes tyrannically obsessive to the point of overshadowing his life, almost taking the place of it, he is in a hazardous situation. His situation is hazardous for the simple reason that the source, the fountainhead of his work, can only be his life.'[44] It was a prophetic remark, for, to a remarkable degree, that proved to be his fate for the best part of two decades as he fed off his own creative fat. In so far as, like their creator, his characters lost their grip on a world against which they could define themselves, they inevitably lost definition. He and they needed resistance. The subversive power of his homosexuality disappeared with its legalising. His sympathy for the poor and disregarded lost conviction as he himself claimed the rewards of fame. Far from being marginalised, the author was frequently feted. He could even buy a limited immunity with alcohol and drugs in a culture which no longer regarded either as particularly deviant. Dramatic attention, meanwhile, had switched elsewhere – to the hyper-realism, the demotic prose, the forceful metaphors of David Mamet and the lyrical, oblique myths of Sam Shepard. The curious accident of his death (he choked to death on the plastic cap of his medication bottle) itself seemed like a casual afterthought of fate.

But there were real signs of recovery at the end as he began self-consciously to explore the mechanisms of his own art and the ironies implicit in an artistic life whose central strategy was a reflection and extension of that adapted by his characters as they worked their way down their personal Camino Real.

Williams did concern himself with moral value. Indeed he insisted that the 'great and only possible dignity of man lies in his power deliberately to choose certain moral values by which to live', adding, interestingly, 'as steadfastly as if he too, like a character in a play, were immured against the corrupting rush of time'.[45] He knew well enough that, as he said, 'there is no way to beat the game of *being* against *non-being*'.[46] How, then, invoke a moral world? The answer is to be found or at least sought in the paradox that lies in an art that seeks to transcend death by mimicking its processes. In stopping time his characters precipitate their own annihilation, but they also force the moment to surrender its meaning. The imagination which lifts them out of the world simultaneously suggests that things can be other than they are. That is what made Williams's therapeutic gestures have the undoubted public power that they do. His plays are all in some fundamental way debates with himself. He is both Tom Wingfield, the poet who escapes, and Laura, the poet trapped in her own inventions; both the spiritual Alma, in *Summer and Smoke*, and the physical John Buchanan; both Val Xavier, in *Orpheus Descending*, who dies, and Carol Cutrere, who lives; both Brick, the defeated, in *Cat on a Hot Tin Roof*, and Maggie, the survivor. But these personal debates became something more. Concerned, as they are, with a divided self, a split between the body and soul, mind and imagination, the death instinct and the life instinct, they claimed and had a relevance beyond Williams's own divided personality.

The British poet and novelist George MacBeth reminds us of Kafka's remark that a good book is an axe for the sea frozen within us and that even the most private of visions may shed light, like a chandelier, into the dark corners of other lives. But, as he insists, it is not any private authority of the grief or the sense of loss or pain which matters: 'that is the fallacy of those who admire their own sadness too much. One life', after all, 'is much like another. What matters is the shape and pattern provided by the chandelier maker. The light comes from the form, not the substance.'[47] So it proved, for Tennessee Williams.

CHAPTER FOUR

Arthur Miller: the moral imperative

Any account of post-war theatre in America must begin not with the war, which (besides the plays squirrelled away by an alienated O'Neill) produced virtually nothing of any note and was directly shared by only a fraction of the American people (and certainly by none of the major playwrights who were to dominate the next three decades), but with the Depression. It was an experience that shaped both Arthur Miller and Tennessee Williams who began to write not in the forties but in the thirties, the former creating a series of protest plays, the latter working with a radical theatre company. This pre-history formed many of their assumptions, defined their themes and explains something of the pressure exerted on their characters. Often plays apparently set at other times seem to bear the impress of the thirties, from *All My Sons* and *Death of a Salesman* through to *The Price*, from *The Glass Menagerie* and *Orpheus Descending* through to *Sweet Bird of Youth*. The loss of dignity and self-assurance which Miller saw as one legacy of the Crash clearly left its mark on Willy Loman as it did on Amanda Wingfield. The sense of promises turned to dust, of the individual suddenly severed from a world that had seemed secure, underlies much of their work. The shock which both writers express seems to derive from their sense of the fragility of the social world, the thinness of the membrane that separates us from chaos. That conviction was shaped by the events of a decade that began with economic debacle and ended with war in Europe.

Miller has been pulled, again and again, back to that traumatic decade, even in the 1960s and 1970s: *After the Fall, The Price, The American Clock* all return, in part or in whole, to that moment when time ran out on a particular version of America. Williams simply shifted his focus away from society and on to the individual left watching the twentieth century sweep by (a reference to Hart Crane's *The Bridge* which Williams used as an epigraph for *A Streetcar Named Desire* and which refers to more than the train which once rumbled out across America). In his plays the wealthy tend to be afflicted with disease, the pure in heart to fight a losing game with mortality and the material world alike. He understood what it was to be relegated from the great American game, to be a spiritual hobo in a world in love with success. Miller, too, knew the price exacted for too complete an embrace of the ideology which fuelled American expansion. He had, after all, witnessed all too directly its effects on his own family. Somehow what it seems to have done to both men is to convince them that there is an underlying structure of human need which becomes immediately apparent only when the fantasies implode, the surface significances are stripped away. During the Depression social aspirations, class presumptions, national myths seemed suddenly irrelevant. The only imperatives were those to do with survival, the only relationships of value those generated by genuine human necessity. Authenticity was no longer to be confirmed by a social system whose integrity and even practical viability were now profoundly suspect. On the other hand the new myths of Marxist–Leninism exerted no more than a momentary pull. In the end both men looked further back. Miller was drawn to a time when the social system was responsive to individual conscience, even to the extent of trying to negotiate a contract between the individual and the state (*The Crucible*). He looked for a relationship between the self and an environment undamaged by modernity (*Death of a Salesman*), a world governed by ancient principles of justice which are breached only at mortal peril (*A View from the Bridge*). If the banality of evil threatened to dissolve that sense of a human community on which personal dignity and identity depend, then he invoked an individual whose grip on present value was a consequence of his grasp on past tradition (*Incident at Vichy*), as he did an elderly Jewish philosopher to counterbalance the self-dramatising egotism of modern man (*The Price*).

Tennessee Williams chose to step outside of time altogether. The modern world exists as threat. Its political perversions, its physical oppressiveness and its spiritual and sexual debilitations leave the individual with nowhere to go but a reinvented past, a place of the imagination where neither moth nor rust doth corrupt but where life can, finally, only exist as an aesthetic gesture.

Miller has the realist's concern to offer a densely populated social world. His characters are manufacturers, salesmen, longshoremen, lawyers, surgeons, policemen, writers; they constitute the society whose values they both exemplify and betray. Williams's characters are failed typists, dismissed teachers, itinerant musicians, ex-athletes, unrecognised poets, unsuccessful actors, disqualified doctors, defrocked priests;

in short, the neurotic, the betrayed, the discarded, the marginalised. They exist at a tangent to the social world whose centrifugal force has flung them to the periphery. They represent an alternative world which exists on sufferance and only so long as its imperatives do not come into conflict with those of a world whose axial lines are defined by power and money.

Both men challenge the presumptive myths of their society, the one choosing to attack from within, the other from without. Williams's characters are artists or performers who have lost their audience. Laura sets her solitary stage of fragile characters in *The Glass Menagerie* as Blanche Dubois designs the lighting and creates the *mise en scène* for a drama which will eventually plunge her into a world of total unreality in *A Streetcar Named Desire*. Brick, in *Cat on a Hot Tin Roof*, remembers a time when he was in the centre of an arena of attention as, once, Shannon in *The Night of the Iguana* played a central part in the rituals of the church. Chance Wayne, in *Sweet Bird of Youth*, aspires to be an actor, Kilroy in *Camino Real* acts as a clown while Val Xavier in *Orpheus Descending* wears his theatrical costume. Eventually, in *Two Character Play*, the theatrical metaphor becomes the total condition of existence. The writer pitches his imagination against the prosaic and the literal, aware that the price of too complete a commitment to the transforming mind is a loss both of the real and of human connectiveness.

Miller's characters seem always to be defending themselves against an accusation, sometimes spoken (*All My Sons*, *Death of a Salesman*, *The Crucible*, *A View from the Bridge*, *Incident at Vichy*, *The Archbishop's Ceiling*, *The Ride Down Mount Morgan*), sometimes merely implied or self-directed (*The Man Who Had All the Luck*, *After the Fall*). Only in *The Crucible* is there a literal courtroom (though lawyers appear with surprising regularity) but the courtroom is implied in much of his work. Matters of innocence and guilt are debated as the public consequences of private acts are explored. His characters spend much of their time rebutting charges whose justice they acknowledge even as they are rejected. They are people who try to escape the consequences of their actions, who try to declare their innocence even when that involves implying the guilt of others. The process of his plays is one that brings his characters into confrontation with themselves, a confrontation which, in the plays of the 1940s and 1950s, was liable to lead to death, but in the later plays to a grace of one kind or another.

Miller derived from Ibsen and Shaw the significance of social causation; where he felt they fell short was in the degree to which they believed this to offer a total explanation. The essence of his concern seems clear enough and it lies in the necessity to resist such determinism in the conviction that the self is not a product alone of the forces that bear upon it. In that context theatre itself becomes an act of resistance – resistance to anarchy, time, process: in short, to mortality.

The American theatre of the forties and fifties was more intensely psychological than that of the thirties. Energy which had once been directed outwards in a project of social transformation or regeneration was now turned inwards. In a curious paradox, the Depression, which exposed the economic and social determinisms of the capitalist system, inspired a drama which celebrated the resistant spirit and presumed that history would bend to the will and the imagination. All that was needed was to awake and sing and the song was to be one of human solidarity. A similar solidarity had been demanded by wartime urgencies. The war over, and the simplicities of thirties politics cruelly exposed, America resumed its material destiny. But this was now a culture less secure, less able to invest its myths with the force of reality.

The war's legacy was a deeply ambiguous one. For a Jew such as Arthur Miller the lessons of the camps could be nothing less than profoundly disturbing. The arrival of the nuclear age brought with it its own paranoia which stained the political life and social relations of a nation whose centrifugal force had always had to be self-consciously countered by centripetal images, from the flag to a coinage nervously insisting *e pluribus unum*. Insecurity about national identity and social cohesion could only be underlined by the dark force of an investigative committee implicitly charged with the task of defining Americanism by identifying and purging its opposite. The war and the political embarrassments of the decade which preceded it effectively blocked easy access to the past. It was as though the individual were in a temporal void, a mood caught by Saul Bellow's dangling man, in the novel, and by Miller's Willy Loman and Williams's Blanche Dubois in the drama. The past exercised a disabling power but it could not be unambiguously claimed. At the same time such characters were baffled by a present whose urgencies seemed to bear no relation to their needs. In the terms of the sociologists of the period they were profoundly alienated.

As America once again made consumerism a value and went about that business of conspicuous consumption identified half a century earlier by Chicago bohemian Thorstein Veblen, a new bohemianism expressed the unfocused dissent of a group of artists and writers. But the Beats – the primary focus of this dissent – ignored the drama. They preferred the chanted rhythms of free verse or the loose structure of the autobiographical novel whose reveries were subject to fewer formal constraints. Tennessee Williams's bohemianism was of a different kind. The sub-culture of the homosexual could not, until considerably later, openly acknowledge the cause of its disaffection, which was accordingly deflected into metaphors in which relationships bred a terrible vulnerability and the self was threatened with dissolution. Arthur Miller's alienation was different again. Unable to conceive of the individual outside a social context he found himself desocialised, excluded by a political system that regarded his kind of moral conviction as dangerously destabilising.

This was the age of the loyalty oath, in which inclusion in the social community had to be purchased with disloyalty to fundamental tenets of America's democratic heritage. The Orwellian newspeak of the House Un-American Activities Committee served to identify the degree to which language itself became a central issue. The language of the state, of the advertising which fuelled the new consumerism, and of the business corporations, whose own structures offered a substitute for that sense of community increasingly eroded by the fragmenting power of the urban and suburban world, all celebrated conformity. Willy Loman's conversation is sprinkled with references to consumer products and to the advertisements which recommend them. It is a language curiously detached from his being. Indeed he is so prone to reverse himself within the space of a few seconds that it is clear that this language has no real roots in his consciousness. But he feels obliged to deploy it; it is, he thinks, the code that will unlock the life he believes himself to desire. There is, however, a counter-current in Willy's soul, a current that never fully catches him, but which is Miller's reminder of another set of possibilities. His characters, accordingly, have to feel their way back to a language of mutual responsibility and personal identity which owes nothing to the banalities of the Organisation Man (as defined by William H. Whyte) or to the callow sentimentalities of a past reshaped by memory. They have to move towards the moment in which they can speak their lives as Tennessee Williams's characters resist the prosaic language which seeks to contain and define them. They are engaged, in other words, in a debate over the nature of the real.

Against the rather drab background of 1950s America Williams's plays seemed exotic and subversive. They placed sexuality at the centre of dramatic attention and hinted at a connection between that sexuality and violence. The morality of his plays seems to reside not in his endorsement of familiar pieties or even in the acknowledgement of the power of conscience but in the legitimacy of the imagination and the necessity for compassion. When he said of his own work that he wished to escape the constriction of realism because truth, life, or reality is an organic thing which the poetic imagination can represent or suggest only through transformation, through changing it into other forms than those which merely present appearances, he was not only describing his own approach to theatre but also his characters' attitude to their own lives. In his case, denial of realism was also a denial of the authority of the actual. Unlike Miller he grants no presumptive power to the past, no moral demand rooted in simple causality. The contingent is too powerful for that. Like Miller, his characters deny the legitimacy of power born out of political or economic hegemony. Concerned, as they both are, with redefining the real they resist the closed nature of realism, its definitional power, for, after their early works, their characters do not come fully formed into the world of the play. They are in some degree their own invention as they reassemble the fragments of experience in an attempt to track down a meaning that evades them.

Miller himself began with a frontal assault on the evils of capitalism. His early, unpublished plays, written when he was a student and struggling writer, equate big business with gangsterism and corruption. Virtue resides in the individual who lends his weight to the cause of the common man. Family loyalties defer to social needs; the union movement stands between the worker and those who would exploit, degrade and destroy him. Motives are clear; language is crystalline, a glass through which we can observe social process; dramatic plot mirrors the plot of history. These are social plays in the sense that they conceive of society as an object, a mechanism whose workings can be exposed by the processes of theatre. They are analytic in intent. There is little doubt as to the nature of the real which is slowly exposed to the protagonist's developing consciousness. The space for human activity seems drastically reduced, defined by the work-bench, the factory floor, the prison cell. But another world exists in embryo, struggling to be born. It exists, however, only at the level of rhetoric – a series of abstract propositions having to do with a restored sense of human unity to be won in the face of a dehumanising system – but the promise is enough to inspire sacrifice, the surrender of the self for the self's true redemption.

Then, something changed. Even *All My Sons*, written during the war, though produced after it, revealed a sense of ambiguity, not, perhaps, dramatically functional but intellectually undeniable. To be sure, the logic of business still cut a vector across human necessities, but the confident moralism of the earlier plays began to fade. As a result *All My Sons* is far closer in spirit, and in detail, to Ibsen (most especially *The Wild Duck*) than were any of those earlier plays. Suddenly, the demand of the ideal, as Ibsen's character had called it, was itself seen as suspect, as stemming from a sensibility determined at all costs to sustain its own innocence. The ideal becomes tainted and the very Manichaean vision that had generated the energy behind those early, unpublished works, reveals itself as deeply suspect. It was a theme he could not then develop. The urgencies of the war suggested other priorities, urged a more absolute morality. But the end of the war, the morally ambiguous fact of two atom bombs exploded over major Japanese cities, and the slide towards what had once been called normalcy, changed the context and the force of Miller's drama. Joe Keller – an industrialist who allows faulty engine parts to be forwarded to the Air Force rather than prejudice his contract – fails to acknowledge a basic human tenet. Until the final moment of his life he refuses to accept his responsibility to a wider community than that constituted by his own family, to ideals beyond the pragmatics of business. However, his son Chris also fails, and that failure is the more significant because he is in direct line of descent from Miller's own earlier protagonists who had so confidently called the world to moral attention. He fails because in accusing his father he seeks a personal ambition. Righteousness and self-righteousness become confused. His father's guilt becomes entwined with his desire to declare his own innocence and, as Miller has said in his autobiography, innocence kills. So it is that a play that seems to recreate the mood and tone of Steinbeck's *The Grapes of Wrath*, a work that also celebrates the community of man, becomes, at least potentially, something else. The ideal is exposed as tainted, motives are seen as confused and suspect, social justice as compromised by private desires. The smooth surface of social commitment is pitted with ambiguity, but then for Miller betrayal has always been a central concern, the betrayal of the individual by social values, of social values by the individual, of the self by its own necessities.

Arthur Miller's father was all but illiterate; his mother loved books. His father was a businessman, committed to the values of business; his mother despised those for whom business was a total world. As Miller explained, his mother and he were linked not only in appearance but in 'our outspoken conspiracy against the constraints and prohibitions of reality'. It might almost have been Tennessee Williams speaking, but where Williams tended to celebrate the individual in recoil from the real,

Miller, from the beginning, acknowledged society's claim on the self, though in many of his plays the divergent values which he associated with his parents are dramatised through pairs of characters who represent the material and spiritual poles of human experience (Abe and Arnold Simon in *They Too Arise*, Joe and Chris Keller in *All My Sons*, Happy and Biff Loman in *Death of a Salesman*, John and Elizabeth Proctor in *The Crucible*, Moe and Lee Baum in *The American Clock*), even if by the 1960s these binary pairings were suffused with irony. It is almost as though he were trying to strip the sensibility into its component parts, to stage the contending elements not only in his own nature but in a human nature divided against itself; and though his plays are scarcely Shavian they do share with Shaw's a dramatic strategy that turns on contending interpretations of experience brought into conflict. There is, buried none too deep in his work, a debate which gives plays such as *All My Sons*, *The Crucible*, *The Price* and *Incident at Vichy* their polemical edge; but, unlike Shaw, Miller seldom allows the dialectic to dominate character.

In becoming a writer, Miller was aware that he was choosing sides between his parents. 'To become a reader meant to surpass him [his father], and to claim the status of a writer was a bloody triumph; it was also a dangerously close identification with my mother and her secret resentment, if not contempt, for his stubborn incapacity with words.'[1] But guilt can prove as ineluctable a bond as love, or so it seemed in his first two Broadway successes, while the contention between his parents was still exercising its power over his imagination in the 1960s, with *After the Fall*, and the 1980s, with *The American Clock*.

Nor is *All My Sons* the only one of his plays in which articulateness is itself seen as profoundly suspect, for in a way that seems to be his inheritance, a suspicion of thought that makes its way too completely into language; an acknowledgement of the reality and power of the deeply inexpressible.

In his autobiography, *Timebends*, Arthur Miller recalls Archibald MacLeish's remark that the essence of America lies in its promises. Himself the son of an illiterate immigrant father, who had risen to wealth only to lose it in the Depression, Miller absorbed the double lesson offered by hope and disillusionment.

His own flirtation with communism as a student was simultaneously a blow struck at his father – an enthusiastic capitalist – and an act of absolution, as he simultaneously offered him an explanation for failure which required no complicity in his own fate. Feeling his father to be a failure, he felt, too, a kind of freedom to begin anew, undefined by a past which anyway lay partly in another country – the Poland from which his parents derived. Indeed, Miller is prone to see in this a general principle equally applicable to Fitzgerald, Faulkner, Hemingway, Wolfe, Steinbeck, Poe, Whitman, Melville and Hawthorne. It is, he suggests, as though

the tongue had been cut from the past, leaving him alone to begin from the beginning, from the Creation and from the first naming of things seen for the first time . . . American writers spring as though from the ground itself or drop out of the air all new and self-conceived and self-made, quite like the business-men they despise. It is as though they were fatherless men abandoned by a past that they in turn reject, the better to write not the Great American Novel or Play, but verily the First.[2]

This was a process which the Crash seemed to validate, proof that the past – its values, its promises, its supposed realities – had very little rele-vance to a new generation that had to construct itself in the knowledge that all gods were dead, all faiths void, all promises mere deceptions. The animating myths of American society, which had sustained it through its years of growth and plenty, seemed the first and primary victims of a collapse which might be economic in form but which was more pro-found and more disturbing than a mere betrayal of financial hopes. As Miller insists, the Depression 'was only incidentally a matter of money. Rather it was a moral catastrophe, a violent revelation of the hypocri-sies behind the facade of American society.'[3] One response was to embrace the secular faith of Marxism – an absolute in a relativistic world in which even the tenets of that most American philosophy, pragmatism, suggested the inutility and hence the falsity of American capitalism. The rapid failure of that new social god, which had promised a brotherhood apparently so compatible with American notions of equality as laid down in the Declaration of Independence, resulted in a double disillu-sionment for many. But though Miller flirted with Marxism he was never committed to it and therefore never experienced the sense of profound disillusionment that disabled so many. His commitment was never to ideology but to a vision of human solidarity which he saw as intimately related to his Jewish identity:

I had somehow arrived at the psychological role of mediator between the Jews and America, and among Americans themselves as well. No doubt as a defense against the immensity of the domestic and European fascist threat which in my depths I interpreted as the threat of my own extinction. I had the wish, if not yet the conviction, that art could express the universality of human beings, their common emotions and ideas.[4]

In his autobiography Miller says of himself that he should have taken heart from Ibsen's line in *An Enemy of the People* that 'He is strongest who is most alone.' 'But the Jew in me', he explained, 'shied away from private salvation as something close to sin. One's truth must add its push to the evolution of public justice and mercy, must transform the spirit of the city whose brainless roar went on at both ends of the bridge.'[5] The image comes from *A View from the Bridge* whose title implies precisely this need to focus on the human need which exists below the rush of social events.

He might have found a more native source in Emerson's conviction that it was necessary to ride both the private and the public horse, like a circus performer, but whatever its source the essence of Miller's liberalism and his drama is that private and public are finally inseparable. It is the basis of his social critique – his sense that a world of self-regarding, self-seeking isolatos must finally also be self-destructive. Perhaps, he seems to imply, the Jew is a natural existentialist. There is no action without consequence and no consequence that can be contained within the self, no self outside the community which gives it both its context and meaning. McCarthyism invited the individual to deny any responsibility towards others, to refuse the moral logic that connected confession with betrayal, to seek safety in privatism, a disengagement from the communal. Myth became dogma, denial piety, prejudice conviction. Words reversed their meaning so that 'loyalty' indicated a willingness to betray, 'idealism' complicity in conspiracy, 'Americanism' intolerance and a denial of freedom. If Miller was a social dramatist by choice, however, he was also a social dramatist *force majeure*, as in the 1950s the political system thrust him into a public space and denied him the right to private commitments and concerns unless they were the simple ones of material enrichment. The irony was that part of the animus of the various investigative committees against Miller, against writers and actors, derived from the fact that they were in many ways the embodiment of the American dream, the possessors of wealth and fame, who nonetheless seemed discontented with such rewards and the system that generated them. McCarthy had no interest in chasing the committed but socially insignificant. This was largely, of course, an aspect of his insatiable desire for the publicity that was the sole source of his importance, but there was more to it than that, more even than the power to be measured against and in terms of the significance of those who could be so casually destroyed. Beyond the genuine paranoia about a world empire seemingly slipping away no sooner than it had been constructed was an anti-intellectualism that de Tocqueville had warned against more than a century before, a suspicion of those who swim against the current, a genuine feeling of betrayal which had little to do with spies and a great deal to do with the conviction that New Deal liberalism had challenged essential American myths having to do with self-sufficiency and individual acquisitiveness. Ironically McCarthy seems to have given Miller what the collapse of fascism had deprived him of – a resistant force against which his drama could pull.

Miller is, beyond everything else, a moralist, and the basis for his morality lies in the free admission of responsibility for the consequences of one's actions. The public world of social relations and political policy has its roots in a fallible human nature. If the evidence for the autonomy of the individual is not strong, in view of what he calls 'the devouring mechanisation of the age', of deterministic ideologies or the literal reductivism of war, then the theatre would place the individual back at the centre of attention: 'Attention, attention must be paid.' Causalities must be insisted upon. As Quentin observes in *After the Fall*, evil derives from denial, for 'we conspired to violate the past, and the past is holy and its horrors are the holiest of all'.[6] Like other Jewish writers working in the aftermath of a genocidal war, he refused to conspire in apocalypse and absurdity. Victim and oppressor, he insists, are separated by more than experience. The defence offered by those who operated the Nazi killing-machine was that they were the will-less agents of a hierarchy and thereby absolved of responsibility and guilt. A primary task, then, was to refuse this consolation, to reconstruct the logic no less than the necessity for morality. At first, in *All My Sons*, he seemed content merely to identify that connection between past and present, the individual and his society, action and consequence, whose disruption had betrayed the whole notion of private and public morality. Later, the picture would become more complex, but for the moment he was still drawn to the assumptions, no less than the strategy, of the Greek theatre, intent on urging the reality of the *polis*. As he insisted, 'Society is inside man and man is inside society',[7] the water is in the fish, the fish is in the water. It is not for nothing that Miller has always been intent on locating his characters in a clearly definable social situation: society is not the context in which his characters exist; it is implicated in their very beings, as the shape of that society is intimately related to their necessities. Beckett might locate his characters in a social and temporal void, ironising power-relationships by reversing their polarities (as in *Waiting for Godot*) and projecting the individual as the victim of a cosmic joke; Miller felt

the need to place his characters in a precisely delineated world of causality and social symbiosis. To be sure, he was aware that, as one of his
characters observes in *Incident at Vichy*, 'even the Jews have their Jews',[8]
but such ironies create rather than subvert moral demands in his work.

He is aware, too, that time has its own distorting power but has tended
nonetheless to locate his plays in identifiable historical moments,
knowing full well that past and present are not opposing terms, while
insisting that actions derive their meaning and moral content from the
extent to which they are acknowledged to take place in time.

All My Sons, then, is, in a way, his Greek play, as it is his Ibsen play. The
substance of the *polis* is re-established by driving out the one who denied
its very basis, Joe Keller. He redeems himself and his society by dying.
His son, Chris Keller, has presented what Ibsen's Dr Relling calls his
'demand of the ideal' to his father and thus precipitated his death with
that same blend of 'acute rectitudinal fever' (Ibsen's expression) and suppressed self-interest which had so fascinated his Scandinavian mentor.
Beyond that, in this, his first publicly successful play, he does not go. The
details of the plot are subordinated to a moral drive which can seem as
moralising as that of Chris Keller himself. The ambiguities are stated
rather than explored, Miller later explaining this as a product of the exigencies of wartime. The real exists; it simply has to be exposed by the
processes of the play, and once revealed it provokes action. Though language may be used for deceit it is ultimately proposed as an analytic
instrument. It is itself, of course, not only a link between the past and the
present, but a demonstration of the extent to which the past invades and
shapes the present. This was not yet, however, something he was keen to
engage. In *All My Sons* Joe Keller has to learn that the 'consequences of
actions are as real as the actions themselves'.[9] The question that this play
does not address, however, is the problematic nature of reality or the
extent to which the issues of power, moral responsibility and self-
definition finally resolve themselves into a debate over the nature of the
real. Miller might remark, later in his career, that while 'I can't say that
I believe you can ascertain the real I do believe in the obligation of trying
to do so', since 'to give it up is to create a kind of anarchy of the senses
which believes that there are no consequences of any determinable type'
and 'everything becomes a question of taste, including the hanging of
innocent people';[10] but in fact reality does become more problematic in
his plays. Are Willy Loman's dreams less real than his prosaic life? Is the
debate in *The Crucible* not in part at least a contention over the nature of
the real that is not wholly resolvable? What are Eddie Carbone's feelings

towards his niece in *A View from the Bridge?* Plainly, in *After the Fall* the
ineluctable facts of the concentration camp and the House Un-
American Activities Committee become part of the kaleidoscope of
memories and reconstructed relationships that constitute Quentin's
debate with himself, but by the time of *The Archbishop's Ceiling* and 'Some
Kind of Love Story' the real is beyond either simple definition or full
recovery. *The Price* acknowledges a degree of self-deceit that makes it
difficult, if not impossible, to stabilise an agreed version of the past and
hence of the identities laid down in that constantly shifting, re-invented
other country.

All My Sons marked the real beginning of a career that was to dominate post-war American theatre and the emergence of a talent that was
to mature with amazing rapidity. It ran for 328 performances. In all
essentials it is a well-made play, somewhat mechanical in construction
and with a plot that depends on the timely flourishing of concealed
letters and suppressed information (though Miller has pointed out the
artifice of classical Greek theatre and defended the suppression of information as a function of character rather than plot). He has also, interestingly, suggested that its real theme may be 'the return of the
repressed' as individuals and societies struggle to deny truths which
threaten an equanimity born out of compromise and denial. There is no
doubt that this is evident in the play, as is that desire for vengeance on
the part of Kate whose life has been distorted by her husband's moral
failings. These are, however, trace elements in a play whose plot was so
powerfully responsive to the immediate context of the war. Its contrast
between human values and a distorted commercialism made it many
years later the most successful play in Israeli theatrical history. But today
the most striking thing is the distance between this play and the work that
was to follow, *Death of a Salesman*, in which form became a crucial
concern. Though he remained convinced that 'there could be no aesthetic form without a moral world, only notes without a staff'[11] at the
same time he wanted to open 'a path into [his] own chaos',[12] a chaos that
lay in some respects on the other side of morality where reality was constructed from the fragments of memory and desire.

Miller has always been concerned with questions of guilt and innocence, which is to say he is concerned with the moral life. But quite the
most interesting aspect of his work has been his awareness that the desire
for a world at moral attention carries its own dangers: 'It was our desire
for a moral world, the deep wish to assert the existence of goodness, that
generated, as it continues to do, political fantasy.'[13] And what is true at

a political level is true equally of individual lives. For though he has continued to insist that 'man could not act at all without moral impulses, however mistaken its identification with any particular movement might eventually turn out to be',[14] he is aware, too, that idealism carries the risk of a selfrighteous disregard for the lives and needs of individuals; indeed, that it may well be the justification of the tyrant as well as the motivation of the reformer. Innocence comes into clear focus only when confronted with guilt.

Arthur Miller is not interested in the photographic reproduction of a reality which anyway will not offer itself up for so casual an analysis. His is a realism of the structure of experience and thought. It is not simply that form and theme are intimately related but that he wishes to create a dramatic form which does justice to his sense of how private and public history cohere. Art may give shape to chaos, but if it is to bear witness to the truth of lives that are fragmented, protean and uncertain it must resist as well as assert those coherences. As he wrote in the notebook in which he was testing ideas for *Death of a Salesman*,

Life is formless – its interconnections are connected by lapses of time, by events occurring in separated places, by the hiatus of memory. We live in the world made by man and the past. Art suggests or makes the connections palpable. Form is the tension of those interconnections, man with man, man with the past and present environment. The drama at its best is a mass experience of those tensions.[15]

Death of a Salesman, Miller has said, is 'a love story between a man and his son, and in a crazy way between both of them and America'. It is true of the play and true, too, of Miller, for whom America has proved a wayward mistress worthy of redemption. Believing, as he does, that the artist is by nature a dissident, committed to the necessity of challenging the given, he is equally compelled by a country which, despite its conservatism, is paradoxically committed to transformation. An immigrant society, what else could it propose? Its animating myths all cohere around the proposition that change is a central imperative. The true American is protean. The problem is that the imagination – the seat of personal and social change – is too easily usurped by facile fantasy, that urbanisation and the brittle satisfactions of the material world breed spiritual inertia and a failure of will. It is for this reason that Miller finds in his most self-deceiving and marginalised characters a dignity that derives from their refusal to settle for simple accommodation – figures such as Eddie Carbone in *A View from the Bridge* or Willy Loman in *Death of a Salesman* of whom he has said, 'there is a nobility . . . in Willy's struggle. Maybe it comes from refusal ever to relent, to give up . . . People who are able to accept their frustrated lives do not change conditions . . . You must look behind his ludicrousness to what he is actually confronting and that is as serious a business as anyone can imagine.'[16]

In creating *Death of a Salesman* Miller deliberately reached for a style that would accommodate his sense of the concurrence of experience, that would express his conviction that while past and present are causally connected (a narrative logic implying moral coherence) they are also co-existent realities informing and deforming one another. Forty years later his autobiography would be constructed along similar lines. In a way he was simply generating a structure that would serve the purpose of a play in which the self fragments along the fault line of personal history. Beyond that, however, he was asserting a conviction about the processes of thought, the constant reinvention of the real and the pressures of memory that shape a world whose inevitabilities are our own unconscious creation. As he explained in the significantly titled *Timebends*, he wanted a play that would do for an audience what a chance encounter with a former acquaintance had done for him, a play that would 'cut through time like a knife through a layer cake or a road through a mountain revealing its geologic layers, and instead of one incident in one timeframe succeeding another, display past and present concurrently, with neither one ever coming to a stop. The past' he saw as 'a formality, merely a dimmer present, for everything we are is at every moment alive in us'. What he looked for was a play 'that did not still the mind's simultaneity, did not allow a man to "forget" and turned him to see present through past and past through present, a form that in itself, quite apart from the content and meaning, would be inescapable as a psychological process and as a collecting point for all that his life in society had poured into him'.[17] It was an effect enhanced, in Elia Kazan's production, by Jo Mielziner's special skills as a stage designer (working to Miller's brief): his concealed lifts enabling Willy's sons – Biff and Happy – to move in space and hence in time, his fragmentary set creating thin dividing lines between past and present, a membrane easily ruptured by a protagonist unable to hold himself back from the vortex of his memories. But in a sense Miller was only capitalising on the virtues of theatre – its ability simultaneously to present appearance and reality, action and reaction, dissonance and harmony.

As he confessed,

All My Sons had exhausted my lifelong interest in the Greco-Ibsen form, in the particular manner in which I had come to think of it. Now more and more the simultaneity of ideas and feeling within me and the freedom with which they contradicted one another began to fascinate me. I even dabbled with the notion of studying music in the hope of composing, for the only art in which simultaneity was really possible was music. Words could not make chords; they had to be uttered in a line, one after the other.[18]

This may be a 1980s sensibility recreating the thought-processes of a 1940s playwright but it does suggest the extent to which analyses of *Death of a Salesman* as simply a social play are to a degree beside the point. To be sure Willy Loman, a salesman in his sixties, is tossed aside by his employer when his social utility is exhausted, but his job has long since ceased to be a central concern to a man whose bafflement has to do with the failure of his life to render its meaning up to him and with his own failure to inscribe either his needs on experience or his identity on an indifferent world. The irony is that he has communicated his values only too completely to his sons whose lives have accordingly been warped and whose own identities have been threatened. If Willy has 'all the wrong dreams' he dies in an attempt to pass these dreams onto his sons. But, as Willy's next-door neighbour, Charley, observes, 'a salesman's got to dream'. And not a salesman alone. When Miller suggests that in a sense these men live like artists, like actors whose product is first of all themselves, forever imagining triumphs in a world that either ignores them or denies their presence altogether, he is describing a process of self-invention which is not theirs alone. The consistency with which this figure of the salesman or his near kin crops up in American writing suggests a near paradigmatic role (from Melville's Confidence Man and Twain's Colonel Sellers, through Lewis's Babbitt to Updike's Rabbit Angstrom; from O'Neill's Hickey and Inge's Rubin Flood to Williams's Stanley Kowalski and Mamet's real estate salesmen).

Death of a Salesman is no more an indictment of the American system than *All My Sons* had been. The latter called, if anything, for a kind of moralised capitalism while the former offers two characters – Charley and Bernard – who show that a full-hearted commitment to capitalism is not incompatible with humane values. Indeed Bernard stands as a justification of the Puritan ethic. Beyond that, as a successful lawyer modestly off to plead a case before the Supreme Court, he is in a sense an embodiment of a principle of justice and coherence which Willy has betrayed in the name of a fantasy, partly of his own making and partly the product of a system in which the self is carefully sculpted to serve social needs. Willy's desire to be 'well liked', his effort to go through life on a smile and a shoeshine, is evidence of his confusion of illusion and reality. What *Death of a Salesman* does dramatise is the power of myth to confer a spurious significance. Willy's infinite capacity for self-deceit has

its social correlative, but that was scarcely less true of the characters in
All My Sons, and would be true of those in *The Crucible* or *A View from the
Bridge*; indeed, self-deception lies at the heart of most of Miller's plays.

There is something very recognisable in Willy's desire to pass something to his sons. Miller's own father had the immigrant's desire to see
his children make their mark, partly to justify his own abandonment of
another world. He wanted, in Miller's words, 'a business for the boys'.[19]
It was an inheritance the playwright had to refuse if he was to survive as
a writer. In a sense this was only a re-enactment of a familiar generational tension. Here, however, it becomes something more. Biff represents a spiritual potential in Willy Loman which he willingly sacrificed
to the material as embodied in his other son. They are aspects of his sensibility and indeed in Miller's original design for the play – then to be
called *The Inside of his Head* – that was to have been a quite literal fact.
Willy is a confused and frightened man. Indeed, we have Miller's assurance that his last name, rather than being a pun on his social status, in
fact derived from the character of Lohmann in Fritz Lang's *The Testament
of Dr Mabuse*, 'a terror-stricken man calling into the void for help that will
never come'.[20] But though this play is far from being a simple indictment
of the American system it is tempting to see a more generalised
significance for Willy's divided self in a society in which the framers of
the Constitution hesitated between the pursuit of happiness and the possession of property as a definition of the individual's inalienable right,
as though the two were roughly interchangeable concepts (indeed a
number of state Constitutions did indeed substitute the word property).
When Linda, at the end of the play, stands bewildered at the suicide of
a man who has just completed payments on the mortgage on his property, we see, therefore, not only the depth of her own failure to understand the man she has loved and fought so hard to protect but a
confusion of realms fundamental to the culture.

Yet this play, which Miller himself has described as 'quintessentially
American' has had no difficulty finding an international audience, often
being produced in countries whose own myths are radically different,
where, indeed, the salesman is an alien and exotic breed. However fixed
the script of a play (though translation already radically destabilises this)
its text (that is, all those elements which combine in a production to generate a field of meaning) is liable to quite radical acts of reinterpretation. On one level it is a vindication of Miller's hope and insistence that
'there is one humanity', on another it is evidence of a pluralism of
meaning which can never be patrolled by an author nor restricted by a

critic. Certainly, no country seems to have been baffled by a play in which an individual creates his own fate while believing himself to be an agent of social process. No audience seems to have had difficulty in responding to the story of a man distracted from human necessities by public myths.

There is, though, perhaps an element of sleight of hand in the logic of a play which suggests that some resolution has been reached through the redemption of a man – Biff – who comes at last to understand the falsity of his father's values and who is, ironically, released from the ties of guilt and love which had bound him to that father by a suicide designed to commit him irrevocably to those values. For Biff in turn, it seems, is to opt for another myth, another set of values at odds if not with the real then with the drift of history. Turning his back on one version of the American dream he seems on the verge of embracing another – an agrarian dream that suggests some moral connection between the individual and the land, a western myth which sees in space a freedom in which to arrive at self-definition. After all, the play's set, in which a tree-filled area gives way to an 'angry glow of orange' from 'a solid vault of apartment houses around the small, fragile seeming home', suggests that time has already invalidated such an option. Though Miller later pointed to the rural drop-outs of the 1960s as offering some kind of justification for Biff's action, he also confessed that his later film, *The Misfits*, could legitimately be seen as dramatising the fate awaiting Biff Loman as he presumably sets out for the ranch which alone seems to satisfy his needs. In *The Misfits* Biff becomes Gay, an ageing cowboy reduced to rounding up wild horses to be turned into dog food while refusing to acknowledge the collapse of his dream. Biff, moreover, seems to resolve his dilemma by moving out of the social world. In moving west he will in effect be turning the clock back, opting for the past, lighting out for the territory ahead of the rest, much as Huck Finn had done, or Fitzgerald's Nick Carraway. In both those cases, however, the apparent resolution was tainted with irony. That irony seems absent here, though earlier in the play we had been told that the whole story had begun with Willy's abandonment by his father and brother Ben's scramble for wealth – both of which took place not in a city but the rural world for which Biff seems about to opt. The resolution of the play thus lies less with the characters or the logic of their actions than with the audience and with the logic of imagination.

Death of a Salesman was an attempt to 'deploy past and present concurrently, with neither one ever coming to a stop'.[21] Neither past nor present, however, is secure and wholly knowable. When Willy Loman walks through the walls of his house, when the apartment houses that surround him dissolve, when his family transmutes before our eyes, what we see is not the past but what use the present makes of the past. It is the theatre that Willy makes of his life, neurotically restaging it in an attempt to discover the moment of lost authenticity. Wishing to feel the author of his being he replays his performances, vaguely aware that self and role have never come into real alignment. Biff and Happy, too, have reinvented their pasts and perform the roles in which they imagine themselves to have been cast. Willy plays his part to its inevitable conclusion, a salesman to the end, selling myths to his son and himself alike. Not for nothing is the play called *Death of a Salesman* rather than *Death of Willy Loman*. The question is whether Biff will lay aside his role or merely choose another.

Speaking of *All My Sons* Miller has accused himself of leaving too little space and time for the 'wordless darkness that underlies all verbal truth'.[22] In *Death of a Salesman* we glimpse that darkness, as we do more completely in his next play, *The Crucible*.

Death of a Salesman ran for 742 performances, nearly twice as long as *All My Sons*, and won all the major prizes, establishing a reputation later to be consolidated by a play which nonetheless prompted an uneasy response from an audience which now found his strictures on American values dangerously disturbing. If *Death of a Salesman* had, in Miller's striking phrase, set before the captains of what he took to be a new American empire in the making 'the corpse of a believer' he now prepared to offer it the corpse of a sceptic. Willy Loman had battled with mortality and anonymity; John Proctor battles for his soul and thereby for the soul of his society.

America was insecure in the 1940s and 1950s. The loss of China to communism and the shock of the Soviet Union's explosion of its own atom bomb initiated a frenzied search for traitors. It was a blow both to prestige and to a sense of the real. China was declared to be a phantasm, while a new demonology was summoned into being to explain the inexplicable. Suddenly the Right had both the justification and the mechanism to initiate a redefinition of the past. The long years of radical government, overseen and sponsored by Roosevelt, that had to be suffered in silence so long as the country faced economic and then military threat, could now be reinterpreted as laying the foundation for treachery. The past was summoned before the present and there required to reshape itself to satisfy immediate needs. The primary agency for that alchemy was the House Un-American Activities Committee and a relatively minor Senate Committee presided over by the junior senator from Wisconsin, Joseph McCarthy. As Miller observed,

the political, objective, knowledgeable campaign of the far Right was capable of creating not only a new terror, but a new subjective reality, a veritable mystique, which was gradually assuming even a holy resonance . . . There was a new religiosity in the air . . . New sins were being created monthly. It was very odd how quickly these were accepted into the new orthodoxy, quite as though they had been there since the beginning of time. Above all, above all horrors, I saw accepted the notion that conscience was no longer a private matter but one of state administration. I saw men handing conscience to other men and thanking other men for the opportunity of doing so.[23]

His first reaction was to adapt Ibsen's *An Enemy of the People*, whose basic concern he regarded as 'the central theme of our social life today . . . the question of whether the democratic vision of the truth ought to be a source of guilt at a time when the mass of men condemn it as a dangerous and devilish lie'.[24] But he would soon have a more literal application for a language of demonology and for the sense of alienation which he had dramatised in the Ibsen play.

The wider context for the political mood of the fifties was the collapse of a particular form of radical-liberal faith. Hard or soft Marxism had been replaced for a while during the war by the communal effort to defeat the Axis. With the end of the war, in Miller's words, the 'dispossessed liberals and leftists in chaotic flight from the bombarded old castles of self-denial', unable, anymore, to regard themselves as the cutting edge of history, turned with some relief to Freudianism which seemed to justify a protective privatism. Certainly, this was a path which Miller himself followed, briefly undergoing analysis. However, if such liberals were prepared to adopt a passive stance with respect to society, society, apparently, was not prepared to return the compliment. One after another of Miller's idols and friends found themselves called before the House Committee and asked not merely to confess their own 'sins' but to name names. The list included the writer whom Miller had most admired in the thirties, Clifford Odets, together with Elia Kazan, director of *Death of a Salesman* and Lee J. Cobb, who had played Willy Loman. Betrayal became the price of citizenship, confession the rite of entry to an American state purged of its Levellers and free-thinkers. The final irony was that there were few who had not long since abandoned their faith in Marx. There was thus little for them to disavow. The question of collaboration or resistance thus seemed at times like a branch of meta-physics. But there was an issue. The Orwellian notion of an un-American act could scarcely itself have been more un-American, implying, as it did, a model of the state at odds with its own history and ideology. The integrity and future of that state were at risk, but not from those who had once been attracted by economic and political theories now two decades out of fashion. The issue was indeed betrayal, but betrayal which had little to do with microfilms discovered in pumpkins. The faith those called before the Committee were asked to break was more profound, having to do with destroying the lives of others in order to secure immunity for oneself. Miller – himself later invited to collabo-rate – was actually driving back from Salem where he had been research-ing *The Crucible* when a radio news bulletin itemised those named before the Committee by Elia Kazan. The shock that he felt reverberated through the play that was beginning to cohere in his imagination.

This, then, was the background against which Miller wrote his play. It was also the background against which it was received. One night, indeed, audience and cast stood in silence as the Rosenbergs were electrocuted in Sing Sing. *The Crucible* ran for only 197 performances, towards the end being kept alive by a cast willing to work for little or no pay. In subsequent years it was to become Miller's most popular play, its relevance to McCarthyism giving way to other urgencies as it was per-formed in China, in Poland and around the world. But in 1953 Miller felt 'more and more frighteningly isolated, in life as in the theatre', believing, as he did, that time was running out, 'not only on me but on the traditional American culture'.[25]

The Crucible centres on a witchhunt which took place in Salem in 1692. A group of girls playing at summoning up devils, with a West Indian servant called Tituba, become suddenly vulnerable when one of their number, the daughter of the Reverend Parris, slips into a form of trance. The Reverend Hale is called in to explore the possibility of witchcraft. Tituba and the girls defend themselves by accusing others. In court their hysteria slowly envelops the community, as personal vengeance and venality are dignified as civic policy. In particular Abigail Williams, one-time servant to John and Elizabeth Proctor, and Proctor's former lover, accuses her mistress of witchcraft. Summoned into court Proctor seeks to defend his wife by confessing his adultery, a confession neutralised by his wife's protective refusal to betray him. Failing in this he is offered life in exchange for a public recantation and the naming of further victims. Tempted, he nonetheless finally takes a stand, sacrificing his life for a sense of personal dignity: 'I am John Proctor still.' It is a play which raises questions about power, about authority, about language, about definitions of the real. Here, as elsewhere in his work, sexual betrayal operates as an image of other denials of the human contract. Here, as elsewhere in his work (most notably *After the Fall*, *Incident at Vichy* and *Playing for Time*), evil exists as some final and implacable mystery.

Nor is it fanciful to see other pressures behind this play than those generated by contemporary politics. Only some eight years after the full and detailed revelations of the Holocaust had forced a reevaluation of human nature and potential, an account of the irrational persecutions, the pseudo-scientific justifications, the murderous rigours, the self-serving activities of the witchhunters was bound to carry overtones of another evil, a darkness which, like the unquenchable thirst for victims on the part of Puritan judges and congressional investigators alike, remains in some profound sense impenetrable. To that degree Miller himself shares in a vocabulary which includes the satanic. But where Jean-Paul Sartre, in the French film adaptation, chose to make the play an epic drama culminating in revolution, a class revolt, Miller's focus was more clearly on the individual. As he wrote of the play in his notebook, '*It has got to be basically Proctor's story*', and the mechanism of that story was to be guilt. So it is Proctor's all but debilitating sense of guilt which first inhibits him from intervening and which subsequently makes him vulnerable. It is guilt that prevents the judges from acknowledging the deception in which they have become accomplices, but the structure of the play no longer depends upon the revelation of guilt, as in his earlier work. Now it is seen as a destructive force, distant from and inhibiting that sense of responsibility with which it is too easily confused.

It is a play about power in so far as it concerns the degree to which authority lies with those who define the nature of the real, who establish the grammar of human relationships, who determine the vocabulary in which the social debate is conducted. Proctor tries to resist the language of his persecutors, to deny their cosmology, but in the world of Salem there is no other available. It is a dilemma felt equally, of course, by those in the 1950s for whom even silence was taken for guilt; but ultimately, like most of Miller's work, it was in essence a play about an individual's struggle to sustain a sense of dignity and meaning in a context in which both are threatened. Proctor is destroyed but not defeated – Hemingway's definition of the tragic – and quite plainly Miller is still reaching out for a modern tragedy which can make sense of a threatening chaos.

Three years later he found himself called before the House Un-American Activities Committee and invited, like Proctor, to become complicit in a prevailing moral anarchy. Ironically, the immediate cause was the State Department's refusal to renew his passport to enable him to attend the Belgian premiere of *The Crucible*, doubly ironic in that, when asked, like Proctor, to name names he replied with a virtual paraphrase of Proctor's own speech. But for Miller, no less than for Proctor, in a perverse way the moral chaos is what permits self-definition. His own self-doubts, which had led to his period of analysis, Proctor's sense of himself as a worthless sinner, lose their significance in the face of an external challenge. The personal dilemma, however, is also essentially a public one. As he pointed out in an interview many years later, speaking of *The Crucible* in the context of Greek drama:

I think they were trying to organise some moral basis for society in those plays. Take a play like *Oedipus*, it's not just a personal, psychological, or psychiatric story; it's also the story of the legitimacy of authority and the irony of authority seeking evil outside of itself when evil is right in it, in the authority. These are political ideas *par excellence* . . . I think I go further back than the recent bourgeois tragedies which are deep, personal psychological works exclusively . . . and have no reference beyond the little worlds that they present.[26]

Authority and power reveal a hunger for a singular reading of experience. If Puritan society was a text, as in a sense it surely was (certainly the canonical power of the Bible, the Word, was assumed to offer the only legitimate decoding of events), the clerics and judges seek to impose a single meaning on it. Proctor constitutes a threat because he will not speak the required words, because he refuses to interpret events along the lines required. He insists upon a perverse reading. Judge Danforth's primary accusation against him is that he seeks to undermine the court, to deny its authority as sole legitimate interpreter of truth. 'What signifies a needle?'[27] he asks sceptically, confronted with the assumption that it constitutes plain evidence of witchcraft. 'I have wondered if there be witches in the world', he admits, pointedly adding, 'I have no knowledge of it.' Though he acknowledges that 'the Bible speaks of witches, and I will not deny them' he chooses to read the world through his own direct experience. He is joined in this by his wife, Elizabeth. 'I cannot believe it', she insists; at which Proctor pointedly warns her, 'Elizabeth, you bewilder him!'[28] That, indeed, is the heart of the threat which they jointly pose. For what they challenge is a singular reading of the world, a reality constituted by those who claim to possess or interpret the Word. When Proctor replies to the Reverend Parris's insistence that 'There is either obedience or the church will burn like Hell is burning!' with 'I may speak my heart, I think', he is told, 'We are not Quakers here yet.'[29] The Quaker's inner light is too close to sanctifying a pluralism of interpretations for those whose authority depends on over-determined readings. When asked to confirm a conspiracy of evil Proctor again replies, 'I have no knowledge in that line.'[30] When the villagers inscribe their names on a document attesting to the good character of Rebecca Nurse, whose life is at risk, their text becomes evidence of their challenge to the writ of the court and another text is inscribed to summon them into court, a warrant which echoes their names, turning testament into accusation. When Giles Cory prepares a deposition, that text, too, is authoritatively interpreted as an attack on the court, an attack that can only be absolved if he is willing to offer a name. His only recourse is to 'stand mute', but not to speak the required words is to stand condemned, as is to fail to inscribe one's name to a confession dictated by others. Mary Warren, tempted to tell the truth, to tell a story whose plot is at odds with that offered by the authorities, is intimidated to the point at which she confesses to having signed her name in the devil's book – a sin once again to be redeemed only with another name, only by subscribing to the authorised text of Salem in 1692.

So it is that the fourth and final act of *The Crucible* begins as 'writing materials' are brought into the jail. Proctor is offered the opportunity to escape his confinement by entering the prison house of authorised language. If, as the Reverend Hale remarks, 'We cannot read His Will'[31] it is, he implies, for his servants in the ministry to read it for him. Elizabeth Proctor tells her husband that 'I have read my heart.'[32] Private interpretations, though, are unacceptable, a challenge to be resisted. Thus Proctor is required to confess in a public form. He must subscribe – in the literal form of writing under or underwriting – to orthodoxy. When he asks, 'Why must it be written?' the answer is that he must lend his name to the narrative, to the plot, which the judges indict. To sign will indeed be a sign whose significance lies precisely in the extent to which his name will complete the prepared document. When he tears the paper containing his signature he rejects also the social text into which they would absorb him, even as he asserts his right to interpret the world in terms of his own beliefs and experiences. For a writer who was to be asked to 'name names' and who had inscribed his own name on numerous petitions there was a special significance in what was in effect, in part at least, a battle for the linguistic as well as the moral high ground. But, beyond this, there is an instructive distrust of the written word. It is true that Abigail's lies expose the fragility of the spoken word but the various legal documents are consistently antipathetic to human values.

The Crucible is a play in which text interleaves with text. Indeed, Miller himself chooses to inscribe the published text of the play not only with conventional stage directions, but also with extended prose passages in which he offers a gloss on the events which he dramatises. In particular he adds density to the historical and social situation and implicitly suggests a connection between Puritan New England and the America of the 1950s. On the one hand these passages emphasise the continuing conflict between the needs and rights of the individual and those of a society which feels itself under threat; on the other they stress the perversities of a contemporary demonology. As he insisted,

In the countries of the Communist ideology all resistance of any import is linked to the totally malign capitalist succubi, and in America any man who is not reactionary in his views is open to the charge of alliance with the Red hell. Political opposition, thereby, is given an in-human overlay which then justifies the abrogation of all normally applied customs of civilized intercourse. A political policy is equated with moral right, and opposition to it with diabolical malevolence.[33]

What is at stake, in other words, is interpretation, a reading of the past and the present. Senator McCarthy, holding aloft a sheaf of papers supposedly inscribed with the names of traitors, flourished an implied history from which he offered to liberate America. Still other lists were to deny people their livelihoods, to make them non-people, to remove their names from the credits of films, or the doors of offices. Miller's play is a text in which a man writes his own history by destroying the document which had been designed to incorporate him in a public history. The 'John Proctor' signed to a piece of paper is not the 'John Proctor' which sounds out confidently even in a prison cell.

The Crucible may be a product of the time; it has not proved limited to its time. Perhaps we should not be surprised by a successful production, in the 1980s, in the People's Republic of China. There, too, the people had been required to subscribe to a text – Mao's little red book – there, too, the self was required to redeem itself through immolation. There, too, a single truth, a single history, a single interpretation was asserted by a society whose demonology was different but no less implacable. Its politics aside, however, *The Crucible* is thematically of a piece with Miller's other works in which an individual struggles to reconcile himself with himself, to discover the terms on which he can survive the knowledge of his own failures.

Theatrically, the play might seem to lack the originality of *Death of a Salesman*. A contention over the shape and substance of the real is conducted in a drama whose approach to character and motive is as unproblematic as its staging. That is not, however, without its justification. For the debate is essentially one between the foursquare, commonsense pragmatism of John Proctor and those for whom even the spiritual world can be domesticated into a prosaic banality. The power of *The Crucible*, indeed, lies in large part in its insistence that evil subsists in the translation of abstract power into routine process, in that very denial of ambiguity which is equally the substance of faith.

When Miller was casting the part of Eddie Carbone, in *A View from the Bridge*, he offered the role first to Lee J. Cobb. It was an offer fraught with ambivalence. Cobb had only recently agreed to collaborate with the House Un-American Activities Committee, informing on his friends and associates. He was now being given the chance to play the part of a man who informs on his relatives. From Miller's point of view it was an attempt to import into the theatre an emotional truth generated outside the play. It was also a piece of casting which offered an opportunity for psychotherapy and expiation. Unsurprisingly, Cobb rejected the offer, by now terrified of political harassment. Nine years later, with Miller's next play, the irony repeated itself as Elia Kazan was asked to direct a play – *After the Fall* – in which he himself was a character, a man, once again, who places his own career, and, more significantly, his own need to declare an unprejudiced innocence ahead of the security of others and ahead of the demands of friendship. But, as with several of his plays, *A View from the Bridge* is not best viewed in the context of its initial production. The idea had been seeded some years earlier, when he was engaged in writing *Death of a Salesman*. 'The Italian play [about] X, who ratted on the two immigrants', as he described it in a notebook of the 1940s, grew from an anecdote told to him by a friend from the Brooklyn waterfront. To a man whose imagination was still drawn to the Greek theatre, it was a story of tragic potential. As he wrote in his notebook: 'The secret of the Greek drama is the vendetta, the family ties incomprehensible to Englishmen and Americans. But not to Jews. Much that has been interpreted in lofty terms, fate, religion, etc., is only blood and the tribal survival within the family. Red Hook is full of Greek tragedies.'[34] Thirty years later he would describe its theme in other terms, locating it against a deepening sense of alienation and anomie:

the play's significance for me lay in its unpeeling of process itself, the implacability of a structure in life. For around me I felt a wasting vagrancy of mind and spirit . . . The much celebrated 'end of ideology,' which some influential ex-Marxists were elaborating, seemed to me to dissolve the very notion of human destiny. At bottom, people were left to their loneliness, each to himself and for himself, and this compounded the sadness of life, although it might liberate some to strike out on their own and make more money . . . How to live and how to relax were not the same problem, not if you had children and the anxiety, which would never leave me, that something lifemocking and mean was stirring in the American spirit – something that had to be outmanoeuvred and thwarted by the strategies of art.[35]

In Europe Harold Pinter and Samuel Beckett created a drama which proposed a profound disruption in experience, a disruption reflected at the level of plot, character and language. It was a direction Miller could not follow. If he, too, was concerned with the disjunction between desire and fulfilment the ironies which he chose to pursue were quite other than those generated by the discrepancies of class, on the one hand, or those derived from a desire to read meaning into an existence blankly resistant to interpretation on the other. To be sure he, too, was aware of the disruptive gap between word and act and of the extent to which motives remain opaque even to the individual concerned, but his main concern, here as elsewhere, is to recuperate meaning, to offer the tragic consolation of signification.

An image which recurs in Miller's autobiography is that of a bridge across which an anonymous stream of traffic sweeps by 'endlessly' and 'blind'. At a time when, in his view, 'a perpetual night of confusion was descending',[36] it became an image of the disregard both of the individual and of the underlying structure of human experience. Whatever else his theatre has concerned itself with it has been centrally concerned to restore to the individual a significance quite apart from social role and hence to underline his conviction that personal responsibility remains an ineluctable reality and public morality the accretion of private decisions. Thus, *A View from the Bridge*, the story of Eddie Carbone's desperate and unacknowledged love for his niece, Catherine, and his betrayal of his wife's illegal immigrant cousins when one of them proposes marriage to her, becomes the celebration of a fatally illusioned but perversely compelling figure enacting an archetypal drama. Not for nothing did he think of the play as his Greek tragedy. Eddie does, after all, share with Oedipus an obsession that leads him towards self-destruction. He, too, comes to the edge of a kind of madness and is tempted by that same sin against nature (although Eddie's relationship to Catherine is literally that of uncle to niece Miller has confessed to thinking of them as father and daughter). The first version was even written in verse.

What is finally compelling about Eddie Carbone is not his fitness or otherwise to be regarded as a tragic hero; it is his total commitment to a single vision, no matter how tainted that vision may be. In that sense he is distant kin to Melville's Ahab and Fitzgerald's Gatsby. As Miller himself has said, 'however one might dislike this man, who does all sorts of fearful things, he possesses and exemplifies the wondrous and humane fact that he, too, can be driven to what, in the last analysis, is a sacrifice of himself for his conception, however misguided, of right, dignity and justice'. The figure of the lawyer, Alfieri, to whom Eddie appeals and who broadens the significance of the action, is, indeed, an equivalent to the chorus in Greek drama, commenting on the action but unable to deflect it. Seen from the perspective of the Brooklyn Bridge, which arches over the Red Hook district of Brooklyn, described by Alfieri as a slum, the gullet of New York, Eddie is a nonentity, of no significance. In fact, in a grey world, he compels attention by the totality of his commitment, his willingness to sacrifice everything to sustain his conception of himself. For in seeking to prevent Catherine's sexual maturity he is trying to preserve both her innocence and his own. Eventually his death serves the same purpose. Indeed, perversely, the arrival of Marco and Rudolpho offers a solution – a form of suicide – to a crisis which could not have been evaded. What, crucially, Eddie lacks is any sense of tragic self-awareness; in fact self-awareness is precisely what must be refused. Though the retribution which he suffers seems to imply a moral world, he himself goes beyond morality. What he challenges is not a social code but the natural order of things. The risk, at least in the first Broadway production, was that Miller was pressing his characterstowards abstraction. Rewritten for its London run, the play became more clearly grounded in a social and psychological reality. As Miller himself observed,

I had originally conceived Eddie as a phenomenon, a rather awesome fact of existence, and I had kept a certain distance from involvement in his self-justification. Consequently he had appeared as a kind of biological sport, and to a degree a repelling figure not quite admissible into the human family . . . In revising it I found it possible to move beyond contemplation of the man as a phenomenon into an acceptance for dramatic purposes of his aims themselves.[37]

In his autobiography Miller speaks of feeling that he was 'disowning the play even as its opening approached'. His own life in turmoil, as his marriage threatened to collapse in the face of his growing love affair with Marilyn Monroe, 'I was turning against myself, struggling to put my life behind me, order and disorder at war in me, in a kind of parallel of the stress between the play's formal, cool classicism and the turmoil of incestuous desire and betrayal within it.'[38] In that context he became very aware of the irony of trying to describe to Van Hefflin, playing the role of Eddie, 'the sensation of being swept away, of inviting the will's oblivion and dreading it', when precisely that sensation was pulling him towards his own fate. How, he asked, 'could one walk toward the very thing one was flying from'.[39] Perhaps it is not entirely mischievous to note, either, that this story of a sexually charged relationship between uncle and niece must have seemed disturbingly close in spirit to a love affair in which Marilyn Monroe seems to have been looking for a combination of lover and father, even calling him 'papa'.

Miller himself ascribed the relative failure of *A View from the Bridge* and its companion piece *A Memory of Two Mondays* (and he might have added the absolute failure, at that time judged by commercial standards, of *An Enemy of the People*) to the images of privation and desperation which they deployed in a society committed to success. In England, not merely was it literally a different play – rewritten in a two-act version, its verse abandoned or transposed into prose, its social density intensified in a production which stressed the physical reality of the Red Hook setting and a community which created the context for Eddie's actions, an objectification of his conscience – but it was performed in a different social world with different cultural assumptions. It may indeed, as Miller had suggested, have seemed exotic in relation to an English theatre he characterised as middle class and bloodlessly polite, but that theatre was on the edge of change, Osborne's *Look Back in Anger* running in London at the same time. Such passion as Eddie's, however, was a shock. Indeed its theme – its hint at incest and homosexuality – drove it from the public stage into a theatre club, a device for circumventing the censorship not abandoned in England until 1968.

In an essay called 'On Social Plays', which appeared in 1955 (as a preface to the one-act version of *A View from the Bridge*) Miller expressed his conviction that plays are indeed essentially social. Had it not been so for the Greeks? Was it not, he might have added, for another of his models, Henrik Ibsen? It was not that individual psychology was irrelevant or without a transfixing compulsion but that the line to be traced was that which linked private feeling with public values. Indeed his drama, and in some ways theatre itself, was predicated on the assumption that what we call social morality is in some degree the sum of individual acts – which is to say that his early Marxism had given way to an existentialism more in the American grain. Thus to commit an act of individual betrayal was, in Sartrean terms, to vote for betrayal as a mode of social behaviour.

Miller is under no illusion that modern society acts on shared assumptions in the way that the Greek world had done; indeed ancient Greece itself had experienced that fragmentation which is now a presumed fact of social life. But the acceptance of responsibility for one's actions, the acknowledgement that, in Miller's often repeated phrase, the birds will come home to roost, is the minimal requirement for any social life.

It is an acknowledgement that not all his characters can make. Willy Loman in *Death of a Salesman,* cannot allow the fact of his betrayal of wife and sons (let alone himself) to enter his soul because the price of doing so is the dissolution of a world whose substantiality he can never question. Likewise, Eddie Carbone must die rather than admit to himself the truth of his feelings and the fact of his actions. As Miller himself said:

What kills Eddie Carbone is nothing visible or heard, but the built-in conscience of the community whose existence he has menaced by betraying it . . . A solidarity that may be primitive but which finally administers a self-preserving blow against its violators. In [*A View from the Bridge*] there is a search for some fundamental fiat, not moral in itself but ultimately so, which keeps a certain order among us, enough to keep us from barbarism.

And that barbarism took an immediate and practical form in the early 1950s to such an extent that Miller, referring specifically to McCarthyism and its fundamental challenge to civilised modes of behaviour, insisted that the pressure of the time's madness is reflected in the strict and orderly cause-and-effect structure of *A View from the Bridge*. Apart from its meaning, he suggested, 'the manner in which the story itself is told is a rejection of that enervated "acceptance" of illogic which was the new wisdom of the age. Here, actions had consequences again, betrayal was not greeted with a fashionably lobotomized smile.'[40]

A View from the Bridge was written at a time when Miller felt wholly out of tune with his society. Indeed this was to be his last play for nine years, as he had come to believe that he and his country were so fundamentally at odds as to have little to say to one another. It is by no means, however, simply a displaced response to McCarthy. If it were, why did the theme of betrayal predate it and why has it remained central since? It has been said that Miller wrote this play to denounce the informer, as Elia Kazan went on to make the movie, *On the Waterfront*, which justified the informer. Whatever truth of that the force of the play lies elsewhere. As Miller has said, 'any such considerations lie to one side of an evaluation of any play as a play'. Indeed a decade later he saw a new production and was struck by

how the passage of time, the shifting of social context and even the theatrical context, both reinforces the original impulse behind the writing of the play and distorts it . . . the question of informers no longer means very much [but] something human is working all by itself, sprung free of the original context, perhaps even purified of any of its author's preoccupations at the time of writing. And yet one knows that, while this purely human spectacle is the ultimate fruit of any work, one will, nevertheless, sit down and write again at a particular hour pressed by the unique weight of a particular day, addressing that day and that hour whose consequences will not even appear to the audience a year or two hence, to say nothing of a decade or in another country. It is the kind of lesson one must remember and forget at the same time.[41]

When Miller returned to the American stage in 1964 it was with a play that tried in part to replicate the processes of memory, to search through the detritus of the past in an effort to identify a coherent plot, to discover a narrative logic in private and public life. Its central character is a lawyer who comes to plead his case before an absent judge, a penitent in an empty confessional, a patient who generates the analyst who will offer a rational explanation for contingent events and a benediction that will make future life possible. Since the mind that seeks restlessly to filter meaning from the continuum of experience becomes a historical consciousness as well as an individual psyche acknowledging its own fallibility, we are exposed, at the level of metaphor, to the trauma of the Holocaust and the evils of the House Un-American Activities Committee no less than the details of personal betrayal.

Quentin, standing on the brink of marriage to a woman who has herself barely survived the horrors of the past, feels the need to reconcile himself both to his own failures and to the fallibility of the human mind and imagination that have made betrayal a constant in human affairs. Attacked at the time for what was taken to be his tasteless portrait of Marilyn Monroe, in the character of a young singing star called Maggie, and for what seemed his attempt to absolve himself of responsibility for her death, he was in fact concerned with broader issues. There is no denying the private dimension but that is the least interesting aspect of a play whose strengths and weaknesses are both factors of its ambition. The link between public and private world is not always convincingly established. Like any synthesising account of history it rests on generalisations about human experience whose plausibility is at times suspect. Heavily influenced by Camus's *La Chute*, it nonetheless moves towards a resolution which is not without its sentimentality. But this is a play whose structure and scope suggest the scale of Miller's imagination, his determination to escape the parochialism of much American drama.

In a later screen scenario, never turned into a film, much of the play's originality is set aside. Nevertheless it offers an insight into Miller's conception of the character of Quentin and the way in which his personal dilemma is to be linked to issues that take us out into the public arena. Fundamentally, he suggests:

the story must follow the unravelling of Quentin's self-illusions, his descent into despair and his ultimate grasp on certain values for himself and society.

This process involves three levels of his life. His legal practice, his psychological background, and his life with Maggie. These are strands of one rope, analogues of each other, even though detailed action on each level is concrete and detailed.

He begins as a man nagged by a sense of inauthenticity, a man unfree, carrying out his moral and ethical duties as a defender of people arraigned by the Un-American Activities Committee. He is being pressed by the rising atmosphere of intolerance and fear so that his own position is gradually menaced more and more. This threat to himself, remote at first, then more actual, presses him to search out his own real rather than sentimental position as a man in society.[42]

The problem is that having, in common with those he defends, abandoned his youthful idealism, his sense of a coherence in personal no less than in social affairs, he no longer knows in what name he lives his life other than his own and egotism, he recognises, is no principle for an authentic life. That authenticity he believes he finds in the person of Maggie, who has no regret for the past and simply lives for the moment. She, in turn, sees in him an authentication of her value, independent of her career as an entertainer. The relationship founders, each determined to defend an image of his or her own innocence. The screenplay ends with Maggie surrounded by fans and sycophants, clutching a drink, her eyes desperate, frightened, lost, all but blind, while Quentin watches from a distance, his own life drained of its original commitments but redirected to a vague belief the need for greater tolerance:

Before the Committee he refuses to destroy other people with his testimony. He sees, and says, that the country must not do this; that we are too capable of destroying one another whatever our social opinions and moral justifications. And that is what the law [is] for – to stake out the bounds of tolerance through which the state must not venture or Power be permitted to break, or we are lost, man against man, unguarded from ourselves.[43]

He joins forces with a group of young demonstrators on the courthouse steps. They are calling for a world without hypocrisy, a world full of truth where people might be human again. This, however, was an optimism he denied himself in the play – a passing concession to a youth movement that had played no role in the stage drama. The screen treatment also diverges sharply from the play in its concentration on the figure of Maggie and in its complete excision of material relating to the concentration camp. Gone, too, is the structure that made *After the Fall* in part a contemplation of time. Where the film was to be linear, Quentin's disillusionment being slowly exposed, the play folds past and present together. Such power as the play has derives from the co-presence of different time scales and different levels of experience, from the intensely personal to the profoundly social. Though the primary agency is Quentin's memory, it is less a play about an individual sensibility than one about a fundamental flaw in human nature; less a work about personal psychology than one about consciousness and the nature of the real. Fragments of experience are brought together in an attempt to see what meaning that juxtaposition might generate. If there is a logical connection between these fragments it is not a causal one. The link is associational. Nor is memory inert or pure. The full meaning of the concentration camp was not part of Quentin's literal experience, though he had visited it in an attempt to penetrate its mystery. It is summoned into being as part of a developing argument. It is a construction in two senses. So, too, are those other nodal moments from the past, edited from the continuum of experience and bevelled into shape until they cohere into a form which renders up significance.

The key word here, as in so many of Miller's plays, is betrayal. As Quentin sorts through a private and public past, as he assiduously edits and reformulates events, the one constant is provided by the need to defend oneself by denouncing others, to pronounce racial purity by finding impurity in others, to lay claim to innocence by declaring guilt. To go forward – as an individual whose most personal relationships have failed, as a society that has chosen to take vengeance on its own history, as a race which has been both victim and victimiser – it is necessary to confront the past, and to do that it is necessary first to construct that past.

After the Fall is Miller's most ambitious play. Its anxious ransacking of the national psyche and of human frailties is what amounts to a psychoanalysis cast in a theatrical form which mimicks its own methodology. The past may be sacred but it is not immutable. We are the product not of the past but of what we choose to make of that past and that is the grace which this play offers and his earlier works did not. This is the first major play in which he does not consign a major character to death. Quentin is redeemed not merely by virtue of acknowledging his own guilt but by accepting guilt itself or, more strictly, responsibility. But that brought Miller close to a dangerous paradox, for if Quentin was to be liberated from his own dark self through confession – the confession that is the play – was the same grace to be extended to the concentration camp guard and the wilful agents of the House of Un-American Activities Committee who, if we are to take his comments about Judge Danforth in *The Crucible* seriously, confirmed him in his conviction that evil is more than a rhetorical trope? Was Quentin a man who in his need for private justification and redemption would take all to heaven with him, however stained their hands might be? For the fact is that there is a massive disproportion between Quentin's guilt and that of those others whose crimes he identifies. If we are all born after the Fall are we all equal in our guilt? Not so, insists Miller. Besides, human betrayal, on the scale of genocide, must begin somewhere. Small acts of personal betrayal are not just cut from the same cloth, they are themselves the first evidence of a denial which becomes massive and definitional. That may be true but dramatically the logic is not easy to establish.

After the Fall roams restlessly through history and personal experience in an attempt to find justification for a hope not suffused with irony. Alarmed at the potential sentimentality implied by a life redeemed by love, he rests the play, instead, on an acknowledgement of human imperfection overcome by confession and knowledge. All actions are self-serving, all gestures potentially suspect unless it be the love which the play's logic wishes to embrace but dare not offer without caveat. That he nonetheless wishes to acknowledge the possibility of altruism, the reality of personal sacrifice and the survival of values not corrupted from within or without is evident from the play's companion piece, set during the Second World War, *Incident at Vichy*. Here, a number of men, picked up at random, await inspection by the German authorities in order to determine whether they should be consigned to the oblivion reserved for those whose supposed racial purity is to be rewarded with liquidation. In the very antechamber to hell, dignity and honour are allowed to shine in the dark as one of their number, whose origin and status guarantee his immunity, voluntarily surrenders that immunity rather than become indirectly complicit with murder. *Incident at Vichy* suggests the extent to which Miller resisted his own analysis in *After the Fall*.

More powerful is the third work in which he chose to confront the meaning of the Holocaust – *Playing for Time*. The story of a half-Jewish Parisian nightclub singer sent to Auschwitz and there kept alive to play in the camp's orchestra, like *After the Fall* it rests on the conviction that the sheer enormity of Nazi crimes has revealed something about human nature which we had never previously been required to face. Redemption here does not rely either on love or self-sacrifice but on acknowledgement of a guilt which implies the persistence of values which if abrogated still exert their pressure on the psyche. Under stress betrayal, it seems, is a natural instinct, a survival mechanism; but beneath that is some residual moral sense which may be suppressed but not eliminated.

After the Fall (and its companion piece *Incident at Vichy*) seems to have succeeded in laying various ghosts for Miller. Certainly the plays that followed were different in mood. Comedy, always an essential element in his work, though curiously invisible to critics, became more central. In *The Price*, indeed, he created a full-blown comic character, an 89-year-old furniture dealer who acts as an ironic counterpoint in a drama in which the past presses on the present and the present reinvents the past. Meeting among the stored furniture of the family home, two brothers reenact old antagonisms and slowly expose the tracery of misunderstanding and self-deceit which have defined their world. Time collapses, memory proves fallible, the substantial realities, implied by a sturdy realist set, prove deceptive and deceiving. Where once the past concealed truths whose unveiling would precipitate moral crisis, now it offers little more than a distorting mirror denying the very notion of a recoverable truth. History, once assumed to render up its meaning under pressure of events, now resolves into a tangle of motives and actions beyond true analysis.

As its title suggests, *The Price* reflects Miller's concern with the crucial relation between past and present, a logic which implies private and public responsibility. There is, indeed, a price to be paid. But the past is no secure territory. It is a fiction constructed to serve psychological and social needs. The contention between the two brothers thus becomes a dispute over the nature of the real no less than an argument over moral necessity. They fail to meet in the past of memory as they fail to meet in a present itself invaded by the past. The self in whose name events are interpreted, motives ascribed and meaning asserted thus itself becomes fictionalised.

Something happened in America in 1929. The birds came home to roost. A price-tag was finally placed on a decade in which payments of all kinds had been deferred. When the stock market crashed it took with it many of the illusions and myths that had fuelled American society. A contract had been broken, a certain innocence ended. After ten years of tickertape and tinsel, suddenly, there were realities. Though the engine of American expansion slowly began to turn again, and the same myths were born out of the flames of the Depression, there were those who never forgot that once they had felt their feet touch bottom, that under pressure necessities had finally been acknowledged. One such was Arthur Miller.

In the 1950s, America was to try to purge the memory of that decade, seeking publicly, through the mechanism of the House of Un-American Activities Committee, to force people to deny the lives they had lived. Arthur Miller resisted and out of that resistance was born first *An Enemy of the People* and then *The Crucible*. But it is not only the state which chooses to deny the past or rewrite it. We are all our own historians, our own biographers. The world we see is in part the world we choose to see, while memory itself is frequently in the service of present need.

The 1930s have cast their shadow over many of Miller's plays: *The Man Who Had All the Luck*, *Death of a Salesman*, *After the Fall* and *The American Clock*. *The Price* is no exception. Indeed, though it was first produced in 1968, he had known the story since the thirties but, as he said, I can't imagine writing a play just to tell a story. My effort is to find the chain of moral being moving in a hidden way. If I can't sense that I don't know where to go. It took him nearly thirty years to find it. He tried in the fifties, jotting ideas for the play in a notebook, but it wasn't until the late sixties that he recognised a shift in cultural values which reminded him of an earlier age. In the midst of the idealism of the anti-war movement and the black awakening he saw the seeds of a coming disillusionment and detected an unconcern for personal morality deepening towards the egotism and greed which would characterise the next two decades. To his mind, the twenties had been built on smoke, on the assumption that a whole society had been granted total immunity to process and moral demands. As the sixties came towards their end he felt the same mood, and, therefore, the same urgent necessity to confront fundamental realities. As he explained: the whole question arose as to whether any kind of life was possible that wasn't completely narcissistic, whether there was any truth in any emotion that wasn't totally cynical.[44] *The Price* had found its moment.

The Price effectively begins in 1929, though it is set thirty-five years later. It was in that year that the Franz family began to be displaced from the American dream. Financially ruined by the Crash, they gradually found their values placed under pressure. What happened to them then, and what they chose to do, shaped their lives.

As in so many other Miller plays the key relationship is that between a father and his two sons, though here the father is present only in memory. It is a relationship which embodies the debt which the past owes to the present and vice versa. It is itself a link in that 'chain of moral being' for which he looked, a reminder of causality, of obligation and responsibility. Here, as in *All My Sons* and *Death of a Salesman*, the two sons – Victor and Walter – represent two different approaches to life. In that sense they are the continuation of a debate in Miller's work about the qualities necessary not only for survival but for survival with dignity and meaning. In *Death of a Salesman*, Happy Loman was the materialist, the womaniser, the man for whom self lay at the centre of every action; Biff was the poet, aware of values beyond those paraded by a society in love with appearance. Together they made up the warring sides of their father's bewildered sensibility. Here, the debate seems to be one between idealism and self-sacrifice, on the one hand, and cynicism and self-concern on the other. That it is never quite that simple is what gives the play part of its fascination and integrity.

When his father retired into himself, shocked at the collapse of his world, one son, Walter, continued his medical training. Brought up to succeed, he becomes a surgeon, 'an instrument that cuts money out of people, or fame out of the world'. The other, Victor, apparently convinced of his father's destitution and unable to persuade his brother to help him, abandoned his education, pounding the beat as a policeman. In his own eyes he sacrificed his future for his father's. How far, however, are either of these adequate descriptions of the two men who now meet for the first time in sixteen years?

With their father long dead and the building in which the family furniture is still stored about to be torn down, the two brothers come together to arrange for the disposal of that furniture, piled up like the memories and hostilities which they have also squirrelled away against a day of reckoning. This is that day. So it is that they meet and expose the tracery of misunderstandings and self-deceits which have defined their relationship.

Miller has suggested that Victor is 'a thin reed' but perhaps 'all we've got . . . an idealist of a sort' who has 'carried the weight of his idealism through his life'. His brother, apparently more ruthless, is nonetheless, as a surgeon, creative and, though cruel, necessary, for without such men 'we're going to stand still'.[45] But the production, Miller insists, must 'withhold judgement', presenting both men from their own viewpoints. Indeed, when the second-hand furniture dealer, Gregory Solomon, suggests that 'the price of used furniture is nothing but a viewpoint, and if you wouldn't understand the viewpoint, is impossible to understand the price', he describes equally a fact of human nature and Miller's own theatrical strategy. At least in his own eyes Walter has changed, while in the course of the play we watch as Victor is forced to reassess his own motives and values. When Walter says of his brother and himself that 'It's almost as though . . . we're like two halves of the same guy. As though we can't quite move ahead – alone'[46] the question remains as to what those elements so joined will be. Nor can there be any suggestion of moving ahead until the past has been acknowledged and embraced. However, in a situation in which, as Walter reminds us, 'We invent ourselves', what is the past and how may we know it?

The Price begins and ends with laughter. It could scarcely be more appropriate. Though scarcely a comedy, it is a play in which humour has a vital role. That it is so is in large part because of Gregory Solomon, one of the great comic inventions of post-war American theatre. A vaudevillian, a comic archetype who self-consciously treads the edge of stereotype, he shambles onto the stage, a figure from another age. Dragged out of retirement at the age of eighty-nine to make an offer on the accumulated furniture, he is a survivor whose humour is the mechanism of that survival. Like the other characters he has paid a price for his life – a daughter dead by suicide, a chain of failed marriages and half-forgotten passions – but he leans into the future because he has come to terms with his past. Victor wears his failure like a badge of honour; Solomon recites his bankruptcies merely as a prelude to his account of an equal number of recoveries. Walter proposes a cynical deal of borderline morality which turns on a wilful deceit: Solomon offers the advice that 'it's not that you can't believe nothing, that's not so hard – it's that you've still got to believe it. *That's* hard.'[47]

I doubt whether Arthur Miller could have created such a figure as Gregory Solomon earlier in his career. No Jewish character appeared in his published work until *After the Fall* in 1964. The Holocaust, likewise, was an unspoken fact until that play and its companion piece, *Incident at Vichy*. It took that long to assimilate the meaning both of genocide and survival. Now the guilt of the survivor gives way to the celebration of the survivor. Solomon is the result, a man who at the very end of his life can now believe in possibility again.

There is, however, a kind of laughter in the play other than that generated by Solomon, or that inspired by an old record played on an ancient phonograph. This too, though, comes from the past. It is the laughter which haunts Victor's memory, the laughter with which his father had greeted his request for help to finance him through college. This laughter is cruel and self-mocking. That in the end it is blotted out by present laughter suggests that Miller is offering a certain grace. The present may be the price we pay for the past but it is not perhaps without its redemption.

The play ends with Solomon about to enter his nineties, as we have just entered ours. Already, in the final decade of the century, the birds are again coming home to roost. Across the world a price is being paid for half a century and more of cruelty, betrayal and self-deceit. For us, too, the past has suddenly erupted through the present. There is laughter in the air, though not wholly drained of irony. Once again, something has happened. Now a divided world, like a divided sensibility, yearns for reconciliation. The price of such reconciliation is truth and an acceptance of mutual failure. It is a price which, historically, has proved too great for those individuals and states too firmly wedded to their own myths of innocence. We are left with nothing more than possibility, but that, too, may be a faith worth embracing.

Miller's comments about the mystery of time . . . memory, self-formation, the degree to which We're all impersonators . . . impersonating ourselves, the extent to which 'We've all become actors',[48] not only reflect the subject and method of his 1977 play, *The Archbishop's Ceiling* (not given an adequate production, based on the original text, until two British companies performed it in the 1980s), they also suggest the extent to which it is worth considering his earlier work in this context. For the debate over the nature of the real did not begin with that play anymore than did his sense of character as a construction, a negotiation with social myths internalised as psychological necessities.

The Archbishop's Ceiling takes place in eastern Europe in what had once been an archbishop's palace. Drained of its original function, it is now home to Marcus, a writer whose contacts with authority lead to suspicions that he may be an agent of that authority and that he and his companion, Maya, a fellow writer, might be involved in compromising their fellow artists. It is suspected, in particular, that microphones are in the ceiling. Into this situation comes Adrian, an American writer anxious to justify, to Maya, his inclusion of her in his new novel. But in this situation fiction and reality are so interfused that there seem no certainties.

Certainties, however, seem called for as Sigmund – conscience of his nation – has his manuscript seized and has to decide whether or not to bow to pressures and leave the country in exchange for the return of his book.

The past – in *All My Sons* so implacable – is here uncertain, ambiguous, vague. Old relationships have to be redefined in the light of presumptions about motives which are themselves constantly in flux. The microphones that may or may not be hidden in the ceiling turn them into actors as they address a hidden audience whose existence they can only presume. But then, the presentation of the self is also plainly a tactic of everyday experience, the conscious construction of the self being particularly apparent to a group consisting, as this one does, of fiction writers. In part this is what it appears, a play about the schizophrenia which is the condition of life in a totalitarian state which has destroyed the very meaning of privacy, though there were other models rather closer to home. But Watergate and the apparatus of the totalitarian state have done more than expose corruptions at the heart of the state; they have underlined the theatricality of political and social behaviour. Several years after Miller wrote the play the ballroom of the Mayflower Hotel in Connecticut Avenue, Washington, was redecorated. The painters and plasterers found twenty-eight hidden microphones. The Mayflower, for long popular with politicians, diplomats and businessmen, had been turned into a kind of permanent theatre by the FBI, or whatever other agency was interested in the alchemical transformation of knowledge into power. But beyond the politics of meaning lies another realm which the play explores. For if all the characters in the play are contained within the fiction of the state – which ascribes meaning to actions and offers to define the reality within which they must live their lives – they are also contained within a fiction inscribed by Arthur Miller, and their very status as writers serves to underline the metatheatrical element. But if he is a kind of god who observes the characters he creates it is worth recalling that the action of the play takes place in an archbishop's palace, its baroque splendour now lost in the gloom. Once it was presumed that no action, no event was too small to command the attention of a deity whose celestial plan gave coherence to lives which would be without meaning or purpose if that god were to absent himself. Not a sparrow could fall from the sky but that He would acknowledge its fall. Everything could be decoded in terms of metaphysical significance. The individual might not be free but he was secure in the conviction that his life was charged with meaning. The absence of

privacy was the guarantee of an ever-present help. Remove that hea-
venly audience, deny the hearing ear and the seeing eye and what would
remain? A text with no author.

Not the least of the ironies of the play lies in the questions which it
raises on metaphysical, social and psychological levels. The characters in
The Archbishop's Ceiling derive their sense of their own significance precisely from their conviction that there are microphones in the ceiling,
that they merit attention, that their personal decisions have more than a
personal meaning. The eavesdroppers, the distant audience, represent a
coercive or manipulative principle but also the root of their personal
identities. The real fear, perhaps, is to find oneself an actor in an empty
theatre – the situation of Tennessee Williams's characters in *Outcry* – or,
like Beckett's characters in *Waiting for Godot*, to discover that the world
sends back no echoes, that there is no one to affirm or deny one's actions,
no one to embrace or deny, no one inscribing a plot. A courageous act
publicly performed requires less courage than one done in a privacy that
drains it of its social meaning. Perhaps it is worse to know that there is
no judge sitting on the Bench, but was that not the situation in *After the
Fall, Incident at Vichy* and *Playing for Time*? Was not John Proctor debating
whether there were powers unseen who possessed the sanction to define
the real? And were Willy Loman's dreams less substantial than the myths
to which his society subscribed? Who did Willy address in his reveries if
not the self in which he wished to place his faith? He is a salesman, an
actor whose performance falters when he can no longer gain access to
his audience. Miller may have said that he would never have written for
the theatre if he had not believed he and it could change the world – a
conviction which faltered with time – but in fact his work has always
been concerned with transformations. Like so many of his characters
Willy is searching for some foundation to his life, some irreducible reality
to which he may subscribe. The problem, given the factitious nature of
experience, is to find the basis for moral action.

In the 1980s Miller turned back to his own past, as he was to do, more
formally, with his autobiography, *Timebends*. *The American Clock* was in
effect the Depression play that he did not write or at any rate did not
have produced in the 1930s. It was no accident that he should have
turned to the subject in 1980 in that then, and in the decade that followed, many of the conditions of the Depression were recreated in an
America which to his mind had once again drifted away from underlying realities. *The American Clock* is an epic drama which sets out to turn

back 'the American clock . . . in search of those feelings that once ruled our lives and were stolen from us all by time'.[49]

The Great Depression, Miller suggests, was one of only two genuinely national catastrophes in American history to be felt by virtually everybody – the other being the Civil War. The gods had spoken. Some kind of judgement had been made. Reality had been changed and a hidden principle had revealed itself: 'It transformed the world from one in which there was an authority of some kind, to one in which you were convinced that there was no one there, that there was no one running the store.'[50] There is something almost Calvinist in his diagnosis of the period. The chickens were indeed coming home to roost: 'America had been on some kind of obscene trip, looking to get rich at any cost right through the 20s, at any cost to the spirit, and had elevated into power the men who could most easily lead that kind of quest. And that aggrandisement is what led to the disaster of '29 and the Crash.' From the perspective of the mid-1980s it was a world in the process of recreating itself. 'They were sharks dealing not only with the economy but the spiritual side of the country. And there's a bit of that today not only here, but all over the world. There's never been a more materialistic moment since I've been around.'[51]

After the 1920s, a decade of hucksterism in which reality was defined by pieces of paper (share certificates, bonds, and, above all, money) suddenly you could hear the sound of America breaking apart. Miller heard that sound as clearly as anyone, certainly as clearly as that poet of decline, F. Scott Fitzgerald. Both stressed the insubstantiality of the twenties. Thus where Fitzgerald observed that 'the snow of 1929 wasn't real snow. If you didn't want it to be real snow you just paid some money and it went away', Miller has a character in *The American Clock* declare that 'they believed in the most important thing of all – that nothing is real! That if it was Monday and you wanted it to be Friday, and enough people could be made to believe it was Friday – then by God it was Friday.'[52] The thirties brought if not reality then necessity.

Back in the thirties, however, the two men stood at different ends of their careers and viewed the world differently. For Fitzgerald, 1929 marked the end of something, confirmation that his portraits of spoiled priests, faltering idealists and self-betraying artists reflected a society which was similarly flawed: for Arthur Miller, it was the beginning of a new world in which causalities were revealed and hence responsibilities confirmed, in which a new democracy of suffering suggested a possible democracy of social and moral action. It was clear enough in the plays that he wrote in the 1930s, plays he wrote as he was going through college or working briefly for the Federal Writers' Project; it is clear, too, in the play he wrote fifty years later, a play written in the late seventies, in 'a country that had no relationship to any I knew', in which 'there was no definition to the society'. Writing after the sixties, in which once again the real seemed to be held at arm's length, and the seventies, in which self-absorption became a value, he felt the need to assert certain truths: 'What I wanted to do was tell people that there is such a thing as necessity. I wanted to tell them that underneath the surface there is a skeletal structure of human relations which is still there. And you find that when the surface collapses.'[53]

The American Clock looks back on the thirties from the perspective of half a century. It identifies the potency of fictions celebrated as realities; it announces the breaking of a spurious authority. It acknowledges the solidarity which was a product of shared suffering, but stresses, too, a fundamental caesura in experience, the radical discontinuity that left so many adrift: 'The structure of the world shook', he has explained. 'What could you believe in?'[54] But while offering to capture the mood of a nation at a critical historical juncture it is, perhaps, at its most vital when it comes closest to Miller's own life, when memory is reshaped as image. Like O'Neill and Williams, in this late play he chooses to return to his own youth and to enter his own drama. In part this is a public drama, which recreates a world of failed financiers, ruined businessmen and bankrupt farmers, but it is also Miller's odyssey in time as he travels back to his own youth, pulling into some kind of shape events which had once appeared merely contingent. So, his long-ago stolen bicycle is transformed from social fact to social symbol. Worries about college tuition, once immediate and practical issues, are now seen in the context of a national experience in which personal dilemmas render up a public meaning. In the original American production the character who comes closest to being a portrait of his mother (though Miller is inclined to dispute this) was actually played by his own sister, herself an actress of some considerable reputation.

There is something of the thirties, too, about the structure of the play, an Odets-style family drama embedded in a social play which offers cameo portraits of an America in which the lives of the rich and poor momentarily coincided. It is a play which still reflects something of the idealism and optimism of that period. Indeed, *The American Clock* comes close to concluding with the word 'Sing', which inevitably brings to mind Clifford Odets's *Awake and Sing*, a play to which Miller had responded with enthusiasm forty years earlier. It is a play, too, which somehow retains his youthful confidence and offers some kind of benediction. It is, after all, he insists, 'ultimately about survivors'. At the same time it is a play that acknowledges that 'there is a clock running on all civilisations. There is a beginning and an end. What is the hour? That is the question. The job of the artists', he insists, 'is to remind people of what they'd rather forget.'[55]

Nor is the emphasis on time merely an indication of social urgency. As he has explained, 'I've become more interested in what is real . . . the mystery of time. I could reduce the history of cultures to how they deal with time, memory, self-formation. We're all impersonators. We're all impersonating even ourselves. We've all become actors.'[56] The connection between time, memory, identity and performance, indeed, became increasingly central, the one-act plays of the 1980s making such concerns their central theme. But while Miller acknowledged fragmentation, dissolution and the coercive pressure of unreality, he also stressed the need for recuperation, for the reassertion not so much of values, though those were implicit in the structure no less than the themes of his works, as of continuity and connectiveness, of that very sense of community that makes theatre possible and necessary. Both *The American Clock* and *The Archbishop's Ceiling* 'were hard-minded attempts to grasp what I felt life in the seventies had all but lost – a unified concept of human beings, the intimate psychological side joined with the social-political. I wanted', he added, 'to set us in our history by revealing a line to measure from. In *Clock* it was the objective facts of the social collapse; in *Archbishop*, the bedrock circumstances of real liberty.'[57] To his mind art had come to prize and to celebrate disconnectiveness for its own sake. That disconnectiveness was genuine enough but art in some fundamental way is surely, he insists, a denial of the very chaos it observes and the artist is one who peoples desolation and inscribes the meaning he suspects may not exist.

Casually dismissed as a realist, in fact Miller has experimented with form, disassembled character, compressed and distended language, and seen in the theatrical plot a paradigm of other constructs having to do with identity and social form. His commitment to a morally accountable and socially responsible self has not inhibited him from exploring the contingency alike of character and public myths. But in a fundamental way his theatre exists to bear witness to those human necessities which survive a knowledge of their fragility. The coercive fictions of the state or the self are nonetheless corrosive for their fictiveness and the theatre nonetheless real for its theatricality. It is that reality which Miller serves.

In *Two-Way Mirror* he created an emotionally powerful drama in which the very substance of reality disassembled as character proves unstable, and this work, which contains two one-act plays, simultaneously underlines the continuities in Miller's work and the extent to which, in terms of style, approach to character and plot, and his sense of the fragility of language he has proved very much our contemporary. As its name implies *Two-Way Mirror* takes us into a world of images, a place of appearances in which things are not quite what they seem. Realities exist but are refracted through memory and approached through guilt and self-concern.

In the first play, *Elegy for a Lady*, a man is revealed, motionless, as yet a character without substance or meaning. Then he begins to act, entering what seems to be a boutique where it transpires he has come to seek a gift for a dying woman. Inside the story is another figure, also motionless, like an actor waiting to go on stage, to enter the drama about to be played out. She, the proprietress, greets the man as a stranger. Then, in assisting him, she slowly raises doubts both about his relationship to the absent woman and the nature of that woman's condition. Is she dying? If so, of what? And how close is he really to the person he claims to love?

By degrees some kind of identity between the absent woman and the person who confronts him begins to emerge before, one by one, they slip out of our vision. The woman becomes motionless, then disappears in the dying light. The man leaves the stage, alone. Are they both real or does one exist only in the mind of the other? Are we watching an elaborate charade, a game played out for their mutual satisfaction or perhaps even for the author's pleasure in constructing character, language and story only to dissolve them again with equal arbitrariness? The questions proliferate.

In the second play, *Some Kind of Love Story*, a detective interrogates a woman who may hold the key to a five-year-old murder. She has called him to her, as she has in the past. Former lovers, they come together apparently to reconstruct the details of the crime. But under what is evidently extreme psychological stress her identity constantly threatens to collapse as she slips into a series of different roles: street-corner prostitute, high-tone lady. What is at stake is her own sanity, her relationship with the detective and perhaps even the state of society itself. For the truth she hints at, but will not confirm with hard evidence, suggests a corruption so deep as to destroy the very notion of law and justice. But is this paranoia or the truth? Are detective and call-girl linked by a common pursuit of justice or by love? And how do we disinter motives which may lie too deep even for those involved to uncover?

The two plays were written, and can plainly be performed, separately. They contrast in tone and style. *Elegy for a Lady* is elegiac, its characters summoned into existence to explore an experience which perhaps evades definition. It is elusive, a subdued piece for two voices, stylistically formal and located in a setting which is rendered impressionistically. *Some Kind of Love Story* is socially situated. The functional realism of the set, with its bed and telephone, its clutter of clothing, locates character in a specific milieu. The play takes place in a world that seems entirely familiar, if remote from our own experiences. A detective sets about the task of discovering facts, and facts, surely, are the pathway to truth. What is a crime story, after all, but a demonstration of the power of rationality over feeling? But does truth really offer itself up quite so easily? Not so here, it appears. The facts are squirrelled away in the mind of a psychotic and therefore are suspect. The detective is, or has been, in love with his witness, and it is love not crime which the play's title chooses to emphasise.

So the contrast between the two plays is perhaps not as sharp as it appears. *Elegy for a Lady*, for all its stylised relationships and allusive language, conjures up a world which is not remote from daily experience. There is, surely, something recognisable about the manner in which the man projects his anxieties, invests his emotional and psychological needs with substance and in part seems to invent the woman he wishes to regard as his lover. Something, too, not entirely outside our experience in the way in which the woman presents herself in more than one guise. In *Some Kind of Love Story*, contrariwise, the apparently rational process of investigative logic slowly dissolves, as character proves too fragile to sustain itself. Social certainties, psychological consistency and moral necessities are all placed under pressure.

In 1991 Miller chose to open his new play, *The Ride Down Mount Morgan*, in London's West End rather than New York. It was a decision which reflected his dismay at the decline of a Broadway theatre which at that time, he insisted, was staging only one play with any serious pretensions, and that a Neil Simon comedy. But there were other reasons why Britain had become a more receptive environment for his drama.

In effect he had been driven from the public stage from the mid-1950s to the mid-1960s. Political reaction meant that there was no longer an audience for a playwright dedicated to testing American values. When he returned the theatre itself had changed. The sixties saw a revolt against the playwright and against language itself. Artaud-influenced theatre groups chose to privilege the actor and to treat with some suspicion those distinguishing marks of a Miller play: rationality, lucidity and the sequential logic of morality. Theirs was a theatre in which the body was legitimised and the Reality Principle subordinated to the Pleasure Principle. This was never true in Britain, where for cultural, class and educational reasons, language remained central and physicality was distrusted. Miller's theatre, resolutely committed to the word, was readily embraced.

Then again, Miller has always been concerned with the flawed self, the tragic sensibility, and this in a culture whose central myths have to do with innocence, optimism and perfectibility. Europe has quite other myths and a history which offers a different vision of human nature, one which finds in Miller's serious engagement with moral issues, as in his increasing fascination with the nature of the real and the substance of identity, a writer of genuine power and fascination. In the seventies and eighties when much (though not all) American theatre, reflecting changes in the culture, had turned towards privatism, Miller remained committed to an exploration of social issues in a way which found a response in Britain whose theatre had, since the fifties, been socially oriented and in a continent in which notions of private guilt and social responsibility had a clear historical referent. Perhaps not only because of his admiration for Greek drama and the work of Ibsen, but also because of his Jewish background, Miller has always insisted on the reality of the *polis*, the notion that the individual is ineluctably part of the social system and derives his or her identity from interaction with others. From this derives a moral responsibility. This truth, however, he offers in a culture profoundly suspicious of social systems. Nixon's and Reagan's America, which forms the setting for *The Ride Down Mount Morgan*, seemed to many to be based on a denial of the social contract and a legitimising of a self detached from personal and public responsibility.

The Ride Down Mount Morgan is a play about a man with no morals but, at least in his own mind, complete integrity. Lyman Felt is a bigamist who has convinced himself that, as a result, he has given two women what they wanted, bearing the burden of knowledge himself. One night, returning to one of them down a snow-covered mountainside, having removed a warning barrier, he crashes and ends up in a hospital bed where the two wives come together, though whether in his mind or actuality is never conclusively established. If Miller's drama is based on what happens when one of his characters can no longer walk away then Lyman's circumstances, immobilised in a plaster cast, ensure that he must now confront his situation.

The play has ironic echoes of *Death of a Salesman*. In the earlier play a man called Loman had tried to claim the American dream, reaching for success in material and sexual terms, only to find himself with nothing. In *The Ride Down Mount Morgan* a man called Lyman appears to have everything, money and sexual possessions, but now has to confront himself. In the earlier play a shadowy figure called Uncle Ben warns against fighting fair with strangers. In this one a similarly shadowy figure – Lyman's dead father – warns him not to trust or forgive. Lyman is part poet, part businessman, a division equally apparent in *Death of a Salesman*, though there, as in *The Price*, these qualities are divided between two brothers, almost as though they are enacting a schism at the heart of the American experience, a culture born out of a spiritual and material impulse. The themes, so apparent in all his plays – guilt, betrayal – are at the centre of this play, too. Even the structure of *The Ride Down Mount Morgan* resembles that of *Death of a Salesman*, *After the Fall* and *Timebends*, as time is collapsed and events are summoned into existence by a mind in which memory and desire are merely two witnesses brought before a court in which the audience alone constitutes the jury.

For all that, this is a play which speaks out of its own moment even as it speaks to others. Written in the seventies and eighties it has elements of both decades, an original reference to Nixon's election being replaced in the course of rehearsals by one to Reagan's. Thus, Lyman voices both the 1970s slogan, 'believe in your feelings' and a 1980 cynicism: 'We're all ego plus an occasional prayer.' As Miller has remarked of Lyman,

he's the quintessential Eighties Man, the man who has everything, but there's no end to his appetite. He keeps saying he's telling the truth about himself, but in fact he's had to conceal everything . . . he discovers that betrayal is the first law of life, that you can either be loyal to yourself or to others but not to both. Your only hope is to end up with the right regrets.[58]

It is, he insists, 'a completely political play'.[59] So, in a sense, it is, but, for Miller, the political is of a piece with what he has called 'the biology of morals'. There is no politics not rooted in individual decisions, while private morality and public morality are of the same flesh. Lyman has collapsed his world into a privatism whose politics he chooses not to address. For Miller he is 'the apotheosis of the individualist who has arrived at a point where the rest of the world has faded into insignificance'.[60]

Lyman wishes to live without guilt and without unsatisfied longings. Convinced that a man can be faithful to himself or to others but not to both, and that the first law of life is betrayal, he sets out to follow the logic of his own desires, seeing this as a form of integrity. In doing so he exults in escaping definition, becoming one person with one wife and another with the other. Theodora, the older of the two, is deeply conservative in all things, tense, possessive; Leah is relaxed, considers abortion, lives life in the fast stream. In one sense, they are literally what he makes of them; in another, what he fears or suspects.

In the play's present Lyman is fifty-six years old, just a year short of the age at which his father (deleted from later texts) died. That father's appearance, trailing a length of black cloth in which he offers to ensnare his son, is thus an expression of Lyman's mortality and an explanation, perhaps, for his desire to resist habit and definition alike. The shifted chronology hardly undermines this, merely changing its political context. For the fact is that by the end of the play he seems close to discovering some kind of meaning in the very banalities which he had fled, in the insignificant details of daily living and continuing relationships. In the meantime, though, he has sought in danger an antidote to routine, only to discover that there is a routine even to betrayal.

The Ride Down Mount Morgan poses director and actors with a major challenge. It is comic without being a comedy and tragic without being a tragedy. You might say that bigamy implies a touch of farce while adultery suggests a level of pain: those, at any rate, have been their theatrical connotations. Here, the humour slowly darkens towards irony. The actors have to shift from one mood to another. Lyman himself, who at times steps out and away from the plaster encased figure on the bed, has both to be able to look down on himself with a sense of detachment and remain passionate about the women he purports to love and the life he wishes to redeem through action. As an audience we see partly through his eyes, his memory, which sometimes reproduces the past, sometimes stylises it, and partly, or so it seems, independently of the man who has perhaps staged this drama out of his own sense of doubt and incompletion as out of his desire for the danger of crisis. Judgement is thus no easy matter.

Because of this double vision it is difficult, too, to make definitive judgements on the two women, for if they seem to represent, at times, too clear a polarity, this is in large degree because they are presented to us through the transforming imagination and memory of Lyman. The real is no more stable here than it had been in *Two-Way Mirror*, and yet, of course, since Lyman inhabits the world he invents and responds to the women he projects there is a reality to memory and to those constructions which he makes of those he encounters. Indeed, from *The Golden Years* onwards Miller has been concerned to acknowledge the degree to which myths are no less real than the diminished world which inspires their creation.

The Ride Down Mount Morgan is a portrait of an imperial self, absorbing others, colonising their lives. Staged at a time of other collapsing empires – this time public and political rather than private and psychological – it offers a diagnosis and perhaps even a prognosis of a culture itself appropriating moral rhetoric to disguise moral decay. Greed and self-righteousness co-exist. Sensuality is a temptation, an isolating appetite which leads to the breaking of personal contracts. In play after play that small fracture widens into a radical dislocation of social responsibilities. 'Why are our betrayals what we remember?' asks Miller, 'because those are the acts that bring the world down.'[61]

There is no resolution to *The Ride Down Mount Morgan*. If betrayal is indeed bred in the bone perhaps there could be none. There is, however, in the play's structuring device, a reminder that the past is never the past; it lives on into the present as evidence of the link between action and consequence and hence between will and moral being. And though such continuities may be the basis of ethical demands they are not suggestive of a static self. Lyman Felt is various. What he seeks is some constancy beneath his various selves. Like many of Miller's characters he wants to drag the world into alignment with his self-image. The world is no less resistant in his case than in that of Willy Loman and Eddie Carbone, but, where they die, he lives on. Possibility survives. Comedy asserts a restraining pressure on the tragic potential, a liberating force on the closed world which seals off the fate of many of his protagonists.

From 1968 onwards, with the production of *The Price*, comedy has played a more central role in his work than in the early plays, touched with humour though they are. His own response is to suggest that with age 'it gets funnier'. Perhaps. There was always irony, born out of a gulf between reality and appearance. Now, though, his sense of the protean nature of identity and the insubstantiality of the real leaves him with moral certainties which can only be sustained with an awareness of their fragility. Late plays have a way of drifting in the direction of comedy, albeit for Miller, as for O'Neill before him, touched with a leaven of darkness. Comedy becomes value. So it does here. But then, so, too, does theatre itself:

Watching a play is not like lying on a psychiatrist's couch or sitting alone in front of the television. In the theatre you can sense the reaction of your fellow citizens along with your own reactions. You may learn something about yourself, but sharing it with others brings a certain relief – the feeling that you are not alone, you're part of the human race. I think that's what theatre is about and why it will never be finished.[62]

It is certainly what Miller's theatre has been about and continues to be about, for to his mind it is an antidote to that very privatism, that concern with the self over others, which is the temptation offered to us all and which makes possible private and public betrayals.

Miller followed *The Ride Down Mount Morgan*, a play that he revised later in the 1990s, with *The Last Yankee* (1993), set in a mental hospital where three women are in a state of recoil from their lives. One remains catatonic throughout; a second, Karen, married to a businessman who barely understands her, seeks oblique strategies that may heal whatever wounds she bears; the third, Patricia, is on the verge of rejoining the world.

Patricia is the child of immigrants and has, like the rest of her family, bought into the American dream though, like them, at great cost. Two brothers, who felt that their lives did not match up to the dream, committed suicide. She herself is bewildered by her fate and frustrated by her husband, Leroy's, refusal to join the American search for success. He is a carpenter, in part building the world he inhabits. For him, the peremptory demands of a materialistic society matter less than other values.

For Karen's husband, a local wholesaler, time is money. He merely sells while Leroy builds. He is restless, upwardly mobile. He sees the world as a competitive arena where people fight for advantage. The subtler needs of human relationship pass him by. For Leroy there are other imperatives. Time is locked up in the things he builds. This is human time. Much the same goes for his relationship with his wife. He has, in her eyes, wilfully failed to seize what America has to offer, settling for something less than he should aspire to. From his point of view, however, he already possesses what he values. The play is an account of Patricia's slow realisation of this fact and his gradual acceptance of the price he has asked her to pay in marrying him.

A deceptively simple play – made for the economics of 1990s theatre, with its simple set and five characters – it is a subtle portrait of those struggling to adjust to their failure to become what they or others wished them to be and their slow understanding of the extent of their true possibilities. A blend of humour, irony and occasional sentimentality, *The Last Yankee* was, perhaps, a final comment on a decade in which a resurgent American dream had been invoked to justify the subordination of older values to do with civility, human contact and a direct relationship to the world.

The Last Yankee has all the affecting simplicity of a fable. It ends, however, ambiguously. Patricia leaves the hospital with her husband, no longer on medication but not yet fully reconciled to a seemingly diminished world. Karen may or may not forge a new relationship with her husband and the world that bemuses her, while the third woman remains inert, as she has throughout, too deeply damaged, it appears, to reconcile herself with life. And it is with this figure that we are left, the lights slowly fading on this image of inertia, though audiences, plainly, at times, wish Leroy and Patricia's departure to mark the true end, a desire sometimes acceded to by directors or nervous lighting technicians unwilling to allow the elevating applause to die down to uneasy silence.

Miller's major play of the 1990s, however, was undoubtedly *Broken Glass* (1994). Largely ignored in America, it was staged by the Royal National Theatre in Britain and won the Laurence Olivier Award as best play of the year. It was a sharp divide that emphasised his contrasting reputation in the two countries, Britain regarding him as a major voice at the end of the century and his own country as a writer of the 1940s and 1950s who had, unaccountably, survived for another half-century. The 1999 production of *Death of a Salesman* on Broadway put him back at the centre of attention but still as a writer of classic plays for another era.

Broken Glass was itself set in the past, in 1938, the year of Kristallnacht, when Hitler unleashed his blackshirts against the Jews and showed the world what was in store. The world responded by doing nothing. But this play of forgotten wounds and past cruelties was not offered as a piece of dark nostalgia, for as ever it was present circumstances which prompted Miller's return to the past. For the fact is that ethnic cleansing was again a reality in Europe, as was the desecration of Jewish graves. The spiralling cruelties of the former Yugoslavia were acted out as he wrote the play and it went into rehearsal.

Broken Glass is set in America but the shadow of events in Europe falls on its characters. Sylvia Gellburg, married to a man who is both proud of his achievement as a Jew and desperate to deny his Jewishness, is terrified by Kristallnacht with its sudden evidence of a broken human contract, not least because it has an echo in her private life, her husband having withdrawn from intimate contact with her many years before. She suddenly loses the use of her legs, becoming paralysed.

The paralysis is quite literal but plainly has symbolic force. Fifty years earlier Miller had written *The Golden Years*, in which he had responded to the paralysis that had characterised America and the European powers in the face of fascist aggression and anti-Semitism, choosing to displace this into an historical drama about Montezuma and Cortes. Now he responded to the new paralysis in the face of genocide (and Rwanda, no less than Yugoslavia, provided evidence for this).

Sylvia is unsure whether it is the shock of the news from Europe that lies at the heart of her problem or her relationship with her husband, who, in denying his own identity, denies, too, the woman he still loves but with whom he can no longer connect. The play went through several titles, including *The Man in Black* and *Gellburg*. The emphasis, in other words, was on the male character. In the final version Sylvia moves much closer to the centre as the emphasis falls on the broken relationship which characterises both private and public intercourse.

The play's ending changed several times, even in rehearsal. In one version Philip suffers a heart attack but is still alive. In another it is unclear whether he is alive or dead. In the final published version it seems that he is indeed dead. It is a crucial matter for the play ends with the paralysed Sylvia rising to her feet. The risk is that the play will imply that she can only assume responsibility for her life when released to do so by the death of her husband rather than as a result of her own self-realisation. It is a difficult scene to play. In the end, perhaps, we are left simply with a sense of ambiguity.

Broken Glass – laced through with comedy as well as pain – is a deeply affecting study not simply of the ease with which we collude in our fate, accede to a spurious sense of inevitability, but also of those continuing Miller concerns: betrayal and denial. Philip Gellburg will not acknowledge who he is and hence his kinship with those, the relevance of whose fate he wishes to deny. Sylvia will not accept that she has put her life on hold in the name of nothing more than habit or convention. Like *All My Sons* and *Death of a Salesman*, *The Crucible* and *After the Fall*, indeed like virtually all of his plays, *Broken Glass* is about the need for individuals to acknowledge responsibility for their lives and thereby for the society of which they are a part. It was not the message of the 1980s, in which money seemed the only reality and greed a sanctioned value; it was not the message of the 1990s, in which blame could be displaced on to others and sanctioned with litigation. It was, however, the central conviction of a playwright for whom political and social policies were an extension of individual decisions and history the agent and not the master of man.

Arthur Miller's plays turn on metaphors – the salesman, the crucible, the bridge, the fall, broken glass – and are themselves metaphors. He condenses narrative into image and expands image into narrative. His is a moral theatre, a liberal theatre, in that it insists on the reality of those connections which tie action to consequence, past to present, self to society.

Interestingly, his final play of the 1990s, *Mr Peters' Connections* (1998), expressed precisely these assumptions. Mr Peters finds himself in what appears to be a disused nightclub in New York City, without quite knowing how he came to be there or who the people are whom he encounters. He is, it appears, in that unreal time which comes on the brink of sleep but also, perhaps, on the edge of death, in that this is a man looking back on his life, and trying to make sense of it, looking back on his society and trying to understand what it has added up to. His repeated question, 'what's the subject?' is the lament of a man who has lost the plot of his life and suspects that the same could be said of his society. The conviction that time would prove the agent of revelation has proved unsustainable. Life seems to have added up to little more than a series of events, encounters, individuals, places, swept away by the passing years.

This is not Miller's *Krapp's Last Tape*. The ironies do not strike as deep. The humour is of a different order. We are not treated to the sight of a man running his finger along the razor-blade of his life. Mr Peters simply contemplates a life whose forward momentum seemed to imply a destination but which has brought him to a place where the past seems to offer no meaning, and he is detached from the passions that once dominated his life and gave some shape to the quotidian.

We are back where Miller took us in *Death of a Salesman* and *After the Fall*, inside the mind of a man desperate to justify himself. The connections between one moment and another, one person and another, no longer seem as clear as they once did. The world is changing and the change leaves him stranded. Once an airline pilot for Pan American, he has lived to see that business, once emblematic of a country on wing to the future, collapse and disappear. Nonetheless, there are moments in that past which still flood his life with light – a lover, the beauty of the sky – so that perhaps the true connections are not those that imply some unfolding pattern of significance but the epiphanies, the transcendent moments that, finally, are what justify life to itself.

For all his recognition of the relativity of truth, for all his acceptance that reality may be no more than a series of performed gestures, Miller is unwilling to let go of certain fixed points. The rocks beneath the waves are not figments of our imagination and the responsibility to indicate their presence remains. There are certain human necessities which must be acknowledged. It may no longer be possible to believe that below the mud is solid granite but, for Miller, beyond the fantasies, the self-deceptions, the distortions of private and public myths are certain obligations which cannot be denied. The present cannot be severed from the past nor the individual from his social context; that, after all, is the basis of his dramatic method and of his moral faith. For if the chickens do not come home to roost we are no longer tied to our actions. A world without consequence is a world without meaning and to a writer who began his career as an admirer of the Greek theatre such an assumption renders theatre itself null. What else is theatre, after all, than a shared apprehension of a common condition, an acknowledgement that there is a level at which the experience of one is the experience of all? It is that simple truth which lies at the heart of Arthur Miller's drama and which, outside of his writing, has led him to speak out in the face of investigative committees in his own country or the oppressed around the world. His real achievement, however, is as a writer whose plays have proved so responsive to the shifting pressure of the social world and whose characters embody that desperate desire for dignity and meaning which is the source of their wayward energy, their affecting irony and their baffled humanity.

CHAPTER FIVE

Edward Albee: journey to apocalypse

In 1959 something was coming to an end. The Eisenhower years were drifting to a close. A man whose status as wartime commander linked him to the urgencies of another age was giving way to someone who self-consciously presented himself as a harbinger of the new, projecting a new frontier in space and promoting style as a value. The empty materialism of the 1950s, in which consumerism was its own justification, now, under Kennedy, apparently required a moral justification, at least at the level of political rhetoric. And if liberal endeavour was still in the service of cold war politics, as conservative Republicanism had shown itself willing to engage at least some of the political implications of domestic social injustice, the shift in direction was clear. Age was handing the torch to youth. New possibilities were on the agenda.

This was no less true on a cultural level. In the theatre new writers emerged: Jack Gelber, Jack Richardson and Edward Albee. Jack Gelber's *The Connection* disturbed theatrical as well as social conventions. Here was a play that seemed to allow the temporal sense as well as the social reality of the drug addict onto the stage. Ostensibly improvised, it offered an urban existentialism denied by its own dramatic strategies, as character and plot were drained of content, and language was deformed by context and subordinated to music which alone was genuinely improvised. *The Connection* had its social roots on the streets and its theatrical roots in Pirandello and Beckett. Nor should the impact of Beckett be forgotten.

With the emergence of the theatre of the absurd in Europe the theatrical balance had seemed temporarily to tilt towards Europe in the fifties. Beckett, Ionesco, Adamov and, more tangentially, Pinter, seemed to be placing the conventions of theatre under pressure, to be issuing a challenge to a drama rooted in psychology and sociology. The self was no longer presented as secure, menaced from within and without, but a resistant centre where conflict implied resolution. Now the self appeared costumed in irony, deflated by context, diminished by situation. The theatre of the absurd, like the *nouveau roman*, was a logical product of a post-war Europe still numbed by the implications of a conflict that had left the assumptions of liberal humanism as devastated as its cities. America never had to confront the evidence of genocide and betrayal. Beckett's defoliated tree and deserted landscape, like Robbe-Grillet's privileging of setting over character, had its literal correlative, to a degree unsuspected by those who had emerged from the war materially prosperous and with the conviction that the human spirit had prevailed.

America was anyway ill-suited to the absurd in a number of respects, despite O'Neill's late plays. Its actor-training was committed to psychological veracity, its theatrical tradition at odds with the absurd's denial of social conflict. But, more fundamentally than that, the absurd was in radical conflict with basic American myths having to do with the integral self and the inevitability of progress.

Both Gelber and Albee bore the marks of the absurd but neither, finally, settled for its radical revisioning. Nonetheless, 1959 did turn out to be a significant year for the American theatre. The success of Off-Broadway opened access to new writers and audiences. Miller's and Williams's plays had opened on Broadway. They were thus dependent on audiences whose own values were likely to be fundamentally at odds with their own, but audiences which at least gave the impression of homogeneity. The small theatres of Off and Off-Off Broadway, scattered as they were in less fashionable parts of town, required greater commitment from their audiences and a predisposition to respond to new work moving in new directions. It was in 1959, too, that the Ford Foundation began making grants to theatre, a theatre which was beginning to decentralise. Thus, across in San Francisco the Actors' Workshop and then the San Francisco Mime Troupe began a process which was to continue throughout the next two decades. Meanwhile, back in New York, the 1959 production of *The Connection* marked a new stage in the development of a key company of the 1960s, the Living Theatre, while the production of Albee's *The Zoo Story* suggested the emergence of a major new talent.

Edward Albee is, in his themes and concerns, a post-nuclear writer. Apocalypse and eschatology are in the air. His fundamental theme is the collapse of communality, the Other as threat. The overwhelming mood is elegiac. His subject is loss, desolation, spiritual depletion. But where in Beckett's work that would breed irony, here, at least in the early plays, it generates a faith in the possibility of redemption. The despair, the more corrosive, the perhaps more self-regarding irony lay ahead. For the moment his was a drama which called for a renewal of the spirit and the revival of liberal values. In that sense he was a product of the Kennedy years.

Viewed from the perspective of the 1990s, Albee's career has been a disappointing one. Early promise was followed, in the seventies and eighties, by a succession of public and artistic failures. His tone became petulant, his language pedantic, his characters pure constructs drained alike of function and conviction. His early plays were powerful and original. The energy and precision of his language was in the service of dramatic metaphors which were convincing precisely to the degree that they were rooted in characters and situations which sustained belief. This is not to say that his was a realist's talent. Some of his later works effectively explore a language detached from context, indeed a language which is all that remains of a civilisation that had destroyed itself through its lack of civility and concern. But he is at his best when the ironies which he explores are grounded in social and psychological substance: *The Zoo Story*, *Who's Afraid of Virginia Woolf?*, *A Delicate Balance*. His is an acute intelligence. His fascination with language – its evasions no less than its precisions – is never less than compelling. But a growing abstraction, a deepening privatism, a concern for the arcane and the tendentiously oblique began to erode his support in the theatre. Though his refusal to repeat early success was admirable, in the quarter of a century which followed *Who's Afraid of Virginia Woolf?* few of his plays came close to achieving either the public impact or the consistency of achievement of his early work.

Thematically, that work was a reaction against materialism drained of transcendence, the confusion of human with exchange values. It responded to an apocalypticism alive in a culture in which nuclear annihilation was felt to be a real and immediate political possibility. At first that took the form of powerful metaphors of human alienation, a drift towards isolation which carried the threat of private and public dissolution, to be neutralised and resisted by a desperately belated renewal of love. The potential for sentimentality in this prototypically 1960s resolution is obviated by a brutally direct language and a model of character which leaves little space for casual epiphany. Religious faith might be specifically rejected in *Tiny Alice*, but faith of some kind remained. However, a clock was running on Albee's limited optimism and the death of Kennedy seems to have set the alarm bells ringing. Vietnam and Watergate marked the end of 'a period in which people in the United

States thought anything and everything was possible'. What happened next was a growing national cynicism which led Albee himself to 'become less and less certain about the resiliance of civilization'.[1] The result was reflected in the black ironies of *A Delicate Balance*, the post-apocalyptic elegy which was *Box* and *Quotations from Chairman Mao Tse-Tung* and the social, moral and political implications pointedly reflected by the title of another of his plays, *All Over*.

When Albee first appeared he seemed what he claimed to be – a 'demonic social critic'. By indirection he dramatised a deeply uncommunal people, alienated from one another and from the public world whose authority they denied but whose imperatives they seemingly acknowledged if only in the nervous determination with which they recoiled from them. With *The American Dream* he naturalised and domesticated European absurdity into expressionistic satire. In *The Death of Bessie Smith* he offered an apparently realist account of personal and institutional racism. In these terms *The Zoo Story* might seem to stand as an indictment of materialism and *Who's Afraid of Virginia Woolf?* as a portrait of a defunct liberalism and a bankrupt but threatening scientism. All of these things seem to be true. There are even ten years' worth of plays – which remain unpublished, unperformed and unacknowledged – that reinforce this model of Albee as a social dramatist. But from the beginning, too, there was another commitment – to the word, to the idea of character as a product of language. He was also as concerned with the structure of myth as he was with the form of social or even political thought. The same unpublished plays which toy with satire, allegory and moral debate also explore the manner in which language bears on social thought and private behaviour. More than one is written in verse and interestingly one of the first of his works to be produced – a joint venture with William Flanagan – was an opera based on Herman Melville's 'Bartleby the Scrivener', Bartleby being a figure whose social refusal is rooted in and expressed by an equal refusal of language. His simple statement, 'I would prefer not to', is as far as he will advance into a linguistic world which expresses precisely that community which he wishes to resist.

The language of Mommy and Daddy in *The American Dream*, like the functional claims of their names, denied in action, is evacuated of meaning, conventionalised to the point at which it becomes self-annihilating. In *The Zoo Story* the clash of ideolects has more than a sociological function. Peter and Jerry, who meet in the no man's land of Central Park, inhabit separate linguistic universes; they meet only in the theatrical interplay, the performative environment created by Jerry – a playwright who selects the *mise en scène*, elaborates the dialogue, devises the metaphors and dictates the rhythms of their encounter. It is he who self-consciously deploys the language and underscores the symbolism of Christian sacrifice. It is he who enacts a metaphor of which he is the principal victim but also the principal beneficiary. Peter is now required to play his role within a ceremony conducted by Jerry. He is to be the central character in his own drama. Indeed, he leaves the play carrying a text in which is inscribed the very precepts for which Jerry has chosen to sacrifice himself.

It is tempting to see Albee's earlier flirtation with verse as reflecting an influence which became increasingly dominant as his career advanced – namely that of T.S. Eliot. It is possible to see the shadow of Eliot's verse and drama from *Who's Afraid of Virginia Woolf?* ('Prufrock'), through *Tiny Alice* (*The Cocktail Party*) and *A Delicate Balance* (*The Family Reunion*) to *Listening* (*The Four Quartets*). It is an influence not always fully digested. What in *Who's Afraid of Virginia Woolf?* remains an ironic comment, hinting at a wider significance, had by the time of *Listening* resulted in a mannered prose, poetised and serving neither character nor action, although by that stage in his career the possibility of action had itself been all but exhausted. What Eliot gave him was a theme, a plot, a structure and occasionally an image. This is not to imply that he was derivative but that to a writer as concerned as he has been with interleaving fictions, which he increasingly came to see as constituting the real, intertextuality had its own informing ironies.

When Albee was at his best – in *The Zoo Story* and *Who's Afraid of Virginia Woolf?* – he hardly needed models. The demotic force of the former and the articulate wit of the latter were *sui generis*. Later in his career this was less clearly the case. In a way it was a logical development. In his first plays he presented a model of the real that proposed a substantial reality to human affairs, a history concrete enough to be denied and to be redeemed by sacrifice (Jerry of himself; George of his fictive son). Later he was more inclined to see reality itself as a product of language: contingent, fictive. The break seemed to come with *Tiny Alice*.

The American Dream could be said to be derivative, an American version of Ionesco's *The Bald Prima Donna* accommodated to the function of social satire. The fatuity of character and aridity of language, which in Ionesco's play tend to reflect an absurdity endemic to human affairs, in Albee's work serve to reflect and amplify a conviction that social forms and public myths have corrupted the self. So the American Dream, predicated on the inevitable rewards awaiting thrift and godliness, has devolved into simple acquisitiveness. Exchange value has replaced human value; appearance is mistaken for substance. It is, as he explained in an introduction to the original text, a play about the substitution of artificial for real values. But those real values have to be inferred from their absence. As in *Who's Afraid of Virginia Woolf?* he explores the fate of those animating principles to which America laid claim and which here and elsewhere he suggests have been systematically abrogated. The American Dream becomes a superficially attractive young man sexually incapable of realising the promise which he seems to offer. It is an image which recurs in his work as he establishes emasculation, impotence and incomplete sexual gestures as a metaphor for unfulfilled aspirations and misdirected personal and social energies. Albee seems uncertain as to when this process began. Here the only character who seems to stand aside from the general collapse of personal identity and moral purpose is Grandma, who steps outside of the frame of the action (though not the play), but even she is infantilised. Nonetheless somewhere in the past is, he implies, a world in which language once aligned itself with social fact. The problem is to find a cure for this alienation.

The American Dream is a slight work. Not so *The Zoo Story*, which must be the most impressive debut ever made by an American dramatist. A potent fable of social anomie, it concerns the encounter of Jerry – a solitary who lives alone in a rooming-house in Greenwich Village – and Peter, an executive in a publishing house, equally solitary despite a family which offers the appearance though not, as it turns out, the reality of communal life. The encounter takes place in a kind of no man's land, in Central Park. Here, Peter comes to be alone. It is an isolation irrevocably ended by Jerry who seems himself to have suffered a revelation. What he has come to understand is that his isolation has merely served to grant him 'solitary free passage' through life, that the immunity from experience which he imagined to be a necessary protection was in fact a self-imposed imprisonment; that a life lived without pain is a life without consciousness. It is this lesson which he attempts to pass on to Peter using what are in effect the resources of theatre: narrative, action, symbol, proxemic communication. He casts Peter in the role of convert and disciple and precipitates the death which will turn denial into faith. It is a play whose rhythms are compelling and which, in the character of Jerry, offers the actor a seductively compelling role, its melodramatic excesses balanced by subtle passages in which power and control are exercised through the indirections of metaphor and the almost musical tonalities of language. The play's one weakness lies in the figure of Peter, who would sit more easily in *The American Dream*. Indeed, Albee has conceded that the character is badly underwritten, and certainly some of the tension in the play is dissipated through the reduction of this character to little more than conventionalised remarks and actions. It is, after all, difficult to believe in his potential transformation by experience unless he can be assumed to understand the nature of the metaphoric role he has been offered.

Jerry seems to understand himself and his function only through narration. The story that he unfolds is not only a parable told for the benefit of Peter, it is the means whereby he arrives at the meaning of his own experiences. The drama which he improvises not merely crystallises a coherent theme from the otherwise random experiences which he invokes, it is the mechanism whereby he can fulfil his new sense of responsibility. Theatre, in other words, becomes the source of meaning rather than simply the mechanism whereby it is identified, more especially since a language which is merely verbal is seen as denatured, drained of genuine communicative power. Jerry thus develops a series of images and we have Albee's assurance that metaphor rests at the heart of his theatre. Indeed when Jerry explains to Peter that 'sometimes it's necessary to go a long way out of your way in order to come back a short way directly',[2] he is simultaneously offering a justification for the indirections of art, the analogical power of metaphor.

In Albee's plays characters are brought to the brink of change; transformations are implied but not realised. He seems to find it difficult to imagine the social reality of the world to which he wishes to restore his characters. Indeed redemption and apocalypse seem to be possibilities with almost equal potential. In some degree, perhaps, that is the source of their power. It is what works against his capacity for sentimentality.

In *Who's Afraid of Virginia Woolf?* that apocalypticism is spelled out in some detail, past and future contending for the present. George is a professor of history who, though married to the daughter of the college president, has refused to embrace the new pragmatics whereby success becomes its own justification. Nick, a new member of faculty, a biologist who, to George, represents the future, shows himself willing to do whatever is necessary to succeed. Both men, however, have lost touch with the real. George and Martha, unable to have children, have invented a fantasy child. Nick, meanwhile, has already begun to elaborate a myth of his own genius designed to serve his psychological and social needs.

In the course of the evening George speaks of the apocalyptic implications of this betrayal of the real as he and Martha are forced by the logic of their own myth to surrender the child who, though the product of their own imagination, has now reached the age of majority. Either they must break the logic of the fantasy or surrender to it. Whichever option they choose will necessarily transform their lives.

As the evening wears on so George and Martha dismantle their myth in a ritual which strips them of illusions. Nick and his wife, Honey, are slowly drawn into this process in which they finally recognise their own strategic withdrawal from the real: her fear of sexual contact, his of failure. Nor is this a private drama of personal trauma. We are plainly invited to recognise a connection between the elaborate and detailed fictions which George and Martha have created as an alternative to confronting the reality of their lives and the equally elaborate fictions of society. And just as those fictions designed as a compensation and a unifying consolation become the source of alienation for George and Martha, so they are, by implication, for the society they represent. That parallel is enforced by references to Spengler's *Decline of the West*, Anatole France's *Penguin Island* and Shakespeare's fictional Illyria. Penguin Island is a capitalist state which destroys itself, while Spengler elaborates a theory whereby decline is marked by the collapse of values in an Age of the Caesars – a period in which money and power become the only realities, an age typified in the ancient world by Carthage and in the modern world by America. Albee's play takes place in the university town of New Carthage, and we have his assurance that George and Martha derive their names from the first president and his wife and that he sees the play as an examination of the fate of American values. As such it seems to imply a wilful erosion of communality and trust whose implications extend beyond the self and into the culture.

George has surrendered principle to accommodation. In describing a boy who, seeking to avoid a porcupine, drives into a tree, he describes himself. The boy spends his life in a kind of suspended animation. So, too, does George, denying and hence negating the past, choosing fantasy over reality. A professor of history, he has chosen to deny history; a liberal, he has substituted equivocation for principle.

For George, language is a substitute for the real. His fantasy son exists only in language; he is a literary construct, a character brought into existence by his joint authors, George and Martha. Indeed there is even a suggestion that George may have written a novel, a novel which fictionalises his own life. In a way the fantasy son is a reproach for the writer who can only address the real through fiction, for whom, indeed, fiction is a substitute for the real. The more their language specifies the details of a life which in truth has no reality outside the words which they use, the more evident it becomes that language itself has become a substitute for the world it purports to describe. George deploys his linguistic skills in a pyrotechnical display which he nonetheless recognises for what it is – a parody of communication. He is, he insists, walking what's left of his wits while Martha is a 'devil with language'. Even Nick is apparently incapable of realising in fact what he boasts about in words. George and Martha admire one another's style and simulate in words, in the calculated crescendos and diminuendos of their arguments, a sexuality which has itself become parodic because drained of its meaning. Intellect seems to serve no purpose beyond a stimulation of jaded sensibilities. George shifts the battle onto the plane of language precisely because he believes he can function there as he cannot in a world of causalities. He and Martha fill the air with sound because without it they would have to confront one another without protection; they play their characters because performance has replaced being. They perform and praise one another for the qualities of their performance, two actors whose audience is Nick and Honey and beyond them their own selves too terrified to emerge from behind the mask. But there is a seductive energy in these performances. In his own productions of the play Albee was at pains to stress the fact that in their verbal battles 'they were both using their minds very, very inventively', stressing both their intelligence and creativity.

George and Martha finally come together in a moment of genuine contact only when they abandon the splendid articulateness and verbal games which have otherwise defined their relationship, when they begin to abandon performance for being. At the end of the play George and Martha converse in monosyllables; language drains away and we are left with a tableau in which the two emerge from night into day, from dream into reality. It was an optimistic gesture which Albee would not permit himself again. He has insisted that 'the only optimistic act in *Who's Afraid of Virginia Woolf?* is to say, admit that there are false illusions and then live with them if you want and know that they are false. After all, it's an act of public exorcism.'[3]

Albee has explained the mood and tone of the play as a product of the early 1960s, the Kennedy years. By the time of *A Delicate Balance*, three years later, the image of a new dawn bringing enlightenment and grace had become merely parodic, one more convenient illusion, one more metaphor behind which to shelter.

There is something static about Albee's plays. *Who's Afraid of Virginia Woolf?*, *Tiny Alice*, *A Delicate Balance*, *All Over*, *Seascape* are all conversation pieces. There are rarely more than four characters on stage. His subject – the substitution of language for experience – is equally his theatrical method. It is in and through language that his characters must find whatever salvation they can. Language is thrown back and forth as though in some game. There is a space between his characters which is literal as well as symbolic. Experience seems curiously intransitive. Albee has been increasingly drawn to Beckett's minimalism. His plays are not compacted with event; they do not, for the most part, turn on revelation. His, too, are characters for whom habit has become a substitute for being. The past presses on his characters not as in a Miller play, where it is evidence of a betrayal for which some atonement must eventually be offered (though betrayals there are), but as the source of an irony which must be neutralised.

There is a social pressure in the early plays that comes from Albee's belief in the urgent necessity to resist the very attenuation of feeling and value which is his subject. Like F. Scott Fitzgerald he seems to feel an intimate connection between the collapse of individual integrity and the structure of the state, but the possibility of resisting this process has slowly diminished.

Beckett has said of Proust's characters that they are

victims of the predominating condition and circumstance – Time . . . victims and prisoners. There is no escape from the hours and the days. Neither from tomorrow nor from yesterday. There is no escape from yesterday because yesterday has deformed us, or been deformed by us. The mood is of no importance. Deformation has taken place. Yesterday is not a milestone that has been passed, but a daystone on the beaten track of the years and irremediably part of us, within us, heavy and dangerous.[4]

For Arthur Miller such a perception is at the heart of the tragic sense of life. For Tennessee Williams it is the root of a romantic sensibility which he both celebrates and laments. For Edward Albee it becomes initially the basis for a drama which suggests the possibility of recuperating lost values, since, as Beckett suggests, 'We are not merely more weary because of yesterday, we are other, no longer what we were before the calamity of yesterday . . . So that we are rather in the position of Tantalus, with this difference, that we allow ourselves to be tantalised.'[5] So, epiphany remains a possibility. Jerry, in *The Zoo Story*, George in *Who's Afraid of Virginia Woolf?* change because they are anyway no longer what they were. Transformation is both fact and possibility, and what is true of the individual psyche is true, too, of that society which is the aggregation of such individuals. This is a world of self-created victims. But Albee has changed in two important respects. Just as Beckett remarked that 'the only world that has reality and significance' is 'the world of our latent consciousness',[6] so Albee has become increasingly concerned with the process whereby we constitute the real. In *Tiny Alice*, *Box* and *Quotations from Chairman Mao Tse-Tung* and *Listening* he explores the degree to which we can construct the reality to which we choose to ascribe authority and opacity, a concern equally of *The Zoo Story* and *Who's Afraid of Virginia Woolf?*, where the capacity to create myths was equated with evasion. In the later plays, however, the emphasis shifts and the real is no longer presented as external and verifiable. His subject becomes consciousness itself. Beckett's observation that 'the world [is] a projection of the individual consciousness'[7] finds an echo in plays which are no longer rooted in time and place.

Beckett speaks of the moment when 'the boredom of living is replaced by the suffering of being', a moment in the life of the individual which he characterises as 'dangerously precarious, painful, mysterious and fertile'.[8] This is precisely that moment which had concerned Albee in both *The Zoo Story* and *Who's Afraid of Virginia Woolf?*, in which 'consciousness in pain' and 'the learning emotion' is a product of being shocked into reality. So, George admits to a 'gradual, over-the-years going to sleep of the brain cells' until everything is simply 'reflex response', as Beckett speaks of 'the pernicious devotion of habit' which 'paralyses our attention'. But Beckett also imagines the transformation which may be effected when 'the atrophied faculties come to the rescue, and the maximum value of our being is restored'.[9] In the early plays Albee creates plays which bring his characters to this point, a painful moment in which a false security is surrendered. Consider the conclusion of *Who's Afraid of Virginia Woolf?* in the light of Beckett's observation that

The old ego dies hard. Such as it was, a minister of dullness, it was also an agent of security. When it ceases to perform that second function, when it is opposed by a phenomenon that it cannot reduce to the condition of a comfortable and familiar concept, when, in a word, it betrays its trust as a screen to spare its victim the spectacle of reality, it disappears, and the victim, now an ex-victim, for a moment free, is exposed to that reality.

'Suffering', he suggests, quoting Proust, 'opens a window on the real.'[10] So it proves for George and Martha. The question is whether they will choose to look through it.

Interestingly, Proust adds that suffering 'is the main condition of the artistic experience',[11] and it is worth recalling that George is, if we can believe it, a novelist. His acquiescence in the suppression of that novel is an act of evasion which is of a piece with his choice of accommodation in preference to conflict. Buried in the play, perhaps, is something more than advocacy of the real. Indeed Albee's parody of both Eugene O'Neill and Tennessee Williams, in the text of the play (playwrights he believes to have created works – *The Iceman Cometh* and *A Streetcar Named Desire* – which endorse illusion as a legitimate retreat from the real) is perhaps an indication of another of the play's concerns, George and Martha's fiction-making skills offering a comment on another kind of fiction-making. The games they enact are as formally plotted as a play, indeed they are 'scenes', performances, staged for an audience – Nick and Honey. And these scenes – witty, articulate but, ultimately, an evasion – are perhaps in part a comment on the theatre with which he found himself in contention.

Albee has reacted against simple realism, what Baudelaire called 'the miserable statement of line and surface' and what Beckett, in quoting that phrase, called 'the penny-a-line vulgarity of a literature of notations'.[12] He has never been a realistic playwright even when as in *The Death of Bessie Smith* and *Who's Afraid of Virginia Woolf?* – he appeared to be. The reaction against such vulgarity, though, became extreme. There are, after all, other vulgarities and metaphor needs one foot on the ground for the other to be in the air. There is a fussiness, a pedantry, which is functional in *Who's Afraid of Virginia Woolf?* but merely mannered in *Listening*. The spill of words which characterised the early plays, an articulateness of which he was thematically suspicious, gave way to a language drained of human content, a brittle language which splintered on its own assurances. But since his concern was increasingly with consciousness, the way in which we constitute the real, it was likely that he would focus less on character as social and psychological fact than as construction, as artifice; less on plot as sequence of event than as performance; less on language as speech act than as a means to give shape and form to experience. Not for nothing does the search for God begin with the word, and, perverse though the suggestion may seem, Albee's drama, no less than T.S. Eliot's, can be seen as religious in the sense that from *The Zoo Story* onwards it was concerned with accounting for the mechanisms whereby we compensate for a sense of abandonment, adjust to an awareness of death and accommodate to a fear of contingency. His is a world whose order has decayed. God is dead.

A new one must be constructed by the mind and imagination operating through a language which itself offers evidence of decay. If that god turns out to be only man himself no wonder his plays moved in the direction of metatheatre as the search for transcendence, for a world on the other side of language, brought his characters back to themselves. In *The Zoo Story* and *Who's Afraid of Virginia Woolf?* language exhausts itself, as its evasions defer to the authenticity of physical contact. From this point on Albee no longer found this piety convincing. Reality could not be so easily defined. What he sought now was to explore the means whereby we reconstitute the world in such a way as to deny its arbitrary nature, and that led him in the direction of religion and politics as it also led him to a concern for the shaping power of story, metaphor and language.

In his 1951 essay 'Poetry and Drama' T.S. Eliot remarked that 'it is ultimately the function of art, in imposing a credible order upon ordinary reality, and thereby eliciting some perception of an order *in* reality, to bring us to a condition of serenity, stillness and reconciliation'.[13] More than thirty years later, Edward Albee observed that 'the usefulness of art in a more general sense has to do with the fact that it makes us understand consciousness and bring some order into the chaos of existence. That is the useful function of art – to direct our attention to a sense of rhythm, to a sense of order – to a comprehension of what it is to be, to be aware of oneself.'[14] But awareness is not all. Eliot's essay ends by suggesting that the process of adducing coherence and form is merely provisional for it 'leaves us, as Virgil left Dante, to proceed toward a region where that guide can avail us no further'.[15] For Eliot the only guide thereafter became faith, as revealed order implied concealed purpose. For Albee that final step became impossible. The stillness and reconciliation of *Who's Afraid of Virginia Woolf?* proved only momentary; *Tiny Alice*, which followed it and which explored the nature of religious conviction, having more to do with need than revelation.

Tiny Alice marked a radical change from the plays that preceded it. An enquiry into the nature of religious belief, it risked being as abstract as its subject. Certainly director, actors and audiences had their difficulty with a play in which character itself seemed little more than an exemplary gesture in a debate over meaning.

Tiny Alice proposes a model of the real more problematic than that presented in anything he had written up until that time. Jerry and Peter, Martha and George had learned to abandon fantasy for the reality of human contact. In *Tiny Alice* that humanity – tangible, psychologically rooted, energetically expressed – is never established. Here identity and role are congruent.

Julian is a lay brother (itself a pun, reliant on the ambiguity and plasticity of language) and as such is both in and out of the church, trembling on the edge of belief. He is sent to meet Miss Alice, apparently an old lady, who wishes to donate a sum so large as itself to seem unreal. When she throws off the appearance of an old crone to appear as a desirable woman this is an indication of the difficulty of determining reality. But she herself is only one element of a conspiracy which also consists of a lawyer and a butler. Since those roles are themselves assumed, however, necessitated by their function as conspirators, there is no stability to character, no secure reality to which audience or reader can cling. Meanwhile the action takes place in a room which contains a smaller version of the mansion of which it is a part. But is this paradigm or model, the original or the copy?

Tiny Alice is concerned with the need for coherence and order. It enacts the process whereby, in search of an explanation for existence, we create an abstraction called God which we then personify, substituting symbol for supposed reality. Drawing heavily on Eliot's *The Cocktail Party*, and perhaps more remotely on Nigel Dennis's *Cards of Identity*, Albee created a play whose intellectual fascination did not finally compensate for its dramatic inertia. For Eliot's verse Albee substituted a mannered prose, much as Eliot admitted that he had given attention to versification at the expense of plot and character.

A Delicate Balance could have taken as its epigraph two lines from Walt Whitman's 'There Was a Child Went Forth' for it, too, is about:

> The doubts of day-time and the doubts of night-time, the
> curious whether and how,
> Whether that which appears so is so.[16]

But in fact another poet provides a more direct source, a poet turned dramatist, T.S. Eliot.

Agnes and Tobias, whose own grasp on reality is tenuous at best, find their 'well-appointed suburban house' invaded by friends Edna and Harry who are haunted by some nameless terror, much as the characters in Eliot's *The Family Reunion* are pursued by the Furies. Sheer contingency immobilises them, sending them not to God but to those who share their predicament, if not their immediate anxiety. Albee's play addresses the fear which lies behind the assurances of civility and the confident urgencies of daily routine, just as the Chorus in Eliot's play acknowledges the anxiety betokened by unlooked-for noises in the cellar, the unaccountable open window, the suddenly opened door, the accumulated evidence that disturbs our sense of the real and makes us cling desperately to the conviction that 'the world is what we have always taken it to be'.[17] This is a play, set in what Eliot called 'the night time . . . the nether world' where the meshes we have woven bind us to each other, a play about those 'To whom nothing has happened, at most a continual impact / Of external events.'[18]

Its characters, like Eliot's, have 'gone through life in a sleep, / Never woken to the nightmare'; they are people for whom 'life would be unendurable if they were awake'.[19] Tobias, in his late fifties or early sixties, has allowed his life to drift. He has become detached, Claire, his sister-in-law, has sought oblivion through alcohol, Julia, his daughter, through what passes for love ('comfort and snuggling is what you really mean, of course').[20] Their experience has been defined by what Agnes calls the 'demise of intensity, the private preoccupations, the substitutions',[21] and what Harry defines as 'disappointments, evasions . . . lies', confessing that they have settled for 'so little'.[22] Now they confront what Eliot's identically named Harry describes as the noxious smell 'that has its hour of the night',[23] the unspoken voice of sorrow at three in the morning. So it is that Tobias speaks of the 'metallic smell' of the house 'at three, or four'. Indeed the echoes from Eliot's play are so loud and precise (Eliot's Harry, for example, speaks of the simplification which takes place in memory as Albee's Claire remarks on the way memory corrects facts and makes it tolerable) that it is almost as though he had deliberately set out to create an American prose equivalent for Eliot's verse dramas. Certainly he could well have chosen as an epigraph for *Who's Afraid of Virginia Woolf?* Agatha's observation in *The Family Reunion* that 'the future can only be built / Upon the real past.'[24]

In particular *A Delicate Balance*, with its ironic wit and ominous concerns, could be seen as the 'nightmare pantomime' which the Chorus identifies in Eliot's play, a play in which the theatrical metaphor is deployed as clearly as it is in Albee's, for just as the Chorus speaks of the characters playing unread parts so Claire talks of Julia 'playing' early-morning hostess while Harry and Edna plainly perform the roles of Agnes and Tobias as they take over the family home. Indeed it is tempting to see *A Delicate Balance* as in part an image of the theatre itself, a world in which, in Tobias's words (speaking of his own sense of detachment), you can play it out again . . . you can sit and watch. You can have so clear a picture, see everybody moving through his own jungle . . . an insight into all the reasons, all the needs . . . And you watch it as it reasons all with a kind of . . . grateful delight, at the same time sadly, 'cause you know that when the daylight comes the pressures will be on, and all the insight won't be worth a damn.[25]

Eliot's Chorus speaks of amateur actors, of the rustling of the stalls, laughter in the gallery, while another character asks how his fellow performers can sit in a blaze of light for all the world to see. For both writers, experience easily devolves into theatre and the factitious nature of theatre is potentially a denial of the very reality which it urges. In the same way the suspension of time, which is equally an aspect of the theatrical moment, what Eliot, in another sense, calls the 'loop of time' when the hidden is revealed and the spectres show themselves, is potentially itself an evasion, for just as Eliot's characters are afraid that time would 'stop in the dark', so the primary fear with which Albee's characters grapple is that 'Time happens.' To arrest it, even with the revelations which theatre can offer, thus becomes a suspect act. Certainly the qualified optimism which characterised the ending of *Who's Afraid of Virginia Woolf?* now gives way to irony. Agnes's observation that with the night we 'let the demons out',[26] is an accurate-enough account of the process of the play; her conviction that the return of daylight will mark the restoration of order is simultaneously an admission of the fragile nature of that order and an admission on Albee's part of the equally fragile nature of the theatrical moment, its limited ability to disturb our sense of the real. A space has opened up not only between people, between language and its function, but between metaphor and its consoling purpose.

In *Quotations from Chairman Mao Tse-Tung* those spaces are psychological, social and political and they generate a text whose fragmentations offer a correlative of those spaces. It consists of a number of deliberately fragmented monologues, from the political observations of Chairman Mao himself to a recitation of 'Over the Hill to the Poorhouse' by the nineteenth-century sentimental poet, Will Carleton. A third voice – the only one speaking words written by Albee – that of an old lady, tells the story of her own decline and the eclipse of love. A fourth figure – a priest – remains silent, his silence nonetheless representing the final element in a quartet whose meanings lie not in reconstructed coherences but in the incompletions, caesuras, aporias which are generated by Albee's interleaved text.

Public and private not merely co-exist but interpenetrate. The senti-mental poetry of Will Carleton, concerned with the collapse of familial values, is intertwined with Albee's equally fictional narrative of decline. Fiction interacts with a supposed reality, time scales overlap, generic forms meet. At times occasional assonances between the different voices create a meaning independent of either voice, congealing in the space between words, between differing discourses. At times one voice creates an interference pattern in another, tone and rhythm generating ironies beyond those which exist in the individual texts. Images in one text are transformed by the context created by the others. Thus the Old Lady's account of someone's fall into the ocean is magnified by Mao's invoca-tion of nuclear war. The effect of this process is to draw attention to the individual texts' status as texts, constructions with their own rhetorical stance, polemical force and stylistic mannerisms. They occupy the same theatrical moment but not the same political, social or linguistic instant. At one stage Albee even played with the notion of the voices sounding simultaneously in a kind of dadaist cacophany which would nonetheless, of course, have had the virtue of reflecting that simultaneous babel which is the collective substance of social reality. But he was not finally interested in a dadaist implosion of sense. What seems to have fascinated him was, on the one hand, the creation of a work which reflects the copresence of the fictive and the supposedly real and, on the other, the degree to which the construction of the real – in art and in life – is a product of mind and imagination; in other words the subject of art is consciousness and the real and the fictional not opposing terms. Seen thus, Mao's special constructions are no less contingent than are Will Carleton's or Albee's; they simply have the sanction of power. Words make reality. But then so, too, did those of the church, now reduced to the role of mute observer, a role drained of function.

All the voices, however, are subject to a reality which governs them, an apocalypse conceived and defined in language but executed beyond that language. Thus it is that *Quotations from Chairman Mao Tse-Tung* is not merely preceded by the post-apocalyptic voice of *Box* but interpreted by it – a constant potential, a logical projection of that failure of humanity evidenced at all levels in a kaleidoscopic text. What has died is a will to action.

Though *All Over* focuses on the dying of a central character, who we never see – surrounded in his final hours by his family, his mistress, best friend and medical assistance – the dying that concerns Albee has less to do with physical extinction than the decay of passion, commitment, meaning. *All Over* is an elegy for lost innocence, for the process of adjustment which is life. The key words and phrases are 'winding down . . . betrayal . . . withdrawal . . . adjustment, loss'. There is a suggestion that history is similarly infected, the death of the Kennedys and of Martin Luther King draining it of hope and energy. And where earlier he had identified a resistant spirit, the possibility of some limited grace and redemption, now that seems itself an assumption that has succumbed to an irony built into the structure of experience.

Character is no more than a gesture; language, indeed, is parcelled out between the various characters with little attempt at differentiation. The Nurse's speeches sound remarkably like the Wife's which in turn resemble the Mistress's. In a play which highlights the squandering of language, its misuse as a weapon and a concealment, Albee comes close to collaborating in the process which he identifies.

In *Who's Afraid of Virginia Woolf?* he articulated his faith in a particular model of the individual. George, who had allowed himself to be reduced to little more than a cipher, to conniving in his own impotence, is restored to himself as America is called back to its liberal principles. In that play, as in *A Delicate Balance*, evasion of the real is presented as wilful. In *All Over*, as the title implies, that historical and psychological moment has passed. Character is no longer a coherent and resistant force because energy has been bled from the system. Entropy is now presented as a central fact of experience. The individual can no longer find definition through resistance, society no longer be redeemed by individuals restored to a sense of their own responsibility to one another and to the real.

A characteristic of drama is that the voice of the playwright is silenced in favour of his/her characters who alone are permitted to speak. Yet this is not wholly so. The voice does remain, albeit inaudible to the theatre audience except as mediated by the actors. It remains in the stage directions. In the case of O'Neill these had expanded until they constituted a parallel text – a commentary, at times almost an independent narrative, going far beyond a system of notations for actor and director. In the case of Beckett or Pinter such interventions are brief, attenuated, instructions which indicate irony through insisting on a necessary space between words or a disjunction between word and act. Such directions indicate a radical diminution of possibility. In the case of *All Over*, Albee, for the most part, seems content to indicate a tone of voice, an attitude, a mode of behaving. But there is a consistency here which suggests something more. Consider, for example, the following:

not a rebuke, none too pleasant, not forceful, no urgency, not pressing, not unkindly, not hurt, not angry, not unpleasant, not sure, not loud, not sad, not hostile, not loud, no expression, without expression, without moving.

The prevailing tone is one of qualification or negativity. Speeches, actions, sentiments, tone are indicated less by what they are than by what they are not. It is as though there were a counter-current working against the logic of feeling and word. At times this hints at that conscious use of understatement, that sense of irony implied in litotes (as in the expression 'none too pleasant', meaning 'unpleasant'), but it is seldom that positive. In fact the primary note is one of tentativeness, of modification piled on modification as simple assertion is avoided. Consider these further examples:

a gentle admonishment, faint distaste, quietly indignant, faintly ironic, fairly arch, mildly mocking, slightly incredulous, rather helpless, mildly annoyed, mildly assertive, somewhat chiding, slightly bewildered, quite annoyed, mild anxiety, almost a reproach, some delight, mildly mocking, mildly biting, a little unsteady, a little sad, mildly impatient, mildly amused, almost unused, quite serious, controlled rage, slightly triste.

It is true that these are characters who lack a clear outline to their lives, who have slowly accommodated to the diminution not only of feeling and convictions, but of possibility, but this is also a writer who lacks the moral certainties of an Arthur Miller, who looks for meaning in nuance and tone. It is true that there has always been something a little arch about Albee. Here, as elsewhere, he calls for a '*tiny laugh*', a '*small smile*', a '*tiny pause*', but now the diminutives proliferate: *a little impatient, a little breathless, a slight smile* and so on, a diminuendo which relates directly to his own sense of a diminished world.

The characters in *All Over* are all literally waiting for the end. Nothing 'happens' in terms of action, and, since we see nothing of the man who is the focus of concern for the other characters, or, more strictly, lack of concern, we focus not on him but on those who squander their lives in their deference to his significance. All are named here for their relationship to him: wife, daughter, mistress, best friend, son, doctor, nurse. But what is their significance when this 'god' they worship is dead? The meaning of their lives will be placed back into their own hands, but they have long since incapacitated themselves to seize that moment. It is a play about waiting in which the process of waiting is synonymous with a deferment of meaning. Each has surrendered an autonomy which was his or hers, a capacity to act and thereby to be. They stand around, witnesses to their own decline, collaborators in their own deepening irrelevance. But where once Albee would have permitted an epiphany, moved the action to a moment in which revelation and transformation were logically related, now no such moment occurs – at least not within the context of the play itself. Something is indeed all over.

At the time of publishing *A Delicate Balance* in 1966, Albee announced that he was writing two short plays called *All Over* and *Seascape* which had a joint working title of *Life and Death*. It was nine years before both were staged. They were no longer short but they did conform to their joint title, for *Seascape* turns the dark assumptions of *All Over* into comedy.

Two reasonably intelligent middle-class Americans sit on an empty beach and debate the meaning of their lives, first with one another and then with two large green creatures who emerge from the sea. Charlie is content to do nothing, to wait out his time. Nancy is appalled by a life of habit, of repetition without purpose, though she has nothing to propose beyond travelling from resort to resort, beach to beach, an ironic reversal of evolutionary process, just as her husband had dreamed as a child of living under the sea. She resists the notion of doing no more than waiting out her time, 'that purgatory *before* purgatory', in which 'the temporary becomes forever'.[27] From Nancy's point of view Charlie has 'caved in . . . closed down'. He prefers to see it as a 'settling in'. Jointly they 'make the best of it'. This much is familiar Albee territory. What is less familiar is his decision to explore human failings by invoking the non-human.

Nancy and Charlie's conversation is interrupted by the arrival of Sarah and Leslie, two large reptile-like creatures fluent in English but unversed in the ways of the world or those who inhabit it. The conceit allows Albee to place the evolution of a relationship – that of Nancy and Charlie – in the context of the evolution of the human race. Thus a debate about meaning in individual lives becomes an amusing exploration of meaning in human life. Distant past and present are brought together in such a way as to make apparent the nature of human development. To Albee, 'it is merely a speed up examination of the processes of evolution' in which 'the sea creatures have come to the point of no return. They have learned about mortality and love and therefore they can't be what they were; they have got to continue their evolutionary process.'[28] The play ends with the word 'Begin', but since the end-product of that evolutionary process, in the context of this play at least, is Charlie and Nancy, spinning out their lives on the edge of civilisation, it is hard to see this as more than an ironic remark, for Nancy has discovered that 'words are lies', or rather that 'they *can* be, and you use them'. Meanwhile, overhead a jet plane roars and the appearance of a stranger prompts a natural resort to a weapon.

Perhaps perversely Albee has insisted that this is 'a completely realistic play, absolutely naturalistic', adding that 'it is just that two of the characters are lizards'.[29] The humour of the play stands in contrast to the portentousness of *All Over*. In a sense, that humour is itself a value implying and relying upon a detachment, a perspective which works against the implacable logic of an evolutionary process coeval with spiritual decline. Here, as elsewhere in his work, it is love which offers to neutralise a sense of abandonment and despair but here, as elsewhere, it is a deeply suspect resource as the basic condition of experience. But then, in a world in which neither history nor science, social pattern nor individual psychology can provide the kind of patterning structure which offers coherence and the possibility of meaning, neither can art. No wonder *Counting the Ways*, his next play, is presented as a vaudeville, a redundant form, as exhausted as the naturalism which Albee has consistently shunned.

Counting the Ways (a reference to Elizabeth Barrett Browning's poem which offers to enumerate the many facets of love) is subtitled a 'vaudeville', and indeed it is a performance, a double act in which a man and woman debate love and its decline. The theatricality of the piece is emphasised when the actor and actress improvise an account of their concerns and private lives and suspend signs announcing the details of the play's author and director. Humorous and ironic, it still echoes Albee's central theme, as the man remarks, 'it's really *loss; loss* is what it's *really* about'.[30] In this world everything collapses into parody. Beneath the banter, the stand-up comedy, there lie a disintegrating relationship and references to death. The title becomes ironic as love dwindles. In the words of *Listening* (1976), his next play, 'It's an old vaudeville act now . . . except not very funny.'[31] *Listening*, originally commissioned as a radio play and first performed by the Hartford Stage Company in January 1977 as a companion piece to *Counting the Ways*, is also about decline – a collapse of purpose and order.

It takes place in a garden, once 'formal . . . trained . . . planned . . . personal', presided over by a fountain whose water comes from a sculpted figure, a 'God'. Now it is marked by decay. The garden is overgrown. No water flows from the god. What was once a home is now, it seems, a mental hospital. The wall which once ensured protection against anarchy is now a denial of freedom containing that anarchy. The change came 'Oh, turn of the century', much as Virginia Woolf had nominated 1910 as the year in which human nature changed. As the Man says, 'How do we know what we had until we lose it?'[32] He is joined by a woman with whom he may or may not have had a relationship and a girl who eventually slits her wrist and may or may not be a patient.

Eliot is once again a major influence here with *Four Quartets*. Even the central image of the garden, the fountain and the garden god come from 'Ash Wednesday' as the mental hospital derives from 'East Coker'. Albee, though, is not in search of faith, an act of will and imagination that can restore a fractured unity, heal a fundamental breach. He is concerned, to the point of obsession, perhaps, with the dissolution of form, the collapse of order, the decay of metaphor. But the decay of metaphor is a threat to art itself and in a sense Albee's own theatre becomes evidence of the loss which he explores. His characters are increasingly severed from context, abandoned in a plotless structure, located in a problematic private and public history. They converse with that same archness, that same irony that interviewers have grown to expect from Albee himself. The question is – what remains? The answer seems to be, very little, beyond voices modulated like instruments in a chamber piece. Indeed, *Listening* is described by Albee in just such terms.

It takes place in a fictional space, a stage set in which the scenery and props have lost their function. The characters can barely agree on a shared script, prompt one another, self-consciously play out a drama whose inevitabilities nonetheless fail to offer reassurance. *Counting the Ways* is in twenty-one 'scenes', the divisions being marked by placards suspended or placed, vaudeville-style, on an easel. *Listening* is in twenty scenes, each one announced by a voice. The sequenced signs and announcements are interventions by the author, literally so in the case of the latter, where Albee's voice was recorded for the radio version. The effect is to underscore the theatricality which confronts us. In *The Lady from Dubuque* this becomes clearer still, with the audience addressed directly. Life has become performance, style has replaced substance. If art offers to shape a meaning out of experience it shares in that aestheticising of reality which is his subject and that leaves him trapped in that paradox identified by Frank Kermode when he insists that 'Words, thoughts, patterns of words and thought, are enemies of truth, if you identify that with what may be had by phenomenological reductions.'[33]

The Lady from Dubuque is like a compendium of Albee's earlier plays – a touch of *Tiny Alice*, an element of *Box* and *Quotations from Chairman Mao Tse-Tung*, more than an echo of *All Over*, of *Listening* and even *Seascape*.

We have the conspiratorial figures from *Tiny Alice*, easing a central character towards death, two outsiders challenging our sense of the real, as in *A Delicate Balance*. Here, as in *Box* and *Quotations from Chairman Mao Tse-Tung*, we are evidently in a post-apocalyptic world in which the decay of love, of simple human connectiveness, has found its logical projection in apocalypse. As in *All Over*, we are offered an elegy for a society slipping towards oblivion, an existence which, as in *Seascape*, has evolved to the point at which meaning seems to have drained away. Beyond the apparent security of a bland suburbia lies that threat of pure anarchy which had invaded *A Delicate Balance*. Consistency or self-parody? It is hard to care overmuch, hard to feel that Albee himself does. Certainly his casual description of a character as 'your average blonde housewife' and another as 'brunette, ripe' and yet another as 'balding, perhaps; average', hardly suggests a commitment to careful differentiation. In a play in which a character remarks that 'the thing we must do about loss is, hold onto the object we're losing',[34] the play itself seems primary evidence for the failure to do so.

Jo, a woman in her thirties, is dying. She suffers spasms of pain, seeking comfort from her husband, Sam. Perhaps to distract her, friends gather in the house, playing games which in fact do little to conceal the tension. Even in the face of such evident need, however, self-concern still predominates. Then into this situation obtrude Oscar and Elizabeth, the latter claiming to be Jo's mother, a lady from Dubuque, her companion an elegant black man in his fifties. They, it appears, are present to ease Jo through her dying, in the process hinting at a wider cataclysm that has already occurred: 'the eastern horizon was lighted by an explosion, hundreds of miles away no sound! And then another to the west – no sound! And within seconds they were everywhere, always at a great distance – the flash of light, and silence.' As Elizabeth remarks: 'Perhaps we were already dead.' To the suggestion that this had been a description of the end of the world, she replies, 'I thought that's what we were talking about.'[35]

In *The Lady from Dubuque* the characters address the audience directly, 'In other words, the characters are aware of the presence of the audience, and since the audience has always been there, the characters are not upset by it.'[36] These are characters trapped in theatre, self-conscious performers aware of their roles, without access, it seems, to the very human values whose loss Albee continues to lament. The lady from Dubuque herself is derived from the figure popular from the *New Yorker* magazine, a fiction now invoked in the name of the real. The cry of pain, ignored or never quite understood for what it is, is no easier for the audience to believe in, reminded, as they constantly are, of its factitious nature, a paradox which seems to leave Albee stranded, identifying but not transcending the contradiction which lies at the heart of his work – how to urge the centrality of the real through the medium of fiction: 'things are either true or they're not', one of the characters remarks; to which the only answer is, indeed, 'Really.'[37]

Edward Albee has chosen to explore territory which lies outside the social and psychological concerns which have dominated American drama. Though he does offer a critique of American values and, in *Who's Afraid of Virginia Woolf?* and *A Delicate Balance*, suggests the price paid for too completely absorbing those values, he is more concerned with examining the way in which we constitute the real. On the whole, from *Tiny Alice* onwards it is difficult to conceive of the reality of his characters, in the sense that psychological plausibility is plainly not a main concern. Indeed they seem to resist their own three-dimensionality, deny the notion of a substantial and fully shared past, and speak a language which strains away from naturalism. Increasingly, he seems concerned to orchestrate the voices of his characters, modulating rhythm and tone, creating harmonics and dissonances. His figures are incomplete; their sexuality is compromised, their values betrayed, their hopes abandoned, their relationships attenuated. As a consequence they become hollow men and women, evidence of their own spiritual emptiness. With each successive play movement diminishes to the point eventually of near stasis. In *Quotations from Chairman Mao Tse-Tung* he interleaves other texts than his own with a fragmented monologue by a character who exists only through the sentimental story which she unfolds. Like Beckett he seems deliberately to eschew the fecundity of theatre, to ironise the potential for an expansion of language into a profusion of meanings consequent upon three-dimensional form and social density. Typically, his plays have a severely restricted number of actors, though no others quite so severely restricted as *Box*. With *Listening* he had reached a stage where the fact that the play was commissioned for radio merely corroborated a process already under way.

But if Albee's weakness has lain in the sometimes arcane nature of the experiments which he conducts that is also the source of his strength. He could plainly have chosen to repeat the effects of *Who's Afraid of Virginia Woolf?* and been rewarded for doing so. In fact, each play took a new direction, often, it has to be said, something of a cul-de-sac. *Quotations from Chairman Mao Tse-Tung*, beyond its concern with the catastrophic collapse of communality at all levels, the parallel and interpenetrating betrayals which he sees as having typified private and public life and which he implies has stained its art, is also an experiment in forcing the audience to play an active role in the generation of meaning from a work whose coherences can only partly be controlled by the playwright. The painterly tableau of *Listening* is a gesture in the direction of visual metaphor, as the carefully counterpointed sonorities of voice in many of his plays suggest the degree to which the musical analogy influenced his method of work. The surreal juxtaposition of giant sea creatures and two middle-class Americans in *Seascape*, though to my mind resulting in a disappointing play, was the kind of experiment that few of his contemporaries would make, though with *Gnädiges Fräulein* Tennessee Williams tried something of the kind.

As Albee's audiences began to decline so he began to declare his independence of them. The communality of the theatrical moment was willingly traded from something more private.

As opposed to many other people who feel that plays are complete only when they are performed, I am convinced that they are complete as a literary art which one can understand merely by reading . . . when a person reads a play, he's reading it by himself. I'm convinced that he can have the complete experience of the play without having to be in the community of a lot of other people . . . Your informed reader is going to be doing exactly the same things as an audience is doing who is watching the play.[38]

Flaubert dreamed of writing a book which 'would entail only the writing of sentences . . . which would be held together by the internal strength of style, just as the earth, suspended in the void, depends on nothing external for its support'.[39] Albee's objective seems similar. The strength is linguistic. What is missing is passion. John Updike recalls Seymour Glass's remark to his brother that while *Madame Bovary* may have been a masterpiece, the literary advice which led to its creation 'killed his chances of ever writing his heart out'.[40] What seems to be missing from Albee's work after those first dynamic plays is that level of commitment. A thin irony betokens detachment but not one deeply felt. Early in his career that irony bit deeper. He was an ironist whose acute awareness of the failed project which is social life is neutralised by a faith which trembles on the brink of sentimentality. It is what earths the high-voltage exchanges of *The Zoo Story* and *Who's Afraid of Virginia Woolf?*. The surviving will to make contact invests even a deracinated language with some meaning. Later he becomes a high modernist, pitching art against life, the severe disciplines of language against the anarchy of experience.

This is a language, though, which it seems, has to be purified, pedanti-
cally refined until, finally, he takes refuge in words from which the taint
of humanity has been all but evaporated.

Except that in 1994 he won a Pulitzer Prize for *Three Tall Women*, a play
plainly rooted in his own life, which explored, with his customary
humour, and also with a deal of human insight, a woman with whom he
had always had a particularly difficult relationship – his stepmother. She
– rich, politically right-wing, unforgiving in her response to any deviation from a supposed norm – represented everything he despised and it
is tempting to see her domineering figure behind his fascination with
dysfunctional families and aggressive women. As he has said,

I knew my subject – my adoptive mother . . . I knew I did not want to write a
revenge piece . . . We had managed to make each other very unhappy over the
years, but I was past all that . . . it is true I did not like her very much, could not
abide her prejudices, her loathings, her paranoias, but I did admire her pride,
her sense of self. As she moved toward ninety, began rapidly failing both physically and mentally, I was touched by the survivor, the figure clinging to the
wreckage only partly of her own making, refusing to go under.[41]

That is the essence of *Three Tall Women*. It is both the process of ageing
– with its shuffling off of ideals, its compromises, its humiliations but also
its victories, or half-victories in the face of such – and the tenacity with
which we cling to a life which is equally capable of offering consolation
and momentary epiphanies, which fascinates Albee. He has commented
on the horror and sadness he was '(re)creating' in writing the play but
that does battle with something else, for he has also commented on the
extent to which audiences find fascinating a woman whom most people
felt to be repellent in person. He has, then, invested her with qualities
which transcend the original, though he plainly has a grudging respect,
at least in retrospect, for her resilience, her refusal simply to capitulate.
The writing, he has insisted, is detached, 'objective'. It was also an exorcism. He was not seeking self-catharsis but did feel that he had finally
laid a ghost, but only in the sense that this was true of all of his characters once they had moved from the imagination to the page and thence
the stage. The silent young man, who constitutes the fourth figure in the
play, is plainly Albee, observing, present yet not a full player in a drama
in which the old woman is the primary actor, staging her death as she
has her life.

But the play is a good deal more than a private act of exposure and,
ultimately, reconciliation, for much of its fascination lies in its central
conceit, the origin of its ironies and perceptions. In the second act, three

actresses who, in the first, had played the roles of an incontinent old woman, her nurse and a young lawyer, become three versions of the same woman seen at different stages in her life. The conversation between these three – one naive, one experienced, one cynical and worldly-wise – generates much of the play's humour, as also its pathos and human understanding. Things were not as the young woman had imagined they would be. The light has darkened; disillusionment has transformed her. By the end of her life she is cruel but her cruelty is tempered by a sense of irony. She is alone – the fracturing of the self into parts suggesting the profundity of an isolating hermeticism that leaves her in dialogue only with her former selves, though since a dummy version of her is propped up in bed, complete with oxygen mask, this dialogue would seem to take place within the mind of the dying woman. She does, indeed, as she suggests in the play's final speech, think about herself in the third person. And though she implies that happiness finally lies in the whole thing coming to an end 'when we can stop',[12] this is not a Beckettian play in which the absurd is beaten only by succumbing to it, for she is equally able to take a kind of perverse pleasure not simply in survival but in precisely the detachment that gives her a perspective that, in spite of everything, she relishes. The world was not what she thought it to be. She has made her own contribution to the pain of her existence, but she is also capable of being surprised by a gesture of reconciliation as she watches herself battle on with a humour which makes her something more than mere victim.

The very structure of the play makes this a portrait of an egotist. In the first act she buys the attention she receives, just as Albee had implied in *The American Dream* that the couple had bought their adopted child for their own gratification. In the second act the conversation is conducted within the mind of a woman who deploys memory to insist on her current self as a product of that self's former guises. It is almost as though the only dialogue worth having is that which takes place within her own psyche. No wonder, then, that the young man never speaks. There is nothing he can say that will interest her while he is no more than a character in a play of her own devising. It was, presumably, why the young Albee had left home. His parents had no interest in granting him autonomy. That came when he sat down to write a play in which what he had seen and heard was reshaped into a drama in which he could finally speak the woman who effectively silenced him. And though this play has much in common with so many of his earlier works, in its portrait of decline, dying, of a self no longer secure in its direction or purpose, there is a counter current evidenced partly in the fact of his protagonist's ability to shape that decline into form, to construct a dialogue itself generative of humour and sustaining irony, and partly in her persistence, to the very end, which earns, as Albee admits, his 'grudging respect'.

Three Tall Women tells the story of a life. It is, however, as its form suggests, the story of many lives and not merely those of the protagonist. We are plural. We contain different selves. The arc of our lives is common to all and this is a play which stares cold-eyed at the cruelties in store. But at the same time it is a play about reconciliation, not, Albee insists, between himself and the memory of his stepmother, but, he would seem to imply, between ourselves and the life (lives) we live. As the old woman says: 'There's a difference between knowing you're going to *die* and *knowing* you're going to die.'[43] In many of his earlier plays the emphasis was on the former. Decline and apocalypse, in the private and public world alike, provided a primary subject. In *Three Tall Women* an acknowledgement of death as the end of the journey does not invalidate the fact of the journey. The old woman spreads little light but in her amused contemplation of the stages of her life she does transform it into a game which is not without its pleasures and ambiguous satisfactions.

In some senses *Three Tall Women* picks up a concern expressed in Albee's earlier play, *Finding the Sun* (originally copyrighted in 1983), in which a man in his seventies announces,

I get frightened sometimes. Don't you? About dying, I mean? What is the age we become aware of it? That we *know* it's going to happen, even if we don't accept it? It differs with the person, I'm told. The earlier on the better . . . somewhere in the thirties – forties at the . . . most tardy . . . When you reach *my* age you . . . well, you get a little frightened sometimes. Because you're alone.[44]

There are echoes, too, of *Marriage Play* (1987) in which a marriage begins to crumble when the husband becomes suddenly aware that he is increasingly detached from his life, 'hanging there, above myself – as they say we do in dying, or can: hang above ourselves, observe ourselves as we die'.[45] 'We come to a moment,' he insists, when 'we understand that nothing has made any difference. We stare into the dark and know that nothing is enough, *has* been enough, *could* be enough, that there is *no way* not to have . . . wasted the light; that the failure is built into us.'[46] The play ends ambiguously but the key phrase is perhaps 'wasted the light', for if there is an enduring theme to Albee's plays it is the need to live consciously. That was a central concern in *Who's Afraid of Virginia Woolf?* and *A Delicate Balance*, and it is the sub-text of the dialogue in *Three*

Tall Women. The greatest enemy, as in *Marriage Play*, is habit, the dull, unquestioning acceptance of process. For Albee, the unexamined life is, indeed, not worth living; it is not living at all. Reconciliation, in his plays, is not a mere acceptance of the given, a recognition of the authority of the real, but a decision actively to acknowledge the terms of the contract and live through and within its contradictory demands. Death may be the one dominant and dominating truth, but it is not the only truth.

He peoples his plays with those who, while aware that they are subject to the peremptory irony of existence, and feeling the occasional terror or vertigo which that inspires, nonetheless construct their own dramas, not simply out of fantasies but out of a resilience, a sense of the comedy no less than the pain of existence. Indeed language itself, with its communicative essence, its inner coherences, its plasticity, its playful pleasures, becomes something more than a resource, a mechanism, a means, an artful evasion of truth and human connectivity. It stands as a denial of the isolation feared by his characters and becomes an embodiment of that communicative drive which has always been a central theme of Albee's plays.

For the most part his characters do not communicate fully, indeed fear the implications of such communication. They are conscious of the deconstructive implications of a life whose only destination is the grave, aware of the ironies within which they must live and uncertain of the status of the real beyond a simple biological logic. There is, however, a tension between their stance and that of the writer, as there is in the work of Beckett. That tension, indeed, is definitional.

The problematic nature of the real was no less a concern for Edward Albee in the late 1990s than it had been earlier in his career. In *Who's Afraid of Virgina Woolf?* there had been an acknowledged real, beneath the illusions and evasions of his characters and the fantasies which seemed to direct American foreign policy no less than domestic values. It was a conviction which quickly collapsed. His 1998 work, *The Play About the Baby*, which, like several of his later plays, opened in Europe, has, at its centre, a baby whose existence is, to say the least, problematic. A play which features two couples, one, perhaps, an older version of the other, it seems, in some ways, to recapitulate themes from his earlier work. He disavows what might seem the most obvious connection, that with *Who's Afraid of Virginia Woolf?*, in which a non-existent child had proved a desperate strategy for its protagonists and a central trope for its author. There is, though, more than a little of *A Delicate Balance* about it, of *The Lady from Dubuque*, itself a compendium of earlier plays, and of *Three Tall*

Women. There are the same invading figures, threatening a supposed reality, the same address across the footlights, an ironic conspiracy with those who, like the characters, are desperate to decode what they see. There is the same exemplary performance by one generation for the benefit of another. This is not to suggest that he is resorting to self-plagiarism but that his works are linked by a basic theme while the ironic self-referentiality suggests something of the hermeticism which he identifies as a feature of characters who never quite make the leap from their own sensibilities into those of others.

What is at stake in *The Play About the Baby*, however, as in so much of his work, are questions about the nature of the real, about the anxieties which infect the individual, anxieties to do with ageing and death, with the coherence or otherwise of experience. The pedantic linguistic attitude of many of his characters, and, occasionally, of their author, is an expression of their, and his, desire to hold the world still for a moment to examine it. It is an expression of the desire for some order, even if it is that imposed by language or, indeed, art. That order can have no final authority. It cannot deny the entropic nature of experience or human life but it is what creates the tension between a threatening absurdity and an arbitrary but nonetheless engaging and potentially redemptive humanity. Edward Albee's work exists within that tension. It may, indeed, be that 'nothing is enough', but the greatest failure is to have 'wasted the light'.

CHAPTER SIX

A Broadway interlude

From *Who's Afraid of Virginia Woolf?* onwards Edward Albee chose to present his plays on Broadway. After all, was this not synonymous with the American theatre? He remained loyal to that decision even when the public response scarcely seemed to justify it. *Tiny Alice* fared poorly, while even his Pulitzer Prize-winning *A Delicate Balance* ran for only 132 performances. Others received more peremptory treatment: *Malcolm* and *The Ballad of the Sad Cafe* folded after brief runs, *The Lady from Dubuque* ran for twelve performances, *Lolita* and *The Man with Three Arms* failed ignominiously. Broadway could be inhospitable to innovation and experiment. Increasingly this was banished to the scatter of small theatres, church halls, lofts and basements of Off and Off-Off Broadway.

Broadway did not, however, cease to exist. Albee was not the only writer to persist with it. Arthur Miller opened *The Price* there in 1968 and *The Creation of the World and Other Business* a few years later (it lost a quarter of a million dollars). Michael Cristofer staged *The Shadow Box* in 1976. It remained a magnet, attracting writers, actors and directors, but now plays were likely to receive their first performances not in the over-large and over-priced theatres of mid-town New York but elsewhere. Arthur Kopit's *Indians* opened in London and received its American premiere at the Arena Stage in Washington before moving to Broadway, where it had a run of ninety-six performances and that for an original work which managed simultaneously to engage history and to make an oblique comment on the deeply flawed enterprise of Vietnam. David Rabe's *Sticks and Bones*, which dealt more directly with Vietnam, began life at the New York Shakespeare Festival Theatre, where Joe Papp's commitment to new voices made this a crucial organisation. It later moved to Broadway where it proved mismatched to its audience. Christopher Durang's *A History of the American Film* reached Broadway by way of four regional theatre productions, while Lanford Wilson's *5th of July* moved from New York's Circle Rep and had lost $135,000 on

Broadway by the end of the season. David Mamet's *American Buffalo*, which began life in Chicago before moving to Off-Broadway, lost an estimated $100,000 when it was produced on Broadway. By the 1970s A.R. Gurney was only one writer to establish his reputation beyond the bright lights and faded glory of America's supposed theatrical heartland.

Arthur Miller and Tennessee Williams, however, were not the only writers to have succeeded on Broadway. For a few brief years a man from Kansas managed to find an audience for plays whose sentimentalities blended with a sense of profound anxiety and disturbing alienation – William Inge.

William Inge did not tackle the issues of McCarthyism or the tensions of a society in which the artist seemed increasingly to define himself as an outsider. He dealt with the world which lay behind the *Saturday Evening Post* covers. While celebrating a particular kind of Americana he managed to convey a sense of the terrible loneliness and frustrations of ordinary life. His characters – in such plays as *Come Back, Little Sheba*, 1950, *Picnic*, 1953, *Bus Stop*, 1955, and *The Dark at the Top of the Stairs*, 1957 – are essentially victims of their own needs. They long to escape, respond to the mournful call of the passing locomotive, plan a future which slowly slips away from them. His was the realist's urge to tell the small truths which accumulate into a larger truth. So, small-town America becomes an image of life itself as aspirations are blunted, possibilities denied and those relationships which seemed to offer meaning and consolation decline into bitterness and anarchy.

Inge's characters are caught in the web of their own sexuality. The more they struggle to escape the more thoroughly are they trapped. He dealt in stereotypes, but seemed to suggest that such stereotypes exist in the world, that they are the final stage of lives in which other options have been exhausted. There is a power in his work that comes from his respect for the details of daily living and simple need. Tighten the screw a few more notches and you would have Eugene O'Neill. His plays have a bleakness which the vitality of some of his characters throws into ironic relief. He stays his hand. His characters are put under stress but not pressed to breaking-point. They have to live on affecting those small compromises which are the stuff of life, hardly noticing the drip-by-drip erosion of purpose as dreams become fantasies before fading into dull habit.

Inge was a pure product of the Midwest. Born in Independence, Kansas, he was a graduate of the University of Kansas at Lawrence and was a broadcaster in Wichita, Kansas. As a drama critic he strayed only as far as the neighbouring state of Missouri and, though later in life he was to move to California, it was those early years which shaped him. His plays were about the suffocating determinisms of small-town life. On the surface they had a gentle humour as innocents struggled with emotions new to them and tried to match ambitions and hopes to the diminished world of possibility. Underneath was a kind of despair born out of that same mismatch of need and experience.

These plays were written in the 1950s. America was on the move. This was the age of the car and the refrigerator as the stairway to the stars turned out to lead through suburbia. The small town was celebrated in the magazines. A man from Independence, Missouri, who had once been a farmer, then a clerk and finally a haberdasher, gave way as President to a man from Denison, Texas. And if, as Auden had suggested, this was also an age of anxiety, and suburbia had always inspired disquiet (from Sinclair Lewis's *Babbitt* through to John O'Hara's *Appointment in Samarra*), nonetheless the material world seemed to promise a better life which drew increasing numbers of Americans to the cities and to the West Coast. It is that promise which draws the curiously innocent Cherie, in Inge's *Bus Stop*. Like so many of Inge's other characters, however, she is distracted by love, a love which seems as unlikely to be her redemption as is that of Madge in *Picnic*.

For all their apparent gregariousness, Inge's characters are solitaries. Like the figure in Andrew Wyeth's painting *Christina's World*, they seem to reach out for something they can never really hold. There is something of the bitter-sweet tone of Thornton Wilder's *Our Town* about these plays but there is a deeper bitterness, perhaps rooted in Inge's own fragile sensibility which led him to the bottle, the psychiatrist's couch and, ultimately, to suicide. Beneath the civilities of daily life and the sentimentality engendered by accounts of young love and passing time he took as his subject loneliness and the compromises we effect in order to deny it. His Midwestern townships are no Egdon Heath but they render as little sustenance for the mismatched couples who struggle to survive there as does Hardy's rural Dorset. His are not characters who immolate themselves in some grand passion, who remake the world which they inhabit, like characters in a Tennessee Williams play, or pitch themselves against their fate, like Miller's John Proctor or Eddie Carbone. Perhaps that is what gives them their appeal. When Marilyn Monroe was cast as Cherie, in the film version of *Bus Stop*, it seemed oddly appropriate. So many of Inge's characters are close to what she seems to have been. Like her they carry a sense of doom. They seek in personal relationships a solution to insecurities which are exacerbated by those relationships.

His characters have an innocence which survives experience; they seem a little stunned by the life which slowly absorbs them. Above all they want to escape but there is no refuge. The Montana ranch to which Cherie and her cowboy lover set out with such naive hope in *Bus Stop* can hold nothing but disillusionment, and the play ends with that cowboy's abandoned friend staring into a future which sends back no echoes. But he never pushes through the pathos to tragedy. In some sense he seems to feel it too large a concept for his characters to bear or perhaps it offers a redemption which he was not prepared to grant. Never permitting himself to wander far from the stereotype, he largely denies his characters the density which would give weight to their individual suffering. But that is perhaps the irony of their situation. They live in a world of pure process and largely lack the self-knowledge which could elevate personal failing into archetypal fact. He offers a closely observed world which is realistic without being real. His characters suffocate in the thin air of their setting.

America's grand dreams have here dwindled to mere domesticity. Somewhere beyond the backyard or the roadhouse the plains stretch out towards a promise which once animated the individual and the nation. Occasionally, in *Bus Stop* and *Picnic*, his characters set off into that world but time has already rendered it meaningless. As in Miller's *The Misfits* the myths have collapsed of their own weight, while those who cling to one another do so in a world which they can no longer understand. In a curious way, indeed, it is not the familiarity of the small-town setting which interests Inge; it is its strangeness. His characters are born out of time. They are travellers who have come to a halt, dreamers who have woken to a radically diminished reality. They perform the ceremonies of daily life without any clear idea of what those ceremonies might mean. They fill the void in their lives with words, like Beckett's characters, and walk the edge of despair with a kind of uncomprehending courage which is not without its fascination.

Inge was a playwright who could so easily have become something greater than he permitted himself to be. Had he done so, however, he might well have lost the Broadway audience who, for a few years in the 1950s, responded to his images of rural alienation and adolescent anxiety. The power locked up in those plays and so seldom released was evident in *The Dark at the Top of the Stairs*, perhaps the best of them all. It was the play that might have become his *Death of a Salesman*. That it stopped short is because of an innate conservatism in form and conception, but also because he hesitated to drive through fact to image, through individual psychology to social reality, through the physical to the metaphysical. Even so, there is a counter-current which constantly threatens to disturb that equanimity to which Broadway audiences supposedly responded.

In 1962 Inge wrote a naturalistic play set in a small Chicago apartment which ended in a spasm of violence. It was specifically a response to what he saw as the violence and brutality of modern life. As he explained,

It was a violence I felt in having to deal with the brutal fact that our life seemed designed to gratify man's greed instead of his happiness and that most of us, as a result, end up feeling rejected as people. Almost all violence, I believe, comes from our feelings of rejection in a world which continues to make a man feel less and less important. The terror or rejection seemed to me the cause of violence everywhere.

It was a comment which had an ironic application to Inge himself, who felt rejected and turned to violence against himself. In *Natural Affection*, however, he created a play which owed more to the 1940s than the 1960s. A teenager, rejected by his mother, murders another woman. To Inge's mind, 'in all murders, we kill substitutes. Even in war. We never know whom we're killing.'[1] It is an observation which carries no greater conviction for its demonstration in a play in which the characters are seen externally. The violence which he understood was not that of the young murderer in 1960s Chicago, but that generated by the pressure of circumstance and character back in the Midwest of the 1950s.

In the mid-sixties he tried to make a comeback with a brittle and fashionable comedy, *Where's Daddy?* (1966). A mild satire on contemporary mores, balanced by an ironic comment on social conservatism, it offered little beyond a whimsical comedy of manners. What it did was underscore the importance of place in his work of a decade before. *Where's Daddy?* has no roots in experience, no purchase on emotional or social realities. Offered as a critique of those who disavowed human commitment, it managed to evade those commitments itself but in doing so acted as a reminder of the quality which had distinguished his earlier plays, a compassion which managed to triumph over a sometimes formulaic sense of character, an engagement with a genuine sense of bafflement and despair in the face of events. His denunciation, in *Where's*

Daddy?, of a hedonistic generation seems to carry conviction but does so in a play which does not. It was not simply that the times had left Inge behind but that he had lost his grip on a world whose real betrayals had nothing to do with fashion and everything to do with a desperation born out of the process of life and the unrelenting context of a particular part of midAmerica at mid-century.

But if Inge's somewhat sombre exploration of private lives could no longer find a place on Broadway, Neil Simon's comic exploration of familiar family dramas and personal anxieties could. Starting with *Come Blow Your Horn* in 1961 he created a seemingly unbroken line of success-ful comedies. As a former gag-writer he tended to pepper his plays with effective one-liners, but the social observation was sharp and the situa-tions simultaneously reassuring and disturbingly familiar. Almost invar-iably the angry blow is deflected, the wounding remark parried, the trauma avoided but the vulnerabilities are identified with such accuracy that from time to time there is the suggestion of another playwright locked inside the Jewish comedian. It is that fact which, perhaps para-doxically, has sharpened the edge of his humour, as in *The Odd Couple* and *The Sunshine Boys*.

Trying to explain the basis of his art he recalled an argument with his wife in which their very relationship made them adepts at the wounding remark. At the height of their exchange his wife had thrown a frozen lamb chop at him, striking him a glancing blow. The absurdity of the sit-uation defused the pain. It seems a particularly telling observation, for that is the quality of his work which is most compelling. He is as accu-rate as his wife in hurling lamb chops and as adept at recognizing vul-nerabilities and absurdities as he had proved on that occasion. By the same token his technique of deflecting pain through humour accounts for both his popular appeal and the critical suspicion that he inspires. Where Beckett's and Pinter's humour leads to the centre of the pain Simon's leads away from it. When he speaks of 'two people on a stage, both of whom cared for each other, but were unable or unwilling to yield or to submit without having first gained some small vicious victory' he identifies a human truth which too often becomes his comic means rather than his dramatic end. The blood in a Neil Simon play is seldom real blood and it is a rare pain which does not come with an analgesic of wit. Just as Simon described himself in his argument with his wife, as outside looking in, 'no longer involved as a man in conflict, but as an observer, an audience, so to speak, watching two people on a stage',[2] so there is a sense in which his characters become vaudevillians – in *The*

Sunshine Boys, literally so – self-consciously performing their lives as an alternative to living them.

In looking for an analogy for his own ability to step back from a situation in order to take a detached view of human absurdities, Simon referred to Lord Cardigan and Lord Raglan in the Crimean War. The choice was an interesting one, for the fact is that there is a battle of sorts in most of his plays, a fencing, a manoeuvring for advantage which is the root of the comedy and equally of the pain which the comedy denies. Though many of his plays have large casts there is a tendency for him to focus on the sparring between two individuals who use language as weapons, and who need one another to give meaning to their repartee. That need, which goes beyond language, is a hint of something in Simon's plays which continues to fascinate.

Neil Simon's is a Jewish wit, though you only have to place it beside that of David Mamet to see that it is less the streetwise, sharp-edged humour of those attuned to urban rhythms that interests him than the quick-fire one-liners of the script-writer. This is Woody Allen without the angst. This is not to say that he has always contented himself with exploring the comic potential of marriage, or those pseudo-marriages between two men who in effect assume the roles of husband and wife (*The Odd Couple*, *The Sunshine Boys*). In *The Prisoner of Second Avenue* he focuses on those who suddenly lose their jobs, while *The Gingerbread Lady*, despite its inevitable and funny one-liners, explores the life of a character evidently based on the fragile Judy Garland. *Chapter Two* came even closer to home as he dealt with the loss of his first wife to cancer. Later plays – *Brighton Beach Memoirs*, *Biloxi Blues* and *Broadway Bound* – stay close to Simon's own experiences and explore slightly less conventional modes of presentation.

Neil Simon's humour is generated out of character and situation. Relationships are problematic. Though accused of sentimentality, in fact he offers little evidence of the victory of love over experience. His is a world full of egotists, defending themselves against other egotists, alert to incursion on their private space and using language to hold others at bay. This is the New York tone which critics have detected. Though now his plays tend to open elsewhere in the country he is the quintessential Broadway writer, highly skilful and creating plays which probe anxieties in such a way as to cauterise the wounds which he momentarily opens. By the 1990s he was one of the few American playwrights who could virtually guarantee a run on the Great White Way.

Broadway's dominance in the 1940s, 1950s and into the 1960s was nowhere more evident than in the musical. Indeed it seemed at that time a uniquely American form, British attempts looking and being anaemic and unadventurous by comparison. The American musical is the residue of nineteenth-century melodrama, European operetta and a black musical originality focused through the creativity of some prodigious talents. It is a theatre which invites its audience to meet in a realm of shared emotions that bridge social differences. Many of the songs generated by the period have become standards precisely because their sentimentalities could be so easily detached from character, plot and setting. However, since *Showboat* in 1927, the musical had shown its capacity to address social issues, albeit obliquely. *The King and I*, *South Pacific* and *West Side Story* all engage with the question of racism, if only in sentimentalised form.

Simply to list the succession of hit musicals of this period is to become aware of the nature and extent of the achievement of America's musical theatre.

1943	*Oklahoma!*	Rodgers and Hammerstein
	On the Town	Bernstein, Comden and Green
1945	*Carousel*	Rodgers and Hammerstein
1946	*Annie Get Your Gun*	Berlin and Fields
1947	*Brigadoon*	Lerner and Loewe
1948	*Kiss Me Kate*	Porter and Spewack
1949	*South Pacific*	Rodgers and Hammerstein
1950	*Call Me Madam*	Berlin, Lindsay and Crouse
	Guys and Dolls	Loesser, Swerling and Burrows
1951	*The King and I*	Rodgers and Hammerstein
	Paint Your Wagon	Lerner and Loewe
1954	*The Pyjama Game*	Adler and Ross, Abbott and Bissell
1955	*Damn Yankees*	Adler and Ross, Abbott and Douglas
1956	*My Fair Lady*	Lerner and Loewe
	Candide	Bernstein, Hellman, Latouche, Parker, Wilbur
1957	*West Side Story*	Bernstein, Robbins, Laurents, Sondheim
	The Music Man	Willson
1959	*The Sound of Music*	Rodgers and Hammerstein, Lindsay and Crouse

1960	*Camelot*	Lerner and Loewe
1961	*How to Succeed in Business Without Really Trying*	Loesser, Burrows, Weinstock and Gelbert
1962	*A Funny Thing Happened on the Way to the Forum*	Sondheim, Shevelove and Gelbert
1964	*Hello Dolly*	Herman and Stewart
	Funny Girl	Styne and Lennart
	Fiddler on the Roof	Bock, Stein and Harnick
1965	*Man of La Mancha*	Leigh, Wasserman and Darion
1968	*Hair*	McDermot, Ragni and Rado.

But that was about it. An astonishing line of successes came to an end. Already the sixties represented something of a falling-off in quality and the seventies opened with a warning of things to come: *Jesus Christ Superstar* by Andrew Lloyd Webber and Tim Rice. The British and the French conquest of the musical was about to begin. *Two Gentlemen of Verona* (1971), *Grease* (1972) and *A Little Night Music* (1973) hardly matched their predecessors, though *A Chorus Line* (1975) perhaps came close. Otherwise the seventies and eighties were a thin time with *Side by Side by Sondheim* (1973), *Annie* (1977), *La Cage Aux Folles* (1983) and *Sunday in the Park with George* (1979)

In the 1969–70 season half the musicals ran for a week or less. In that respect the musical theatre merely reflected the condition of Broadway. Rapidly rising costs conspired to make production a high risk, low-return business. Curiously the greatest number of musicals to open in a single season, twenty, was achieved in 1971–2, a figure matched in 1979–80; neither season, however, produced anything of lasting value. By contrast, in 1984–5 only five opened and in 1988–9, six. That same year saw thirty new theatrical productions open on Broadway, two fewer than in the previous year which had itself established a record low. Perhaps this is not surprising given an average ticket price of $34, one musical, *Jerome Robbins's Broadway*, charging $55.

In 1989 Arthur Miller remarked that:

When I began to write, the illusion, which was partially based on reality, was that you were writing for the whole people . . . You felt that you were addressing the whole city, and therefore the whole country, and for that reason the plays we were writing had a story, they had some psychological depth, they were translatable into common experience.

That collapsed partly because of an increasing sense of alienation on the part of intellectuals and partly because prices were driving out the less well off:

at that time [the late fifties] the prices went from four dollars to ten dollars and it seemed to me a scandal. I didn't know many people who could pay ten dollars to go into a theatre, or who would want to pay ten dollars to get into a theatre . . . I was even instrumental in getting a meeting going between all the crafts in the theatre in the hope that we'd all take less money, the unions, the playwrights and everybody, and keep the costs down. Nobody was interested. Now we are without an audience at all. We have zero audience, for what you could call significant or serious theatre. Even when plays get good reviews people don't come . . . We don't have a theatre . . . We have shows . . . But nobody discusses the central question: where's the audience? I remember the scandal among us when the *New York Times* took the theatre news off the front part of the Sunday paper and put it in the middle, and put the movies and the television ahead of it. That was a shocker! But they were reflecting reality; really. It was gone, the thing was gone.[3]

Where it had gone was, in the 1960s, to Off-Broadway and, in the 1970s and 1980s, to the regional theatre. Broadway success was still sought, but increasingly it was a rare play whose reputation was not first made elsewhere. No new playwright, after the 1950s, seemed likely to open on Broadway as Williams and Miller had done. The future now lay beyond Broadway and, as the sixties gave way to the seventies, beyond New York.

In 1987 Marsha Norman declared Broadway closed to serious drama, while Lanford Wilson suggested that there had been no more than two good plays on Broadway for a quarter of a century. But elsewhere, he insisted, the situation was different: 'We're building a strong theatre literature that is being done across the country . . . We can't be bothered about New York theatre.'[4]

CHAPTER SEVEN

Sam Shepard: imagining America

The climber and writer M. John Harrison speaks, in his novel *Climbers*, of cutting through a nylon rope suddenly to discover, hidden in its interior, brilliant reds and blues, 'as if you had cut into a sparrow only to find beneath its skin the colours of the macaw'.[1] Peter Brook has spoken of the theatre in similar terms as the place where the invisible can appear. As he observes, 'We are all aware that most of life escapes our senses' and that a powerful explanation of various arts lies in their power to detect and present the invisible through rhythms or shapes. It should not surprise us to see Sam Shepard, an admirer of Peter Brook, express much the same sentiment.

Shepard has no desire to stage the bland exterior of experience. He wishes to slice through the rope. For Peter Brook, the knife was provided by ritual, which had to be rediscovered and rearticulated; not the rituals borrowed or adapted from primitive tribes (though he was to conduct his own experiments in that direction) but those which touch a contemporary nerve. He found an example in pop music; so did Sam Shepard, whose own experience as a musician alerted him to the importance of rhythm in more ways than one. Peter Brook looked for a 'holy theatre'; Sam Shepard played with a group called the Holy Modal Rounders. The rhyme was accidental; the intent less so.

Peter Brook suggests that a search for an underlying unity implied in the notion of ritual might, in an age of images, require resort to the image before language could re-emerge as a primary mechanism; Sam Shepard enacted that process in plays in which character and language were indeed subsumed in image. It is not, particularly in his early plays, that he chose to abandon language but that it played another role than that of communicating character, forwarding plot, articulating mood or value. His was what Peter Brook had called 'a language of actions, a language of sound – a language of word-as part-of movement, of word as lie, of word as parody, of word as rubbish, of word-as-contradiction, of word-shock or word cry'.[2] What he pursued was what Brook described as a 'more than literal language'. And if for the British director that led in the direction of poetry, so at times it was to do for the American writer, not always, it has to be said, working consciously or in conscious control of his imagination.

One of the weaknesses of the American experimental theatre of the 1980s lay in the failure of some of its exponents to realise that movement can be as conventionalised as language, that it is simply not true to suggest that the body tells truths which words deny. Bad faith awaits us on all levels of experience and no deceit is as primary or debilitating as self-deceit. Shepard was seldom guilty of this, though in a work such as *Operation Sidewinder* he was to prove capable of a curious mixture of sentimentality and condescension in his use of native Americans as an image of the holistic grail which he sought. His skill was to acknowledge the conventionalities of language and to play games with the cliche, the ideolect, the aphasic aria without solemnising the body as a sign of transcendent truth. If the early plays were spontaneous images, unelaborated scenes, scarcely ever rewritten or submitted to rational reinterpretation, the later ones were confidently honed (there were fourteen drafts of *True West*), language and action being carefully modulated.

Peter Brook's attempt to describe the object of his own experiments has more than a passing relevance to Shepard's work, for, as he explained, he and his actors were 'trying to smash the apparently watertight divisions between the private and the public man: the outer man whose behaviour is bound by the photographic rules of everyday life, who must sit to sit, stand to stand – and the inner man whose anarchy and poetry is usually expressed only in his words'.[3] It is always a mistake to be over-solemn about Sam Shepard. As a young writer his own aesthetic principles were as closed to him as to the critics he baffled, but it was in essence anarchy and poetry he wished to release, though in his case not by any means only through words. He was, more and more deliberately as his career progressed, concerned to explore what was repressed. Brook wished to deny psychology. Shepard did not. And, thematically, that took him in the direction of incest (*Fool for Love*), violence and unreason (*A Lie of the Mind*). The energy of his work can be primal and anarchic but not, after the early plays, random. The danger which he dramatises and courts came to be carefully scored. Its rhythms are as important as its precise manifestations. In that sense his 'holy theatre', like Brooks's, is earthed in what the British director called the 'rough theatre', a theatre in which the grit of experience scored itself across the world of the subconscious and repressed.

Shepard is a man of divided loyalties: a musician, an actor, a writer. All three careers have informed one another. Few Shepard plays are without music – another way of making the invisible present. Few of his plays fail to set the actors a series of challenges as they are required to break through the carapace of naturalism. His career as a writer began Off-Off Broadway, more or less by chance, as a newly established experimental theatre company announced its need for new plays when he had just arrived in the city. Since then, however, he has chosen to have his work premiered just about as far from Broadway as you can get without leaving the continental United States, at San Francisco's Magic Theatre. It is a revealing choice which says something about the natural home of his sensibility, something about the kind of theatre he is interested in creating and the relationship between performer and audience he wishes to see. The Magic Theatre is a small theatre, an intimate theatre. Audiences are unprotected by space, by distance, and though Shepard had no interest in assaulting his audience in the crude way that the Living Theatre at times chose to do, he did wish to disturb and disorient. As he was to find with a subsequent performance of *Operation Sidewinder*, a theatre such as Lincoln Centre was not likely to be the ideal venue.

There is a visceral power to Shepard's work, a sense of the unexpected. You feel the pressure of an imminent violence which presses against character from within. There is a physical menace in the plays, sometimes an almost sadistic revelling in conflict, a battle for dominance; but the real violence is an internal pressure which threatens to implode character, disassemble it along lines of primitive fears, needs and desires. His characters frequently tread the very edge of insanity. Figures from the past occupy the same space and time as those who inhabit an uneasy present. Reactions are magnified, sensibilities heightened to the point that, in *Fool for Love*, sound reverberates abnormally and lights pierce the darkness with a disturbing intensity. In *True West* the improbable is acted out as though a dream fantasy had been infiltrated into everyday experience, a scene, incidentally, which appropriates the aesthetic values of the Hollywood world it appears to parody. And parody is a breath away as characters play out their roles in a drama which presses towards the grotesque.

Shepard's characters often seem borderline psychotics. On occasion they have already crossed the border. Their insanity lies precisely in the fact that they are obsessive. In the case of Travis, in the film *Paris, Texas*, guilt, self-hatred, a desire to opt out of a complex world of desire and competing needs, leads him to abandon language and seek a form of self-annihilation in a world stripped entirely of social demands. In *Fool for Love* and *A Lie of the Mind* a sadomasochistic passion drives out all other concerns. In *True West*, a self divided wrestles itself to a standstill, transforming a banal setting into a battlefield in which the dead are so many discarded electrical appliances and the concluding blackout more than an indication of the play's completion. Under stress, his characters tend to simplify. Like a computer facing overload, they revert to primary function, refuse extraneous data. They have no peripheral vision. The focus narrows and becomes intense. They are neurasthenically sensitive. But this hyper-reality does not exclude fantasy. Isolated in a radically fore-shortened moment, they reach back into memory and project possible future tracks which become part of that moment. Reality is dense in a Shepard play; it resonates, reverberates. Even Travis's silence, in *Paris, Texas*, is compacted with an unarticulated past and simultaneously charged with a kinetic energy. In one sense he quite literally sees the world through a glass darkly; in another, he exists in a timeless moment, afraid of time because of its logic.

Sam Shepard is a performer. So are his characters. In the words of a poem written in Los Angeles in 1981, 'people here I have become / the people / they're pretending to be'.[4] They act out their lives as though they are minor figures in a national drama of decline. Theirs is a world where 'far off you could hear the sound of America cracking open and crashing into the sea',[5] a world in which myths of masculine independence and existential truth have collapsed into anomie, psychosis and a destabilising violence. This last is 'a tangible presence [which] you feel ... everywhere in America'.[6] His characters, like Tennessee Williams's, are drifters, seekers after a truth in which they can no longer believe. On occasion they reach out a hand, hoping to find some momentary consolation, only to find that passion carries its own virus of violence and despair. There is in Shepard, and to some degree in his plays (and maybe only partly coincidentally, in the roles he plays on screen), a romantic attachment to those who once sidestepped American ambiguities by living mythically – cowboys in harmony with the natural world, farmers feeling the soil run through their fingers – but something has tainted that purity. A dream has died and now lives on only as fantasy. Men and women meet across a great divide of experience. He once remarked that the sadness of American country music derives from the fact that it speaks 'of the true relationship between the American male and the American female' which is 'terrible and impossible'.[7] The family – another American myth – is now a metonymic parody of the culture. Fathers, like Tom Wingfield's in *The Glass Menagerie*, have fallen in love with long distance. Brother fights brother, mothers are off-stage voices or oppressive presences, conspirators in the dissolution of love.

Character is hollowed out in these plays as men and women alike fight to deny the past and inhabit a present drained of symbolic content. There is no consistency. Moods, dress, identity can switch in a second; characters are fractured, divided, doubled until the same play can contain, as independent beings, what are in effect facets of a single self. Even male and female elements of individual identity are flung off as separate elements which then fight to reunite, a struggle which underlines Shepard's desire to reach back beyond the social to the archetypal. But if this fluidity contains a threat of anarchy the opposite is equally menacing. As a writer, Shepard has spoken of his desire 'To not be fixed'. This is what keeps his characters on the move. Again like Tennessee Williams's figures they fear stasis, overdefinition, even the trap of language. When Shepard said of his own father that he did not 'fit in with people' he was in effect describing many of his characters.

Against the aphasia of his characters Shepard pitches his own poetic sense, reshaping their broken language into arias which find an assonance even at the heart of disharmony. But often that language is itself second-hand, consisting, as it does, of cliches, powerful emotions, finessed into words already processed through myth and media. Its meaning lies less in individual words than in the rhythms of speech. Coherence is shaped by the writer so that the poet becomes the one who rescues from silence and who finds a shape in formlessness. In *Motel Chronicles* he speaks jokingly of being an Osiris pieced back together by a young girl; but in effect that is the role he plays in relation to the fractured characters whose lives he dramatises. His problem is that he more than half believes in the myths whose underside is violence, is more than half a convert to the supremacy of incident over story. His prose works – *Hawk Moon* and *Motel Chronicles* – consist of expanded anecdotes, brief poems, random thoughts, memories; for the first ten years of his career he showed a preference for the one-act play. He felt the spontaneous fragment to hold such an integrity that it was not to be tampered with. He subscribed to a sixties faith in the authenticity of the subconscious and the power of the moment which seemed a compressed image of truth. By the eighties he had come to fear that fragmentation was the enemy.

There is a confessional element to Shepard's work. His father reappears in various guises – an alcoholic who deserted the family, a man in love with space, a bewildered guide to a son who fears above all that he will metamorphose, become the man he feared as well as loved, become as constant in his inconstancy as the person he despaired of loving until he wandered to his death one day. His grandfather 'who always sat in a hole of his sofa wrapped in crocheted blankets facing the TV' on a farm that 'looks abandoned'[8] appears in *Buried Child*. The family, he has said, is what 'you never really get away from – as much as you might want to try'[9] and that is the role it plays in his work, an image of a fate as inescapable as one's DNA. The grandson who returns to visit his grandfather and who climbs the stairs to look through the family photographs in *Buried Child* is obviously close kin to the Sam Shepard who did the same thing. But in writing of broken love affairs, of the cynicism of Hollywood, of moving on, he reshapes private material into public form. The family becomes important because 'It's a thing that everybody can relate to.'[10] In the same way his experience with a drug-shocked Joyce Aaron (an actress and for a time Shepard's companion) surfaces in *A Lie of the Mind* where a character is plunged into an autistic silence by violence rather than drugs.

In *Motel Chronicles* he speaks of feeling 'the demonic attachment of a man for his only woman'.[11] It is a telling phrase and one which, with its blend of cliche and precision, accurately describes the relationships which generate the energy of, for example, *Fool for Love* and *A Lie of the Mind*. There is no gentleness in any of the pairings in his work. They are all touched with doom, driven by a need which language can neither define nor contain. Two fears of equal force create a terrible balance – the fear of presence and the fear of abandonment. These people cannot survive together and cannot exist apart.

His prose collections are full of dreams and visions and this is a key to his drama, which has precisely that quality of heightened experience structured not by rational process but by the logic of the subconscious. When he says that 'Small moments open for me sometimes in crossing the kitchen when the sun hits a particular color in the paint job. I go into a reverie from pastel blue of a time of Dairy Cows, a very few people, all who knew each other, in a small isolated American village',[12] he identifies both a method and a point of reference. The names of cars and musicians, of film stars and small towns, are stepping-stones to an adolescent personal and national past that predates the alienation which makes such visions simultaneously necessary and the root of irony. Now he inhabits a world in which the definition of insanity, in the words of a 1979 poem, is someone who chooses not to conceal 'His desperate estrangement from people', and rock and roll becomes a kind of encoded violence, albeit one whose rhythms represent a freedom denied 'the dance trapped in form, the actor trapped by the script'.[13] Characters in his work are liable to set fire, literally or symbolically, to their few possessions and walk out into the desert land, away from the pain of relationship and being. The drama begins when they cannot permit themselves this doubtful consolation or when they return to find a world bereft of love and hope. They are in a sense doing what the figure in one of the episodes in *Motel Chronicle* does following a brain operation – mourning the loss of their lives. The world Sam Shepard describes is running down. In the words of a poem:

> The motion animal breaks down
> A little at a time
> Broken horse time
> Gelding with swollen fetlocks
> Hoof rot from standing in the marsh grass too many days
> The winged animal begins to swing in lower circles
> Not looking for prey
> Just praying not to crash
> In Science talk it's called entropy.[14]

In Shepard's work men are violent, striking out at one another, at the women they love and at inanimate objects. Like so many demented Billy Budd's they are unable to articulate their feelings, unable even to understand their own motives. They seldom have a job or if they do it is occasional or marginal. They are failed farmers, minor rodeo performers. They ride on the intensity of their emotions. They take the inside track. Something is missing from their world, above all a rational control. They live by instinct. The subconscious becomes the conscious. What is buried is disinterred. What is felt must be enacted. Even the past becomes a present reality, a memory, a three-dimensional fact. His is predominantly a male world but not a world of male camaraderie. He has suggested that men are more interesting than women, since the real mystery in American life lies between men, not between men and women. But while it is true that in terms of American myth male relationships have been seen as keys to the cipher of national identity, in fact Shepard began to get more interested in the relationship between men and women as his work progressed.

In Shepard's plays families are divided against one another yet are unable to escape the fact of that relationship. There is no friendship.

They are, in Melville's terms, 'isolatos'. Shepard's women characters, meanwhile, are the baffled witnesses of male aggression or victims of an uncontrolled passion. The glass which separates male from female in *Paris, Texas*, in less tangible form separates all his men and women. They are the embodiment of need, but the magnetic power which attracts them to one another in his plays also repels. A swiftly changing polarity creates an irony which darkens towards the absurd. But that division infects all his characters who themselves contain contradictions, fracture into complementary figures (as in *True West*), or divide along gender lines. As he explained in an interview in 1988,

life is made up of contradictions. The tricky part is to stay in the middle and not take sides, not walk over to one side in preference to the other. If you can stay right in the middle of a contradiction, that's where life is. Exactly where it is . . . It's when you're torn that things start to fall apart . . . But to be right in the middle of a conflict . . . and let it play itself out where you can see . . . well, that's where things begin to get exciting. You can't avoid contradictions. You can't avoid paradoxes.[15]

Far from avoiding them he has sought to inhabit and explore them.

All the circumstances of Shepard's life have had to do with the temporary, with division and separation. Parental divorce, a constantly shifting home, a lifestyle which led to a succession of personal relationships have all shaped his perceptions. It is scarcely surprising that his plays should reflect this nor that he should generalise his experience as social fact. In the early plays fragmentation is an aesthetic principle no less than a fact of character or social relations. Increasingly it becomes an aspect of a deeper alienation, a division within the self which relates to a division between the self and its context. In that same 1988 interview he explained that he had arrived at a point

where I'm not interested in anything that doesn't have a kind of wholeness to it. I'm not interested anymore in little fragmented bits and pieces of stuff that might be interesting for five minutes. I need something that has more of a definite wholeness to it. That has a sense of being a story that's already been told . . . and that you're just coming to it . . . What's most frightening to me right now is this estrangement from life. People and things are becoming more and more removed from the actual. We are becoming more and more removed from the Earth to the point that people just don't know themselves or each other or anything. We're this incredible global race of strangers . . . *That's* terrifying. Things are so dispensable now. People live together for a while . . . then they split, and they never see each other again. Then they get together with somebody else – split. Have kids – split. Then the kids never see each other. It's absolutely frightening – this incessant estrangement . . . People are being amputated from each other and from themselves.[16]

It would be difficult to imagine a better description of the world of Shepard's plays. His characters are, indeed, estranged from one another and from themselves. The space between them seems unbridgeable. Emotions are intense but unsustained. The hand that would caress, balls into a fist. Husband and wife, father and son, lovers, brothers, are all strangers. But beneath this drama of alienation is a unifying repetition. His reference to a story 'that's already been told' is a hint at the significance of ritual and myth in his work for in so far as his plays are accounts of the rivalry of sons, of the son's search for the father, of men and women caught in the contrarities of emotions, they are, indeed, stories that have already been told. In that sense Shepard's plays are best seen as fables, re-enactments of myth.

His is certainly a recognisably American world. It is compacted with popular folklore, the familiar stereotype, the cartoon, the bric-abrac of modern living, the theatrical properties of American experience. His plays have settings which are themselves part of a familiar iconography. His characters often speak a language which has already been processed through the media and shaped by recognisable American concerns; but it goes deeper than that. His spiritual migrants and social outcasts, charged with a dangerous kinetic energy, are involved in a restless search whose object evades them. Like Beckett's characters they are drawn equally to silence and to a neurotic volubility. The one secures a limited immunity: it is the choice made by Travis at the beginning of *Paris, Texas*. The other is a means of staving off extinction: as Tilden observes in *Buried Child*, 'You gotta talk or you'll die.'[17]

Sam Shepard was a sixties invention. His enthusiasms were those of a generation – movies and rock and roll, two democratic arts. It was a music that belonged to the young, who were the new consumers; it was a music that belonged to those on the edge of society, to the blacks, to poor whites, like Elvis Presley. Sam Shepard had never felt incorporated into America, except at the level of myth. Like the Beats he admired, he had no roots. They lived mythically, in search of some spiritual grail. Their trips were partly literal and geographical, partly metaphorical and psychological. In one mood they chose the road: in another, marijuana. Sam Shepard, bounced from place to place as a child and from town to town with the drama group he joined, was about the same business. The movies, meanwhile, offered an alternative history, not a world of fact tied into time but a world of myth, rooted in place. Shepard was the first playwright to construct his drama out of the materials of the popular arts, to infiltrate the sounds and images of popular culture into work which rendered up its meaning less to those who approached it with an analytic mind than to those who chose to inhabit its images and respond to its rhythms on an emotional or visceral level.

There is something of the romantic about Sam Shepard, who chose to enter a world of visions through a door that would have been known equally by Coleridge and De Quincy. His sense of a unity lying on the other side of fragmentation is likewise not without its romantic implications. There is an air of the temporary about the world of his plays, which tend to take place in motel rooms, parks, apartments, rooms cluttered with the junk of modern living or stripped to their anonymous essentials. His characters are similarly either assemblages of fragmenting memories, disconnected experiences, or radically simplified sensibilities seared by a single dominant emotion. As he remarked of *Angel City*, the term 'character'

could be thought of in a different way when working on this play. Instead of the idea of a 'whole character' with logical motives behind his behavior which the actor submerges himself into, he should consider instead a fractured whole with bits and pieces of characters flying off the central theme. Collage construction, jazz improvisation. Music or painting in space.[18]

Such an approach was very much in tune with the experiments of the Open Theatre with which he worked for a while, concerned as they were with developing the craft of acting, with exercises which required actors to effect abrupt changes of character and context. But what for the Open Theatre was a means, for Sam Shepard was an end.

Later in his career, beginning, perhaps, with *Buried Child* (1978) and continuing with *True West*, *Fool for Love* and *A Lie of the Mind*, the set tends to become realistic ('Old wooden staircase down left with pale, frayed carpet laid down on the steps'), as it does in *Buried Child*, or starkly bare ('Deep, wide, dark space') as it does in *A Lie of the Mind*. Either way the characters are thrown into relief. These are not, however, realistic plays in any conventional sense. Reality expands to incorporate fantasy, dream and myth. Sensibilities are pressed to extremes. There is a gothic element to Shepard's imagination as his characters focus their lives to a single point. Theirs is not a stable world. Violence is a constant possibility, love the source of an anarchic energy. Passion destabilises identity and distorts perception. Shepard's characters tend to be neurotically hypersensitive. Everything in their interior and exterior lives is magnified, amplified. He is prone to employ music much like the soundtrack of a film, literally underscoring moments of emotional intensity.

Music 'with an American backbone',[19] as he describes it in a note to *A Lie of the Mind*, it also serves to reinforce the specifically American world of his fables of failed love and buried dreams.

Shepard has talked of the need for a playwright constantly to re-evaluate the nature of his work, to strip it down to its essentials. He may, he suggests, know a great deal about 'timing, rhythm, shape, flow, character(?), form, structure' but still know nothing about what he calls 'the real meat and potatoes'.[20] But that list is in some sense the meat and potatoes in Shepard's work. Consider the order which places timing and rhythm first, which emphasises flow and ends with form and structure. This seems an accurate account of his own priorities. Consider, too, the question mark significantly placed after the word 'character'. The figures in Shepard's plays are not stable or easily definable. They are not rooted in a social or psychological world which defines them with any precision. They are their performances. They come into being through the rhythm of their language as much as through its lexical meaning, or, rather, meaning is generated out of tone, rhythm, inflexion, volume, cadence more than through a literal verbal expressiveness. And where is plot in his list? That, too, has a low priority if we mean by that action which serves a narrative function. There is action in Shepard's plays. There are stories. But more than anything else they are explorations of emotional states, expressions of anxieties, disturbing journeys into the individual subconscious or the collective psyche of the tribe. No wonder he has said that he feels the pull of 'the ancient'. After all, someone who 'strips everything down to the bones and starts over'[21] is liable to find himself going back in order to begin anew. Speaking of the experimental theatre, he defined it as that which lay outside a familiar world in which theatre could indeed be adequately defined through its ingredients: 'plot, character, set, costume, lights'.[22] This list, instructively, includes precisely those elements relegated from his own work or presented there as problematic.

The power of words, for Shepard, does not so much lie in the delineation of a character's social circumstances as it does in the capacity to evoke visions in the eyes of the audience. It follows that he has no interest in the literal transliteration of speech, but he also resists descriptions of his language as symbolist or surrealist. For him language is intuitive, expressive in the way that improvisational music can be. Like music it comes out of a sense of an instinctive harmony, an energy which is spontaneous and explosive. Words, he explained, are 'not thought [but] felt. They cut through space and make perfect sense without having to hesitate for the "meaning".' His objective is to penetrate to a 'world behind the form', to address not only the mind but also the body and the emotions and that leads him towards myth, since that 'speaks to everything at once, especially the emotions'.[23]

Generational conflict has been a central motif of drama from Aeschylus to Shakespeare, Chekhov and Ibsen through to Arthur Miller. Father and son wrestle for possession of the past and the future. At stake is the question of responsibility and the nature of identity. It is a battle for power and self-knowledge as the father stares into the mirror of the son and sees himself, and vice versa. It is an argument about the nature of reality and the extent of freedom. For few dramatic literatures, however, has that concern been as significant as it has proved for the American.

Eugene O'Neill's relationship with his father dominated some of his most powerful plays. Tennessee Williams's uneasy relationship with his father resulted in a series of portraits of domineering and destructive authoritarians. For Arthur Miller, from the very beginning of his career, the father-son conflict proved the nexus for his psychological and sociological concerns. Perhaps for a society so dedicated to the ideology of new beginnings, of a future untainted by history and of the individual as independent moral force, this was bound to be a crucial theme. It certainly proved so for a dramatist born in 1943 who first made his impact in the Off-Off Broadway of the 1960s and became a key figure in the 1970s and 1980s.

Sam Shepard Rogers III, the seventh to bear that name, was born into a service family. Theirs was an unsettled existence as they moved from base to base before arriving in Duarte, California. His father was a violent alcoholic, though also a man with a love for poetry. Shepard's escape lay through theatre. He joined Bishop's Company Repertory Players, a travelling group, and with them moved to New York. He did not, however, thereby escape his father, whose presence haunts a number of his plays and films. It was his father who introduced him to the work of Federico García Lorca in the original Spanish and who first interested him in jazz. But his father also represented an incipient anarchy. The vertiginous threat of violence was never far away. For Shepard himself there was a way of drawing on that double inheritance without succumbing to it – music: 'Rock and Roll is violence manifest without hurting no one.'[24] In terms of writing he was drawn to the Beats – to Jack Kerouac, Gregory Corso and Lawrence Ferlinghetti – and then to Samuel Beckett. Later it was to be Bertolt Brecht and Eugene O'Neill.

Shepard's change of name to the one that 'would be the name [he'd] die with' was itself a declaration of independence, later reflected in a speech in his play *The Holy Ghostly* in which a father upbraids his son for just such a betrayal of the past and rejection of himself: 'I know ya' set out to hurt me . . . Right from the start I knowed that. Like the way ya' changed yer name and all. That was rotten . . . That name was handed down for seven generations, boy.'[25] It was a break symbolised by his move to New York City but it was never a complete break, psychologically, in so far as then and throughout his career he has been drawn, in his drama and in his work for the cinema, to the world he left behind. The very restless impermanence of his early years, trailing from Illinois to South Dakota to Utah, became an image of a rootlessness which was both threat and redemption. The figure of the cowboy, which provided the title for his first play, was to recur as image and fact throughout his work. The cowboy was both free and irresponsible, walking away from those whose commitment he had won. That doubleness, the rhythm of attraction and repulsion, is the mark of many of his plays. The sense of some regenerative force in heartland America is strong, but it is a world that conceals not only mystery but also threat.

Shepard arrived in New York in 1963, precisely at the moment when theatre there was undergoing a profound change. Broadway was virtually defunct as a source of new work. Off-Broadway had begun to price itself out of a market which was itself changing. Suddenly new venues were opening: cafes, lofts, church halls. One such was Theatre Genesis, at St Mark's in the Bowery, founded by Ralph Cook, headwaiter at the Village Gate, a jazz club where Shepard worked cleaning dishes and waiting on tables. On 10 October 1964 a double bill of Shepard's plays opened there – *Cowboy* and *The Rock Garden*. The latter, about the alienated members of a family, he saw as autobiographical. Like many of his early plays it offered a series of tableaux or images, though some of what seemed their originality of structure was, he confessed, a result of simple ignorance, while some of the alogical juxtapositions seem to have been a result of disorienting drugs.

The most accomplished of his early plays was *Icarus's Mother*. Inspired by a Fourth of July celebration, it sets image against image; the rising rush of a rocket is balanced by the precipitate dive of an aircraft, the celebratory detonation of fireworks matched by an ominous explosion. There is a sense of threat and terror as the surface begins to crack under pressure. Past violence, the underside of an historical celebration, finds an echo in possible future violence. But the images which interest him are less those which are presented on stage (as Tennessee Williams makes the glass menagerie a central prop and symbol or Arthur Miller the clutter of old furniture in *The Price*) than those which cohere in the mind. The apocalyptic imagery of *Icarus's Mother* only works because it activates an anxiety already deep in the sensibility of its audience. It is in the mind that the otherwise disparate images come together, the scattered references to 'fire' and 'burning' acquire their significance. As he has said, 'When you talk about images, an image can be seen without looking at anything . . . You can see things that don't appear on stage . . . The fantastic thing about theatre is that it can make something be seen that's invisible and that's where my interest in theatre is . . . that's the image . . . that I'm looking for.'[26]

These early plays have little in the way of linear narrative. Character is not conceived as dense with social experience, language not as exposing truth or clarifying relationships. It was a theatre that seemed in tune with the times. Shepard had arrived in a New York in which the 'happening', formally structured events which developed a series of images out of objects and people, offered to bridge the gap between art and performance. He was surrounded by writers, directors and actors determined to construct a new drama commensurate with an age in which the unconscious was to be liberated and consciousness become a subject. This was a theatre of visions which developed an interest in the body as object as well as the object of desire. As he later explained:

To me the influence of the sixties and the off-off-Broadway theatre and the Lower East Side was a combination of hallucinogenic drugs; the effect of those drugs and the perceptions of those I came into contact with, the effect of those drugs on my own perceptions, the Viet Nam war and all the rest of it which is now all gone. The only thing which still remains and still persists as the single most important idea is the idea of consciousness. How does this idea become applicable to the theatre? For some time now it's become generally accepted that the other art forms are dealing with this idea to one degree or another. That the subject of painting is seeing. That the subject of music is hearing. That the subject of sculpture is space. But what is the subject of theatre which includes all these and more.[27]

The answer seems to lie not only in a combination of all these elements, but also in myth and ritual as mechanisms of understanding.

Shepard's early plays do not lend themselves to rational analysis. He was suspicious of formal structure ('A resolution isn't an ending; it's a strangulation').[28] His characters are liable to dissolve or fracture into opposites. Style becomes subject. Seeking an analogy for his approach to language he found it in music, something he saw, too, in the Beats: 'I've practiced Jack Kerouac's discovery of jazz-sketching with words . . . following the exact same principles as a musician does when he's jamming.'[29] Experience is presented as fragmented ('Everybody's caught up in a fractured world . . . what's happening to them is unfathomable.')[30] The figures who move through these plays are cartoon-like (in *La Turista* they are deliberately clichéd and named after brands of cigarettes). They have their roots in popular culture. They are cowboys, rock stars, shamans, mobsters. He plunders contemporary myth, the unifying images of a society lacking a centre. Long before he turned to the screen as writer or actor he was fascinated by the cinema, whose two-dimensional characters nonetheless had a compelling reality. Literally an art of surfaces, a projection, film nonetheless plainly tapped into and generated anxieties, needs, dreams in a way that made its images common currency. This was where modern myths were constructed, projected and reinforced.

Shepard is aware of the ambivalence of the images on film. He fantasises a Hollywood cowboy, face thick with make-up, horse decked out in silver studs, sinking to his knees and screaming: 'Forgive me Utah!' The very doubleness of film, though, is a clue to its fascination. Speaking of Buster Keaton, he remarked on the extent to which his art depended on a passive, unyielding face contrasting with a body 'performing more things than a body can perform'. It is, he remarks, 'a double action with two opposites happening simultaneously'.[31] As a description that remark could be applied to much of Shepard's own work, which deals in fractured sensibilities, divided selves, polarised relationships. Father and sons, brothers, husbands and wives are expressions of a radical split in experience, an alienation which has its correlative in the social world. But balancing the alienation is an equally powerful drive towards unity.

In a *Village Voice* review Edward Albee noted that 'what Shepard's plays are aboul is a great deal less interesting than how they are about it',[32] and this was particularly true of plays which came to him as images or which grew out of drug-induced visions. As he explained of *Chicago*, staged in 1965, 'The stuff would just come out, and I wasn't really trying to shape it or make it into any big thing. I would have a picture and just start from there. A picture of a guy in a bathtub, or two guys on stage with a sign blinking, you know, things like that.'[33] There was a gnomic quality to this early work which left not only audiences but also actors baffled. Initially resistant to rewriting, he saw the problem as one of finding the appropriate production style. But gnomic or not his imagistic plays began to find a critical following with Obies for *Red Cross*, *Icarus's Mother* and *Chicago*, all elliptical pieces. His concern seemed to take a new turn, however, as he was employed by Michelangelo Antonioni to script, along with several other writers, his film *Zabriskie Point*, an unhappy experience for Shepard but one which involved him in the film world to which he was later drawn. He even saw one of his plays – *Operation Sidewinder* – staged at New York's Lincoln Centre.

Operation Sidewinder was his first three-act play. In some respects a showcase for the rock band with which he played, it managed to interweave a number of familiar Hollywood genres – science fiction, the crime movie, the western – with rock music in a parable about the conquest of a destructive scientism by those in tune with spiritual values, the latter represented by a group of Hopi Indians. Theatrically inventive, it nonetheless failed to spark much interest, though Shepard was now plainly interested in extending his plays beyond simple, vivid images. Indeed he found himself at some kind of crossroads. After a precocious beginning he had continued to build his reputation Off-Off Broadway, but few productions of his work satisfied him, nor had he succeeded in breaking through to larger audiences or in finding consistent critical support. More importantly he felt ambiguously about a number of his plays. In 1971, he decided to leave America.

As a musician he was aware that for the best part of a decade Britain had been a key centre for rock and roll. In the end his move there proved something of a mistake but the distance from America did do something to free him theatrically. The Open Space Theatre in London staged *The Tooth of Crime* – though not without fierce arguments with Shepard – and the Royal Court, responsible for encouraging and developing the careers of a number of young British playwrights, produced *Geography of a Horse Dreamer*, two of the best of his early plays.

The Tooth of Crime stages a battle between two rock stars, a style war in which each battles for psychic territory. Described as a 'play with music', with Shepard writing both lyrics and music, it begins with a song sung by Hoss, who enters in a black leather outfit with silver studs and black kid gloves, a combination rock star and cowboy. This, in effect, accurately describes Shepard's aesthetic principles:

> You may think every picture you see is a true history of
>   the way things used to be or the way things are
> While you're ridin' in your radio or walkin' through the
>   late late show ain't it a drag to know you just
>   don't know you just don't know.

So here's another illusion to add to your confusion
Of the way things are . . .
All the heroes is dyin' like flies they say it's a sign
    a' the times
And everybody's walkin' asleep eyes open – eyes open
So here's another sleep-walkin' dream.
A livin' talkin' show of the way things seem . . .
So here's another fantasy
About the way things seem to be to me.[34]

His plays have precisely the quality of dreams, a jumble of fantasy and reality, of the familiar pressed to the extreme and of emotions no longer contained and repressed. The heroes have indeed outlived their time, existing now only as pure performance, as gesture and style. In *The Tooth of Crime* the heroes are the great rock stars, models, for Hoss, of those who created their own codes and lived by them, the great cowboys and movie stars, artists and musicians. What is left, however, are only echoes. Hoss is a killer who has lost his instincts, under pressure to stay at the top of his profession. It is tempting, indeed, to read both this play and *Geography of a Horse Dreamer* as Shepard's own sense of artistic crisis, unsure as he was at the time of the direction of his career and yet expected to top his earlier success. In *The Tooth of Crime* Hoss is harassed by 'The bookies, the agents, the Keepers',[35] as in *Geography of a Horse Dreamer* the protagonist, who has the ability to dream the winners of horse races, is urged to come up with more winners, to dream dreams for those who stand to benefit from those dreams. Hoss debates with his father, as the protagonist of *Fool for Love* was to do, and is advised 'The road's what counts. Just look at the road. Don't worry about where it's going.'[36] That could stand both as a description of Shepard's own approach to writing, certainly early in his career, and as a piece of rationalisation for a man whose future was indeed uncertain at that moment. A character's observation that 'The image is my survival kit',[37] perhaps also has more than a passing relevance to a playwright who, for all his public performances, remained a private person.

The fight between Hoss and his rival Crow, also dressed like a rock star, is fought through language as they challenge one another on a lexical battlefield. They switch between ideolects, challenge one another with jargon, exchange repartee, flourish abuse, search for weaknesses exposed and exploited by words, invent a past which can be invoked as weapon. In a scene which is a genuine *tour de force* they hone language to a sharp edge. At a time when the American theatre, under the influence of Antonin Artaud, was reacting against words, Shepard was a poet committed to their power, regarding them as 'tools of imagery in motion', with the power 'to evoke visions in the eye of the audience'.[38] Language, he insisted, has the potential of making 'leaps into the unknown'.

For actor/monologist Spalding Gray, who appeared as Hoss in the Performance Group production of the play, the key lay in the language which he described as 'sheer contemporary poetry . . . music that I perform with the instrument of my body'.[39] For Shepard himself the play had, indeed, begun with language, 'a certain sound which is coming from the voice of this character, Hoss',[40] while music enabled the audience to come to terms with an emotional reality. In the case of *The Tooth of Crime* it was to be a 'sounding board' for the play. For him, music could achieve immediately what it might take several pages of dialogue to create verbally. Its impact was also direct, by-passing the mind. Not an enthusiast for the kind of experimental theatre which required physical contact between performers and audience or the literal breaking of the barrier between stage and auditorium, he was interested in provoking a different kind of involvement.

Shepard's route into *Geography of a Horse Dreamer*, written during his stay in England, was also language, though this time the idiom was that of 1930s thriller. The points of reference are Raymond Chandler and Dashiell Hammett. If *The Tooth of Crime* was 'built like *High Noon*', *Geography of a Horse Dreamer*, subtitled 'A Mystery in Two Acts', takes the cowboy hipster into the mean streets of London. Its central character, who is significantly called Cody (after Buffalo Bill Cody), is kidnapped from Wyoming by gangsters who learn of his ability to dream the winners of horse races, while Doc (named after Doc Holliday) plots to remove from his neck the organ presumed to be responsible for his powers. The play ends as Cody is rescued by his brothers, who kill most of the gang responsible. Once again we are offered a fable of lost heroes. Some magic has gone, destroyed by venality and time: innocence has been corrupted by those who have no understanding of or respect for mystery.

In *Operation Sidewinder* the US Air Force and its technological inventions had broken a primitive contract between man and his environment, man's physical and spiritual sides. A similar betrayal lies at the heart of *Geography of a Horse Dreamer*. In so far as the play is also a comment by Shepard on his own work, it stands as something more than a reaction against critics who appropriate his art and attempt to explain

its mechanisms. It is true that he has seldom been happy with productions of his plays and it is tempting to see this work as a comment on the
uses to which other people had put his insights. But beyond that there is
an element of self-criticism, for in drawing on private experience he
potentially devalues it by deploying it in the context of a public art with
its own economic imperatives. As he has said, in speaking of his work, 'I
feel a lot of reluctance in attempting to describe my part of a process
which, by its truest nature, holds an unending mystery.'[41]

Shepard's career seemed to take a new direction with *Curse of the
Starving Class* (1977) and *Buried Child*, which was first performed in 1978,
one winning an Obie Award, the other a Pulitzer Prize. Both three-act
plays, they appeared more realistic. Certainly the sets indicated a kind
of detailed realism which had seldom characterised his work before, but,
rather as in Pinter's work, this merely served to foreground the non-realistic treatment of character. Indeed, within moments of *Curse of the
Starving Class* opening we are offered a speech in which Wesley describes
his feelings on listening to his father's drunken attempt to break into the
house, a speech which begins as naturalistic narrative but quickly
devolves into something else, as its rhythms reenact the crescendo and
diminuendo of a violence refracted through his sensibility:

I was lying there on my back. I could smell the avocado blossoms. I could hear
the coyotes . . . I listened like an animal. My listening was afraid. Afraid of
sound. Tense . . . Feet coming. Feet walking toward the door. Feet stopping.
Heart pounding. Sound of door not opening. Foot kicking door. Man's voice.
Dad's voice. Dad calling Mom. No answer. Foot kicking. Foot kicking harder.
Wood splitting . . . Then no sound. Then softly crying. Soft crying. Then no
sound. Then softly crying.[42]

The speech, which lasts a full five minutes, is ostensibly addressed to his
mother but is in effect an interior monologue. It ends with him impersonating the sound of his father's car driving away or of the cars on a
distant freeway. It is a speech, moreover, which shows Shepard at his best
as a poet of the theatre. The function of the speech is to convey information. In its essentials it simply recapitulates what we have just been
offered in the conversation between Wesley and his mother. Its meaning
lies partly in its rhythms, partly in the way the language is placed under
strain, reflecting a sensibility under pressure. The narrative logic of the
speech suggests that the threat is external; the grammatical structure
locates it also in the self which observes.

The family inhabit a run-down farm. Wesley is an alcoholic, violent,
in debt, a victim and a victimiser. His wife, Ella, is as determined to

escape as is Wesley. Both husband and wife try separately to sell the property and abandon a family which exists more in name than in reality. In the course of the play their two children turn into versions of themselves. This potential is evident in their names which echo those of their parents: Emma and Weston are children to Ella and Wesley. Indeed at the end of the play Weston dresses in his father's clothes and masquerades as him. In much the same way Vince, in *Buried Child*, turns into a version of his father, the brothers exchange identity in *True West* and the son in *Fool for Love* repeats his father's act of desertion, as his love affair with his half-sister suggests a reflexive world from which there is no escape.

It is tempting to root this concern in Shepard's own difficult and extremely ambiguous relationship with his own father, also an alcoholic who abandoned the family. Plainly there is a risk of becoming the thing you fear. The family becomes a closed system replicating its tensions and contradictions. The prevailing sense is one of claustrophobia. Not only are his characters, like Tennessee Williams's, trapped inside their own skins for life, they are caught in a biological trap which condemns them to re-enactment. They are also trapped in the absurdity of relationships on which they rely for meaning and survival but which are equally the source of their pain. Thus Wesley tells the story of an eagle which swoops down and lifts a cat into the sky: 'they fight. They fight like crazy in the middle of the sky. That cat's tearing his chest out, and the eagle's trying to drop him, but the cat won't let go because he knows if he falls he'll die.'[43] This is the essence of the relationships in Shepard's plays, certainly of that which lies at the heart of *Buried Child*, which opened not long after *Curse of the Starving Class* and which won him the 1979 Pulitzer Prize.

Buried Child is about a homecoming and shares something with Harold Pinter's play called *The Homecoming*. There is the same sense of menace, the same sense of a buried past pressing on present behaviour. Vince takes his girlfriend Shelly to see his grandparents whom he has not visited for six years. His grandfather, Dodge, sits on a faded sofa watching a flickering television screen and drinking. His grandmother, Halie, dressed wholly in black as though in mourning, dwells on thoughts of her dead son, Ansel. Neither shows any sign of recognising Vince, any more than does Tilden, his father, a man who carries vegetables into the house from a backyard which has formerly grown nothing. For a writer who had never received the recognition or acknowledgement of his own father this is a play rooted deep in his own psyche. But Shepard is not an autobiographical writer in the simple sense of dramatising his own experiences. He is concerned with the failure of relationship, the space between those who should be physically and emotionally close. As Dodge remarks to Shelly, 'You think just because you propagate they have to love their offspring. You never see a bitch eat her puppies?'[44] The child buried outside the house is his own, a child whose red hair matches that of its mother, Halie, as a young woman. It is in that sense an image of the past, the past which Dodge wishes to deny: 'This is me', remarks Dodge, 'Right here. This is it. The whole shootin' match.'[45]

With a play set in a farmhouse in the shadow of 'dark elm trees' it is difficult not to think of O'Neill's *Desire Under the Elms* particularly given the dead child and the sense of sexual threat which both plays have in common. Indeed, the irony implicit in a closed world which breeds only continuing further entrapment might seem to pull them closer together. But Shepard's concerns are rather different. The dead child is an echo of its mother as Vince is of his father and grandfather. As in *Curse of the Starving Class* we are confronted with repetition as a kind of hell. As in O'Neill's late plays we are faced with a world in which the family is the source of pain and consolation alike. Both Tilden and his brother Bradley had left only to be drawn back again. Tilden, like Travis in *Paris, Texas*, had drifted into the desert, trying to survive without speaking. Outside of speech he imagined himself equally outside of the ironies of experience. 'I was alone. I thought I was dead . . . I thought I was dying but I just lost my voice.' He comes to the conclusion that 'you gotta talk or you'll die.'[46] At the same time he confesses that he cannot 'figure anything out'. Dodge's response 'There's nothing to figure out. You just forge ahead'[47] – is both a Beckettian irony and an echo of his earlier advice to concentrate on the road rather than the destination. This might almost be a comment on *Buried Child* itself, which, as its first director pointed out, has elements of the detective story about it except that the 'solution' – Dodge's culpability – is no solution at all. The detective story is invoked, if at all, at the level of parody. The search for meaning, the attempt to 'figure it out', leads nowhere. As Dodge says, tauntingly, of Shelly, 'she thinks she's going to get it out of us. She thinks she's going to uncover the truth of the matter. Like a detective or something.'[48] It is tempting to see this both as a taunt directed at the dramatic critic and, more profoundly, as an observation about the hunger for meaning and coherence.

In *Suicide in B♭*, first produced in 1976, he had created, in the figure of Laureen, a woman who stands poised before a window contemplating her death, a divided sensibility debating with herself. Her cry, 'If only I don't die before I find out . . . Just let me live five minutes longer',[49] merely prefaces her apparent plunge to the street below. The desire for meaning coincides with the absence of meaning. This is Beckett's irony and Shepard's. Likewise the final speech of *Buried Child* is deeply ironic. As Tilden enters the house carrying the corpse of the dead child, Halie is heard celebrating the beneficence of nature: 'You can't force a thing to grow. You can't interfere with it. It's all hidden. It's all unseen. You just gotta wait til it pops up out of the ground. Tiny little shoot. Tiny little white shoots. All hairy and fragile. Strong though. Strong enough to break the earth even. It's a miracle . . .'[50] A religious minister watches events unfold, as powerless to intervene as the minister in Edward Albee's *Quotations from Chairman Mao Tse-Tung*. His ineffectualness merely serves to underline the irony of Halie's desperate assertion that 'We can't not believe in something. We can't stop believing. We just end up dying if we stop. Just end up dead.'[51] In a play dominated by images of disso-lution – one brother is buried, another has been killed, a third is an amputee – the vegetables heaped upon the stage seem to have much the same significance as the leaf which appears on the tree in *Waiting for Godot*.

The buried child, it appears, is the incestuous product of Tilden and his mother. As in *Fool for Love* incest serves to underscore the hermetic nature of their world. There is, indeed, a kind of autism about Shepard's characters, who pay little regard to the world beyond themselves. They become alternative versions of themselves, doomed to re-enactment. The fact of incest is an embracing of the self in another guise. Life, as Vince comes to realise, is replication without meaning, re-enactment without purpose. Thus he describes driving in a car and seeing himself in the windscreen:

I studied my face. Studied everything about it. As though I was looking at another man. As though I could see his whole race behind him. Like a mummy's face. I saw him dead and alive at the same time. In the same breath . . . I watched him breathe as though we were frozen in time . . . And then his face changed. His face became his father's face . . . And his father's face changed to his grand-father's face. And it went on like that. Changing. Clear back to faces I'd never seen before but still recognized. Still recognized the bones beneath . . . Straight back as far as they'd take me. Then it all dissolved.[52]

In *Suicide in B♭* the woman similarly stares at another version of herself as do the characters in *Fool for Love* and *True West*.

True West, which appeared at the Magic Theatre in 1980, is set in what

Shepard himself has called the temporary world of California. The action takes place in a suburban house, where synthetic grass is not the only touch of artifice. Austin is a successful Hollywood scriptwriter. His older brother, Lee, is a semi-derelict petty thief whose rivalry with Austin leads him to develop his own idea for an authentic western, a project which he sells to a somewhat stereotypical Hollywood producer, complete with pink-and-white flower print sports shirt, white sports coat and matching polyester slacks. Close kin to Mamet's mogul in *Speed the Plow*, he proves equally gullible when confronted with Lee's bizarre proposal. By this time Shepard was entirely familiar with Hollywood kitsch, which he had already parodied in *Angel City*, but here this is merely the background for a play which explores the two central characters. In a stage note Shepard stresses the need for realism in the *mise en scène*. Attention was to be focused on the two brothers, with only the sound of a coyote yapping in an ever more intense and maniacal way offering a commentary on a situation which itself gradually becomes more anarchic.

Austin works on his script while his brother continues his life of petty larceny, taunting his brother with his lack of courage. Yet another of Shepard's characters who has spent time in the desert before returning to supposed civilisation, he has a menacing authority. There is a constant threat of violence as he slowly dispossesses his brother, securing a commission from Austin's producer and leaving his brother nothing to do but develop the idea which Lee lacks the ability or skills to do himself. By turns comic and threatening, the play explores the dissolution of identity as the two men slowly exchange roles. Lee suggests that he had 'always wondered what'd be like to be'[53] Austin while Austin says of the producer that he thinks 'we're the same person', and confesses that when drunk 'we all sound alike'.[54] The staid Austin ends up battling to leave a world where 'nothing's real' to go to the desert from which his brother had emerged. They wrestle amidst the debris of a house they have wrecked. Now Austin has become the thief and Lee the Hollywood writer. The play ends as the brothers prepare to continue their fight in a desert landscape while in the background a coyote howls. They seem, in other words, about to live out the screenplay which Lee has just sold to Saul Kimmer, a contemporary western in which two men do battle in a desert landscape:

they take off into an endless black prairie . . . what they don't know is that each one of 'em is afraid, see. Each one separately thinks that he's the only one that's afraid. And they keep ridin' like that straight into the night. Not knowing. And the one who's chasin' doesn't know where the other one is taking him. And the one who's being chased doesn't know where he's going.[55]

The irony is the greater when the two are merely aspects of the same self, drawn equally to solitude and the public world of social action, to the construction of artistic form and the celebration of anarchy. No wonder their mother tells Austin that he 'can't kill' his brother. The reflexiveness of a text in which the characters re-enact a screenplay of their own devising suggests a world in which reality is modelled on fiction rather than the other way around, a world which is hermetic, echoic, apocalyptic.

But into this Sisyphean absurdity there intrudes the figure of the mother, who wanders through the action largely oblivious to the mayhem around her, like the comic drunk in movies who survives bar brawls intact. The fact is that *True West* is extremely funny. Its absurdities and *non sequiturs* breed humour as well as violence. Lee's attempt to feed bread to a line of stolen toasters, like his brother's assault on a typewriter with a golf club, is surreally funny. It is also something else. The attack on the typewriter stems from Lee's inability to find a language for his thoughts, and that has been a continuing theme of Shepard's work. It certainly lay at the heart of the pieces which he developed with the actor and founder of the Open Theatre, Joseph Chaikin. *Tongues* (1978) and *Savage/Love* (1979) both explore the inadequacy of language in the face of feeling and experience. Thus the voice of a mother, in *Tongues*, is heard saying: 'They told me what kind of pain I'd have. How the spasms would come. How to deal with the pain. How to push. Nothing they told me was like this.'[56] Different tones of voice drain words of their apparent meaning. In *Savage/Love*, a title devised and defended by Shepard, love proves not merely undefinable but the source of an exultation, a despair, a doubt, an incomprehension, a fear, a need which words can hardly even approximate. And that irony lies equally at the heart of his next play, *Fool for Love* (1983), whose epigraph was taken from Archbishop Anthony Bloom: 'The proper response to love is to accept it. There is nothing to do.'

Fool for Love is set in a low-rent motel room on the edge of the Mojave Desert. Shepard describes it with a detailed realism, but realism has a special meaning in this play. One of the characters (a device familiar from Pinter's *Old Times*) is himself a fantasy who exists only in the minds of Eddie and May, two lovers who play out the drama of their passion in this bleak setting. When that character their – father – claims to be married 'in my mind', he adds 'That's realism',[57] and, indeed, in this setting reality and fantasy are two aspects of the same experience. May accuses Eddie of fantasising a rural dream; he accuses her of fantasising a rival. Both accusations are the product of real anxieties and fears. These are two characters whose emotional sensitivities are so acute that they are neurotically responsive to every action. In a stage direction Shepard indicates the need for sounds to be distorted and magnified by means of a bass drum hidden in the door frame and microphones concealed within the set. Likewise their movements are carefully choreographed. They circle one another like animals, pressing themselves back against the walls which become an image of the emotional world from which they cannot escape. They are simultaneously attracted and repelled by one another. The gentle touch and the violent blow are merely two possibilities present in the same moment. An early encounter proves paradigmatic:

They stand facing one another for a while. She crosses slowly to him. She stops. He takes a few steps towards her. Stops. They both move closer. Stop. Pause as they look at each other. They embrace. Long, tender kiss. They are very soft with each other. She pulls away from him slightly. Smiles. She looks him straight in the eyes, then suddenly knees him in the groin with tremendous force.[58]

Eddie, a rodeo rider, is described as having 'a peculiar broken down quality about his body'. May, a short-order cook, has a 'tough drabness'. They are as marginal as the setting. Together, though, they generate an energy whose intensity is reflected in the amplification of sound for which Shepard called. Indeed May transforms herself, changing clothes on stage until she becomes seductively attractive. She has two fears of equal force: that Eddie will stay and that he will go. Either way she is tense with a mixture of fear and longing. For his part Eddie slowly dismantles a shotgun and drinks tequila, an implied threat registered by May but immediately ironised by a story told by the Old Man who sits on a reclining chair on a small extended platform at the edge of the stage. He recalls an occasion from the past when, as a baby, she and he felt threatened by mysterious creatures only to discover that they were nothing more than cows. As he tells the story so she crawls on hands and knees and hugs a pillow, regressing to the childhood he invokes.

Eddie and May are half-brother and sister but in another sense they are two parts of a divided sensibility. The schizophrenia which afflicts so many of Shepard's characters here becomes an aspect both of the relationship between men and women and of a self which contains both elements. When Eddie and May jointly recount their past the Old Man insists, 'I wanna' hear the male side a' this thing.'[59] The story they tell is of the death of May's mother. In despair at losing the Old Man she had killed herself with a shotgun. Since Eddie now owns a shotgun and appears to abandon May at the end of the play, they seem to be re-enacting that experience, participating in a ritual of attraction and abandonment. The man wishes to move on, not to be tied down. The woman craves a home. For once, in a Shepard play, the struggle is a near equal one. As he explained, he had to sustain a female character and have her remain absolutely true to herself, not only as a social being, but also as an emotional being. He has to 'sustain both sides of the issue' so that 'They're just who they are.'[60]

Cutting a tangent across this are two sub-plots. May's date, a country boy called Martin, blunders into the motel room where he becomes an audience to their revelations, while Eddie is pursued by anonymous and violent forces who shoot out the windscreen of his truck and eventually blow it up, leaving an apocalyptic glow in the sky. The former is the source of humour; the latter of menace. These are the twin poles of Shepard's world.

Two epigraphs to his 1985 play *A Lie of the Mind* define the parameters of his concerns. One, taken from H.L. Mencken's *The American Language*, identifies a public world of individuals adrift in an America which has lost its direction, a world of space and unthought resiliency:

Most were bankrupt small farmers or down-at-heel city proletarians, and the rest were mainly chronic nomads of the sort who, a century later, roved the country in caricatures of automobiles. If they started for Kentucky or Ohio, they were presently moving on to Indiana or Illinois, and after that, doggedly and irrationally, to even wilder and less hospitable regions. When they halted, it was simply because they had become exhausted.[61]

What remains is the possibility of connecting with others, but that relationship, particularly that between men and women, is itself the source of a paralysing irony as need creates its own vulnerability. So it is that the second epigraph, taken from the work of Cesar Vallejo, addresses a private world in which another kind of space denies fulfilment:

Something identifies you with the one who leaves you, and it is your common power to return: thus your greatest sorrow. Something separates you from the one who remains with you, and it is your common slavery to depart: thus your meagerest rejoicing.[62]

And what is true of two selves in thrall to the necessities they would deny is true equally of a self inwardly divided, with solitude and companionship its twin irreconcilable goals. The same play's 'music note' calls for music with 'an American backbone' and its set description for a design which will convey a sense of 'infinite space, going off to nowhere', thereby underscoring the extent to which Shepard sees himself as writing America and dramatising the lives of those who walk the vertiginous edge of experience. Again and again they walk off into the desert which will take them out of an anxious social context at the cost of annihilating their identity. It is the world from which Travis emerged, in *Paris, Texas;* it is the world to which he returns, like the cowboy who exists only when he enters a public world in which there is no place for him, when he enters time and a story in which he has a ritual role to play.

The opening stage direction of *A Lie of the Mind* might be a description of the psychological and spiritual situation of many of his characters: 'Impression of huge space and distance between the two characters with each one isolated in his own pool of light.'[63] The play opens with a character further isolated, having apparently lost the power of coherent speech. Shepard has twice had experience of people rendered aphasic, once by drugs and once by catastrophic illness. In *Paris, Texas* he turned the slow acquisition of language, by a character who had deliberately desocialised himself, into an ironic account of the repossession of social responsibility and the enactment of a profound and damaging anxiety. Language becomes a social tool but also a mechanism of deceit and a reminder of betrayal. In *A Lie of the Mind* language has been beaten out of Beth by her husband Jake. From stuttering incomprehension she moves to a sudden and equally alarming fluency, rendered bizarre by its illogicalities. Such coherence as she can muster is associative. In struggling for the name of the man who has damaged her she arrives at the word 'love', a connection which many another Shepard character might have made.

The lie of the title refers in part to the alternative reality constructed by Jake. The play begins with a lie as, standing alone in a pool of light, he insists that Beth is with him, though in so far as she can never be purged from his mind this is a lie with an inner truth. He constructs scenarios which are born out of anxiety. His jealousy feeds on images which he creates to taunt himself. Her wearing of perfume becomes evidence of her infidelity. She is an actress but to him the line between pretence and reality is blurred. By the same token, to her, too, if his account is to be believed, acting 'is more real than the real world'.

Beth and Jake are like mirror-images of one another. If she is an actor he, we are told, is 'always playacting'. The second scene, in which she expresses her love for Jake, and pleads with her brother to stay with her, is immediately reflected in the following scene in which Jake declares his love for Beth and pleads with his brother to stay. This becomes a pattern for the play. In scene six Beth lies on a bed, 'her face turned away from the audience' in a way which Shepard pointedly describes as 'almost the identical position and attitude of sleep as JAKE in previous scene'.[64] In scene five Jake's mother purports to know nothing of his wife, as in scene six Beth's mother uses identical words to express her ignorance of Jake's existence. Jake insists that he has killed Beth; Beth that she has been killed by Jake. They are like twins; to be apart is to lose part of themselves. Indeed, in a state of physical decline and mental confusion which directly parallels Beth's, Jake mistakes his sister for her. As in *Fool for Love* the relationship, despite its sexual reality, seems essentially that between brother and sister.

A Lie of the Mind is another of Shepard's enquiries into the nature of love. Its most eloquent moment is also one of its least fluent. Beth, whose brain is damaged, nonetheless registers an emotional truth which exists beneath the evasions and deceits of daily existence:

This is my father. He's given up love. Love is dead for him. My mother is dead for him. Things live for him to be killed. Only death counts for him. Nothing else . . . This is me. This is me now. The way I am. Now. This. All. Different. I – I live inside this. Remember. Remembering . . . I know what love is. I can never forget. That. Never.[65]

And if the language is fractured, as it often is in Shepard's work, it is not brain damage alone that accounts for it. As one of his characters remarks, 'Soon's it gets normal we'll talk normal.'[66] For the truth is that it is not only Beth who is 'kinda – shattered'. There was once, it appears, another kind of existence, but 'That was a whole other time.' The question asked by Jake's mother – 'Is there any reason in this Christless world why men leave women?'[67] – echoes throughout his work. To her, love 'is a disease that makes you feel good. While it lasts. Then, when it's gone, yer worse off than before you caught it.'[68] The echo of Hemingway is unmistakable. The only authentic response is to 'resist'. For Beth's mother, 'we're so different that we'll never be able to get certain things across to each other'.[69] The problem is that 'the female one needs – the other' while 'the male one – doesn't really need the other. Not the same way . . . The male one goes off by himself. Leaves. He needs something else. But he doesn't know what it is. He doesn't really know what he needs. So he ends up dead. By himself.'[70]

At one stage Beth, who her mother says has 'male in her', wears a man's shirt which makes her 'feel like the man . . . Like father . . . Like brother.'[71] Indeed, in a reverie Beth suggests to Frankie, Jake's brother, whose voice she believes is like her brother's, that he should 'pretend to be in love with me . . . This shirt is a man to you. You are my beautiful woman.'[72] For all that Shepard's work is male-dominated he seems fascinated by the androgyny, the doubleness of the individual sensibility.

In 1991, during the Gulf War, Shepard staged what one critic described as a fierce anti-war play and another an exercise in nostalgia which took the audience back to the 1960s. It was neither. Like his earlier plays it was about an America whose inner coherence was lacking. Its title – *States of Shock* – might be equally applied to any of his immediately preceding plays underscoring, as it does, the extent to which Shepard's America continues to crack open along the fault lines of violence and failed love.

  States of Shock is set in a restaurant which becomes a kind of no man's land on a mental battlefield. The restaurant, which still has the remnants of a faded civility about it, becomes the stage for a post-apocalyptic drama, an image of an America which has slid from war into a boredom which threatens to devolve into anarchy. Once again this is a play about a father and son, the difference being that it is the son rather than the father who is, apparently, dead, killed in a war whose traumatising impact is apparent in the characters as in the almost featureless space which they inhabit. The Colonel has brought Stubbs, a veteran confined to a wheelchair, into the restaurant as his guest. The wheelchair is decorated with American flags, a touch of irony which deepens as the play develops. Neither Stubbs nor the Colonel is in full control of himself, the former being prone to blow a whistle and expose a war wound, the latter to probe into the past as into an exposed wound, at times screaming in an alarmed and alarming way.

  The Colonel has brought his guest to the restaurant in order to mark the death of his son, killed at the moment of Stubbs's wounding, though at times Stubbs and the son seem to blend into one another. With the aid of toy soldiers and restaurant cutlery the Colonel restages the event. The stage is lit, from time to time, by the flashes of what seems to be incoming fire, while explosions are mimicked by offstage percussion instruments. Stubbs, it transpires, had been wounded by his own side and, whether true or not, it is clear that this is a society which is destroying itself. To the side of the stage sit a middle-aged couple waiting, mostly in vain, to be served and finally turning to obsessive behaviour. They are the witnesses, the embodiment of a society which sees without perceiving, imagining that the routines of American life will insulate them from inconvenient truths. Their own slide from the banal to the psychotic suggests otherwise.

In *States of Shock* the father is bewildered by the fact of a lost son in the context of a society which insists on its victories. It is a dilemma which underlies much of Shepard's drama in so far as loss is a central theme and violence a concrete image of the pressures which place myths and realities under strain. This gap between the American values to which he is drawn and an American present – fragmented, incoherent, attenuated – from which he is repelled generates an energy which is discharged through his plays. *States of Shock* shows that conflict at its most acute. American flags can no more conceal the reality of a wheelchair-bound victim of war than could President Bush's campaign visit to a flag factory distract from the reality of economic and spiritual decline. Then again, perhaps they did. *States of Shock* certainly had a very abbreviated run.

The 1990s seemed to mark a change of emphasis. From the destructive nature of male–female relationships, the fragmented and fragmenting family unit, Shepard seemed to turn his attention to the pressures exerted on men, pressures that left them maimed, scarred, in psychological and social confusion. In *Far North* (1988), a film that he wrote and directed, men appear to have lost their roles and their direction. Lying in hospital beds, they can only watch the world on television or through a window. They can act, if at all, only through the women who are no less confused but are in control. In *States of Shock* women have no place except as observers of a brutal and brutalising encounter, as two men perform their dysfunctional relationship, disabled as they are by a shared history of trauma as much as by the trauma of history. In *Simpatico* (1995) two men, co-conspirators in a criminal enterprise, see their identities placed under increasing pressure. For Shepard, the American male is cut off from a past in which the national story gave him a central position and adrift in a present in which he is unsure of his role. Violence, once sanctioned by frontier realities no less than frontier myths, is now turned against those who represent a seductive but constraining love or against the self which duly fractures. In a world in a state of flux everything is temporary. And that is no less true of *Simpatico* than of his earlier works.

Indeed, even the circumstances of its composition suggest the extent to which there is no still centre. Shepard claims to have written it on the steering wheel of a car as he drove towards Los Angeles on Highway 40. It is set, in part, in one of the towns strung out along the San Bernadino

Freeway, places that he has characterised as being on the edge of nowhere, towns where people have simply lost the will to continue. Indeed, in some ways the characters inhabit less a place than a psychological space. Certainly, they seem to move between California and Virginia almost instantaneously as though that were an expression of a rootlessness which is almost definitional.

Carter and Vinnie were once partners in a racing scam. In order to protect themselves they framed a racing commissioner, called Simms, with pornographic photographs, employing the services of Rosie to do so. She subsequently switched her affections from Vinnie to Carter, who left with his partner's woman and car, two facts which have worked increasingly on Vinnie's mind in the fifteen years since the crime and what he sees as his desertion. Carter becomes rich; Vinnie has been surviving from moment to moment on handouts from his former partner. He lives in obscurity under a series of assumed names while the commissioner, also under an assumed name, has been secured a job on the fringes of the racing industry. When the play opens, however, this arrangement begins to come unwound as Vinnie decides to reveal its details to the disgraced commissioner, even handing over the photographs, evidence, incidentally, of Carter's involvement.

Vinnie's life seems in spiralling decline. He lives in some squalor, fantasising about life as a private detective. As his new woman, Cecelia, observes, what seems to be missing is continuity: 'Everything seems so busted up to me. Like I've lived a dozen different lives.'[73] Vinnie has done precisely this himself, switching from alias to alias and losing any sense of himself.

Despite the fact that some of the play's key statements are made by women their comments seem to bear most directly on the men. Thus it is Cecelia who comments on the fact of 'people drifting apart', insisting that it is 'worse than death',[74] and Rosie who observes that 'Everything has already happened! It's already taken place',[75] but it is the men who most directly evidence these facts. Paradoxically, though, the relationship between Vinnie and Carter seems akin to a marriage. As Vinnie observes, it is 'kinda like marriage . . . a *lot* like marriage',[76] as what once joined them becomes the cause of their alienation.

Vinnie's threat, however, comes to nothing. As it happens, Simms has no interest in revenge or self-justification. But by then Carter has himself begun to collapse, repeating Vinnie's decline. Indeed, in effect the two men, like the brothers in *True West*, exchange places, an expression, perhaps, of a single fractured sensibility. Only Simms, it seems, facinated by bloodlines, committed to a racing industry in which continuity, at least at the level of heredity and genetics, remains a central truth, is perhaps outside this entropic logic.

The irony of *Simpatico* is that the title word can be applied to no one in the play, except possibly Simms. The characters inhabit a world without character, see human relationships, Mamet-like, as simple agencies. The past is only the site of events that have destabilised them. The present is temporary: the future unimaginable. Even identity can no longer be sustained. Causalities are broken. They are performers no longer secure in their roles or certain of their lines. In that sense they reflect one of Sam Shepard's fundamental concerns. In 1983 he wrote to Joseph Chaikin saying that,

Something's been coming to me lately about this whole question of being lost. It only makes sense to me in relation to an idea of one's identity being shattered under severe personal circumstances – in a state of crisis where everything I've previously identified with in myself suddenly falls away. A shock state, I guess you might call it. I don't think it makes much difference what the shock itself is – whether it's a trauma to do with a loved one or a physical accident or whatever – the resulting emptiness and aloneness is what interests me. Particularly to do with questions like *home? family?* the identification of *others* over time? people I've known who are now lost to me though still alive.[77]

That shocked state effectively defines the mood of much of Shepard's work, from *Curse of the Starving Class* and *Buried Child* through *Paris, Texas, A Lie of the Mind, States of Shock* and even *Simpatico*. Identity, meanwhile, fragments, metamorphoses. Of *Simpatico* Shepard has said: 'identity is a question for everybody in the play. Some of them are more firmly aligned with who they are or who they think they are. To me a strong sense of self isn't believing in a lot.'[78] That last remark is interesting, for Shepard's sense of character has very little to do with a resolute self defined through its encounter with the world. Despite his own nostalgia for a rural world (and the corruption of horse racing in *Simpatico* is equally a betrayal of nature and tradition), frontier existentialism in which a resolute and implacable identity emerges from an encounter with nature plays no role in his work.

In another letter to Chaikin he had spoken of a '*characterless* character . . . hunting through various attitudes and inner lives for a suitable "character" – one that not only functions in this world but one that is really "himself"'.[79] That self, however irreducible, the core of being, is, it seems, unsustainable, and increasingly Shepard was to concern himself with the multiple selves compacted within 'character'. Vinnie and Carter, in *Simpatico*, are actors, confidence tricksters, changing names and clothes. Their lack of substance is the key to their success, to their

power. But the price is a sense of crisis as the anonymity of their surroundings invades them, performance substituting for being.

As the 1990s came to an end Shepard, encouraged by a year-long
exploration of his work by New York's Signature Theatre Company,
revised an earlier play and premiered another. Having already rewritten
Buried Child for Chicago's Steppenwolf Theatre, demystifying it, he
rewrote and renamed *Tooth of Crime*, which became *Tooth of Crime (Second
Dance)*. The new play was *When the World was Green* (1996), in which an
old man on death row is interviewed by a young woman. The murder
for which he is to die, we learn, was a consequence of a two-hundred-
year-old insult, a vendetta which he has in all probability botched, possibly killing his young interviewer's lost father. Like *States of Shock* it
perhaps addresses a contemporary issue since precisely such vendettas
were at the time convulsing the Balkans. Beyond that, however, there are
echoes of earlier Shepard as the man and woman circle one another,
haunted by an ambiguous past, uncertain as to their true relationship in
a world in which identity remains deeply problematic.

There is something of Tennessee Williams in Sam Shepard. His characters, too, inhabit a broken world. They cling to one another with the
same desperation, damage one another with the same inevitability.
Moving on carries the same seductive consolation while simultaneously
offering the same threat of annihilation. Meanwhile in the background,
for both writers, is the flicker of violence as character threatens to disassemble and language degenerates from poetry into formless prose. Both
are romantics observing the collapse of form and beauty. They acknowledge the power of love, but, in a world so inhospitable to selflessness, see
it distorted in the direction of egotism and insanity – an insanity which
on occasion offers a coded glimpse into truth. Both have created plays
in which heroes inhabit a world drained of the mythic context which
gave such lives meaning and exemplary power. Both acknowledge the
force of sexuality but insist on the all-but-unbridgeable gulf between
men and women who perceive reality differently. Both have split their
characters in two, choosing to dramatise as external tension an internal
conflict; both have been drawn to the androgynous as an image of a
divided self. Both have found in performance a symbol of lives which are
the enactment of stories with their roots in the distant past of ritual and
myth as well as in a present in which role and being have become confused. Somewhere back in the past a unity was destroyed, language came
into being and a space opened up which has never been closed. It was
out of that experience that comedy and tragedy were born. It was out

of that experience that art assumed the responsibility for reinventing order and meaning while never escaping the ironic knowledge of their contingency. In the words of *The War in Heaven*, a radio play by Sam Shepard and Joseph Chaikin:

> There was a time
> when I felt I had a destination
>
> I was moving
> toward something
> I thought I understood
>
> There was an order
> that was clear to me
> a lawful order
>
> Then we were invaded
> all the domains were shattered
> connections
> were broken
> we were sent
> in a thousand directions.[80]

The Angel who narrates the story concedes that on occasion the connections are momentarily re-established – 'maybe sometimes / love . . . sometimes together / both / changing / moving / into each other . . . sometimes music / music / that will clear things / away . . .'[81] Both Tennessee Williams and Sam Shepard acknowledged the power and reality of such moments, but recognise, too, the truth of the words spoken by the Angel in *The War in Heaven*:

> Every minute I'm here
> something's changing in me
> something's diminishing . . .
> Every second I'm here
> I'm weakening . . .
>
> I have a partner
> the partner
> is me
> the partner
> has a partner
> in me
>
> Turn me loose . . .
>
> there are no days
> there is no time
> I am here by mistake.[82]

For Tennessee Williams, whose Kilroy, in *Camino Real*, clings to the love which mocks him on the very edge of a desert called Terra Incognita, a world once shaped by myth can now only be redeemed by love and the poet's eye. For Shepard, too, a certain grace may light up the darkness and redeem the past, no matter how flawed or mysterious it may be, no matter how attenuated. In the final words of *A Lie of the Mind*: 'Looks like a fire in the snow. How could that be?'[83]

CHAPTER EIGHT

David Mamet: all true stories

In an essay on 'Fiction and Reality' Mario Vargas Llosa spoke of the effect of abolishing the novel in Spanish America for three centuries as those in power set themselves to create 'a society exonerated from the disease of fiction'. Their failure he ascribed to the fact that the realm of fiction was larger and deeper than the novel. As he explained, they could not

imagine that the appetite for lies – that is, for escaping objective reality through illusions – was so powerful and rooted in the human spirit, that, once the vehicle of the novel was not available to satisfy it, the thirst for fiction would infect – like a plague – all the other disciplines and genres in which the written word could freely flow. Repressing and censoring the literary genre specifically invented to give 'the necessity of lying' a place in the city, the inquisitors achieved the exact opposite of their intentions: a world without novels, yes, but a world into which fiction had spread and contaminated practically everything.

It was an observation designed simultaneously as an assault on the corruption of the state and as an explanation of the nature of much South American fiction. Magical realism, he implied, was a natural product of societies which 'still have great difficulty . . . in differentiating between fiction and reality'.[1] But America, too, is a fiction. More than most societies it existed as idea before being realised as fact, and fact had then to be pulled into line with myth. As a character in David Mamet's *The Water Engine* asks: 'What happened to this nation? Or did it ever exist . . . did it exist with its freedoms and slogan . . . Where is America? I say it does not exist. And I say it never existed. It was all but a myth. A great dream of avarice.'[2] What Vargas Llosa says of South American countries – that they are 'in a deep sense more of a fiction than a reality' – is equally true of America. His description of his own country as an 'artificial gathering of men from different languages, customs and traditions whose only common denominator was having been condemned by history to live together without knowing or loving each other' is close enough to an

American anxiety to find an echo for Vargas Llosa's remark that 'Le Perou, ce n'est pas Perou.'[3] America, too, is not America. It is compounded of myths to do with freedom and equality, of yeoman farmers and sturdy individuals, of spirituality and material enterprise. It propounds a dream of increasing wealth and perfectibility; it propounds a singular identity forged out of difference. It talks to itself in the dark for reassurance about its special status. No State of the Union Address is complete without its celebration of a special grace which has made it the peacemaker, the international frontiersman, the one bright light in a dark world. No wonder American writers, from Cooper, Hawthorne and Melville to Fitzgerald, Faulkner and West have set themselves to explore its myths. No wonder playwrights, from O'Neill through Miller to Shepard and Mamet, have done likewise.

David Mamet explores the myths of capitalism, the loss of that spiritual confidence which was once presumed to underpin individual identity and national enterprise alike. The language of liberal concern and humane principle echoes through plays in which rhetoric seldom if ever matches the reality of character or action. Nor are rapacity and greed presented as the decadent products of history. In America, he implies, they were its motor force. Sam Shepard is more ambivalent. His characters are scarcely less the alienated products of their society than are Mamet's. The characters in *True West*, surrounded by the detritus of a technological society, planning petty thefts and engaging in spasmodic bouts of violence, seem close kin to the figures in Mamet's *American Buffalo*. The peepshow in Mamet's *Edmond*, in which characters are physically separated from one another and sexuality is alienated as product, has its echo in Shepard's film *Paris, Texas*. For both writers the urban world is bleak and denatured. But Shepard is drawn to the mythical world of heartland America as his characters act out mythic roles, the embodiment of a culture hooked on dreams. There is no reality outside the imagination of those who perform their dramas in a world which is an extension of their own psyches. Reality is never stable in Shepard's plays. The America his characters manufacture serves the purpose of their own needs, which are rooted less in history than in a private set of anxieties or images. Like Mamet's characters, however, Shepard's seek to close the spaces in their lives. They are obsessive. A single dominant idea determines their actions. The frontier they explore has less to do with the landscape they inhabit than with their own state of mind. The country of which they are alienated citizens is one contaminated with fiction.

The Brazilian writer João Ubaldo Ribeiro prefaces his novel *An Invincible Memory* with the observation that 'The secret of Truth is as follows: there are no facts, there are only stories.'[4] It is tempting to suggest that much the same could be said of David Mamet's work or of Sam Shepard's. The reflecting mirrors of their plays throw back images not so much of a substantial reality as of a world transformed by the presence of the mirrors. Their characters live mythically. They live by exclusion. In the case of Mamet's characters what is excluded is everything that does not sustain the myth; in the case of Shepard's, everything that cannot be pulled into the vortex of emotion. In both cases, though, story, myth, fantasy have a power which renders the banality of surfaces null.

In some ways Mamet's first film as director, *House of Games*, can stand as a paradigm of his plays. A group of confidence tricksters conspire to rob a woman, a psychiatrist, of her money. In an elaborate 'sting' they trick her into surrendering her money in the belief that they need her help and that she is in some ways guilty for their situation. When she sees through the operation she is told that there is 'nothing personal' since it is 'only business'. Offering to let her in on their methods so that she can study what she calls 'the *confidence* game' they then ensnare her once again, winning her trust by apparently offering her their own. Their game merely reflects hers as psychiatrist. As she confesses, 'It's a sham, it's a con game.' The implied motto of them all is that identified by one of the conmen: *semper fidelis*, a motto on which he adds his own gloss – 'Don't Trust Nobody.' But this warning is itself a ploy designed to win the confidence of its victim who ultimately reverses the sting by herself employing those methods of deceit which she has learned. We leave her, a murderess who has killed with impunity, a successful woman whose last act is to steal.

House of Games stands as a paradigm in that in play after play Mamet presents us with characters who turn moral virtues into vulnerabilities, justify criminality in terms of business, generate plots and perform roles with consummate skill, trade friendship into advantage and generate a language out of phase with experience. Like a blend of Eugene O'Neill, Arthur Miller and Tom Stoppard, he combines a concern with the underside of the American dream with a powerful social vision and a brilliant linguistic sensitivity to create plays of genuine originality.

Mamet's is a world in which people are not what they seem. The petty gangster in his film *Things Change* is not the Mafia leader he is taken to be; the card-players in *House of Games* not simply gamblers. They are all, like the figures in *A Life in the Theatre*, actors. It is not that they conceal substantial selves beneath their masks. They are their masks. They exist in and through their performances. Everyone, it seems, exploits everyone else and when it appears otherwise, as, briefly, in *Speed the Plow*, this proves illusory. Reality is deconstructed. It is not that human needs or fears are denied. Quite the contrary. Mamet's tricksters freely acknowledge them; they show a perception, a sympathy, an insight which is startling. It is simply that such an awareness is a tool of the trade. Just as advertising, pornography or Hollywood make fundamental human needs serve the purpose of commerce, so Mamet's confidence-men do the same. In doing so, of course, they thereby acknowledge the reality of those needs as they do the equally powerful impulse to exploit them. They also show the power of the imperial self, which wishes to subordinate other people, to colonise their imaginations as do Madison Avenue and Hollywood. It is, as the supposed psychic in *The Shawl* correctly identifies, the sense of 'loss', the need to 'believe', a feeling of 'fear', a desire for 'order,' which brings his victim to him and delivers her into his hands. It is, as he says, a question of trust, of confidence, but, and here is another twist to the tale, he, too, feels the same things, knows the same needs. As an actor is tied to his audience, and derives not only his living but his meaning from that relationship so, too, are Mamet's salesmen, confidence-men, tricksters. They are wordsmiths whose lies are transmuted into a kind of truth by those who need a story which will give meaning to their lives. As Ibsen's characters cling to their 'life lies', or Tennessee Williams's characters flare into life within the magical circle of their own inventions, so Mamet's embrace the fictions which are paraded before them by the new priests of a post-industrial society, selling reassurance, forgiveness and grace to those in terror of an empty universe or an empty life. The final irony is that those salesmen/priests are themselves in search of grace and have to discover it in the sheer professionalism of the performances which they deploy, in the insights which are the weaponry of their particular trade.

David Mamet's theatre essays are full of references to truth, authenticity and reality; he speaks of responsibilities, values, the community. Discipline, work, dedication are assumed to generate an experience that can engage human aspirations and acknowledge deep psychological needs. Words hold a magical power to command experience; they are the tacit meeting-point where desires and fears are embraced and controlled. His plays are something else. In them authenticity is more usually traded in for performance; reality is a construct devised by those afraid to believe themselves its product. The language of communality and mutual responsibility is deployed by those who have no faith in it other than as a tactic to ensnare the unwary. Words have no weight except as elaborate mechanisms of deceit. His is a world full of petty criminals, dubious salesmen, gangsters, actors, urban cowboys, speaking a language which shatters on its own uncertainties. In this world, indeed, language is intransitive, gestures are incomplete, relationships self-serving and temporary. The individual has no substance beyond the masks he wears. And yet somewhere in this inchoate swirl of inauthen-ticity there is a truth – about human need, about the human capacity to construct meaning out of chaos – and that truth is as much the essence of his drama as is the caustic analysis of the collapse of purpose and value.

Mamet began writing in the 1970s, a decade which had the air of the day after the party. Kennedy's commitment to defend any friend, fight any foe, his call to the service of one's country, had devolved into a squalid war which killed 50,000 Americans and spiritually maimed as many more. The political idealism which led a generation onto the streets to fight racism and into the Third World to fight poverty ended in the 'me' decade, in which self-interest and self-exploration were offered as values to those embarrassed by their time on the barricades. A Vice-President had been indicted for corruption, a President of the United States forced to resign for betraying his public trust. It was hard to relate the My Lai massacre (and the rush to absolve those responsible), or Watergate, to American values or to accommodate a murderous high-tech war waged against a low-tech enemy to American myths of the city on the hill, the beacon to the world, the land of the self-sufficient indi-vidual. Even the sexual freedoms of the sixties were reinterpreted in the light of a new conservatism and feminism. Every decade is liable to be a reaction to the one which precedes it (the political earnestness of the thirties to the supposed political frivolity of the twenties, the moralising consumer-oriented fifties to the wartime freedoms and relative austerity of the forties), but the sixties, which finally died around 1972, left a more ambiguous legacy than most.

Viewed in one way, Mamet's attempts to breathe life into American values, by exposing the extent to which they had been betrayed and sub-verted, might make him seem a product of his times. After all, the ren-ovation and reassertion of American principles was going to be high on the political agenda, at the level of rhetoric if not reality, for the next

decade and a half, and there is something of the civics teacher about
David Mamet, as there is a sentimentalist. The theatre essays often look
back to his own early years as, implicitly, he seems to identify a time when
corruption had not yet started. As he says in an essay ostensibly about
the theatre, but in fact an assertion of moral no less than theatrical 'First
Principles', in a

morally bankrupt time we can help to change the habit of coercive and frightened action and substitute for it the habit of trust, self-reliance and coopera-
tion. If we are true to our ideals we can help to form an ideal society – a society
based on and adhering to ethical first principles – not by *preaching* about it but
by creating it each night in front of the audience – by showing how it works. In
action.[5]

But though he talks about Americans as being 'recipients of the boon of
liberty' this is no sixth-grader or America firster for, he insists, Americans
'have always been ready, when faced with discomfort, to discard any and
all first principles of liberty, and further, to indict those who do not freely
join us in happily arrogating those principles'.[6]

David Mamet addresses a public world which carries the impress of
history and myth and a private world invaded by public values. For
Arthur Miller the past is holy. It has to be addressed and embraced. His
plays are full of revelations and confessions which redeem if not the
characters then the idea of the moral self. Mamet's characters have no
functional past. They are stranded in the present. The past is inert, dis-
functional, like the discarded objects in Don Dubrow's resale store in
American Buffalo. It does not inform the present except as the origin of a
now degraded language or as the source of a set of decayed and disregarded values. His characters look out over a polluted lake (*Duck
Variations*) or encounter one another in a junk store (*American Buffalo*), a
wrecked office (*Glengarry Glen Ross*), an alienating singles bar (*Sexual
Perversity in Chicago*) or the brothels and peepshows of a decadent city
(*Edmond*). The dominant image is one of decay. Like the celebrants of
some religion whose principles have long since been forgotten, they echo
phrases drained of meaning by time. The Constitution, vaguely
recalled, is seen as a justification of greed, the frontier as a cover for
rapacity. Individualism has collapsed into an alienated solitariness and
enterprise into crime. Revolutionary rhetoric has dwindled to aphasia,
love decayed to an aggressive sexuality and brotherhood to simple paranoia. His characters come together as conspirators in temporary alliances which form and dissolve and which are motivated by greed and
egotism. Men and women meet across an all-but-unbridgeable divide

and deploy a language as secondhand as anything in Don Dubrow's store. Yet there is redemption. It lies in the persistence of need, in the survival of the imagination, in the ability to shape experience into performance and in a humour born out of the space between the values of the characters and those of the audience.

His plays feature man as an endangered species. His characters have forgotten how to make contact and have ceased to ask themselves the reason for their existence. Theirs is a life without transcendence, spiritually arid, emotionally bankrupt. Yet the plays themselves expose the deformed logic of such characters as they do the desperation with which they struggle to conceal it with platitudes and self-revealing appeals. Mamet is every bit as much a moralist as Arthur Miller. It is just that he seldom if ever allows his characters to perceive their own failures or to identify the implications of their personal betrayals. In Mamet's case the membrane between the self and an alienated and alienating society has become permeable. That self has accordingly been invaded by the language and assumptions of an aggressive capitalism in which value is determined by price and relationships turn on commodity exchange. The fantasies of adspeak and the media world define the parameters of experience and provide the vocabulary of a need easily satisfied by consumption – the possession of an object (*American Buffalo*, *Glengarry Glen Ross*) or a person (*Sexual Perversity in Chicago*, *The Woods*). Yet there is, Mamet insists, an irreducible reality. There is 'a way things are irrespective of the way we *say* things are',[7] and we become aware of that in the moment when a residual human need makes its presence felt. In both *American Buffalo* and *Glengarry Glen Ross*, no matter how briefly, characters place a personal relationship ahead of personal advantage. Just as in Edward Bond's *Saved* or *Lear*, the smallest gesture assumes a disproportionate significance. His characters desperately wish to connect. They have simply forgotten how to do so. Their need has been alienated from them and offered back as sexual encounter or business relationship. But we are offered a glimpse of selflessness as, in *American Buffalo*, Don's concern for his young helper, Bobby, momentarily overcomes his self-interest and, in *Glengarry Glen Ross*, the victim of a confidence trick apologises to the trickster for reneging on the deal and a salesman refuses to buy himself goodwill through betrayal.

The central theme of Mamet's plays is loss. His characters look for some kind of meaning to random events and try to generate order out of a threatening chaos. Their paradox is that they fear those who might neutralise their solitariness: they deceive those from whom they demand trust. They are the victims of self-generated ironies. They know and deploy the language of a humane and moral world. They acknowledge the reality and persistence of fear and need. Yet that language is deployed with a cynical awareness, that knowledge exploited in the pursuit of advantage.

In *The Education of Henry Adams*, Adams conceded that 'The human mind has always struggled like a frightened bird to escape the chaos which caged it.'[8] History was evidence of that failed enterprise, science a gesture of faith. The myth of human progress was itself born out of denial. If progress, then direction, if direction, then purpose, if purpose, then meaning. Once that meaning lay in a relationship with the natural world and through that to some underlying and unifying principle. Then technology and tools seemed to promise mastery before, in a post-industrial world, the self becomes a primary value, hedonism a logical result, power and money, as Spengler predicted, a means and an end, and experience aestheticised. Mamet's characters inhabit this last world. Nature has failed man or man nature. Lakes, in his work, are polluted, woods associated with mildew and decay. The great technological achievements of the nineteenth century, celebrated in Chicago's World's Fair Century of Progress Exposition, a point of reference in two of his plays, have turned into junk. Money is, in many of these plays, a motivating force and a metaphor. What can be taken by force or by guile acquires a greater significance than that which is freely given. Daniel Bell, in his book *The Coming of Post-Industrial Society*, identified the loss of a sense of transcendence as a primary fact of such a period. Indeed he has summarised a process which in Mamet's work is collapsed into metaphor. For most of history, he insists '*reality was nature*, and in poetry and imagination men sought to relate the self to the natural world. Then *reality became technics*, tools and things made by men yet given an independent existence outside himself, the reified world. Now *reality is primarily the social world* . . . what does not vanish is the duplex nature of man himself – the murderous aggression, from primal impulse, to tear apart and destroy; and the search for order, in art and life.'[9] This is Mamet's world. These are the contradictions which he dramatises. He is the poet of post-industrial society.

In *The Shawl*, first presented in 1985, a woman in her late thirties visits a man who claims to be a mystic. In fact a confidence trickster, he understands what drives her to consult him: 'you want me to exhibit my *power*. Is this not the truth? . . . For the question is WHAT POWERS EXIST? . . .

This is a rational concern. *Is there an order in the world?*[10] This was equally the question debated by the two old men in *Duck Variations*. Even the petty criminals in *American Buffalo*, alarmed at the chaos of which they are the primary evidence, look for a rational principle behind seemingly arbitrary events and themselves generate a plot whose own structure hints at coherence, no matter how farcical or contingent. The final irony of Mamet's plays, however, is that the very faith which makes individuals vulnerable to exploitation and deceit is primary evidence of the survival of a sense of transcendent values for which otherwise he can find no social correlative. That might seem to suggest a sense of the absurd but Mamet will not permit that irony to become the only note sounded in his plays. Something in the relationship between Don and Bobby survives the reifications of *American Buffalo*; James Lingk is not simply ridiculous, in *Glengarry Glen Ross*, retaining his faith in the man who duped him. In *The Shawl* confidence trickster and victim share more than their roles in an elaborate fiction. They need one another for reasons which go beyond the drama of deceiver and deceived which they enact. Indeed there are hints that some non-rational connection between them may exist, that beyond language there may lie a surviving, instinctual mutuality.

For David Mamet, the closest analogy to the theatre and the cinema is the dream. As he has explained,

Even in the most rational plays, the element which has the power to move us is not the rational element or the polemic element but the mythic element. It is the unresolved, not the resolved conflicts which matter. We see this in our everyday society and in the decay of disparate mechanisms: Government, Religion, Theatre. We have seen them decay into rational organisations, each one of which thinks its purpose is the same: to determine by force of reason what is right and then do it.[11]

The logic of theatre, he suggests, should be that of the dream, addressing anxieties and needs which the rational mind sublimates. So, too, with the cinema which is, he insists,

the least literal medium. The great film makers are those who understand that it is the medium that most closely approximates to the nature of dream. Because anything can happen; because you can't perceive distance in a movie; because the light that falls on people is quite artificial . . . as film makers became more acquainted with the nature of the camera, they discovered cutting and juxtaposition of images the better to tell the story. They understand that in the juxtaposition of the temporal and the plastic, they could conjoin things in a way that could only happen in one other place: the Dream . . . The great movie makers evolved at the time of Freud's thinking: Eisenstein, for instance, the vast power of whose films comes from the ability to juxtapose simple and uninflected images.[12]

An ironic and entirely self-conscious homage to Eisenstein and his deformation of reality occurs in his script for *The Untouchables*, as a pram bumps down a flight of Potemkin-like steps in a sequence whose temporal logic is disturbed. But his plays are apt to play similar games, whether it be the carefully focused juxtapositions of *American Buffalo* and *The Water Engine*, the jump cuts of *Sexual Perversity in Chicago* and *Edmond* (the one exploring fantasy, the other nightmare), or the overlapping on and off stage performances of *A Life in the Theatre*. The tendency to 'read' his plays naturalistically, to praise or deplore them in terms of their literal accuracy, he sees as in part a result of ignorance – not knowing how petty gangsters, street corner voyeurs or salesmen speak, critics tend to see his poetic restatement of their language as the thing itself – and in part a resistance to metaphor. He is no detached naturalist, dissecting the body politic, but a writer offering images of alienation, moral dislocation and spiritual decay for which those characters offer a dramatic correlative. He resists equally realism, which he sees as mundane, and a self-conscious experimentalism, since a play 'concerned essentially with the *aesthetic* politics of its creators may divert or anger, but it cannot enlighten'.[13]

   In the concluding decades of the twentieth century a number of writers have begun to move, in their work, towards a concern for spiritualism. The failure of ideology to inform or shape the world satisfactorily, of psychology convincingly to offer a secular route to self-understanding, or self-interest, of materialism or the rituals of social form to offer a structure to experience or a destination worthy of the journey, left them standing at the doors of faith. It was a logic which unfolded in as heterogeneous a group of people as George Steiner, Doris Lessing, Iris Murdoch, Alice Walker and August Wilson. The rise, internationally, of religious fundamentalism, though plainly at odds with the non-doctrinaire, non-authoritarian politics of such writers, may have been responding to a similar process. David Mamet has, perhaps, been on a similar pilgrimage. Not for nothing does he quote from Ecclesiastes in his essay 'A National Dream Life' – 'For man also knoweth not his time: as the fishes that are taken in an evil net, and as the birds that are caught in a snare; so are the sons of man snared in an evil time when it falleth suddenly upon them.'

   What his plays all, in very different ways, explore is the damage that has been done to the spirit, the loss of meaning in the lives of those who have been taught that such meaning lies in the alienated products not of their labour but of their desires. The theatre, with its roots in the church (and he as a child performed exemplary religious dramas), offers another version of the community gathered around the domestic table. For the moment other roles are laid aside and the audience share an experience which, in the case of his own plays, takes us beyond a model of theatre as mirror to the times. In a sense you could say much the same of the work of Arthur Miller and Tennessee Williams, neither of whom, like Mamet, could identify a social mechanism to reshape the social world whose alienation had in part generated their drama. Like Eugene O'Neill before them they were liable to use the word 'soul' in explaining that human quality placed under most pressure by modern society: in that sense Mamet seems a natural inheritor of a basic theme of the American theatre. He is prone to refer to the human spirit: 'Every reit-eration of the idea that *nothing matters* debases the human spirit . . . Who is going to speak up for the human spirit?' His answer is 'The artist. The actor' who works on 'that stage which is the proponent of the life of the soul'.[14] The theatre, he insists, affords an opportunity uniquely suited for 'communicating and inspiring ethical behaviour'.

Mamet's plays, unlike his theatre essays, are neither polemical nor didactic. His spiritual concerns have not led him, as at times they have led Doris Lessing or Alice Walker, to generalise his characters to the point at which they dissolve individual identity in the generality. His concern with unity does not lead him to unhinge the door of time, as it does them, though the poet is invoked as ironic commentator. He is com-mitted to the moment, to characters who exist in time and who must find their redemption in the present, like the audience who confront them in the theatre: 'The magic moments, the beautiful moments in the theatre always come from a desire on the part of artist and audience to live in the moment, to *commit* themselves to time.'[15] He is interested in what binds people together. The fact that his characters use scatological lan-guage, inhabit a diminished world, are scarcely able or willing to decode or respond to one another's needs, has led some critics to see him as com-mitted simply to rubbing our collective noses in the squalor of contem-porary existence. In doing so, however, they miss a greater commitment. As he explained, Kafka once observed that 'one always has the alterna-tive of ignoring and choosing not to participate in the sufferings of others, but . . . in so doing one commits oneself to the only suffering that one could have avoided'.[16] Since the very condition of theatre is 'that which *unites* the actor and the house, a desire to share something',[17] the theatre stands as a paradigm and metaphor. This does not, of course, suggest that theatre is immune to egotism, ambition and falsity. *A Life in the Theatre* offers a comic demonstration of art decayed to artifice and harmony broken by rivalry. But the need for such unity sounds like a constant note beneath the dissonance. As he observed in an essay which he wrote about that play: 'We certainly all need love. We all need diversion, and we need friendship in a world whose limits of commitment . . . is most time the run of the play.'[18] Reminding us that, for Camus, the actor is the embodiment of the Sisyphean nature of life he also implies the extent to which the actor stands as an image of those temporary alliances and desperate performances which are the stuff of daily life.

Hemingway observed that all true stories, if continued long enough, end in death and yet the story, as Scheherazade knew, is itself a defence against death. Not only in childhood fairy-tales is there an ever after. So long as the story continues, so long as there is a teller and a listener, we are not alone and we have imaginative control over our experience. At the heart of all Mamet's plays are story-tellers whose stories shape their world into something more than random experience, decay and inconsequence. That is why even his most morally reprehensible characters command his respect. They are in the same business as he is. They create drama and by so doing give themselves a role.

Shaped into myths such stories become the structuring devices of a society, a way of encoding its values, of shaping its dreams which, Mamet insists, are the figures of our desire. The theatre is concerned with such stories. They are both its means and the focus of its analysis.

An early play, *Dark Pony*, has all the simplicity of a bed-time story. A tale told by a father to his daughter, it tells of a pony who can always be summoned to the rescue. The words 'Dark Pony' themselves have a magical effect, language being able to hold fear and anxiety at bay. Yet even here the story is stained with the need of the teller, a need more sharply defined in *Reunion*, its companion piece. This is a portrait of a man who holds his life together, rather as does the protagonist of Hemingway's 'Big Two-Hearted River', by an act of radical simplification. As a reformed alcoholic, a member of Alcoholics Anonymous, he will have learned to take one day at a time. His language is similarly foreshortened. Simple declarative sentence follows simple declarative sentence. He seems consciously to avoid the complex sentence as he does the complex thought. Indeed the speeches in the early part of the play seem to fall into a short-lined, non-rhyming verse form. There are few conjunctions, a fact which accurately reflects a life of many beginnings, of actions that have never generated continuous meaning. The reappearance in his life of his daughter, a daughter whose own life is unsatisfactory, is a threat because it reminds him of causality, of time that has passed without meaning emerging, because it hints at a story which ends badly. This may or may not be the relationship which was the focus of *Dark Pony* but either way it is a reminder of the incapacity of story to keep the real at bay, of the inchoate nature of experience which story is designed to deny.

Even here, in these early plays, then, the story carries a virus. Bernie's narratives in *Reunion* are of random violence, those in *Dark Pony* shaped by the unexpressed need of the teller. There is a vacancy to these lives, an emptiness circled around with words, and that void is reflected, too, in the space between speaker and listener. Private need is never quite enough to close the gap between those who feel alienated from themselves and from others. These first plays could apparently scarcely be simpler. A third, *Duck Variations*, consists of an inconsequential dialogue between two old men, an exchange whose unmentioned subject is death. They are conversation pieces. There is no movement, no plot except the unravelling of character. *Reunion*, *Dark Pony*, *Duck Variations* could be radio plays, except that the unbridgeable physical space between the characters is a clue to another gulf, psychological, spiritual.

Sexual Perversity in Chicago is also a conversation piece, except that this time there is a neurasthenic rhythm, an urban pace to a play in which random energy is substituted for a purposeful life. Owing something to Mamet's experience of Chicago's Second City revue group, it consists of a series of short, rapidly presented scenes in which two urban males, Bernie and Danny, discuss their sexual fantasies and attempt to act them out with two women equally bemused by sexuality in a world in which it has become fetishised, an alienated product of commodity exchange, a key component of a myth of consumption. Much of the play's humour derives from the characters' failure to understand themselves or other people, the ironic space between a confident language of sexual aggression and a fumbling incompetence when confronted with the reality of potential relationships. Bernie's view of women is pornographic, metonymic: 'Tits and ass.' He acts as mentor to the apparently more naive and sensitive Danny. It is an approach born less out of desire than fear. Safely mythicised as willing collaborators in their own seduction, women cease to threaten. Safely displaced into fiction they lose their power to engage his confused and vulnerable emotions. Accordingly, when

Danny finds himself involved with a real woman he is unable to function, incapable of adjusting to the complexity of relationship.

Sexual Perversity in Chicago explores a world in which language generates action and public myths invade private lives. Mamet dramatises a
world drained of beauty, purpose and meaning, a world in which aggression is a mode of communication and words have become denatured.
Its principal currency is sexuality but a sexuality devalued, counterfeited,
to the point at which it neither buys immunity from solitude nor offers
satisfaction for needs. The singles bar becomes an effective image of a
society in which alienated individuals market themselves, seeking the
very companionship they fear, as they substitute lifestyle for life. Lacking
real intimacy, they substitute only simple physicality.

Mamet has talked of his struggle to construct a play which consists of
something more than a series of short scenes, but in fact the style of
Sexual Perversity in Chicago could hardly be more apt. Its discontinuous
scenes accurately reflect the fragmented experiences of his characters
who have no plot to their lives and are terrified alike of causality and
commitment. Past and future are transformed into fantasy. Only the
present moment has any force and that is void of meaning. The broken
rhythm of their exchanges is itself an expression of the intransitive
nature of language and experience alike. The play won an award as best
new Chicago play and Chicago is plainly its setting as it is of his first two-
act play, *American Buffalo*, a work which ultimately established his national
and international reputation.

American Buffalo is set in a junk store in Chicago. The characters are surrounded by the detritus of the city's Century of Progress Exposition
which, in 1933, looked back over a century of development and forward
to the following hundred years of achievement. The characters inhabit
the ironies which stem from the juxtaposition of material progress (whose
products have turned into junk or simple curios) and moral regression.
The apparently naturalistic set is charged with significance, just as much
as that of a Tennessee Williams play. Indeed Mamet has rejected those
readings which would reduce the play to simple naturalism:

I don't think it's a naturalistic play at all. It's a fairly well stylised play. The language is very stylised. It's very strict rhythmically. Structurally, it's classical. It's
divided into two acts. It takes place in twenty-four hours and adheres to all the
unities. Certain things about the play are misleading. For example, the fact that
it has a lot of four-letter words might make it difficult to see that it's written in
free verse. The fact that it takes place in a junkshop might make it easier to

mistake it for a kitchen play. The fact that these three people happen to be thieves might make it easier to say that this is not a play about ourselves because the playwright isn't employing traditional theatrical devices of character.[19]

For him, though, character and setting offer a metaphor which the audience is invited to decode in terms of their own experience. It is a play 'set deeply in the milieu of capitalism', an idea which he suggests has exhausted itself. Speaking at the time of the London production of *Glengarry Glen Ross*, also its world premiere, he described capitalism as an enabling myth rooted in greed. Quoting W.C. Fields's observation that you can't cheat an honest man, he indirectly identified a central motif both in that play and in *American Buffalo*, a play in which petty criminals plan to rob a man who has purchased a buffalo-headed nickel for $90. Previously unaware of its rarity value, they now assume that even this purchase price must have understated its value. Greed breeds resentment and provokes criminality; but the point is that, morally speaking, the criminality is seen by Mamet as implicit in capitalism. When one of the three, an emotionally unbalanced and paranoid man called Teach, defines free enterprise as 'The freedom . . . of the individual . . . To Embark on any Fucking course that he thinks fit . . . In order to secure his honest chance to make a profit',[20] he is hardly wide of the point.

The planned crime, however, never occurs, as Godot never comes. It simply provides a future objective, a marker which, once passed, will be replaced by another. In effect the characters simply pass the time torn between a paranoid suspicion of one another and a desperate need for contact. Indeed, the characters form a kind of family group, with Don, the store-owner, as the father, and Teach as his son, a kind of half-brother to the mentally damaged Bobby. Somewhere in that relationship is real affection as well as need, but in the world of *American Buffalo* values are inverted. Criminality is described as business, theft as an extension of national principles. Only in the fantasy world of their planned crimes do they come together, gain significance and status. Rather like the figures in O'Neill's *The Iceman Cometh*, they project themselves into fictions which alone can grant them meaning.

We know little about the characters in *American Buffalo*, but that is the essence of Mamet's approach. For him 'leaving out . . . is the whole trick'.[21] In part that is a reflection of fundamentally simplified lives, a series of radical denials whereby normal human responses have been suppressed along with the language which describes those responses. In part it is an aspect of Mamet's attenuated realism:

We don't want to hear where he or she went to college unless that is essential to what they are trying to get . . . leave it out . . . no matter how revelatory of character it seems to be there isn't any character except action. Action and character are the same. The character in a play can't reveal anything more about his character by telling things gratuitously about himself than a character at a party can reveal anything gratuitously about himself.[22]

And if that sounds remarkably like Pinter then we have Mamet's assurance that 'he was the greatest influence on me, as a young actor and a young student and a young writer. Absolutely!'[23]

Ostensibly, the play concerns a developing criminal conspiracy rendered increasingly farcical by the thieves' incompetence and by their evident fear of the action which they propose with such apparent confidence. They have no idea how they will break into the apartment where the coin collector lives nor how they will locate and open the safe or even identify the coins which they assume, on the basis of little or no evidence, will be stored there. An accomplice fails to arrive, having been mugged on his way to the store. Don, otherwise so assured, assembles a team of misfits and incompetents. Teach insists on his commitment and courage and then arrives late, possibly in the hope that that courage will not be put to the test. In fact the crime is an irrelevance. What they are doing is passing the time, enacting their need for purpose to their lives, for companionship. They do so by creating a fantasy, a fiction, a story, elaborating the details of a man about whom they know nothing and of his apartment, of which they are wholly ignorant. Within the story they feel both secure and alive.

Beyond the parameters of the story, however, is a threatening world. Police cars circle the block while every gesture has to be inspected for its concealed menace. As played by Al Pacino in New York or Jack Shepherd in London, Teach is a highly neurotic individual, hypersensitive to slights, neurotically alert to condescension and threat. Every gesture is over-interpreted. His model of the world is one of naked competition in which advantage to one must spell disadvantage to another. He sees himself as a frontiersman for whom survival is a prime necessity and life a process of seeking supremacy over others. The motive for the crime is less financial reward than punishment for what is presumed to be the customer's momentary advantage. The play, in Mamet's words, is 'about the American ethic of business'. His point here and elsewhere is that the morality of institutions is not that of the individual, that corporate morality justifies unacceptable behaviour. Here, Teach sees the planned crime as 'business' and as such not subject to normal restraints.

Indeed, when he suspects that they may have been betrayed by the young man, Bobby, he beats him viciously and is himself beaten in turn by Don. It scarcely needs Teach's confused references to American principles to remind us that the slaughter of the buffalo – a central and ambiguous symbol in the play – was itself justified as a business activity, as, incidentally, was the harrying of the Indian who found himself inconveniently situated across the pathways of an American progress celebrated in the Chicago Exposition. Indeed the Chicago setting is a reminder that this city ('hog butcher to the world', as the pig-sticker among the assembled junk perhaps reminds us) was itself created out of business (trade with the Indians) and was home to Al Capone who turned crime into business as, Mamet suggests, others turned business into crime.

Teach, Don and Bobby, known to one another by their first names but denying the intimacy which that implies, are surrounded by the remnants of America's promise. They have inherited a language evacuated of meaning and principles distorted and deformed by greed and suspicion. They deploy the rhetoric of American revolutionary virtues but deny them in practice. Indeed Teach is barely in control of language as, like a Pinter character, his vocabulary outstrips his comprehension. He deplores the rising tide of violence, while arming himself and threatening to unleash a murderous assault himself, a paranoid response which is perhaps not without its political implication in a play in which he carries a weapon, 'Merely as a deterrent.'

But beyond a social critique of American business values, *American Buffalo* is a play about failed relationships, about the gap between people whose need for contact is as real as their evasion of it. There is a real affection between Don and Bobby, albeit one betrayed when it conflicts with business. Teach has as great a need to be 'well liked' as had Willy Loman, except that he can never permit anyone access to his inner life or acknowledge the genuine sense of vulnerability which he feels. Bobby, too, desperately craves affection. Not the least of the ironies of the play, however, is that need can never align itself with action. The characters never quite allow themselves the openness necessary for genuine contact. Something has destroyed their sense of being part of a community of selves. If this is in effect a kind of family then it is as broken as are the families in *Reunion*.

Mamet's dialogue is fragmented, its syntax broken. His characters often converse in incomplete sentences, substitute nonsense words, find language draining away in the face of experience. In part this is an accurate reflection of how conversation works, but it is something more than that. Despite his observation that American speech falls naturally into iambic pentameters, the shaping of his prose is quite conscious. As an actor at the Neighborhood Playhouse in New York he had learned the significance of rhythm. From Stanislavsky he had derived the conviction that 'rhythm and action are the same . . . words are reduced to the sound and the rhythm much more than the verbal content and that's how we communicate with each other'.[24] Praised for dramatic conversations which seem simple transcriptions of demotic prose, in fact he contrives that language with great care. The spaces which open up in the language of his characters open up equally in their lives. Their linguistic incompletions reflect psychological and social incompletions. This is an intransitive society in which thought and feeling fail to leap the gap between individuals who fear the very communication they seek. To communicate fully is to become vulnerable and the fear of vulnerability is finally greater than the fear of isolation.

Mamet's characters are liable to reverse themselves within a matter of seconds. Thus Don defines business as 'common sense, experience, talent', only to redefine it moments later as 'People taking care of themselves.'[25] Teach insists that he never complains about those who cross him, after an obscene tirade against someone who has. Such reversals are the sign of a self-cancelling language.

Teach's language turns round on itself with a comical bathos. When their co-conspirator fails to turn up he suggests that he 'should be horsewhipped with a horsewhip'.[26] Language here is a closed system, self-consuming. The disproportion between cause and effect (what Teach takes as a hostile inflection precipitates a cascade of violent but essentially meaningless obscenity), between rhetoric and fact (Teach describes his decision to carry a gun as 'A personal thing of mine. A silly personal thing',[27] inadvertently borrowing the trivialising vocabulary of manners), underlines the failure of language to give them any leverage on experience, while stressing the gap between word and meaning. The one character who appears genuinely selfless – Bobby – speaks the least and though he tells a critical lie (alleging that he had seen the target of the planned robbery leaving his apartment) he does so out of love for Don.

For the most part dialogue consists of brief, sporadic bursts, monosyllables, simple questions, abbreviated statements, as though no thought can be sustained. Even in the context of this aphasia, however, the last pages of the text are particularly spare. Only one or two speeches exceed a single sentence. For the only time in the play Teach is called by his first name, indeed a diminutive of his first name. After an orgasmic outburst of violence they are left, their plans in ruins, with nothing more than one another. Teach begins the process of blotting out memory, erasing action, thereby detaching himself from responsibility for that action. He places a paper bag on his head ('I look like a sissy'), behaving like an animal signalling his subservience to the pack leader, Don, who is left alone, as the play ends, with Bob. Some ritual has been completed. The tableau is of two men, like father and son, briefly together, no longer even separated by language, an echo of the opening scene but now uncorrupted by the greed and paranoia which had generated such disharmony.

Roland Barthes speaks of 'the shudder of meaning' which language generates sometimes completely independently of its formal coherence. Just so you might describe the sounds produced by Beckett's characters, whose words circle around a void which cannot be named. Just so you might describe Mamet's characters who deploy a language whose literal meanings are lost to them but who communicate with total clarity their sense of need, loss and fear, their defensive aggression.

American Buffalo opened at Chicago's Goodman Theatre in November 1975, reaching Broadway fifteen months later in a production featuring John Savage, Robert Duvall and Kenneth McMillan, where its reviews were, in Mamet's words, 'mixed to mixed'. Its language, its tenuous plot, its deracinated characters, its disturbing metaphor of social alienation left critics confused and uncertain. Seizing on what they took to be his naturalism, they responded to it as in part a message from the lower depths and praised or rejected it for its authenticity, or otherwise, of language. In fact, like a super-realist painting, the play presses language and character beyond a surface precision. Nor is this an account of a deterministic social environment. The failure of Mamet's characters to understand themselves or one another is scarcely a product of environment, fate or genetics. They have created their own context by conspiring in their own irrelevance and generated their own identities through taking as real and substantial what in fact is only myth degraded into fantasy.

Nearly a decade later, in 1983, Mamet wrote what is in some senses, intellectually, a companion piece to *American Buffalo*. *Glengarry Glen Ross* is set in and around a real estate office and was inspired by Mamet's own experiences in a Chicago real estate agency: 'I sold worthless land in Arizona to elderly people.'[28] The characters in this play are indeed confidence men, tricksters, and that very phrase is a key one for it under-lines a vital ambiguity in human experience which seems always to have fascinated Mamet, for the confidence trickster depends on a human need to believe which in turn creates a sense of vulnerability. It also implies a greed which invites exploitation. The epigraph to the play is the shop-keeper's slogan: 'Always be closing.' A closing-down sale implies that the buyer has an unfair advantage over the seller. The response is greed rather than pity. As indicated earlier, not for nothing has the salesman or confidence trickster emerged as a central figure in American writing, from Melville's *The Confidence Man* and Twain's 'The Man Who Corrupted Hadleyburg', *Huckleberry Finn* and *The Gilded Age* through Sinclair Lewis's *Babbitt*, O'Neill's *The Iceman Cometh*, Miller's *Death of a Salesman*, Inge's *The Dark at the Top of the Stairs*, O'Hara's *Appointment in Samarra* to Ellison's *Invisible Man* or Updike's Rabbit Angstrom books. He becomes the image of a society hawking dreams for hard cash, selling a model of the real, of the ideal, for a two-dollar bill. When they sell real estate it is not the real that they sell. In some ways, perhaps, it is a reflection of an ambivalence rooted deep in the culture, a reflection of the eighteenth-century consti-tutional debate as to whether America should commit itself to the pursuit of happiness or the possession of property. O'Neill saw it as an American desire to possess one's soul by possessing the world.

There is, however, a function which goes beyond this, for the salesman is a story-teller and no matter how corrupt the salesmen in *Glengarry Glen Ross* they are consummate story-tellers, actors of genuine skill who respond to a deep human need for reassurance, companionship, order and belief. And if we are left at the end of the play with a powerful sense of betrayal, of human need turned against itself, corrupted by a society which has made money a value and exploitation a virtue, we are also left with a sense that the victory of materialism is only provisional. There is a residual and surviving need not addressed or satisfied as there is a faith not wholly destroyed by betrayal. As Mamet has insisted of one of the victims of the real estate salesmen, he 'wants to believe in someone, that's all he wants. So, finally, at the end of the play, even though he's been robbed of his money, or almost robbed of his money, the impor-tant thing is that he won't even believe that because he wants to believe in someone, that he's found a friend.'[29] Likewise, when one of the sales-men is in a position to betray one of his friends he fails to do so 'because it's more important to him to keep a promise'.[30] These are fragile foun-dations on which to construct an alternative society, but in the context of the play such gestures have to be sufficient.

Glengarry Glen Ross concerns a group of real estate salesmen whose company has imposed a ruthless regimen. The most successful will receive a Cadillac, the runner-up a set of steak knives; the loser will be fired. It is a neat paradigm of a competitive capitalist society. The key to success lies in securing the addresses of likely buyers. Since priority is given to the successful, this is a world in which success breeds success. Such is the pressure that it encourages unscrupulous methods with respect to the clients and ultimately with respect to the company. Increasingly desperate, one of the salesmen, Shelley Levine, breaks into the office and steals the address list of potential clients. The crime is investigated by the police. The salesmen's own fraudulent activities, by contrast, in deceiving their customers, is regarded simply as good business, sanctioned by the ethics of a world in which success is a value and closing a deal an achievement.

The play is in two acts, the first being divided into three scenes, each of which takes place in a Chinese restaurant. The second is set in the real estate office, following the robbery. It is in part a play about power. Just as Pinter (to whom the play is dedicated) once observed that in all human relationships at any given moment one will be dominant, the other subservient so, here, the first act consists of three conversations whose sub-text is to do with power and its manipulation. In the first, Shelley Levine confronts David Williamson, whose job it is to assign the addresses, or 'leads'. They speak in a code impenetrable to the audience, deploying the jargon of the trade. As a result, other signals are foregrounded. As Mamet has said: 'if you see a couple in a restaurant talking at the next table and you can't quite hear what they are talking about but it's evident that what they are talking about is important, that fact, and the fact that you don't quite understand the vocabulary, makes you listen all the harder'.[31] It also means that the audience fall back on, and hence are sensitised to, tone, rhythm, volume.

Williamson says little: most of his speeches are restricted to a single word, an incomplete sentence. Levine's, by contrast, betray a growing hysteria. For the most part, Mamet restricts his stage directions to the word 'pause' or the simplest indication of movement, but Levine's speeches are sprinkled with italicised or capitalised words and with obscenities. He is the petitioner afraid to stop speaking in case the answer is the one he fears. It is Williamson who breaks off the conversation, leaving Levine alone. In the second scene, Dave Moss tries to ensnare his fellow salesman, George Aaronow, in a plot to steal the 'leads' from the company office. A conversation which begins with the camaraderie of prejudice ends with Moss threatening his colleague as an accomplice to a crime as yet uncommitted, on the grounds that 'you listened'. Language becomes a trap: simply to listen is to become guilty, as the skills honed on salesmanship are turned against one another. Having wrung a promise from Aaronow not to betray him in the event of his committing the crime, Moss himself is immediately guilty of such a betrayal.

Betrayal, indeed, is a central theme in a play in which human need is turned against itself, the third scene offering a particularly telling example of this process. Two men in a restaurant booth discuss morality, authenticity and need, or they appear to do so, since the conversation is in fact remarkably one-sided. Only in the final sentences does it become clear that one is a salesman and the other his mark. In a reversal of the first scene, power lies with the speaker. The potential client is permitted only an occasional word. The skill lies in the mixture of hokum and truth offered by the salesman, Richard Roma. He acknowledges the centrality of loss, deplores greed, identifies the reality of insecurity, as in a later scene another salesman closes a deal by urging the need to believe and insisting on his need to 'convert' his clients. Then, in a deliberately bathetic climax, he begins his sales pitch: 'Listen to what I'm going to tell you.' The story begins.

These are consummate story-tellers; actors of genuine accomplishment. When the need arises they can improvise a drama or create stories of total plausibility. It should not be assumed that their ethical failure loses them Mamet's sympathy nor yet that of the audience.

Not for nothing was Thorstein Veblen an early influence. It was the bohemian radical who, in *The Theory of the Leisure Class*, underlined the extent to which, for the businessman, 'Freedom from scruple, from sympathy, honesty and regard for life, may, within fairly wide limits, be said to further the success of the individual in the pecuniary culture.'[32] It was in Veblen that Mamet could have found the salesman apotheosised as the quintessence of dishonesty. There, too, he would have found a surviving religious commitment generalised in the direction of a concern for the human spirit. In Veblen's work, as in Tolstoy's, he could and did find an instinctive hostility to the institution which seemed to absolve the individual of his moral responsibility. Indeed, to list the writers most frequently quoted by Mamet – Veblen, Tolstoy, Freud, Kafka, Bettleheim – is to identify certain constants: a concern for the individual alienated from his own nature and from his fellow man, a fascination with the desire to find pattern in chaos, and a belief in the centrality of story, this last, in a sense, subsuming the others. For it is the stories his characters tell, the myths they elaborate, the performances they stage, which constitute their attempt to deny that alienation and discover form in mere contingency.

For Mamet the natural focus of drama seems to be the irreducible component of the speaker and the listener. This is true not only of such plays as *Reunion, Dark Pony, Duck Variations, The Woods* and *A Life in the Theatre*, but also of *Sexual Perversity in Chicago, American Buffalo, Glengarry Glen Ross* and *Speed the Plow* in which the characters group themselves into pairs. It is the relationship between two individuals which not only provides the skeletal sub-culture of his plays, the basis of a tension which generates its electrical charge, but also offers a mirror of the relationship between the writer and his audience.

For Mamet 'the artist is the advance explorer of the societal consciousness'.[33] But, more than that, in so far as the theatre offers a model of social action, of meaning generated through and by the interaction of individuals who serve a meaning beyond their own, the artist can become an agent of moral if not social change. What is celebrated is mutuality: 'We live in an unhappy nation . . . one way to alleviate the moral pall and the jejune super-sophistication of our lives is by theatrical celebration of those things which bind us together.'[34] Yet celebration is scarcely the keynote to his drama. Relationships are seen as attenuated, exploitative, competitive, destructive; society is dramatised as a series of temporary and self-serving alliances, a community held together only by the mutuality of need and ambition, and dissolved when it ceases to serve its purpose. Betrayal is a constant possibility. The fact of the dramatic portrayal of an alienated and alienating world is thus played against the assumption of alienation. There is a redemption in the form which seems beyond the imagination of the characters. The irony is very consciously deployed by Mamet, as his plays sustain that very sense of moral coherence denied by their action. The need is acknowledged by characters who reach out to one another, who conspire in sustaining a myth which will offer them meaning even if it closes down possibility, but they can find no way of turning need into satisfaction. They seem victims of their own capacity to refuse the consolation of relationship. The theatre itself, however, is an assertion of possibility. What cries out from these plays is need. The problem is that their characters have learned to distrust the very source of possible grace: 'The urge to support each other's social position has atrophied . . . we expunge direct reference to that which *we* desire most, which is love and a sense of belonging.'[35] This, rather than planning a robbery, devising a new machine, buying real estate property, is the real subject of *American Buffalo*, *The Water Engine* and *Glengarry Glen Ross*. The rituals which his characters enact, from *Sexual Perversity in Chicago* to *Speed the Plow*, are the remnants of a need for shared experience which had once been reflected in religion, ideology or myth.

If his characters pervert language, distort values and divert profound psychological needs into temporary social objectives, this is no more than do those who direct national policy or construct the fantasies of commercial and political life. But because we are permitted to see a space between the evident need of such characters for meaning and companionship, and their equally evident denial of both, we become aware of the inadequacy of their response. The English playwright David Hare has said that the theatre is ideally designed to expose the social lie, as word can be played against action. Mamet deploys it to suggest the disproportion between need and fulfilment for, as he has explained, 'My premise is that things do mean things; that there is a way things *are* irrespective of the way we *say* things are, and if there isn't, we might as well act as if there were.'[36]

Mamet has spoken of himself as an outsider. As a child of immigrant Jewish parents he feels that he has inherited the role of observer. Whether true or not it seems possible that it does have something to do with his almost irrepressible optimism. If that seems a strange way to describe the work of a man who has produced a series of plays which seem to add up to an excoriating assault on American values it is because too often the plays are only seen in terms of pathology. The fact is that, outside of a fellow Jewish playwright, Arthur Miller, it is hard to find anyone in the American theatre, or, indeed, American literature, who has quite as much faith in fundamental American principles, as well as quite such an acute awareness of the threat to individual identity implicit in the compromise of language and the denial of community. The comedy, which is a vital component of his work, depends for its effect precisely on the persistence of those very values in the audience which are being denied by the characters on the stage. It is a comedy generated by contradiction, a comedy at the expense of characters who have evacuated a saving irony from their lives. Laughter and judgement are related and the fact of judgement is an affirmation of values. Perhaps there is something Jewish, too, about an apprehension of such a rhythm of moral ebb and flow. What is true politically and morally is true, too, metaphysically. 'All plays', he has said, 'are about decay. They are about the ends of a situation which has achieved itself fully, and the inevitable disorder which ensues until equilibrium is again established.' This, he insists, 'is why the theatre has always been essential to human psychic equilibrium. The theatre exposes us to decay, to the necessity of change.'[37] Mamet does not write tragedies. Nobody has ever died in a Mamet play, except offstage and by report in *The Water Engine*. His concern does, indeed, lie with the tenuousness of our social state, but as much as any writer of tragedy he is committed to a belief in fundamental values which can only be betrayed at great social as well as psychic cost.

Mamet returned to the Century of Progress Exposition of the Chicago World's Fair with *The Water Engine*, a play written originally for radio but subsequently performed by the author's own St Nicholas Theatre Company in Chicago in 1977 and, in New York, at Joe Papp's New York Festival Public Theatre the following year. Subtitled 'A Fable', it is a comic-strip drama which tells the story of a man, Charles Lang, who invents an engine which is fuelled only by water. It is the perfect American invention: free energy to fuel the American machine; something for nothing. To Mamet it is a fable about the common person and the institution. Paraphrasing Tolstoy, he wrote that, 'We have it somehow in our nature . . . to perform horrendous acts which we would never dream of as individuals, and think if they are done in the name of some larger group, a *state*, a *company*, a *team*, that these vile acts are somehow magically transformed, and become praiseworthy.'[38] In that sense it is a variation on the theme of *American Buffalo* and the still-to-be-written *Glengarry Glen Ross*.

Once news of the invention leaks out, Charles Lang finds himself threatened by the criminal agents of the industry which that invention will displace. Eventually, indeed, he and his sister are killed by the agents of monopoly capitalism. However, this is less an anticapitalist tract (a form which, in keeping with its 1930s setting, it partly parodies) than an exploration of myth and, as he has said, 'The only profit in the sharing of a myth is to those who participate as storytellers or as listeners, and this profit is the shared experience itself, the *celebration* of the tale, and its truth.'[39]

The plot identifies divisions of class and money power. It dramatises the fate of the individual, isolated, threatened, excluded by those who have commandeered American enterprise. But the form – a radio play, a public fable – asserts the opposite. It joins together actors and listeners as collaborators in a common world. The human contract denied by

institutions which absolve themselves of human responsibility is reinvented by a theatre (in this case a radio drama) which relies on the survival both of communality and a shared sense of justice for its effect.
The particular drama, moreover, turns on what Mamet insists is an
instinctive distrust of the institution, a distrust which indicates a shared
apprehension of the world. As he explained in a note to the published
version, the result of a play which was presented partly realistically and
partly as a self-conscious radio production, is 'a third reality, scenic truth
which dealt with radio not as an electronic convenience, but as an
expression of our need to create and to communicate and to explain –
much like a chainletter'.

The stage version retains the radio station conventions of the time,
the drama being partly enacted in front of microphones. The action
intercuts between the studio, a lawyer's office and the World's Fair. The
voice of a chain-letter – mixing promises and threats – is intercut with
that of a soapbox speaker analysing national decline, an elevator oper-
ator whose staccato statements offer an ironic commentary on the
action, and a newspaperman – truth-teller and myth-maker combined.
In effect he stages a debate about an America which is scarcely less
fictional than the characters who implicitly define it. As the soapbox
speaker remarks, 'Where is America? I say it does not exist. And I say
that it never existed. It was all but a myth. A great dream of avarice . . .
The dream of a Gentleman Farmer.'[40] The Fair itself is a fiction, a myth
of American progress which, like the other competing myths in the play,
emphasises the evident need for story.

There is an irony, however, unstated but present. The company which
presents this radio drama is itself a part of the commercial world which
it indicts. Indeed a companion piece, *Mr Happiness*, added to the
Broadway production, features a radio agony aunt, close kin to
Nathanael West's Miss Lonelyhearts, who, following an apparently
sincere and humane programme of advice to the lovelorn and the
suffering, most of whom are trying to absolve themselves of responsibility for their lives, ends up with a sales pitch for his book.

Mamet wrote *Lakeboat* in 1970. It was a decade before it was staged. It
is a cross between an early O'Neill sea play and a series of sketches from
Chicago's Second City. A play in twenty-eight scenes, it offers an impressive account of shipboard life on a Great Lakes boat as seen through a
series of conversations. These slowly create a portrait of the private lives
of those for whom the society of the ship becomes an image of a wider
world. The language is frequently banal or self-cancelling. Thus one

sailor, whose job it is to make sandwiches, remarks that 'I don't want to make these sandwiches . . . Not that I mind it. I just fucking hate making sandwiches.'[41] When a crew member fails to turn up one of the characters insists that he knew him but 'Not overly well.' By the end he is asserting that he 'knew him *very* well . . . very well'. Another sailor denounces the missing man as a 'gambling degenerate' while celebrating the purity of the racetrack. A former cook is described as 'not married' by a man who thirty seconds later insists that he is or has been. Their language is by turns bathetic and obscene – the Mafia being a 'very property-oriented group' and women 'soft things with a hole in the middle'. But beneath the male camaraderie and pointless banter is another world. Slowly we learn that one sailor is divorced, while another, who has a blind mother and a father killed by drink, is himself suffering pains which lead him to consider suicide, admissions which ring no response from his colleagues. They are more interested in the fantasies they elaborate from the movies or the dramas which they invent for themselves. When not developing their sexual fantasies they construct a story to account for the missing member of their crew. In the course of the play he becomes in turn a derelict gambler robbed by a prostitute, a high-spending gambler attacked by the Mafia and a man who has to be silenced by the FBI. He is injured or, more likely, killed. There is no evidence for any of this. The reductive truth is that he had overslept and missed the sailing. The fictions which they elaborate, and which they subsequently abandon without regret, are their protection against boredom. Like Beckett's tramps they pass the time by talking.

Mamet's plays tend to be predominantly male. There are no women in *Lakeboat*, as there are none in *Duck Variations*, *American Buffalo*, *A Life in the Theatre* or *Glengarry Glen Ross*. They have, however, a parodic relationship to that equally male tradition of American writing which celebrated the independent, self-defining individual, creating an identity out of his encounter with the natural and social world. In Mamet's plays the men enact ironic versions of these encounters. Cooper's forests have become real estate developments, Melville's open sea a lakeboat sailing on an endlessly repeated voyage around domestic ports.

It is that absence of women and still more the differing needs and perceptions of men and women that he chose to address with *The Woods*. Another two-hander, it concerns the relationship between Nick and Ruth, a relationship which is slowly exposed not so much through action or plot as language. Ruth, sensitive, anxious to cloak sexual need with a sentimental vocabulary, speaks in a free-verse form. Her speeches are lyrical, over-extended as she tries to construct a world out of words, displacing Nick's blunt physicality into language. *The Woods*, Mamet insists, is a play about intimacy but it is, for the most part, about failed intimacy, a will for connection which is frustrated. Nick's response to Ruth's romanticism, her desire to reshape her world linguistically, is a series of blunt, prosaic interjections. The rhythm of the play is a mirror of its theme as Nick resists the sentimental, thrusting through Ruth's protective chatter and carefully elaborated fantasies with reiterative interjections, brief spasms of language. From time to time she succeeds in pulling him into her world and briefly his prose is reshaped as verse, but for the most part his speeches barely extend beyond a few sentences. Ruth has twice as many lines as Nick and many of his are little more than monosyllables, blunt and resistant. Something is plainly breaking up. Their relationship is collapsing and she tries to hold it together with a nervous flow of words, to hold truth at bay. Her comments range from the banal – 'our *appetites* are just the body's way to tell us things we may need'[42] – to the revelatory, as her fears about the relationship bubble to the surface in seemingly random remarks about male aggression. She is increasingly desperate to accommodate herself to a situation which she instinctively resists: 'It all is only things the way they are.'[43]

She looks for permanency, continuity. She deals in symbols – rings, bracelets – which bind people together, and a natural world which she sees as validating their relationship. She explores the past because 'This is the best / This is the best thing two people can do. / To live through things together. If they share what / they have done before.'[44] She asks him to tell her a story because, as she later promises, 'I will tell you a story . . . a bedtime story.'[45] She presents herself as lover, child, mother, offering reassurance, comfort and love. He counters with stories of violence and betrayal. On the rare occasion he does appear to share her vision, imagining himself living happily with someone, protected from the elements, she is absent.

Afraid to broach the question of their relationship, to acknowledge her fear that it has failed to engage him, she speaks elliptically: 'sometimes things are different than the way you thought they'd be when you set out on them. This doesn't mean that, *you* know, that they aren't . . . that they aren't . . . Wait. Do you know what I mean?'[46] Her repeated appeals – 'Do you understand me? . . . Do you know what I mean? . . . Do you know what I mean? . . . Do you know what I mean? . . . Do you know what I meant?' – simply break on his intransigence. Indeed, in a parody of her need for contact he launches on a crude sexual assault, forcing her to abandon the gentility of her protective language: 'You tore 'em, will you hold on, for chrissakes?'[47] In terms of the basic rhythm of the play this is a moment of defeat for Ruth. Increasingly desperate, she is reduced to bizarre legalism: 'If you come up here with me, that means you are . . . when you come up here that means you are committed . . . If you are a man. Because I am your guest.' Nick's response is to underline a central truth of the play: 'You talk too much.'[48]

Her next attempt to secure the commitment which she craves is to give him an inscribed bracelet which announces her love. He declines it. Desperate, she falls back on narrative: 'I'm telling you this story.'[49] The image she offers is of aliens who appear on earth simply because their absence has created a need which can only be satisfied by their appearance. Once again he refuses the metaphor. She now becomes the rationalist; he the one belatedly aware of emotional truth.

In this third and final scene the balance of power has shifted. Her decision to leave gives her momentary advantage. Frustrated, he strikes her. In a spasm of guilt and regret he reveals that his brutally simplistic approach to their relationship had been rooted in a fear of his own emotional vulnerability. He confesses to being confused by his own need for a companionship which goes beyond mere physicality. In moving his characters outside the cityscape, which is the context for many of his plays, he strips them of social role. What interests him here is the gulf which exists between male and female experience, language and needs. Set, very deliberately, against a background of the natural world ('Down in the City everything is vicious . . . I come up here, I see things'),[50] it strips them of their posturing. Nick, indeed, seems driven almost to the borders of breakdown. Slowly his language is infiltrated by metaphor, shaped into the verse which, until then, had characterised Ruth's speeches. For what is probably the first time he speaks of love rather than sex. The play ends as Ruth begins to tell a story, a story of two lost children who cling to one another for comfort, a story in which the two characters also come together. The evidence of their contact lies in his urging her to continue the story. The play ends with three words which project the story and their relationship forward: 'The next day . . .' His fear of death, repeatedly expressed in the play, is neutralised, Scheherazade-like, by story, and the relationship on which story depends.

Duck Variations is in fourteen scenes, as is *Reunion. Sexual Perversity in Chicago* is in thirty-four, *Lakeboat* twenty-eight, *A Life in the Theatre* twenty-six and *Edmond* twenty-three. Experiences are presented in a series of vignettes, revue-style acts ending in a blackout. In part this is a product of his Chicago experience of Second City ('My first plays were a bunch of dramatic blackouts. For a long time I wrote very episodic plays as if I'd been forever fixed by the six-minute blackout'),[51] but beyond that it says something about the structure of experience in these plays, an experience marked by discontinuities, radical incompletions and isolated moments. The plays discover patterns which are invisible to the characters themselves. If the scenes are short, so are the speeches. More often than not there is a staccato rhythm to his work, with dialogue consisting of abbreviated bursts of language. Character dominates plot, which is in turn compressed into dramatic images. As he said at the time of the first production of *Glengarry Glen Ross:*

There are two kinds of plays that I've been writing for the past fifteen years. One of them is an episodic play, one which is done in a lot of short takes, short scenes, where one sees various aspects of the lives of these people and where there is perhaps very little causal connection given the audience between one scene and the next. And it's true that in those plays there isn't a lot of plot. There's a spine to them; there's a certain progression but these are basically one-act plays. The difference between a one-act play and a two-act play deals with the development of character, the change of character. I think that those episodic one-act plays deal with the revelation of character and there is in most of them very little plot. On the other hand the plays that I've written that are traditionally structured, that have a two or three-act structure, have a lot of plot in them. It's just that the subject of the action is one that we're used to seeing as a traditional plot.[52]

Edmond, produced in 1982, managed to be both episodic and concerned with the development of character. Described by Mamet as a play he likes about a city – New York – which he does not, it is, as he has said, 'very, very spare, with words of one syllable, kind of harsh'. He was, he explained, 'rather surprised' that he had written it. It is a play, in his view, about a man who is looking for a place where he can be saved. Asked whether it might not be a play about death he replied, 'Maybe it is. It is about a man resigning. In every scene he casts off more and more of the veil of the world.'[53]

Overwhelmed by the pointlessness of his daily existence and of a marriage that has lost its meaning, he sets off on a personal odyssey, looking for experience which will cut through the banality of his life, stimulate a sensibility dulled to the point of torpor. Like Nathanael West's Lemuel Pitkin, in *A Cool Million*, he is systematically abused and deceived but, unlike Pitkin, he fights back, screaming invective at a woman on the subway, beating a pimp-turned-mugger and murdering a waitress after a brief sexual encounter. It is a journey stimulated, as elsewhere in Mamet's work, by a confidence trickster, one of many in the play. A fortune-teller, whose words have the same plausibility as those of the salesmen in *Glengarry Glen Ross*, the supposed clairvoyant of *The Shawl* or the accomplished tricksters of *House of Games*, assures him of the special status and significance in which he wishes to believe. Her analysis of Edmond's alienation is accurate enough: 'The world seems to be crumbling around us. You look and you wonder if what you perceive is accurate. And you are unsure what your place is. To what extent you are cause and to what an effect . . .'[54] Once again, though, the perception of need is merely a prelude to deceit. Edmond's experiences lead him not from naivety to knowledge but from ignorance to self-defeat as he himself becomes a false teacher, parading banalities as truth.

For Dennis Carroll, in his book on Mamet, the final scene indicates Edmond's new-found vulnerability and personal growth as he forges a new relationship with his black cell-mate, a relationship which he sees as 'clearly an authentic one marked by genuine rapport, a fact underlined by a dialogue which moves in consonant images'. The ending, in which the two men kiss and go to sleep in separate bunks, he sees as indicative of 'deep love and affection'.[55] It is hard to agree. The relationship is based on an act of homosexual rape, which is an inversion of his own earlier sexual aggression, while the space between the two men is emphasised not only by the separate bunks but by the rhetorical distance between them, with Edmond quoting Shakespeare and the black prisoner reduced to echoing his words ('There is a destiny that shapes our ends . . . PRISONER: Uh-huh . . . EDMOND: Rough-hew it how we may. PRISONER: How'er we motherfucking may')[56] or developing theories about spacemen or crazy gurus blessed with second sight. The play ends as they swap banalities: 'Do you think we go somewhere when we die? / I don't know, man. I like to think so. / I would, too. / I sure would like to think so. / Perhaps it's Heaven. / I don't know. / I don't know either but perhaps it is. / I would like to think so. / I would, too.'[57] It is a dialogue which resembles nothing in the play so much as its opening: ('The girl broke the lamp. / Which lamp? / The antique lamp. / In my room? / Yes. / Huh.').[58] The circle is closed

Edmond is Mamet's *Woyzeck*, with the city playing the same role as in Buchner's play and the central action once again the stabbing to death of a woman. The question which hangs over *Woyzeck*, moreover, is the one with which *Edmond* opens; is its protagonist a free agent or the victim of a logic that escapes him? The most bleak of Mamet's plays, it presents a world in which hell is not so much other people as the degradation of human relationships into soulless transactions. In a series of variations on a theme Edmond visits a clipjoint, a peepshow, a pimp and a brothel. The dominant realities are money and sex. We see him in the lobby of a hotel, in a subway station, a coffee house, the doorway of a mission, the interrogation room of a police station. He is always passing through, temporary, unrooted, in the anteroom of life. In a sense that is the condition of most of Mamet's characters as they ricochet off one another in a search for something that can seldom find its way into words. In fact the language of *Edmond* is not quite as spare as Mamet remembers it being, but when characters do elaborate beyond a simple question or statement it is to become articulate in the language of self-deceit as they offer hand-me-down advice as wisdom or elaborate theories born out of paranoia. The need for human contact, the desire to penetrate the mysteries of experience, is as apparent here as in any of his plays, but where elsewhere we are allowed to glimpse the survival, no matter how vestigial, of other values, here they are corrupted at source. Perhaps Mamet's surprise at having written the play comes from a recognition that *Edmond* is indeed harsher than anything else he has created.

For those in the American theatre Hollywood has always stood as an image of success and corruption. Mamet feels much the same ambivalence, speaking of it, as does one of his characters in *Speed the Plow*, as a sink of iniquity, while rejoicing in its possibilities.

The dialogue in *Speed the Plow* is a blend of cant and hypocrisy; the characters are self-serving and cynical. They look for material reward but flavour private ambition with the language of public responsibility. They want credit for sustaining the very values which they betray. Bobby Gould is a Hollywood executive charged with approving scripts for production. Faced with a pretentious script by a well-known author, on the one hand, or a 'buddy movie' featuring a star lured from another studio on the other, he has no difficulty in deciding on his priorities. The deal is brought to him by a long-time associate, Charley Fox, who holds a 24-hour option. It nearly comes unstuck, however, when a temporary secretary trades her sexual favours in a bid to support the 'art movie'. Fox rescues his deal by forcing her to confess her strategy to Gould, who had convinced himself that she acted out of love or at least respect.

It is patent that both films are devoid of redeeming features. The one, written in a witheringly mannered prose, is a post-nuclear fantasy about the regeneration of mankind by radiation; the other is a formula movie whose details interest no one precisely because its success is guaranteed by its adherence to formula. This is not, in other words, a question of art versus the market, integrity betrayed by venality. *Speed the Plow* is a comic play whose humour is generated by characters who switch from self-serving cant to arrogant honesty with breathless speed. Thus, Gould sentimentalises over the fact that theirs is a 'People Business', that 'people . . . Are what it's All About', only to add, 'It's *full* of fuckin' people.'[59] It is, indeed, the very speed of these changes of direction in the levels of discourse which is the basis of Mamet's comic method: 'If you don't have principles', explains Gould, 'then each day is hell, you haven't got a compass. All you got is "good taste"; and you can shove good taste up your ass and fart "The Carnival of Venice".'[60] That disjunction functions, too, at the level of character. Karen, his secretary, appeals to '*principles*', wishes to 'Talk about purity' while planning to screw her way to influence. Gould, meanwhile, plans to screw her to win a $500 bet. The fun is to watch three confidence tricksters each determined to trick each other. Bobby Gould, arch manipulator, is himself manipulated in every sense by his secretary. His evident need to be loved for himself rather than for his influence makes him vulnerable to those who realise how to exploit that need, in just the same way as does Hollywood itself, whose buddy movies are a celebration of that very need to believe in the significance and value of friendship and love which make the exploitation of that need possible.

In *The Day of the Locust* Nathanael West used Hollywood for his satire on an America in the process of moral implosion, as did F. Scott Fitzgerald in *The Last Tycoon*. In both books character has collapsed into role, art been debased into commerce, principles traded on the open market. In both books, Hollywood, in pandering to grosser appetites, had become an image of a debased American dream. *Speed the Plow* lacks West's paranoia and anger, his apocalypticism, as it does Fitzgerald's sense of tragedy, of the final curtain being rung down on the liberal dream and on an art which could no longer sustain itself in the face of corruption. Aside from a brief assault by Fox on Gould, it lacks the violence of West's and Fitzgerald's novels. But there is a sense here, as in those works, of real need met by artificial satisfactions, of dreams colonised by commerce, of sexuality become simple currency, of language drained of its function. Life, in *Speed the Plow*, is aestheticised; it becomes a badly plotted script. But as ever in Mamet's plays there is a counter-current: an irrepressible energy to the characters, a wild inventiveness to their dialogue and a persistent confidence that drives them. And though that energy is neurotic, that inventiveness paranoid and that confidence shot through with irony, we are never quite left, as we are in West's book, with apocalypse or, as we are in Fitzgerald's, with a planned entropy. For West, life as pure performance was life denying itself. For Mamet, performance retains a more positive quality which if it cannot quite redeem can at least fascinate.

'I hope that what I am arguing for, if I'm arguing for anything', Mamet has said,

finally and lately has been an *a priori* spirituality, saying 'let's look at the things that finally matter: we need to be loved, we need to be secure, we need to help each other, we need to work.' What we're left with at the end of the play or the end of the day is, I hope, courage to look at the world around you and say, I don't know what the answer is but I'm going to try to reduce all of my perceptions of the terror around me to the proper place. After all is said and done we're human beings and if we really want to we can find a way to get on with each other, if we have the great, almost immeasurable courage to be honest about our desires and to not institutionalise and abstract our relationships to each other.[61]

Challenged to confess to a certain sentimentality in such a view he pleaded guilty but insisted, with equal conviction, that there is no alternative.

There is little sign of sentimentality, however, in *Oleanna* (1993) which is, first and foremost, a study of power. The particular circumstances of the battle between the characters, John and Carol, is provided by a university in which he is a professor and she a student. Institutional authority comes up against gender politics: the language of political correctness impacts on that of a presumed liberal humanism. Such was the sensitivity of the issues, indeed, that the play was frequently received by partisan audiences dividing along gender lines.

Carol, apparently bemused by her studies, comes to see her professor. Her language is confused and confusing. She seems to have only the most tenuous grasp not only of the course but of human relationships. The professor, meanwhile, is preoccupied with his own affairs. His marriage seems under pressure. He is buying a new house and awaiting confirmation of his tenure. The conversation between the two is interrupted by the telephone. For his part he does little more than offer a few mildly patronising remarks, placing an apparently consoling and, it seems, avuncular hand on her shoulder, a gesture whose ambiguities fuel the dramatic confrontation of the second act. She seems to fail to understand what he is telling her, or respond to his attempts to put her at her ease.

In the second act she returns, her language and attitude transformed. She is now aggressively confrontational, retrospectively interpreting his earlier gesture as an assault and deploying the jargonised language of militant feminism. The play ends with his marriage and career in ruins as, in a spasm of violence, he strikes out at the woman who has destroyed him, thereby apparently validating her accusations.

The playwright Paula Vogel regarded this as such a partisan piece that she set herself to create a work in which audiences' sympathies would be genuinely equally divided: *How I Learned to Drive*. It is certainly true that the faults are not evenly divided. Carol plainly speaks a language which is not her own. She over-interprets words and actions and pursues her quarry with what she sees as detachment but what, in truth, seems closer to vindictiveness. For his part, John is unprofessional, patronising, remiss in his duties, but scarcely worthy of an attack which is plainly disproportionate. This, however, is not the point. The play is not designed as a delicate balancing act but an exploration of the mechanisms of control.

Both characters possess power. John's derives from his role as a teacher and from the knowledge he possesses. Carol's is based on an authority derived from her gender at a moment when that is invested with social and political force. The battleground on which they meet, however, is largely linguistic. Each deploys his or her own jargon to which they seek to make the other subject. With the exception of the ambiguous physical gesture of the first act and the physical assault that concludes the second, the battle is waged entirely at the level of language. It is that which shapes them as it defines the nature of their relationship. They are both the victims of language and its arch-manipulators.

The vulnerabilities of each are exposed obliquely, as much through John's one-sided conversations on the telephone and Carol's baffled circularities as through directly confrontational linguistic encounters. *Oleanna* is a deeply disturbing play not simply because it touched on an issue that was genuinely dividing society at the time or even because, like Miller's *The Crucible*, it inverts the power relationship between youth and age, thereby destabilising normative values, but because it is a reminder of the power of interpretation, of the fact that language defines the nature of the real and hence human relationships. It was a point that Mamet had made in another context in *Sexual Perversity in Chicago* and *The*

Woods. In the latter, a man and a woman see the world differently, deploy different images, encode language differently, using that language to ensnare or distance one another, to close off the avenue to true intimacy, an intimacy which both, in different ways, fear. They inhabit different experiences. Language may appear to be shared but is, finally, not wholly transitive. There are no true dialogues but simply overlapping privacies. In a world in which reciprocity carries implications of a feared mutuality, words are weapons or shields in an undeclared war. Beyond the immediate politics of the play, then, is a more profound irony, a deeper sense of dismay. As in *Sexual Perversity in Chicago*, men and women meet across an apparently unbridgeable divide, a gulf reflected at the level of language and, in part, created by language.

In one of his essays, Mamet asks whether all communications between men and women are negotiations. The answer is 'yes'. *Oleanna* is a flawed negotiation not least because, as he has also remarked, society has fallen apart and nobody knows what they should be doing. That anxiety is clear in *Oleanna*. Carol and John step out of their roles but fail to discover others that satisfy.

In the London production, Harold Pinter chose to begin the play with the song from which the title is derived: 'Oh, to be in Oleanna – that's where I would rather be. Than be bound in Norway and drag the chains of slavery.' It is a song whose vision of utopia is plainly at odds with the reality of a republic whose own vision of perfection has foundered. Mamet's fragmented speeches provide a correlative for a society whose dialogue with itself is flawed. It is not just that below the surface the old Adam survives, that American images of a new Eden sit uneasily alongside a manifestly fallen mankind, but that something has disappeared from American life. These characters are now rootless people for whom the old maps no longer apply. They are adrift. John is not destroyed by Carol. He is already insecure in his relationship to the world. Carol is neither a victim nor an avenging harpie. She genuinely does not understand the world in which she moves and eagerly grasps at anything that seems likely to render it into her hands. The power that both seek and deploy is no more than a sublimated desire to feel that they command their lives. The irony is that to exert that power is to lose what they most seek, some sense of consolation, harmony and peace.

There is a kind of power working, too, in Mamet's next play, *The Cryptogram*, which opened in London in 1994. This power derives from suppressed knowledge, from truths withheld, from betrayals. Things are coming to an end – a friendship, a marriage, a young boy's innocence.

The ground is moving beneath the feet of those whose assurances are now slowly destroyed. A three-way conversation between a boy, his mother and a family friend, circles around a vacant centre. The boy's father is absent. Father and son are due to go on a trip to the woods. The clothes are packed. Everything is ready, except that there is a tension in the room that seems to have no point of reference. The boy cannot sleep, indeed hears voices. His mother is tense. Everyday objects seem to acquire disproportionate and obscure significance. A teapot is dropped, a blanket is torn, either now or in the past. A knife is flourished. Every effort at normalising the situation fails. The conversations are fragmented, the characters never quite engaging with one another, each with his or her own unexpressed fears. The words 'spilt', 'broken', 'torn', punctuate the action as though there were, indeed, a code to be read. In the distance is the Second World War (the events occur in 1959), a correlative for present anxieties.

There is a sense that they are all in thrall to something over which they like to believe they have no control. Thus the male friend insists that 'things unfold . . . independent of our fears of them'.[62] But he, it turns out, has a vested interest in promulgating such an idea, as if his own treachery were in some way unwilled or inevitable.

In fact, we slowly learn, he has lent his hotel room to the woman's husband, thus facilitating the adulterous affair that has led to his decision to abandon the family. Her response – 'Things occur. In our lives. And the meaning of them . . . is not clear'[63] – is in part a genuine expression of the gnomic nature of experience and in part a defensive response, a distancing of herself from an all too clear betrayal.

The play ends with each wrapped in his or her own privacies, unable to reach out. The male friend, an ageing gay, is sent spinning back to the isolation of his hotel room home. The boy's mother prepares to move on, still unable to make sense of what has happened. The boy himself, in some ways the true centre of the play, edges closer to psychosis. He has witnessed without seeing, heard without understanding. Aware that the fixed points of his existence have been removed, alert, indeed, from the very beginning, to a feeling of insecurity he nonetheless could not earth in true meaning, he looks for a consolation he is plainly not going to be afforded.

The Cryptogram, which would seem to have a clearly autobiographical dimension, Mamet himself being the product of a broken home, is a spare, elliptical, disturbing work. Its indirections indicate the existence of a black hole to be detected only by the effect it has on those drawn to the very edge of self-extinction. That corrosion of communality which has characterised all his work here moves beyond the proto-families of *American Buffalo* and *Glengarry Glen Ross* into the very family itself, the family about which he had, perhaps, been speaking all along.

The Old Neighborhood (1997), which followed – three linked plays, two of which had been written and, indeed, published some time before – served to underline his sense of a community long since decayed, of relationships which have thinned to transparency.

Apart from anything else, *The Old Neighborhood* is evidence of Mamet's increasing fascination with the nature of Jewish identity, and though the decade and century ended with his Wildean comedy *Boston Marriage* (1999), it is that aspect of his career that was becoming most evident, as he broadened his work to include novels and poetry. A novel, *The Old Religion* (1997), centred on a Jew framed for a murder in 1913 in Georgia. In the course of the book he slowly finds his way back to his faith, losing his life but discovering the meaning of that life. Mamet's work now included not only a movie, *Homicide* (1991), in which a policeman finds his way back to his Jewish identity, a television film, *Lansky*, which explored the Jewish roots of a Mafia figure and a volume of poetry, *The Chinaman* (1999), which includes a poem called 'Song of the Jew', but also coffee-table, richly illustrated books called *Passover* (1996) and *Bar Mitzvah* (1999). The writer who had first appeared a quarter of a century earlier as the author of plays exploring the collapse of language, community, the moral self, now stood as an essayist, theatre and film director, screenwriter, poet and novelist increasingly concerned, as individual and artist, with the nature of faith and the Jewish self.

There is in David Mamet's work a yearning for that very sense of trust denied by every betrayal he documents. His characters are the victims of the language they speak, evidence of the paranoia they express. But somewhere, at the very heart of their being, is a sense of need which is the beginning of redemption. Their words may snap, like so many brittle shards, under the pressure of fear or greed; they may anxiously try to adjust themselves to the shape of myths and fantasies, deny or exploit the desire for companionship. Deep down, however, below the broken rhythms of speech, beyond the failed gestures at contact, is a surviving need for connection. The plays enact the failure of that urge but are, in their very being, an announcement of its possibility. Their energy is generated by that ambiguity.

CHAPTER NINE

The performing self

At a time when we live fragmented lives, have accustomed ourselves to anomie, are increasingly alienated from one another in an urban environment in which we teach our children to distrust the friendly stranger and suspect the request for help, when we bar our door against the unexpected visitor and fear the dark, the theatre represents a world in which a lost sense of community is momentarily restored. Here, the dark contains no terrors that are not controlled. The community of actors – interdependent, occupying the same moment and sharing the same linguistic world – offers a paradigm of communality echoed by the audience similarly conjoined to share if not a single experience then at least a field of meaning.

How much more true is this of the avant-garde theatre whose performing spaces – from the Provincetown Players to the Performance Group – have been intimate areas into which the individual is welcomed as an acknowledged member of a select community. Certainly that was how the playwright Paul Goodman, later produced by the Living Theatre, saw things in 1949: 'the essential present-day advance garde is the physical re-establishment of community'.[1] In the 1960s, that community was increasingly to be enacted through a physical contact between audience and performer, a feature of the Living Theatre's *Paradise Now*, the Open Theatre's *Viet Rock*, and the Performance Group's *Dionysus in 69*.

The Living Theatre began by self-consciously celebrating modernism which Julian Beck, one of its co-founders, admired for putting language under strain and thus provoking a new perception of the real. Its first plays were by Gertrude Stein and T.S. Eliot, by Alfred Jarry and Pablo Picasso, by Kenneth Rexroth and William Carlos Williams, a blurring of genres which was itself a modernist gesture. In a way that modernist logic was continued, in that there is a clear line connecting Pirandello's *Tonight We Improvise* with William Carlos Williams's *Many Loves* and then, crucially, *The Connection* (1959) by Jack Gelber, which drew attention to its own theatricality much as the postmodern fiction writer (Coover, Barth, Federman) drew attention to his own fiction-making. Heavily influenced by Beckett's *Waiting for Godot*, *The Connection* presented a group of addicts waiting for their connection – the man who will give their lives momentary meaning, who will fix them, not only in the sense of bringing them drugs but by giving them location, identity, definition. Though this Godot does arrive it is only to set his Sisyphean crew climbing back up the hill of their own authenticity in a parody of the routines of daily life. The play is presented as being improvised by 'real' addicts who resist the text offered to them by the supposed author. In fact only the jazz, which punctuates the action, is actually improvised, a jazz which, interestingly, Julian Beck related to the automatic writings of surrealism: otherwise the text remains implacable, the freedom illusory. Only art, it seems, offers the possibility of transcendence, itself a modernist stance.

The avant-garde of the sixties, seventies and eighties turned, very self-consciously, to the achievements of modernism. The creators of happenings – which occupied a kind of no man's land between theatre, ballet, art and music – related themselves to the dadaists and surrealists. The Living Theatre and others turned back to Antonin Artaud, a French theatre theoretician and practitioner who himself had links with surrealism, while Richard Foreman derived a number of his techniques and concerns from Gertrude Stein. What they had in common was a problematic attitude to language, to the simple causalities of plot, to the notion of theatre as an arena for the exploration of character. Theatre was deconstructed, disassembled and recuperated in an attempt to redefine the real. The past was to be denied, ignored or remade in a present moment, which became not merely the occasion but the focus of and justification for theatre.

There were those in the sixties who believed that the same objective could be achieved chemically. For Ken Kesey the virtue of LSD lay in the fact that it enabled people to live permanently in 'the here and now', while Timothy Leary's Psilocybin Project offered the opportunity to pass 'beyond the Door' into another realm of being, to be reborn, to go beyond the self, an experience re-enacted by the Living Theatre, whose performers celebrated drugs and sought self-transcendence through encounter rituals. But drug-taking, too, has its history, the fifties Beats celebrating ego while purporting to annihilate it as they pursued the mystical on a literal trip across America. Beyond Aldous Huxley, whose *Island* became a crucial text, lay the romantics, Whitman and Blake, whose own blend of the physical and the mystical appealed. And romanticism, of which surrealism had in some ways been a child, was very much alive in a period in which the physical could dissolve into the spiritual and the spiritual rematerialise as the physical under the pressure of a heightened sensibility.

It was a time of visions. If Artaud seemed to validate their experiments so, too, did the Polish director Jerzy Grotowski whose book, *Towards a Poor Theatre*, was published in the magical year of 1968 and whose desire for a 'theatrical reality' which would challenge normative values was conveniently dislodged from its political context. Once again here was a theatre practitioner who insisted that the function of the actor is not to tell a story or create an illusion but to be there in the present, denying the fact of alienation and incompleteness and negotiating a unity between the individual and the collective. The objective, he explained, was to experience and discover the real. Art and life were to become one. The theatrical act and the social act were likewise to become one.

Because the moment was to be holy we are not left with texts, or such texts as we are left with are little more than the discarded skins of some exotic animal. Just as the political dramas of the time were to expend their energy in the process of transforming the self and then society, their residue, the evidence of their effectiveness, being a radically reconstructed reality, so, too, with these groups which hoped to make a gift of a world remade, a familiar enough American objective. It was an illusion cruelly exposed in the two decades which followed and which led Richard Schechner in particular to denounce himself and his fellow practitioners for failing to sustain the momentum of their revolt. In seizing the day they forgot not only yesterday but also tomorrow and where once private epiphanies were to be the beginnings of public transformations, in fact, politically, they ushered in a period of intense self-concern. Theatrically there followed an era in which the avant-garde concerned itself with the processes of consciousness, turned to the monologue, disavowed the physicality and exuberance of public spectacle and closed down the multi-channelled experience of total theatre. Beyond the avant-garde, the dramatist, with the marked exception of David Mamet, increasingly concerned him- or herself with the family, the private, the domestic, the psychological. Politically, revolt and social reform were followed by a conservatism which reinstated materialism as a value and invoked self-sufficiency and self-improvement as primary virtues.

For Artaud it was necessary to break through language in order to touch life. His was to be a theatre of symbol and archetype which would restore the gesture, movement, spectacle and resist the merely social or psychological. He wanted to reinstate the mystical and the religious. He was suspicious of the authority of the text, being distrustful of the functionalism of language in a western theatre which 'employs speech not as an active force springing out of the destruction of appearances in order to reach the mind itself, but on the contrary as a completed stage of thought which is lost at the moment of its exteriorization'.[2] It was an interesting point, for his argument was that the theatre had dealt in conflicts which were clearly accessible to spoken language. As a result it had focused on questions of morality while denying itself access to experiences which evade language. He wanted what Mary Caroline Richards in her translation called a 'plastic' theatre, precisely the word used by Tennessee Williams.

It is not hard to see why Artaud appealed. His sense of social, psychological and moral dislocation, his belief that 'there are too many signs, that everything that used to sustain our lives, no longer does so',[3] chimed with the image of a decade of youth that proclaimed the bankruptcy of old ideas and forms. His desire to engulf the spectator in the action, to refuse to acknowledge a distinction between audience and performers, was likely to appeal at a time when barriers of all kinds were under attack. He denied dualism, sought to reinstate belief, saw theatre as a process of discovery rather than the revelation of predetermined insights. He believed theatre could be a mechanism of release that would flood the sensibility with experience. Just as Marcuse was advocating regression to simpler modes as a progressive move, so Artaud had called for things to be broken apart in order to begin anew – a new theatre, a new society. In the 1930s such hubris led straight to the mental hospital. In the 1960s, with R.D. Laing declaring psychosis a social construct, Artaud was celebrated as a high priest of the new theatre. His resistance to the achievements of the past was one shared by those in the 1960s who wished to reconstruct theatre for the new age. It was a denial of the past that repelled Arthur Miller, who saw it as a refusal of moral responsibility. The anarchy of the senses for which the Living Theatre called was precisely the root of a modern evil for Miller, who heard echoes of Nuremberg. Indeed, when the Living Theatre visited Berlin their performance was accused of being fascist. Had not Camus's *Caligula* dramatised a world in which experience substituted for morality? But if there was a threat in this theatre, as formulated by Artaud, there was also a generosity.

It was to team with an unexpected energy released through the body made suddenly articulate. The conscious and subconscious, body and soul, were to join in a celebration of possibility. If Artaud turned his back on humanism, for its moralistic drive, he was nonetheless committed to the realisation of human potential, simply seeing that potential as lying in other directions. It was a potential which Julian Beck and Judith Malina came to feel they were denying, precisely because their improvisations were simulated. True spontaneity was denied both performer and audience. The text seemed increasingly restrictive. Like Gelber with his characters, Beck and Malina wished to liberate themselves from the simple enactment of the given. If this sounds like a familiar American existentialism, as the self struggles to liberate itself from constraints in an act of definitional resistance (in fact the contending force in Gelber's play), the immediate inspiration lay elsewhere, in the France not just of Jean-Paul Sartre but fundamentally of Antonin Artaud, whose classic work, brought back from France by the composer John Cage in the 1950s, was translated by Mary Caroline Richards and published in America in 1958, an advance copy going to Beck. It was to prove a key document for the following decade.

Ironically the breakthrough, for the Living Theatre, came with Kenneth Brown's *The Brig* (1964), ironically because this was a work that made restriction a central image and fact. It consists of a cacophony of sound and a flurry of activity, the audience being subjected to an assault on the senses of the kind called for by Artaud. Its characters are trapped more completely than Gelber's had been, to the point at which their identities have been sandblasted away by an implacable system. Set in a Marines detention centre, it presents a powerful and protracted image of the destruction of the individual. Those in detention are permitted only to request permission to cross the many white lines drawn on the floor. They are referred to by numbers, are allowed to make no acknowledgement of their fellow prisoners and can only leave to an anonymous and invisible other world when their sentences are finished or madness has completed the immolation of the self by other means. Seen at the time as primarily a social statement, it was in fact a powerful image of the absurd which operated directly on the sensibility. Its text is rudimentary. Verbal language defers to movement and spectacle. It invites less an intellectual decoding than a visceral response, and though its very relentlessness, the sheer unforgiving rigour of its vision, was one that the Living Theatre would shortly reject, it did ironically allow for improvisation as the actors spontaneously responded to any infraction of the rules which structured the lives of their characters. It was, however, a purely ironic freedom, and as such a pure paradigm of Artaud's 'theatre of cruelty' in which the job of theatre was to teach us that 'we are not free'. But though the play was an exemplary text in other ways, too, operating as Artaud had wished, through 'crushing and hypnotising the sensibility of the audience',[4] de-emphasising the significance of verbal language, Artaud's vision was at odds with the Becks' essentially American optimism and their desire to create a Dionysian theatre, open, celebratory, anarchic.

The Brig was followed by Mysteries (1964), Frankenstein and Paradise Now (1968), public ceremonies in which language was to be broken down as a means of revealing and forcing other forms of communication. Paradise Now drew on the I Ching and R.D. Laing. It proposed a revolution in sensibility and in politics, the latter to be accomplished by means of the former. Members of the cast spelled out the words 'PARADISE' and 'ANARCHIST' with their bodies, literally making the body inscribe its own meaning, making language shape itself to their own being. This theatre was to release the libido and the subconscious, to welcome an anarchy of the senses that would overthrow a theatre and a society that had paid the price in sublimation and neurosis (the subject of much American drama) for an ordered social system that had in fact become repressive and repressing. The Reality Principle had had its day; it was time for the Pleasure Principle to redeem an anally retentive, ego-centred world whose repressions had, in society, generated social conflict and psychosis and, in the theatre, tragedy and its bourgeois shadow, the problem play. The ludic and the carnivalesque were to liberate those in thrall to the word (and hence the writer), to the past, to convention, to authority and, indeed, to the notion of theatre as an experience distinct from life. Texts were not abandoned, Beck believing in the power of theatre to reinvest verbal language with meaning, to renovate words, but they were fragmented, exposed as constructs, decontextualised, itself a modernist gesture learned from Artaud. Such productions did cut a vector across a strongly verbal, deeply psychological American drama. They resisted the formal framing of an art whose circumstances of production had seemed to disavow a social continuity between the theatre and the street. Indeed as the Living Theatre became highly politicised in the sixties and thereafter, so the street became increasingly attractive, since there the state obligingly demonstrated its innate repressiveness, arresting nude members of the Living Theatre as they spilled onto the sidewalks of New Haven or challenged the authority of the government in Brazil.

The Becks' was a theatre that chose to see in the actor a potential which lay beyond the vivifying of a verbal text fixed in its structure and its rhythms. Theirs was a theatre confident, absurdly confident, of its ability to transform the individual sensibility and the social system. It was a hubris that bred arrogance and eventually an exclusivity at odds with its objectives, but for a time it seemed to reflect the mood of a society increasingly at odds with what seemed an alarmingly repressive system, at home and abroad, in which an anonymous technocracy developed and prepared engines and agents of control and destruction.

By sheer chance members of the Living Theatre found themselves at the Odéon theatre in Paris when it was taken over by revolutionary students in 1968 and made the centre of revolt, a revolt which, interestingly, recuperated the slogans of the surrealists. In the circumstances it is not difficult to understand their conviction that the theatre was itself the stage on which revolt would act itself out. They were, however, quickly overtaken by events and the intellectual deficiencies of a theatre which had sought to by-pass the intellect became increasingly apparent. The attack on authority was often specious. The authority of the writer was denounced only to be replaced by that of the director or his group. Rationality was deplored in the name of a sensual and emotional style that became dangerously programmatic and prescriptive. Political orthodoxies were challenged in the name of racial and sexual archetypes which proved equally oppressive and limiting. In other words, the subtext remained power and its distribution; and that implied faith in a reality which it had set out to confront.

The Living Theatre did play a significant role in questioning the direction and functioning of the American theatre. Its efforts to bring into that theatre poets, new writers, those concerned with the exploration of form, language, structure, the theatrical space, represented a new direction and a new source of energy. That in the end it proved so much a product of its time and so incapable of inspiring a new generation was a cause of regret to Richard Schechner, himself director of the Performance Group, who, in *An End to Humanism*, sought to write the epitaph for the avant-garde of the sixties and early seventies. But it stands as evidence of one of those relatively rare occasions in the history of the American theatre when a group has chosen to examine the constituent elements of their art, when plot, narrative, language, character have been called into question or redefined, and when the audience has been assumed to be something other than figures in the dark who stare through a missing fourth wall at people who ostensibly remain unaware that they are observed.

The Open Theatre, another key group of the sixties, was born out of a concern for the ensemble experience, for the exploration, by the actor, of his or her own capacity in relation to others. Its founder Joseph Chaikin, who had played in the Living Theatre production of *The Connection*, was concerned to develop a series of exercises which would enable the actor to move beyond the naturalism at which actor training in America had aimed. For him, too, community was to be both the method and objective of the work as it was the gift which the theatre offered to a world characterised by alienation: 'Ensemble asserts the way that people are alike. We live and die separate. But there is a point where we are completely interlocked, a point where we are brought together . . . two by two, or in threes or fours, by our participation in something larger than each of us.'[5] Like the Living Theatre it also wished to explore ways in which the actor could become something more than a reciter of texts and the embodiment of other people's meanings. Theatre was to be more completely live than was possible in an art which turned on the reiteration of prescribed actions and words in the service of a sociology or psychology of the individual.

The Open Theatre was not originally established to perform publicly nor was it politically committed. But just as the Living Theatre moved steadily from its modernist concern with language as object and the theatre as a mirror of its own processes to a more directly intervention-ist stance, so Chaikin and his fellow actors entered the public arena with productions that engaged the political realities of sixties America. As with the Living Theatre their very first productions included modernist works by Eliot and Brecht. It was, however, with a play inspired by the Vietnam war that they first made a major impact. *Viet Rock* was a collab-orative venture, with playwright Megan Terry first providing an outline and then elaborating on this in response to the input of the group. The writer, however, remained central for Chaikin as he/she did not for the Becks while, after an initial experiment in audience–performer contact, he preferred to avoid that physical interaction which was a basic strat-egy and, at times, an essential weakness of the Living Theatre. Where the Becks had placed their faith in the actor exposing, often quite liter-ally, a naked self, stepping out of role, Chaikin saw the actor as working in a 'third person present tense'.

The writer with whom the Open Theatre is most associated is Jean-Claude van Itallie, Belgian-born but raised and educated in America. His *American Hurrah* offered a satirical view of an America in which language has become denatured, performance and being, fiction and reality hopelessly confused. A triptych, whose separate elements are 'Interview', 'TV' and 'Motel', it dramatises a society in which individuals are alienated from themselves and others, the war in Vietnam becomes an extension of television soap opera and the individual moves towards automaton. Indeed, in a final segment specifically inspired by Artaud, van Itallie creates three huge dolls: a motel-keeper and two guests, one male, one female. The guests never speak but engage in a parody of sexual contact and slowly destroy the room; the motel-keeper's voice, meanwhile, comes from a loudspeaker, language and experience now separated from one another. The play ends in a cataclysm, with wailing sirens and bright lights which dazzle the audience, as Artaud had called for characters enlarged to the size of gigantic manikins and 'intensities of colors, lights, or sounds'. His prediction of a time when 'the basest instincts' would be liberated seems realised in *American Hurrah*. The play in part grew out of Open Theatre exercises and presented a series of images in which paradoxically, the refusal to permit the actors either a transitive language or a physical integrity exposed precisely that failure of feeling and community which had lain behind the group's creation. In other words, it is a play that relies on absence rather than presence, that implies that the cataclysm with which it concludes is simply a logical extension of spiritual collapse.

Van Itallie's later work, *The Serpent* (1968), also deploys a series of images, tableaux in which the biblical story of the Fall is blended with contemporary myth – the killings of President Kennedy and Martin Luther King. It is a play in which ritual, sound and movement replace plot, dialogue and action. The text, of course, is only the starting-point in drama but here that is more plainly true, as the physical co-operation of the actors who collaboratively create meaning is pitched against a language of alienation, detachment and despair. The actors, in other words, redeem the text, resist the plot in which they are seemingly entrapped.

It is a play that can only be 'read' in terms of a physical performance which is not designed simply to articulate a given text but in large part to subvert it. Indeed the play began not with that text but with the improvisational exercises of the group. The tension which gave it something of its force was thus in part a product of production history. Its social logic was despair; its emotional impetus was towards a recuperation to be achieved through co-operation. The tableaux, like frozen frames in a film, can only generate meaning through the collaboration of the actors who form part of its structure.

The following year, after the creation of another work, *Terminal*, by Susan Yankovitz, the group debated whether the political situation was such that they should be committed primarily to theatrical or political change, with Chaikin dissolving and then reforming the group in an attempt to resolve the problem in the direction of theatre. A final complete work, *The Mutation Show* (1971) pressed even further towards a drama that communicated through movement, mime, and proxemic relationship. The text itself was slight as became a work which invoked Kaspar Hauser, the boy kept imprisoned in a cellar for the first sixteen years of his life (a subject that also fascinated Peter Handke). Himself deprived of language, his journey back to speech is a mutation paralleled by his loss of real autonomy. Yet there is another transformation as actors who begin by identifying their offstage identity assume other roles as required – as assertion of the possibility of change implicit in theatre.

Following a final production – *Nightwalk* (1973) – Chaikin declared the Open Theatre closed. He did so out of a fear that means might become ends, as training and development were at risk of giving way to the pressures of production. Anxious to avoid the group falling into a destructive routine he opted to end one of the more interesting theatrical experiments of the sixties.

What the Open Theatre offered was a rigour lacking in the Living Theatre. The only American group that Grotowski praised, it managed to sustain a disciplined approach that inhibited the sentimentality into which the Becks' romanticism so easily devolved. Its insistence on the significance of the text, albeit a text which bore the imprint of its own improvisational exercises, created a structure and a context for its experimentation. Its objective, to widen the emotional and intellectual range of the American actor, to break with the Method's psychological orientation – rooted as it was in turn-of-the-century Russian realism – had slowly broadened into a commitment to new writing and, to some degree, to a new politics. But Chaikin was finally unwilling to allow the group to lose touch with its original impulse and as a result it never suffered the lingering death of the Living Theatre or the Performance Group.

The Performance Group was created in 1967 to explore the possibilities of theatre, and in particular to investigate the dynamics of a group of actors who, instead of subordinating themselves to a part, were to discover aspects of themselves and ways of relating to one another in a way which would liberate meanings contained within and even inhibited by the literary text. This, too, was to be a Dionysian theatre and it is no coincidence that their first production, in May 1968, should be called *Dionysus in 69*. Physical contact was to by-pass inhibitions. This was not to be an illusionistic theatre. Indeed not only were the mechanics of the occasion to be openly acknowledged but individual members of the audience were inducted into the theatre space with a ceremony designed to signify their passage into a special environment.

The Performance Group drew on the insights and frequently the language of anthropology. The 'training-rehearsal-preparation process' was to draw actors into 'other ways of seeing' and perceiving reality. In other words, there were to be elements of ritual and ceremony (sometimes plundered – in the sense of decontextualised from other cultures), which had to do with altering the state of mind of the participants. It followed that the audience could not be regarded in quite the same way, since it had to be liberated from what was seen as a merely voyeuristic role. Strictly speaking there can be no audience to ritual, with theatre now to be regarded as a secular rite, and perhaps not all that secular, the word 'holy' being bandied around, audiences being invited to undergo rites of passage and a new cultural priesthood emerging. Nor was the line between drama and therapy a clear one. Body and mind were to conjoin. A primal wound was to be healed. A birth ritual in *Dionysus in 69* re-enacted that trauma, with the actors naked, delivered forth to announce their own names as though that self were pure, uncluttered, free of the artifice of the role then to be assumed. Nudity was assumed to be a purified state. No room for deceit there. But nudity and deceit are, one might say, familiar bedfellows, while Schechner's assumption that excellence in art is 'a function of wholeness as a human being' is sadly, or perhaps reassuringly, wide of the mark.

For this group, too, language was to be liberated from its role as signifier. It was to be broken down into sound units, fragmented into syllables, explored for its sonorities, tonalities. In *Dionysus in 69* three different texts were interleaved, with lines from Elizabeth Wycoff's translation of *Antigone* and David Grene's translation of *Hippolytus* being integrated into Arrowsmith's version of *The Bacchae*, thereby diminishing the authority of any single language or perspective. Meanwhile other texts, those generated by actors exploring their own literal and private experiences, were allowed to infiltrate the action as theoretical role and personal identity were counterposed, thereby, you might suppose, exposing the fictionality of both; but this was the sixties and Schechner's group underwent regular therapeutic encounter sessions designed to put them in touch with themselves and their fellows, to reach for a level of authenticity ironically denied by the text of a play which warns against the mutability of the self.

Arthur Miller once praised Elia Kazan for his awareness that plays contain the history of other plays. In a sense what the Performance Group did in their next production was to extend this logic. *Commune* (1970), incorporated elements from Shakespearian and Jacobean drama, from nineteenth-century American literature and from the Bible, an intertextuality designed to expose an associational logic to experience. The production was developed over the course of nearly a year through improvisation. There was, indeed, no single author, as befitted a play which, as its title implied, explored the nature of community. It was to be a work that rejected the notion of a coherent narrative in favour of shared images and dynamic action. As Schechner observed, theirs was to be 'No longer a theatre of telling a story – or even doing a story.'[6] The audience was to be enrolled in the generation of a performance to be experienced directly by those pulled into the action by the requirement that they should perform certain prescribed actions. *Commune* professed a clear ideology. It rested on the conviction that American history is one of violence and oppression. The Sharon Tate killing, in which a drug-crazed Charles Manson murdered the film star Sharon Tate, is related to the My Lai massacre in Vietnam in which Vietnamese peasants were murdered by American troops, both being presented as evidence of a specifically American villainy. The problem is that the intellectual substructure for this argument is lacking, that it begins with its conclusions. Like *Dionysus in 69* it evidences a refreshing honesty, in that both plays explore the dangers implicit in a group that come together in a revolt against the rational and the moral. What is lacking is any attempt, dramatically, to relate theme to methodology. Distrust of authority – the authority of the writer – suspicion of rationality and distaste for illusionism have their virtue, in a system and a theatre which have rested perhaps too completely on them. But the Performance Group was not without its own coercive strategies, while its own capacity for self-deceit was considerable.

The Group continued to experiment, the writer gradually playing a larger role, until it began to disintegrate, Schechner eventually pulling out. Reborn as the Wooster Group, under Elizabeth LeCompte, it moved in a new direction. It was a direction which saw the playwright,

the director, the designer and often the actor subsumed in the same sensibility, as group ethos began to defer to the monologist or to pure autobiography. Later the group would concern itself with deconstructing
literary texts: *Our Town* in *Route 1 and 9* (1981; the last act), *The Crucible* in
LSD . . . Just the High Points (1985), *Three Sisters* in *Brace Up* (1990) and *The
Hairy Ape* (1995). For the moment, though, as the 1970s gave way to the
1980s the private began to dominate in the work of Spalding Gray and
Jack Smith, Leeny Sack and Bob Carroll. And while Gray denied that
the personal excluded the public Schechner saw an era as having ended,
one, however, that had transformed our sense of theatricality as the imi-
tation of an action, as secondary to other processes – psychological,
social, political. The Performance Group, in particular, he thought, had
staked its claim to see theatre as a mode of behaviour, as a means of
understanding, as a primary human activity. That assumption took
Schechner and others in the direction of myth and ritual, where that
proposition seemed most literally true, and by definition these excluded
a single governing intelligence, the writer, but did invoke the notion of
community and a functioning priesthood. However, the importation of
such rituals from other cultures or attempts self-consciously to identify
the iconography of contemporary myth could all too easily become an
artificial exercise. Feeling the lack of such shared myths they set out to
construct them from the fragments not so much of American experience
as those of the Third World or ancient Greece. By simulating the ritual
– precise actions, resonant sounds, communal rites, symbolic gestures –
they hoped to reconstitute an element drained alike from theatre and
society. Not the least ironic aspect of these groups was the degree to
which in working to move theatre and thereby society in a new direction
they turned to the past. But then where else would the logic of a lost
organicism, an alienation born out of modernity, a division between
mind and body, performer and community lead but to the past?

Beyond that was another irony, a product of the times, in that theatres which began as largely apolitical experiments in testing the potential of theatre, in exploring the dynamics of the group and working for
a restored unity within the self and the community, should co-exist with
other groups and other writers for whom such divisions were rooted less
in an abstract sense of alienation than in clearly identifiable political,
social and economic realities which would not defer to sentiment.
Indeed, for many, distinctions of race and gender, in particular, were
crucial to a sense of identity and purpose; reality was neither problematic nor transformable through vatic rites, and social change was more

urgent than spiritual transformation. The Living Theatre, the Open Theatre, and the Performance Group addressed a social and educational elite already in tune with calls for a transformed consciousness: the black theatre, women's theatre, Chicano theatre and other groups who defined themselves in terms of racial, political or social allegiance sought out audiences who were often not attuned to the indirections of theatre, but who were part of a community which needed no lessons in the deceptions of language, the virtues of body language, the urgencies of change or the significance of solidarity. In another period the audience for Julian Beck, Joseph Chaikin or Richard Schechner would, like those individuals themselves, have been drawn to the achievements of Brecht and Lorca, Beckett and Pinter. The audience for Amiri Baraka and Luis Valdez, the San Francisco Mime Troupe or the Bread and Puppet Theatre would probably not have been found in the theatre at all. These latter were less concerned with developing techniques of acting or methods of releasing the individual from the constraints of the ego than with identifying and urging a liberation more easily defined. The Living Theatre's assaults on the bourgeoisie were the bohemian's revolt against conventional morality and conventional art. Baraka and Valdez attacked them as the source of an historic injustice.

But if the avant-garde theatre of the sixties and early seventies was characterised by a transformed sensibility, that of the seventies and eighties took a more cerebral path. The exuberant spirit of theatre groups who spilled off the stage and into the auditorium and from there onto the street chanting imprecations against a positivist world, invoking the body against the mind, gave way to those – such as Lee Breuer, Richard Foreman and Robert Wilson – who tended to place the action of their works securely back on the stage, reinstate the conscious mind and turn the animate sensual body into art object. The audience, invited by Beck and Schechner to leave their seats and become a part of the action, were now required to stay in their places and become aware of the degree to which they were collaborating on the level of the mind and the imagination. The focus now was to be on consciousness itself, on the process of perception, the way in which the real is summoned into being by the mind that perceives it. Performance theatre invited the audience to look beyond the surface of the real, to feel and respond to experiences which never made their way fully into language. What Bonnie Marranca has called the 'theatre of images' wished the audience to become so aware of the surface that it can no longer be dismissed as an irrelevance. Indeed by slowing the action down, by creating tableaux which draw attention to detailed surface reality, Foreman and Wilson, in particular, hoped to force an awareness of every element of a figure or scene. In Richard Foreman's words, the world of signs was to be replaced by a world of perceptions. In terms of art the analogue would be Richard Estes or George Segal; in literature, Alain Robbe-Grillet and Walt Whitman. We are not invited to look beyond but at. However, if we do so for long enough we are liable to move into a trance-like state which takes us off into a mysticism not contained in or implied but provoked by the object.

In 1965, John Hawkes pointed out that he had begun to write fiction on the assumption that 'the true enemies of the novel were plot, character, setting and theme'.[7] Five years later, Robert Wilson was asking of the theatre 'is it necessary to have a story, is it necessary to have characters, is it necessary to have . . . symbolism?'[8] The questioning came out of a doubt about the logical coherences of narrative, the subordination of moment to flow, of simultaneity to sequentiality, and out of a wariness about the supposed substantiality of character, a self whose complexities were presumed to be beyond appearance. The power of the symbol ostensibly lay in the assumption that manifest reality had only a second-order status; theme implied a hidden structure; setting, a context whose social associations leached into the figures it contained. In fact, whatever they may have said, both Hawkes and Wilson did retain all the elements whose necessity they had questioned. But their centrality was diminished. Neither, as Hawkes said of himself, was 'socially oriented'. What did interest them was the dissembling of conventional structures. Thus Wilson became, as he himself explained, interested in paying inordinate attention to small detail, in movement, in the juxtaposition of object and figure. Put another way, he tended to break action up into small fragments, to separate form from function, to offer a collage of simultaneous events creating what he called 'overlays of visual correspondences'.

You might well ask what is left after you have thrown out plot, character, setting and symbol. Hawkes's answer was 'totality of vision or structure' and Wilson would seem substantially to agree, the acts of dislocation, or deconstruction, in which both engage, being, they would claim, anything but perverse. Indeed John Hawkes has sought to present his own work as a romantic concern for the ideal. Thus, to him, 'destruction or derangement', far from being 'gratuitously offered up as rare specimens of perverse thinking . . . constitute . . . the only serious condition there is, the constant inversion of the ideal'[9] in the sense that André Breton's locomotive in the forest, 'the vine covered rusted engine that's forever inert, forever immobile, dead, somehow conveys more of "locomotive" than the enormous slick black machine roaring down the track'. The destructive image thus 'posits the ideal' in the sense, perhaps, that the ruined abbeys of the romantic painter did much the same. A similar idea seems to lie behind the 'theatre' of Richard Foreman and Robert Wilson (whose work was itself drawn to Breton's attention), a theatre which in part seeks to recover the ideal through what might indeed reasonably be called derangement, through just such a slowing down or arresting of movement as Breton had created, stilling the rush of action and event in order to recuperate not so much meaning as form and structure. The 'obsessive quality' which Hawkes identified in his own work, an obsessiveness characterised by 'repeated form', is there, too, in Wilson's work, as it is, incidentally, in that of the composer Philip Glass whose music formed an integral part of Wilson's *Einstein on the Beach*.

Susan Sontag, in 'Against Interpretation',[10] had rebelled against the tyranny of meaning which evacuated the moment and implied the dependent status of appearance. She wished to restore an interest in form in the sense that Roland Barthes, in *L'Empire des Signes* (1970), had expressed an admiration for those Japanese arts which saw in the surface an opacity which was its own justification. In the same way, Alain Robbe-Grillet chose to reject the literary speleologists who wish to pass through the surface of his work in order to reinstate a density it was his purpose to deny, believing, with George Santayana, that words and images are like shells, no less integral parts of nature than are the substances they cover. Interestingly, precisely this passage was used as an epigraph by Erving Goffman in his book *The Presentation of Self in Everyday Life*, which itself drew on the theatre as a central image for social interaction.

The implication is that if we create the world through our consciousness we are also a product of that consciousness in the sense that Rimbaud believed that 'I am thinking' should be rendered as 'one is thinking me'.[11] This emphasis on consciousness, and through consciousness, on the self, however, was one that Susan Sontag was not prepared to countenance, in an essay called 'On Art and Consciousness', published in 1977, deploring its solipsism. To her it seemed to imply an hermetic world whose asocial nature led in the direction of autism and mental illness, of which repetition and abstract or distended notions of time (both deployed by Robert Wilson, who also relied on the insights of a brain-damaged boy) were primary evidence. It is not hard to see what she means, as audiences are invited to make what they will out of isolated images whose only authority lies in the fact that they have come unbidden and unrelated into Wilson's mind (though the surrealists required no more justification). His faith in the communicative power of the mentally damaged was denounced, in another context, by Arthur Miller, for whom the refusal of the rational mind and the articulate voice was a wilful sentimentality and a denial of one's full humanity.

But even an avowedly asocial art disturbs the social world in which it has its existence. As Georges Braque observed, 'the vase gives shape to emptiness, music to silence',[12] a remark admiringly recalled by John Hawkes and reflected in Wallace Stevens's poem, 'The Anecdote of the Jar'. Art not only has an internal structure but its pressure creates a resistant form in the world beyond its parameters, which takes us through modernism back to a romanticism for which a revived attentiveness to immediate reality, a reality which only renders itself up fully as a result of concentration, a slowed-down apprehension, is the key to a transfigured and transfiguring consciousness. There is something of Keats's negative capability about Wilson's and Foreman's desire to resensitise the mind almost to a neurotic degree, while John Hawkes's observation that the imagination 'is always and inevitably erotic' finds its justification in the work of Richard Foreman, as in the romantic sensibility. There is something of the romantic, too, in Wilson's flirtation with trance-like states. In *Deafman Glance* (1971) he and his group consciously worked at inducing trance through the reiterative actions of the performers and hallucinations were, indeed, by no means rare amongst his audiences. At times Philip Glass's music seems to come close to provoking a similar response.

Language is marginalised as Wilson reacts against 'words in a dried out, flat, one-dimensional literary structure' in so far as 'fragments and hidden detail become without words suddenly transparent'.[13] But these fragments do not relate to some predetermined whole. If they cohere it is in the mind that generates relationships which are hidden by the simple logical coherences of plot, character and language. Indeed, in an attempt to evade even his own control over those images Wilson opened the performance up to images provided by others in his group and finally to those which cohere in the mind of the observer, a partner whose active involvement, at the level of mind and imagination, is required.

The humanism of this theatre lies not in its subject or its procedures but in the degree to which it makes the audience an active collaborator. The irony, however, lies in the fact that an art which relies for its completion on the active intellectual involvement of the audience should be quite as wilfully gnomic as it frequently is and, indeed, through its trance-inducing repetitions, quite as manipulative.

Not that language is excluded. In *Overture to Ka Mountain and Gardenia Terrace, a Story about a Family and Some People Changing* (1972) a number of texts – William Demby's poetry, Nijinsky's autobiography, a script of Wilson's own devising and a monologue by his grandmother – were juxtaposed, fragmented in such a way that lexical meaning was subordinated to sound, rhythm, tone. Language becomes an object among other objects, rather as in a dadaist performance though without the dadaists' anarchic impulse. His slowing of language, like his slowing of movement, was designed to draw attention to the surface; in the case of words, to break a conditioning which subordinates word to meaning or object to function. The intertextual gesture suggests a refusal to privilege any particular discourse.

In *A Letter for Queen Victoria* (1974–5) he took the process a stage further, language being arbitrarily assigned to performers who were instructed that their function was to transcend the language they uttered. In the name of what? That was less clear. The public might be invited to provide what was missing in the performance, otherwise they were ignored. The figures on the stage seldom interacted. History, if invoked, was only acknowledged as a series of dislocated images. There was a privatism about this art that brought it to the edge of absurdity. These, after all, were the Vietnam years. Assassination, racial strife, social disorder, foreign wars, political corruption never penetrate the carapace of this art. Ostensibly radical, in aesthetic terms, it could be accused of a fundamental conservatism. It was a theatre which had something in common with fifties happenings, sixties pop art, or seventies kinetic art, as it did with therapeutic methods and contemporary dance. In a way his is a poet's strategy, bringing together, as he does, different orders of experience, elements precisely controlled but which in combination generate something no less powerful for being imprecise. If that process operates he stands justified; if it does not his increasingly grandiose and expensive 'operas' seem little more than fashionable gestures for a fashionable international audience. *The Life and Times of Joseph Stalin* lasted for twelve hours and featured nearly a hundred performers. By the time of the Los Angeles Olympics, however, he had created a work which defied the combined efforts and financing of several countries.

This is a world drained of depth, which resists interpretation – a world of signs without significations. Indeed, he acknowledged the influence of the formalists. Instead of multiplying the dimensions of the self – as performance theatre had done – this theatre reduced them until the human figure became a barely animate object among other objects, deprived of full mobility, an element in a design whose total structure remained gnomic. The aesthetic seems to be derived from the world of art and indeed a number of individuals and groups had their origins in the art world, most particularly Christopher Hardman, once of the Bread and Puppet Theatre and then of the Snake Theatre, and Robert Wilson himself. It is a theatre in which archetype becomes stereotype. The voice is detached from the figure which supposedly generates it.

Performers become in a sense living sculptures – not yet the automatons popular with street entertainers in the late eighties who mimicked the spasmodic actions of machine-men (rather like Woody Allen in *Sleeper*), but figures deprived of narrative role, psychological depth or social relationship. The return to the picture-frame stage was not without its art-historical association.

Both Wilson and Foreman filled the canvas of their stage like artists for whom the placement of a figure, the composition of a scene, the balance of colour and texture was as much the subject and object of the work as the figures themselves. The intensity of the work derived precisely from a control over the speed with which information is released to the observer, the amplification of sound, the extent to which the repetition of sound or image makes the smallest variation apparent. The demands made by their work derive less from a fear of physical assault, always a non-insurable risk in sixties theatre, than the degree of concentration required of an action deliberately prolonged to the point of boredom or enhanced perception.

Until the mid-seventies, Richard Foreman was concerned with defamiliarisation. By locating an object (which might also be a human figure) on stage, decontextualised, isolated from its social context, he hoped to force new levels of perception, rather as Andy Warhol had done in his seemingly interminable film of a man sleeping. In a later stage, he became more interested in the process of consciousness, more particularly his own. In a sense it was an echo of Gertrude Stein's belief in the centrality of the artistic mind, shaping fragmented experience into conscious form, and indeed Foreman acknowledged her inspiration. No longer subordinated to the elaboration of story or meaning, no longer committed to the exploration of character, he, like Stein, created a series of images, moments, tableaux, which turned the mind back on itself. For her, drama was a 'bright filled space'; it was 'sight and sound and its relation to emotion and time, rather than in relation to story and action'.[14] Anyone who has read Gertrude Stein's work knows that her sentences edge their way forward with a terrible slowness, forcing attention onto the surface of language. Each proposition is countered by the opposite in a virtual parody of precision and balance. Her language is less concerned with knowledge (which she tautologically defines as 'what you know') than with 'deciding about knowing'. Foreman shares the same conviction working by juxtaposition and if that seems reminiscent of the surrealists then they, too, were indeed a point of reference, though he rejected them as genuine models. Foreman's is an anti-illusionist theatre in which empathy is deliberately inhibited. The fragments of sound are often deliberately processed so as to become detached from their individual human source; the moments of action, the vestiges of implied character, cohere, if at all, only in the mind of the observer. And that coherence is deferred as long as possible for fear of inhibiting a full exploration of individual moments. And because Foreman is so abstemious, so minimalist in his effects, the observer has to become hyperaware. Rather as John Cage sought to sensitise his listeners to their environment, amplifying sounds normally filtered out by the sensibility, so Foreman sought at first to provoke a sensitivity towards sound, movement and surface blunted by familiarity – a 'concrete theatre' – and then to explore ways in which those elements, external to the self, are drawn into the self and transformed. Initially he aimed at a tension between mind and object, deliberately disrupting efforts to incorporate that object into a narrative context by the deployment of various alienating devices (elastic chords are stretched across the stage, the action is slowed down or speeded up). Later that tension is relaxed.

His plays – *Angelface* (1968), *Total Recall (Sophia = (Wisdom)*, *Hotel China* (1971–2), *(Sophia = (Wisdom): Part 2* (1972–3), *Café Amerique* – fail to exemplify the rigour of his theories. Meanings, whose tyranny he wished to avoid, proved remarkably persistent, if evasive, and the narrative gesture survives. In some ways these are works more interesting theoretically than practically and as such share something with certain postmodern novels. Foreman later directed classical plays and operas. In 1991 he established the Ontological-Hysteric chamber theatre at St Marks in the Bowerie. Later works include *Samuel's Major Problems* (1993).

Robert Wilson came to theatre by way of art and architecture. In 1988 he became director of the Byrd Hoffman Foundation which itself ran workshops in dance, movement, theatre and the related arts. That mix is evident in Wilson's *The King of Spain* (1969), which presented a series of 'moving pictures', slowed-down actions, choreographed movements, as it was in *The Life and Times of Sigmund Freud*, a four-hour presentation which incorporated the earlier work, a production which Wilson called a 'hybrid dance play'. In his case these were projections of a private world, personal visions, and if he did include recognisable historical figures – here Freud, as later, Stalin – he had no interest in plumbing their psychological depth or exploring their historical significance. He also avoided the use of professional actors. The emphasis was to be on the visual. Language is de-emphasised not, as with performance theatre, because it involves deceit or because it distracts from the warm, sensual body, but because it earths meaning too resolutely. The stage abounds with fantasy animals or patterned reversals, as men 'play' women or those with black skin play those with white. In describing his work Wilson tended to fall back on the vocabulary of art and architecture, rather than theatre. He is interested in method rather than content and there is in effect no plot, character or coherent language. With *Einstein on the Beach* he worked with Philip Glass, and indeed his works began to resemble operas in their blend of music and movement, not to say their vast expense. *Overture to Ka Mountain* lasted for 24 hours in Paris and 168 hours in Iran, where it incorporated *Deafman Glance* and *Overture*, a length which immediately makes clear that this is not a production which relies on linear logic since the audience, which anyway spoke very little English, could not be expected to sustain their presence let alone their concentration over such a period.

With time Wilson's productions became so large in scale that they proved difficult or even impossible to stage in their entirety. The avant-garde, more usually associated with the small-scale and the inexpensive, now became epic in scale and highly fashionable, Madame Pompidou jetting into Munich in 1982 for a performance of *The Golden Window*. *CIVIL warS*, a contemplation of war through history, followed in 1984. Later work included his version of Ibsen's *When We Dead Awaken* (1992), *The Black Rider* (1990; text by William Burroughs) and *Alice* (1995), based on *Alice in Wonderland*.

Like Wilson and Foreman, Lee Breuer has links to modernism and a concern for the allied arts. His fables are self-consciously related to Kafka's, while one of his works was part of a programme subtitled 'A Valentine for Marcel Duchamp'. He had worked with Ann Halprin's Dancers' Workshop, while the first works that he wrote and produced for Mabou Mines (the name deriving from a Nova Scotia mining town) were staged in art galleries and were directly influenced by developments in the art world. The group, which worked in Europe in the late sixties, took its name in 1969 and, after working as the resident company at the La Mama Experimental Theatre Company, performed the same role in the early eighties with the New York Shakespeare Festival. *The Red Horse Animation* was first performed at the Guggenheim Museum in New York City in 1970. *The B Beaver Animation*, the second part of what Breuer considers a trilogy, opened at the Museum of Modern Art in 1974. With the third part, however, *The Shaggy Dog Animation*, the premiere took place in a theatre. But if it had roots in modernism it also owed something of its aesthetic to pop art, the cartoon strip, the cinema. *The Red Horse Animation*, in which actors, in a minimal setting, summon into being the consciousness, sensibility and tactile sense of a horse, was actually published in a comic-strip version and, in another version, printed so that the photographs appeared like the frames in a movie. *The B Beaver Animation*, in which a beaver tells its story of struggle and decline, a story which a series of author's interventions describes, cinematically, as 'takes', relates that story to human destiny, seeming simultaneously to offer and deny the modernist notion that art may redeem life until we are left with the Beckettian logic of personal destiny: 'EAT. CRAP. SCREW. CROAK.'

The Shaggy Dog Animation offers a parody of Hollywood, the pop world, radio and the west coast sensibility, deploying the whole array of theatrical possibilities from amplified music and pop groups through to puppets, as we are offered the ironic account of a dog's love for its master.

Breuer's work is parodistic, ironic, fabulous in the sense of generating fables. *A Prelude to a Death in Venice* (1979), a work which consists of a single actor, a puppet which he endows with life, and a phone booth, is surprisingly affecting, though once again its aesthetic, as well as its title, derives from the world of movies. So, a police car is suggested by a huge wheel, a representation of a camera distortion. The play stands both as a critique of the notion of an easily recoverable real and, like many of his other works, as an observation about the artist and the process of an imagination which works by indirection, analogy, displacement, doubling, self-interrogation. He deals in metaphor whose very literalness he explores with humour and willed naivety. Like Wilson and Foreman, on occasion he detaches voice from character, itself a gesture which generalises his fables. Also like Wilson and Foreman, his work gradually fills out, a pregnancy which brought forth a plenitude of sound, movement and energy previously constrained and muted. This was not the world of performance theatre. All three continued a rigorous control of all aspects of their theatre. The emphasis was still on the mind that observed, that sought to find or generate order, and not on the body. This was the 1970s. Truth was taken to lie in fragments, in discontinuities and disjunctions, as in the sixties it was presumed to lie in the denial of dualism, the recovery of innocence and a holistic serenity. This did not make the work of Wilson, Foreman and Breuer the enemy of humanism. It could be challenged for its resolute avoidance of those substantial realities then in the process of affronting both mind and imagination – the facts of racism, poverty, war, Watergate – but it was less concerned with the substantiality of the given than with the process whereby we recuperate the real. But, to a degree, concern with the processes of art, besides linking their theatre back to the modernists they all admired, also explored the extent to which we are complicit at the level of the mind, in the way that performance theatre had suggested that we are at the level of the sensibility, in the construction of the world we choose to call reality.

Yet there were still those for whom the physical self was taken to be the route to truth or truths, while beyond the theatre lay a tangible world whose physical locations might serve both to break with the factitious assumptions of drama and to bleed other realities into performance. Thus in 1978 Meredith Monk formed the Vocal Ensemble to explore the potential of the human voice (later works include *Atlas: an Opera in Three Parts* (1991) and *Politics of Quiet* (1996)), as Laurie Anderson had in her John Case-influenced performance pieces. Meanwhile, Carolee Schneeman used her (frequently naked) body to tell stories as, at a later date, did Karen Finley (*We Keep Our Victims Ready* (1989)). In the 1980s Anne Hamburger founded En Garde Arts, concerned with producing site-specific plays (an early work was *At the Chelsea* (1988)), as, at times, was Ping Chong, whose work explored Oriental myths and traditions (in, for example, *Deshima* (1990) and *Chinoiserie* (1995)). One of En Garde Arts' best known playwrights was Mac Wellman, who set plays in Central Park (*Bad Penny* (1989)) and a former theatre (*Crowbar* (1990)) and whose work was extensively praised by another playwright equally committed to language, an exploded language, oblique, equally in revolt against naturalism: Eric Overmayer. Both were concerned to explore a new kind of theatricality to which a non-naturalistic language was the key. This, in turn, was to give them an affinity with Suzan-Lori Parks and Len Jenkin, who declared that he wished 'to see theatre energetically stomping around the USA and the rest of the world', and whose vision of that theatre called, at least at the level of metaphor, for playwrights to 'put on plays by the highway side'.[15]

It sounds as if he were dedicated to offering populist works, but it is not the nature of the avant-garde to do that. And whether it was Karen Finley or Mac Wellman, Ping Chong or Len Jenkin, there remained a space between the performed self and the audience which shifting the location of the performance changed but did not necessarily close. This is not the theatricalised society of the 1960s. It has its politics – Mac Wellman, in particular, took pleasure in attacking a reactionary funding agency while Suzan Lori-Parks had a racial agenda – but what was at stake was less a transformed society than a transformed sensibility. This was not the warm, sensual communalism of the Performance Group, or the edgy anarchic communitarianism of the Living Theatre. It was a theatre in which the voice, the body, the specified site, a liberated language free of naturalistic functionalism, were to unlock perception. The question was, whose? The theatrical avant-garde, after all, is a minority within a minority. There were those, however, for whom the urgencies of the political and social world were of central concern and those are, in part, the subject of the next chapter.

CHAPTER TEN

Redefining the centre: politics, race, gender

The political theatre of the sixties and seventies seemed a long way removed from the avant-garde concerns of the Living Theatre, the Performance Group and the Open Theatre. In fact they had a good deal in common. Not merely were those groups politicised in due course but black theatre, women's theatre, Chicano theatre were also in the business of transformation. For them, too, language was suspect. They, too, sought a closer identification between performer and audience. If performance theatre wished to strip away illusion and deceit in order to expose the real, then so, too, did a theatre for which that process was both a therapeutic and a political act. If the Living Theatre spilled out of the theatre onto the streets, as a deliberate act of provocation, then this was also a logical move for those whose natural audience associated the theatre building with the very system against which they were in revolt. On the west coast the San Francisco Mime Troupe fought a legal battle to secure the right to perform its political fables in a public park as El Teatro Campesino staged its agit-prop sketches in the fields of California's agro-businesses; on the east coast no anti-war rally was complete without the Bread and Puppet Theatre or the more ephemeral groups presenting agit-prop allegories of the urban guerilla confronted by the technological American ogre. Ralph Ellison has said that when American life is most American it is apt to be most theatricalised. That has never been as true as it was in the 1960s, a decade in which performance was a cultural and social imperative, whether it was the theatricalised costuming of a generation in kaftans and psychedelic clothes or the public display of political commitments in marches and demonstrations.

Vietnam disturbed more than a political equanimity. It challenged fundamental myths having to do with personal and public integrity, the clarity of moral concern, technology as an agent of progress, America as a symbol of democratic freedoms. It was not only a political consensus that dissolved with the 1968 Tet Offensive in South Vietnam and the massacre at My Lai. When North Vietnamese soldiers penetrated to the heart of the American Embassy compound in the New Year offensive, they infiltrated the American consciousness on another level, too. When American troops butchered innocent civilians they also killed America's self-image as guardian of the good and the true.

Vietnam was America's *Heart of Darkness* and later, in Francis Ford Coppola's *Apocalypse Now*, was seen very self-consciously in those terms. The hard, integral self, far from sustaining its integrity in an alien world, as frontier myths had proposed, collapsed into a corruption that proved socially and morally corrosive. Raised to expect inevitable victory, Americans found themselves confronting a defeat whose implications went beyond military debacle. It was difficult even to find a language in which to express a sense of loss. The Vietnam Memorial, long delayed, had a Hemingwayesque minimalism as though the country, like Frederic Henry in *A Farewell to Arms,* had come to distrust the abstract virtues which had sent 55,000 Americans and many more Vietnamese to their deaths, and could only place its faith in the integrity of a list of names. Meanwhile, at home, American cities burned, incandescent with centuries of racial injustice.

There are few occasions when an individual year can be said to mark political, moral and social tensions on an international scale. One would be 1989, the year of the revolutions. Another would undoubtedly be 1968, which saw change bloom and shrivel in Europe, the American fate in Vietnam foreshadowed, and social revolt emerge in psychedelic colours in a country which also saw a Civil Rights leader and a presidential candidate shot dead by assassins.

The war, however, infiltrated American drama at an early stage. Robert Lowell's trilogy, which appeared, under the collective title *The Old Glory*, in 1964, offered an account of American history, refracted through the work of Nathaniel Hawthorne and Herman Melville, which presented that history as the creation and consolidation of empire. To Lowell, American messianism became the source of corruption and ultimately of cataclysm, its own idealism, whose symbol and justification was the flag, generating an arrogance born out of self-righteousness. In rooting his work in nineteenth-century literature Lowell was implicitly claiming an alternative tradition, offering a critique of power, challenging a singular reading of experience, while its own poetic form asserted the resources of a language not yet entirely denatured by power. Its density, its allusiveness, its plurality of meanings stood as a denial of an authorised text. Thus Captain Delano, in *Benito Cereno*, Lowell's version of Melville's story, fails to recognise social injustice or the potency of revolutionary forces precisely because of his chauvinism and his desire to see the world at moral attention. He is the victim of his own reading of experience, a reading which he has absorbed along with an American rhetoric of superiority. To him, blackness is impenetrable, an implacable fact which invites neither understanding nor acknowledgement. As a result his life falls under its shadow, as it does under the shadow of the violence which he unleashes against a world that must be made to conform to his Manichaean vision. That violence, indeed, braided together with a terrible naivety, creates the pattern for the cloth of *Old Glory* and links the three parts of Lowell's play – *Endecott and the Red Cross*, *My Kinsman, Major Molyneux* and *Benito Cereno*. A response in part to the racial situation in America and in part to an imperial history, *The Old Glory* was produced by Jonathan Miller in such a way as to enhance its irreality. Its style was influenced partly by the political cartoon and partly by *Alice in Wonderland*, a choice which proved entirely appropriate as the morass of Vietnam tended, in subsequent years, to be reflected in works whose principle image was one of surreal confusion.

In the movies the war was restaged as a western in *The Green Berets*, and the parallel was acknowledged from a different ideological perspective in *Soldier Blue* and *Little Big Man*, as it was later in *Apocalypse Now*. A similar parallel struck the poet Robert Bly, so that it is scarcely surprising that the theatre should also have embraced this analogy for a war in which high technology took on low technology, the US Cavalry was once again confronted with guerilla warfare. Certainly Arthur Kopit's *Indians* and Sam Shepard's *Operation Sidewinder* suggested some such parallel. But the war's greatest impact was its radicalisation of the theatre. Groups which had previously been apolitical or whose politics had been vague and diffuse now began to see their theatre as more directly interventionist. In a way it was ironic that the Open Theatre should have begun its public career with *Viet Rock*, by Megan Terry, given its earlier commitment to the development of purely theatrical skills. Less surprising, perhaps, was the Living Theatre's choice of the American military as its image of the oppressive and destructive nature of experience in Kenneth Brown's *The Brig*, or the Performance Group's production of *Makbeth*, which presented America as a fascist society, *Commune* (1970), in which the My Lai killings were seen as integral to America's history of violence, and *Mother Courage and Her Children* (1974).

The San Francisco Mime Troupe turned from its performance orientation, which had resulted in productions of *Tartuffe* and *Ubu King*, to domestic social concerns and thence, in 1967, to the war, Goldoni's *L'Amant Militaire* being staged for its anti-war stance and *The Dragon Lady's Revenge* exploring the link between the war and drug trafficking. The Bread and Puppet Theatre, founded to explore the possibilities inherent in large-scale puppets, quickly became so involved in the anti-war movement that it became difficult to imagine a public demonstration without the mute, accusing figures developed by Peter Schumann, their classic anti-Vietnam presentation being *A Man Says Goodbye to his Mother* (1968). Even El Teatro Campesino, the Chicano theatre directed by Luis Valdez, turned to the war in *Vietnam Campesino* (1970) in which the Vietnam peasant, menaced by the American military, was seen as a natural brother to the Chicano fieldworker threatened by American capitalism.

The single playwright whose work bore the most obvious imprint of Vietnam, however, was David Rabe, who had himself served there. His works were not offered as anti-war plays. It is simply that the war lies behind all other experiences, making them translucent. The past shines so clearly through the present that it distorts it. His characters find themselves in situations that make no sense. Disoriented, they try to reconstruct their lives from fragmented memories. In *The Basic Training of Pavlo Hummel* the central character is initiated simultaneously into the skills of killing and first aid, the two so contradictory that it adds to the irony which frames the play as he lies wounded by a grenade thrown by a fellow soldier. In *Sticks and Bones* (1972) the protagonist, David, is literally what his society is symbolically – blind. He returns from the war physically and mentally wounded but, unlike Hal Ashby's movie, *Going Home*, this is not a work about therapy and reconciliation. In a perverse way the fantasies which haunt him – including a Vietnamese girl he has left behind – are more real than the society to which he returns, at least as represented by his family, consciously modelled, by Rabe, on a long-running radio and television situation comedy, 'The Adventures of Ozzie and Harriet'.

They come out of the world of Albee's *The American Dream;* he out of *Heart of Darkness*. He sees his nightmares as reality; they see their dreams as reality. His family is happy to embrace him as returning warrior; they are not willing to accept him as a demented and confused victim who accuses himself and them of cruelty. This was, of course, precisely the fate awaiting America's servicemen who returned traumatised, often bemused by drugs, suicidal and transfixed by guilt. David's drift towards suicide is encouraged by his family who wish only to be relieved of such an embarrassment. The play is part farce, part situation comedy, part absurdist drama. Moments of occasional lyricism counterpoint a language drained of content and function. Yet if Vietnam set this particular drama in motion it was not its cause. For that Rabe looks to an America raised on fantasy, an America for which reality appears through the viewfinder of a camera (David's brother aimlessly photographs the scene). When language and reality conflict it is reality that must defer. Where the bland equanimity of daily routine is disturbed by pain or tension they must be wished away. These qualities are not a product of Vietnam; Vietnam, it is implied, was made possible by them. The conflicts between and within the characters are conducted through a style which moves with deliberate unease between what passes for realism and what is evidently fantasy. For part of the time it borrows its aesthetic from the world of soap opera only to disturb that untroubled realism with elements from another world. Invited to 'Just be happy', David replies, 'You mean take some old man to a ditch of water, shove his head under, talk of cars and money till his feeble pawing stops, and then head on home to go in and out of doors and drive cars and sing sometimes.'[1] On one level Rabe seems to imply that if television played its role in ending the Vietnam war, it also played its part in accommodating its images of violence to the continuum of entertainment and fantasy. But, beyond that, *Sticks and Bones* dramatises a world in which euphemism and platitude, popular myth and bland routine have eroded a sense of the real, a world in which language has been drained of its power to carry knowledge or to communicate anything which threatens to intrude awareness of suffering or pain.

Much the same could be said of *Streamers* (1976). Though set in an army barracks, early in the war, and focusing on the lives of a group of soldiers for whom a posting to Vietnam is a constant threat, it is not a play fundamentally about Vietnam. The soldiers are already profoundly neurotic, alienated from one another and from themselves. The title refers to parachutes which fail to open and the play implies that this is a given, not only for this group of misfits and psychotics but for those outside the claustrophobic world of the military. Vietnam represents the threat of death which renders their daily rituals pointless. Their tentative gestures at control take place in the context of a contingency that can terminate their lives at any time. Their need is clear; their ability to satisfy that need, less so. The irony is deeper, however, than those generated by the war itself. Indeed to characterise Rabe simply as a Vietnam playwright is misleading. It is true that in many of his plays the war proved his point of reference, that its trauma has exercised a powerful pull on his sensibility, but the uncertainties he addresses go beyond that. Strategically it is the pressure which fractures character, exposes the fissures in experience, reveals the inadequacy of language, identifies the gap between individuals who share their circumstances if little else, but his plays in part offer a critique of American society, profoundly uncommunal, in retreat from the real, disturbed alike by the demands of personal and social life. Beyond that, he addresses more fundamental dislocations in experience.

Perhaps, though, that is the point about Vietnam. It disturbed an equanimity which was not merely social. The divisions it opened up in society may have healed with time but what it exposed about national values and the integrity of the self under pressure was not so easily forgotten. Behind the cliche of nightmare was a genuine sense that reality was not perhaps as self-evident as it appeared and the moral world more profoundly ambiguous than suggested by national myths of the City on the Hill or frontier fortitude. And because conscious parallels between Vietnam and America's past were drawn, the stability of that past was threatened. Much the same point was made by Tom Cole in *Medal of Honor Rag*, in which a white psychiatrist interviews a black Medal of Honor winner whose mind has given way under the contradictions of a war that was 'Brutal without glory, without meaning', in which he 'was trained to kill people of another world in their own homes, in order to help them'.[2] His faith in logic, morality and personal integrity destroyed, he allows the anarchy to enter his own being, as does the reporter in Amlin Gray's *How I Got that Story* (1979), slowly exposed to the corrosive nature of a world in which every structure is in a state of collapse, not least those of the play whose own stylistic dislocations mirror those of a society in trauma – a trauma which, in the hands of James McLure, in *Lone Star* (1977) and *Pvt Wars*, is presented as mordant humour. The latter, set in a mental hospital, creates characters for whom fantasy and reality are no longer separable and for whom language is in a state of near terminal collapse. The humour might suggest a degree of detachment, as the war itself began to recede, but the ironies are not redemptive. Fragmented lives never do come together.

It was evident from these plays and from the plethora of Vietnam movies in the 1980s – *Hamburger Hill, Platoon, Full Metal Jacket, Good Morning Vietnam* being merely the better known – that, unlike Korea, this was a war whose implications would still be explored several decades later. For a country whose national myths had to do with success, the integral self and a Messianic role, defeat, corruption and international obloquy were difficult to take. Far more than the Second World War, it disturbed a sense of the real and it is scarcely surprising that the theatre – described by David Mamet as the 'dream life of the nation' – should reflect this both in terms of subject and style.

Walter Benjamin's remark that 'every epoch dreams its successor'[3] may have inspired the wrath of Theodore Adorno who thought it smacked of utopianism, but it is hard not to feel the pressure of such a conviction behind much sixties theatre in America. The transformations of theatre, in which the actor can dissolve the self in the name of role, became a clue to, indeed a paradigm of, social transformations. This was an exemplary theatre designed to show the freedom of becoming rather than the stasis of being. That is why character is so often smashed, presented not as a series of actions continuous with the self but as a range of performed gestures. Sometimes, as in gay theatre, Chicano theatre, black theatre, or native American theatre, archetype is pressed in the direction of stereotype as evidence of the pressure of history, social prejudice or economics, as proof of the self's surrender of density. Sometimes, though, that stereotype becomes the mask to be torn away by the reborn self or, particularly as is the case in gay theatre, consciously deployed by the rebel inhabiting and hence colonising an identity designed to demean (Charles Ludlam's gay Ridiculous Theatre Company, Ronald Tavel's *Lady Godiva*, Harvey Fierstein's *Torch Song Trilogy*).

Adorno offered his own epigram. The recent past, he suggested, 'always presents itself as though it has been destroyed by catastrophes. *Hic et nunc* I would say that it thereby presents itself as pre-history.'[4] So it is for the writer for whom history implies its own transcendence. The assumption is that the black American, the Chicano, the native American and, in a sense, women have been excluded from history if not from its consequences and that the articulation of that fact is an essential step towards change. This is a theatre of transformation, in which the spiritually, socially and emotionally emasculated man comes into his own (Lorraine Hansberry's *A Raisin in the Sun*, 1959), the slave becomes the rebel (LeRoi Jones's *The Slave*, 1964), the campesino the radical activist (Luis Valdez's *La Quinta Temporada*, 1966), the victim the principal (Marsha Norman's *'night, Mother*). The fact that the theatre, by its very nature, deals in transformations is perhaps one reason why it proved the central genre in the sixties and early seventies, a period, anyway, when performance was a primary trope, metaphor and political reality.

The splintering of the audience and its reformation as a series of groups allied by race, gender or political persuasion was a reminder not of anomie but of communal strength, of a realignment with clear social and political implications. For Luis Valdez, for Amiri Baraka, for the Bread and Puppet Theatre or the San Francisco Mime Troupe, the theatre was in large part a means to an end, a way of clarifying process into image, of displaying the mechanisms of manipulation and suppression and thereby identifying the possibility and direction of change. It was a theatre designed in some sense to dissolve in its own social realisation. Far from seeking access to the literary canon, such writers and groups turned their back on the literary world, were uninterested in the response of critics or a sophisticated audience and sought their justification on the streets, in the city parks or in those cultural centres whose primary objective was recovering a usable past (El Centro Campesino Cultural). They plotted a radically transformed future.

In a curious way many of these theatres depended, at least initially, for their relevance, their energy, their power, on the very system which they opposed. For Sartre this is the essence of rebellion. Speaking in the context of his study of Baudelaire, he remarked that: 'The rebel is careful to maintain intact the abuses from which he suffers in order to rebel against them . . . He wants neither to destroy, nor transcend, but only to stand up against the order of things. The more he attacks it, the more he secretly respects it; the rights that he openly contests, he preserves intact in the depths of his heart.'[5] This is a proposition which those who challenged the racial, patriarchal, social and economic structure of American society would instinctively and fiercely have rejected. After all, what was their theatre about if not radical change and a rejection of historic injustice? But in fact in many of the early plays by radical playwrights or theatre companies, personal and group identities were born out of the moment of confrontation and in that sense power was still conceded to those they would resist.

Political and social victory would thus drain their drama not only of its relevance but ultimately of its meaning, a consummation devoutly to be wished, perhaps, but inevitably those who turned to theatre for the expression of their beliefs were liable to have a double commitment: to the reality which they transmuted into theatre and to the theatre into which they transmuted reality. It is not that such people are careerists but that their commitments of necessity included a commitment to the mode in which they chose to express themselves. They were the products not only of a social history but of an aesthetic history. It is not so much that they wished to preserve the power system which perversely conferred meaning on those who rebelled against it but that the theatre was itself in part a product of that power system and encoded its meaning.

The price of revolt was often a shrinking of language, a simplification which was partly a response to the new audiences they wished to address and partly a suspicion of articulateness as the source of alien values and of an ambiguity inimical to action . What, after all, is our status as eavesdroppers on a drama shaped for other ears? The use of Spanish in Chicano theatre may have its practical implications, but it is also exclusionary. Amiri Baraka's black revolutionary plays may strike a response from black audiences while being rejected as simplistic by white ones. Can we hope to derive the full implications of Hanay Geiogamah's *49*, which draws on native American traditions, while not sharing or fully understanding the history and context of those traditions? Gay theatre may have one meaning for gays and quite another for those who view that world from the outside.

A character in T.S. Eliot's *The Family Reunion* rightly observes that 'the particular has no language'.[6] Nor it does. The unique is hermetic, incommunicable. Its expression is its denial. In that sense language itself is a denial. Between the thought and the word falls the shadow. Language is, in its very origin, an act of translation and translation is a search for equivalence. An experience generated by or inscribed in one language can only be rendered into another by identifying or asserting an analogical relationship and, as Alain Robbe-Grillet has said, 'All analogies are dangerous.'[7] They are, however, all we have got. Moreover, this is also the process underlying the construction of metaphor. Thus translation – between languages, between people, between experiences – partakes of the metaphorical. It is, in that sense, in its essence poetic, which is to say an act of faith. But that is its point. It is born out of a will to understand, to believe that understanding is possible. Not for nothing are the roots of theatre in religious ceremony. As members of an audience we are never mere observers, and sixties theatre capitalised on that fact, turning the audience either into communicants or into the accused.

But the co-opting imagination may risk denying the very liberal spirit which gives it birth just as the centrifugal force of American culture can homogenise those for whom their distance from the centre and their distinction from the norm is the essence of their being. The problem is that

American culture is a vortex which draws into the centre whatever begins on the periphery. To rebel against America and its values is seen as quintessentially American. As Saul Bellow has remarked, 'There's hardly anything that can be invented by any American rebel which won't be incorporated into the general cultural effort of the country and be richly rewarded.'[8] Well, perhaps not richly but otherwise, for a while at least, this proved as true of black drama as it did of the random energy of sixties performance theatre, of nudity and scatological language.

When Robert Lowell said of Diana Trilling's distaste for sixties demonstrations that she was a 'housekeeping goddess of reason, preferring the confines of her mind to experience',[9] he was pronouncing the basic principles of a decade. To be authentic it was necessary to act and to feel. Ratiocination seemed too close to rationalisation. The search for an authentic self lay on the other side of a search for an authentic society. At the Fourth Congress of Czechoslovak Writers, in June 1967, the novelist Ludvik Vaculik declared that art and power were 'not suited for each other',[10] simultaneously a plea for irresponsibility, as art liberates itself from mere functionalism, and a call for rededication, as it regroups to annihilate its persecutors. It was a statement that had less to do with historical accuracy – art and power, Plato notwithstanding, having not merely co-existed but sustained one another in all societies – than with a conviction that art should be oppositional (two decades later Vaclav Havel, a playwright, became the first president of a newly free Czechoslovakia, art and power coming into creative alignment).

When Robert Lowell refused to enter the White House for a reception during the Vietnam years it may have been a gesture tainted with a curious kind of hubris but it was also a symbol of his refusal to see art co-opted by power. Art was itself to be a countervailing force and the theatre in particular became a focus for revolt, not least because of its public nature. In Paris in 1968 a sign outside the Odéon theatre, occupied by students and other political and cultural insurrectionaries, read; 'When the General Assembly becomes a bourgeois theatre, we must make bourgeois theatre into a General Assembly.' The question was to be whether a decade with a special fondness for the slogan would prove capable of producing an art or indeed a society in which the slogan justified itself through its own immediate obsolescence.

For Milan Kundera his was a culture in which 'the guarding of frontiers is still regarded as a greater virtue than crossing them'.[11] But, suddenly, the crossing of frontiers became a political and cultural imperative on an international scale and nowhere more so than in the United States where racial, social and gender limits were transgressed and the boundaries separating art from society, audience from performer and theatre from the street were consistently and energetically penetrated. And where would the revolt against constraint, against history, against the delegitimation of feeling, a spontaneous communality, end, and an instinctive and pre-linguistic awareness of truth and justice begin, except with the word?

When in *Vanity Fair* Becky Sharp decides to subvert the world into which she has been born and in which she has suffered injustice, she begins by flinging a dictionary at the feet of her first oppressors. She rejects the grammar, the vocabulary, the lexis, the etymology, the history of power locked up inside the language which has contained and threatened her, in favour of another system of signs. Her life becomes a consistent sequence of lies as she shows a contempt for language and through language for those who have shaped it and the world they have bequeathed her. It is through her body that she articulates her meaning and negotiates her reality. So, too, in the sixties and early seventies, those excluded from the mainstream of American society, those marginalised socially and economically, those who found themselves the victims of language no less than of social action, turned to physical being as a denial of the irrelevance and social impotence presented to them as their fate. The ethos of the era was being there. The sign of authenticity was presence, whether that was the faith of a performance theatre, suspicious of the deceptions of language and anxious to explore the possibilities of secular ritual, or the conviction of those who wished to change the shape of social action. The one wished to redefine the nature of the real, the other to expose its mechanisms and alter its direction. Not to have been on the Selma march, the march on Washington, the Vietnam protest rallies was to have missed the party, to have denied yourself an authenticating experience. This was precisely the accusation levelled at James Baldwin who failed to attend the rally at the United Nations protesting the killing of Patrice Lumumba, who did not go to Oakland, California, when the Black Panthers came under deadly assault. His excuse was that he was writing, that he was sitting alone at his typewriter, a double sin at a time when propinquity was virtue and the writer's necessary act of withdrawal suspected as an act of betrayal. This was the time when the Living Theatre took its romantic message onto the streets of New Haven hoping for the clash with police which would validate its model of a coercive police state. It was the time when demonstrations were very self-consciously offered as street theatre, frequently with theatrical groups playing a major role. Beyond the authenticating power of the moment lay a hidden audience, an audience who stayed at home but watched the drama unfold on television, a self-consciously staged melodrama in which the leading characters were often very deliberately paraded as caricatures, puppets whose very form implied their manipulation by forces and ideologies readily identified and objectified. This was the medieval play writ large with virtue and vice portrayed in homilies enacted on the city streets, sometimes in wordless pantomime, at other times in a language deliberately simplified or amplified for polemical reasons. The image on the screen – whether it be the Pentagon failing to levitate at the behest of a sea of people or marchers huddled against the policeman's club – spoke more clearly than words.

Yet for those anxious to deploy the power of theatre in the cause of social and political change language was a central issue, not least because it contained and expressed the very history that had to be challenged. Just as Carlos Fuentes has spoken of the way in which the 'Renaissance language of the conquest hides the Medieval marrow of the colonizing enterprize'[12] in Latin America, so writers became sensitised to the irony of articulating their experiences through a historically stained language which had itself marginalised that experience. Thus it was that LeRoi Jones warned against black writers becoming 'fluent in the jargon of power', while Luis Valdez infiltrated Spanish into his Chicano plays and the native American playwright Hanay Geiogamah supplemented the word with a physical solidarity which had its own imperatives and, it should be said, ambiguities.

In his autobiography Jean-Paul Sartre described his sense of being inhabited by the dead, those whom he did not know but whom he saves from annihilation through his being. That sense of redeeming the past through the present, of giving voice, through present being, to those silenced by time, is strong in the black writer, more especially since the dead were silenced – socially, economically, politically, culturally – when in life. So it is that the past is revisited, reinvented by the writer who thereby asserts more than the simple existence of ancestors. The past has to be redeemed before the present can be claimed and the future plotted. It is the task which Ralph Ellison and John Williams, Toni Morrison and Alice Walker have set themselves in the novel. Alex Haley's odyssey (whether a purely accurate or partly mythical reconstruction of a link to the past) in *Roots* re-enacted a journey implicit in the present identity of every black American. So, too, in the theatre, Theodore Ward's *Our Lan'* projected backwards in time that articulate resistance necessary to present rebellion, as LeRoi Jones's *The Slave* revealed the rebel hidden at the heart of the slave. The community celebrated by the black writer (or, indeed, by the feminist) is not one bounded by the moment. Solidarity extends backwards to embrace those whose suffering released the present to assume its responsibilities and acknowledge its debt. To free oneself from history it is necessary first to confront it and in confronting it charge it with significance. When, in Alice Walker's *In the Temple of My Familiar* one of her characters speaks in tongues (like a character who does likewise in Canadian author Margaret Laurence's *The Jest of God*) she does so because suppressed voices have been suddenly released, voices from the past which become the voice of the present. That is what black theatre has in part concerned itself with doing, from LeRoi Jones to August Wilson; it has also been a significant sub-theme in women's drama (Lavonne Mueller's *Little Victories*, 1983, which brings together Susan B. Anthony and Joan of Arc, Ruth Wolff's *The Abdication*, 1969, set in 1655, Eve Merriam's *Out of Our Father's House*, 1975, which ranges from the eighteenth to the twentieth centuries, or Joan Schenkar's *Signs of Life* which includes the figure of Alice James). In much the same way the Kiowa playwright, Hanay Geiogamah, takes us into the past in *Foghorn* (1973) as, in a different sense, does the Chinese-American playwright David Henry Hwang in *FOB*. The past is not to be preserved as an icon but assimilated, recast, restructured to serve the exigencies of the present.

The theatre offers the black American a multiplicity of selves denied in the social world. The myths of white America celebrate possibility, an identity which can be reshaped to meet each new contingency (Natty Bumppo dissolving and reforming as Leatherstocking, Long Rifle, Hawkeye, Deerslayer); the history of the black American is one in which possibility is denied and identity fixed and defined by a society which feared the black Proteus. It was Strindberg who pointed out the power of the theatre to deny fixity: 'I lived and I live multifariously the lives of all the people I describe . . . I live in all ages.'[13] In the case of the black writer that multifariousness stands as social fact.

For a time, LeRoi Jones (reborn as Amiri Baraka) chose a form of silence, laying aside drama in favour of direct intervention, not out of Rimbaud's despair at changing the world but out of a distrust of his own articulateness and of the indirections of art. George Steiner quotes Thomas Carlyle's remark that 'Speech that leads not to action . . . still more that hinders it, is a nuisance on the Earth.'[14] This was a conviction held by an increasing number of those in the sixties and early seventies who saw social change as imperative, and certainly by Amiri Baraka. It was a conviction that at times created a bias against the aesthetic, a distrust of the ambiguous, the oblique, the self referring, the rational, the verbal, the psychological. So it was that a number of black writers and critics who patrolled the boundaries of black self-definition with an unrelenting zeal and distrust of detachment, perspective and ambiguity, turned not only James Baldwin but also Ralph Ellison into figures of suspicion.

In a search for a wider audience (or sometimes a narrower one defined by race, gender or sexual persuasion) and for social utility, subtleties of speech were sacrificed to broader gestures, the stereotype,

The archetype. A crudity of form and expression was seen, at times, as evidence of authenticity and incorruptibility. It is not that the imagination gives way to the authenticity of fact – though, for a brief, inglorious period the ill-named 'theatre of fact' staked a claim of that kind – but that the imagination also had a history which had to be confronted, a history articulated by those in a position to enforce meaning. It was that hegemony that was now to be challenged.

Joseph Brodsky has suggested that it is language that best survives the collapse of empire and that often it is the language of those from the provinces or the outskirts that, paradoxically, sustains if not the system then the culture. In America it could be doubted if there was such a centre to be preserved but, as the American empire began to slip into decline in the 1960s and thereafter (the nervous bombast of John F. Kennedy being quickly exposed), so the marginal, the dispossessed, the outcast, the disregarded moved to the centre. In a paradoxical way America began to feed off the energy of those who contested its values most directly and who had been denied access to its promises.

Theatre can enact what the novel can only describe. It invites our literal collaboration, in real time, with events whose fictional status is balanced by the physical fact of their presentation. James Baldwin's *Blues for Mr Charlie* (1964) may dramatise a reality (Emmet Till's murder) transposed into fiction, but that fiction is then recast as the reality not of murder but of shared experience. On the stage we see the black and white world divided – the stage itself being offered as a paradigm of social divisions – but we know that the interracial cast has collaboratively joined together to dramatise those divisions and the play's ambiguous ending, in which a white liberal, guilty of betrayal and bad faith, may or may not be permitted to work with a black civil rights group, is effectively resolved, given that this was an Actors Studio production, by the presence of an interracial audience who, at least for the purpose of this production, have joined together in their response to the drama. The audience, in other words, is an actor in this drama, as is the reader. What the reader lacks, however, is the sense and reality of being part of a group whose whole is greater than the sum of its parts. This is a vital aspect of theatre and never more so than in the 1960s.

By the same token, for black theatre groups to deny access to whites, for Chicano, gay or feminist theatre groups to perform for audiences who define themselves in terms of race, national origin, gender or sexual preference, is to propose another model of community, a resistant group who discover and assert their solidarity precisely through their presence on such occasions. Elsewhere in the world the subversiveness of theatre is readily apparent as groups foregather in a theatre who would be arrested if they chose to come together anywhere else. The mere act of assembling is subversive. Vaclav Havel's revolt began in a theatre, though the logic of that revolt would one day take him out of the theatre and into the Presidential Palace.

The fact that the theatre operates in the present tense gives it a special appeal to those who wish to mobilise present action, to become actors in their own drama. That presentness, as opposed to the past tense of the novel, lends an immediacy to work which is designed to provoke present action. A book finds its individual audience. A play must summon into existence a community of selves who mutually agree to one another's co-presence. For a white reader to engage an aggressive novel by a black novelist in the protective and even resistant context of his or her own home is wholly different from joining an audience in which that person may be in a racial minority, in a theatre which may be located in an area which breeds its own insecurities.

In the 1960s the theatre sought to recuperate the community which was its own condition of being. It celebrated the coming together of actors on a stage and the conjoining of actors and audience. At a time when community was threatened – socially, politically – it offered itself as paradigm. At a time when those pressed to the margin of the social world could feel themselves displaced, alienated and disregarded, the theatre chose to move them to the centre of dramatic action. For few was this as true as for the black American who for too long had played only a walk on part in society no less than in theatre.

Alain Robbe-Grillet has pointed out that 'Flaubert wrote the new novel of 1860. Proust the new novel of 1910. The writer must proudly consent to bear his own date, knowing that there are no masterpieces in eternity, but only works in history, and that they have left the past behind them and heralded the future.'[15] Lorraine Hansberry's *A Raisin in the Sun* bears its own date. It is a work in history. Its history, however, is not congruent with that of her contemporaries who were contemporaries in time but not experience. Her own references to a kinship between her central character, Walter Younger, and Arthur Miller's Willy Loman, in *Death of a Salesman*, merely underscores the differences between them. Miller's play concerned its protagonist's obsession with the past, a past which holds the clue to his sense of failure; but in terms of form the play leans into the future, its dislocations evidencing that formal innovation which constituted the logic of Robbe-Grillet's celebration of the new. The form and style of Hansberry's play takes us further back, to the realistic drama of Clifford Odets; but that realism is not accidental. It is the essence of its claim to our attention. It is an exercise in truth-telling in which subject takes precedence over form. As she herself remarked, 'The realistic playwright states not only what is, but what can and should be.'[16]

For the black American, history had been projected in slow motion. The franchise, social freedom, economic independence, educational equality, individual autonomy were endlessly deferred. Access to the theatre itself was first severely restricted and then inhibited. The urgencies of the black writer were, accordingly, not those of the white. Black history was a kind of parallel universe, related to white history but out of synch with it. There was a black audience, not yet fully attuned, perhaps, to drama as a mirror to social experience and an agent of social change, but increasingly looking for self-images, publicly enacted, which offered something more than a pathological view of their experiences. *A Raisin in the Sun* does lean into the future, then, but at the level of plot and character. New commitments and new resources are identified, new sources of energy. In Miller's play no such vision is held out. The only advance seems to lie in Biff's retreat to an earlier stage of social development as he leaves the city to work on a farm. Walter Younger and family move off towards suburbia. Lorraine Hansberry has to have a commitment to the future. It is a cultural and political imperative. Those who possess even a limited autonomy, who can at least plausibly lay claim to the myths no less than the substance of a material life, can afford to question the meaning of such myths and realities; those who are a step and more behind cannot. Willy Loman ends his life owning his own home but suffocated by suburbia and vaguely aware of the inadequacy of a life mortgaged to a dream of success. Walter Younger is denied access to that suburbia and desperately needs to retain his faith in the possibility and ultimately the reality of the American dream. The Younger family are closer kin to Odets's Berger family than to Miller's Lomans. They, too, are called upon to wake and sing.

A Raisin in the Sun was a key text. The first play by a black woman to win the New York Drama Critics' Circle Award, the first play by a black woman to be performed on Broadway, the longest-running play by a black writer on Broadway for a quarter of a century and a production which launched the career of a number of major black actors, it marked the beginning of a new direction in the American theatre. The black American was not a stranger to Broadway, though the Great White Way was not inappropriately named. Langston Hughes's racial melodrama of 1935, *Mulatto*, secured a successful run, while Theodore Ward's *Our Lan'* appeared in 1946 and Louis Peterson's *Take a Giant Step* in 1953–4. Broadway, however, was hardly a natural home for dramas that contested, as Hughes's and Ward's drama had done, the values and practices of American society. But the mood was changing. During the fifties and sixties the plight of black Americans was back on the agenda, put there by ordinary black Americans no longer willing to accept second-class citizenship. In a way *A Raisin in the Sun* was a classic statement of civil rights liberalism. A black family is poised to move to the suburbs in order to escape the determinism of inner-city life. But confronting them is an urbane racism, backed up by the threat of violence, and their own failure of will and imagination. The women of the family are determined, the man less so. His spirit has been so thoroughly eroded by years of social disregard that he places a low value on his own integrity. The play is an account of his recovery of will, supported and provoked by a family that now seems united in its desire to challenge the white world. The struggle of the black writer has always been for the right to articulate his or her own life. So it is that the protagonist of Theodore Ward's *Our Lan'* is pointedly described as the son of an 'inarticulate father' and a 'mute but undaunted mother'. His strength lies in his ability and willingness to argue his case and if necessary to underpin this articulateness with action. The same is true of *A Raisin in the Sun*.

There is a parallel between the setting and those who inhabit it which makes the later decision to move house equally a decision to remake those who inhabit it. So we are told that its furnishings are 'tired', that, once the embodiment of 'love and even hope', they have had to 'accommodate' over time. The carpet shows its 'weariness', a 'depressing uniformity'. We are told that 'all pretenses but living itself have long since vanished from the very atmosphere of this room'. When Walter's wife,

Ruth, appears we are told that, once pretty, she is now a 'settled woman', her hopes frustrated, while 'disappointment has already begun to hang in her face'. The single window which provides the sole natural light which the family enjoy, and which allows only a faint glow to 'fight its way through', is a parallel to the hope which has never quite been extinguished. Like the plant which Mama nurtures, 'they ain't never had enough sunshine'.[17] They have been relegated to this overcrowded Southside apartment as they have been pressed to the edge of the social system. It is, as Ruth observes, a 'rat trap', perhaps, like the ringing alarm clock which opens the play, an implicit reference to Richard Wright's classic novel, *Native Son*, also set in Chicago's Southside, whose opening pages also present a cornered rat as an image of black oppression, a reality and a metaphor to be transcended.

The play carries an epigraph from Langston Hughes which asks what happens to a dream deferred. The two options which he proposes are the collapse of all hope or apocalypse. Lorraine Hansberry dramatises a third option – personal renewal through social action. In doing so she created a play which accurately reflected the mood and strategy of a civil rights movement for which the desegregation of housing, along with the desegregation of education, transportation and all public services was a major objective. An inheritance suddenly offers the Younger family the opportunity to transform their circumstances. For Walter Younger it is a chance to redeem his manhood, to buy a liquor business which will restore a sense of pride. For his daughter, Beneatha, it is the cash necessary to finance her medical training. For his mother, beyond aiding Beneatha, it is the key to a new life in the white suburbs. In the hierarchy of values which the play proposes it is this last which represents the desirable in so far as it is their implied challenge to the white power structure which gives them a sense of unity and purpose. The fact that Lorraine Hansberry's own family had been involved in efforts to secure the desegregation of housing suggests a degree of personal involvement in the play's ostensible subject, but *A Raisin in the Sun* is not offered as social paradigm. As Theodore Adorno observed of committed art, it 'is not intended to generate ameliorative measures, legislative acts or practical institutions . . . but to work at the level of fundamental attitudes'. For Sartre, its task is to 'awaken the free choice of the agent which makes authentic existence possible at all'.[18]

A Raisin in the Sun is rooted in personal experience, an experience which turned on Hansberry's racial identity, and though the struggle of the Younger family for a sense of dignity, for a space within which self-definition can become possible, was not restricted to race, it is clear that for Hansberry the play rests if not on the fact of race then on the meaning ascribed to it. As she explained,

From the moment the first curtain goes up until they make their decision at the end, the fact of racial oppression, unspoken and unalluded to, other than the fact of how they live, runs through the play. It is inescapable. The reason these people are in a ghetto in America is because they are negroes. They are discriminated against brutally and horribly, so that in that sense it's always there, and the basis of many things that they feel – and which they feel are just perfectly ordinary human things between members of a family – are always predicated, are always resting on the fact that they live ghettoized lives . . . but overtly it isn't introduced until they are asked by the author to act on the problem which is the decision to move or not move out of this area.[19]

The feminist writer Adrienne Rich, while acknowledging Hansberry's publicly stated feminism, her awareness, expressed in an interview with Studs Terkel in 1959, that 'Obviously the most oppressed of any oppressed group will be its women . . . since women . . . are oppressed in society, and if you've got an oppressed group, they're twice oppressed',[20] nonetheless criticises her women characters. She notes, in particular, that her second play, which was to have been called *The Sign in Jenny Reed's Window*, mysteriously metamorphosed into *The Sign in Sidney Brustein's Window*, while a central figure in her posthumous work *Les Blancs* underwent a similar gender transformation. She hints at a discontent with the women characters in *A Raisin in the Sun* but forbears to identify the nature of that discontent unless it be her concern that here, as elsewhere in Hansberry's work, the focus moves to the man – to Walter Younger. It is hard to agree. Walter may declare a new level of commitment but he does so under pressure from the women who challenge him and who between them represent a courageous past and a determined future.

A Raisin in the Sun is a celebration. It celebrates not merely endurance, sheer survival, but possibility. As a writer Hansberry set her face against despair or cynicism. In a prospectus for the John Brown Memorial Theatre, to be constructed in Harlem, she denounced what she called the 'idle, impotent and obscurantist efforts of a mistaken avant-garde',[21] as in *The Sign in Sidney Brustein's Window* she was to include a self-pitying absurdist playwright who generalises personal disappointments into a dramatic strategy and a social philosophy. Hers was not to be an art of victims. Each one of the characters in *A Raisin in the Sun* is self-deceiving. The pressures of the eternal world have pressed them in the direction of stereotype because they have internalised that narrowing of possibility which is a fact of their social circumstance. Walter has become shiftless and unreliable, his mother the domineering matriarch, his wife the doggedly enduring drudge, his daughter the self-concerned naif. What they learn in the course of the play is the danger of becoming trapped in their roles as absolutely as they appear to be trapped in their physical surroundings. Indeed by the end of the play it is evident that the crucial change has less to do with location than sensibility. They have allowed themselves to be contained and defined by a history which only seems implacable. It is a potential awkwardness of the play, however, that these transformations depend upon a *deus ex machina* in the form of an insurance policy whose proceeds alone seem to provoke change. In Miller's play the policy is a chimera, final evidence of Willy Loman's failure to understand his life; here, as in *Awake and Sing*, it is the catalyst of change.

Lorraine Hansberry died in 1964, her death effectively closing her second play, *The Sign in Sidney Brustein's Window*, which had otherwise been sustained, for over a hundred performances, by the support of friends and admirers. Though it had taken several years to write it is almost as though she knew that her death were impending in that the play is over-crowded with ideas. At its heart is a concern for commitment in all its guises – political, racial, sexual – and an awareness of betrayal as a central motif of human existence. Pressed together in a single Greenwich Village apartment we find a homosexual absurdist playwright, a failed actress, a reformist political candidate, a call girl, a Jewish bohemian, a betrayed wife and a black ex-communist. In one way or another they debate, rather too articulately and self-consciously, the meaning of existence, the possibility of action, the virtue of flawed faith versus cynical despair. Each character is weighted with a personal history generalised into a philosophy of life. Each character is tempted to recoil from a moral life by an experience of rejection or an ambition which places the self at the centre. Something has gone wrong. Each one has failed and not only in personal dreams. Each one has been failed, by others, by the social system, by human nature. The debate, therefore, is over the legitimacy of despair, of which corruption is merely a symptom.

At the centre of the play is Sidney Brustein, histrionic, a performer. His wife is an actress, his neighbour a playwright, his sister a sexual performer who enacts fantasies for the men who thereby sustain her fantasy.

Everyone in the play, in other words, is an actor – a deceitful politician, a wife sustaining the facade of a happy marriage, a man pretending to be free of prejudice. But here performance is evasion. The sign in the window is not an accurate account of the truth. This is a world in which compromise is presented as wisdom, cynicism as logical tactic, self-pity as legitimate, betrayal as inevitable. The prejudice which the Younger family had encountered in *A Raisin in the Sun* is here presented in a wider context, for in a world of moral detachment there are no imperatives which transcend the self. Sidney Brustein's belief, articulated by the cynical reform politician, that 'Politics are . . . compromise-ridden exercises in futility'[22] is matched by his wife's refusal to involve herself in other people's lives: 'Live and let live, that's all.'[23] Meanwhile, her sister Gloria has sacrificed her moral being in the name of nothing more than a fancy life-style. Explaining the context of the play, Lorraine Hansberry located it in terms of the Sartre–Camus debates of the post-war years. As she explained,

The silhouette of the Western intellectual poised in hesitation before the flames of involvement was an accurate symbolism of some of my closest friends, some of whom crossed each other leaping in and out, for instance, of the Communist Party. Others searched, as agonizingly, for some ultimate justification of their lives in the abstractions flowing out of London or Paris. Still others were contorted into seeking a meaningful repudiation of *all* justifications of anything and had, accordingly, turned to Zen, action painting or even just Jack Kerouac.[24]

It was her response, in other words, to what she saw as the betrayal implicit in absurdist thought – which she mocks in a stylised scene between Sidney and his sister Gloria in which 'each speaks . . . stiffly and unnaturally' in a 'fragmented delivery beyond sense or sequence, as if lucidity no longer required logic. An absurdist orgy . . . a disintegration of reality to parallel the disintegration in SIDNEY's world.'[25] In the papers she left behind on her death there was a parody of Beckett's *Waiting for Godot*. On the other hand she rebelled equally against the coercive logic of communism and the restrictive language and thought generated by a view of the world bounded and defined by race. We are shown where such interpretations of experience may lead as Gloria commits suicide, the logic of her own life, her rejection by her black lover and the casual uninvolvement of those around her, leading to self-destruction. It is a play which urges commitment less at the level of political action, which is merely one aspect of experience, than at the level of human engagement.

The Sign in Sidney Brustein's Window is not without its sentimentalities. It is overly schematic, the various betrayals being self-consciously developed in parallel. Too much is compacted into a work in which characters prove all too articulate, spelling out their political, social and literary philosophies in a way which is not always convincing. The play is Hansberry's *Ship of Fools*, representative types being brought together to debate issues rather than enact them. At the same time she had begun to experiment with form, to explore the state of mind which made the events of *A Raisin in the Sun* possible. It was not a desertion of black concerns nor even a refusal to be constrained by them, but an attempt to locate them in terms of a wider historical and philosophical context. It was a strange play to float on Broadway; that it did not immediately sink was a result of the financial support of those who were both aware of the tragedy of a dying playwright and touched by a play which addressed dilemmas which were real enough for a generation wary of a commitment which might prove personally and artistically destructive but socially and morally redemptive.

Lorraine Hansberry wrote other works, works which specifically engaged the realities of the black experience. *The Drinking Gourd*, a play for television about the 'peculiar institution' of slavery, was never made; *Les Blancs*, partially reconstructed by her husband Robert Nemiroff, and set in colonial Africa, was not produced until six years after her death; a post-nuclear play, *Where Are the Flowers*, was never performed and a planned drama on Mary Wollstonecraft never written. Other projects included an opera about Toussaint L'Ouverture, a musical based on native American Oliver LaFarge's novel *Laughing Boy* and, reputedly, a play about Abe Lincoln. Lorraine Hansberry's creative life was a short one. She completed work on *A Raisin in the Sun* in 1957. Seven years later she was dead of cancer. Theatrically, she was not an innovator; her experiments with form were no more radical than her politics. With her first play, however, she succeeded in achieving dramatically what the Civil Rights movement was achieving socially. If the play's occasional sentimentalities made it recognisable Broadway fare, its social concerns did not. In this play the white world is marginalised, its hypocrisies being deftly exposed without being caricatured. The potential for action lies not with the representatives of a morally corrupt society but with those black Americans who construct their lives out of decisions made.

James Baldwin showed the same ambiguity in his drama as he had in his prose. Thus, where in his essays his pronouns claimed an identity with the white American he threatened with apocalypse, in *Blues for Mr Charlie* he wished both to castigate and embrace the white liberal. If in *Another Country* he equivocated over a black protagonist consumed by his own rage, in *Blues for Mr Charlie* he did much the same thing. Richard has returned from the North, carrying with him photographs of white girls, symbols of his desire to revenge himself on history. Unwilling to accede to a southern code which requires him to subordinate himself to white racists, he precipitates a clash. The result is his murder, legalised when his assailant is freed by a white jury, a white liberal newspaperman, Parnell, failing, at the last moment, to stand by those for whom he claims sympathy. The play ends with preparations for a Civil Rights march which Parnell begs to join.

Blues for Mr Charlie is a confused play. Baldwin's thumb is securely on the scales. The only white liberal is severely compromised not only by his last-minute betrayal – insufficiently motivated – but by the sexual rather than moral motivation which he is given. The ending thus becomes merely ironic as the interracial co-operation is undercut by Baldwin's unwillingness to concede that moral foundation for liberalism which alone would make sense of the play's concluding moments. It is unclear, too, whether Richard is killed because he chooses to press the confrontation or because the woman he loves has persuaded him to lay aside his gun. His father, Meridian, speaks of the Bible and the gun as representing two possible futures, but there is little in the play, except at the level of rhetoric, to suggest that anything but the latter can effect change. The Civil Rights marches are to continue, but his identification of the incorrigibly corrupt nature of liberalism and the implacable corrosiveness of southern racism makes it difficult to see how they are to succeed.

It is true that the play is called *Blues for Mr Charlie* and that its focus, therefore, is designed to be in part on the white community whose historical failures have precipitated the present confrontation. It is a community, however, which for the most part he seems content to parody, often very effectively, and whose only critic can be dismissed as a man corrupted by his own fantasies. There is an element of parody, too, in his treatment of the black community. The minister is equivocal, the rebel consumed by anger, the redemptive woman sexually ubiquitous. And since the only alternative to Old Testament retribution, the fire next time, symbolised by the gun, is New Testament love it is at least confusing that that love should take a sexual form and be dispensed with such undiscriminating generosity.

Blues for Mr Charlie is unashamedly presented as a melodrama not least because the world it dramatises is itself inherently melodramatic. The South has, after all, chosen to theatricalise itself, preferring to stage history as myth. Whether costumed as cavaliers or white-sheeted members of the Klan, its inhabitants have presented themselves as actors in a drama in which race played a central role. Baldwin's play begins with a gun-shot. The stage is divided along racial lines. His characters play out roles which seem to have been handed to them, speaking their lines self-consciously as though, even in private confrontation, they are aware of an unseen audience. The Civil Rights march is itself a piece of theatre. In his essays Baldwin is restrained by his own rhetorical strategy. His carefully balanced sentences, rooted in the calm language of the King James Bible, tended to displace into language what was born in the pain of dislocation and injustice. His grammar denied the threat of dissolution which he identified. His very reasonableness was a denial of the urgency of his warnings. In the theatre that voice disappears to be replaced by a pluralism of voices, while violence is permitted to break open what the prose style of the essays contained and controlled. For the fact is that the reality of southern experience was that the sophistication of language and the subtleties of art alike had been met with the crude finality of the gun-shot too often to sustain confidence in either. In that sense the surrender of subtlety in *Blues for Mr Charlie* is deliberate and calculated, while in the context of the South the fact of segregation – recreated in the division of the stage into blacktown and whitetown – had indeed proved more powerful than the tentative attempts at reconciliation which are shown as surviving only in intent, not fact.

For LeRoi Jones colour was a frontier of experience, the point at which language and myths break down. The experiences of the different races, he implied, are contiguous but not congruent. To move from one world to another is to necessitate a rite of passage – in his case, as in that of so many others, a change of name. In his black revolutionary plays he insisted on the need to reject the style and substance of white aspirations. The danger, he recognised, was to permit the corruption of experience by language. Reborn as Amiri Baraka he deliberately coarsened his effects, eschewing the ambiguities of *Dutchman* and *The Slave* and turning character into polemical gesture. It is as though he wished to deny a potential white readership/audience a purchase on works designed to resist that indeterminacy of meaning privileged by the literary critic. These plays have their indirections, being essentially didactic fables. What they do not permit is a perverse reading. They are in the service of personal and social transformations which make the plays themselves merely means to a social end. They deny density, ambiguity, opacity. The aesthetic becomes suspect. He began, however, in another mode and in another genre.

His journey from LeRoi Jones, poet, influenced by Charles Olson and Robert Creeley, by William Carlos Williams and Ezra Pound, to Amiri Baraka, playwright, expressed his conviction, prompted initially by a visit to Castro's Cuba, that 'It was not enough just to write, to feel, to think, one must act! One *could* act.'[26] Drama interested him because he 'wanted some kind of action literature, where one has to put characters upon a stage and make them living metaphors'. To his mind, indeed, 'Drama proliferates during periods of social upsurge, because it makes real live people the fuel of ideas' and because it is 'a much more popular form than poetry'.[27] If he was not, in his own words, strong enough to act, he would be strong enough to speak.

The assassination of Malcolm X, on 21 February 1965, marked a radical shift in his attitude and values: it was the event which finally provoked his break with his white wife, his Greenwich Village/Lower East Side existence and his commitment to a literary life detached from the urgencies of social revolt. He moved uptown to Harlem and established the Black Arts Repertory Theatre/School on 130th Street, becoming what he later characterised as being 'a fanatical patriot' for black nationalism. Using the income from two of his plays (*The Toilet* and *Experimental Death Unit #1*, then running at the St Marks Theatre before white audiences paying $20 a ticket), he renovated the building which was to serve the interests of the black community.

If the example of Africa and its successful rebellions against colonial rule was in part the inspiration of his own commitments to cultural nationalism, a later visit to Africa would serve to provoke the abandonment of that stance, since both here and in Newark, he saw that a simple change in the complexion of power would not bring about the transformations for which he looked, a change in outlook which he dated to 7 October 1974 when he first publicly acknowledged his new faith in revolutionary socialism. His new commitments, it seemed, could always be dated with an amazing precision. His subsequent Marxist-Leninist work lacked dramatic power and political utility. A few years earlier, however, as he struggled with the implications of his own ambivalence, he had created a drama of genuine power which addressed those very ambiguities which came close to destroying him as an individual and making him as an artist.

Dutchman (1964) is a fable. Set on a subway train, it delves below the

surface of racial and sexual relationships. The elementally named Clay,
a young black man in buttoned-down collar and suit, is challenged by
Lula, an apple-eating white temptress. He aspires to invisibility, taking
on the protective colouration of middle-class America. He seeks safety
in words. She provokes him, dislodging him from his lexical refuge.
Given the history of black–white relations in America she represents
that sexual temptation once punishable by death. She wishes to destroy
that which attracts her. Reinvented as sexual threat or black rebel he
becomes dangerous and vulnerable. At first he resists being pulled into
this interracial dance of death, refuses to collaborate in the myth in
which she would entrap him, but, ultimately, provoked, he becomes a
powerful and dominating presence. Abandoning both his disguise as
would-be white man and the language which has been his protection, he
strikes her. Right is in the act. But his own ambivalent loyalties draw him
back to the word he had abandoned for action. There is, however, to be
no such escape. She kills him, and the anonymous whites, who have
slowly filled the carriage and mutely observed the action, now throw his
body onto the tracks and await the next black victim.

Dutchman is a play which directly expresses LeRoi Jones's own
dilemma. Just as Clay insists that Charlie Parker's music had been a
product of repression, his refusal to enact the logical violence of a victim
of racism, so he sees his own poetry as a product of a similar repression.
Jones was himself ambiguously balanced between a career as a writer
and a more active involvement in the black movement. Married to a
white woman, he was also in process of questioning that relationship.
The ambivalence of *Dutchman* was thus deeply rooted in his own sensibility and his own description of the play – 'it is about how difficult it is to
become a man in the US' – a personal *cri de cœur*. As he has said, 'the
contradictory motions of my life must make it obvious how confused I
was. I had to read *Dutchman* again just to understand it. And those words
led in all directions, away from the page and into my life and memory.'[28]
The power of *Dutchman* came partly from its rhythms, shaped with a
poet's sensibility, and partly from the pressure of history which lies
behind its mythic encounter. It is, however, the ambivalence of Clay,
generated out of Jones's own experience, which gives it an authority and
integrity.

Its companion piece, *The Slave*, which his wife called 'Roi's nightmare', was also, he admitted, 'close to our real lives'. The play concerns
a black revolutionary on the eve of a race war who takes time out to confront his former wife, a white woman, and her white professor husband.

This play, too, reflected his sense of having reached a moment of crisis as he toyed with the idea of abandoning his own wife to commit himself to a cause into which she would have introduced a potentially disabling ambiguity. In the play, however, that ambiguity is itself crucial, an ambiguity evident in the title. The play begins with a shambling field slave who is suddenly transformed into a contemporary black rebel, a social transformation effected by white racism and liberal equivocation. But that black rebel remains in a crucial sense a slave to other commitments. To have abandoned his troops on the eve of battle is to acknowledge the genuineness of his relationship to his former wife; to engage in debate with her husband is to acknowledge the continued attraction of words. He knows that his new commitment has required a series of sacrifices. One is his relationship to his wife and children; the other is his respect for a literary tradition which, as a writer, makes sense of his present. He is aware, too, of the ugly logic which seeks to replace one dominant group with another through the mechanism of force, with no more sophisticated justification than the fact that 'you had your chance . . . now these other folks have theirs'. As Baraka, he later offered his own interpretation of the play:

Walker Vessels suffers from an ego-worship. He's hung up on his own ego syndrome, his individualism. That's why I call the play 'The Slave,' because if he is the general, the commander of the revolutionary army, he has no business being in that white man's house. He has no business talking to these people. He is supposed to be out leading his brothers. He is supposed to be fighting . . . And this is why, essentially, Walker is a weak man. But his intentions are close to the reality that I believe in. That is, he believes if an equitable social structure is going to be reared in America, it will probably be by force.[29]

The play is rather less certain on this point.

Though *The Slave* is not such a convincing work as *Dutchman*, the debate which it stages, a debate less between Walker Vessels and his ex-wife or her husband than within Walker Vessels himself, has an openness which was about to disappear from his work as, in the late sixties, he began to write his black revolutionary plays, works which added up to little more than agit-prop sketches, the identification of heroes and villains in that revolutionary war which *The Slave* had prophesied. Pragmatic and frequently simplistic, they were designed to raise consciousness, to politicise, to generate images commensurate with his racially defined politics, politics he would himself reject within a few years when he came to regard such nationalism as an evasion of a situation which lent itself more directly to Marxist analysis. Unfortunately that new commitment would in turn bring new constraints as he produced plays which seemed reminiscent of thirties melodrama.

Even in this period, however, one production stood out. *Slave Ship* (1967) combined stereotypical characters with radical theatricality, collapsing history into a powerful image of black suffering. Later criticised by Baraka himself for failing to identify capitalism as the root of slavery and for opposing to it a 'petty bourgeois' nationalism, it was in fact an attempt to discover a way to express, in theatrical terms, both the experience of slavery and the continuity of black suffering. In effect an extended image, it reached towards a kind of theatre displaced first by racial and then by Marxist homilies. Though imperfect it is a reminder of what was lost when Baraka decided to sacrifice his talent to dogma.

The principal question posed by his early and best plays was, as he himself identified it in referring to a little-produced play written in 1964 – *A Recent Killing* – 'Is the Act as Legitimate as the Word?' He later came to regard this question as 'absurd', the product of a bourgeois society, since 'Now we know the act is more legitimate, it is principal!'[30] For a writer such a question can never be so cavalierly dismissed. Sartre resolved it by defining his own work as a literature of praxis. For him, to write was to act. Baraka has never been able to convince himself of the legitimacy of such a suggestion, distrusting the very qualities which constitute his talent. The consequence has been if not quite silence then at least a wilful surrender of those qualities which once distinguished him as a writer. Once his debate with himself reflected so accurately and painfully the debate with his society that his work had a moral force and aesthetic integrity that made it seem central. Today he remains wedded to a social analysis whose bankruptcy has been a central fact of twentieth-century history.

Ed Bullins was a product of the black movement of the sixties, but he was also capable of offering a critique of its excesses. In an age of rhetoric he distrusted the coercive language of those who would reduce experience to slogans. For the most part he was committed to exploring the urban ghetto world from which he had come, a world of numbing determinisms and startling lyricism. As August Wilson was to do two decades later, he set himself to detailing the psychic history of those placed under pressure by a social system whose brutalities he acknowledged but which, for the most part, he chose not to dramatise. Like Wilson, he set himself to write a cycle of plays which would capture his sense of the black community in the twentieth century. Like him, too, he finds in music a unifying element, frequently incorporating it into his plays.

His scepticism towards the more simplistic consciousness-raising aspects of the black movement surfaced in *Dialect Determinism* (1965), which challenges its own reductive rhetoric, *It Bees Dat Way* (1970), in which anti-white sloganeering is exposed, and *Death List* (1970), in which a black assassin is identified as the enemy of the black people, a product of the very racism which he opposes. Throughout his work he has reserved his greatest scepticism and even contempt for those who choose to appropriate the lives and experiences of others in the name of a cause whose righteousness is regarded as too self-evident to make itself available for examination.

Unable to find anyone to stage his early plays he co-founded the San Francisco Drama Circle and subsequently Black Arts/West, later leaving it over an argument about its future direction. He opposed those who saw it primarily as a weapon, an arm of revolutionary activity in which radical blacks and whites would use it as a base for their activities. His interest lay elsewhere, in the creation of a theatre which would emerge from and engage the black community, an objective which he shared with Robert Macbeth's Harlem-based New Lafayette Theatre, to which he moved in 1967.

Bullins's landscape is urban. His characters are warped, sometimes, as in *Clara's Ole Man* (1965), to the point of becoming grotesques. Their possibilities are restricted, their dreams unrealised, their hopes forlorn. Theirs is a world whose parameters are defined by a threatening violence. The sexuality which offers release from such determinisms is itself tainted with violence. Yet within this bleak environment need generates its own beauty. Denied any other form of transcendence, his characters find it in one another. Beneath the broken rhythms of their experience is another harmony, heard only occasionally, often unrecognised by those who seek elsewhere for meaning. It is a harmony generated by mutual need.

Clara's Ole Man is set in the 1950s and portrays a hermetic world. Much the same could be said of *In the Wine Time*, the first of his cycle plays, and of *The Corner*. There is nothing here of Lorraine Hansberry's quiet confidence in inner resources which lend plausibility to an open challenge to the white world, a challenge which will itself generate meaning. Here, escape remains a dream. *In the Wine Time* (1967) presents 16-year-old Ray as torn between desire for a fantasy woman and enlisting in the Navy. Cliff, who himself feels trapped, urges him to abandon his sexual fantasies and escape from the Philadelphia ghetto where he feels entombed. The play ends with a spasm of violence as Cliff murders a neighbourhood hoodlum. We are offered, it seems, a choice between, in the words of the play's central character, a 'world of dreams and lies and fairy tales' and 'a jungle or a desert'.[31]

In the New England Winter (written in 1967 and produced in 1971) moves the action into the sixties while retaining a foot in the previous decade. Cliff is released from prison. His wife Lou has deserted him, and his brother, Steve, has moved into Cliff's home. When a friend, Bummie, tells Cliff that his brother had once fathered a child by Lou, Steve kills him. Like Ray in the earlier play he clings to a woman who he reinvents in his mind, a woman he had known, in New England, a woman who was in all probability psychotic.

Bullins's characters are never simply elements in a naturalistic drama of emotional and spiritual desperation. They are people who look for an order, a structure to experience, a meaning to their lives, for which they can find no evidence. They are not offered simply as images of social and psychological deprivation. Their needs could never be satisfied by a house in a white suburb or by political revolt. They believe, along with Beckett's characters, that 'there must be order . . . there must be form . . . something . . . besides this emptiness' or else there is only 'emptiness'.[32] Their failure to identify such order is the root of the irony of which they are victims. The only form is the shaping imagination of the writer, but this is at the heart of another irony, as he explained in *The Duplex* (1970), set in Los Angeles, in which Steve is himself a writer, the author of *In the Wine Time*. He reads this story, with its account of the fantasy girl, to the woman he now lives with and who carries his child. But she shares little with the fantasy, being regularly raped and robbed by her husband, a man who dominates both his wife and Steve. It is tempting, then, to read this play as Bullins's admission of the ultimate inability of art to provide that sense of order missing from experience. Indeed, in a sense many of his characters are themselves close kin to the writer, generating their own alternative but fragile worlds.

In the other plays of the cycle – *The Fabulous Miss Marie* (1971) and *DADDY!* (1977) – Bullins shifts his attention further up the social scale. The former deals with a middle-class existence in which sexual betrayals are merely public evidence of the collapse of relationships. The latter takes us into a Central Park apartment, home now to a successful black musician and his girlfriend, a place in stark contrast to the Newark ghetto home of the wife he had abandoned more than a decade earlier.

This time, however, the shattered family ties are allowed to re-form, the possibility of personal relationships, untainted by betrayal, envisaged as a possibility.

In a career stretching over more than twenty years Ed Bullins has experimented with agit-prop sketches, absurdist one-acts, naturalistic social plays and powerful poetic dramas. While working to consolidate the black theatre, creating black theatre groups and developing black audiences, he has resisted those who sought to enrol his work as simple adjunct to political movements. He has remained suspicious of those who would substitute polemic for perception, who demand that black theatre should restage the social dramas of America as simple morality plays. He has taken as his subject the lives of those for whom daily existence is its own drama. Nor, despite appearances, has he concerned himself only with the pathology of ghetto experience. It is true that the lives he places on stage have been distorted by drink and drugs, scarred by violence, marked by sexual betrayal, ironised by unattainable fantasies. Beyond this, however, he celebrates the resistant spirit, listens for an assonance hidden at the heart of discord, and, in confronting the evidence of dissolution, begins the process of reconstruction. The world which he places on stage is airless, the individuals deprived of transcendence. The act of placing them on stage and of assembling a community of individuals to observe them, however, is a denial of the necessity of despair. As Bullins himself explained of his 'Twentieth Century Cycle', he wished

to recreate reality in a new atmosphere – [give] . . . a fresh illumination, a fresh view of things . . . extend your vision . . . It will just tell the stories it tells, in the hope that the stories will touch the audience in an individual way, with some fresh insight into their own lives – help them to consider the weight of their experiences.[33]

One of the most powerful black voices of the 1980s was August Wilson, a man who had encountered racism at an early age. At his first school he was the only black child in 1,500 pupils. On his desk every day was a note reading: 'GO HOME NIGGER.' At lunchtime he ate alone. No one would join him. He left high school when a teacher refused to believe that he was indeed the author of a term paper on Napoleon. Wishing to conceal this from his mother he continued to leave the house every day, going to the library rather than to school. There he learned to 'crawl inside words'.

In 1968, on the tide of black cultural nationalism, he co-founded the

Black Horizons Theatre in Pittsburgh, but failed in his attempts to write plays because of his inability to construct dialogue to his own satisfaction: 'The reason I couldn't write dialogue', he explained in an interview in 1989, was 'because I didn't respect the way blacks talked; so I always tried to alter it'. But, in 1978, on leaving what he described as a 'neighbourhood of fifty-five thousand blacks' to live in St Paul, Minnesota, with its much smaller black community, 'for the first time I began to hear the voices I had been brought up with all my life and I realised I didn't have to change it. I began to respect it.'[34] He first became involved in theatre in 1982 when he started to write scripts for the local science museum's children's theatre while submitting work to the O'Neill Theatre Center. When one of these, *Ma Rainey's Black Bottom*, finally made its way to Broadway, it proved the first of a remarkable series of successes. It won the New York Drama Critics' Circle Award and the Pulitzer Prize. When *Joe Turner's Come and Gone* joined it in 1988, August Wilson became the first black playwright to have two plays running concurrently on Broadway.

He did not originally set himself to write an historical cycle, but there came a time when he realised that that was in effect what he was doing. His first play, *Jitney*, had been set in 1971, his second, *Fullerton Street*, in 1941. It was not until *Ma Rainey* (set in 1927) however, that he recognised the logic of his own work.

August Wilson chooses deliberately to situate his characters historically, but his are not historical dramas in the sense that the past is treated as icon, faithfully reconstructed in its detailed realism. For him the past constitutes something more than a series of way-stations on a journey towards the present, though it is that, too. The past is the present. It provides the images, the language, the myths which we inhabit, with which we debate and against which we define ourselves. He has set himself to recreate the emotional, psychological and spiritual history of a people, to identify the way in which the individual has struggled to sustain a sense of self in the face of pressures, internal and external. As Wilson himself has explained: 'I'm taking each decade and looking back at one of the most important questions that blacks confronted in that decade and writing a play about it . . . Put them all together and you have a history.'[35]

To construct your history is, as Wilson himself has observed, 'doubly important if someone else has been writing yours for you';[36] but this is not polemical drama. It is offered neither as appeal nor exhortation but as celebration. This is not to say that he deals with victories but that he chooses to focus on the often losing battle of individuals placed under the kind of pressure which makes personal meaning so difficult to sustain.

His approach to history is tangential. The major events of each decade find no more than an echo. Thus, *Ma Rainey's Black Bottom* is set in 1927 but there is no reference to Marcus Garvey, deported that year by Calvin Coolidge and probably the most famous black American of his day; no hint of the Ku Klux Klan, which had been a key issue in the 1924 election, as it was to be in the 1928 one. *Fences* takes place from 1957 to 1965 but there is no reference to Little Rock, Arkansas, the first use of Federal troops in the South since the Civil War, nor to any of the Civil Rights activities of the early sixties. It is not that histoty which Wilson sets out to tell. He looks not at the centre of social and political action but at the margin: 'the plays . . . deal with those people who were continuing to live their lives. I wasn't interested in what you could get from the history books.'[37] Those he chooses to focus on confront history not in its public and political form but in its day-to-day effects. They exist on the margin. *Ma Rainey* is even set in a side room, as *Fences* takes place in a ramshackle house on the edge of a city and focuses on the life of a man whose job it is to handle society's garbage. *Joe Turner's Come and Gone* deals with the literally dispossessed and is set in a down-at-heel boarding-house.

August Wilson has defined his objective with clarity:

I write about the black experience in America and try to explain in terms of the life I know best those things which are common to all cultures. I see myself as answering James Baldwin's call for a profound articulation of the black experience, which he defined as 'that field of manners and ritual of intercourse that can sustain a man once he has left his father's house.' I try to concretise the values of the black American and place them on a stage in loud action to demonstrate the existence of the above 'field of manners' and point to some avenues of sustenance.[38]

Ma Rainey's Black Bottom began as a one-act play called *The Homecoming*. It involved two black scouts for a white record company and its theme was economic exploitation. By 1980 he had decided to bring the musicians themselves on stage, so 'I opened the door to the bandroom and there were these four guys there. Then I realised that it had to be about more than economic exploitation. I had to show the content of their lives in order to show where the blues came from.'[39] In that sense there is something emblematic about the stage set for *Ma Rainey's Black Bottom* (1984). Set in a recording studio, the action takes place partly there and

partly in a basement band room to which the black musicians are relegated. High above is a 'control booth' from which the white company
literally controls them. Public history, in the sense of political developments, may be excluded from the play but it is faithfully recreated in
terms of a stage set which replicates its polarities while the appropriation, by a white recording company, of black talent and the black experience as expressed in black music stands not only as an historically
accurate fact but also as an exemplary image of the relationship between
the races.

This is a play which uses music as fact and image. On one level it is
concerned with the recording, by Ma Rainey and a group of black musicians, of a number of songs. That music exposes the tensions between
black and white and amongst the black musicians. But it is also a
resource, a meeting-ground, the source of a harmony which briefly pulls
together those separated by ambition, need or experience. Indeed the
play has as an epigraph, a verse from a song by Blind Lemon Jefferson:
'They tore the railroad down / so the Sunshine Special can't run / I'm
going away baby / Build me a railroad of my own.' As Wilson remarks,
his concern is with those who live out their lives on Chicago's Southside,
'their values, their attitudes, and particularly their music', a music that
'connects' those 'for whom this music often lies at the forefront of their
conscience and concerns'.[40] The qualities which he ascribes to the music
– blues music – are equally the qualities of those who create it or rely
upon it. So, it represents 'warmth and redress . . . braggadocio and
roughly poignant comments – vision and power'. It is what allows them
'to reconnect, to reassemble and gird up for the next battle in which they
would be both victim and the ten thousand slain'.[41] James Joyce once
asked 'why should not a modern literature be as unsparing and direct as
song';[42] in August Wilson's case, it is. Alice Walker has spoken of her
attempt to achieve in prose what black musicians achieve with their
music. August Wilson has come close to succeeding in this.

Ma Rainey is based on the 'Mother of the Blues', Ma Rainey. She
expects, and for the most part receives, deference from her fellow black
musicians and is tolerated, for her financial value, by the white record
company. But things are changing. Sturdyvant, the white owner of the
company, has neither respect for nor understanding of her music.
Indeed he is already looking for a more popular sound, something with
'a lot of rhythm'. The band itself reflects this changing world, though
each man's ability as a musician is in a sense an extension of his character. Cutler, the leader, is 'sensible' and his playing 'solid and almost

totally unembellished. His understanding of his music is limited to the chord he is playing at the time he is playing it.' Slow Drag is 'bored by life' but is 'deceptively intelligent' and plays 'with an ease that is at times startling'. Toledo, the piano player, who, Wilson suggests, 'throughout the play has been set up as a substitute for the White man',[43] understands that the limitations of his instrument 'are an extension of himself'. The final member is Levee, younger than the others, flamboyant, rakish and 'somewhat of a buffoon'. His trumpet-playing is 'totally dependent on his manipulation of breath. He plays wrong notes frequently' and 'often gets his skill and talent confused with each other'.[44] The tensions within the group reflect those in the black world as those between the group and Sturdyvant reflect those between black and white.

Much of the play's effect comes from comedy undercut by glimpses of the reality which underlies the music no less than social relationships. Thus Levee, to some extent a figure of fun, recounts a story of his mother's rape and his father's lynching, a story followed by Slow Drag's rendering of 'If I had my way / I would tear this building down.' Ma Rainey's banter suddenly gives way to a clear statement of her own bitterness at her treatment by the whites. So, she comments on a white manager who, in six years, had only allowed her into his house on one occasion and then to entertain his friends: 'If you coloured and can make them some money, then you are all right with them. Otherwise, you just a dog in the alley.'[45]

The blues themselves mark a division between the black and the white worlds. For the one it is 'life's way of talking . . . a way of understanding life';[46] for the other, entertainment. This is the essence equally of a story told by Cutler about a black minister forced to dance for a crowd of southern bigots. In a way this is the position in which they find themselves, a fact which provokes Levee to a denunciation of a white god, indifferent to black suffering. Once again a blues chorus offers a commentary: 'You want to be my man / You got to fetch it with you when you come.'[47] The play ends when Levee, betrayed by Sturdyvant's refusal of his compositions and rejection of his planned recordings, turns against his fellow musicians. Unable to strike out at the white man, he kills Toledo, and the play's final moments are accompanied by the sound of Levee's 'muted trumpet struggling for the highest of possibilities and blowing pain and warning'. As Wilson remarks, 'Levee is trying to wrestle with the process of life the same as all of us . . . His question is, "How can I live this life in a society that refuses to recognise my worth, that refuses to allow me to contribute to its welfare, how can I live this life and remain a whole and complete person?'"[48] Compared to the figure of Loomis, in the later play *Joe Turner's Come and Gone*, Levee 'has a firmer sense of who he is – where Loomis is more clearly on a search for identity, on a search for a world that contains his image'.[49] Here, as throughout, the music provides an ironic commentary, an expression of the conflicting pressures which define black life.

For Wilson

the blues music is terribly misread. It is the carrier of the philosophical ideas of black Americans. It is their cultural response to the world. In coming from the oral tradition one passes along information orally and the best way to do that is to make it memorable so that if I tell you a story it's something you want to pass on to someone else. Music and songs were a way of doing that. You had a bonus. The music provided you with an emotional reference to the material and the information and the ideas in these songs.[50]

Together with a planned play on Otis Redding which was never written, he had originally decided to call the combined works *Dangerous Music*. It is a title which reflects his sense of the subversive power of the blues.

In *Fences* the central character is a 53-year-old one-time baseball player, now garbage collector, Troy Maxon. The setting is a small dirt yard framed on one side by a decaying porch and on the other by an unbuilt fence, expressive, as we discover, of Troy himself, whose youthful promise has been frustrated and distorted and who has failed to construct a secure identity. The time is 1957 when, as Wilson explains, 'the hot winds of change that would make the sixties a turbulent, racing, dangerous, and provocative decade had not yet begun to blow full'.[51] Yet the signs are there. Troy has just challenged his employer to tell him why whites drive the garbage trucks while blacks do the heavy lifting, not to him a political question but one which is a sign of his frustration and evidence of the man he might have been.

Troy is a bitter man, a bitterness which comes from his sense of failure and exclusion. Rejected as a youth by the white baseball leagues, he is trapped. The son of a sharecropper who had left home at fourteen and turned to crime only to be redeemed by a wife who represents the stability which he simultaneously needs and fears, he drifts to another woman who flatters an ego crushed by a lifetime of disappointments. Troy frustrates the sporting ambitions of his own son partly out of jealousy, partly out of a desire to protect him from the disappointments which he himself had suffered, and partly because once he has secured the boy a safe job he will feel absolved of responsibility. Meanwhile he is caught, unable to realise himself and desperate for a respect denied him daily.

The play follows Troy from 1957 to 1965, eight years in which his life winds down. An affair with another woman results in her death giving birth to his child, and an alienation from both his wife and son. Having protected his brain-damaged brother he now commits him to hospital, apparently to his own financial advantage. He dies while practising a baseball stroke in his backyard, a parody of what had once promised him fame and security. In a coda, as the family gather for his funeral, the son he had alienated and driven away is finally reconciled to him. A Marine, he has clearly traded in his dreams for a regulated life, and already we can see a hint of discontent and disappointment. The play ends with Gabriel, Troy's brain-damaged brother, who believes himself to be the Angel Gabriel, attempting to blow the trumpet which he has carried since his injury. He fails to sound a note. Unlike Troy, however, he can adjust to the abrupt collapse of his illusions, improvising a wild dance in its place, a dance designed to open the gates of heaven to his dead brother. The fence, meanwhile, comes to stand for his wife's attempt to keep Troy in, to bind him to her; it also stands for Troy's attempt to hold knowledge at bay, knowledge of his own betrayals, his own failures and his own mortality.

It is tempting to see August Wilson as doing for a black underclass what Lorraine Hansberry did for the aspiring middle class. But where she created characters who self-consciously forged their frustrations and dreams into social action or political significance, he does not. There is an anger in the plays but it never shapes itself into polemic. Indeed, he is interested precisely in that space between suffering and its articulation, between need and its expression. His characters seldom make a connection between their individual sufferings and the necessity for social transformation. Their lives express that need; their words, their actions, seldom do. They want to be at ease with themselves and their world but fail in that ambition. They are fenced in and if, unlike Lorraine Hansberry's family in *A Raisin in the Sun*, they do not choose to break through that containment in a public way, finding the meaning of their lives in that conflict, they are aware that a barrier exists. As a result the anger and aggression bounce back and are turned inwards. The barriers are so implacable they seem organic. Troy questions the practices of his employer but his victory is to move himself from the rear to the front of the garbage truck. In the end that victory is far less important than others. He leaves behind a child, his daughter Raynell, and when he is dead the son he had alienated joins with his illegitimate half-sister to sing his father's song – a song that had grown out of his experience. The man who had spent his life seeking his 'song', his identity, the shape to his life, was that song. He worked with what he was given and through the tangle of loyalties and betrayals, cruelties and kindnesses, became a person who others could join in mourning: 'Troy has a willingness to live life with zest and vibrancy . . . that is what I discover in the blues. Vitality and life affirmation whatever the subject is.' As Wilson has said:

Each of the characters in *Fences* has to make a reconciliation with Troy. The 'illegitimate' child represents hope for the future. Everyone in the play is institutionalised: there's the army, the jail, the hospital and the church. The only one free from any constraints is the 17 year old daughter with her garden. That's the new life and the future. All hope is represented with her.[52]

From the perspective of the 1960s such writing would seem conservative. It explores and in some senses celebrates the given. Lives are not shaped into weapons nor laments into diatribes. His characters do not serve meaning; they are not subordinated to social purpose. They speak their lives and sometimes sing them. The music is the blues, not the protest song. Wilson has said of *Fences* that 'I had to write a character who is responsible and likes the idea of family . . . We have been told so many times how irresponsible we are as black males that I try and present positive images of responsibility . . . I started *Fences* with the image of a man standing in his yard with a baby in his arms.'[53] Yet, of course, that moment is a profoundly ambiguous one. His responsibility in accepting his illegitimate child is balanced by his irresponsibility in engendering it. His enthusiasm for his new family is a denial of the loyalty demanded by his old one. This is the pressure which dismays and bewilders Troy. But the play, which is set in the constraining limitations of the backyard and which flirts with stereotype is, ultimately, celebratory. As Wilson has explained

What I tried to do in *Ma Rainey*, and in all my work, is to reveal the richness of the lives of the people, who show that the largest ideas are contained by their lives, and that there is a nobility to their lives. Blacks in America have so little to make life with compared to whites, yet they do so with a certain zest, or certain energy that is fascinating because they make life out of nothing – yet it is charged and luminous and has all the qualities of anyone else's life. I think a lot of this is hidden by the glancing manner in which White America looks at Blacks, and the way Blacks look at themselves. Which is why I work a lot with stereotypes, with the idea of stripping away layer by layer the surface to reveal what is underneath – the real person, the whole person.[54]

The choice of musicians and a former sportsman as central characters in *Ma Rainey* and *Fences* was a conscious attempt to explore and expose key areas of supposed black freedom. As he explained, 'the two roads into white American society traditionally open to blacks, entertainment and sports, fail the characters'.[55] Since they do fail them the meaning of their lives is generated out of their own actions. In *Fences* the white world is a defining absence in so far as it sets the parameters of black freedom, determines the economic context, shapes the hopes and aspirations of those it casually relegates to the margins of experience. But where in the 1960s black playwrights were prone to see identity as a product of conflict, a challenge to the white world openly delivered, Wilson is concerned to dramatise those who look for meaning in the daily business of living. It is not that the white world is irrelevant. Its corrosive power is evident. It could be said to lie behind many of the personal betrayals and jealousies, the bitterness deflected from social action into psychological fact. Wilson writes in the mode of Ed Bullins's later work rather than that of Baldwin, Hansberry or Jones. He is interested in what the black individual and the black community makes of its own experience. As Wilson has said, 'As a whole our generation knows very little about our past . . . My parents' generation tried to shield their children from the indignities they suffered . . . I think it's largely a question of identity. Without knowing your past, you don't know your present – and you certainly can't plot your future . . . You go out and discover it for yourself.' That past lies in large degree in a black sensibility forged out of more than an American experience of persecution or disregard. As he insisted, 'if black folks would recognize themselves as Africans and not be afraid to respond to the world as Africans, then they could make their contribution to the world as Africans'.[56] This is very much the theme of a play which opened at the Yale Repertory Theatre in 1986, and Broadway in 1988, *Joe Turner's Come and Gone*.

The play was inspired by a series of poems that Wilson had been writing called 'Restoring the House', in which a man sets out in search of his wife who had been sold from Mississippi to a family in Georgia some five years before Emancipation. From this grew the idea of, people being separated and then restored, which generates both the plot and the theme of *Joe Turner's Come and Gone*.

In August Wilson's plotting of black history, this play takes us back to 1911. It is set in a boarding-house in Pittsburg. The African heritage is that much closer than it had been for Troy or Levee, though it has been partially burned away by the experiences of slavery. As Wilson explains in a note to the published version, 'From the deep and near South the sons and daughters of newly freed African slaves wander into the city.

Isolated, cut off from memory, having forgotten the names of the gods and only guessing at their faces, they arrive dazed and stunned, their heart kicking in their chest and a song worth singing.' It is a crucial moment. They carry with them a double heritage, symbolised by their Bibles and guitars, and confront an ambiguous reality. They are free and carry with them the hope engendered by that freedom and yet what awaits them as they arrive in Pittsburg are the 'crooked cobbles and the fiery blasts of the coke furnace' and this is to be the crucible which they hope will shape 'the malleable parts of themselves into a new identity as free men of definite and sincere worth'.[57] They travel, separate people whose primary experience has been one of dispersement, united only by their joint condition of slavery and now in search of some other connection, some 'song' which can express their lives even though that, too, is bound to be rooted in an ambivalence – 'a wail and a whelp of joy'.

There is some stability. The action takes place in a boarding-house presided over by Seth, son of northern free parents and, in his early fifties, married for over twenty-five years to Bertha. Around them is a series of literal and spiritual transients: Selig, a white man who travels the country selling pots and pans and searching for lost people, bringing them back together; Bynum, a conjure man who insists that his name comes from his power to bind people ('Just like glue I sticks people together');[58] Harold Loomis, a man in his early thirties, travelling with his daughter in search of his wife, and Mattie, a young woman looking for her lost lover, as Jeremy, a young man, is searching for a woman to love. They are all, in other words, searching for a sense of completion.

Bynum claims to have a 'powerful song', by which he means his ability to bind people together, but in fact the musical imagery continues in the stage directions. Jeremy, who travels with his guitar, has a spirit 'yet to be moulded into song'. Loomis, in search of a world 'that speaks to something about himself' is, we are told, 'unable to harmonize the forces that swirl around him'.[59] That harmony is in essence the Whitmanesque lesson that Bynum tries to teach Jeremy, whose attraction to Mattie seems purely sexual: 'You just like a man looking at the horizon from a ship. You just seeing a part of it. But it's a blessing when you learn to look at a woman and see in maybe just a few strands of her hair, the way her cheek curves . . . to see in that everything there is out of life to be gotten.'[60] The harmony of which Bynum and Wilson speak is that identified by Alice Walker when she explains that 'I am trying to arrive at that place where black music already is; to arrive at that unselfconscious sense of collective oneness; that naturalness, that (even when anguished "grace").'[61] Indeed you could say of Wilson what Alice Walker says of herself in that he, too, is 'preoccupied with the spiritual survival, the survival *whole*'[62] of his people. For both of them that concern leads back in time as they explore a past which is part factual, part mystical.

Behind the dislocations of an American experience lies another world which exists at a tangent to the apparently implacable reality of history. In *Joe Turner's Come and Gone* the characters are, for the most part, wanderers, their restless journey – physical and psychological – a correlative of that other diaspora forced by slavery. Underneath, however, there is a deeper harmony which becomes apparent, particularly through music. Here the scattered individuals who make up the temporary lodgers in Seth's boarding-house come together in the Juba, a dance which, we are told, is reminiscent of the 'Ring Shouts' of the African slaves. Song becomes a metaphor for identity: group identity and personal identity. As Bynum observes,

I used to travel all up and down this road and that . . . looking here and there. Searching . . . I didn't know what I was searching for. The only thing I knew was something was keeping me dissatisfied . . . Then one day my daddy gave me a song. That song had a weight to it that was hard to handle. That song was hard to carry. I fought against it. Didn't want to accept that song . . . But I found out it wasn't his song. It was my song. It had come from way deep inside me – I looked back in memory and gathered up pieces and snatches of things to make that song – I was making it up out of myself . . . When a man forgets his song he goes off in search of it . . . till he finds he's got it with him all the time.[63]

Wilson has remarked that 'I certainly identify with the attempt to heal. This attempt to bind together.' As with Alice Walker it is a desire which leads him back in the direction of Africa. He feels the need to urge black Americans to recognise the fact that

they are African people . . . There's something that's part of the blood's memory. There's a sensibility that's still African, despite the fact that we've been on the north American continent for three hundred and seventy years. We walk down the street differently. There's a certain style. We decorate our houses differently, our ideas about the world are very different, and those things have survived for hundreds of years.[64]

The play is named after Joe Turner, brother of the governor of Tennessee, whose habit it was arbitrarily to seize Negroes and imprison them for seven years as a free workforce, a fact recorded by Bynum in song. Loomis is one of those so imprisoned, an experience which broke up his family and so damaged him psychologically and spiritually that,

Bynum insists, 'you forgot how to sing your song'. This seven-year detention comes to stand for slavery itself and Loomis's alienation for its
effects. As Loomis replies, 'I been wandering a long time in somebody
else's world.'[65]

Joe Turner treads a dangerous path. The potential for sentimentality is
clear both in the assumption of a recoverable unity and in its suggestion
of a continuity imprinted on the race. So Bertha moves as in a dance
'centuries old . . . to which she is connected by the muscles of her heart
and the blood's memory'. When she laughs we are told that it is 'a celebration of life, both its pain and its blessing'.[66] What resists this potential sentimentality is his success in creating a work with the shape and
authenticity of a folk-tale. It ends with Loomis reconciled not only to his
lost wife but, more significantly, to himself. So, we are told in a stage
direction, that having 'found his song, the song of self-sufficiency, fully
resurrected, cleansed and given breath, free from any encumbrance
other than the workings of his own heart and the bonds of the flesh,
having accepted responsibility for his presence in the world, he is free to
soar above the environs that weighed and pushed his spirits into terrifying contractions'.[67] As Wilson himself has said, 'Blacks in America have
been wrestling with ghosts of the white man for decades, trying to exorcise them from their lives. Loomis learns that he is responsible for his
own salvation and presence in the world.'[68]

In her book *In Search of Our Mothers' Gardens* Alice Walker called for a
work that 'exposes the subconscious of a people, because the people's
dreams, imaginings, rituals, legends are known to be important, are
known to contain the accumulated collective reality of the people themselves'. This, a work 'of black people' rather than 'limited encounters
with a non-specific white world' was, she insisted, likely to be the key text.
August Wilson's work would seem to be concerned with just such an
attempt to engage a collective reality through 'the relationships between
members of a black family – or between a man and a woman', rather
than through an engagement with 'white people as primary antago-
nists'.[69] In pursuance of that, in *Joe Turner* he used what he is inclined to
call an 'African story telling mode', a form in which the story, myth and
music are shaped into exemplary tales which dramatise both the collapse
of personal, familial and social structures and their reconstitution
through shared experience. As he himself has suggested these are plays
informed by his own background as a poet and if he chooses to sidestep
black–white confrontations he can do so both because that territory has
already been cleared for him by others – 'I can only do what I do because

the 60s existed . . . I am building off that original conflict'[70] – and because, writing in the 1980s, he can claim a perspective denied to those for whom writing implied the evasion of a responsibility which properly took one onto the streets in protest. Hansberry, Baldwin, Baraka were concerned with making history, with intervening in the social and political process. They offered exemplary figures whose value lay in their effectiveness in dramatising issues which were extensions of an immediate political and social reality. They explored the psychological effects of social strategies and identified the connection between private meaning and public revolt. August Wilson is a recorder of history as it is written in individual lives and invented by a community broken by time but reforming itself through experience. His 1988 play, *The Piano Lesson*, explores a series of historic ironies as a brother and sister argue over the legacy of a family piano. Is it to be preserved as a reminder of a violent past, a totem, or is it to be sold to finance the purchase of land on which their father had worked as a slave? Two versions of history contest with one another. That is the essence of Wilson's work. History is not inert. It is not simply what happened but what is made of the past.

He speaks of and to the black community in his desire to show the extent to which 'there is a whole and complete culture that is black America', but he quotes approvingly the black artist Romane Beardon who has said, 'I try and explain in terms of the life I know best those things which are common to all cultures.' That, Wilson insists, is 'what I do. I write about the dispossessed.' Yet at the same time he has said that 'You have to make a decision about where you're going to go, whether you are going to assimilate or separate. I offer my plays as parts of that debate.' The fact of his success on Broadway and in the country's regional theatres where his were sometimes the first black plays to have been staged should not blind us to where he locates himself in that debate:

The theme I keep coming back to is the need to re-connect yourself. Having been uprooted from Africa, an agrarian land-based society and taken into the South, again rural, after a couple of hundred years an African-American culture was born. Then, right in the middle of that to uproot yourself and to attempt to transport that culture to the pavements, to an urban industrialised world which was not welcoming was a terrible mistake. I think it would have been better if we had stayed in the South. When we left we left people back there . . . that connection is broken, that sense of standing in your grandfather's shoes. This is simply what I'm trying to do with my plays. Make that connection. Because I think it's vital. Having shared a common past we have a common past and a common future.[71]

Two Trains Running, set in Pittsburgh in 1969, and the sixth cycle play,
opened in New York in April 1992. It is set in the 1960s, a period of assassination and riot. America's cities were aflame. The Vietnam war was
taking a disproportionate number of black lives. National leaders were
being murdered. Yet none of this makes its way, except indirectly, into
Wilson's play. It exists off-stage. A black power rally is being held nearby.
Malcolm X's name is invoked. But there is no sense that this bears
directly on the lives of the characters. As the play's central figure,
Memphis, remarks, 'These niggers talking about freedom, justice, and
equality and don't know what it means. You born free. It's up to you to
maintain it. You born with dignity . . . Freedom is heavy. You got to put
your shoulder to freedom. Put your shoulder to it and hope your back
hold up.'[72]

Despite Wilson's personal allegiance to black power, and its function
in transforming a sense of personal and group identity (and he has said
that black power was 'the kiln in which I was fired'),[73] Memphis's rhetoric is shot through with ambiguity. He had effectively been driven out
of the South by a blend of corruption and injustice and now insists that
'There ain't no justice. Jesus Christ didn't get justice. What makes you
think you gonna get it? . . . Talking about black power with their hands
and their pockets empty. You can't do nothing without a gun. Not in this
day and time.'[74] But, as another character observes, in a time of police
violence, 'You can't use the word "nigger" and "gun" in the same sentence.'[75] For his part, though, Memphis has no intention of taking up the
gun. He intends to challenge the white system by forcing the city officials
involved in urban renewal to give him a fair price for his house and then,
possibly, take one of the two trains running back to the South each day
to reclaim his birthright. It is a journey he may or may not take but, like
the other characters in the play, he has not given up on life. Indeed, this
is another dimension of the play's title for as Wilson has said, 'There are
always and only two trains running. There is life and there is death. Each
of us rides them both. To live life with dignity, to celebrate and accept
responsibility for your presence in the world is all that can be asked of
anyone.'[76]

The action of the play takes place in a restaurant, across the street
from a funeral parlour and meat market, but such a restricted setting (not
without its metaphoric significance as life and death are divided only by
the breadth of a street) belies the breadth of Wilson's concerns. Each of
the characters seeks to survive and prosper on his or her own terms. For
West, the funeral business is his route to wealth and success; for

Holloway it is the supernatural; for Wolf, the numbers game. But, as Holloway suggests, 'all you got around here is niggers with somebody else's money in their pocket. And they don't do nothing but trade it off on each other . . . Until sooner or later . . . somebody's gonna take it and give it to the white man.'[77]

But here, as elsewhere in Wilson's dramatic saga, the political logic of this observation is never extended into the action. This is the given within which his characters live and have their being. These are the terms within which they define themselves. They live at a time of change. Some are rich, some poor, though mostly the latter, but while money remains a central theme, this is not the essence of their lives. Their struggle is to become something more than victims, to relate to their lives in some other way than that determined by a white world that we never see but which exists as some seemingly implacable reality that determines the parameters of their experience.

In a sense Wilson plays a dangerous game. One of his characters here is a petty criminal, another a gullible fool, yet another an exploiter of his own race. Life seldom seems to extend beyond the regular business of playing the numbers, of getting by from day to day. If there are those, off-stage, who wage a public battle, who join their efforts with those of others to secure social or political justice, his characters seem to see this as marginal to their own concerns. They have their dreams but those dreams are intensely personal. They are, though, what enable them to survive, and out of their privacies, their individual yearnings and pragmatic solutions, something else emerges as Wilson creates an underlying harmony, weaves a tapestry. It is the rhythms of this community, the point and counterpoint, the variations on a theme, that interest him. The mentally damaged Hambone can only reiterate a single phrase, but that provides an ironic refrain (doubly ironic when he is persuaded to substitute the slogans of Black Power) to the music of this group of people who may sound different notes but who come together in their needs.

Justice never comes to Hambone, who dies before he receives his just deserts; it does to Memphis, who secures the money he has been seeking for his restaurant. When Memphis offers fifty dollars to buy flowers for Hambone's funeral, feeling, we are told in a stage direction, 'all the cruel and cold ironies of life', he instructs that the dedication should say that 'it's from everybody . . . everybody who ever dropped the ball and went back to pick it up.'[78] He himself plans to return to the South to demand restoration of the property stolen from him, but, beyond that, his dedication is close to echoing Wilson's own desire to celebrate the lives of those who dropped the ball, because of injustice, of a failure of will, of the nature of a life which seldom fulfils what it seems to offer.

There are moments in *Two Trains Running* when the action can seem a deal too pat, a touch sentimental, as Memphis receives his just deserts, as Sterling's number comes up and a young woman, called Risa, perhaps finds the consolation she seeks. Nonetheless, while the city's renovation project may have its casualties, the renovation that interests Wilson is to do with the survival of individuals and of a community whose extraordinariness lies precisely in the ordinary nature of the needs and dreams of those who constitute it.

It is an approach that he explained in a note to the published version of the next play in his sequence: *Seven Guitars* (1995), set in 1948.

Despite my interest in history, I have always been more concerned with culture, and while my plays have an overall historical feel, their settings are fictions, and they are peopled with invented characters whose personal histories fit within the historical context in which they live. I have tried to extract some measure of truth from their lives as they struggle to remain whole in the face of so many things that threaten to pull them asunder. I am not a historian. I happen to think that the content of my mother's life – her myths, her superstitions, her prayers, the contents of her pantry, the smell of her kitchen, the song that escaped from her sometimes parched lips, her thoughtful repose and pregnant laughter – are all worthy of art.[79]

Hence, as he adds, *Seven Guitars*. This is concerned precisely with personal histories, though these not only fit within the historical context, they constitute that history which, finally, has no less authority than that conducted by those who determine the nature of national politics or the structure of the economic and social system. Indeed, ironically, the character who most stridently warns against living at the end of 'a white man's boot', who insists that somebody needs to emerge to lead the black man out of bondage, and for whom everything is 'a plot' against the black man, is himself deranged, finally, in his delusion, killing a friend.

Yet the irony is deeper than it seems, for this man, whose heroes are Toussaint L'Ouverture and Marcus Garvey, speaks truths in his simplicity that others ignore. It is not that his bewildered state of mind invalidates his views but that his story is one among many, that the myths which drive him are different from those that animate a guitar player driving for success or a young woman looking for a man to take her away from a run-down apartment in Pittsburgh.

Seven Guitars centres on the figure of Floyd 'Schoolboy' Barton. The play begins with his friends returning from his funeral before we move back in time to witness the events which led to that death. Floyd seems on the verge of success in the white-dominated recording industry but has no money to get his band together. Like *Ma Rainey*, however, this is not a play about white exploitation. The focus is clearly on Floyd and his friends. Like the rooster which crows in the next yard, they strut around, displaying for the women who essentially find their own destinies through the men to whom they commit themselves.

Wilson himself has said of this period, 'The situation of blacks was hopeful after the war. We thought, "When we fight and die for our country, we will no longer be second-class citizens." But we quickly found that we remained stigmatized by color and culture.'[80] That is the context within which his characters live their lives but it is not presented as determining those lives. The men do arm themselves but those are not the means by which they will achieve real power. Indeed, the weapons are turned against themselves, as in *Ma Rainey*.

For Wilson, the back yard in which the action is set is a place of death but also a place of new life. *Seven Guitars*, he has said, 'is about people battling society and themselves for self-worth'.[81] It is a song of lament and achievement. From the very first moments of the play the air is full of music, ironic, humourous, sad: the blues. And as Wilson insists, 'The blues . . . is simplicity and profundity at the same time. It's a cultural response to the world that contains our world view and our ideas of life. If we disappeared and someone found these recordings, they could tell about our pain, our pleasure, our God, our devil.'[82] That is the nature of this and his other plays. Like the blues they are designed 'to give clear and luminous meaning to the song which is a wail and a whelp of joy'.[83]

Seven Guitars is full of stories, songs, myths, the small change of life. It is sensual, lyrical, polyphonic, comic and at moments violent. It stages rituals of courtship and displays of male aggression. It orchestrates the voices of those who sing their lives, who reach beyond disillusionment and despair in search of a future which they spin out of dreams and fantasies.

Wilson is not about the business of forging revolutionary heroes, honing racial polemics or generating theatrical energy out of confrontation across racial divides. Like Floyd 'Schoolboy', he is a blues player anxious only to sing. That his songs are in part a product of the pressure under which all his characters live their lives, the pressure of racism, is true enough. But they are also a product of something beyond that, of the effort to make sense of flawed relationships and a flawed life in which the fact of death has the power to threaten all coherences and corrode all dreams.

His characters are resisters on the grand scale, no matter the circumstances of their lives. They are survivors whose survival depends on their own capacity to create meaning, moment by moment, out of pain no less than pleasure. The seven guitars of the title are the seven characters each of whom makes his or her own music but who, taken together, create a complex symphony. That is Wilson's theatrical strategy: that is, equally, his social and even metaphysical conviction. Through drama his community extends beyond that assembled on the stage.

For Suzan-Lori Parks, writing in 1995,

the history of History is in question . . . a play is a blueprint of an event: a way of creating and rewriting history through the medium of literature. Since history is a recorded or remembered event, theatre, for me, is the perfect place to 'make' history – that is, because so much of African-American history has been unrecorded, dismembered, washed out, one of my tasks as playwright is to – through literature and the special strange relationship between theatre and real-life – locate the ancestral burial ground, dig for bones, find bones, hear the bones sing, write it down.[84]

That may seem like a description of August Wilson's strategy. He, after all, has set himself to hear the bones sing, re-remember history and then reintegrate it into a past whose membrane remains permeable precisely because history can never be a finished project. But Suzan Lori-Parks's approach is rather different. While insisting that theatre is 'an incubator for the creation of historical events',[85] that history is, in fact, to be shaped by the way in which it is constructed, by the language through which it is explored, a language refigured to acknowledge incremental shifts in meaning and experience. Hers is a theatre in which reiterative riffs of language are deployed, an approach which confessedly owes something to Gertrude Stein in one direction and jazz and oral tradition in another. As she has explained, 'for me, language is a physical act. It's something which involves your entire body – not just your head. Words are spells which an actor consumes and digests – and through digesting creates a performance on stage.'[86] A spell, to Parks, is also 'a place of great (unspoken) emotion . . . a place for an emotional transition'[87] in her work. It is tempting to recall that the title of one of Ntozake Shange's works was *Spell # 7*, though her sense of the incapacity of language to achieve what music or dance can suggests a different emphasis. On the other hand, Parks does advocate 'dancing around as you write',[88] implying that movement, too, has a history and the body a memory.

Given the success of Wilson it is a little odd to see her wondering 'if a drama involving Black people can exist without the presence of the White' even when she refines her statement to substitute 'interest' for 'presence.' For other dramatists, it seems, 'Blackness' becomes 'merely a state of "Non-Whiteness"',[89] as though the lives of Black people could only make sense in terms of the absent but ultimately defining oppressor. It is a familiar dilemma, identified by Jean-Paul Sartre, for whom the risk was that rebellion would be shaped by what it opposed. The fact is, though, that Wilson, for the most part, avoids this temptation. Parks's rebellion, meanwhile, is not against white America, whose sins of omission and commission she nonetheless notes, and not merely in passing, it is against forms of representation that can themselves be enslaving or at least which, for her, fail to unlock a world of possibility. That world of possibility may itself have social and even political implications, but, more significantly, it unlocks words, ways of thinking and feeling, and hence ways of being.

There is more than an element of fable as there is of ritual in her work as she substitutes her own myths for those which have been validated as history. She is a subversive writer but not in a directly political sense. Her humour, her irony, her sometimes subtle, but more often deliberately broad and caricatured characters, are aimed to subvert conventional responses. Aware that language itself has a history, that locked up within it are presumptions, attitudes, values, that it determines as well as expresses the user, she foregrounds it as subject as well as an agent of thought. Thus, as she says, 'Each word is configured to give the actor a clue to their physical life. Look at the difference between "the" and "thuh." The "uh" requires the actor to employ a different physical, emotional, vocal attack.'[90]

Behind Parks's comments is a determination to stake out new territory, to explain her own aesthetic, for which she proposes the following formula:

BLACK PEOPLE $+$ x $=$ NEW DRAMATIC CONFLICT
(NEW TERRITORY)

where x is 'the realm of situations showing African-Americans in states other than the Oppressed by/Obsessed with "Whitey" state; where the

White when present is not the oppressor, and where audiences are encouraged to see and understand and discuss these dramas in terms other than the same old shit'.[91] She doth protest too much. Her undoubted originality does not turn on her avoidance of such situations (while Bullins, Shange and Wilson, for example, do not write 'the same old shit') but on her attitude to language, which shapes character as it does event. For her, an infiltration of the past involves its linguistic reconstruction.

Her attitude to the past, meanwhile, is more usually ironic and comic than angry. As she has said, 'I can get more out of history if I joke with it than if I shake my finger at it and stomp my feet. The approach you take toward your subject really determines what you're going to get. So I say to history, "Anything you want. It's okay, you can laugh."'[92]

Suzan-Lori Parks came to public attention in 1989 with *Imperceptible Mutabilities in the Third Kingdom*, which won an Obie Award the following year for Best New American Play. Other plays include *Greeks* (1990), *The Death of the Last Black Man in the Whole Entire World* (1990), *The America Play* (1991), *Devotees in the Garden of Love* (1991) and *Venus* (1996).

The very linguistic freedom of her plays – she develops her own language, based on a black demotic which, ironically, she glosses as 'foreign words and phrases' – reflects the freedom she claims to reinvent the past less on a literal than an imaginative level. She circles her subject, offering oblique insights, developing disturbing metaphors and metamorphoses. Clichés are inhabited and transformed, tragedy is restaged as comedy. The fact of slavery and transportation, the assassination of Lincoln, the impact of Vietnam, exist as points of reference, defining experiences and events, but their meaning is absorbed into the incantatory rhythms and exuberant inventiveness of works whose meaning lies, in part, in their form and method. The freedom which begins on the level of language is emblematic of a more radical revisioning of past, present and future. Character and plot do not exist in a conventional sense. They are so many brush strokes, markers, figures in a design whose incompletions and spaces are as important as the shapes they seem to form. While respecting the forms used by others, she distrusts linearity and the implications of naturalism, with its presumptions about the self and social structures. She deliberately dislocates the supposed fixities of identity and history alike, developing an aesthetic which turns on accretion, accumulation, incremental change.

Interrogating her own style she asks, 'What does it mean for characters to say the same thing twice? 3 times? Over and over and over and oh-vah . . . How does that effect their physical life? Is this natural? Non-natural?' Her answer is that, in *Betting on the Dust Commander* (1987),

the 'climax' could be the accumulated weight of the repetition – a residue that, like city dust, stays with us. After years of listening to Jazz, and classical music too, I'm realizing that my writing is very influenced by music; how much I employ its methods. Through reading lots I've realized how much the idea of Repetition and Revision is an integral part of the African and the African-American literary and oral traditions.[93]

She is, she has said, interested in how 'Rep and Rev – a literal incorporation of the past – impact on the creation of the theatrical experience'.[94]

Explaining the origin of *The America Play* (1990–3), she identifies the route from her fascination with language to her concern with history. She wanted, she explains, to write about a hole. 'You can riff off the word, you can think about that word and what it means and where it takes you . . . You think of h-o-l-e and then w-h-o-l-e and then black hole, and then you think of time and space and when you think of time and space you think of history.'[95] The opening stage direction, in a play whose epigraph is John Locke's statement, 'In the beginning the whole world was America', is thus, 'A great hole. In the middle of nowhere. The hole is an exact replica of the Great Hole History.'[96]

Suzan Lori-Parks is an acquired taste. Her statements about her work can often seem wilfully naive. Her theatrical experiments – and she is aware of herself as marking out new territory – can indeed be liberating, and were received as such by many reviewers. But like Gertrude Stein, or, in another direction, the Stein-influenced Richard Foreman, she can also be somewhat gnomic and tangential. What carries audiences through and beyond such concerns, however, is the vividness of the language, the moment by moment inventiveness and a humour which can be as broad as that in those theatrical forms which once traduced black life but which in her hands celebrate it.

A rather different approach to history is adopted by Anna Deavere Smith, who has set herself to tape conversations with ordinary Americans for a performance called *On the Road: A Search for American Character* (1993). An actress as well as writer, she has presented this material in the form of a monologue. A section of the larger work, *Fires in the Mirror*, derived from material about the clash between blacks and Jews in Brooklyn Heights, led to an Obie citation. She followed this with *Twilight Los Angeles* (1992) about the 1992 riots. In contrast to August Wilson, however, her objective lies in a broader presentation of the American dilemma. As she has explained,

There are so many twists and turns in our race drama. It's no longer black and white. It's harder to define ourselves merely along racial lines. How will American theatre, which has, in the past, shaped itself around an ethnocentric aesthetic, respond to the drama of America . . . Will the theatre respond by creating a language, a way of seeing, an audience, an artist who has the facility to perceive . . . the obscured, to see the twists and turns, to see inconsistencies, ambivalences, ambiguities?[97]

When black drama began to make its mark it was predominantly as a male activity. The key anthologies of the sixties and early seventies – *New Plays for the Black Theatre*, *New Black Playwrights*, *The Black Drama Anthology*, *Black Drama in America: An Anthology*, *A Black Quartet* – between them published fifty-four plays. Only four were by women (Elaine Jackson, Sonia Sanchez, Salamu and Adrienne Kennedy). The most promising new voice, that of Lorraine Hansberry, had been stilled; that of another, Alice Childress, a woman who had been writing for the theatre for some time, tended to be lost in the stridency of the moment. Even Adrienne Kennedy was marginalised, her surrealistic style proving difficult to accommodate to a new orthodoxy favouring work which addressed the racial situation through realistic or symbolic dramas or through the agit-prop simplicities of revolutionary art. In fact, a glance at the bibliographies will reveal that historically women writers had played a key role. Nonetheless, Alice Childress's *Gold Through the Trees* (1952) was the first play by a black woman to receive a professional performance on the American stage.

Childress appeared as an actress in a number of key productions by the American Negro Theatre in Harlem, *On Striver's Row* (1940) and *Anna Lucaster* being among them. She also wrote a one-act play –*Florence* – for the company. Sensitive to the pressures on black actors and writers she has been concerned to create her own models of black life, resisting alike those offered by the white world and, as the sixties progressed, by a black revolutionary literati in search of exemplary figures. So it is that she received the first Obie Award for her play *Trouble in Mind*, which dramatises the dilemma of a black actor who tries to invest the stereotypical roles he is required to play with some humanity and dignity, while her 1969 play, *Wine in the Wilderness*, stages the problem of the black artist in creating images of black life which have truth rather than mere utility. Alice Childress's drama is direct, even melodramatic. Her concern is with the relationship between men and women, often in the context of a racially charged situation. Stylistically unadventurous – her play *The*

Wedding Band (1972–3), about an interracial love affair is a piece of sturdy realism she nonetheless creates theatre which is compelling by virtue of its human commitments. As she has said, 'I concentrate on portraying have nots in a have society . . . The Black writer explains pain to those who inflict it. Those who repress and exclude us also claim the right to instruct us on how best to react to oppression.'[98] Her work, however, is rooted in particular experiences, experiences based in race and gender but not wholly defined by either.

Adrienne Kennedy is stylistically at the other extreme. Unlike Childress a university graduate, she studied creative writing at Columbia in the mid-1950s. Her first success came with *Funnyhouse of a Negro*, presented in 1962 as part of a workshop presided over by Edward Albee. It won an Obie Award. Part of Albee's enthusiasm stemmed from the play's stylistic originality. Its central character, Sarah, fragments into a series of roles, white and black, male and female. She is a product of the pressures brought to bear on her. As Kennedy explains:

It was a huge breakthrough for me when my main characters began to have other personas – it was in fact my biggest breakthrough as a writer . . . I had many recurrent dreams . . . I started to let the images accumulate by themselves. When I made the breakthrough where I discovered that the character could have other personas, the images seemed more indigenous.[99]

Character is reconstituted as image or explored for its dissonance and harmony. On the literal level the pressure on character proves unsustainable and Sarah dies, a suicide, but the tension which destroys her does prove sustainable in art. The play contains and shapes contradiction as she cannot.

The style she developed for *Funnyhouse of the Negro* proved the key to what followed. A note to *The Owl Answers* (1963) explains that 'The characters change slowly back and forth into and out of themselves, leaving some garment from their previous selves upon them always to remind us of the nature of she who is Clara Passmore who is the Virgin Mary who is the Bastard who is the Owl's world.'[100] A similar note to *A Rat's Mass*, performed in Boston in 1966 and in New York three years later, explains that 'BROTHER RAT has a rat's head, a human body, a tail. SISTER RAT has a rat's body, a human head, a tail. ROSEMARY wears a Holy Communion dress and has worms in her hair.'[101] There is no stable surface, no confident sub-text. *The Owl Answers*, like *Dutchman*, is set on a subway train, but where in LeRoi Jones's play that setting is the literal

context for a symbolic action, in Kennedy's play even that dissolves. She
has explained her own approach in terms of image and dream:

I see my writing as a growth of images. I think all my plays come out of dreams
I had two or three years before; I played around with the images for a long
period of time to try to get the most powerful dreams . . . *A Rat's Mass* was based
on a dream I had once . . . in which I was being pursued by red, bloodied rats
. . . I was just haunted by that image for years . . . I try to take these images and
. . . find out what the sources for them are. All this is unconscious . . . I'm not in
that much control of it . . . there was always great confusion in my own mind
of where I belonged, if anywhere . . . I struggled for a long time to write plays
– as typified by *Funny House* – in which the person is in conflict with their inner
forces, with the conflicting sides to their personality, which I found to be my own
particular, greatest conflicts. I had worked for a long time before I did *Funny
House* on having people in a room with conflicts. I was very much in awe of
Tennessee Williams at the time and so I imitated him. Somehow it just didn't
work. It didn't have any power. I just didn't believe it when I read it. Starting
with *Funny House*, I finally came up with this one character, Sarah, who, rather
than talk to her father or mother, talked with these people she created about her
problems. It's very easy for me to fall into fantasy.[102]

It is, indeed, but it is not always as easy to interpret that fantasy in terms
of metaphor.

As Alice Childress reminds us, black Americans are the only racial
group within the United States ever to be forbidden to learn to read and
write. Yet, at the same time, as slaves it had been necessary to master an
alien language the better to be able to perform their required duties.
There was, in other words, a doubleness to language. It was simultaneously the badge of enslavement and a key to liberation. The slave narrative, an articulate claim to hegemony over experience, constituted a
crucial assertion of intellectual accomplishment and stood, hence, as a
moral demand. Yet that narrative was shaped by other traditions than
those born out of the history and prehistory of slavery. In a broader
sense that has always been a major paradox for the black writer.
Language is a product of history; there is a syntax, a grammar to power
that is congruent with that of speech or, still more, the written word. To
address the Other in his own language is already to concede a hierarchy
of values, to deny the equality which is the implied meaning of the discourse. The central character in Alex Haley's *Roots* at first refuses to
speak the language of his captors or to utter the name which they have
imposed on him; he thereby refuses to acknowledge not only their power
but the legitimacy of that power. The alternative, however, is silence. It

was not an alternative claimed by Alex Haley who chose to live with the paradox and invest it with irony.

James Baldwin was attacked in the late sixties and early seventies because his language was controlled, tamed. The balanced sentences implied rational debate where passion was required. His rhetorical style seemed shaped for a white audience with which he seemed to identify himself at least for the purposes of literary strategy. His studied articulateness seemed itself to be an appeal for inclusion in a world whose experiences were not his own. Ralph Ellison, too, was attacked as a writer who admired Melville and Twain, whose novel, *Invisible Man*, incorporated quotations from James Joyce, who, in short, looked outside the black world even in the act of seemingly celebrating that world. Whatever language might be spoken by the characters in the black novel the voice that narrated, that contained these characters and shaped the narrative, was barely distinguishable from that which controlled the fictional world of *The Grapes of Wrath* or *Tender is the Night*. Alice Walker was to attempt to address that problem in *The Color Purple*, handing the narrative to a character – Miss Celie – whose own imperfect command of written language is the mark of a crucial integrity which distinguishes her even from her missionary-educated sister.

Drama has no mediating voice or only implicitly so. The characters speak or do not out of their own created consciousness. They have a physical presence which simple description can only approximate and may indeed deny. Their co-presence on a physical stage which is a condition of drama is an enactment of community, which in the novel must be asserted or established through narrative. For Ntozake Shange, who felt that both her social origins and her gender were of fundamental importance, this aspect of theatre was crucial.

Growing up in St Louis in the 1950s she had encountered racism: working in women's studies programmes in California had alerted her to the historical reality of sexism. Her own interest in dance served to underline not simply the importance of the physical dimension of her work but also the extent to which that physicality was expressive of her double identity as black and woman. What resulted was a series of poems, inspired by Judy Grahn's *The Common Woman*, dramatising aspects of the lives of seven women, which she performed to musical accompaniment, first in Berkeley, in 1974, and subsequently at the Public Theatre in New York and on Broadway. Under the title *For Colored Girls Who Have Considered Suicide/ When the Rainbow Is Enuf* it celebrated the emergence of the black woman into a full sense of her own strength and potential. Very deliberately at odds with conventional dramatic structures, it proposed music, rhythm, song, physicality, sensuality as liberating and defining qualities for black women and hence as necessary elements of any theatrical experience which offers to celebrate and present such women. It sets out, in the words of one of the characters, to

> sing a black girl's song
> bring her out
> to know herself
> to know you
> but sing her rhythms
> carin' / struggle / hard times
> sing her song of life
> she's been dead so long
> closed in silence so long
> she doesn't know the sound
> of her own voice
> her infinite beauty
> she's half-notes scattered
> without rhythm / no tune
> sing her sighs
> sing the song of her possibilities
> sing a righteous gospel
> let her be born.[103]

The performance inhabits dangerous territory. Far from resisting stereotypes about black sensuality and rhythm, it embraces them. Far from denying the significance of emotion and intuition to women it asserts them. The pathology of the urban ghetto is not refuted; it is transcended. All of this seems a little easy, but we are not invited to 'read' the play in terms of realism. Shange deals in archetypes. Her concern is to break other models – social models, dramatic models and to deny the power of a language which she declares she wishes to 'attack, deform . . . maim'.

Her later work, *Spell #7: geechee jiboana quik magic trance manual for technologically stressed third world people* (1979) had similar ambitions, reconstructing and then subverting the minstrel show image of blacks and seeking in its own methodology – once again dance, music, verse a method of building an identity not usurped or shaped by whites. Shange's work, like that of Alice Walker in the novel, was evidence of a broadening of concerns by black women writers beyond that of race. The feminist movement may, historically, have had its roots in the fight for racial justice in the nineteenth century no less than the mid-twentieth century, but it was also a reaction against the sexism which, particularly in the sixties and early seventies, came to afflict the black movement. As some of the public battles for racial equality were won, it became increasingly evident that other battles still lay ahead for women effectively relegated to support status in the civil rights movement and regarded as chattels or queens in the black power movement. If black dramatists saw their theatre as an extension of their battles for dignity and identity in the 1960s, redefining the audience for their plays and creating works which bore the weight of social action, in the 1970s it would be women who discovered in theatre a powerful device for analysing and presenting their anxieties in a public arena, for placing at the centre of dramatic attention those formerly relegated to the margin, economically, socially, politically and theatrically.

If social and economic power has historically resided with men, in America and elsewhere, the drama constructed out of social life has tended to reflect this fact. In *A Raisin in the Sun* Lorraine Hansberry focuses on a man, Walter Younger, precisely because the myth which he internalises is essentially a male one. The American dream, which requires the individual to dominate his environment and seize a promise of economic and social advancement, constitutes a fiat which he cannot bring himself to deny. The denial of his social role is also a denial of his familial and sexual one. It is in this sense that Hansberry feels that it is '*his* ambition, *his* frustrations and *his* decisions . . . which decisively drive the play on'.[104]

In a culture in which political destinies have been shaped and public myths generated by men it is hardly surprising that they should have equally dominated its popular culture, its literature and its theatre. The taming of a continent, the struggle with nature, the accumulation of wealth, the pursuit of status has, as that language suggests, been seen as a function of maleness. And was that not the business of America, its manifest destiny? Until enfranchised, women were quite literally seen as the mere observers of history, not its engine. Their realm was a private one as that of men was a public one. For Lillian Hellman this had some basis in reality, whether that behaviour be rooted in gender difference or role: 'I think women almost have to be more . . . interested in a personal life than men have to be . . . I think women, no matter how liberated they are, feel more pressed to look for a personal life, whether it's a husband or a lover or a house or children or whatever it is, than men feel pressed

318 Modern American Drama, 1945–2000

to.'[105] It is certainly true that a great deal of women's drama in the seventies and eighties chose to explore emotional life, the relationship between mother and daughter, that between sisters; its central subjects were the fear of and yet desire for abandonment, and the threat of cancer. Thematically these plays were concerned with the necessity for self-definition, for the acceptance of the burden of freedom. But as that should make clear, such themes, no matter how much they are approached through the acting out of private emotional crises, are by no means privatist. Just as Willy Loman's struggle with private demons simultaneously dramatised a public dilemma, so, too, did that of the characters in many of the plays written by women at last encouraged to participate in a theatre which had not always previously proved hospitable.

A 1973 *New York Times* survey suggested that family responsibilities inhibit women from working in the theatre, Judith Barlow subsequently noting how few of America's earlier women dramatists had children. For playwright Honor Moore, women dramatists anyway existed only in the 'nooks and crannies'. But, as Julia Miles, director of the Women's Project has pointed out, women have in fact been a significant, if partly invisible presence in the American theatre. In the 1902–3 season women wrote 22 per cent of the new original plays. It is also true that more than half the plays produced by George Pierce Baker's Harvard Workshop 47 between 1913 and 1917 were by women, while a third of the ninety-two productions staged by the Provincetown Players between 1915 and 1922 were written by such women as Neith Boyce, Louise Bryant, Edna St Vincent Millay, Djuna Barnes, Edna Ferber and Susan Glaspell. The same could scarcely be said, though, of the Group Theatre, the Theatre Guild or even the Federal Theatre, while Broadway remained to a remarkable degree largely a male preserve. But when Gerald Bordman, in what is claimed as the standard one-volume reference book on the American theatre (*The Oxford Companion to American Theatre*), lists only just over forty women playwrights between Otis Warren (born 1728) and Marsha Norman (born 1947) this is, to put it mildly, an understatement. Nevertheless in the seventy years of the Pulitzer Prize for drama (beginning in 1918) the award has only gone to women on six occasions (Susan Glaspell, Zoe Atkins, Mary Chase, Beth Henley, Martha Norman, Wendy Wasserstein). In 1935, partly out of dissatisfaction with the Pulitzer Prize, the New York Drama Critics Circle Award was instituted. It, too, however, managed to reward only four women in the period to 1983 (Lillian Hellman, Carson McCullers, Lorraine Hansberry, Beth

Henley). It was also seventy years before Actors Equity – founded in 1912 – elected its first woman president – Ellen Burstyn.

The emergence in the seventies and eighties of a significant number of women's theatre groups – including the Women's Project which, in its first six seasons, produced 160 workshop and rehearsed readings, 22 studio productions and 4 mainstage productions – suggests that the relative paucity of women playwrights has less to do with their marital status and maternal roles than with attitude of mind, encouragement and production possibilities.

As with many black theatre groups of the 1960s, some of the newly created women's theatre companies had an ambivalent function. Concerned to effect a transformation in consciousness and thereby in social behaviour they saw themselves as fostering a drama designed specifically to raise consciousness, to offer a supportive environment. With such names as the New Feminist Repertory, It's All Right to Be a Woman, Womanspace Theatre, Circle of the Witch and, indeed, The Women's Project, they signalled their priorities. As Helen Keyssor has suggested in *Feminist Theatre*, 'characters in feminist plays only rarely transcend their contexts'.[106] This is partly because they see themselves very self-consciously as laying foundations. Far from wishing to transcend their contexts they wish to make those contexts translucently clear. The communality of the theatre thus becomes a tool, an image, an exemplum. In the words of the It's All Right to Be a Woman Company,

We make theatre out of our lives, our dreams, our feelings, our fantasies. We make theatre by letting out the different parts of us that we have pushed inside all our lives . . . Making theatre out of those private parts of ourselves is one way we are trying every day to take our own experiences seriously, to accept our feelings as valid and real.[107]

Theatre may thus become a means rather than an end, a mechanism for validating feelings and concerns otherwise marginalised by society. As with so much political theatre of the thirties this may give such plays a social energy not matched by their theatrical sophistication or dramatic power. Writers of less than compelling talent are welcomed for their commitment rather than their skills. But, just as August Wilson could not have written as he did without the black theatre groups of the 1960s who engaged in the necessary task of challenging assumptions and models of black identity, so it seems likely that the women's theatre groups of the seventies and eighties will prove to have served a similar function.

For the anarchist Emma Goldman, writing in 1914 on the social significance of modern drama, the artist was or should be what Auguste Strindberg had called a 'lay preacher, popularizing the pressing questions of his time'.[108] Twenty-two years later, the director of the Federal Theatre Hallie Flanagan saw the virtue of that theatre as lying in the fact that 'it is impregnated with facts of life commonly outside the consciousness of the theatre worker'.[109] They spoke in the context of a theatre self-consciously seeking to address the social issues of the day, albeit a theatre concerned with economics rather than gender. Thirty years on, once more women insisted that drama open itself up to those issues which were felt on the pulse. Now, though, those were more likely to be to do with the role and identity of women in society.

It was in the 1960s, with the growth of Off and Off-Off Broadway, that the woman playwright began to find some space to occupy. A new audience emerged, younger, more open to experiment, less committed to orthodoxies of form or subject. Adrienne Kennedy, Irene Fornes, Rosalyn Drexler, Rochelle Owens and Megan Terry found a ready response. In the decade that followed a more self-consciously feminist theatre emerged. The co-founders of the Women's Experimental Theatre (Clare Ross, Roberta Sklar and Sandra Segal) explained their philosophy in a manifesto published in Karen Malpede's 1983 book *Women in Theatre: Compassion and Hope:*

The work of the Women's Experimental Theatre is predicated on the belief that women have a separate and distinct experience. Our plays give testimony to the uniqueness and stature of that experience. We see through feminist eyes. We rigorously focus on women's lives and are engaged in developing forms of research and presentation that reflect and create women's culture. We call upon the woman in the audience to experience herself as a woman at the center of her own life, to acknowledge the validity of her experience, to feel her commonality with the other women in the theatre, to reflect upon her separateness, to consider change, to celebrate. Most theatre is male theatre – men talking to other men about what is important to men. Our theatre is by, about, and for women.[110]

The objective is that outlined by Helene Cixous in her essay 'The Laugh of the Medusa':

By writing her self, woman will return to the body which has been more than confiscated from her, which has been turned into the uncanny stranger on display – the ailing or dead figure, which so often turns out to be the nasty companion, the cause and location of inhibitions. Censor the body and you censor breath and speech at the same time. Write your self. Your body must be heard.[111]

One playwright who benefited from the emergence of a reinvigorated Off and Off-Off Broadway theatre was Rochelle Owens. Though her performance play, *Futz* (originally written in 1958), had its initial performance at the Tyrone Guthrie Workshop in Minneapolis in 1965, it was New York's burgeoning alternative theatre which provided a stage for the poetic, surrealist metaphors which were the essence of her work. She herself has explained that her primary interest is

in the flow of imagination between actors and the director, the boundless possibilities of interpretation of a script. Different theatrical realities are created and/or destroyed depending upon the multitudinous perception and points of view of the actors and director who share in the creation of the design of the unique journey of playing the play. There are as many ways to approach my plays as there are combinations of people who might involve themselves.[112]

That injunction applies equally to the audience exposed to works whose allusiveness and occasional opacities resist simple interpretation.

The play takes us into elemental passions and bizarre experiences. *Futz* concerns a man's love for a pig, *The String Game* a priest's self-defeating attempts to control the sexual appetites of his Eskimo flock. In *Istanboul* we move in a world of Norman men and Byzantine women, a world, like that of her first two plays, marked by grotesque deaths and sensual appetites. *Beclch*, set in a mythic Africa, centres on a Queen who explores and transcends the limits of excess, of sexuality and violence, while a later work, *He Wants Shih!*, set in the China of the Manchu dynasty, features the dismembered head of the last Emperor which disconcertingly continues to speak. To Owens, 'If *Beclch* is about the doom of excess then *Shih* is about the doom of total renunciation – an excess, too, in a way.'[113] It hardly needs saying that Owens deals in a surreal, gothic universe. Her plays offer bizarre images, dream-like structures with an associative logic. Even when her work seems grounded in a tangible history – *The Karl Marx Play* and *Emma Instigated Me* both deal with historical figures, the latter with Emma Goldman – this is a history that dissolves, takes the impress of the mind which imagines itself into being.

As Rochelle Owens has explained, she sees her function as a playwright as being the necessity to challenge established categories of theatre. This, indeed, in part explains her fascination with Emma Goldman: 'I became excited about the idea of Emma Goldman describing herself as an anarchist . . . the process of artmaking is linked with random and accidental happenings that the artist encounters, a state of confusion and disorder, which is what anarchy is. One creates out of the disorder.' As a poet she is concerned 'to explore "meanings made anew"'. Indeed it is precisely 'the rhythms and tonal meanings as well as the inspired imagery of the language',[114] which compel her attention. As a woman she is committed to investigating the nature of the relationship between men and women, reinterpreting her own early work as a series of feminist statements in the light of a developing feminist criticism which unlocked aspects of her own plays even to herself. By the time of the Obie Award-winning *Chucky's Hunch* (1981), however, this dimension of her drama was explicit, her principal male character, a failed artist, being described by Owens as 'a type of self-pitying male that a lot of women recognise as having known, married or lived with, at one time or another. These men always regard women as support systems of one kind or another . . . The very last thing they want in a woman is a competitor.'[115] Behind this remark lies a certain bitterness at the response of theatre reviewers, themselves almost exclusively men, to work whose elliptical qualities they profess to find baffling, but whose response she suspects to be rooted in a sexism which will accept such indirection from Beckett or Shepard but not from her. Her risk-taking, however, is more radical in certain respects and the price of risk-taking may be failure fully to communicate. Her associative logic is not always easy to follow and there is a gnomic quality to some of her plays not satisfactorily resolved by critical exegesis.

Equally resistant to realism was Maria Irene Fornes who arrived in the United States from Cuba in 1945 at the age of fifteen. Her interest in theatre was sparked by the French production of *Waiting for Godot*. She began writing with *Tango Palace* (1963) and the influence of Beckett seemed clear enough. First produced by the San Francisco Actors Workshop, it features two figures, one of whom begins the play in a canvas sack, while the other 'is a mixture of man and woman'. Together they act out a ritualised game, enacting a sequence of different roles while, like Beckett's Vladimir and Estragon, they try to understand their situation. Maria Irene Fornes has explained that the play derived from 'a feeling about their relationship between a mentor of some sort and a student'.[116] It is a 'play' in several senses. The tone is playful, as the characters play a series of games and enact a number of mini-dramas. One of the characters is described as 'an androgynous clown' and here, as elsewhere in the work, character is fluid. These are not figures who represent any consistent psychology. Indeed in *The Successful Life of 3* (1965) the characters are named He, She and 3, as in *Prominade* (1965) they are either denoted by numbers (105, 106) or by letters (Miss O, Miss U, Mr

R, Mrs S). Speeches, in these early plays, are rarely sustained for more than a single sentence or re-form into verse.

Her approach to character is reminiscent of the Open Theatre's transformation technique, in which radical and sudden changes of character were the basis both of their acting exercises and of plays developed out of the company's work by such writers as Jean-Claude van Itallie and Megan Terry. It is hardly surprising, therefore, to find her work produced by the Open Theatre. But, dissatisfied with the surrender of control implicit in the author's handing of the text to others, she quickly moved to directing her own plays.

Though some of her work has responded to political events, notably *A Vietnamese Wedding*, performed in 1967 as part of a week of protest against American involvement in Vietnam (though in truth more lyrical, more celebratory than protesting), and some has been characterised by critics as feminist (for Bonnie Marranca *Fefu is* deeply feminist in its perspective and guiding spirit) Maria Fornes has herself tended to resist too casual a labelling of works which remain essentially personal and idiosyncratic. Hence her own account of her 1983 play, *Mud*, insists that 'it is not an anti-male play . . . It is also not a feminist play.' Her feminism, particularly in this play, consists of making women central to her work and perhaps in the freedom with which she focuses on sexuality. Of *Mud* she has remarked,

It says something about woman's place in the world, not because she is good or a heroine, not because she is oppressed by men or because the man 'won't let her get away with it,' but simply because she is at the centre of that play. It is her mind that matters throughout the play . . . It is because of that mind, Mae's mind, *a woman's mind*, that the play exists. To me that is a more important step toward redeeming women's position in the world than whether or not *Mud* has a feminist theme, which it does not . . . I believe that to show a woman at the centre of a situation, at the centre of the universe, is a much more important feminist statement than to put Mae in a situation that shows her in an unfavourable position from which she escapes, or to say that she is noble and the men around her are not.[117]

In many ways woman's drama, whatever its subject, whatever its tone, constitutes a statement, an assertion. It is an argument for the relocation of the centre. In a male cultural imperium the woman is liable to be seen as marginal, a province of an empire whose power, language, authority and coherence lies elsewhere. The assumption of significance to women's experience is an attempt, by women writers, not only to address the details of their lives but to think themselves out of a centre defined by default. They are, in effect, resisting a culture of appropriation which gives meaning to women only as they are seen in relation to men. Not concerned with writing back to that centre, they have implicitly asserted the existence of a different hierarchy of values and concerns. For the ardent feminist that may constitute the creation of a new imperium; for others it is simply to imply the legitimacy of different, co-existing and interpenetrating systems. That may suggest an effort to decolonise the mind, and a significant number of plays by women have taken as their subject women who emerge from the power of men, much as countries have emerged from the paternalism of empire. The struggle for independence and a separate identity seems to carry with it that same anxiety and vulnerability which African writers have acknowledged in newly emergent countries. It is almost certainly to reach for a new language in a competitive language system; it is to insist on a space in which new meanings can cohere and new relationships be negotiated.

For Sue-Ellen Case, in *Feminism and Theatre*, Freud's emphasis on the self as a male self had fed into theatre via Stanislavsky and Method acting: 'The techniques for the inner construction of a character rely on Freudian principles, leading the female actor into that misogynistic view of female sexuality.' More specifically, 'In building such characters as Amanda in Tennessee Williams's *Glass Menagerie*, the female actor learns to be passive, weak and dependent in her sexual role, with a fragile inner life that reveals no sexual desire.' This is contrasted with the character of Alan Strang in Peter Shaffer's *Equus*, where 'the young man's sexuality is blatant and aggressive, giving the male actor a complex and active internal monologue.'[118] It is a curious comparison which seems to begin with its conclusions.

In the case of Amanda we are offered a portrait of a woman in her fifties, shaped by the assumptions of her own culture, who, like that culture, has chosen to deny the reality of experience, to refuse to allow into language realities which conflict with the myths which she embraces as her defence against self-knowledge. Infinitely more subtle and complex than Shaffer's protagonist, she displaces her own sexuality onto a daughter who she wishes both to protect and surrender. By wrenching these characters out of their cultural contexts, by failing to locate them in terms of dramatic context or psychological function, Sue-Ellen Case builds a model of women characters and their portrayal which is unsustainable. Thus, we are told that 'From Antigone to Blanche Dubois, the female actor works on the passive, broken, sexual development of their characters, which isolates them from the social community rather than integrating them into it.'[119] Assertions about Method technique blend into assumptions about gender roles in world drama which are surely unsupportable and which certainly make no useful distinction between male and female playwrights (what, after all, are we to make of Susan Glaspell, Lillian Hellman, Carson McCullers or Lorraine Hansberry in these terms?).

Is it helpful to be told that the relationship between Blanche and Stanley in *Streetcar*, the mother and the father in *Long Day's Journey Into Night*, and the dancer, Rosalyn, and cowboy, Gay, in *The Misfits*, portray women's sexuality as 'subordinate and derivative in relation to that of the leading male characters, reflecting the subject position of male sexuality within the Freudian-based theatrical domain'?[120] There is no sense in which Blanche, one of the most powerful characters in American drama, derives her sexuality from or is sexually subordinate to Stanley Kowalski. Her sexuality has a longer and more complex history, being rooted in denial: a denial of time, of death, of reality. Stanley's victory is Pyrrhic. Gay, in *The Misfits*, is a man whose whole system of values has collapsed, who enacts ancient rituals only barely aware that they have been voided of meaning. The moments of contact between him and Rosalyn are moments of mutuality. Mary Tyrone, in *Long Day's Journey Into Night*, a portrait of O'Neill's own mother in a play in which character is rooted at least as much in O'Neill's biography as in the theatricality which invested that biography, is scarcely best understood through a subordinated sexuality. Each of the characters in the play is subordinate – to role, to myth, to fate or memory. In a male household Mary does locate herself in terms of those whose lives have focused her needs, but her sexuality is no more insecure than that of the men for whom her morphine addiction is an image of their own evasion of the real. And does it really advance the analysis of drama or of the role of women in the theatre to be told that realism is a 'prison house of art' for women, reifying the male as sexual object and the female as the sexual 'Other', or that linear narrative is masculine? Not the least of the problems implicit in this kind of analysis is that it results in the rejection not only of those plays which have provided some of the finest women characters in drama but also of those women who have produced powerful and original work. Susan Glaspell's *Trifles*, both realist and linear, is a skilful and effective feminist work, while few playwrights have been as influenced by Freud. Lillian Hellman is attacked for presenting lesbianism as 'a painful, defeating experience' which occurred within a heterosexual rather than lesbian community, and this in a play in which such a lesbian experience is in effect problematic. Lorraine Hansberry is treated with suspicion for placing men at the centre of her work, while Marsha Norman is distrusted for creating inappropriate role models. There is no doubting the justice of observations about the marginalising of women and women's experience in American drama, no doubting either the degree to which the American theatre has, in terms of theatre ownership, authorship, direction, design and reviewing, been a substantially male affair. The creation, from the mid-1970s onwards, of new women's theatre groups thus played a crucial role in permitting a pluralism of voices into the theatre. But the reinvention of plays in a bid to reveal their bias, a bias which reflected that of the society which generated them, has little to offer, more especially when it is conducted with little respect for context or for psychological consistency.

As the 1970s progressed, so the decentralisation of the American theatre came to be reflected in the increasing number of Broadway successes which had received their initial productions elsewhere. It was no longer a case of out-of-town tryouts but of plays by regional dramatists whose talent was fostered by local theatres. Broadway production might still be the ultimate accolade but the economics of Broadway, and the failure of nerve which was a consequence, meant that the initiative passed elsewhere. One impressive product of that process was Marsha Norman. Born and raised in Louisville, Kentucky, she was encouraged to become a dramatist by the artistic director of Louisville's Actors Theatre, subsequently the home of an annual New Plays Festival. Best known for her Pulitzer Prize-winning 'night, Mother, she made her debut with a play if anything more original and compelling and, incidentally, set partly in Louisville, Getting Out (1977). Drawing in part on her experience of working with disturbed children, she dramatises the experiences of Arlene, a woman in her late twenties, just released from an eight-year prison sentence for murder. To this point her life has consisted of little more than prostitution and a bitter assault on the world around her. The child of inadequate parents, she is one of a family of misfits and petty criminals. Brought back from the prison to her home town by a guard whose feelings for her are a confused mixture of sexual aggression and simple human need, she has to decide between a dangerous and possibly well-paid existence on the streets or a menial and poorly paid job working in the kitchen of a local café.

The power of the play derives not only from the ambiguous reality of that choice, whereby a decision to opt for an honest living is simultaneously a decision to choose an anaesthetised existence, as degrading in its own way as prostitution, but also from the play's authenticity of language and originality of conception. Marsha Norman is a musician. As a child her piano was the source of support for a girl whose family's religious fundamentalism led to her isolation from the community. Indeed, at one time she considered enrolling at the Julliard. It is an influence which shows in her work.

As she herself has said, 'rhythm and tone . . . are . . . things you learn best through music, not language'.[121] Certainly, *Getting Out* shows something more than a sensitivity to the rhythms and tonalities of urban speech. It is a play for voices. Arlene exists both as her new self – the self released from more than the prison experience – and her old. As the playwright's notes make clear, this other self, who moves through the action and speaks, is 'Arlene's memory of herself, called up by fears, needs and even simple word cues'. Both characters are vivid, three-dimensional, present, but they contrast with one another. This is a contrapuntal drama in which the two selves are played against one another. Arlie, the younger self, is vital, aggressive, streetwise, foul-mouthed, angry, vindictive, resistant; Arlene is suspicious, guarded, potentially withdrawn, vulnerable, indecisive. Between the two selves lies a prison experience and a single relationship which had brought meaning into her life – a relationship with the prison chaplain. The voices – a past voice and a present voice – contend with one another for the future. There is an underlying continuity. Arlene was born out of Arlie, but the space between them is considerable, the dissonance crucial. No relationship in the play is as vital as this one. Other voices exist: that of the mother, the prison guard, the pimp, the upstairs neighbour, as well as an assortment of high school principals, doctors and wardens. They each represent coercions, influences, threats. They are authority figures offering her a role, a direction, a set of possibilities. But the central need which motivates Arlene is the need to seize control of her own life. The difference in tone between her two voices is vital to her survival, but it is also necessary that she should find a way of coming to terms with her own past. The key moment of the play is thus that in which, finally, both voices sound in unison. Arlene does not deny her former self. She integrates her into her own future.

The problem which confronts Arlene is in a sense the problem which confronts playwright and audience alike. The future which she chooses to embrace is one characterised by blandness and habit. Her horizon

shrinks. The price of her survival – a central theme of this and other
Norman plays – is a menial job and a life whose parameters are bounded
by the supermarket, the television and an occasional game of cards. The
self which she finally outgrows had been destructive but compacted with
energy. Her new freedom contains more than an element of resignation.
The figure who drifts through the play as an image of destructive
anarchy may have a compulsion and an attractiveness lacking in the
older, seemingly broken figure who must make her choice between two
unattractive futures. Not the least achievement of *Getting Out is* that
Arlene's struggle for possession of herself, a battle waged externally with
society and internally with her own destructiveness, is as compelling as
it is.

If this is a play in which male violence and oppression define the
boundaries of experience in one respect (Arlene's mother had been
beaten by her father, as Arlene is the victim of her pimp and potentially
of the prison warder), this is not a play which responds to a simple
gender analysis. The voice of the prison loudspeaker is specified to be
that of a woman. The school principal who rejects her is a woman, while
the person whose kindness and respect begin the process of recovery is
male. Yet at the same time a key relationship here, as in *'night Mother*, is
that between mother and daughter, while the stress on survival, mental
and physical, is one that Norman herself has seen as carrying a specific
meaning for women. The mere fact of placing a woman at the centre of
attention becomes itself a significant step in a national drama and,
indeed, a national literature which has seldom chosen to see the experience of women as culturally vital:

> the appearance of significant women dramatists in significant numbers now is
> a real reflection of a change in women's attitude toward themselves. It is a
> sudden understanding that they can be, and indeed are, the central characters
> in their own lives . . . the problem [is] that the things we as women know best
> have not been perceived to be of critical value to society. The mother–daugh-
> ter relationship is a perfect example of that . . . Part of what we have begun to
> do, *because* of the increasing voice of women in the world, is redefine survival.
> What it means is the ability to carry on your life in such a way that it fulfils and
> satisfies you.[122]

The process of *Getting Out is* precisely one in which its protagonist
struggles to become the central figure in her own life, to escape external
difficulties; hence the ambivalence of its title. That her victory should
itself be hedged around with ambiguity, that the life which she reclaims
seems so void of meaning and direction, is a function of our own ten-

dency to view that life, as the school principal, the warden, the psychiatrist, the pimp and the guard have done, from the outside. In a play in which the very structure denies the legitimacy of such judgements, we are caught in our own bad faith.

There is no condescension in *Getting Out*. But that has not stopped critics from finding such condescension in Marsha Norman's work in so far as both here and in *'night, Mother*, we are offered portraits of psychologically disturbed women who appear to break under pressure. What she chooses to dramatise, it is said, is not women's experience but a pathological version of that experience. It is true that her central technique is to place her characters under pressure, but that is because she is interested in the strategies which they develop to handle the emotional tensions which threaten their stability. They are emotionally vulnerable but that vulnerability is not simply disabling.

In *Third and Oak*, originally produced by the Actors Theatre in 1978, she generates comedy out of the encounter of two women in a laundromat and two men in a pool hall, albeit a brittle comedy that covers the pain of betrayal and loss. A middle-class woman comes to wash her husband's clothes in the middle of the night. By the end of the play we discover that he had died a year earlier and that it has taken the intervening period for her to work up the nerve to deal with the situation. The woman she meets comes from a different world and a different class but she, too, has been abandoned, this time for another woman. For both women, men had been the key to the meaning of their lives. Both are fighting to adjust to the removal of that key. But the laundromat section of *Third and Oak is* balanced by the pool hall section in which a past death and a threatened death precipitate the same sense of abandonment, the same sense of alarm at the disintegration of meaning. This time, though, the focus is as much on men. Men and women may find different methods of handling the emotional crisis in their lives but Marsha Norman resists a simplistic distinction along gender lines.

These early plays reveal a playwright of keen observation, a subtle wit and a sensitivity to the nuances of language. *Getting Out* was moderately successful while the laundromat section of *Third and Oak* was later filmed for Home Box Office, but her real breakthrough came with *'night, Mother*, which opened in Cambridge, Massachusetts in 1982 and moved to Broadway the following year. The play concerns the struggle by Thelma Cates, a woman in her late fifties or early sixties, to prevent her daughter Jessie committing suicide. The play is a duologue. Its simple set is charged with significance in that we learn that Jessie plans to shoot

herself in an adjacent room. The door to that room thus becomes the
route to her death but also, in her mind, to her release. Struggling to
make sense of the failure of her life – her marriage has crumbled, her
son is delinquent, her relationship with her mother is empty and without
consolation – she sees her deliberately willed death as marking a
moment of control. By choosing to die she can choose retrospectively to
shape her life. She must thus resist her mother's effort to deflect her as
one more attempt to snatch that control from her. Her mother, for her
part, must prevent the suicide, partly out of a love which she has never
been able to articulate, partly out of fear of desertion and partly out of
guilt, a sense of responsibility and complicity. Jessie's objective, beyond
a good death, is to relieve her mother of guilt; her mother's objective,
beyond saving her daughter, is to do the same. Ironically this struggle
achieves what they have never achieved before, a sense of closeness.
What has been concealed, denied, evaded is exposed and ultimately
accepted. It also, ironically, gives meaning to both their lives. Jessie, in
taking her life, thereby becomes its author, while her mother is freed
from the banality of her existence. Real feeling animates her. As Marsha
Norman has said, 'the experience of this evening . . . will belong only to
her forever. Probably for the first time, Thelma has something that is
securely hers, that she does not need for anybody else to understand and
would not tell anybody. She has a holy object.'[123]

These are characters who have occupied the same physical space but
not the same emotional world. As in many other of her plays her characters tend to speak past one another in a series of overlapping monologues. Somehow pain can only communicate itself indirectly. For most
of the time it remains locked up within the self. The theatre, to Marsha
Norman, is about the moments in which the barriers briefly collapse. As
she has explained of 'night, Mother, 'It's the moment of connection
between them . . . it is a moment when two people are willing to go as
far as they can with each other . . . This is exactly the kind of meeting
the theatre can document, can present and preserve.'[124]

As with all her plays, 'night, Mother is about survival, and if that seems
a strange way to describe a play in which one character eventually takes
her own life it merely underlines the fact that the survival that concerns
her is the effort to make sense of experience and embrace it. Jessie has
lived her life at one remove. She has been shaped by other people. Now,
with a sudden detachment, she reclaims her life. The fact that she uses
her new sense of power to take her life is, at least in her own mind, the
proof of its reality. As for her mother, rather like Peter, in Edward

Albee's *The Zoo Story*, she has been changed, if not redeemed, so that her survival has become something more than mere repetition and habit.

Marsha Norman's *'night, Mother* has a musical structure: it is

written in sonata form. And works that way . . . When I realized that the piece had basically three parts, suddenly I recognized the musical equivalent was right there and ready . . . In each of the three movements of *'night, Mother*, you'll see that it builds and then settles down and stops, there's a moment of silence and then that second movement picks up.[125]

Certainly it is a play that reveals all her skills with language, not the streetwise talk of *Getting Out* and *Third and Oak* but the competing languages of mother and daughter, language systems which rarely intersect. Jessie wants to use language to open up her life; it is a scalpel cutting away dead flesh. Her mother wants to use it to smother reality, to deny it. Their rhythms are different. Yet the relationship is a central one to Marsha Norman as to other women writers, a territory vacated by male writers. As she has explained,

The mother–daughter relationship . . . is one of the world's great mysteries; it has confused and confounded men and women for centuries . . . and yet it has not been perceived to have critical impact on either the life of the family or the survival of the family, whereas the man's ability to earn money, his success out in the world, his conflicts with his father – these are all things that have been seen as directly influencing the survival of the family. Part of what we have begun to do, because of the increasing voice of women in the world, is redefine survival. What it means is the ability to carry on your life in such a way that it fulfils and satisfies you. With this definition of survival, Mother looms large. What you hope for your life, how you define the various parameters of what's possible for you, those are all things with which Mother is connected . . . As women, our historical role has been to clear chaos, and I will not stop until I have it.[126]

In view of this assertion of the centrality of the mother–daughter relationship in *'night, Mother*, it is surprising to discover that it was attacked by several feminist critics who saw it as capitulating to stereotype and hence being rewarded for its conservatism.

The main thrust of the feminist assault grew out of a rejection of Norman's suggestion that identity could be affirmed through its ultimate denial, and the fact that women were represented in the play by a mother whose narcoticised state was in some way seen as a legitimate response to abandonment, and by a daughter who has allowed herself to bear the burden of other people's betrayals and who sees the only way of handling her problems as lying in self-destruction. No wonder, the argument went, that the, largely male, theatrical establishment had rewarded her, since the play confirmed a model of women as inadequates whose lives drained of meaning once the stereotyped gender roles of wife and mother proved fallible or insupportable. Since, moreover, both women were portrayed as neurotic, in flight from the real and denying themselves, its effect was likely to be reactionary. Such a response denied the irony of Norman's work and the complexity of her characters. The overlapping clarity and self-deceit, characteristic of Jessie, her insistence that suicide will give her a retrospective key to her life yoked to her simultaneous awareness that it will do damage to her mother (why else the events of the play, the struggle to justify herself and absolve her mother?), reveal the playwright concerned with the contradictions of experience and fully alert to the weaknesses no less than the strengths of those whose struggle for survival she depicts. Alive to those areas of women's experience denied by male dramatists, she has no interest in creating consciousness-raising exemplary texts for those wishing to use drama as a means of fostering sisterly solidarity. The attack on her play said a great deal more about divisions within the women's movement than about her supposed betrayal.

A later play, *Traveller in the Dark* (1984), concerned the struggle between a doctor and his minister father for the mind and soul of his son. In choosing to focus on the relationship between men she seems to have moved into a world in which she operates with less assurance. At least to this point it seems that her special strength as a writer is to dissect the motives, feelings and anxieties of women charged with the task of inventing themselves in a world which offers them so little in the way of a personal or public role which they can embrace with assurance or dignity.

Norman's next plays were both comedies. *Sarah and Abraham* (1992), which focuses on the story of the biblical Sarah, Abraham and Hagar, as presented by an improvisatory theatre company, slowly reveals the off-stage drama of a group of actors whose private sexual behaviour manages to intertwine with the work they are presenting. *Loving Daniel Boone* (1992) is set in a Kentucky museum, one of whose exhibits has the power to whisk people back to a past in which they discover as much about themselves as about the period in which they so surprisingly materialise. Both are whimsical works, comedies, and while even her earlier, more powerful dramas were never without humour, here that humour seems to serve little but the conceit out of which it springs. The result is amusing and inventive but not, like *Getting Out* or *'night Mother*, moving.

In *Trudy Blue*, her last play of the decade, humour still exists but is undercut by a central truth. Ginger, the figure at the centre, is dying. The action takes place on a single day but into that day tumble a wealth of memories, a kaleidoscope of fantasies and future projections. This is an imagined as well as a lived life. The past is not finished business. The future consists of more than the threatening oblivion. She is a writer, and fiction, therefore, is a part of her. She summons it to her aid, seeking to comfort herself with inventions. In the book she is writing she creates a man who will offer her the consolation she needs, as, beyond the text, she generates a fantasy guru who will lead her to peace and reconciliation.

The play apparently ends with the death of the protagonist and the publication of her novel, which is named for its central character, Trudy Blue, herself a version of the author. But there are moments when it seems we have left the sensibility of the woman whose memories and imaginings otherwise constitute the play, as though we were projected into the future beyond the moment of her death.

Trudy Blue is, in essence, a defence of the imagination as a resource, as the root of meaning. It is through it that Ginger makes sense of her life, pulls together all the disparate threads of her experience. Afraid of her approaching death, she looks for meaning and finds it, at last, precisely in those threads, those experiences, those connections with others. But it is through the imagination that such patterns become clear. The multiple aspects of her personality and her life can finally be celebrated in themselves but also as they find expression in others and in the dreams, fantasies, fictions which also form part of the woman who now confronts her end with a rediscovered dignity.

The fragmented self of *Trudy Blue* looks back to the fragmented self of *Getting Out*. The struggle for meaning on the edge of death recalls *'night Mother*; the struggle to reconcile competing necessities replays something of the dilemma of *Traveler in the Dark*; the consoling fictions and enlivening fantasies echo those in *Loving Daniel Boone*. This is not to say that Marsha Norman revisits her earlier works but that there is an underlying theme within the variety of her plays. This has to do with the struggle to justify life to itself, with the need to discover how to continue with dignity, the grounds on which survival will be something more than habit and routine, but equally how to face the end contented that some meaning has emerged out of contradiction and failure as out of those moments, rarer, perhaps, of consonance and harmony.

Beth Henley, like Marsha Norman, effectively began her career at the Actors Theatre in Louisville. Her particular gift as a playwright is the

ability to deal with pain and desperation through humour. Her characters are frequently uncertain of themselves, aware of inadequacies, alert
to the precariousness of their identities. They choose to deflect this
awareness, though, with the flip remark, the sardonic aside. At her best
she sustains this tension, allowing the humour to thin out momentarily,
offering a glimpse of the underlying fear and neurosis; at her worst she
allows her work to slide in the direction of sentimentality. She is drawn
to the comic grotesque, pressing character and action to extremes, but
frequently withdraws from the implications of her own vision. The result
can be a release of tension and dramatic conviction.

Her first play, *Am I Blue?* was a product of her sophomore year at
Southern Methodist University, Dallas. Refined over the years, it was
later performed by the Critics Repertory Company in New York in 1982.
An encounter between two teenagers on the verge of sexual initiation,
it has something of Salinger's wry humour and psychological insight, but
the sheer familiarity of her characters – a tomboy girl and an adolescent
boy who hints at a sexual experience which he lacks – gives it a derivative feel. It was her second play, *Crimes of the Heart*, premiered in
Louisville, Kentucky, which brought her attention and success. It won
her both the New York Drama Critics Circle Award and the Pulitzer
Prize when it moved to Broadway in 1981.

Crimes of the Heart is essentially concerned with the relationship
between three sisters. Each of them has failed, emotionally. The world
has not turned out to be what they wished it to be. In the past is a shared
trauma, their mother's death by hanging. This is the temptation they
must each resist. One sister has just turned thirty and sees an emptiness
to her life; another has returned from Hollywood where she failed to
launch her career as a singer. The third sister, married to a successful politician, has just shot him in the stomach rather than shoot herself, having
been caught having an affair with a 15-year-old boy. The ingredients are
in place for a serious drama of women's alienation and there is a suggestion that male insensitivity has driven more than one of them to the
verge of self-destruction, but, instead, the play takes a comic direction,
albeit one that never entirely heals the wounds opened up by experience.
Henley has explained that

Writing always helps me not to feel so angry. I've written about ghastly, black feelings and thoughts . . . The hope is that if you can pin down these emotions and
express them accurately, you will be somehow absolved. I like to write characters
who do horrible things but who you can still like . . . because of their human needs
and struggles . . . I'm constantly in awe of the fact that we still feel love and kindness even though we are filled with dark, primitive urges and desires.[127]

Men play only a marginal role. Two key male figures never appear: the father, whose desertion of their mother seems to have precipitated her death, is present only in name. The husband, shot in the stomach by Babe, remains offstage, his own emotional distance underlined by his absence. The male characters are simply romantic props, images of the paths the women might have followed in their emotional lives.

Beth Henley comes out of a recognisable southern tradition. She deals in the eccentric and the grotesque. She fuses together the violent and the humorous. As she herself has said,

> I've always been very attracted to split images. The grotesque combined with the innocent, a child walking with a cake, a kitten with a swollen head . . . Somehow these images are a metaphor for my view of life . . . Part of that is being brought up in the South; Southerners always bring out the grisly details in any event. It's a fascination with the stages of decay people can live in in this life . . . the imperfections.[128]

The desperation that had led the sisters' mother to commit suicide has left them with psychological wounds, but it has also left them with a determination to survive. Together again, briefly, they generate, in their harmonies and dissensions, a solidarity which, while not denying the past, suggests at least one antidote to their pain, albeit only momentary.

The Wake of Jamey Foster (1982), Beth Henley's next play, was altogether cruder. It ran for only a week on Broadway and is a slight piece. The balance so carefully sustained in *Crimes of the Heart* is sacrificed to the exaggerated humour of comic grotesques who lack that contact with real feeling that had distinguished her earlier play. Much the same was true of *The Miss Firecracker Contest* (1984), where even the comedy began to disappear to be replaced by pathos. That tendency had also been clear in *Am I Blue?*, but in the context of a brief and affectionate character-sketch it had not then proved disabling. In *The Miss Firecracker Contest* her touch is less sure.

Tina Howe may be an admirer of Beckett and Ionesco but her comedy is very much of her own making. She deals in comic grotesques. A self-confessed enthusiast for extravagance, she creates plays in which satire and parody erode even the ground on which she stands. She can, after all, hardly attack the pretensions of the art world, as she does in *Museum* (1976), or those of cookery, as she does in *The Art of Dining* (1979), without being aware that her art, too, is designed for consumption and is vulnerable to the consumer. It is that realisation, indeed, which gives her work its ironic edge. Her plays owe something to vaudeville, with a series of stand-up, or, in the case of *The Art of Dining*, sit-down routines building to a crescendo. In a world of fast-talking, larger-than-life characters, whose conversations overlap and repeat, anarchy is never far away. The platitude begins to acquire a manic edge and hysteria is constantly threatening to erupt. Language offers the first warning tremor. In a consumer world the names of artists, wines, foods become weapons blindly wielded in a battle for status and an elusive satisfaction. Words seem to spill involuntarily from those whose fears and desires are barely under control. A blend of Woody Allen, Ionesco and Elaine May, Tina Howe dramatises the comedy of those who have no grasp on value but a profound anxiety about their own identity and social standing. Both *Museum* and *The Art of Dining* are choreographed like a French farce and indeed much of the humour is generated by the pace at which the action moves, a pace which matches the frenzied drive of those anxious to miss no experience presumed to be fashionable or satisfying.

Her most popular, though not strictly speaking her most original, work to date is *Painting Churches* (1983) in which, once again, art and the making of art is at the centre. This time character is not allowed to slip so far in the direction of parody. Here a poet, his wife and an artist daughter are about to move house. Their lives, in the form of their possessions, are scattered around them preparatory to removal. Father and daughter alike use their art to express their lives. She, though, handles the world obliquely. Her portraits look for truth through distortion, rather as do Howe's plays. Art becomes a means of knowing, a mechanism of reconciliation, a way of giving shape to perceptions and feelings which can otherwise scarcely be articulated. The play, in other words, stands as a justification of Tina Howe's own method, though ironically does so by modifying that method in the direction of realism. The lyricism hinted at in the earlier works moves closer to the centre: the artist is now viewed with less irony.

Though her central character here is the woman artist, as in her next work, *Coastal Disturbances* (1986) it was to be a woman photographer, hers is not a feminist drama (indeed she was attacked by feminists for her play *Birth and After Birth*, 1986). The absurdities which she both identifies and makes the basis of humour is not rooted only in the relationship between the sexes. Her target is the pretension which invades all social intercourse, the uses to which art is put by those who fail to grasp its human potential. She is interested in the comedy of human affairs, the rituals which we solemnly enact as though they were the essence of our relationships instead of the games we play. She has said that she sees the theatre as an arena for celebrating excess and that is indeed her strength as a playwright. She is at her best when she mirrors social absurdity, our voracious appetite for experience and self-inflation, in a drama which is comic and wildly inventive.

That invention hardly flags in *Approaching Zanzibar*, which followed in 1989, but now the focus is on a fear of death. After a series of plays set in enclosed spaces – even the beach of *Coastal Disturbances* is such – she writes what seems to amount to a road drama as a family set out across America to visit a dying woman. Herself now fifty, Howe had had to face one of the implications of that age as an increasing number of relatives began to die. She was aware, too, as she has explained, of the prevalence of AIDS and decided to write a play that would engage with both the reality of death and the means by which that fact could somehow be integrated into life.

The Blossom family's journey across the country is thus simultaneously a voyage into understanding, a painful but necessary confrontation with the barely sustainable reality of a human experience dominated by the knowledge of decline and death. Wallace is a composer who seems to be losing something of his talent. His wife, meanwhile, is caught up in the menopause and struck by the fact that her child-bearing days are over. Their children are poised on the edge of life, unsure and even neurotically insecure.

At journey's end they encounter Olivia, herself, significantly, an artist, on the edge of death. Here, the old woman and the young child come together in a ceremony which effectively celebrates the journey through life that one has completed and the other is about to begin. The different ages of that life are thus brought together in a play which begins as a comedy and ends as a poetic rite. It is a play which plainly places special emphasis on the anxieties, pain and sublimities of women's experience but that is integrated with larger concerns, and it should be clear that if Beckett was once an influence at the level of style – and Howe sees her attitude to language and event in this play as evidence of her absurdist roots – there is nothing absurdist about the implications she draws from a life engendered above the grave. Indeed, if anything, there is something decidedly American, even sentimental, about her determined optimism, about the epiphany to which she leads her characters. Like the artists in this and her other plays she may be aware of the fragility of art, anxious about her own power to command words or shape experience into convincing form, but the resilience that she celebrates is of a piece with the satisfactions of art as her characters discover meaning in the seemingly random and even reductive.

Following *One Shoe Off* (1993), a more directly absurdist work related to her earlier somewhat disastrous *Birth and Afterbirth*, she once again turned to the metaphor of the journey for *Pride's Crossing* (1998), which has, as its primary point of reference and conceit, a cross-Channel swim by its central character, Mabel Bigelow, but which also takes us on a trip through time, through, that is, the life of that character and the experience of a culture. It is a life that seems to spiral down towards old age and impending death. The action which gave meaning to Mabel's life now lies far in the past. Infected with cancer, she is, at ninety, the last of her line. But she is a survivor, now retrospectively putting the pieces of that life together as, in memory, she revisits her younger self.

The swim across the English Channel is not the only crossing in the play. Pride's Crossing is the name of the town where the action is set but, beyond that, Howe is interested in those other liminal experiences, those transformations, changing roles, breaching of boundaries that are an aspect both of private experience and unfolding history. Yesterday's confident social structures dissolve, the child becomes the adolescent, the young woman, the frightened but courageous person on the brink of the end. Meanwhile, pride, too, functions differently. For some it is no more than a class arrogance, a reckless disregard. For others it is rooted in a sense of self. In some ways Mabel herself is a victim of pride, or if not exactly pride then of the social rules which she momentarily confuses as such. She refuses to breach decorum, the rules of the tribe, and marries the wrong man. She lives her life in the shadow of that mistake and yet never succumbs to self-pity, except, perhaps, in so far as she replays that life now, acknowledging the many people she has been and the people she might have become.

Mabel summons memories into her reductive present, indeed her mind is no longer able to keep past and present apart: another crossing, another breached boundary. We are almost, but not quite, in the realm of dream. And, indeed, the play ends with an epiphany that takes place not in a tangible world of reality but a fantasy born partly out of need and desperation and partly out of a life redeemed by its own moments of pure consonance when, briefly, metaphor and fact came into momentary alignment. She dives once more into the waters of the Channel, except that now those waters are charged with a symbolic force as she sets out on her last journey, reconciled with who she is and what she has done. She is a survivor who has survived her own mistakes and the pain, as well as the exultances, of life.

Tina Howe has said that with *Pride's Crossing* she wished specifically to celebrate a woman's life and women's capacity to survive and transcend their circumstances. In a sense that has been the underlying theme of many of her plays. Laced with comedy, stylistically inventive, sometimes absurdist but more often, in latter years, lyrical, they have explored aspects of women's sensibilities, acknowledging profound anxieties but also celebrating their resilience. This is not to say that she writes only for and about women. She writes about the human comedy, which is always only a short crossing away from the human tragedy.

Her plays have often mirrored her own state of mind, reflected the various stages of life through which she was passing. In doing so, however, they were not so much documenting her own circumstances as exploring the implications of a shifting perspective. Her plays are now much more rooted in a sense of character than they were at the beginning of her career and yet much more epic in scope. She reaches out across time and space, seeking a correlative for the life journeys which she stages and celebrates.

The politics of feminism engaged many women writers. Politics in a larger sense tended to be as absent from their work as from the American theatre as a whole in the seventies and eighties. The pressure of the real, however, was such as to force at least one woman writer in the direction of documentary. Emily Mann, who trained as a director at Harvard and the Guthrie Theatre in Minneapolis, began her career with *Annulla, An Autobiography* in 1977, a play based on an interview with survivors of the Holocaust. She followed this, in 1980, with *Still Life*, focusing on a Vietnam veteran, and, in 1984, with *Execution of Justice*, an exploration of the trial in San Francisco of Dan White who shot San Francisco's mayor, George Moscone, and the liberal homosexual city supervisor, Harvey Milk. In 1986 she became the first woman to direct her own play on Broadway when *Execution of Justice* opened at the Virginia Theatre.

Emily Mann's father had been head of the American Jewish Committee's oral history project on the survivors of the Holocaust and it was reading the material he gathered which inspired her to start work on *Annulla*. Her plays, however, are not simply edited transcripts. They work by juxtaposition and assonance; they rest on a conscious musical rhythm.

Though *Anulla* is presented as the story of a woman whose wartime experiences are the justification for the play's existence, in fact there is more than one story told in this play. For Mann, or the figure she becomes in the play, called simply the Voice, has in fact been seeking to understand something of her own family history and, hence, something about herself. At the same time the woman she interviews has an agenda of her own, since she is in process of writing a huge, disorganised play, called *The Matriarchs*, about the need for women to rule the world. In other words, *Annulla* consists of a series of stories which sometimes complement and sometimes intertwine with one another. It is something considerably more than a documentary.

We are asked to see the figure of Annulla as legitimising a version of history but the more we learn of her the less secure that history becomes. Her survival, it turns out, depended on her ability and willingness to dissemble. In a play about the necessity of remembering we have a central figure for whom continued life seems to turn on the ability to forget. It was once Annulla's ambition to act and it was her skills as an actress that facilitated her survival. The line between her reality and her performance has, it seems, blurred a little, at least with time. Now she writes a play but one that seems to lack any coherence. In that sense she is self-deceiving. How, then, is she a reliable witness, how then a validator of the 'play' in which she unknowingly now finds herself? Her own life, meanwhile, would seem to contradict her assurance that women can transform the world for the better. The Women's Party which she plans seems invalidated by her own behaviour.

The Voice, meanwhile, follows a track of her own, lays down a plot at a tangent to that which she had herself proposed in coming to England to seek out this woman with her secret cache of memories. What she has really been searching for, it appears, is some understanding of her own family and hence of herself. There is a connection between the two stories, a connection which slowly reveals itself, but the subject is not what it appears. This is not an unmediated memoir. It is a crafted piece, a play with its own inner dynamic, its own conscious shape.

That is equally true of *Still Life* (1980), in which Mann explores not simply Vietnam, which seems its ostensible object, but American violence, the capacity of individuals for self-deceit and the pluralistic nature of the real, as refracted through different sensibilities. It is true that it is built from the separate but overlapping stories of three real people, a man, his wife and a lover. It is true, too, that they exist in the world, recount their experiences, offer their own insights, voice their own needs. But those voices are orchestrated by Mann and hence the meanings that emerge are a product of her thematic concerns.

She arranges the pieces to construct her picture. She works, very consciously, by juxtaposition, ironic comment, repetition, to forge a meaning that is independent of that offered by any of her interviewees.

Thus, she herself has said that she wanted to 'make people feel and experience the other side of the Vietnam War' but also that she found in the war 'a metaphor for how we have to adjust to our lives'.[129] She also finds a parallel between the violence in war and that in society at large, a violence which is not merely physical. Without the raw material produced by the interviews the play would not exist. Without the shaping of that material by Mann, without the themes which she teases out of the material, the 'characters' she creates by her own acts of juxtaposition or simply by the choices she makes in the material to include, the play would not exist. Her themes are not those of her 'characters'. She follows her own track. And if there is, perhaps inevitably, an element of therapy in a process which leads her interviewees to face their own experiences and acknowledge their fears and suppressed memories, then that therapy, that confrontation and transcendence, is equally an objective of Emily Mann, playwright.

In *Execution of Justice* (1984) she took even greater liberties, relying, now, not just on interviews, transcripts and reportage but invented material designed to reflect general opinion. She also summons, for the judgement of the audience, what she calls 'uncalled witnesses' who are partly based on actual people and partly imagined.

Given that at the heart of the work is a crime (the murder of San Francisco's mayor, George Moscone, and city supervisor, Harvey Milk, by Dan White), a crime which never resulted in a satisfactory conviction, there is no doubt that the play is, in effect, offered as the trial that never happened in that it attempts to read into the record material never presented, to offer insights excluded by a system of justice which seemed to serve no one's interest – hence the play's ambiguous title.

As in her previous play, too, she wished to locate the personal testimonies in the wider context of society at large. Acknowledging a connection between the theatre and the courtroom, she stages a play in which justice is as much the subject as the object. But in this play she enters the text more directly, calling for particular sound and lighting effects, consciously distorting the real in order the better to present the real.

And what is true of this work is also true of *Greensboro* (1996), in which, once again, there is a crime, the shooting to death of members of the Communist Party demonstrating against the Ku Klux Klan and the American Nazi Party. And we have her assurance that she sees *Greensboro* as 'a trial', and the audience as 'the jury', but what she is after is less a detached consideration of the facts than a visceral response to the events and their aftermath. And to achieve that she offers polemical arias, moving music and a melodramatic and contrasting representation of victims and villains.

Perhaps the least subtle of her plays, it nonetheless, like her others, underlines the extent to which hers cannot be seen as a documentary theatre merely offering to present fact, to summon before audiences the actual, the real. Knowledge of the factual basis of the work does import into it a feeling of authenticity but that authenticity is deliberately used as one element in a creative process that puts Mann firmly in control. It is, in the end, she who 'creates' the characters, shapes the plot, forges the language. The themes are those she chooses to elaborate. She is a playwright and not a mere recorder of fact.

Her dramatisation of the lives of the Delany sisters in her 1995 play *Having Our Say: The Delany Sisters' First Hundred Years* was a considerable success, drawing as it did, once again, on real experiences and real events, but it was different in kind from her earlier work, being in part an adaptation of a book by the Delany sisters themselves. The fact is that Mann's claim on our attention lies in her crafting of found materials, the extent to which she uses testimonies as the starting point and not the final destination of her dramatic concerns. She herself has claimed that the form she has chosen is, in some way, related to 'being female', in so far as women, rather than men, are liable openly to share their experiences in conversation, to address anxiety and pain directly, to listen. But this suggests a kind of passivity that does less than justice to plays which are the product of her own imaginative and moral concerns and which derive their power from that rather than merely from their roots in fact, more especially since facts, in these plays, prove so ambiguous, so much a product of perspective, so expressive of unaddressed needs.

A smaller group of women, concerned to write from a specifically lesbian point of view, saw in the theatre a way not merely of expressing and thereby publicly validating their own sexuality, but of creating a new sense of solidarity. When a first collection of lesbian plays was published in 1985, it was a self-consciously pioneering effort. The marginality of the texts was underlined by appeals for production both by 'mainstream' theatres and by those groups looking for works which would reflect their own sexuality and serve as ceremonies bringing together those who felt alienated from themselves no less than their society. They were works which endorsed the sexuality of those taught to regard themselves as aberrant and which offered, through public performance, that very openness discouraged by mainstream society. Perhaps the best known of a group of plays which were in fact little known or performed was *Dos*

Lesbos, by Terry Baum and Caroline Myers, a play ironically subtitled *A Play By, For, and About Perverts*. Using a mixture of realism and revue, it offers an amusing account of the problems, private and public, encountered by lesbians.

If America could afford to regard lesbian theatre as marginal to its concerns, however, it could no longer regard women's theatre in the same light. At the beginning of the sixties there were few women dramatists in a position to have their work staged either in New York or beyond Broadway. Lillian Hellman, who for long had seemed the only visible representative, had fallen silent. Lorraine Hansberry was regarded as a phenomenon who said more about race than gender. In the next twenty years, though, the situation was transformed. A voice that had been silenced could now be heard with clarity. It was a voice, moreover, which was not without wit.

By far the funniest woman writer to emerge in the seventies was Wendy Wasserstein. Her early plays – *Any Woman Can't* and *When Dinah Shore Ruled the Earth* (the latter written with Christopher Durang) – were satirical sketches with a touch of the cabaret about them, but with *Uncommon Women and Others* (1977), *Isn't It Romantic* (1981) and *The Heidi Chronicles* (1988) she created what was in effect a trilogy of plays which traced the dilemma facing women in America from the 1960s to the 1980s. In the first she follows the career of a group of undergraduates plotting their lives in the security of a women's college (Mount Holyoke) in 1972, to a meeting six years later. The play is narrated by an unseen woman whose comments are ironised by the action, as their views are ironised by time. In the second, she explores the life choices of Harriet and Janie as they battle to reconcile their desire to fulfil themselves through work and through love. The world has changed. They want to claim the freedom which they now believe to be their right and yet other commitments have not faded with a redefinition of gender roles. *The Heidi Chronicles*, like *Uncommon Women and Others*, moves around in time, juxtaposing attitudes and values as it dramatises the developing selfhood of its central character.

Wendy Wasserstein's dialogue is sharp and witty and if her dramatic structures generate a sentimentality born of nostalgia, as well as an irony generated out of failed aspirations, few writers have been as responsive to the shifting social and sexual realities of late twentieth-century America.

The Heidi Chronicles dramatises the life of a woman from her high school days through years spent at Vassar and Yale and on to a career as an art history professor. The play traces Heidi's relationship with two men, Peter Petrone and Scoop Rosenbaum, and with her fellow women. Peter becomes a pediatrician, opening an AIDS clinic; Scoop, ironic and randomly attracted to Heidi, marries her friend, Susan. Her friends become successful in different realms. Susan makes it in Hollywood, laying aside her earlier idealistic politics and retreating from feminism. Heidi goes through a personal crisis and, at the age of thirty-nine, adopts a Panamanian baby. She herself, as an art historian, retrieves women artists from obscurity for her students but insists on her essential humanism rather than any commitment to a specifically feminist view. The play touches on a changing political, cultural and social world, finding humour in the discrepancy between frivolity of attitude and seriousness of situation, between ideal and actuality. It is a satire whose commitment is to the confused emotions, thoughts and aspirations which her characters try to shape into coherent form.

The play won the Pulitzer Prize and, like 'night, Mother, ran full tilt into feminist critics. Alison Solomon, in the Village Voice, described it as 'just the kind of show Susan would love to produce. It assures us that [intelligent, educated women] are funny for the same traditional reasons women have always been funny. They hate their bodies, can't find a man, and don't believe in themselves.' Laurie Stone, meanwhile, attacked Wendy Wasserstein, on National Public Radio, for demeaning feminism by having Heidi prefer the word 'humanist', thereby implying that the latter word diminished the former. Both responses were embraced and quoted by Phyllis Jane Rose in an article in American Theatre in 1989. She accuses Wasserstein's character of going 'to the heart of male domination' on her own initiative, becoming complicit with the status quo. The attack was the fiercer because the women's theatre movement by then seemed to have passed its peak and to be facing a crisis. As she pointed out, whereas in 1980 there were 110 women's theatres in America, by 1988 there were fewer than 10. The presence at Buffalo, in that same year, of 291 women playwrights from thirty-four countries at the First International Women Playwrights Conference merely served to underline the talent which, at least on an international scale, was available, not its success in sustaining women's theatre groups or reversing female stereotyping.

Quoting Audre Lorde's remark, in 1979, that 'Difference is that raw material and powerful connection from which our personal power is forged',[130] Rose called upon Wasserstein to use her work to 'empower' women. There is a point here; humour can, of course, be ingratiating.

It can be a means of claiming kinship with one's oppressors. It can, however, also be liberating, warning of the price which may be paid for abandoning one stereotype in order to embrace another, more socially useful one. Nor were the attacks justified. Susan's self-deceits, her trading of ideals for success, of feminism for power, is wittily exposed by Wendy Wasserstein, while the self-doubts which afflict her protagonist serve to underline the degree to which she wrestles not just with public images but with the private tensions which shape the individual's response to the world. Nor should a claim to humanism be seen as a diminishment of women in the context of this play. We should not forget, either, that Heidi is a fiction and that a writer's responsibilities extend beyond the creation of exemplary fables.

In a sense *The Sisters Rosensweig* (1992) might seem a continuation of *The Heidi Chronicles*, in so far as it addresses the question of the life choices of women in a changing world. Wasserstein herself regards it as her 'most serious effort' and affected to be surprised when audiences responded to the humour rather more than they did to what she thought of as the more serious dimensions of the play. But, in fact, that serious-ness emerges from the humour which, as elsewhere in her work, is an agent of social analysis.

The Rosensweig sisters are Jewish and middle-aged. They come from Brooklyn but meet up in London to celebrate the birthday of the eldest, Sara. Each of them has apparently secured a degree of success, Sara in banking, Gorgeous as a talk-show hostess and Pfeni as a journalist. Yet each of them is insecure in some respect, having effected a compromise with life that leaves them incomplete. They trail failed marriages behind them. The fake designer clothes which Gorgeous wears are symptomatic of the deceits they have practised on themselves. They are in retreat. They feel in some sense detached from themselves and their lives. They are in denial.

Sara has denied her Jewish identity and in some sense her involvement in life. Now living in London, she feels detached from who she was. A series of marriages has left her with someone else's name and a sense of having exhausted her possibilities. Gorgeous, too, bears someone else's name while Pfeni has had her first name given to her by a man who is, finally, as detached from life as she. Outside the house the world is chang-ing. The Soviet empire is collapsing. Countries are regaining their names. The process of the play is one whereby the sisters do the same. In coming together they perform a ritual in which they rediscover them-selves. In celebrating Sara's birthday, they in fact experience their own rebirth. When Sara Goode announces that she is Sara Rosensweig, the daughter of Rita and Maury Rosensweig, she reclaims her own identity and her kinship with her sisters. Each takes a step forwards.

Sara is helped in this by Merv, whose own wife has recently died and who is himself looking for a route back into a life from which he has been in recoil. He is the origin of much of the play's humour and a catalyst in Sara's recovery. Like so many of Wasserstein's characters these have, in some senses, drifted into being observers of experience and have to become protagonists in their own lives once again. Comedy, so often both a product of detachment and a means of redemption in her work, is such again here. That element is less central, however, in her next play, *An American Daughter* (1997).

Inspired by what seemed to Wasserstein to be the attacks suffered by successful women (the abuse directed at Hillary Clinton when she campaigned for an extension of health care and the attack on Zoë Baird, nominee for Attorney-General, being cases in point), the play focuses on the figure of Lyssa Dent Hughes, nominee for the post of Surgeon-General. Having once ignored a jury summons, she finds herself attacked from all sides by feminists and liberals no less than conservatives. It is tempting to see a personal element to the play in that Wasserstein has herself been attacked by a similar, and equally unlikely range of critics, but she is less concerned with this than with the plight of women in a supposedly post-feminist America. For alongside the plight of Lyssa she places the dilemma of her friend, Judith Kaufman, an African-American oncologist, childless and likely to remain such.

In the end what matters is only in part the confused nature of a society that has never attained the unity which it boasts, never truly granted that freedom of opportunity which it announces. It is only in part the conflict between idealism and the flawed nature of those who believe themselves to be idealists while in fact driven by self-concern and a soulless pragmatism. What drives the play is the effort of two survivors, Lyssa and Judith, to reconcile themselves to their possibilities and to continue. In that sense it is close to her earlier plays. Where it differs is that the comedy is now subdued.

Wasserstein's plays are political, in that they engage with the individual's struggle to make sense of changing times, to live according to principles that are generated not out of fashionable beliefs or pragmatic adjustments but out of genuine convictions rooted in a sense of self which is a product of experience. Her heroines show what Hemingway called grace under pressure, but that pressure comes from the struggle to balance biological drives, social ambitions, political commitments with the need to discover the basis on which life can be lived with some dignity. For much of the time she generates humour out of these conflicts, but beneath that humour there is a real battle going on which that humour only partly obscures.

Wasserstein has moved from Off-Broadway to Broadway and takes pleasure in having done so, not least because thereby she feels she has played a role in opening up possibilities for women writers and actresses while laying before American audiences the dilemmas, needs and perspectives of women in a society which has not always regarded these as worthy of being placed at centre stage.

The suspicion which her work has generated among some feminists, strengthened here by a caustic portrait of a post-feminist young woman, for whom gender politics and career seem closely allied, may be understandable but is surely paradoxical. If Wendy Wasserstein and Marsha Norman are really to be seen as threats to feminism rather than as writers in some ways liberated by and contributing to it, then it is difficult to see how feminism is to reach the theatrical audience it wishes to address, for it is their very success which makes them suspect. Had they not received the Pulitzer Prize they may well have attracted less animosity.

So the history of the black theatre movement is replayed by the women's theatre movement. First, demands for exemplary figures, conscious-raising fables, then the rapid establishment of theatre groups principally designed to address those defined by race or gender, and then the decline of such groups and the emergence of writers freed to embrace an ambivalence and an irony which would have once been seen as treachery but which has in some degree been enabled by those who preceded them.

A writer's double commitment to language and the real, to the shape of the imagination and that of society, to transformations effected in the mind and the world, to doubt and certainty, image and fact, must leave him or her suspended between competing demands which are definitional. The terms of that negotiation alter; in time the notes change the stave. The tension never disappears. Where more natural for those seeking transformation to turn than the theatre where transformation is the essence of the form? And there are moments when the theatre has blazed with an inner light which has the power to change those who experience it. By the same token, however, we know little enough how art communicates or even how we relate to the world we inhabit to be sure of the effect of staging our anxieties or dramatising our private and public needs. Alison Solomon, Laurie Stone and Phyllis Jane Rose are right to question the effect of Wendy Wasserstein's play, but wrong to be sure that they know the answer.

It was Brecht who reminded us of the stunning if ironic truth that 'You can make a fresh start with your final breath.' The theatre can never do less than hold that fact at the centre of attention but it can also not subordinate itself to ideology and live. It can, however, confront us with images of ourselves which shock by virtue of their truth or falsity and out of such shocks is born at least the possibility of a new life. America never ceases making itself. It is a construction whose central project is itself. The same could be said of theatre. No wonder that those who have played a full role in inventing the one should demand a full role in inventing the other and see both projects as deeply implicated in one another. A stage which gives back no echoes, as for many groups in America it has not, or echoes so distorted as to deform the lives of those who listen, may be said to be failing America. Can it also be said to have failed itself? The theatre is a product of its own history and of the culture of which it is an expression but, like an individual, it can transgress its own boundaries and project a future which may begin in the imagination but have its being in the world. In the sixties, seventies and eighties this was the demand made of it by many.

The dominant culture has always retained the power of naming. Thus native Americans were homogenised as Indians and Japanese and Chinese as Asian-Americans. But such language can be inhabited and redirected. So Philip Kan Gotanda, a third generation Japanese-American, claims

Asian American as a 'political term' which harkens back to the time when people from many different cultures and backgrounds – Chinese, Japanese, Filipino, Korean, Vietnamese – found they had something in common. There was a political reason we should work together, given racism and the context of America. We found that under this banner of Asian American we could move forwards.[131]

A beneficiary of the black movement, the Asian-American theatre began to define itself in 1965 with the establishment of the East West Players in Los Angeles, an acting group which by the 1970s had begun to concentrate on plays by Asian-American writers, a move which was pioneered further up the Californian coast by the Asian-American

Theatre Workshop in San Francisco. This was followed by New York's Pan American Repertory and Seattle's Northwest Asian Theatre Company.

It was 1980, however, before the first anthology of Asian-American plays was published, significantly entitled *Between Worlds*. The doubleness experienced by black Americans was felt no less acutely by those who acknowledged the influence of black writers. The Philippine-born Jessica Hagedorn, while identifying the importance of Chinese-American writer Ping Chong, like David Hwang pointed to the influence of Ntozake Shange. By the same token Hwang himself was drawn to Sam Shepard as Ping Chong responded to the work of Meredith Monk. A further influence was music. Philip Kan Gotanda was in a rock band with David Hwang while Jessica Hagedorn played with another rock band originally called the West Coast Gangster Choir.

Laurence Yep, a Chinese-American who grew up in the black area of San Francisco, has explained that 'it took me about twenty years to come to a realization that I could never be white. Then it took me another five years to realize I could never be totally Chinese, that instead I was an Asian American, a Chinese American, a person between two cultures. You can be from more than one culture, and you can draw from the best of both.'[132] Having begun his writing career as the author of science fiction stories featuring aliens, he had come to feel that what he was doing was 'writing about myself . . . developing this emotional vocabulary to talk about myself'.[133] So it was that he began to write about his own heritage, in *Pay the Chinaman* creating a character who denies his past. As he has said, 'it's almost as if he wants to erase himself and if you erase yourself totally there's nothing but a hole there'.[134] Just so, in David Hwang's *Family Devotions*, a character turns to his grand-nephew and remarks: 'Look here, the shape of your face is the shape of faces back many generations – across an ocean, in another soil. You must become one with your family before you can hope to live away from it.'[135]

In Hwang's *FOB*, a Chinese immigrant fresh off the boat (FOB) and hence usually the object of some contempt by those assimilated to American ways, encounters, and tries to win, Grace, a first-generation Chinese-American woman. In the course of the play, however, both ironically enact the roles of two figures from Chinese mythology. The gap between their daily reality and their mythic roles is a source of the play's humour but also a reminder of their double identities: Chinese and American. *The Dance and the Railroad*, set in 1863 during the building of the trans-continental railroad, operates on a similar principle, as a newcomer, also fresh from the boat, undergoes a double initiation – into the America he wishes to find and the Chinese past which he carries with him in spite of himself.

Writing in 1982 Hwang remarked that 'American theatre is beginning to discover Americans.'[136] Not that it had ever been otherwise. O'Neill came from Irish Catholic stock, Arthur Miller from Polish Jewish, Tennessee Williams from southern Baptist. But they were all white and with their roots in Europe. What had changed was not America but America's perception of itself. As Hwang rightly pointed out, the American theatre's attempt to acknowledge the multi-cultural nature of American society was the artistic expression of a political transformation, a transformation which began outside theatre but which theatre both reflected and facilitated.

In the sixties this was a theatre of praxis, with an immediate political objective. Both black theatre and Chicano theatre shaped themselves to a battle which was likely to be immediate and real. The half-life of a metaphor was short indeed. LeRoi Jones's slave was already transmuting into a rebel; Luis Valdez's campesinos into ironic insurrectionaries. But by the mid-seventies, and thereafter, a more contemplative mood prevailed, a suspicion of peremptory dogmatism. The confrontation was now less likely to be between a fictive champion of the new racial enlightenment and a white oppressor than between the individual and his or her own history. Myth was no longer a brittle construct improvised to challenge the confident mythologies of mainstream America but a carefully researched exploration of a past previously ignored or suppressed. The centripetal pull of national identity weakened as a new model of personal and social meaning emerged. Where once America had offered to burn off the past in the crucible of assimilation, and conformity had been elevated into a political imperative, now multiculturalism was acknowledged if not embraced as a defining characteristic.

As David Hwang observed, 'Immigration is making Caucasians an increasingly smaller percentage of this country's population.'[137] He might have added that linguistically, too, America was changing. The immigrant's desire to shuck off the skin of the old culture remained strong. It was an impulse which provides part of the dramatic tension and humour of his plays: *FOB* (1979), *The Dance and the Railroad* (1981) and *Family Devotions* (1981) . But for the second and third generations the past becomes a vital aspect of meaning, the root of a racial identity which is not to be denied or simply reforged into a weapon. As Hwang remarked,

We somehow believe that to be less 'ethnic' is to be more human. In fact the opposite is true: By confronting our ethnicity, we are simply confronting the roots of our humanity. The denial of this truth creates a bizarre world, cut off from the past and alienated from the present, where cosmetic surgeons offer to un-slant Asian eyes and make-up artists work to slant the eyes of Peter Ustinov, 1981's Charlie Chan.

He quotes approvingly a remark by South African dramatist Athol Fugard: 'To me, the curse of theatre today is generalizing. You need a place, you need the reality first.' Hwang's plays, he has explained, are his attempt to 'explore human issues without denying the color of my skin'.[138]

David Hwang's training as a playwright was with an unlikely duo: Sam Shepard and Maria Irene Fornes (herself Cuban-born). From Shepard he learned the power to be derived from the juxtaposition of reality and myth and the significance of a collective history. He was also impressed by an approach to character analogous to that of a jazz musician improvising on a theme: 'almost a collage effect, bits and pieces of the character at different points, butting up against one another'.[139] The impact of such influences seemed clear to him in his first play, *FOB*, as in his later *M Butterfly*. From Fornes, perhaps, he derived his resistance to simple realism. The Asian influence was secondary.

He has explained that in his own early production of *FOB* the ritualised element owed more to the American avant-garde than to Chinese opera. It was the Public Theatre production of the play in 1980 which introduced this facet and in his next play, *The Dance and the Railroad*, he set out consciously to combine western and Asian theatre forms. The emphasis was to be on form. Where other Asian-American playwrights had, as he explained, been trying to create some kind of Asian-American synthesis in terms of the ideas advanced – political notions, even polemics – he was more interested in the merging of forms, a process which is a way of 'making your political statement in a much more theatrical fashion'.[140] But for a Chinese-American writer who had never been to China, a second-generation son of wealthy parents from a family Christianised for generations before their arrival in the United States, the Asian component of his sensibility had already incorporated the West. There was in that sense no purity to be compromised, while the notion of a cultural or social norm in an immigrant society such as America must be a fictional proposition. *M Butterfly*, indeed, addresses the question of the extent to which we require those stereotypes which we agree to treat as archetypes, the degree to which we collaborate in those confusions which bring us to the brink of tragedy. It is a play in which gender no less than racial cliches becomes the basis of personal and national psychology.

It was inspired by a newspaper article which reported a trial in which a French diplomat and the Chinese opera singer with whom he lived were sentenced for espionage. The part of the story which fascinated Hwang, however, was the revelation that the opera singer, whom the diplomat had believed to be a woman, was in fact a man. Twenty years of cohabitation had, it seemed, proved insufficient for him to discover this basic fact. The diplomat's explanation was that he had never seen his lover naked, believing her modesty to be a characteristic of Chinese women. To Hwang this last claim was no less absurd than the sexual confusion and turned on western stereotypes of eastern women. It also recalled the plot of Puccini's *Madame Butterfly* in which a callous American mistreats and abandons a Japanese woman, eventually driving her to suicide. This, too, had seemed to him evidence of western clichés about the East and women. Racism and sexism intersect. What is implied is a form of imperialism, literal and symbolic. *M Butterfly* is a play, Hwang insists, which underlines the necessity to confront the truth rather than to settle for the fantasies and stereotypes which seem so much more seductive. So, he insists,

the myths of the East, the myths of the West, the myths of men, and the myths of women – these have so saturated our consciousness that truthful contact between nations and lovers can only be the result of heroic effort. Those who prefer to by-pass the work involved will remain in a world of surfaces, misconceptions running rampant. This is, to me, the convenient world in which the French diplomat and the Chinese spy meet. This is why, after twenty years, he had learned nothing at all about his lover, not even the truth of his sex.[141]

In this schema the West becomes masculine, the East feminine. It is not that politics is sexualised, but that the process whereby myth and stereotype are invoked to validate attitudes and actions applies to the world of politics no less than to that of sexual relationships. It is in that sense that *M Butterfly* links imperialism, racism and sexism. In terms of form the play borrows from and employs western opera, as the characters simultaneously act out the roles in *Madame Butterfly*, Kabuki, in which men play the roles of women, and, Hwang suggests, a kind of situation comedy.

After a series of poorly received plays, Hwang ended the 1990s with *Golden Child* (1997), rooted in the stories of his maternal Chinese grandmother. Speaking in 1998, however, he was inclined to see his work in terms both of an American and an Asian tradition: 'I think you can see the stuff I write, as well as the novels of Amy Tan and other ethnic Asian writers, as part of American literature. But with the world getting smaller, you can also look at our work as a kind of Pan-Asian literature of the diaspora.' It seemed to him, indeed, that some of the assumptions of an early period had been misplaced:

one thing I think was damaging in the 1970s and 1980s was this fantasy of one true, authentic Chinese-American literary voice, a holy grail uncorrupted by assimilation. Now people are starting to realize that there's a much wider diversity of experience that exists among us. The romanticization, the glorification of the root culture just seems very simplistic to me now, a kind of high school mentality – our team versus their team. Real life is far more complicated than that.[142]

For the Japanese-American writer one event, now fifty years in the past, still has its reverberations. In a xenophobic spasm the United States government, on the outbreak of war, ordered the internment of those of Japanese descent. There could scarcely have been a clearer indication of their perceived status as unassimilated aliens whose loyalties must lie elsewhere. Wakako Yamauchi, whose first play, *And the Soul Shall Dance*, received its initial production in Los Angeles in 1977, was herself brought up in a camp in Arizona where her father died. Philip Kan Gotanda, a Sensei (third generation Japanese-American) whose rock musical *The Avocado Kid* opened in 1979 and whose later play, *Yankee Dawg You Die*, describes a debate between two actors over the stereotypical roles offered to Asian actors, has described that camp experience, suffered by both his parents, as 'a psychic scar, almost like an abused-child syndrome'.[143] Later came *Ballad of Yachiyo* (1995), based on his aunt and set in Japan.

But the real trauma, which links writers of Japanese, Chinese and Philippines background, derives from the immigrant experience itself. It runs through Jessica Hagedorn's *Tenement Lover* (1981), David Henry Hwang's *Family Relations*, Wakako Yamauchi's *And the Soul Shall Dance* (1977) and Laurence Yep's *Pay the Chinaman* (1987).

In the 1960s Richard Schechner and Julian Beck went in search of authentic rituals to reinvigorate their own performances. This quest took them to New Guinea and India, as Peter Brook went to Africa and Grotowski to the Indian sub-continent. But closer to home, for the Americans at least, was a people whose lives had for centuries centred on ceremonies, public rites, performed actions; those who had been accommodated to imperial myth as 'Indians' but whom newly sensitised liberals were learning to call native Americans. They themselves identified tribal loyalties while recognising the value of solidarity in the face of those whose historic injustices were written in the geography of their lands no less than in their depleted numbers and debilitated social conditions. Looking to forge an organic community in which the performing self would derive meaning from and contribute meaning to the group, the Performance Group and the Living Theatre gave little attention to those communities which had found themselves sacrificed to American myths of individual endeavour and manifest destiny. Historically, conventional theatre hardly proved central to the native American. The Indian Actors' Workshop, founded in Los Angeles in the late sixties, was primarily concerned with developing the skills of actors working in Hollywood. In 1968, however, the Santa Fe Theatre Project did produce a number of original plays by native Americans while in 1972, with the assistance of Ellen Stewart of the La Mama Experimental Theatre Club, Hanay Geiogamah, a Kiowa, created what was later called the Native American Theatre Ensemble. The group lasted until 1976, later being reborn as American Indians in the Arts. Though this was the single most important organisation, there were several others: the Navajo Theatre, the Spiderwoman Theatre Workshop, Four Arrows, the Red Earth Performing Arts Company and the Indian Performing Arts Company.

The first collection of plays by a native American playwright, Hanay Geiogamah, appeared in 1980. It showed a writer testing different styles and approaches. *Foghorn*, which opened in Berlin in 1973, was a freeranging satire which, like Amiri Baraka's *Four Black Revolutionary Plays* or Luis Valdez's early work, deployed stereotypes to deconstruct the Indian of popular culture. With visual reminders of the occupation of Alcatraz in 1969 and the violent encounters at Wounded Knee in 1973 (scene of the 7th Cavalry's revenge killing of women and children following its own defeat at Little Big Horn), it drew on figures from history and myth (Pocohontas), from television (the Lone Ranger and Tonto) and from the Wild West Show, the action being interspersed with or accompanied by music from *Rose Marie*. The play is framed by a Spanish sailor's erroneous identification of those encountered by Columbus as 'Los Indios!' and in a series of sketches identifies the process whereby they are deprived of their identity. A teacher punishes a child for communicating through tribal gestures and announces that 'You are going to learn the English language . . . The most beautiful language in all the world. The language that has brought hope and civilization to people everywhere.

The one true language . . .'[144] The Lone Ranger pleads to be acknowledged as the more intelligent of the television duo. The teacher is
beaten; the Lone Ranger has his head cut by his Indian sidekick, Tonto.
But this play is conventional in its unconventionalities. Far more daring
are *Body Indian* (1972) and *49* (1975).

Body Indian, far from proposing role models for a new enlightened and
self-confident native American identity, dramatises the pathology of a
society degraded by drink and wilfully self-destructive. Though
Geiogamah insists that 'it is important that the acting nowhere is conducive to the mistaken idea that this play is primarily a study of the
problem of Indian alcoholism', drink is the primary motivation of the
characters and the primary detail of the staging, with so many empty
bottles littering the stage that they stumble, literally and symbolically, as
a result. The central character, Bobby, has lost a leg in a railway accident. From the moment he enters the apartment which constitutes the
play's set he is seen as little more than a source of fresh funds by the
drinkers who huddle together against reality. Having leased his land out
he is temporarily in funds. Intending to buy himself six weeks in a
detoxification centre he secretes money about his person, in his artificial
leg and his shoe. His companions, however, steal it while appearing
unaware of what they are doing. Finally they steal the leg itself, hoping
to realise enough cash to keep drinking a little longer. The play ends with
the sound of the train rushing towards him, its light glaring as though
their actions were the cause as well as the consequence of his accident.

Body Indian is a brave acknowledgement of the complicity of some
native Americans in the fate which has been devised for them by whites.
From time to time the characters make half-hearted attempts to dance
or play tribal music but these are ironic gestures in a play in which the
only sense of community lies in shared degradation. And yet these are
not isolatos. They are all pulled together by some surviving instinct. Nor
is the play a naturalistic work offering a blank face of determinism. The
action is intensified, exaggerated to the point at which it becomes a
ritual, an anti-ceremony in which the characters enact their own potential for self-destruction. But the play seems offered as a warning. In contrast to Nathanael's West's *A Cool Million*, significantly subtitled *The
Dismantling of Lemuel Pitkin*, *Body Indian* is less absurdist parable or biting
satire than a compassionate rendering of a world diminishing to the
point of extinction. It ends on a note of horror but not without an indication that some vestigial community, some echo of meaning remains.

Geiogamah's *49*, first performed in 1975, offers a more optimistic version of the same conviction. A *49* is a celebration, part music, part dancing, part singing. To the watching policeman it is a disturbance with a potential for violence. Its threat lies in the fact that it brings large numbers of Indians together in the same place. For the Indians themselves the self-same factors are positive. Though only distantly related to the formal ceremonials of a century before and though misunderstood and distorted by those who take part, it is still a link to the past and hence a key to identity. The presiding spirit is the Night Walker, a shaman figure who ties past and present together through his own being and through the stories he tells. In that sense he stands for the writer who performs a similar function. Thus Geiogamah has said that 'More than anything else I wanted the young people to be affirmative in the face of despair and unreasoning force. I had an instinct to minimise the negative and sought to do this even though much of the action is essentially negative.'[145] Thus, despite the degradation of ancient ceremony into modern festival, Night Walker 'is always optimistic, never without hope'. Tribal chants may devolve into contemporary ballads but Apache violins, rattles, ratchets and bull-roarers mix with piano and guitar. So it is that Geiogamah insisted to his actors that 'while taking part in a 49, young Indians are in an extremely heightened state of awareness of their "Indianness",' and achieve 'a group conviviality that is intertribal'. The *49* offers 'not only an emotional release but also a means of expressing thoughts and attitudes difficult to articulate under less stimulating conditions'.[146]

Much the same might be said of Geiogamah's play which itself becomes a *49* and reproduces on stage precisely that sense of physical solidarity which he had seen as the product of such ceremonies. While the full-throated songs and strenuous dances had been contrasted throughout to the thinly mechanical voices of the police who communicate through their radios and sit, isolated, in their patrol cars, it is, finally, the physical solidarity of the Indians which conveys his essential meaning. Threatened by the police they shape their bodies into a barricade which forms and reforms, a living organism. This is the bird to which Night Walker refers as he celebrates the continuity of his people.

> Go!
> Go forward!
> The tribe needs you I go with you.
> I am always with you. We are a tribe!
> Of singers.
> Of dancers who move with the grace of the bird.
> Of people who know color.

Of weavers.
Of hunters,
We pray.
We are a tribe!
Of people with strong hearts,
Who respect fear.
As we make our way.
Who will never kill.
Another man's way of living.[147]

Hanay Geiogamah is Night Walker. His plays are that chant of celebration. His people are the bird which in the face of change, decay, deg-
redation, still exhibits grace because flight is of his essence. When the
Performance Group sought to shape their bodies to the title of the play
they presented they were articulating their convictions about the physical nature of theatre and the redemptive power of the body. When
Geiogamah directs his actors to merge into a figure, to stage their own
capacity for unity, he draws on an already existent symbiosis. Historical,
social and cultural fact coalesce in a moment of theatre which is simultaneously a moment of ethnic truth.

Spanish-language drama was scarcely the invention of the 1960s, though
it was then that Chicano theatre first began to force itself onto if not
national then regional attention. Indeed it seems likely that the very first
dramatic presentations in North America (the rituals and ceremonies of
native Americans aside) were in Spanish, whether it be those performed
in 1567, in what would later be Florida, or the entertainments with which
the conquistadores sought to amuse themselves as they pushed into the
territory which would one day be called Texas, in the concluding years of
the sixteenth century. In the nineteenth century New Mexico and
California were to see Spanish-language theatre. In his book, *Contemporary
Chicano Theatre*, Roberto J. Garza refers to the establishment of the Padua
Hills Theatre in California in 1932 as typifying the various folklore groups
which sprang up as a result of immigration from Mexico in the early
decades of the twentieth century (interestingly David Henry Hwang was
later to begin his career as a playwright as a result of working with Cuban
born dramatist Maria Irene Fornes at the Padua Hills Playwrights
Festival). For the most part, however, such groups were celebrating a folk-
loric Mexico, the Mexico of dance, spectacle and religious ceremony. The
daily experience of the Mexican-American was somewhat different.

In the city all the ills of urban life, exacerbated by the insecurities consequent upon a sometimes suspect legal status, led to a ghetto experience

which could be dispiriting and degrading. In the country the Chicano or Chicana quickly found him or herself regarded as little more than cheap labour to be hired and fired at will. Agro-business's exploitative practices, which had once ensnared the 'Okies' who had struggled out of the dustbowl of the Midwest, now trapped those who moved north rather than west seeking inclusion in an American dream offered as a natural birthright to citizens and as a guaranteed prize to the would-be immigrant. And just as the Okies had tried to organise against the power of the growers in the thirties, so Mexican-Americans tried to challenge that power in the sixties. A series of strikes and boycotts were organised, and it was partly as a result of these strikes that a young man named Luis Valdez emerged as a crucial figure in Chicano theatre.

Valdez, the son of an immigrant worker, majored in English, with a special emphasis on playwrighting, at San Jose State. His first play, performed there in 1964, was an absurdist drama, drawing on Mexican myth, called *The Shrunken Head of Pancho Villa*. From the college he moved to the San Francisco Mime Troupe, which had been founded in 1959 and which had quickly become radicalised, performing in the city's parks in a broad style which owed much to *commedia dell'arte*. In 1965 Valdez began to work with the Farm Workers Union and quickly came to feel that the theatre might have a role to play. He devised a short, comic, agit-prop sketch which identified two men as strikers and one as a strike-breaker. The piece was created to entertain the strikers and to encourage others to join. Following the success of this experiment he founded El Teatro Campesino and for two years this performed within the context of the strike. He called the brief plays, which were presented in fields and meeting-halls, 'actos'. These were plays which challenged public stereotypes with stereotypes. They relied on broad humour and, like the Mime Troupe's performances, required a broad production style.

Later he became more interested in exploring the nature of Chicano identity. In 1971 he and his group settled in San Juan Bautista, in California, where they set out to farm the land as the Mayans had once done. Theatrically, he developed a new form which he called the *mito* (myth), which combined the group's political consciousness with a religious concern. Beyond that, in later years, lay the *corrido*, or ballad, which drew on song and dance. The early work had a strong improvisational element but by 1975 he decided that he wished to develop himself as a writer and, in 1977, invited to write a play for the Mark Taper Forum, he produced *Zoot Suit*, a success in Los Angeles but a failure in New York. Later he took another step into a wider market-place with his film *La*

Bamba. As he explained, in *Zoot Suit*, a play set during the so-called Zoot Suit riots in the 1940s, in which a Pachuco (young tearaway) finds a personal resilience in the face of violence, he had given a disenfranchised people their religion back by dressing his central character 'in the colors of Testatipoka, the Aztec god of education' just as in *La Bamba* the figure of Richie Valens has elements of Quetzalcoatl, the plumed serpent.[148]

Valdez is no spontaneous spirit with a natural talent for raw drama. At college he studied Latin for four years so that he could read Plautus in the original, subsequently incorporating aspects into his *actos*. He admired Brecht and drew self-consciously on his techniques. He has suggested that his conviction that myth is 'the supporting structure of everyday life' makes him more Jungian than Freudian. But at the same time he has confessed to learning a great deal from his experience in working with strikers and performing in the open air.

In 1965, and for the subsequent ten years, his objective was to use theatre to raise the political consciousness of the Chicano community. Thereafter he became more concerned to explore the past – spiritual and mythic – which could give depth to an identity which he had previously attenuated, shaped for immediate social objectives. By 1987 he was taking pride in El Teatro Campesino's penetration of Hollywood and looking forward to the possibility of performing on Broadway. This was not to be a denial of his commitments. He was, he explained, planning a movie about the grape strike, insisting that 'My Vietnam was at home. I refused to go to Vietnam, but I encountered all the violence I needed on the home front: people were killed in the Farm Workers strike.'[149] He had, he insisted, strayed very little from his original objectives.

For Luis Valdez the Hispanic is itself already the product of a melting-pot. He himself is part Yaqui Indian. While looking forward to a time when such differences will no longer be crucial, he believes they will come only when the reality of difference has been acknowledged: 'I draw on the symbolism of the four roads: the black road, the white road, the red road and the yellow road. They all meet in the navel of the universe, the place where the upper road leads into the underworld – read consciousness and subconsciousness. I think that where they come home is in America.'[150]

In Chicano drama language is a crucial indicator of character and attitude. Thus, not untypically, in *Soldier Boy* by Judith and Severo Perez, a work produced by El Teatro Campesino in 1982, we are told of one character that he has fierce and uncompromising determination to make his own way in the Anglo world, a determination reflected in the fact that although he is fluent in Spanish, 'he now speaks only English'. Another is described as speaking English with a heavy accent while feeling 'more comfortable in Spanish'. Yet another 'speaks only Spanish but can understand some English'. In several plays by Luis Valdez the dramatist switches between languages, sometimes as an indication of the extent of his characters' assimilation of political attitudes and sometimes as a reflection of the doubleness of their identity. Much the same is true of *Guadalupe* (1974) and the significantly titled *La Victima* (1976), both products of El Teatro de la Esperanza.

The Spanish-speaking community in America is a diverse one, more especially in New York where Spanish, Cuban and Puerto Rican groups perform largely in the Spanish language, though in the seventies and eighties bilingual productions became increasingly common, while a number of Hispanic-American plays are either translated or written in English. The backgrounds of the writers are widely divergent. Lynne Alvarez, born in Portland, Oregon, is the daughter of Argentinian parents, while John Jesurun's family come from Puerto Rico. Eduardo Machado was born in Havana while Jose Rivera was born in San Juan. Milcha Sanchez-Scott has an even more varied background, being born on the island of Bali, the daughter of parents who claim Indonesian, Chinese, Dutch and Colombian antecedents. They meet not in a language but a way of seeing.

At the end of the twentieth century immigration had changed New York much as it did around the turn of the century. But where once English was the high road to American identity, in the 1990s, as opposed to the 1890s, language communities had an air of greater permanence. It was not only that it had become possible to move from neighbourhood store, to taxi, to restaurant without hearing English spoken, beyond a phatic gesture so heavily accented as to defy translation, but that the pressure to surrender language to social advancement had diminished. The residue of cultural re-enfranchisement, which had been a mark of the sixties and seventies, is new confidence about origins, or simply a diminished necessity to deny origins in the name of some Platonic American self. It is a changed mood which has provoked its own anxieties as a minority of the threatened majority sought to legislate the primacy of English.

The theatre is an arena in which societies debate with themselves. It is where that delicate negotiation between the individual and the group finds its natural context. Its very form and circumstance is an exploration of that relationship. The presumption, once powerful and enshrined in the social organisation of theatre in America, that there is a consensus as to the terms of that debate and that negotiation, has diminished sharply in the concluding decades of a century which ended, internationally, on a revival of lost nationalisms. The breakup of empire, which saw the re-Balkanisation of Europe and the collapse of homogenising ideologies, scarcely left America immune. The English language may have merged victorious and American popular culture have provided a shared reservoir of images but these were no longer so rooted in a clear set of values. In being claimed on a global basis they were in some degree severed from the culture which generated them and whose own confident Messianism, the last spasm of which was evident in the rhetoric of the Reagan presidency, drained away with the conclusion of a Cold War which had frozen its consciousness at mid-century. Now those who arrived from Asia, from eastern Europe and from South and Central America brought with them their own cultural imperatives. On the whole, whatever the experiences of deprivation and suffering which had prompted their departure, they were less willing to engage in that annihilation of history, except as cultural artifact, which had once been the rite of entry to a society which invested so completely in the future: the theatre bore the marks of that. The blandness, the anonymity, the conformity which was America's gift as well as its burden was now to be met with a determination to reach back beyond homogenising myths to a self and a group identity which had their origins in other times and other places. The result was a transformed society whose own anxieties about national purpose and meaning were ironically the very essence of that possibility which remained its greatest gift to the world. The making of America has never ended. That is its dilemma and its strength. It is the primary source of its remarkable energy. The theatre, likewise, is never complete. It, too, requires the collaborative efforts of those who bring to the same stage experiences which differ radically. And what they create there is always provisional. The audience changes from performance to performance as the actors do from production to production. The play lives only by virtue of the transformations upon which it relies for its enactment. The voice of the man or woman is never entirely lost in that of the actor, as the voice of the actor is never entirely displaced by that of the character. We are all multiple selves as America is a multiple country, a kaleidoscope whose patterns change with every demographic tremor. No wonder that it has so often been in the theatre that this drama of national identity has been performed. Of course, it is entirely possible that the science fiction classic *Blade Runner* may prove to have a predictive power and that some time in the next century a hybrid street-babble composed of fragments of half a dozen languages may become the mark of a new technological underclass, but it is equally likely that spaceship America may continue its voyage into inner space with a regular injection of energy from those societies which once seemed so alien. Certainly the theatre has already shown signs of that transforming energy as America has rediscovered the kinetic power of heterogeneity.

For Carlos Fuentes the novel was born from our failure to understand one another as unitary, orthodox language has broken down. From that fact came the comedy and the drama of Cervantes and Tolstoy. To impose a unitary language, therefore, would be to kill the novel but also, he insists, to destroy society. For Salman Rushdie the essence of the novel lies in the fact that it permits languages, values and narratives to dispute, thereby resisting the single voice of dogmatic politics and religion. What they say of the novel is equally true of the theatre, indeed more so since there the pluralism of voices sounds out in an environment in which the disputing languages are given social form. The quarrel takes place in real time, the time which is uniquely the theatre's and not the novel's own – the present. From the 1960s onwards those new voices have sounded out from stages and theatres throughout America. For Mikhail Bakhtin ours is an age of competing languages, and to be sure the primary enterprise of our time has been the effort to challenge the imperial grammar, the presumptive text of orthodoxy. The breakup of empire, the American no less than the British and Soviet, has released a linguistic pluralism, as voices resonate where once there was silence, itself, of course, a kind of language – accusing but powerless. Those voices are the sound of a culture inventing itself, of a world in which the freedom of being remains a central project and endeavour. The theatre sets the stage for that drama, revealing, as it does, the extent to which the imagined can become the actual, the self be reborn in a myriad of guises, a singular thought become a communal truth. The youngest schoolchild knows the feeling of possibility born out of theatre. It is a knowledge which we carry through our lives. Greasepaint and light are not agents of deception. They are means of making visible what is otherwise concealed.

CHAPTER ELEVEN

Beyond Broadway

It seems somewhat incredible today to think that, their early radical work aside, work which surfaced, if at all, in small regional theatres, both Arthur Miller and Tennessee Williams launched and, for some time, largely sustained their careers on Broadway. It was then, as it assuredly is not today, the originator of drama. Broadway openings may have been preceded by out of town try-outs, in which fine tuning, and, occasionally, major surgery was performed, but the Great White Way was assumed to be the midwife of American drama. As midwives go, however, she began to be somewhat pricey, developing expensive habits. Costs rose and nerves started to fray. Over time, managements began to demand some guarantee of success and that could only be achieved by allowing someone else to conduct research and development, increasingly Off-Broadway, Britain and the regional (or, as some, with alarming honesty, preferred to call them, not-for-profit) theatres that were going to burgeon in the 1960s and 1970s. In a sense, then, the title of this chapter is a truism since virtually no new playwright appearing from the 1960s onwards found their first stage on Broadway, which in time became like a rich man employing food tasters. If such flourished the plate was snatched away; if they died it was rejected.

The new theatres, though, were not designed as try-out houses. On the contrary, they served their own constituency, no longer content, like the old theatrical circuit, to recycle Broadway hits. They commissioned plays and, on occasion, nurtured talent (Lanford Wilson, David Mamet, Terrence McNally, August Wilson, among others, benefited from this system).

Besides, where Miller could say that it was possible at least to have the illusion that in presenting your work on Broadway you were addressing the American people, as the 1950s gave way to the 1960s America seemed increasingly at war with itself, fragmenting into different component parts. There simply was no single audience, if there ever had been. Nor was it only a matter of race, Vietnam and then gender and sexual preference creating a divisive agenda. The young began to look for a different kind of theatre, less structured, less invested with what they took be the conventionalities of the mainstream.

In part they found that in the rock concert and the street demonstration, both heavily theatricalised. In part they found it in the small theatres of Off- and Off-Off-Broadway, more reasonably priced, more radical, both aesthetically and politically. And theatre itself was changing. The absurd had arrived from Europe and though *Waiting for Godot* could succeed on Broadway thanks to its cast of Bert Lahr and Tom Ewell, neither of whom, according to its director, Alan Schneider, had a clue as to what it might be about, Becket, Ionesco, Genet and Pinter (not an absurdist but himself influenced by Beckett and a master of the non-naturalistic play), along with those American playwrights who quickly absorbed their influences, found their natural home Off-Broadway and in the new small theatres and theatre spaces then springing up. Beckett never returned to Broadway, except for another high profile *Godot* in the 1990s.

Off-Broadway was acknowledged by Actors' Equity as early as 1950 when it accepted a different contract for theatres with between 199 and 299 seats in an area bounded by Fifth and Ninth Avenues, from 34th to 56th Streets. At that time, however, few original works were staged. Even Julian Beck and Judith Malina's Living Theatre staged European plays. The breakthrough came, in their case, with Jack Gelber's *The Connection* in 1959, while the same year saw the emergence of Edward Albee with *The Zoo Story*. Off-Off-Broadway (fewer than 199 seats) was already underway by 1958, with Caffè Cino, followed by La Mama, which opened in 1962.

Though these plays frequently offered a critique of American values, relatively few of the new playwrights chose to address the major political issues of the age until Vietnam began to drip feed into the national psyche. But, then, relatively few playwrights of the 1950s, outside of Williams and Miller, and, later, Lorraine Hansberry, had chosen to engage with the politics of that decade, and it is worth remembering that, while the 1960s have been mythicised as a political decade, the 1950s, too, saw America engaged in a war in Asia, while witch hunts by right-wing politicians threatened freedoms in the arts, education and the federal bureaucracy, and for the first time since the Civil War Federal troops were sent into the South. Nonetheless, if a recently financially enfranchised youth were disaffected their anger was as unfocused as that of Jimmy Porter in *Look Back in Anger*. James Dean was a symbol of revolt against authority but not of engagement with political issues.

That changed in the 1960s as the civil rights movement went from political progressivism, relying on the courts to secure its objectives, to a highly visible strategy, effectively staging the drama of America's contradictory principles in sit-ins and street demonstrations. Vietnam became an issue as it reached out to those whose families had a purchase on the American political system and that system began, defensively, to realign itself. But it was several years into the decade before the aesthetic adventurers of Off- and Off-Off-Broadway began to follow the logic of their own oppositional stance and the rebel without a cause became a rebel decidedly with a cause.

Nonetheless, values were being challenged. Boundaries that had seemed to have the force not only of tradition but of social and moral conviction began to be eroded and that extended to the theatre. Several of the new writers came from a background in art or were as committed to music as to theatre. The aesthetic of one form bled into another. By the same token, avowedly gay characters began to appear in drama while black dramatists carried their work firstly to Off-Broadway and then on to the streets. The barrier between audience and performer now became permeable. It was virtually a new conventionality for characters on stage to address audiences directly, sometimes within their roles and sometimes as actors, as though thereby to introduce an authenticity apparently denied by their fictional status.

In a country in which social experimentation was firmly on the agenda, at least for the young, theatrical experimentation was attractive. And that, effectively, took Broadway out of the picture though, as the 1960s developed, like Hollywood it showed its enthusiasm for whatever aspects of this new theatre could be alchemised into hard cash. And young playwrights, such as Terrence McNally, did occasionally find themselves accelerated to escape velocity on Broadway, to mutual astonishment and bafflement.

Many of the new writers who suddenly found a stage in the coffee bars, lofts, basements and church halls which constituted the geographically unlocatable Off-Off-Broadway were themselves young. When Tennessee Williams opened *The Glass Menagerie* on Broadway he was thirty-four. Arthur Miller was thirty-one when *All My Sons* opened. By contrast, Arthur Kopit was twenty when his first play was produced, Sam Shepard twenty-one, as was John Guare; Christopher Durang twenty-two, Terrence McNally twenty-five, Lanford Wilson twenty-six,

Jean-Claude van Itallie and Jack Gelber twenty-seven. This was not true
of all the new writers. Edward Albee was thirty when *The Zoo Story*
announced his arrival but, nonetheless, the low costs, and, it has to be
said, low production values of the new theatres, meant that the financial
risks were lower at Joe Cino's Caffè Cino, Ellen Stewart's La Mama
Experimental Theatre Club, Al Carmine's Judson Poet's Theatre or
Ralph Cook's Theatre Genesis, and that, therefore, writers who would
never have commanded a Broadway stage saw their plays produced, and
refined their talents, often untroubled by reviewers, in the limited spaces
and with the limited resources offered by theatres which in part shaped
their aesthetics.

At first the predominant influence was the European experimental
theatre but this was quickly adapted to an American mode. What most
shared, however, was a reaction against the presumptions of realist
theatre. Theirs were plays, at first often comic and surreal, in which plot
was not primary, psychological and social motivation largely absent,
character a free floating signifier and language less rooted in the self than
explored for its own textures, rhythms, ironic contradictions or wild exuberance. The physical body of the actor, the interaction between performer and audience, became primary concerns. Later, some (including
Durang, Guare and Wilson) would move towards a more lyrical theatre,
sometimes realistic but more often metaphoric and even elegiac.

The definition of a play was up for debate while theatre expanded to
include experiments that, on occasion, seemed to lack form and
purpose. Thus Wallace Shawn, who began writing in the 1960s but
emerged as a produced playwright in the 1970s, recalls that at that time
'the whole field of theatre was really a strange sort of *non*-field, in which
the whole business of "standards" just didn't appear',[1] and it is true that
a kind of democratisation of theatre was consequent upon the prolife-
ration of peforming spaces and a genuine attempt to explore and
expand boundaries. Playwrights often laid claim to a spontaneity of
thought, a freedom of invention, which left them unwilling to offer rational analysis. Indeed rationality tended to be seen as limiting the possibilities of the form.

'What was a play,' asked Shawn, answering that no one knew and few
cared. 'In writing a play,' he said, 'one really didn't know whether one
ought to draw one's inspiration from Ballanchine's ballets or Frederick
Wiseman's documentaries – or from Emily Dickinson's verses, Fra
Angelico's frescoes, the songs on the radio, the day's newspaper, or one's
own life.' As a result he decided that he would 'run as fast as [he] could

into the heart of confusion . . . write without any clear purpose, with blurred purposes, or no purpose . . . Instead of deciding what I would try to do, I would only look up to ask what I was doing when it was almost done.'[2] What was true of Shawn was also true of a number of other playwrights. It was not simply that this was on-the-job training (though Terrence McNally regarded his time with director Elaine May in just that way) but that in a decade of radical change, in the arts no less than in political and social thought, theatre itself was not just an arena for change but itself subject to redefinition. The result could often be gnomic gestures which resisted analysis (as with some early Shepard plays), but equally frequently it could be works of true originality. Sometimes both.

Some writers made a transition to Broadway or, more likely, occasional plays were picked up by a commercial enterprise desperate for 'product' and anxious to tune in to new fashions and trends. Thus Terrence McNally's *Bad Habits*, first produced Off-Broadway, was transferred to Broadway in 1974. But despite Broadway productions of *The Ritz* in 1975 and *Broadway* in 1979, he found a more conducive environment Off-Broadway and in the new regional theatres that increasingly offered an alternative to New York and became a breeding ground for new American theatre. Lanford Wilson, many of whose plays would move to Broadway, nonetheless rooted himself in an Off-Broadway company which he had been involved in founding. The Circle Repertory Company set itself to rediscovering what it called the lyric realism of the native voice of American theatre.

Given the fact that Off-Broadway, Off-Off-Broadway and regional theatre between them generated most new American drama, from the 60s to the end of the century, it would be impossible to do justice to the full range of playwrights who emerged in this period. What follows, therefore, is no more than a sample, drawn from different generations of writers who must, in that sense, stand for those many others who have sustained the American theatre in the face of economic challenge and proliferating competition from electronic entertainments. Terrence McNally, Lanford Wilson, John Guare, A. R. Gurney and David Rabe began their careers in the 1960s; Richard Nelson and Wallace Shawn in the 1970s, Tony Kushner and Paula Vogel in the 1980s. For Nelson and Shawn, the British theatre proved crucial. For Vogel it was regional theatre. Widely divergent in style and attitudes, they nonetheless share an engagement with American values, with American utopianism and a belief in the theatre's power to address contemporary reality, often in the context of unfolding history. Others spawned by Off-Broadway, Off-Off Broadway and regional theatres are to be found elsewhere in this book.

TERRENCE MCNALLY

Writing in 1995, Terrence McNally announced that 'The American theater has never been healthier. It's Broadway that's sick. The American theater,' he insisted, was 'no longer Broadway. It is Los Angeles, it is Seattle, it is Louisville, it is everywhere but the west side of midtown Manhattan.' Indeed, he was ready to claim that 'for the first time in our history, we have a *national* theater'; that national theatre was constituted of those theatres all over America which now generated new drama. And that regional theatre also existed in New York. As he explained, 'I wouldn't be a playwright today if it weren't for the regional theater. My regional theater is the Manhattan Theatre Club. I'm a regional playwright who just happens to live in New York.'[3]

There was a time when Off-Broadway seemed to imply radical experimentation, and for many writers it did. Indeed there was a time when simply to experiment seemed enough not only to attract attention but critical esteem. As McNally has said, 'I think our generation of writers went through a period of being overpraised for anything we wrote . . . In the '60s, if you wrote a play and you were under 30, you could get it done in New York. The result was that a lot of young American writers never developed a sufficient technique in playwriting.'[4]

McNally was stage manager at the Actors Studio for two years before his own first play, *And Things That Go Bump in the Night*, a futuristic and profoundly long and wordy piece, received its first performance there in 1962 and then opened, in a revised version, in 1964, at the Guthrie Theatre in Minneapolis, before closing, critically unlamented, at the Royale Theatre on Broadway. He himself recalls a review which read: 'The American theatre would be a better place today if Terrence McNally's parents had smothered him in his cradle.'[5] Full of invention, *And Things That Go Bump in the Night* also falls foul of his own strictures about technique. What it did show, however, was the wit, the social awareness, the fascination with performance that was to characterise much of his work, along with a virtual obsession with opera that was to resurface repeatedly.

McNally wrote his Vietnam plays, including *Botticelli*, but even this was an idiosyncratic piece in which two conscripts play a language game featuring, inevitably, Italian composers, as they wait for a Viet Cong fighter to emerge from a tunnel. He is no radical playwright, however, despite such works as *!Cuba Si!* (1968) and *Bringing It All Back Home* (1969). He is, by nature, a writer of comedy and, for a time, even farce, *Bad Habits* (1971), which contrasted two sanitoriums, one permissive, the other decidedly not, representing the former and *The Ritz* (1975), the latter.

The Ritz used a New York bathhouse as a setting and hence introduced gay characters as comic figures. Gay characters, indeed, would move to the centre of his drama, but no longer in the context of farce. Increasingly he wrote comedies which probed the pain of those who never quite connect with others in the way they wish. McNally dates the shift in his work to the 1982 production of *It's Only a Play*, which was, he has said, 'part satiric and part heartfelt'.[6] The heartfelt element gradually became the essence of plays that lost none of their humour but in which character was no longer merely an agent of comedy but the site of a drama about loss and the will to connect.

In *The Lisbon Traviata* (1985), for example, beneath a brittle humour which turns around one character's obsession with opera, a gay relationship breaks down disastrously. The pain is held at bay with language, one kind of obsession being offered as a correlative of another. In *Frankie and Johnny in the Clair de Lune* (1987) the couple are heterosexual but the anxiety is common. These are people drawn to one another but wary of the pain that may result. The language they deploy to seduce already contains the despair from which their feelings spring and which they fear may swallow them again. *Frankie and Johnny* concerns a moment of contact between two people who thought that their life had passed them by. As McNally has said, it 'examines intimacy and what people who are over forty do about a relationship . . . It's about love among the ashes.'[7] It is about the competing needs of privacy and commitment.

There is no condescension in the portraits he draws, as there had, perhaps, been in his earliest work. All his characters have their limitations – of intellect, taste, humour, judgement – but he acknowledges the needs which dominate their lives, the extent to which desire is both, as in Tennessee Williams's plays, an antidote to death and at the heart of those whose daily lives are finally of less significance than the private moments of consonance they so desperately seek.

In *Lips Together, Teeth Apart* (1991), which McNally, speaking that year, saw as his best play, a brother and sister, together with their spouses, come together on the Fourth of July. One of them, Sally, has inherited a house on Fire Island from her brother who has died of AIDS. Both relationships are under strain. Sally, now pregnant, has a history of miscarriages, her husband is afraid of children, her brother-in-law John, who is sexually drawn to her, has cancer. The fourth character, Chloe, prattles on, confessing that 'I talk too much probably because it's too horrible to think about what's really going on.'[8] Each of them, indeed, has secret fears which they expose only in what amount to soliloquys. They are, in John's words, getting through the business of living, while deeply insecure and frightened. They hesitate to enter the swimming pool because of an irrational fear that it might carry the AIDS infection, until Sally forces the issue. They are unaware that it is precisely their fears and insecurities that they have in common.

Meanwhile, next door, unseen, are gay men, seemingly enjoying life. When they throw a Fourth of July Party their celebration sounds vital, that of the two couples febrile and unconvincing. But both gay and heterosexual characters, the seen and unseen characters, ignore the plight of a man who walks into the sea and drowns. Only Sally shows any alarm, and even she loses sight of him and is distracted by her own concerns. There is, in other words, a desperation to which they all close their eyes, of which they all choose to be unaware. The shadow of AIDS is merely one aspect of that, not the play's subject but a metaphor for the arbitrary and for a pain which they all wish to deny. And when McNally instructs that at the end of the play the house lights should come up to full intensity, the audience, too, is implicated. The play ends as the sound of an ultra-violet bug exterminator announces the death of the mosquitos which flit around the house and Mozart's *Così Fan Tutte* comes to full volume while the characters watch a shooting star. Death and beauty combine.

AIDS is not the subject of *Lips Together, Teeth Apart*, but it suffuses the play, as fact and image, and McNally has said that, 'I don't see how you can write a play today – if you're writing about contemporary life – and, if not mention it, have it as a subtext in the play.'[9] It is in that sense, indeed, that it functions in *A Perfect Ganesh* (1993) in which two middle-aged women friends go on a trip to India, both fascinated and terrified by the culture they observe, but, as in the previous play, in fact suppressing their real fears. Margaret has discovered a lump in her breast. Her friend, Katherine, is haunted by the memory of the homosexual son whom she loved for himself but whose sexuality she could not accept and whose own pain she could not acknowledge. In a non-naturalistic play, in which the Indian god Ganesh has the power to change his form and appear as a number of different characters, that son is allowed to speak for himself:

That's not love. It's guilt that's become a curse. She should have loved me not just for falling down and scraping my knee when I was a little boy but for standing tall when I was a young man and telling her I loved other men. She should have loved me when my heart was breaking for love of them. She should have loved me when I wanted to tell her my heart was finally, forever full with someone – Jonathan! – but I didn't dare. She should have loved me the most when he was gone, that terrible day when my life was over.[10]

Margaret's cancerous lump, like the accidental death of her infant son, like her husband's adulterous affair, like AIDS, like the death of Katherine's son, murdered by homophobic African-Americans, is an unavoidable fact that is avoided but has to be acknowledged. Instead, the two women have allowed life to become a series of defensive tactics. Meanwhile, they are befriended by two young men, one of whom is himself dying of AIDS.

India is a place they go looking to forget or looking for a miracle, for a cure, an India whose own suffering is so easily put out of mind. And they do find a miracle in so far as, led by Ganesh, they reach the point of being able to face their fears. The play ends, as is so often the case with McNally's work, with music and the moment of grace it tends to bring. The journey they go on only incidentally has to do with India. What they discover is that they already held their lives in their hands, that there is a divinity to all things and that those distinctions which divide are the enemy of an essential humanity. As McNally has said, 'I think it's out of terror of one another and of intimacy that we become racist and homophobic and sexist and all these things.'[11] A central theme of all his work is the barriers that people erect between themselves and the means by which they sustain those barriers.

Gay playwrights, once forced to express their concerns and commitments obliquely, if at all, increasingly staked out their territory in the American theatre. For some, such as Charles Ludlam, this involved camp celebration, a technicolour extravaganza. For Harvey Fierstein, in *Torch Song Trilogy*, a series of plays about a drag queen, it was a matter of exploring the almost conventional needs of an unconventional character. For others, such as Lanford Wilson, it was, for much of the time, a question of registering a gay presence in the unfolding story of an America in which personal and communal values alike were under stress. While Edward Albee would attract a certain degree of opprobrium for resisting what he saw as the ghettoising of gay theatre, and for rejecting a definition of himself as a gay playwright (without ever seeking to deny the nature of his identity), Tony Kushner embraced such a definition and sought to create an aesthetic rooted in that identity. In the case of McNally, the reality of gay life moved to the centre of his work but always with a consciousness of what was shared, what was common.

The indirections of his previous two plays disappear in *Love! Valour! Compassion!* (1994), winner of the 1995 Tony for Best Play. Brought together in a farmhouse, eight men work out their fears and passions. Once again, AIDS is a presence but this is only one aspect of the lives of this disparate group of people. We have McNally's assurance that in it he 'wanted to write about what it's like to be a gay man at this particular moment in our history . . . I think I wanted to tell everyone else who we are when they aren't around'.[12] Beyond that, it is an account of love and its vicissitudes. It has moments of near farce but is centrally concerned with shifting relationships, the ever-present fact of being 'a bystander at the genocide of who we are',[13] and with the need to find such solidarity as is available once fears and occluding privacies are addressed.

McNally's plays are, essentially, about love, valour compassion and the multiple and various forms that they take. There is behind them a Whitmanesque respect for the Other, a sense, ultimately, of the divinity as well as the absurdity of all. Indeed, it was that conviction that lay behind *Corpus Christi* (1998), a play which inspired considerable hostility in that it presented the story of Christ as a homosexual, born and raised, in this version, in Corpus Christi, Texas, in the 1950s. It is a play of some wit, and not always subtle ironies, which for all its scatological language and conscious provocations, rests, finally, on the conviction, expressed by John as he baptises the actors who are to perform: 'I baptize you and recognize your divinity as a human being.'[14] That, after all, is essentially the true faith on which McNally's plays are based. He writes of people who ask for respect, who evidence a common humanity, who suffer from the same debilitating fears as one another, who seek the same comfort, who need the same redemption. His drama is not polemical but it does rest on the conviction that whatever different forms those fears may take they demand attention. And if, as here, there are those who stress separation and difference it is not only within the boundaries of the stage that some commonality is to be found. Thus, where Bartholomew quotes the biblical injunction, 'If a man lies with a man as with a woman, both of them have committed an abomination; they shall be put to death, their blood is upon them', Christ, who in this play presides over a gay marriage, recalls another passage which is more to his taste and which embodies his, and it has to be said, McNally's conviction that the divine is to be found in everything: 'And God saw everything that He had made, and behold it was very good.'[15]

Terrence McNally is not a radical playwright. *Corpus Christi*, no matter how it was received, was no attempt to provoke conservative opinion. At base its theme was Christ's: love one another. The conscious blurring of the line between Eros and agape may have laid him open to attack – Pilate's question to Christ is 'Art Thou a queer then?' and his answer, 'Thou sayest I am'[16] – but it was of a piece with his desire to blur other distinctions, to incorporate rather than exclude. And once again, as in all his work, as, indeed, in *Master Class* (1995), the play which preceded *Corpus Christi*, humour is an agent of his humanity, exposing vulnerability and, like music, a vital aspect of most of his plays, itself a root to harmony and transcendence.

Few if any of his plays could be said to be naturalistic. Lighting and sound have their thematic roles (in *Corpus Christi* the sound of the cross being built echoes through the play as a token of approaching death). Characters are permitted to step out of the action to address their private fears. Off-stage action bears on what is seen on stage, magical figures appear, the dead rise. But this is less to disturb our sense of the real than to call all as witnesses to a struggle for life which is, therefore, a struggle with death and which does, indeed, require love, valour and compassion.

LANFORD WILSON

Lanford Wilson, born in Lebanon, Missouri, in 1937, arrived in New York in 1962 and immediately gravitated to Off-Off-Broadway. His first plays, *Home Free* (1964) and *The Madness of Lady Bright* (1963–4), were staged at the Caffe Cino. Both include characters who have no existence outside the needs which generate them. In the case of the latter the central figure is a no longer attractive gay man who recalls those who once drifted through his life, one of the earliest plays to feature a gay character. It was with *This is the Rill Speaking* (1965), however, that he offered a glimpse of the direction his work would take.

This is the Rill Speaking is a play for voices, with actions pantomimed, which offers a portrait of a small Missouri community. Its use of overlapping scenes and elided experiences, its staging of a community of people, even its sentimentality blended with a sense of loss, was to recur in *Balm in Gilead* (1965), *The Rimers of Eldritch* (1966), *Hot l Baltimore* (1973) and, indeed, in much of the work of a playwright increasingly concerned with the loss of values, of the connective tissue which once united individuals and their society.

Balm in Gilead takes place in and around an all-night coffee shop on Upper Broadway. Its customers come from the underside of American life. Buyers and sellers (of drugs, sex, stolen property), they are a degraded version of that larger society to which they have no real access but which, in some senses, they mirror, as did the drug addicts of Gelber's *The Connection*. Non-naturalistic, it stages the repetitions, the reiterative rhythms of what O'Neill would have called a bottom of the world Ratskeller. It is a carefully choreographed piece, in which scenes are repeated and the action occasionally frozen. Within that choreography, however, actors are encouraged to improvise both movements and, in the background and therefore mostly unheard, brief speeches.

In one sense the characters are caricatures but the play's effect comes less from an interest in the origins or fate of individuals than from the emerging pattern formed by this group of desperate survivors. Voice blends with voice as, by accretion, Wilson constructs a world which is itself deconstructing. There are cameo roles, as a figure emerges for a moment from the background noise of desperation, but this is not where the play lives and breathes. These are characters getting by from moment to moment, locked in their own privacies but part of a larger portrait. Echoes of this play were to recur in *Hot l Baltimore*, inspired by the same 76th Street and Broadway hotel that features here.

In *The Rimers of Eldritch* Wilson once again creates a community in decline. This time he is back in the midwest. It is a place of desperate people who watch as their small town falls apart and their lives do likewise. At its heart is a young crippled girl, on the brink of a maturity that simultaneously compels and alarms her, and a young boy as baffled as she by what is happening to him. An inadvertent killing disrupts their world while the town's eccentric finds himself accused of a crime he did not commit.

Once again Wilson is concerned to create a sense of community by layering speeches and scenes, bringing separate stories together. Once again, too, he is interested in the harmonies and dissonances that emerge from voices that sound out in what amounts to a ritual, a ceremony, an elegiac song, a lament. Innocence is lost, relationships are fractured, trust is corroded, security destroyed. At base his characters are the victims of a natural process which destroys the grace of youth and the basis for hope. But they are also collaborators in decline. The poetry of their lives is sacrificed too easily, broken on the rack not only of time but also of self-concern. The final irony, however, is that Wilson hears that poetry still in the interleaved remarks of those who register their separation from one another but no longer recognise the rhyme between one life and another. That poetry, however, survives in the play, which itself offers the consolation of form.

The Rimers of Eldritch took Wilson back to his home territory in Missouri. *Lemon Sky* (1970), one of the best of his early plays, was more directly autobiographical. Set in suburban San Diego, in the late 1950s and the present, it stages the dilemma of a seventeen-year-old boy called Alan, who has sought out the father who had abandoned his family for another woman. He has travelled from the midwest but in fact the journey he goes on is less to do with space or even time, as past and present interact, than with experience and understanding, as he makes discoveries about his father but more fundamentally about himself. The earthquakes which from time to time shake the house stand as an image of more profound disruptions in the life of a boy who is discovering his own sexuality as he does the corruption within his family.

Non-naturalistic, *Lemon Sky* acknowledges its own status as a play. Alan is the narrator who summons the action into being, its distortions reflecting his own state of mind. Characters survive their own death, rather as in Thornton Wilder's *Our Town*, though Wilson's play lacks the easy sentimentality of the latter. The sun shines down on a bleak world in which sexuality is a dark secret and the reconciliation with the past that Alan had sought is never quite achieved because some facts remain suppressed, some keys to truth lie unused and unacknowledged. *Lemon Sky* is a subtle and disturbing work whose form reflects the tensions which give it birth. Seeing the world, as we do, through the sensibility of a character desperate to make sense of his life but aware of the extent to which that life has been distorted by his experiences, certain truths remain impossible to confront. The audience is required to fill gaps left in the text, to infer truths from the shock waves which run through the text.

The most successful of Wilson's early plays was undoubtedly *Hot l Baltimore* (1973), whose action takes place in the lobby of a run-down hotel inhabited by prostitutes, petty criminals, the dying, those bewildered by a life that appears to render up no clear meaning. The building is in decline (hence the missing letter in its display sign and the title,

language itself suffering depletion) and scheduled for demolition, and as
such mirrors the lives of those who inhabit it. It is a temporary home.
All its guests are on a notice to quit, the symbolic significance of which
is clear enough as they stare into a future that seems to have only one
certainty. Yet we are closer to Tennessee Williams, here, than Samuel
Beckett, though Beckett is, perhaps, a presence. Wilson himself cites
Chekhov and *The Cherry Orchard*, as some process, some historical
moment comes to an end and the characters step out into an unknown
future. There are momentary consolations to be found, just as there are
depleting ironies. Some vestige of fellow feeling survives. The light is not
quite extinguished in their eyes as, for a moment, they come together,
even if such moments pass.

These are characters who survive through the stories they tell themselves. They perform their lives, their deceits being directed as much at
themselves as at others. The play, meanwhile, is constructed out of these
overlapping stories, out of voices which blend and separate as the lives
of the characters momentarily touch before a suffocating isolation cuts
them off from the consolation of companionship. *Hot l Baltimore* won the
New York Drama Critics Circle Award and an Obie, the latter being a
prize created in the 1955–6 season for Off-Broadway theatre.

Wilson followed this with *The Mound Builders* (1975), a play about an
archaeological dig in the course of which he lays bare not only the collapse of an ancient civilisation but the collapse of his own, as the group
of archaeologists slowly falls apart out of self-regard, greed and the
primitive instincts which seem to have survived the passage of time.

By this stage in his career Wilson's emphasis had begun to shift. His
involvement with Circle Rep had, he explained, led him to wish to write
parts for actors that were 'fully rounded'. He wished to give greater
autonomy and depth to characters he had earlier been content to regard
simply as voices, lending their own particular notes to a broader score.
The Mound Builders was evidence of this, as, perhaps more significantly,
was a series of plays, beginning with *5th of July* (1977) and continuing with
Talley's Folly (1979) and *Talley and Son* (originally *A Tale Told*) (1981), which
unfolded the story of the Talley family. The first takes place in the 1970s;
the latter two in early July 1944.

Once again, Wilson returns to his home state of Missouri. In the first
play Kenneth Talley, Jr., a paraplegic who has lost his legs in the Vietnam
war and who lives with his homosexual lover Jed Jenkins, is in recoil from
the world. A school teacher, he can no longer teach, except a young boy
as traumatised as himself. He is joined by two childhood friends, John

and Gwen, anxious to buy his house, and who had once, like Kenneth, shared a youthful idealism but now make their money out of business. All of them have a vested interest in forgetting the past, as, it seems, do the children in the nearby school who are taught nothing about Vietnam. The next generation, meanwhile, is represented by fourteen-year-old Shirley Talley, who is, it seems, John's abandoned daughter, and who melodramatically dramatises herself as the last of the Talleys.

This is not a play that offers a sentimental version of 1960s radicalism. A representative of that world survives, a fly in amber, spaced out on drugs. Rather, the action of the play is concerned with the process whereby Kenneth is slowly lured back into life, facing himself and the world from which he had withdrawn. It ends as he succeeds in breaking through to the apparently autistic young boy and resolves to return to school teaching. He will stay in the house, with its family history, and acknowledge the significance of his relationship with his lover. It is a play about healing wounds, about surviving after a trauma that had affected a nation no less than this individual, and it is plainly not without significance that its action is set at the time of Independence Day. In a country built on denial of the past, confrontation with the past becomes a necessary step in reaching for the future.

As elsewhere in Wilson's work, the temptations of sentimentality, of issues too conveniently resolved, insights too readily achieved, are not entirely resisted. Much the same could seemingly be said of the second play in the sequence, which concerns an unlikely romance between Sally Talley, a minor figure in *5th of July*, and the Jewish Matt Friedman. Yet, seen in the context of the other two plays, it is not without its ironies for, though each play is designed to stand alone, taken together they do reflect on one another as the point of view shifts, history, in one form or another, exerts its pressure and the ambiguous force of American values works itself out in terms of a single family.

In *Talley's Folly*, two people meet who bear the scars of the past. Matt is a survivor of the Holocaust, which had claimed his parents and sister, and Sally of an illness that leaves her barren. Neither is young. Their future is in the balance. They have to lay ghosts, get past the differences that separate them. That they do so is in part a consequence of their own resilience, of their humour and of their mutual desire to escape. Taken alone, *Talley's Folly* is a simple love story. In the context of the play which followed, however, the relationship between these two people, honest, privileging feeling over ambition, seems strangely aberrant. For the third play in the sequence, *Talley and Son*, presents a world in which greed, cruelty and ambition determine actions and family relationships are no more than agents of a callow pragmatism.

Talley and Son is a melodrama. Where in *Talley's Folly* the warm-hearted Matt narrated his own story, acknowledging the theatrical nature of the event in which he was involved, much as had the protagonist of *Lemon Sky*, in this we are seemingly offered a realistic drama in which characters oblige by being no more than they appear.

For all the weaknesses of its third part, however, Wilson's trilogy is an affecting portrait of the collapse of American idealism into venality and self-interest, whether it be in the 1940s or the 1970s. The fact that he remains committed to a redemptive logic perhaps shows no more than how American he is, for the fact is that in virtually all of his plays, no matter the evidence that he adduces for spiralling moral decline, there is always a small epiphany, a rededication to the force of the human heart. His work exists within and is in part defined by that tension.

Much the same was true of his 1982 play, *Angels Fall*, in which a group of individuals find themselves stranded in a New Mexico church during a nuclear alert but, for the most part, resolve the various dilemmas that they had brought to this place.

In 1987, however, with *Burn This*, Wilson seemed to move in another direction, with a play of crude passion and excoriating language. Anna, a dancer whose lover is a successful screenwriter, has returned from the funeral of a gay friend, when her apartment is invaded by Pale, that friend's brother. He seems barely in control, on the edge of breakdown, paranoid, violent. It is, as Wilson has said, a love story but a long way removed from *Talley's Folly*. Both characters are vulnerable, damaged in ways they can barely articulate. If they come together, as they do, it is not because they find security and peace. What they do discover is shared pain.

The figure of Pale was created for John Malkovich, who did, indeed, take the part by the scruff of the neck. In some sense, however, the sheer force of the character risks unbalancing the play, his dominance never quite being squared with the mutuality he appears to seek and on which the play's resolution seems in part to turn. Nonetheless, *Burn This* introduced an idiom, more familiar from the work of David Rabe and David Mamet, and naturalised by Pale's psychotic condition, which seemed to counter what elsewhere in Wilson's work can seem a tendency to sentimentality. The brittle and sometimes brutal exchanges reflect a relationship in which the partners wish both to deny and affirm their passion, afraid, as they are, of the vulnerabilities they expose and the needs to which they implicitly confess. They are both emotionally wounded and their language no less than their behaviour is evidence for this.

In some degree that is equally true of his next play, *Redwood Curtain*, a Circle Repertory Company production which opened at the Seattle Rep in 1992. The male protagonist, Lyman Fellers, shares something with Kenneth Talley. He is a Vietnam veteran who has retreated to the redwood forest of northern California, traumatised by his experiences and in retreat from other people. Like his society, which also suffered trauma in that war, he wishes only to forget, to obliterate the past, but the price for that is an existence without purpose or direction, and we have Wilson's assurance that he did, indeed, wish 'to emblematize the whole state of the country'.[17]

Fellers is tracked down by a young Asian-American woman called Geri Riordan, in search of the American soldier who she believes fathered her by a Vietnamese woman who had given her up for adoption. Both have lost something; both feel that it is impossible to pick up their lives because of a past to which they cannot adjust. He is, we eventually discover, not the father she sought but through him she discovers who was. It was the man in whose house she has been raised, a musician who, apparently, died out of a sense of despair. In other words she already possessed what she thought she sought.

The conclusion, however, is not as pat as it seems nor is the play entirely realistic. For the resolution of her dilemma, as of that of the disoriented Lyman Fellers, lies in her return to her music (she is a concert pianist) and his hesitating move into her house where he stands and listens to her play. Both, separately, have heard a music they thought lost to them as a harmony sounds out amidst the dissonances of their lives. They have, in effect, saved one another.

Since he began in the theatre Lanford Wilson has written about those who are scarred by their encounter with the world, people who have retreated, disengaged themselves. He has presented a society that has lost its energy, its sense of direction, its inner coherence. His communities are in decline, relationships are under pressure. The corruption is partly external, a distorting materialism, a fear transformed into aggression and violence, and partly internal, as characters sacrifice feeling to ambition and relationships to narcissism. A connection that once existed between people and the land has been compromised. They are threatend by an apocalypse that is partly of their own making and partly a product of a society that has lost sight of its own reason for being.

But against this he pitches a surviving will for connection. His plays edge towards epiphanies. Sometimes these are earned, rooted in the sensibility of characters alive to the need to break out of their isolation, shaped by experiences that create their own necessities. Sometimes they are gestures of a writer determined to offer the consolation of meaning at a cost to the logic of his own plays.

Throughout a long and continuing career, however, he has created plays distinguished by their language, individual speeches being subtly orchestrated, or driven by rhythms that are revelatory of character, expressive of the complex relationships of those whose lives he stages. He writes about loss and decline but also about those who survive by virtue of their own courage and humour, their acknowledgement that out of need can come resolution. Stylistically, his plays have moved from early experiments, influenced in one direction by European experimental drama and in another by Tennessee Williams, through those dramas in which communities were recreated on stage by means of a kaleidoscope of scenes, a carillon of voices, to works which reflect a harsher, more traumatised culture. If character has increasingly engaged him it is because he has come to believe that the community he celebrates, and on which, as a writer, he depends, begins with the individual, as theatre itself depends on the individual voice as much as it does on the provisional society created on the stage and in the auditorium.

JOHN GUARE

John Guare comes from a theatre family. As a teenager he was an admirer of Chekhov and Tennessee Williams. At Georgetown University in the late 1950s he wrote one-act plays before moving on to Yale, where he studied drama. The emergence of a renewed Off-Broadway and its wilder and cheaper cousin, Off-Off Broadway, gave him a stage. Free of the pressure of reviews he was free, too, to experiment, and did so with plays that showed the influence of, among others, Ionesco, Dürrenmatt, Orton, Pinter and Feydeau. Beginning at the Caffe Cino and subsequently at the Provincetown Playhouse, he also benefited from time at the O'Neill Centre, where he first tried out a section of what would later become his first success, *The House of Blue Leaves*.

He was drawn at first to farce, convinced that it was a form particularly suited to a chaotic social and moral world. He was certainly determined to lay siege to naturalism and reinstate a sense of the poetic, to place language at the centre of his work. Ahead lay the deeply lyrical

Nantucket plays (*Lydie Breeze*, *Gardenia* and *Women and Water*), but for the moment language was to be an agent of comedy, satire and the absurd. In *Muzeeka* (1967), for example, he offered an oblique response to Vietnam and its contaminating influence. Then, in 1971, came *The House of Blue Leaves*, which won him a handful of awards, as it did again when revived at the Lincoln Centre in 1986.

The play takes place on the occasion of a visit by the Pope to the Queens district of New York. For Guare, it was a blend of Strindberg and Feydeau, and certainly the farce is laced with (off-stage) violence. Filled with decidedly secular nuns, insane movie directors, dumb movie stars and assassins – hardly unknown in American society – it is concerned, at least in part, with frustrated dreams and humiliations, with a paranoia which is definitional of a culture in which discontent is factored into the national enterprise. All the characters pursue happiness, locating that chimera in familiar places – religion, success, money. The result is a form of moral anarchy. Indeed, there is something of Nathaniel West about a work in which reality has been so completely colonised by fantasy that it no longer has true meaning, as there is in his portrait of a society which puts no limits on possibility and hence loses any coherent moral shape beyond an unregulated desire.

Following a highly successful adaptation of *Two Gentlemen of Verona* (1971), he celebrated Bicentennial year with *Marco Polo Sings a Solo* (1977), a wildly inventive piece, surreal, apocalyptic, bizarre, and *Landscape of the Body* (1977), a darkly allusive work in which the imminent violence of urban life becomes a metaphor for that greater violence which is implicit in being, as Beckett has a character remark, born astride the grave. In a play which itself constitutes a metaphor, his approach is metaphoric.

His next play, *Bosoms and Neglect* (1979), poorly received on its first appearance but successfully revived in 1999 by New York's Signature Theatre Company, is a finely balanced work which moves from wild comedy, as a young couple flirt and fight, to a beautifully modulated second act which is moving without ever being entirely drained of humour. Indeed, humour is an aspect of the play's humanity. *Bosoms and Neglect* is in part a satire of trendy psycho-babble, of narcissism, of self-regarding bookishness, and in part a comedy of human relationships. It is also a play which addresses those vulnerabilities, fears and anxieties that exist just beneath the surface, as a woman conceals the breast cancer which has been eating away at her body.

In some ways *Bosoms and Neglect* seems a transitional play. It contains elements of his earlier work – comedy verging on farce – but is leaning towards a genuine engagement with character and an acknowledgement of pain. That latter element moved to the fore in a sequence of plays beginning, in 1982, with *Lydie Breeze* and *Gardenia* and continuing, in first draft, in 1984, and then in revised versions in 1985 and 1988, with *Women and Water*, which explored the nature of the utopian impulse. All three (a fourth, *Bullfinch's Mythology*, is promised) are poetic, lyrical works that explore the failure of an ideal community which is plainly offered as a version of that greater venture which is America.

All three plays concern themselves with the fate of a utopian community conceived by a group of people during the American Civil War. *Lydie Breeze* is set in 1895, *Gardenia* in 1875 and 1885 and *Women and Water* in 1861 and 1864. In other words we go backwards in time, just as the name of the community is utopia written backwards. And, indeed, Guare reads American history backwards, tracing failed ideals back to their origin. The utopian impulse, it seems, carries the seeds of its own destruction.

In *Lydie Breeze* we see the consequences of past betrayals as lives have been infected, contaminated by jealousy and self-regard. That infection has its correlative in the form of a venereal disease which itself shows the two faces of love, creative and destructive in the same moment. And so it has proved for these characters, both on a personal and public level. It is the very perfection of the utopian dream that generates its own corruption; the very desire for the purest of love that breeds a desire for vengeance when it is betrayed or frustrated. For some of the group, this generates a cynicism that elides with the very system of power they had conspired to deny. For others, the knowledge of fallibility joins them with those from whom their desire for perfection had sundered them.

The young Lydie Breeze is terrified of life and of the love which will destroy her innocence, but hers, it seems, will be a fortunate fall. Her form of innocence stems from a denial of knowledge, ignorance of the consolations to be offered by others. She must leave this community which has isolated itself on the edge of a continent as if it feared corruption when in fact the corruption was already within.

Lydie Breeze explores a dream by deploying the inner mechanisms of dream, as moment slides over moment, memory folds into memory. Small rituals, the ceremonies of personal relationships, blend into a larger myth as Guare dissects a failure of will and imagination that was not without its relevance to a society which, in the 1980s, seemed precisely to be trading in a vision of moral possibility for the pragmatics of power and money. But Guare does not sentimentalise a utopia which, by definition, is static. The young Lydie Breeze, on the brink of life, afraid of a transformation which she believes to be a betrayal, has to take a step beyond the stasis of this broken community which has already been broken apart, destroyed by its inner contradictions. A couple in the same play walk into the sea and die rather than compromise what they believe to be a new-found perfection. They walk the wrong way. In the other direction lies the land and the unregenerate people from whom they have separated themselves but who, eventually, will prove the redemption of the utopian community.

Gardenia, which followed *Lydie Breeze*, is more prosaic. It offers to document the utopian community, and its very specificity blunts some of the lyricism of the previous play, not least because the banality of the venture stands exposed. Already there are signs of failure. Its members have begun to communicate with the nearby community, which they distrust and which they can only patronise. The manifesto which they have prepared is refused publication. As one of them tellingly remarks, 'maybe our moment of glory came in the moment we dreamed it'.[18]

Their purpose in founding a utopian community was to create a society that would 'shine as a beacon to the world'.[19] This was to be their Manifest Destiny. They would 'examine the purposes of being male and female', and 'search for something higher'.[20] But they are sustained by the proceeds of theft, their end thus being tainted by their means. Then jealousy and violence enter their community. Entranced by the purity of their original vision, by the energy and confidence of their youthful idealism, they are blinded to the moment-by-moment collapse of its inner coherence. Bewitched by their own vision of a perfect future which will gift them the new Eden they seek, they ignore the fact that it is to be constructed by men and women who are themselves flawed and who obey other imperatives than those envisaged in their new philosophy.

If *Gardenia* is more prosaic than *Lydie Breeze*, *Women and Water* restored a genuine lyricism of language, blended with stage metaphors of affecting force and originality. Set during the Civil War, it is a partly expressionist work, reminiscent in some ways of Robert Lowell's *The Old Glory*. This is the moment the grand gesture was formulated. It was born out of the confusion and violence of war, a war here rendered through a series of startling metaphors as the elder Lydie Breeze's skirt is filled with coins, letters, mementoes of those about to die; scattered crates are moved around to form trenches, ships, graves; lanterns shine through the mist and a muslin cloth is transformed from sail to flag to the white sand of a beach. In a disordered world, where dead bodies and wild animals invoke apocalypse, where betrayal is a constant possibility and immediate fact, those who are to constitute the new world come together, their project already blighted not only by our knowledge of its ultimate fate but by the cruelties already exposed in a society itself born of the brightest hopes but moving with such rapidity from the Book of Genesis to the Book of Revelation.

The Nantucket trilogy is not written out of a conviction that the utopian is dangerously deluded, that idealism is necessarily tainted and the possibility of change a simple irony. It is true that this utopia, programmatic and naive, does collapse, that its promulgators are in thrall to the past which they hope so earnestly to escape, scarred by the violence in which their dream was born. But these are not plays without hope and Guare is not a writer concerned with social, political or metaphysical ironies. Even the poetic nature of the language hints at the survival of a consonance that escapes the principal characters, suggests a harmony beyond the dissonance which fractures their community. The rituals of theatre, after all, are themselves not without their utopian assumptions while transformation is of its essence.

The Nantucket trilogy is a considerable achievement. It reaches for, and largely achieves, that poetry of the theatre that Guare had always valued. Meanwhile, at one moment he opts for an affecting simplicity in his staging, as in the language of his characters; at another the stage is alive, as costumes and props become signifiers, actors in a drama which in the end is concerned with something more than the fate of a national dream. For his are characters trying to find some inner core to experience, endeavouring to give shape and purpose to the merely random, and if the struggle is doomed to fail then such dignity and purpose as is available is born out of the struggle as it is out of a faith which drives the individual beyond the normal boundaries of meaning and belief.

These plays never quite achieved the success they deserved but the play which opened in 1990 at the Lincoln Centre did. *Six Degrees of Separation* tells the story of a black confidence trickster who, claiming to have been mugged in nearby Central Park, persuades a rich couple to give him money and shelter. On the basis of a supposed friendship with their son, away at college, he insinuates himself into their household, playing on their liberal guilt. He is a confidence trickster who can only succeed because his victims wish to believe him, wish to absolve themselves of feelings they would deny they have. And this confidence trickster is entirely plausible. He reflects back to them their own beliefs, claiming to share their intellectual interests, their elitism and their belief in the decline of moral values, convictions doubtless also held by the Lincoln Centre audience who are thus equally seduced. His plan fails only when he is discovered inviting a male hustler into the apartment.

The play's title derives from the notion that 'everybody on this planet is separated by only six other people. Six degrees of separation.'[21] And, indeed, it would seem to demonstrate both how close we are to one another, in the sense of sharing the same hypocrisies and vulnerabilities, and how remote, not only from others but also from our own motives, our own lives. It is not the exposure of the young man, Paul, that finally lies at the heart of the play, but the exposure of everybody else. As the play progresses we discover the gulf between the rich couple and their son, the shallowness and self-serving nature of their supposed moral values, the gap between themselves and those beyond the supposedly secure doors of their handsome apartment. In the end it is the con man who has a greater insight into others, albeit an insight which never transmutes into true understanding or compassion.

Nor is art a defence against their human failings. A Kandinsky painting hangs over the stage, one more possession to pile up against a threatening world. Paul, meanwhile, deploys his imagination and his actorly skills to deceive, while himself insisting on his role as an agent of understanding. It is an ironic gesture for Guare to make as his own theatre is equally available for co-option as life-style accessory or avenue to insight and understanding and that, perhaps, is part of the play's concern. Like many of his works, however, it ends with a gesture of hope, as does the play which followed it, *Four Baboons Adoring the Sun* (1992), a modern Greek tragedy whose tragic denouement is deflected as a woman who has suffered loss nonetheless celebrates life in the face of death.

John Guare's work is immensely varied. It includes absurdist sketches, exuberant farces, surreal comedies and lyrical works of genuine poetic force. He has explored American values and satirised aspects of a culture convinced of its manifest virtues. His resistance to naturalism, his fascination with language and the physical resources of theatre, owe something to his early years Off-Off-Broadway, and in essence his work still seems more at home in smaller, more intimate spaces, despite a success that has brought him some of the country's leading awards. Dramatically, he remains as unpredictable as ever, unpredictable and prolific, but among his many plays are several, not always successful on their first appearance, that will surely become part of the canon of twentieth-century American drama.

DAVID RABE

David Rabe is very much a product of Off-Broadway and regional theatre. His career began at Joe Papp's Public Theater and he has opened plays at the Long Wharf and Chicago's Goodman Theatre. His Vietnam plays are discussed earlier in this book but in fact his work has been seen rather too much in terms of his response to that war. For with each succeeding play it began to seem that Vietnam was a symptom rather than the disease. *Streamers* (1976), for example, opened when Vietnam was already if not fading into history then finally and irrevocably over, and the tensions and disruptions in the play go a good deal deeper than those caused by a particular circumstance, no matter how traumatising. There are, indeed, Beckettian overtones, at least to a central metaphor (that of a man plunging downwards, his parachute failing to open) which turns not only on the irrevocable fact of death but a hopeless hope, an irony generated out of need. But if absurdity was a product of an ineluctable circumstance it was also exacerbated by the personal betrayals and social dislocations of society. And it was those that came to the fore in his next work.

Hurlyburly (1984) is a caustic comedy set in Hollywood. It focuses on a group of individuals who serve an industry they despise, trade women like CARE packages and blot out the evidence of decline and impending apocalypse with drink and drugs. The America we glimpse, on a flickering television screen, or mirrored in the lives of those who generate the country's fantasies, is profoundly bleak. All four men in the play have failed marriages while the women trade their sexuality for what passes as comfort. The brutal dialogue, albeit shaped by Rabe into urban arias, slips and slides over a reality that they cannot address. The characters fill the air with noise to blot out their fears. They appear confident but the very brittleness of their dialogue, their shifting allegiances, reveal an underlying psychosis. They see no coherent values. Theirs is a society in which religion, science, politics, culture all seem bereft of purpose, personal relationships are without meaning and everyone is spun off to the margin of a society which in truth lacks a centre. They are, in the words of one character, 'testing the parameters of the American dream of oblivion'.[22]

The central character, Eddie, roots around amidst the detritus, the jumble of images, in search of some coherence. He dreads, and in a sense is right to dread, the dull acquiescence of those who survive by swimming with the tide, and hence finds himself defending the wild and anarchic violence of Phil, a criminal psychotic. He, at least, counters madness with madness, heading towards oblivion with a driving if unfocused energy. The play ends with Eddie deciding not to follow him. Rabe has said that,

> I always thought that once the audience began to see Eddie's distress – the brilliance of his mind and the waste of it, the burning virtue in him turned in on itself – I always felt that the recognition of his ideas, a kind of sympathetic chord in his sensibility being heard and responded to by the audience would draw them to him. He has a kind of innocence and gullibility . . . He's very open, really. I felt that by the end you would be with him completely . . . But somehow that never happened. The play does not get interpreted as if there was a questionable society around it, a sociological context, materialistic and deluded, that in some way might be conditioning and directing the characters.[23]

Perhaps, it is tempting to say, it has something to do with Eddie's studied and callous sexism, his scatological language, his addiction, his anarchic instincts. At the same time there is, in fact, an innocence to this man who despises the society he resentfully serves, who retains a faith in some values uncontaminated by corruption even if he is incapable of formulating what those values might be. He collaborates in the entropy he observes but sets his eyes on redemption, despite the fact that the object of that redemption is deeply suspect.

Nor, as Rabe insists, is he in some way aberrant. As he asks, 'What's in this play that's different from the behavior of certain wheeler-dealers on Wall Street . . . or Washington, D.C. politicians, or football players, athletes? The only common denominator to all these groups is this time and this country. Everybody's addicted . . . cocaine and TV are both drugs.'[24] And that is the point. Like Jack Gelber, in *The Connection*, he is creating an hermetic group who nonetheless stand for the state of a culture.

Rabe's work is distinguished by its rhythms, by a language shaped by those who share their circumstances if little else, a language which, he has noted, they are 'restrained by' but which also reflects their particular vision of the world. In *Streamers* and *Pavlo Hummel*, as he reminds us, it is the language of the army, 'the melting pot of all those different neighborhoods and slang, plus the army jargon . . . a very masculine vision. The way they speak very much makes them who they are.' In *Hurlyburly* 'the characters all talk the language of high tech and Hollywood'. As he claims, the result is, indeed, a kind of stage poetry. He is not in search of naturalistic detail. The words are, he insists, "inventing the stage, and character reality, and event, as they go'.[25] And that is, indeed, a defining feature of his work, which has never settled for offering a slice-of-life realism. He deals in metaphors and the language his characters speak is an agent of those metaphors.

In 1991 he produced a prequel to *Hurlyburly* in the form of *Those the River Keeps*. At its centre is the figure of Phil, who will die in the other play, destroyed by his own rage and in pursuit of a vision he cannot articulate. It is like *Hurlyburly* in its humour but also in its sense of people living in a world devoid of meaning and comfort, a spiritual ice age. It does little more than deepen the ironies of its companion piece since whatever apparent moments of consonance the characters reach is subject to our knowledge of the dissolution that lies ahead.

There is a darkness to Rabe's work which does battle with a need, not quite equal and opposite, to discover some basis for redemption. Sometimes that lies in a humour which suggests a surviving sense of perspective. Sometimes it lies in a will for meaning and connection not quite annihilated by the deconstructive forces at work in society and the human mind. Thus, if, in *Goose and Tomtom*, a play given a workshop production in 1982, he stages a violent and disturbing world in which language is not only implicated in, but an agent of, extremes of cruelty and degradation, he has also written *A Question of Mercy* (1998), a subtle and anguished debate about a doctor's dilemma in agreeing to collaborate in the mercy killing of a man dying of AIDS. It is a play of betrayals, confused motives, compassion not quite commensurate to needs, flawed love, failed hopes: it is also, however, a play in which people try to do what is right without the grace of assurance that they know what right might be.

Perhaps this is to say no more than that David Rabe is a moralist. Beneath the violence, the denatured language, the fragile camaraderie forged out of desperation and necessity, beyond the social and metaphysical ironies to which his characters are subject, is a search for something that will justify life to itself. It is what drives Eddie, in *Hurlyburly*; it is what drives the doctor in *A Question of Mercy*. It is, perhaps, what drives an author whose dramatic world lurches from bleak portraits of a society in moral free fall, mordant comedies of entropy, to works in which the search for transcendence, for some kind of grace and human connection, still survives what seems the evidence of its own futility. The very innocence which makes his characters seem mere victims is the evidence that a light still flickers in the darkness.

A. R. GURNEY

At a time when emphasis was placed on paradigm shifting, innovative staging, radical politics and aesthetic experimentation, when the theatre audience was fragmenting along lines of race, gender, sexual preference and ethnic identity, the work of A. R. Gurney seemed, to some, beside the point. After an admittedly experimental beginning, he came to be thought of as the poet of the middle and upper classes, writing well-structured, usually funny plays which frequently tended to focus on well-off WASP characters located in country houses or colleges. Any revolt was more likely to be the occasion of humorous comment rather than serious subject matter. He seemed to write essentially Broadway plays – at least in their celebratory tone – which for some mysterious reason found themselves performed Off-Broadway or in the country's regional theatres. In other words, from a certain point of view he seemed irretrievably unfashionable, exploring, and in some ways celebrating, a world that might continue to exist but which seemed to one side of current concerns.

If he was not exactly a maker of well-made plays, conventionally structured, formally realist, he did, it was thought, create works in which characters obligingly revealed themselves fully, explicating their motives, confessing to their secret crimes. Plots could be relied upon to work themselves out leaving no ambiguous residue, while language, even if used to deceive, itself seemed crystalline, a glass through which to see a world whose ultimate order was assumed. He was also an unapologetically comic writer who suffered the common fate of comic writers: he was not taken entirely seriously. Meanwhile, his decision to explore the lives of the middle and upper classes was taken by some critics as a sign of his inconsequence and an explanation for what they mistakenly took to be the conservatism of his theatre. For a long time little attention was given to A. R. Gurney. This began to change with the success of *Scenes from American Life* and *The Dining Room*.

Born in Texas, A. R. Gurney, Jr (later the Jr was dropped) was educated first at the University of Texas (*de rigueur* for Texans) and then at Yale, where he joined the Yale Drama School, graduating in 1962, at the age of thirty, when Off-Broadway and Off-Off Broadway were providing stages for young writers in a way not true since the Washington Square Players and the Provincetown Players in the early decades of the century.

In fact, and in contradiction of his later reputation, at the beginning of his career he was a dedicated if not radical experimentalist. Thus he said of *The Rape of Bunny Stuntz*, first professionally produced in 1964 by the Playwrights Unit, under the auspices of Edward Albee, Richard Barr and Clinton Wilder, that it was 'full of experimental fervor', and that he was 'attempting to write a play and create an audience to go with it',[26] a claim not without justification.

A slight work, *Bunny Stuntz* nonetheless suggests the extent to which Gurney was exploring ways of creating plot and character by indirection. To a large extent a monologue, it slowly constitutes the moral and physical world which its protagonist inhabits while the ironic dismantling of her assurance, her uncertain performance, undermined from within, suggests his interest in the theatrical constituent of the real – a concern which, later in his career, would prove a central theme.

Gurney was for a time a teacher of classics at MIT, a fact reflected in several of his plays, including one of his earliest, *The Comeback*, first presented at the Club 47, Inc., in Cambridge, Massachusetts, in January, 1965, and written, as he has confessed, under the influence of Anouilh and Giraudoux.

His continued interest in classical myths, wedded to experimental techniques, was equally evident in *The Golden Fleece* (1967), again a product of the Albee–Barr–Wilder Playwrights Unit, and *The David Show* (1969), produced at the Players Theatre in New York City.

It was not until *Scenes from American Life*, however, which opened at the Forum Theatre in New York, in March 1971, following a workshop production at Boston University, that he attempted anything longer than a one-act play, while acknowledging that even here he was 'having difficulty saying goodbye to the one-act form'.[27] It was also, he explained, his first try at exploring the idea of ethnic identity.

Scenes from American Life is a deliberate attempt to create a virtuoso work, to build a portrait of America by amassing a complicated series of snapshots from different moments stretching from the 1930s into what was then the near future. It was to be the story of a series of families, though two would predominate, and to that end he called for actors playing sons in one scene to play fathers in another, and daughters, mothers. The whole moves with speed and panache, time shifts being signalled by internal references, music or differing technologies. Social values, manners and assumptions change but there are also continuities in terms of attitudes and values. It is a play that engages with the American class system, race, political prejudices, but does so in what amounts almost to a vaudeville as scene gives way to scene in rapid progression.

Scenes from American Life offers a portrait of America's elite over the course of nearly fifty years, exposing its racism, its xenophobia, its anti-Semitism, its nationalism, its assumption that the interests of business and the state are synonymous and subsumed in their own class interests. In other words, it is a radical drama which masquerades as a social comedy.

It has, to be sure, little in common with the radical plays of the 1960s and early 1970s, either in its subject matter or style. But in focusing on the elite it comes far closer to acknowledging the real roots of power in America than did those works which contented themselves with celebrating the rebel or staging the evidence of an oppressive state. Though offering its own simplicities, it attempts a different angle of attack, historising those coercive aspects of American society which derive their power precisely from their refusal to present themselves in a coercive form or to adopt an aggressively overt authoritarianism. His bigots are the more powerful because they are themselves convinced of their lack of bigotry. They lead the nation astray because they seriously believe that they serve its interests and that these interests are synonymous with their own. They value form, manners, decorum, breeding, gentility over justice and humanity. The antiquated nature of their customs, and their apparent remoteness from the concerns of others, makes them appear no more than quaint survivors of another era. But that, too, is an aspect of their power.

If *Scenes from American Life* is a diorama, a moving portrait of mid-century America, the warning that it offers extends even to those who have historically regarded themselves as immune from history, absolved from ultimate responsibility (even while insisting on the virtue of duty), exempted from the common struggle for a life of dignity and purpose, and it is that which gives it its force. *Scenes from American Life* builds on Gurney's earlier comedies and satires but its epic scope and darkening vision distinguishes it from them. It attracted deserved attention, effectively launching his career as a major force in the American theatre.

But if there was a subversive edge to *Scenes from American Life* Gurney was equally capable of using a similar technique to offer a rather more anodyne portrait of America over time. In *The Dining Room*, first performed by Playwrights Horizons in 1982, he comes closer to recapturing the mood of *Meet Me In St Louis* or *The Magnificent Ambersons*: humour mixed with melancholy, whimsy stained with irony. In between, however, came three other plays: *Children* (1976), *The Middle Ages* (1977) and *The Wayside Motor Inn* (1977).

The Wayside Motor Inn is technically challenging and socially more diverse than his earlier work. First produced by the Manhattan Theatre Club in November 1977, this is, as its title suggests, set in an hotel, using a single set to bring together five separate stories. Reminiscent of the theatrical adventurousness of Alan Ayckbourn, whose work, together with that of Neil Simon, provides perhaps the closest parallel to Gurney's, it interweaves these stories in such a way that they appear to comment on one another while sustaining their own logic.

Gurney has obligingly identified his intentions in a play which is brilliantly constructed and which, while bringing together seemingly diverse characters, each involved in resolving quite separate dilemmas, manages to create both a portrait of a society and an account of the individuals' changing concerns over time. His characters range from a teenager wrestling with his father, through students in their twenties exploring sexuality, to a salesman in his thirties whose marriage is placed under strain by his job, a couple in their forties and fifties on the verge of divorce and another couple facing the imminence of old age and death. In other words, though the play is synchronic he manages to embrace the diachronic, finding an alternative to that swift move through time which characterises several of his other plays. As he explains:

The play is about ten ordinary people who find themselves at the wayside inn of their lives, wondering which turn to take. Their difficulties and conflicts are commonplace, but I have attempted to give a dimension and resonance to their situations by presenting them side by side, and in some cases, simultaneously on stage. It is my hope that in this way we can make the ordinary seem somehow extraordinary, just as several melodies enhance each other when they are interwoven in a musical ensemble piece.[28]

He acknowledges the problems he is posing for actors since, unlike musicians, they cannot put their instruments down. They have to remain in character, oblivious to the other stories which are blended with their own, unaware of the assonances, harmonies, disjunctions, ironies, humour generated out of the co-presence of other inhabitants of this literal and symbolic inn. As he insists:

Whenever their scene is being interrupted or amplified by a concurrent scene, they must constantly maintain an organic sense of character, of feeling, being, or doing something appropriate. There must never be a 'choral' tone to this play. Let the actors listen to the rhythms of their role and the role of those acting with them, and all will be well. Otherwise, the play will have a stop-start, artificial, and mechanical tone to it.[29]

As we have seen, nearly twenty years later Edward Albee, in *Three Tall Women*, created a play in which three stages in a woman's life were brought together by the expedient of splitting her into separate characters. Fully aware of each other, they reveal successive stages in a life which moves from youth to decrepitude, from naivety if not to wisdom then to knowledge. Here, Gurney achieves something of the same by presenting the audience rather than the characters with the opportunity to make connections. The latter are deaf to a dialogue which is evident only to those who can see and hear all those momentarily isolated in this wayside inn. Only the audience can see a connection between the would-be student's decision about his future, the actual students' sexual initiation, the casual infidelity of the salesman, the divorce of the married couple and the imminent death of a man as he is shown his new-born grandchild, the wheel thus beginning to turn again.

Gurney followed *The Wayside Motor Hotel* with *The Dining Room*. The play, unsurprisingly, is set in a dining room, with the other rooms only indicated by the merest of gestures. Beyond the room there is nothing. Indeed, his stage direction calls for the two entrances to be masked in such a way as 'to suggest a limbo outside the dining room', further indicating that a 'sense of the void surrounds the room . . . as if it were on display in some museum many years from now'.[30] The action takes place in the course of a single day but that day itself incorporates many such, stretched over time. As in the earlier work, scene flows into scene, time into time, with the actors playing multiple roles. For Gurney, the optimum cast size is six, but between them they play fifty-six parts, which is not only a handy financial saving but constitutes part of the bravura nature of the play, the choreographing of the scenes offering a sense of contrast and flow essential to its effect.

He followed it, in 1986, with another such fable, *The Perfect Party*, a comedy verging on farce in which a professor of American literature and history decides to throw a perfect party, with none of the usual tensions and disasters. The party is offered as a self-conscious image of America, with a society reporter obligingly remarking that 'what you've got here seems to be a kind of microcosm of America itself, in the waning years of the twentieth century'.[31]

It is tempting to see *The Perfect Party*, for all its farcical elements, its metatheatrical gestures (the text is full of quotations and references, theatrical and otherwise), as an ironic but personal play. Albeit in humorous form, it addresses questions about Gurney's own drama, its reception, its thematic concerns. The confession of his protagonist that he finds himself, like his society, burdened by conflicting values seems an accurate enough account of the man who created him. Gurney's plays are parties, celebrations which, while acknowledging the confused lives of those who inhabit a confused society, nonetheless opt for celebration. He is aware that the order which he creates is, indeed, contingent and momentary, that the community which he assembles is itself arbitrary and unsustainable, but nonetheless he, like his protagonist, remains committed to sustaining a 'vital human community in this impossible land of ours'.[32]

His comedy may seem to imply a fundamental conservatism, and in some respects it does. Certainly there is, in Gurney's work, a prevalence of WASP characters, expensive houses and tennis matches, as there is a determination to expose gulfs in experience and perception only to close them. Revelation gives way to resolution, albeit a resolution often drained of confidence and built on a compromise which may lack a final stability. He has not, however, lost his instincts for experiment when it comes to form. His 1987 play, *Sweet Sue*, is a two-character play performed by four actors, each character being doubled. It would, he explains in a note, 'be a mistake to break the parts down into different psychological aspects or alter-egos'; what he is attempting is 'to sketch the human figure from two different perspectives'.[33]

The play's structure and stage design reflect the subject of a play which, beyond its comic force, is also an exploration of the nature and possibilities of art and the contingency of experience. The scenes, Gurney instructs, should overlap, 'even as an artist's sketches might present several perspectives or positions simultaneously. It is,' he adds, 'as if we were leafing through a sketchbook, retaining an image of one drawing even as we move onto the next'.[34] Meanwhile, the set itself is to reflect this sense of sketching, with the suggestion of a window and suburban greenery beyond but nothing so definite as to define the possibilities of those who inhabit this space.

It is tempting to see an element of self-questioning in a play in which the central character accuses herself of being content to produce mere entertainment, of failing to confront the world directly. Gurney, after all, has been accused of much the same. But if it is problematic to make such a link in *Sweet Sue*, it is almost invited in *The Cocktail Hour* (1990), a play featuring a playwright who comes to the family home to seek permission to stage a play based all too closely on the family's actual life. That meta-theatrical interest returned in 1992 with *The Fourth Wall*, staged at Westport County Playhouse, a work in which the characters are aware of their status as actors.

Beyond the humour, the satirical comments on contemporary theatre, the parodies of dramatic and acting styles, *The Fourth Wall* offers an implicit defence of Gurney's own approach to theatre. A recognition of the artifice implied by the stage, the craft involved in play construction, it is also a celebration of artifice and craft, a conjuror's revelation of his methods even while he is in the process of using those methods to bewilder and delight. There is no substance to these characters. They readily acknowledge their factitiousness, confess to the inconsequence of their actions. Yet the fourth wall before which they perform, and which they finally breach, remains a mechanism for exposing the performatic element in the life which they do not so much mimic as magnify and resonate. As with so many Gurney plays, *The Fourth Wall* turns on a single, simple idea, elaborated with wit and a satirical verve. And what was true of this play was true equally of those which followed.

Gurney's 1993 play, *Later Life*, produced at Playwrights Horizons, takes as its premise an idea reminiscent of Arthur Miller's *The Man Who Had All The Luck* and a Henry James short story. Austin has spent his life convinced that something terrible will happen to him. Meeting Ruth, an attractive woman, again, after a gap of many years, he is drawn to her and she to him. However, his very civility, his politeness, his tendency to defer to others, slowly alienates her and she returns to the husband from whom she is separated but who adopts a more aggressive attitude. Austin is a product of a Bostonian society in which everything has to be in equilibrium, in which the slightest deviation from agreed form will bring about collapse. He is without fault and that is his fault. The terrible thing that will happen to him has already happened. He is doomed because he is incapable of recognising the threat to which he has already succumbed. He is unable to acknowledge or embrace the vitality and disorder of life.

Cleverly constructed, *Later Life*, like a number of Gurney's plays, is the dramatic equivalent of a short story, a play which turns on a single idea worked out with adroitness and humour but which deliberately lacks both breadth of scope and depth of analysis. It is an expanded anecdote written with considerable wit which finally does not disturb the equanimity which, thematically, it would seem to criticise as the source of a dismaying conservatism. But that is precisely the kind of irony he is not disposed to address, though here, as elsewhere in his work, we are invited to see a parallel between the theatre and the action of the play. Thus, when, in the first speech, a character informs us that she is 'setting the stage', meaning by that that she is preparing the way for Austin and Ruth's encounter, she is also underscoring a truth of Gurney's work. For he is acutely aware of the degree to which performance invades human behaviour, and sensitive to the artifice which lies at the heart of social convention and, indeed, character itself.

The fact is that his characters seldom threaten to escape their theatrical origins. Indeed, it is their very awareness of their own theatricality which often generates the humour and underscores the pathos of their situation, whether it be the brilliantly funny *Sylvia* (1995), in which a central character is a dog, and we are asked to accept the conceit that it can speak and engage its owners in dialogue, or the metatheatrical games of *Overtime* (1996), which offers an alternative version (rather than the 'modern sequel' claimed in its subtitle) of Shakespeare's *Othello*, without the Moor and with a slatternly Desdemona living in a Venice which has transmuted into modern America. A work whose humour derives both from its comments on contemporary issues and from its knowing, if deliberately dislocated, engagement with the Shakespeare play, it manages to turn Shakespearean tragedy into a Gurney comedy with all the familiar markers of such a play – Jessica longing for a WASP lover and Portia organising the local tennis tournament. Indeed it is tempting to see, in the remarks Gurney gives to Lorenzo, his own ironic commentary on the perceived unfashionable nature of his own subject matter and social origins. Thus, Lorenzo laments his 'pallid, conformist Episcopalianism',[35] the fact that he has lived the 'bland bourgeois life of the suburban country club',[36] that, in short, he lacks the advantages of a modish ethnicity.

Overtime also serves to remind us, however, that Gurney is not a failed tragedian but a writer aware that comedy is the obverse of that same coin. By the same token, and despite his increasing propensity to scatter his work with references to contemporary figures and events, he is not a would-be political playwright who lacks the courage of his convictions. His satire is more generalised than that, more concerned to explore relationships and attitudes which remain remarkably constant, no matter the passing times.

He is a man fully aware of the constraints of the theatre and alive to the potentialities which those limitations paradoxically facilitate. As he has said:

what attracts me about the theatre are its limitations as well as its possibilities. Indeed, its best possibilities may lie in its limitations . . . Anyone who writes plays these days is forced to explore the very restrictions of this enduring old medium. I am particularly drawn to it because I like to write about people who themselves are beginning to stretch out and push against the walls.[37]

That act of resistance could, of course, be the source of tragedy. Instead he has chosen to see in it both a source of humour and of that touching struggle to survive in a changing world which is his essential subject. His is not a sardonic or ironic humour. His plays do not debate moral issues of great moment or offer themselves as revisionist accounts of history or gestures of social protest. Indeed, for that very reason he has at times felt marginalised as from the 1960s onwards the theatre became a stage for America's debate with itself over ethnic, sexual, gender or national identity. Certainly critics, always uneasy in the presence of humour apparently unredeemed by existential despair or social utility, have tended to ignore the achievements of a man whose very prolific output has itself been the source of suspicion.

Yet there is a pathos in his portraits of those whose own values are so at odds with their times that this gives them a relevance that has not always attached itself to the work of those who fought yesterday's battles. There is no doubt, I think, that he shares the nostalgia of some of his characters for the theatrical comedies of the 1930s no less than for the civilities of a society now so evidently at odds with itself. In that sense he is a conservative. But his approach to the theatre has been as radical in its way as that of any self-conscious experimentalist. The fact that that radicalism has been in the service of comedy has distracted from its impact as has his concern for the fate of a section of American society who have managed to retain power over American fact but not over the American imagination. He is the poet of WASP America. But he is the poet of far more than that, for beneath the witticisms, beyond the jokes, the *bons mots*, the pastiche, is a human comedy in which characters try to make sense of themselves, their relationship to others, the gulf which opens up between aspiration and fulfilment. And though he never presses this comedy to the point at which it collapses in the face of genuine pain, contenting himself with exposing the strategies which his characters deploy to avoid genuine feeling, the membrane is, on occasion, a thin one, while the splendid artifice of *Sylvia* reminds us that the theatre is in the business of entertainment.

RICHARD NELSON

There have been times when Off-Broadway has proved a somewhat inexact description of a theatre's geographical location. Instead of audiences venturing a few blocks from Broadway, they would have required a transatlantic air ticket. A number of Edward Albee's plays opened in Vienna while Sam Shepard, David Mamet and Wallace Shawn all chose to première plays in London. And while Richard Nelson did begin his career in America, for more than a decade his plays were first staged in England, by the Royal Shakespeare Company, and this had the curious effect of making him seem barely visible to those who followed the development of American drama.

Nelson was in some ways a product of the 1960s, though it was the mid-1970s before his first plays appeared. He was shaped by that apparently radical decade in that he has seen himself as a political playwright, and has responded to the fascination with theatricality which was a feature of that decade. It is not that he thinks that plays should concern themselves directly with politics, in the sense of urging a particular ideological line, but that politics are a part of experience and hence a vital concern of theatre, while aspects of performance have long since invaded the social and political world. The two, indeed, come together in an early play, *The Vienna Notes* (1978), in which a US Senator, whose life is threatened, dictates his memoirs to his secretary, so concerned is he that his performance come up to the expectations of his audience. History, in other words, is a construct, a drama carefully staged for our consumption, so that any playwright who engages with the one is likely to find himself involved in the other. That assumption has led Nelson to question his own craft, the function of art in a society which has learned to appropriate fiction for its own purposes.

Nelson began to write at a time when the barricades had come down. Vietnam was over, the civil rights movement largely a memory. Public issues seemed to defer to private ones in a period characterised as the 'me decade'. Yet for Nelson, as for Arthur Miller, the private and the public are intimately connected and his theatre has continued to deal with public issues as, like John Guare, he has explored the fate of American utopian impulses.

His career began with *The Killing of Yablonski* (1975), first staged at Los Angeles's Mark Taper Forum. Despite its origin in fact, however (Yablonski was murdered and the head of the United Mine Workers Union put on trial), neither this, nor his next play, *Conjuring an Event* (1976), also produced at the Mark Taper Forum, was a documentary. Both present the writer as problematic, rather more so in the latter, a non-realistic play in which the reporter becomes the generator of events.

Following *Bal* (1979), a play which featured a total 'grotesque', who subordinates others to his own egotism, he wrote a play which is epic in scope (it covers forty-five years and features forty-five characters) and, like his earlier work, non-naturalistic in style. *Rip Van Winkle or 'The Works'* (1981) retains the central irony of Washington Irving's tale, as one political power is replaced by another, power having its own imperatives. But, unlike Irving, he is centrally concerned with change, having, like his own society, experienced precisely that in the course of the previous decades. Thus the transformations of the eighteenth century have their parallels in the 1960s and 1970s. In both periods individuals struggle to make sense of themselves and their society in an age of radical change. In both, too, the struggle between idealism and materialism is acted out by those for whom freedom is both an ideal and a defence of greed.

The shifting realities of the period have their correlative in a stylistic fluidity as Nelson invokes bizarre images and places character under pressure. Nothing seems certain. Identities are suspect. Character metamorphoses. Experience is misread. Language is allusive and sometimes gnomic. Even the land is insecure, dust one moment and enveloping bog the next. For Nelson, the problem of the nature of reality and how it is perceived or defined is deeply implicated in an idealism that must be transformed as it is translated into action. The Puritan ethic so easily degrades into self-aggrandisement and material ambition. Beyond that, the farcical elements that co-exist with the tragic in the play suggest two possible interpretations of the American experience.

Following *An American Comedy* (1983), a relentlessly funny satire both of over-solemn political commitment and callow detachment, and *The Return of Pinocchio* (1983), in some ways an account of the Ugly American, as Pinocchio returns to his native Italy to sell his tainted version of the American dream, he wrote two plays, *Between East and West* and *Principia Scriptoria*, which had a certain symbolic significance for him. Not only did they both address the question of the role of the artist in a time of change but his own career was itself in process of change, both plays opening in England, which he was to make his theatrical home for the following decade and a half.

Between East and West (1985) also concerns change, as it does exile, as a Czech theatre director and his actress wife find themselves in a new country, the United States, unsure of its codes, uncertain of its values. Their command of English is imperfect. In the background, meanwhile, the rhetoric of the Cold War plays itself out on television. They have, it seems, traded a world in which art was granted significance as an agent of public policy, for one in which it is a passing entertainment, their production of Chekhov's *Three Sisters*, a play also, in part, about a sense of exile, being dismissed by critics as 'too European'. Their private lives also seem out of alignment in a play whose scenes are played out of chronological order.

Its companion piece, *Principia Scriptoria* (1986), also stages a debate about the role and significance of art and does so by locating one of its characters in an alien environment. Set in 1970 and 1985, it concerns Bill, a backpack radical from the United States, and Ernesto, a native of the South American country where the action takes place. Both find themselves in gaol in a play which begins as a comedy but shifts into a serious engagement with the pragmatics of power as they are tortured and, in a later scene, meet up again, now in new roles. When Bill returns he and Ernesto are on different sides of a debate about the relationship between the writer and power.

Principia Scriptoria, however, is less concerned to assert the writer's moral superiority, to insist on the writer's right to offer a detached critique of society, than it is to acknowledge the contradictions of which the writer, no less than anyone else, is capable. As in *Rip Van Winkle*, changing times change people. Neither writer is the man he was a decade and a half earlier and if that is so what special insights can either claim? Not merely is there a disjunction between the writer's craft and his moral self – and Ezra Pound is invoked as exemplar – but the writer is as susceptible as anyone to shifts in the political sub-structure.

Nelson's next play, *Sensibility and Sense* (1990), makes essentially the same point as we see a group of radicals from the 1930s meet up again in the 1980s to debate a history which now seems more deeply problematic than it once had done. Seeking funding for a radical magazine, they had, it seems, been entirely willing to compromise by accepting money from a man who represented the very things they affected to despise. Years later, they meet to debate the significance of those earlier times when, as radicals, they saw themselves as standing centre stage in the world's drama. They, too, are exiles, exiled from a time which once seemed to flood their lives with significance and from selves which no longer seem continuous with their present lives. For, slowly, they and we become aware that their grand schemes did not founder on the rocks of a history over which they had no control, but on personal failings that already infected their supposed utopian values.

Two sets of actors play the characters in the two different time periods, but eventually both play side by side as past and present are braided together dramatically, as they are in fact in the lives of people who failed to understand the extent to which their politics were extensions of private needs. The stories which they tell themselves are designed to locate them at centre stage, part of the master story of history and the writer's struggle to engage with it. In fact they slowly expose the extent to which they are the products of their fiction-making skills, the great events which they saw themselves as engaging with and influencing merely existing, as in *Between East and West*, in the background of lives whose significance is not amplified, as they had once hoped, by history.

In a sense it is difficult not to see an element of self-doubt on the part of Richard Nelson, as he looks back to the 1960s, when the political world seemed to resolve itself into convenient polarities, when art assumed an unimpeachable moral superiority and theatre, in particular, insisted on its political function. That self-doubt is, in part, what gives his work its special quality as, in play after play, he explores the way in which history is created, the fiction maker shapes the world and the actor offers that blend of self-regard and poetic insight that is a distinguishing characteristic of his craft.

The theatre, indeed, moved to the centre of his attention in two plays that he wrote for the Royal Shakespeare Company: *Some Americans Abroad* (1989) and *Two Shakespearean Actors* (1990). The first is a comedy, with serious undertones, about American university students and their faculty processing theatre as part of their summer course. The second, set in 1849, focuses on the rivalry between the English actor William Charles Macready and the American Edwin Forrest, a rivalry that led to a lethal riot. And the contrast between two rival performers, who perform offstage as well as on, represents a continuation of Nelson's debate with himself about the nature and function of theatre as well as its relationship with the reality it purports to re-present.

Macready and Forrest are both performers, dissemblers, in their private no less than their public and artistic lives. Outside of the texts which they declaim they tend to incoherence. There is a factitious comfort, security and coherence about the products of theatre that is lacking in the life beyond its doors. Within the theatre time is plastic, indeed it is suspended. Characters die only to live and die again. On the streets it is quite otherwise. The two realms do bleed into one another and certainly have an ambiguous and problematic relationship. Yet while seeming to acknowledge its secondary status, the play also stages moments when the actor disappears in his part, when the language he speaks raises him above his personal fallibilities, when a truth is spoken from the stage which transcends that implied by mere fact. *Two Shakespearean Actors* includes two cut-down versions of *Macbeth*, as played by the rival actors. The effect is for the most part comic, but not entirely so. Nelson is struck both by the inadequacies of theatre, its association with artifice, deceit and self-display, and by its ability to speak a truth inaccessible by other means.

Columbus and the Discovery of Japan (1994), also first staged by the Royal Shakespeare Company, fittingly begins with a theatrical performance, fittingly because the Christopher Columbus who sets sail for Japan and ends up in America, himself has all the qualities of a playwright, an actor, a designer and a director. He creates a fiction and then relies on a willing suspension of disbelief on the part of those who are his audience. In that sense this is a play in which the parallel between a voyage of discovery and the writing of plays is explored, as is the contrast between the apparent order of art and the sometimes terrifying disorder of experience. Columbus, being himself a story teller, admires writers and artists. Both groups are confidence tricksters. And what greater fiction than the idea of a new beginning, a new Eden. The mere power of certain fictions gives them an authority that resists true disillusionment. So, once again, this play is, perhaps, another stage in Nelson's exploration of the utopian impulse, equally capable of summoning America into existence or a play into being, and for some of the same reasons.

Nelson's decision to open his plays in England was a response to what he saw as the diminishing opportunities in America. In a decade whose priorities lay elsewhere – in a vapid materialism, a single-minded drive for success, a right-wing political and cultural agenda – he turned to a society which, though in many ways reflecting the values of American politics, still seemed to regard the theatre as a place in which moral, social and aesthetic debates could be staged. In the Royal Shakespeare Company he also found a theatre with resources that outstripped those of most American Off-Broadway or regional theatres. At the same time,

he was fully aware of British cultural chauvinism and touched on it in
New England (1994), a play which also addressed the issue of displacement, of finding yourself in an alien environment, that he had touched
on in *Between East and West* and which had obvious relevance to his own
situation. This time he located a group of British people in America, all
in some way related to literature, and staged the drama of their mutual
misunderstandings, exiled, as they are, not only from their own country
but from one another and from any sense of genuine values.

In some senses that double consciousness was on display again in *The
General from America* (1996), which focuses on the American Revolution
and which, again, drew on the resources of the Royal Shakespeare
Company. Beneath the epic sweep of history, however, what interests
him are the less than heroic postures of the principal players in the
national drama of history. And the theatrical metaphor is once again to
the fore, not least because one of the characters, Major André, stages a
play within this play, while Benedict Arnold, hero or villain depending
on one's perspective, is himself an actor, or at least a dissembler, performing his treachery, as he tells himself, for a higher cause.

In Nelson's hands history becomes a product of private ambitions and
petty desires. Chance plays as great a role as strategy while language is
deployed to fill the moral vacuum and give a shape to mere contingency.
The battle for freedom teeters on the edge of farce. The past, in his
hands, becomes, in part at least, a convenient construction, a drama
which we stage to serve present interests.

There are no certainties in Nelson's work. What seems fixed and
immutable is frequently a product of interpretation. Things change. In
Goodnight Children, Everywhere (1997), the shift from childhood to adult-
hood takes a group of characters into a new country, destabilising them,
a favourite dramatic tactic. Indeed, often his plays are born out of that
moment of destablisation. He moves the action forward in time or displaces it from one country to another. He frequently pitches expectation
against fulfilment, ideal against pragmatic behaviour, assertion against
actuality. Sometimes his characters are literal actors; sometimes they
merely deceive, others or themselves. Yet his is not an entirely relativistic world. Though fully aware of the extent to which his characters
inhabit an unstable reality, he nonetheless implies the existence of
values, often precisely in the moment they are being betrayed. Indeed,
it is their betrayal that in some way validates them.

His plays are seldom realistic. He is prone to deploy projected titles,
is fond of entering the action at mid point, forcing audiences themselves

to construct the context of the action. His language is at times lyrical, metaphoric, at others comic, self-ironising. Character is by turns a performed gesture and a psychologically coherent truth. Yet, beginning in the romantic-radical 1960s, moving through the privatism of the 1970s, the conservatism of the 1980s and the liberal-conservatism of the 1990s, he has remained convinced of theatre's power to address the moral world, which is, I suspect, what politics, finally, are to him. And if theatre itself, like the history which it mimics and which, in turn, borrows its devices, is a blend of the authentic and the factitious, well, that is the irony with which Nelson's work engages.

WALLACE SHAWN

One of the ironies of Wallace Shawn's career is that for many he is better known as a character actor than a playwright, appearing in films which range from *Atlantic City* and *Manhattan* to *Princess Bride*, and television programmes from *The Cosby Show* to *Deep Space Nine*. Even the work which established him in the public mind, *My Dinner with André* (1980), filmed by Louis Malle, seemed to foreground him as an actor. Indeed, this was a work which essentially seemed to have no writer (and was, in truth, based on actual dialogues), being a dinner-table conversation between Shawn and the theatre director André Gregory. It is a fact best explained not only by the difference between cinema and theatre and their audiences but by the fact that his plays are uncompromising, theatrically challenging and, apparently, provocative of those they address. Shawn does not offer his audiences comfort, or even, on one level, entertainment.

The son of a famous literary editor, Wallace Shawn studied history at Harvard, taught English in India and studied politics, philosophy and economics at Oxford. He began writing plays in high school, though he was in his thirties before he secured a professional production of his work, *Our Late Night* (1975), at André Gregory's Manhattan Project. It won an Obie Award.

Asked about his working method he has said that:

I don't have an idea for a play until after I've finished writing it. I write first, and come up with what it's about later. My technique could be compared to having a large canvas and coming in every day and putting a dot on it somewhere, and after several years – literally – I begin to say, 'That reminds me of an elephant, so I think I'll make it one.'[38]

The process of making it one, however, does result in plays which are sharply focused, the more random process of accretion giving way to a clear intent.

Wallace Shawn approached the theatre with some uncertainty, unclear as to a form which seemed suddenly heterogeneous and in flux. Two of his early plays, *A Thought in Three Parts* (1977) and *Marie and Bruce* (1979), explore what he calls 'the magical forces of sex and love',[39] though it is less magic or, indeed, love which dominates works whose quasi-pornographic actions seem to stem from the narcissism of the characters and disturb less by their insights into human behaviour than by an explicitness which perhaps distracts from other concerns. At the heart of these plays, though, is a concern with the spaces between those who are simultaneously attracted and repelled, the gap at the heart of relationships whose intimacies become, in part, self-mocking, masking, as they do, a deeper solitariness and self-concern. They are uncomfortable works and caused discomfort.

His real achievement, and in some sense the heart of his personal and theatrical commitments, is on display in later works, beginning with *Aunt Dan and Lemon* (1985) and continuing with *The Fever* (1990) and *The Designated Mourner* (1996). With these plays Shawn set himself to address 'what people always with touching hopefulness insist on calling the "mystery" of man's inhumane treatment of his fellows (mass murder, etc)'.[40]

In one sense he is a product of Off-Off-Broadway; in another he owes something to British theatre, especially the Royal Court Theatre. Certainly *A Thought in Three Parts, Marie and Bruce, Aunt Dan and Lemon* and *The Designated Mourner* were all first produced in Britain. Despite that early award, however, he was not an immediate success and, indeed, has proved something of an acquired taste as far as critics are concerned. Before *Aunt Dan and Lemon* (in which he also appeared as actor) most of his reviews were, he confessed, negative, in some cases hate-filled diatribes. Indeed he has acknowledged receiving a few of this kind for *Aunt Dan and Lemon*, although that play, more than his others, also provoked widespread critical enthusiasm.

The fact is that Wallace Shawn has a knack of making people feel uneasy. A Joint Stock production of *A Thought in Three Parts*, in 1977, led to calls for its prosecution on grounds of obscenity. Then the issue was sex; with *Aunt Dan and Lemon* it was politics. He has insisted that the theatre can have a political importance in that good works of art sharpen the awareness. Shawn's drama has a subcutaneous quality to it. It cuts deep.

Aunt Dan and Lemon was written after the Reagan election, an election which contrasted the charm and authority of a right-wing candidate, absolute in his dogmas, with the seemingly equivocal and unconvincing Jimmy Carter, and on one level Shawn suggests that the play raises the question of whether the right-wing might not be more frank than liberals. Beyond that, however, he was interested in the degree to which the smiling apologist for violence frequently has a seductive charm and an assured style significantly lacking in those whose liberal self-doubt can make them seem vacillating and unselfconfident. Not for nothing had Henry Kissinger, paradoxically Shawn's boyhood hero and subject of Aunt Dan's admiration, once spoken of the aphrodisiac nature of power.

And there is a seductiveness about violence, more especially the mechanical efficiency, the apparent technical precision of warfare. The Nazis applied science and technology to the elimination of a people. For those who provided the machinery or arranged the logistics of death the problem was a practical rather than a moral one and was not without its challenges and satisfactions. Lemon's expressed admiration for such procedures and efficiencies provoked some of the controversy that Shawn's play inspired.

This present generation, meanwhile, raised on computer games and virtual reality, knows the deeply suspect thrill that can accompany images sent back by bombs and missiles smart enough to transmit images of their targets if not smart enough to ask why they do as they do. Play Station wars have that same power to abstract us from the implications of actions undertaken in our name.

Aunt Dan and Lemon is a play that seems to have been written out of a sense of anger, though the anger which it, in turn, has occasionally provoked has been paradoxically misplaced in that there is a tendency to mistake the views of characters for those of their creator. Not for nothing has Shawn reminded us of the modernist gesture implied in the unreliable narrator. An opening speech which appears to speak admiringly of the destruction of the Jews is only the first of a series of destabilising gestures in a play which explores the ease with which we acquiesce in evils provided only that they leave us in secure possession of our lives and lifestyles. As Aunt Dan observes: the whole purpose of government is to use force, 'so we don't have to'.[41]

In *Tender is the Night*, F. Scott Fitzgerald describes the degree to which the whole world exists in order to serve the needs of the rich. There came a moment when Wallace Shawn arrived at much the same conclusion. Aware that he is himself a member of a privileged ruling class, he sees the writer's job, therefore, not as entertaining others like himself but as trying to effect change through an analysis of the situation. Perhaps that is one reason he seems to feel more at home in a British theatre that has never quite given up on the idea of theatre as a site for debate. Shawn's objective is, he has explained, to turn people into honest and sensitive observers of the world, and while his personal style is to indulge people who need to escape, as a playwright he insists on grabbing the theatre-goer by the throat and trying to get him to worry about the things that are bothering him. David Hare (who directed *The Designated Mourner* at Britain's Royal National Theatre) is a great admirer of Shawn's work and, given his political and dramatic concerns, it makes sense that he should be.

We suffer, Shawn implies, from an impoverishment of the moral self. We like to believe that political and social systems exist independently of us, that we are not responsible for history and that we have, in some indefinable way, earned the good fortune we are anxious only to maintain. As a result we acquiesce in a political system that sustains our advantages, while 'operating under the illusion that we . . . have no power at all over the course of history'. For Shawn, 'that is . . . the very opposite of the case'.[42]

His proposition is that, as he has said, 'a perfectly decent person can turn into a monster perfectly easily'.[43] In the former Yugoslavia we have watched horrified as neighbours become murderers and rapists, but the murderer is perhaps present in all of us, at least by proxy. There is a logical chain, Shawn seems to imply, that leads from personal acts of moral abdication to an Adolf Hitler.

Shawn is not the only American playwright to close the gap between Hitler's treatment of the Jews and contemporary political events. Arthur Miller does much the same in *Broken Glass* and Tony Kushner in *A Bright Room Called Day*, rejecting the implacable absolutism of the Holocaust. It is a dangerous game to play. But all three writers suggest that there is a dynamic to disregard, a procedure to public acts of cruelty which are rooted in private abdications. We are the creators not the victims of history. Thus, Aunt Dan admires not only Kissinger but an amoral young woman who exploits others to serve her own interests, not something that could be said to distinguish her from others either in the 1980s, when this play was written, or, perhaps, at any other time since self-interest is the acid which corrodes the ethical sense.

There is no writer's point of view in *Aunt Dan and Lemon*, if we mean by that a character who will obligingly draw a moral, underscore an irony. The shock of recognition is for the audience. The play, he has explained, 'suggests, fairly or unfairly, the vicarious enjoyment we get out of violence committed by world leaders. It's about people reading about the exercise of power, rather than being personally involved.' Shawn is a designated mourner for lost values but also an engaged playwright who believes, perhaps unfashionably, that the theatre retains its power to transform.

Having written *Aunt Dan and Lemon*, he came to feel that he had 'to go very much further, and that meant, perhaps, that I had no business being involved in the artistic, quasi-artistic, or semi-artistic world of the theatre at all'.[44] The problem of theatre lay precisely in its conventions, in its oblique methods, in the privileged space, on which it relied, between the performer and the audience, albeit a space challenged, if naively, in the 1960s. His plan was to perform his next work in people's homes. In other words, he was to follow the logic of *Aunt Dan and Lemon*, which was not only addressed to the audience but was in some ways about the audience. By penetrating the personal space of those he wished to challenge he would strip away the associations, the rituals of theatre, which made it seem in some ways separate from the experiences of those who attended.

For a year, accordingly, he performed in private houses and apartments. As he explained,

I had several reasons for wanting to do that, but one of them was that I sincerely doubted that you could ever convince an audience in a theatre that you actually *meant* the thing you were saying; however loud the agonized screams of the clown who's being crushed by the falling scenery, the people in the audience always seem to think that it's 'part of the show' and keep right on roaring with laughter. To put it another way, I didn't want to provide another well-prepared meal for the theatrical season's cultural menu, not even a titillatingly 'spicy' one. I wanted to talk seriously to people, particularly members of my own privileged class. I wanted to intervene in people's lives.[45]

Inevitably, perhaps, he eventually came to accept a contradiction in such a procedure since if he was looking to intervene in people's lives he was unnecessarily restricting the scope of such an intervention by providing a home delivery service to half a dozen people at a time. This awareness led him back to the theatre. It could, as he has acknowledged, equally have led him in other directions, presumably direct action, politics, polemics. In fact he followed it with *The Designated Mourner*.

The Fever was first performed in an apartment near Seventh Avenue in New York, not as far Off-Off-Broadway as London, but a step or two. The play is, in part, an accusation, in part a confession of complicity, in part, perhaps, an attempted expiation. It is also a monologue whose drama derives, by definition, not from conflict, except from within the psyche, nor from the tensions of an unfolding plot. The narrator is on a journey in a poor country but the real journey is into the self and through that self into the assumptions on which his life, his class and, ultimately, his society is based. There is a narrative, as the speaker, given no name, recounts his journey and the details of the society through which he is moving. But it is less this society than his own that provides the focus.

The accusation at its heart is that the price of a comfortable life, an intellectual life, even, perhaps, an apparently secure moral life, is paid by others. There is a chain of logic that connects those who suffer to those for whom such suffering is nothing more than a distant report, if that. There is a chain of logic that connects the daily business of life in a wealthy country to the daily business of death in a poor one: 'The cup of coffee contains the history of the peasants who picked the beans, how some of them fainted in the heat of the sun, some were beaten, some were kicked'.[46] And that logic is, in essence, a moral one as well as a simple product of economics. Indeed, to see it as the latter is to grant a simple and protective determinism which relieves the individual of responsibility.

The very life of the mind, a certain fastidiousness about experience, culture, the theatre, rests on certain disturbing realities. This is not simple Marxism, though ideas of base and superstructure are not that far away. Indeed, the narrator is given a copy of *Das Kapital*, though he reacts against its impenetrable jargon. But he does respond to the simple description of the conditions in which people live. And Shawn delivers this piece in the apartments and homes of those who are ostensibly secure, protected and well-off. Such thoughts, however, quickly fade. The insights of theatre, itself part of the economic system, are easily forgotten. It is, anyway, he suggests, a form in which it is easy, in one's emotional responses, to suppress questions of morality, tears being shed, in *The Cherry Orchard* for example, for a representative of an exploitative class who has lost nothing but an estate that was an expression of her privilege.

The Fever ends with the narrator accepting that he could abandon everything and fight for justice or simply return home. However, even if he should choose the latter, that home will no longer be what it was. As he asks himself:

What will be home? My own bed. My night table. And on the table – what? On the table – what? – blood – death – a fragment of bone – a severed hand. – Let everything filthy, everything vile, sit by my bed, where once I had my lamp and clock, books, letters, presents for my birthday, and left over from the presents bright-colored ribbons. Forgive me. Forgive me. I know you forgive me. I'm still falling.[47]

That same dis-ease is to be felt by the audience, that same need for forgiveness instilled.

Is this monologue a play? Shawn expressed his own doubts on receiving an Obie Award for best play in 1991. But why not? It has all the qualities of a play. Its plot is the moral education of its central character, its dialogue is contained within the self but a dialogue it is. It explores the sensibility of its protagonist. Like all plays, however, its essential dialogue is with the audience except that in Shawn's play that becomes a mute but essential character in the drama.

Shawn followed *The Fever* with *The Designated Mourner*, which, in some ways, acknowledges the significance of that very liberal intelligentsia he had challenged, even castigated earlier. As he has said,

I was writing *The Designated Mourner* very much with an awareness of my previous plays, certainly *The Fever*, and it definitely expresses the thought, at least in terms of this play, that if those people who in this little world are the 'liberal intelligentsia,' if they disappear the world will be much worse off, the hope of a better world will be further away.[48]

Beyond that, he was, he suggested, allowing that interest in love, sex and personal relationships expressed in his earliest plays 'to get mixed up with the more political subjects that were in *Aunt Dan and Lemon* and *The Fever*'.[49] It was also an attempt at accommodating the different stylistic approaches of his other plays.

The Designated Mourner features three characters, one, Howard, an intellectual, another his daughter and the third, Jack, her husband. It is set in the near future in an unspecified country in which tyranny is on the rise and culture on the decline. As the play progresses so Jack becomes increasingly dismissive of the cultural concerns and political commitments of his wife and father-in-law, himself lapsing into a self-obsessed, anti-intellectual stance. The play ends with Howard and his daughter murdered and Jack sitting alone in a park having regressed politically, culturally and morally.

It is, as is apparent, a bleak work. It projects a future that merely extends a logic observable in the present. Yet, in so far as it is a warning it is also a play that identifies values. Jack's self-obsession constitutes a recognisable enough temptation. The onanistic and degraded culture that merely stimulates needs in order to satisfy them is a familiar characteristic of late twentieth-century society, and Shawn does not absolve himself, as we have seen, of the tendencies he recognises. However, though Howard and his daughter do end up as victims the play stands as some kind of Catonian warning aimed directly at the audience for, as he has said, in an interview with Ros Wetzsteon, 'My plays are really about the audience. The main character is you.' Of *Aunt Dan and Lemon*, though with immediate relevance to all his plays, he remarked that 'The audience has to react to this play . . . Otherwise it's a disaster. If they sit like a piece of cheese, it would be a horrible experience.' His description of *The Fever* can thus stand as a definition of the kind of theatre to which he has committed himself, a theatre which, of its nature, is likely to inspire conflicting responses from audiences and critics, for that play is designed as 'some kind of human exhortation which is meant to arouse thought and action, not appreciation or enjoyment'.[50]

PAULA VOGEL

Paula Vogel sees her career as having started when, in 1980, she sent her play *The Oldest Profession* to theatres across the country only to have them reject it, though an earlier work, *Desdemona*, had been successfully staged the year before at the New Plays Festival in Louisville and before that, in 1973, in a staged reading at Cornell University. It was something of a false start and even *Desdemona* had to wait another fourteen years before a successful revival. Effectively emerging as a playwright in the 1980s, in which, it seemed to her, conservatism characterised the theatre no less than the wider society, she found it difficult to secure production, though increasing financial constraints led her to develop works which required little in the way of resources. Very conscious of insinuating herself into what to that point had been a resolutely male profession, she was aware of her own marginality, not least because she was not only a woman but an avowed lesbian. *Desdemona*, indeed, which is a distorted and inverted version of *Othello*, was created precisely in order to see the world from a different perspective, in a sense to invent the tradition from which she felt in certain respects excluded. Even gay playwrights had been men and their protagonists, largely, likewise. Despite their differences they could lay claim to a tradition that went back not simply through Tennessee Williams, Albee, Lorca and Oscar Wilde but through Chekhov, Ibsen and, indeed, Shakespeare. And since theatre works by dialogue she wished to enter into an implicit debate both with her own society and, implicitly or explicitly, theatrical history. As a result, she has written relatively few plays that do not in some way engage with other texts, by Shakespeare, Albee, Mamet and others.

Stylistically, she is drawn to the expressionists and the absurdists, responding to their fragmenting of surface structures and, in the case of the latter, to their legitimising of what she calls a drama of stasis, which, for her, offered an equivalent to Virginia Woolf's stream of consciousness, action being less important than the exposure of a state of being. For Vogel, fantasy is a form of realism, simply displaced a little further along the spectrum.

Desdemona derives part of its aesthetics from film and a note encourages directors to respond accordingly. It features Desdemona as sexually aggressive and vulgar, shaping her own experiences instead of existing only in relation to Othello, who remains off-stage. Interested in works that dealt in negative empathy – she had been reading *Lolita* – she set out to create one. This was to be a play without a male protagonist and one in which the woman protagonist revelled in resisting the role into which she felt herself pushed, by her absent husband and, beyond him and unknown to her, William Shakespeare.

If *Desdemona* was an implicit conversation with Shakespeare, with *The Oldest Profession* (first read in 1981, first produced in 1988), the point of reference was David Mamet's *Duck Variations*, a conversation between two men deflecting their fear of death into stories which seem to offer consolation but which in fact keep circling back to the deaths they fear.

The Oldest Profession concerns five women, four in their seventies, one in her eighties, who are revealed as prostitutes. This reality, and the fantasies in which they consequently engage, are what keep them alive, though, one by one, they slip into death. Like Mamet's characters they, too, are story tellers. Their meaning lies in part in their stories, as in their sense of social utility and shared circumstances. But the commonality on which they rely, actors appearing in the same play, is slowly destroyed as death claims them and the play ends with a Beckett-like moment of silent stasis.

With *And Baby Makes Seven* (first staged in 1984 and then, in 1990, by Circle Rep) the literary point of reference becomes Edward Albee in so far as, like *Who's Afraid of Virginia Woolf?*, it deals with the creation of a fantasy child. At the time its premise seemed somewhat extreme. A decade later and it would no longer seem such, being based on the idea of two lesbians who live with a gay man who has fathered a child by one of them. In advance of the arrival of the child, however, they create a series of fantasy versions, themselves acting the roles they invent. One is supposedly raised by dogs, the second is a young genius and the third a figure based on the child in Albert Lamorisse's film *The Red Balloon*. They are, perhaps, as Vogel has suggested, the libido, the ego and the id. That aside, they are an expression of the anxieties which permeate the household and as such have to be laid to rest. In other words the characters have to set out to kill their own inventions while desperate to embrace them. *And Baby Makes Seven* is thus a comedy generated out of contradiction as they plot to assassinate their own alter egos. The result is a series of slapstick scenes, joky encounters, black humour.

Beyond the question of the child, however, and the inevitable tensions invoked by its impending arrival, is the question of this group of people whose lives and relationships are about to be transformed. And beyond that, in a play which makes constant references to other literary texts and in which the characters are themselves constructors of plot, character and language, lies a reference to the anxieties which attach themselves to the creation of a play. The metatheatrical element, in other words, extends to Vogel's own fantasy child, namely the play itself.

For all the pleasures to be derived from these early plays, however, it was with *The Baltimore Waltz* that she broke through to public recognition. Workshopped in 1990, it opened at Circle Rep in 1992. It was in part a response to the death by AIDS, in 1988, of her homosexual brother, Carl. Her own failure to join him on his last journey to Europe (she was unaware of his illness) left her with a sense of guilt which blended with a feeling of anger. *The Baltimore Waltz* was a last gesture, an act of reconciliation, a proffered grace. In keeping with her brother's character, however, it was not to be solemn but a curious surreal odyssey.

The action takes place in the shocked moment in which the central character registers the death of her brother. Drawing on fragments of travel books, movies, fiction, Vogel deploys mysterious images, oblique symbols, 'lush lighting', Hollywood-influenced music, in a kaleidoscope of scenes (thirty in all) which reflect a mind flicking restlessly through a distorted memory bank. It is a journey that ends back in the same Baltimore hospital where it began but, following that initial second of shock expanded to fill the length of the play, she is now reconciled and dances with her brother in one last fantasy. They meet here, within the fantasy, as they can no longer meet in life.

This is not an AIDS play, as such. It does not dwell on the pathology of the disease or invite audiences to respond sentimentally to the idea of loss, though loss is its starting point and a word picked up and echoed in the text. Indeed AIDS only enters the play in parodic form as Acquired Toilet Disease, a kindergarten disease picked up by a young woman teacher from toilet seats. It is not an angry play, although it acknowledges, still in parodic form, the failure of both politicians and the medical profession to respond with true seriousness: 'if just one grandchild of George Bush caught this thing . . . that would be the last we'd hear about the space program'.[51] It is a play in which the sheer energy of invention is pitched against the finality which gives it birth.

It is a play which, in offering a parodic version of AIDS, risked offence, but that has always been an aspect of Vogel's work. It is not that she sets out simply to provoke, though she does aim to disturb a version of theatre that she sees as too cosily familiar and reassuring. She is simply anxious to offer an oblique perspective, to challenge normal presumptions, and that can lead her into potentially dangerous territory, whether it be offering Desdemona as a sexual predator, staging the dilemma of septuagenarian prostitutes, presenting a paedophile in a less than hostile way or, as in her next play, *Hot 'N' Throbbing* (1993), featuring a woman pornographer and extreme violence.

Like all of Vogel's plays, this is not a naturalistic work. She establishes a lighting convention which indicates the fantasy element in a play which is itself concerned with fantasy. *Hot 'N' Throbbing* concerns a family in which Charlene, mother to Leslie Ann and Calvin, is a story editor for a company producing what she chooses to call 'women's erotica'. Her husband, Clyde, is the embodiment of male violence, kept at bay by a restraining order until he breaks into the family home and murders her. Charlene, in effect, colludes in her own destruction in so far as her work, while seemingly expressing a woman's right to engage with the erotic, also exists in the world, playing its role in the degradation that places her and others at risk. When her own daughter continues the script that her mother has left incomplete she appears to be replicating her error, or at least projecting the ambiguity into a future that seems unyielding.

It is plainly a play that seeks to explore the violence at the heart of sexuality and the sexuality at the heart of violence; which seeks, on the one hand, to validate a woman's sexual freedom, her right to explore her own erotic possibilities, but which is simultaneously aware of the degree to which sexual imagery has a history that is predominantly, if not exclusively, male. Vogel's own work is itself deliberately sexualised. This is the territory she has staked out for herself: this is her Yoknapatawpha County. Sexuality becomes a language, the site of her drama, a central metaphor, a vital aspect of character and even a key to social and political values. She has, however, grown discontented with one aspect of *Hot 'N' Throbbing*, coming to feel that its ending implies the impossibility of breaking into a cycle of violence. Indeed, at the end of the 1990s she planned to change the play's ending in such a way as to further problematise the nature of the relationship between sex and violence. In particular, she proposed to show the daughter standing back from the situation and, as a professor of critical legal studies, herself both offering an objective view and transcending the circumstances of her own reductive experience. Nonetheless, it remains a bleak play in which Charlene's erotic writings never really rise above the banality of pornography and hence the validation of female eroticism is always in thrall to male necessities and images.

With *The Mineola Twins* (1996), which opened in Alaska, she appeared to move into a more directly political arena in that the two principal characters are in turn conservative and radical while the play moves from the 1950s to the 1990s, thus offering scope for commentary on a changing political scene. But those characters, Myrna and Myra, are played by the same actress and, as the play progresses, emerge as aspects of an America essentially at war with itself. It is a device that enabled her to offer a series of ironic comments on changing sexual, social and political values. It is a roller-coaster ride through an America with no clear idea as to its direction. Amusing and perceptive, it stages American history as a mix between melodrama and comic book. It is not, however, an analysis that bites particularly deep, threatening, as it does, to reduce genuine ideological and moral debate to a kind of vaudeville.

With her next play, however, she touched a national nerve. *How I Learned to Drive* (1997) dealt not with politics or even political correctness, though it was inspired, or perhaps provoked, by Mamet's *Oleanna*, but, seemingly, with paedophilia. I use the word 'seemingly' because this is not a play that sets out to offer a denunciation of child abuse, as is apparent from Vogel's suggestion that it was also in part inspired by Vladimir Nabokov's *Lolita*. Technically, it was another attempt to create a character with negative empathy, to find ways of engaging audiences with a character to whom they would feel instinctively hostile. But behind that was perhaps a desire to swim against the tide, to dig her heels in at a time when there were those – politicians and those who administered arts funding – who presumed to define those subjects regarded as legitimate.

The play's title comes from a literal driving lesson, as Peck, a man first seen in his forties, teaches his young niece, Li'l Bit, to drive. But there is another kind of lesson being taught, as he is sexually drawn to a young girl who finds little understanding or comfort from her immediate family. Nor is it simply a play about the psychopathology of abuse, for Vogel is concerned with much more than echoing a contemporary alarm about this sensitive subject. She is interested in the psychology of both individuals, in their separate, and, occasionally, mutual needs, in the nature of love, destructive and healing, in the resilience and despair that determine actions. And there is another kind of lesson as Peck warns his niece about the dangers that face her and, implicitly, therefore, the danger that he poses to her.

We enter the play part of the way through the story. Li'l Bit is almost eighteen. The relationship is, thus, unequal but not wholly unacceptable. Reverse the genders and you have *The Graduate*, what appears to be a compassionate act of initiation into the adult world, an act not without its humour. This is reinforced by the character of Peck, based in part on the figure of Gregory Peck as he appeared in *To Kill a Mockingbird*. The *coup de théâtre* is that Vogel then moves us back in time, regressing the ages of the two characters, until they cross a line, and what was understandable, and even acceptable, transmutes into something else. But by this stage attitudes to the two characters have already been formed. She also instructs that the sexual intimacies which Peck enacts should be performed in mime, against a background of sacred music, a distancing effect that takes the edge off the shock and adds a ritualistic element that inhibits instinctual responses.

Li'l Bit's life is bleak. She lives in a suburban world that has nothing to offer her and in a family that seems to afford neither understanding nor comfort. The larger world, like that of her family, seems tainted by a sexuality that has no connection with genuine needs. A porno-drive-in jostles for space with a revivalist church and an empty motel. She has nothing ahead of her and no one to turn to but Peck. As for him, he is married but his wife neither understands him nor the nature of his pain. She seeks to prop up the marriage with domestic routine, as if he could happily settle into such a bland and comfortless world.

If his own motives are tainted, Vogel gives him not simply a deep sense of vulnerability but also a genuine love for the girl he nonetheless and undeniably abuses. Also, given its roots in *Lolita*, it is scarcely surprising that Li'l Bit is something more than mere victim. Peck works desperately to seduce her, and there are hints of his earlier paedophile activities both with girls and boys, but he never assaults her without her acquiescence, while she gradually comes to understand the power that she herself has in relation to a man to whom she is emotionally drawn.

Vogel then projects the action forwards into a life whose emptiness is in part a reflection of the lack of love that Li'l Bit's family had offered and in part of the vacuousness of the culture, just as it is a consequence of the trauma of her relationship with Peck. Looking back, the now adult woman recalls herself seducing a young man on a bus, acknowledging, finally, the desperation that leads to such acts as well as the sense of power which is a product of seduction. In a sense this is no more than to acknowledge a familiar cycle whereby the abused become abusers, but there is more going on here than that. For she recognises, too, the need which generates such actions, the sexual contact being only a manifestation of that need. Again, reverse the gender and you have an entirely familiar genre of novels and plays in which young boys are initiated into manhood by understanding women, accommodating prostitutes and even aggressive and sex-hungry matrons.

How I Learned to Drive forces audiences to a constant reassessment of their attitude towards the characters and the unfolding story. When Li'l Bit's grandmother was growing up, we learn, a girl was a woman at the age of fourteen and sex entirely legal. This does not make Vogel an advocate of child sex. What she wishes to do is to seduce audiences, disturb assumptions, make the observer aware of his or her shifting moral perspective. The audience, like Li'l Bit, is first made complicit, offered reassurance, and then betrayed. For alongside suggestions of a relativistic morality is set the knowledge that Peck had persuaded his niece to pose nude for him at the age of thirteen and that he had fondled her breasts at the age of twelve. Step by step she leads us to the core of Peck's guilt, the physical reality of his actions, yet at the same time she ritualises this process, and leads us to a greater understanding of the individual nature of both players in this sad and destructive game.

In one sense the play has the air of a conventional morality tale. Li'l Bit survives, reconciling herself to her life and therefore to everything that has happened to her. Peck is eventually destroyed and collaborates in his own destruction. It takes, we are told, seven years for him to drink himself to death. Having waited for his niece to become eighteen and thus legitimise their relationship, he loses her and with her someone who has become vital to his survival. But, for Vogel, morality is a more complex affair. In particular, she does not wish to portray Li'l Bit as simple victim, more especially in a culture which, in the 1990s, seemed happy to encourage people to abdicate responsibility for their own lives. Indeed, the process of the play is coterminous with Li'l Bit's slow acceptance of the fact that she is in control of her life. She now drives her own car, literally and symbolically, and she is happy for the now dead Peck to sit in the back seat, a memory that she has accepted as a part of who she is, just as eventually Peck himself had acknowledged what he had become and, in warning Li'l Bit against himself, enabled her finally to reject him, handing her back her life.

The play itself is in effect Li'l Bit's attempt to go back through that life, acknowledging the extent of her own complicity, the degree to which there came a moment when she not only played this dangerous game but even devised certain of its rules, rules accepted by the man whose love for her had rendered him into her hands. Peck breaks many moral and social rules, but never those devised by Li'l Bit. He is despicable but not without compassion and the fact that he has the appeal he does is because we see him through her eyes and through our knowledge of her acceptance of him. She now has the strength to confront her life and, in contrast to *Hot 'N' Throbbing*, move on.

In a way, *How I Learned to Drive* is a love story. Its story of need, exploitation, shifting systems of power, sacrifice, injury is not restricted to this relationship. The betrayals and occasional transcendences, the loneliness traded for comfort, the intimacy sought and frustrated, the selfishness transformed into selflessness that characterise the relationship between these two people, who feel excluded, alienated and alone, define more than this encounter between a damaged girl and an equally damaged man whose lives briefly touch in the anonymity of the modern world. There is no denying his culpability, no refuting the unspoken accusation, but, for Vogel, there is more, far more, to this relationship than can adequately be summed up in a word not uttered by any of the characters and not in her mind when she wrote it.

How I Learned to Drive was awarded the Pulitzer Prize. The woman whose first play about an immoral Desdemona was turned down by every theatre to which it was initially sent had won one of the country's major prizes without ever compromising on her determination to sail against the current, to challenge theatrical models and moral presumptions alike.

TONY KUSHNER

Tony Kushner's first play, *A Bright Room Called Day* (1985), scarcely suggested the success that lay ahead with the baroque splendours of *Angels in America* (1991 and 1992), surely the most successful play of the 1990s. It is, however, a work of considerable subtlety. Heavily influenced, as he had been, by the work of Bertolt Brecht, this was, he has explained, his attempt both to address and in some sense to purge his influence.

Kushner shares Brecht's aversion to realism, as he does his sense of the power to be derived from foregrounding theatricality. But his own instincts led in a rather different direction, not least because of his own sexuality and his concern both to address that and to allow it to become an integral part of his aesthetic. Thus, *A Bright Room Called Day*, while set in the Germany of the 1930s and featuring a group of Germans on the verge of the apocalypse which was Nazism, was a response to the despair that he felt over domestic politics and the deepening tragedy of AIDS. As a consequence he infiltrates a figure from 1980s America (later, 1990s America) – a Jewish woman in her thirties called Zillah Katz – into a work which is, at least in part, about the failure of the characters to intervene in their own fate, about the failure of political will in the face of coercion. She is an anarchist, which, Kushner implies, is the only form of radicalism America seems capable of producing, certainly in the second half of the twentieth century.

One key feature of the play is Kushner's insistence that it should be regarded as unfinished, a text available for updating since it is designed as a debate between the past and a shifting present. As a result references to Ronald Reagan were later replaced by those to George Bush and the Gulf War. In a British production, Margaret Thatcher was invoked. The play is divided into twenty-five scenes and includes Brecht-like titles and projected pictures, along with a ghost, called Die Alte (the Old One) and the Devil, the latter changing his guise with the times.

Behind the play is the question of whether there are, indeed, lessons to be learned from the past, whether that be distant from us in time or space or rather closer to home. History presents a finished appearance. It is, apparently, about concluded business. Kushner's strategy is to break it open. Zillah, in the decade of the 'Great Communicator', can no longer live in the 'United States of Amnesia'. Hitler may have invented history, substituting myth and prejudice for an inconvenient past; Reagan, to her, has simply sidestepped it altogether, preferring fantasy.

She moves to Germany in order to learn something from its history, to deconstruct that history which otherwise seems to have exhausted its meanings. And that is, essentially, what Kushner himself does with the play, challenging even the seemingly implacable force of the Holocaust as if it were the paradigm, the absolute standard of evil and betrayal. His consequent linking, through the figure of Zillah Katz, of Adolf Hitler and Ronald Reagan/George Bush, invited and received critical opprobrium. His defence was, on the one hand, to remind such critics that the views were those of the character while on the other hand insisting that one of the functions of art is to amplify, to shock, to disturb.

The truth, or otherwise, of that aside, *A Bright Room Called Day* marked an impressive debut. He assembles a group of characters who refuse to believe in their vulnerability, political idealists who put their faith in a solidarity which they themselves fail to exemplify, artists who think it possible to work within a system that recognises them as the enemy, individuals who believe that retreat into private concerns will grant immunity. As scene follows scene so the historical screw is tightened, and Kushner offers a political chronology whose logic seems inexorable, a chronology only interrupted by scenes from the present in which Zillah ponders past and present for the meanings they might offer.

What might seem like a logically unfolding story, however, is further disrupted by the appearance of Die Alte, who exists to carry the story further back still so that the particularities of Weimar Germany and its aftermath are seen in a wider context. The Nazis, after all, were welcomed by a people who thrilled to war, romanticising a violence drained of its true substance, and the fear is that such a response transcends the moment, that it is factored into human responses. Indeed, Kushner grants this character a genuinely moving, lyrical and poetic speech which is chilling precisely because language itself is seen as an agency of violence, recasting it as glorious enterprise, soldiers being granted a glamour that derives from young lives put at risk and from the language with which such gestures are celebrated.

For a play which seems to engage with Brecht, there is a deal of Beckett in the air. The absurd, after all, was surely born in part out of that war. Certainly Ionesco has said as much. The principle characters do escape but since one heads for an America which will one day see Reagan and Bush in power there must, at least in Kushner's mind, be an irony in such escape. The fear is that there is no way out, that the ironies are not a function of politics or yet of human nature but of an existence in which 'When God is good / The hours go, / But the world rolls on,

/ Tumbrel-slow, / And the driver sings / A gallows song: / "The end is quick. / The way is long." [52]

Kushner has explained his own doubts about the power of art to impact on the political world, let alone, one might think, the metaphysical. However, he has also insisted that the point of liberation politics lies in the creation of new systems, and his next play, the two-part *Angels in America*, was an embodiment of that. Provoked by the death of a friend from AIDS, it is a wild, exuberant fantasy which, in some degree, pitches its own inventiveness, its own multi-faceted nature, against the cold rationalism, the seemingly implacable nature of the political and natural world.

Millennium Approaches, the first of the two plays, received a workshop production at the Mark Taper Forum. At the centre of the action is Prior Walter, dying of AIDS, and Louis Ironson, his lover, terrified and unable to offer him the consolation of a continuing relationship. This story interacts with a number of others, including that of Roy M.Cohn, himself a closet homosexual and the lawyer who secured the execution of the Rosenbergs, besides working as an assistant to Senator Joseph McCarthy. The play involves cross-casting and doubling, denying the very boundaries so anxiously insisted upon and enforced by the political system which relegates AIDS sufferers to the margin. Races and religion are promiscuously mixed while desire is pitched against, and in part redeems, the harsh pragmatism and moral failings of society. Fantasy becomes not merely a style but a mode of being. Variety, heterogeneity, unpredictability, transformations, pluralisms, ambiguities, anarchic gestures are contrasted with the arbitrary codes, legalisms, fixities of a society which works by exclusion.

The play is set in 1985, when AIDS was an urgent social and moral issue but not a political priority. Prior represents the human need being ignored by those who command the political system, a challenge to the humanity of everyone involved. There is no antidote to his condition except through the grace extended to him by those who struggle towards a sense of their responsibility towards one another, a responsibility precisely abdicated by Cohn, who wishes to corner the market on the only palliative available, concerned, as he is, and as is the system he represents, to serve his own interest and perpetuate his existence. There is no antidote except that grace and the camp exuberance that refuses limits, creates its own myths, defines and then violates its own boundaries, that, in short, demonstrates possibility. In that sense this is not a play about AIDS and the gay community alone.

It is about an America that has forgotten its own myths, laid aside its communitarian impulses and hence suffers from a sickness of the spirit that needs curing. It is a serious play and its humour is a token of that seriousness. It creates its own language – a language constructed out of performance gestures, poetry, stage metaphors, verbal excess – as a means of locating a different way of seeing experience, a different mode of being. The marginal move to the centre of this universe, those at the centre having decayed of their own disregard. The very theatricality of the piece, its emphasis on a liberated imagination, on emotions given full licence, on a Promethean impulse, is a way of legitimising the kind of freedom to which it lays claim, a freedom from constraints, a freedom to engage with the world at the level of feeling.

Kushner's theatre, he acknowledges, lacks the muscular puritanism, the confident seriousness of much other political theatre. His is a theatre built in part on the work of other gay theatre practitioners, in particular on that of Charles Ludlam. Aware that he exists within the wreckage of history, with the avenue to understanding and grace blocked by those forces that believe themselves to be expressions of historic process, he seeks to blast through with a series of wild and sometimes bizarre gestures, to ease past a prosaic literalness with an insinuating poetry and oblique images. On the other side, as *Perestroika*, the second of the two plays, suggests, is not a utopia to substitute for that which no longer carries credence, though he is unwilling to relinquish his belief in such a world, but an observable truth about human relationships. Everybody in that play, he suggests, finds their way back to reality but that is 'disappointing and small and hard'.[53]

The title is derived from his conviction that Gorbachev was, indeed, heralding the possibility of a new democratic socialism. It was a hope that was to be frustrated, but Kushner refused to change the title since he believed that change was coming about, that a political stasis was being broken open. This play, after all, was written in the aftermath of the fall of the Berlin Wall and the end of a Cold War that seemed to have given authority to those in the political realm who had a vested interest in sustaining the *status quo*. The new has first to be imagined before it can be summoned into being. *Angels in America* was about that imagining. The final words, 'More Life', are both a summary of the plays' methodology and a blessing. Of *Perestroika* he has said, 'the play is about . . . the devastation and a willingness to keep moving in the face of devastation'.[54]

The play ends with an epilogue set five years on from the main action. In doing so it projects the future to which Kushner is as committed as he is to an analysis of the pathology of the past. While offering an account of the failure of American utopianism, Kushner nurses his own utopian impulse. He stages a resistant America, eternally in rebellion against constraint and definition, an America in which religions, races, sexualities co-exist and intermingle. It is a mixed genre work in which the very idea of intermixture carries moral and social as well as aesthetic force and the breaching of boundaries is both method and subject. Even the angel of the title is both an angel of death and of redemption. It is an angel who is less a representative of an omniscient God than a product of need, an epiphany which has its origin in the desperation but equally the instinctive charity of those who refuse to draw the logical conclusion from the betrayals, the divisiveness, the cruelties of history and personal relationships or the apparent absurdities of life.

Kushner chose to follow *Angels in America*, however, with a bleaker work in which the humour which characterises the first act is placed under pressure in the second. *Slavs! (Thinking About the Longstanding Problems and Virtue and Happiness)*, first staged at the Actors Theatre of Louisville in 1994, responds to the collapse of the Soviet Union, the betrayal of another utopian ideal seemingly careless of the fate of those it purported to serve. The dominant metaphor is that of radiation, which has warped the bodies and destroyed the lives of the next generation. Nor is this simply a lament over the past, as the apparatchiks of the old order are replaced by nationalists dedicated to a new repressive order which works by exclusion. The poverty and injustice once to be banished by communism continue to dominate the world. Capitalism, the other master story, equally fails to find a place for the poor and disadvantaged, the pursuit of money carrying a virus no less virulent than that of a once triumphant and now historically irrelevant communism.

Money, indeed, was to be at the centre of his next play, *Hydriotaphia or the Death of Dr Browne*, inspired by the figure of Sir Thomas Browne, whose *Hydriotaphia* or *Urn Burial* was a contemplation of death and its implications. In Kushner's play, Browne clings tenaciously to life on his death bed, as death, in person, impatiently awaits and his own soul is desperate to escape, not least because of the bedlam that surrounds it.

That bedlam is a result of those who are likewise anxious to hasten his departure so that they can receive the financial rewards which they assume will be theirs. Browne's refusal to die, like his literally terminal constipation, is a product of his unwillingness to let go, of his wealth but equally of his intellectual pleasures which he has pursued to the exclusion of those beyond his door who suffer.

Kushner's *Hydriotaphia or The Death of Dr Browne* is a wild, baroque circus of a play, coruscating in its indictment of false values yet pitching against the personal corruptions and contaminating greed of society its own exuberant style. In that it reflects something of his approach to drama throughout his career to date. Even here, though, there is perhaps another acknowledgement that, like Sir Thomas Browne in another sense, the writer may be guilty of his own withdrawal from the immediate imperatives of social and political change.

Yet, in the end, his is, surely, a theatre of praxis. It is action. Its serious concerns and comic methods, its barely controlled exuberance, its pluralism of voices, stylistic hybridity, promiscuous mixing of genders, races, ideologies, its faith, ultimately, in the moral and spiritual resources of the individual and the will to connect, are a manifesto for a utopia which is not a programmatic structure and does not lie in some distant time and place, but is within the grasp of those who understand its necessities.

Notes

I THE ABSENT VOICE: AMERICAN DRAMA AND THE CRITIC

1 David Mamet, *Writing in Restaurants* (London, 1988), p.16.
2 Roland Barthes, *Barthes: Selected Writings*, ed. and intro. Susan Sontag (London, 1983), p.187.
3 *Ibid.*, p.283.
4 M.M. Bakhtin, *The Dialogic Imagination*, trans. Caryl Emerson and Michael Holquist (Austin, 1981), p.3
5 *Ibid.*, p.266.
6 *Ibid.*, p.332.
7 Roland Barthes, *Barthes: Selected Writings*, p.187.
8 *Ibid.*, p.188.
9 *Ibid.*, p.187.
10 Miroslav Holub, *On the Contrary*, trans. Ewald Osers (Newcastle upon Tyne, 1986), p.18.

2 EUGENE O'NEILL'S ENDGAME

1 Nancy L. Roberts and Arthur W. Roberts, (eds.), *'As Ever, Gene': The Letters of Eugene O'Neill to George Jean Nathan*, (London, 1987), p.65.
2 Travis Bogard and Jackson R. Bryer (eds.), *Selected Letters of Eugene O'Neill* (New Haven, 1988), pp.213–14.
3 *Ibid.*, pp.513–14.
4 Jean Chothia, *Forging a Language* (Cambridge, 1979), p.130.
5 Jackson R. Bryer (ed.), *The Theatre We Worked For: The Letters of Eugene O'Neill to Kenneth Macgowan* (New Haven, 1982), p.257.
6 Eugene O'Neill, *Long Day's Journey into Night* (New Haven, 1956), p.178.
7 *Ibid.*, p.131.
8 Eugene O'Neill, *A Touch of the Poet* (New Haven, 1959), p.178.
9 *Ibid.*, p.181.
10 O'Neill, *Long Day's Journey into Night*, p.105.
11 *Ibid.*, p.13.

12 Eugene O'Neill, *A Moon for the Misbegotten* (London, 1958), p.151.
13 O'Neill, *Long Day's Journey into Night*, p.98.
14 *Ibid.*, p.139.
15 Eugene O'Neill, *Strange Interlude* (London, 1928), p.71.
16 *Ibid.*, pp.71–2.
17 O'Neill, *Long Day's Journey into Night*, p.85.
18 Arthur and Barbara Gelb, *O'Neill* (New York, 1973), p.5.
19 Roberts and Roberts, *The Letters of Eugene O'Neill*, p.44.
20 Borges, in Gerard Genette, *Narrative Discourse*, trans. Jane E. Lewin (Oxford, 1980), p.236.
21 Louis Sheaffer, *O'Neill: Son and Artist* (London, 1974), p.534.
22 Gelb and Gelb, *O'Neill*, p.873.
23 Virginia Floyd (ed.), *Eugene O'Neill at Work: Newly Released Ideas for Plays* (New York, 1981).
24 Roland Barthes, *Barthes: Selected Writings*, ed. Susan Sontag (London, 1983), p.187.
25 Eugene O'Neill, *Hughie: A Play* (London, 1962), p.20.
26 *Ibid.*, p.28.
27 Kristin Morrison, *Cantors and Chronicles: the Use of Narrative in the Plays of Samuel Beckett and Harold Pinter* (Chicago, 1983). pp.3–4.
28 Samuel Beckett and Georges Duthuit, *Proust and Three Dialogues* (London, 1965), p.28.
29 O'Neill, *A Moon for the Misbegotten*, pp.115–16.
30 Roberts and Roberts, *The Letters of Eugene O'Neill*, p.202.
31 *Ibid.*, p.174.
32 Ingmar Bergman, *The Magic Lantern*, trans. Joan Tate (London, 1988), p.34.
33 O'Neill, *Hughie*, p.7.
34 Donald Bouchard (ed.), *Language, Counter Memory, Practice: Selected Essays and Interviews by Michel Foucault* (Oxford, 1977).
35 O'Neill, *Hughie*, p.29.
36 Jean Chothia, *Forging a Language*, p.106.
37 Virginia Floyd (ed.), *Eugene O'Neill at Work*.
38 Samuel Beckett, *Endgame* (London, 1964), p.45.
39 Ralph Waldo Emerson, *Essays: First and Second Series* (New York, 1906), pp.231, 246, 248–9.
40 Sheaffer, *O'Neill: Son and Artist*, p.533.

3 TENNESSEE WILLIAMS: THE THEATRICALISING SELF

1 Albert J. Devlin, *Conversations with Tennessee Williams* (London, 1986), p.106.
2 *Ibid.*, p.90.
3 *Ibid.*, p.5.
4 *Ibid.*, p.31.
5 *Ibid.*, p 99
6 *Ibid.*

7　*Ibid.*, p.90.

8　*Ibid.*, p.37.

9　*Ibid.*, p.44.

10　*Ibid.*, p.27.

11　*Ibid.*, p.32.

12　Arthur Miller, *Timebends* (London, 1987), pp.180–1.

13　Williams, 'Fugitive Kind'. Typescript in Humanities Research Center, University of Texas, Austin.

14　Tennessee Williams, *Where I Live* (New York, 1978), p.8.

15　*Ibid*, p 35.

16　*Ibid.*, p.96.

17　*Ibid.*, p.292.

18　*Ibid.*, pp.170–1.

19　Devlin, *Conversations with Tennessee Williams*, p.292.

20　Tennessee Williams, *Four Plays by Tennessee Williams* (London, 1957), p.1 .

21　Tennessee Williams, *Five Plays by Tennessee Williams* (London, 1962), p.127.

22　Williams, *Where I Live*, pp.36–7.

23　*Ibid.*, p.212.

24　Gilbert Debusscher, 'Menagerie, Glass and Wine', in *The Glass Menagerie: A Collection of Critical Essays* (Englewood Cliffs, 1983), p.34.

25　David Jones, *Great Directors at Work* (Berkeley, 1984), p.188.

26　*Ibid.*, pp.150–1.

27　Williams, *Where I Live*, p.346.

28　*Ibid.*, p.51.

29　*Ibid.*, p.49.

30　Richard Gray, *Writing the South* (Cambridge University Press, 1986), p.178.

31　See in *ibid.*, p.272.

32　See in *ibid.*, pp.43, 45.

33　Jones, *Great Directors at Work*, p.144.

34　Williams, *Four Plays*, pp.288–9.

35　*Ibid.*, p.289.

36　Williams, *Five Plays*, p 87.

37　*Ibid.*

38　Vanessa Redgrave, 'The Lady Does What the Lady's Got to Do', *The Independent*, 7 Dec. 1988, p.21.

39　Williams, *Five Plays*, p.324.

40　*Ibid.*, p.338.

41　*The Observer*, 7 Apr. 1957.

42　Tennessee Williams, *Sweet Bird of Youth* (London, 1959), p.92.

43　Tennessee Williams, *The Night of the Iguana* (London, 1963), p.44.

44　Williams, *Where I Live*, p.125.

45　Williams, *Five Plays*, p.129.

46　*Ibid.*

47　George MacBeth, *A Child of War* (London, 1987), p.188.

4 ARTHUR MILLER: THE MORAL IMPERATIVE

1 Arthur Miller, *Timebends* (London, 1987), p.19.
2 *Ibid.*, pp. 14–15.
3 *Ibid.*
4 *Ibid.*, pp.82–3.
5 *Ibid.*, p.314.
6 Arthur Miller, *After the Fall* (London, 1964), pp.100–1.
7 Robert A. Martin (ed.), *The Theatre Essays of Arthur Miller* (Harmondsworth, 1978), pp.8–13.
8 Arthur Miller, *Incident at Vichy* (New York, 1965), p.200.
9 Interview with the author.
10 *Ibid.*
11 Miller, *Timebends*, p.160.
12 *Ibid.*, p.276.
13 *Ibid.*, p.86.
14 *Ibid.*, p.100.
15 Arthur Miller, Notebooks ms. in Humanities Research Center, University of Texas at Austin.
16 Arthur Miller, *Salesman in Beijing* (London, 1984), p.27.
17 Miller, *Timebends*, p.131.
18 *Ibid.*, p.144.
19 *Ibid.*, p.130.
20 *Ibid.*, p.179.
21 *Ibid.*, p.131.
22 *Ibid.*, p.144.
23 Martin (ed.), *The Theatre Essays of Arthur Miller*, p.87.
24 *Ibid.*, p.17.
25 Miller, *Timebends*, p.350.
26 Interview with the author.
27 Arthur Miller, *The Crucible* (Harmondsworth, 1968), p.70.
28 *Ibid.*, p.66.
29 *Ibid.*, p.35.
30 *Ibid.*, p.65.
31 *Ibid.*, p.115.
32 *Ibid.*, p.119.
33 Miller, *Collected Plays* (London, 1958), p.249.
34 Miller, Notebooks ms., University of Texas at Austin.
35 Miller, *Timebends*, p.356.
36 *Ibid.*, p.309.
37 *Collected Plays*, p.51.
38 Miller, *Timebends*, p.356.
39 *Ibid.*, p 370.
40 Martin (ed.), *The Theatre Essays of Arthur Miller*, pp.260–1.
41 *Ibid.*, pp.262–3.

42 Typescript, Humanities Research Center, University of Texas, Austin.
43 *Ibid*
44 Interview with the author.
45 *Ibid.*
46 Arthur Miller, *The Price* (London, 1968), p.110.
47 *Ibid.*, p.37.
48 Interview with the author.
49 *Ibid.*
50 *Ibid.*
51 *Ibid.*
52 Arthur Miller, *The American Clock* (London, 1983),p.10.
53 Interview with the author.
54 *Ibid.*
55 *Ibid.*
56 *Ibid.*
57 Miller, *Timebends*, p.587.
58 Peter Lewis, 'Change of Scene for a Mellow Miller', *The Sunday Times*, 3
   Nov. 1991, p.6.
59 Janet Watts, 'The Ride Down Mount Miller', *The Observer*, 3 Nov. 1991,
   p.59.
60 *Ibid.*
61 *Ibid.*
62 Peter Lewis, 'Change of Scene for a Mellow Miller'.

5 EDWARD ALBEE: JOURNEY TO APOCALYPSE

1 Interview with the author, September 1980.
2 Edward Albee, *The American Dream and The Zoo Story* (New York, 1963), p.21.
3 Interview with the author.
4 Samuel Beckett and Georges Duthuit, *Proust and Three Dialogues* (London,
   1965), pp.12–13.
5 *Ibid.*, p.13.
6 *Ibid.*
7 *Ibid.*, p.19.
8 *Ibid.*, p.19.
9 *Ibid.*, pp.20–1.
10 *Ibid.*, pp.21, 28.
11 *Ibid.*, p.28.
12 *Ibid.*, p.76.
13 T.S. Eliot, *Selected Prose of T.S. Eliot* (London, 1975), p.146.
14 Julia N. Wasserman, *Edward Albee: An Interview and Essays* (Houston, 1983),
   pp.10–11.
15 T.S. Eliot, *Selected Prose*, p.146.
16 Walt Whitman, *Complete Poetry and Selected Prose and Letters* (London, 1971),
   p.334.

17 T.S. Eliot, *Collected Plays* (London, 1982), p.74.
18 *Ibid.*, p.65.
19 *Ibid.*
20 Edward Albee, *A Delicate Balance* (New York, 1966), p.23.
21 *Ibid.*, p.82.
22 *Ibid.*, p.158.
23 Eliot, *Collected Plays*, p.66.
24 *Ibid.*, p.60.
25 *A Delicate Balance*, p.128.
26 *Ibid.*, p.170.
27 Edward Albee, *Seascape* (New York, 1975), p.12.
28 Interview with the author.
29 *Ibid.*
30 Edward Albee, *Counting the Ways and Listening* (New York, 1977), p.26.
31 *Ibid.*, p.104.
32 *Ibid.*, p.126.
33 See Gore Vidal, *Fact and Fiction* (London, 1977), p.82.
34 Edward Albee, *The Lady from Dubuque* (New York, 1980), p.61.
35 *Ibid.*, p.158.
36 *Ibid.*, 'Performance Note'.
37 *Ibid.*, p.134.
38 Wasserman, *Edward Albee: An Interview and Essays*, p.8.
39 John Updike, *Hugging the Shore: Essays and Criticisms* (London, 1984), p.120.
40 *Ibid.*, p.121.
41 Edward Albee, 'Introduction', *Three Tall Women* (New York, 1995), n.p.
42 *Ibid.*, p.110.
43 *Ibid.*, p.109.
44 Edward Albee, *Finding the Sun* (New York, 1994), pp.16–17.
45 *Ibid.*, p.21.
46 *Ibid.*, p.38.

6　A BROADWAY INTERLUDE

1 William Inge, *Natural Affection* (New York, 1963), pp.5–6.
2 Neil Simon, *The Comedy of Neil Simon* (New York, 1971), p.3.
3 Christopher Bigsby (ed.), *Arthur Miller and Company* (London, 1990), pp.179–80.
4 David Savron, *In Their Own Words: Contemporary American Playwrights* (NewYork, 1988), pp.319–20.

7　SAM SHEPARD: IMAGINING AMERICA

1 M. John Harrison, *Climbers* (London, 1989), p.152.
2 Peter Brook, *The Empty Space* (London, 1968), p.49.
3 *Ibid.*, p.52.
4 Sam Shepard, *Motel Chronicles* (London, 1982), p.38.

5 Sam Shepard, *Hawk Moon* (New York, 1981), p.12.
6 Sam Shepard, Interview in *Sunday Times Magazine*, 26 Aug. 1984, p.19.
7 *Ibid.*
8 Shepard, *Motel Chronicles*, p.40.
9 Kevin Sessums, 'Sam Shepard, Geography of a Horse Dreamer', *Interview Magazine*, Sept. 1988, p.78.
10 *Ibid.*
11 Shepard, *Motel Chronicles*, p.42.
12 *Ibid.*, p.57.
13 Shepard, *Hawk Moon*, p.158.
14 *Ibid*, p.159.
15 Sessums, *Interview Magazine*, p.78.
16 *Ibid.*
17 Sam Shepard, *Buried Child, Seduced, Suicide in B♭* New York, 1979), p.25.
18 Sam Shepard, *Seven Plays* (New York, 1981), p.xiv.
19 Sam Shepard, *A Lie of the Mind* (New York, 1986), 'Music Notes'.
20 Bonnie Marranca (ed.), *American Dreams* (New York, 1981), p.211.
21 *Ibid.*
22 *Ibid.*, p.212.
23 *Ibid.*, p.216.
24 Ron Mottram, *Inner Landscapes: The Theatre of Sam Shepard* (Columbia, 1984), p.7.
25 *Ibid.*, p.8.
26 Marranca (ed.), *American Dreams*, p.197.
27 *Ibid.*, p.212.
28 Ellen Oumano, *Sam Shepard: The Life and Work of an American Dreamer* (New York, 1986), p.4.
29 *Ibid.*, p.5.
30 *Ibid.*, p.6.
31 Shepard, *Hawk Moon*, p.87.
32 See Oumano, *Sam Shepard: The Life and Work of an American Dreamer*, p.38.
33 *Ibid.*, p.40.
34 Shepard, *Seven Plays*, pp.205–6.
35 *Ibid.*, p.227.
36 *Ibid.*
37 *Ibid.*, p.250.
38 Marranca (ed.), *American Dreams*, p.216.
39 *Ibid.*, pp.176, 180.
40 *Ibid.*, p.200.
41 *Ibid.*, p.214.
42 Shepard, *Seven Plays*, p.138.
43 *Ibid*, p.201.
44 Shepard, *Buried Child*, p.112.
45 *Ibid.*, p.111.
46 *Ibid.*, p.78.
47 *Ibid.*

48　*Ibid.*, p.63.
49　Shepard, *Suicide in B♭*, pp.146–7.
50　Shepard, *Buried Child*, p.132.
51　*Ibid.*, p.60.
52　*Ibid.*, pp.142–3.
53　Shepard, *Seven Plays*, p.26.
54　*Ibid.*, pp.36, 39.
55　*Ibid.*, p.27.
56　*Ibid.*, p 307.
57　Sam Shepard, *Fool for Love* (San Francisco, 1983), p.27.
58　*Ibid.*, p.26.
59　*Ibid.*, p.73.
60　Mottram, *Inner Landscapes*, p.156.
61　Sam Shepard, A *Lie of the Mind* (New York, 1986).
62　*Ibid.*
63　*Ibid.*, p.1.
64　*Ibid.*, p.28.
65　*Ibid.*, p.57.
66　*Ibid.*, p.52.
67　*Ibid.*, p.86.
68　*Ibid.*, p.92.
69　*Ibid.*, p.103.
70　*Ibid.*, p.185.
71　*Ibid.*, p.75.
72　*Ibid.*
73　Sam Shepard, *Simpatico* (London, 1995), p.39.
74　*Ibid.*, p.45.
75　*Ibid.*, p.102.
76　*Ibid.*, p.21.
77　Barry Daniels (ed.), *Joseph Chaikin and Sam Shepard, Letters and Texts 1972–1984* (New York, 1989), pp.128–9.
78　Don Shewey, 'Entity Dance or is it Identity?' *American Theatre*, July–August 1997, p.17.
79　*Letters and Texts*, p.123.
80　*Ibid.*, p.160.
81　*Ibid.*, pp.170, 172, 175.
82　*Ibid.*, pp.161, 171, 175.
83　Shepard, *A Lie of the Mind*, p.131.

8　DAVID MAMET: ALL TRUE STORIES

1　Mario Vargas Llosa, 'Latin America: Fiction and Reality', in *Modern Latin American Fiction: A Survey*, ed. John King (London, 1987), p.5.
2　David Mamet, *The Water Engine* (New York, 1978), p.64.
3　Vargas Llosa, 'Latin America', p.5.
4　João Ubaldo Ribeiro, *An Invincible Memory* (London, 1989).

5 David Mamet, *Writing in Restaurants* (London, 1988), p.27.
6 *Ibid.*, p.24.
7 Dennis Carroll, *David Mamet* (London, 1987), p.27.
8 See Daniel Bell, *The Coming of Post-Industrial Society* (London, 1974), p.168.
9 *Ibid.*, p.488.
10 David Mamet, *The Shawl and Prairie Du Chien* (New York, 1985), p.5.
11 Michael Billington, 'Dream Sequence: David Mamet talks to Michael Billington', *The Guardian*, 16 Feb. 1989.
12 *Ibid.*
13 Mamet, *Writing in Restaurants*, p.11.
14 *Ibid.*, p.21.
15 *Ibid.*, p.30.
16 *Ibid.*
17 *Ibid.*, p.21.
18 *Ibid.*, p.105.
19 Interview with the author.
20 David Mamet, *American Buffalo, Sexual Perversity in Chicago and Duck Variations* (London, 1978), p.35.
21 Interview with the author.
22 *Ibid.*
23 *Ibid.*
24 *Ibid.*
25 *American Buffalo*, pp.6, 7.
26 *Ibid.*, p.74.
27 *Ibid.*, p.41.
28 Interview with the author.
29 *Ibid.*
30 *Ibid.*
31 *Ibid.*
32 David Riesman, *Thorstein Veblen: A Critical Interpretation* (New York, 1953), p. 187.
33 Mamet, *Writing in Restaurants*, p.19.
34 *Ibid.*, p.30.
35 *Ibid.*, p.36.
36 *Ibid.*, p.69.
37 *Ibid.*, p.111.
38 *Ibid.*, p.19.
39 *Ibid.*, pp.107–8.
40 Mamet, *The Water Engine*, p.64.
41 David Mamet, *Lakeboat* (London, 1981), p.36.
42 David Mamet, *The Woods* (New York, 1979), p.8.
43 *Ibid.*, p.10.
44 *Ibid.*, p.23.
45 *Ibid.*, p.39.
46 *Ibid.*, p.54.

47 *Ibid.*, p.59.
48 *Ibid.*, p.63.
49 *Ibid.*, p.73.
50 *Ibid.*, p.96.
51 Interview with the author.
52 *Ibid.*
53 *Ibid.*
54 David Mamet, *Edmond* (New York, 1983), p.16.
55 Carroll, *David Mamet*, p.103.
56 Mamet, *Edmond*, p.100.
57 *Ibid.*, p.106.
58 *Ibid.*, p.17.
59 David Mamet, *Speed the Plow* (New York, 1987), pp.21–2.
60 *Ibid.*, p.45.
61 Interview with the author.
62 David Mamet, *The Cryptogram* (New York, 1995), p.31.
63 *Ibid.*, p.78.

9 THE PERFORMING SELF

1 See Karen Taylor, *The People's Theatre in America* (New York, 1972), p.206.
2 Antonin Artaud, *The Theatre and Its Double*, trans. Mary Caroline Richards (New York, 1958), p.2.
3 *Ibid.*, p.77.
4 *Ibid.*, pp.82–3.
5 See Robert Pasolli, *A Book on the Open Theatre* (Indianapolis, 1970), p.23.
6 See Arthur Sainer, *The Radical Theatre Notebook* (New York, 1975), pp.218–19.
7 See Malcolm Bradbury, *The Novel Today* (Manchester, 1977), p.7.
8 See Stephen Brecht, *The Theatre of Visions: Robert Wilson* (Frankfurt on Main, 1978), p.28.
9 Bradbury, *The Novel Today*, p.7.
10 Susan Sontag, *Against Interpretation and Other Essays* (London, 1967).
11 Ignace Feuerlicht, *Alienation from the Past to the Future* (Westport, 1978), p.57.
12 Heide Ziegler and Christopher Bigsby, *The Radical Imagination and the Liberal Tradition* (London, 1982), pp.178–9.
13 *Ibid.*, pp.175–6.
14 Gertrude Stein, *Lectures in America* (Boston, 1957), p.104.
15 Anthony Graham-White, 'Len Jenkin', in *Contemporary American Dramatists*, ed. K.A.Berney (London, 1994), p.295.

10 REDEFINING THE CENTRE: POLITICS, RACE, GENDER

1 David Rabe, *The Basic Training of Pavlo Hummel and Sticks and Bones* (Harmondsworth, 1978), p.163.
2 Tom Cole, *Medal of Honor Rag* (New York, 1979), p.20.

3 See Walter Benjamin, *Aesthetics and Politics*, trans. Ronald Taylor (London, 1980), p.111.
4 *Ibid.*, p.112.
5 See Jacques Ehrmann (ed.), *Literature and Revolution* (Boston, 1970), p.87.
6 T.S. Eliot, *The Collected Plays* (London, 1962), p.66.
7 Alain Robbe-Grillet, *Snapshots and Towards a New Novel*, trans. Barbara Wright (London, 1965), p.81.
8 See Ignace Feuerlicht, *Alienation from the Past to the Future* (Westport, 1978), p.86.
9 See David Caute, *Sixty-Eight: The Year of the Barricades* (London, 1988), p.29.
10 *Ibid.*, p.161.
11 *Ibid.*
12 See George Abbott White and Charles Newman, *Literature in Revolution* (New York, 1972), p.118.
13 See Feuerlicht, *Alienation from the Past to the Future*, pp.73–4.
14 George Steiner, *Language and Silence* (Harmondsworth, 1979), p.67.
15 See Gore Vidal, *Reflections Upon a Sinking Ship* (London, 1969), p.20.
16 Lorraine Hansberry, interview with Studs Terkel, *Freedomways*, 19 April 1979, p.184.
17 Lorraine Hansberry, *A Raisin in the Sun and The Sign in Sidney Brustein's Window* (New York, 1966), p.40.
18 Benjamin, *Aesthetics and Politics*, p.180.
19 *Dictionary of Literary Biography* (Detroit, 1985), p.125.
20 *Freedomways*, p.251.
21 *Ibid.*, p.187.
22 Hansberry, *A Raisin in the Sun and The Sign in Sidney Brustein's Window* p.206.
23 *Ibid.*, p.239.
24 *Ibid.*, p.140.
25 *Ibid.*, p.306.
26 Amiri Baraka, *The Autobiography of LeRoi Jones/Amiri Baraka* (New York, 1984), p.166.
27 *Ibid.*, p.187.
28 *Ibid.*, p.188.
29 Werner Sollers, *Amiri Baraka/LeRoi Jones* (New York, 1978), p.137.
30 Amiri Baraka, *The Motion of History and Other Plays* (New York, 1978), p.2.
31 Ed Bullins, *The Electronic Nigger and Other Plays* (London, 1979), pp.138–9.
32 Ed Bullins, *New Plays for the Black Theatre* (New York, 1969), p.167.
33 *Dictionary of Literary Biography*, 38, p.49.
34 Interview with the author.
35 Hilary DeVries, 'The Drama of August Wilson', *Dialogue* 83, 1 (1989), p.49.
36 *Ibid.*, p.50.
37 Interview with the author.
38 *Contemporary Dramatists* (London, 1988), p.571.
39 Interview with the author.
40 August Wilson, *Fences and Ma Rainey's Black Bottom* (London, 1988), p.121.
41 *Ibid.*, p.130.

42 Vidal, *Reflections Upon a Sinking Ship*, p.35.
43 Kim Powers, 'An Interview with August Wilson', *Theatre*, 16, 1 (Fall 1984), p.54.
44 Wilson, *Fences and Ma Rainey's Black Bottom*, p.137.
45 *Ibid.*, p.191.
46 *Ibid.*, p.194.
47 *Ibid.*, p.212.
48 Powers, 'An Interview with August Wilson', p.53.
49 *Ibid.*
50 Interview with the author.
51 August Wilson, *Fences* (New York, 1986), p.18.
52 Interview with the author.
53 DeVries, 'The Drama of August Wilson', p.53.
54 *Ibid.*, p.52.
55 *Ibid.*
56 *Ibid.*, p.54.
57 August Wilson, *Joe Turner's Come and Gone* (New York, 1988), n.p.
58 *Ibid.*, p.10.
59 *Ibid.*, p.14.
60 *Ibid.*, p.46.
61 Alice Walker, *Contemporary Literary Criticism*, 27 (1984), p.453.
62 Alice Walker, *In Search of Our Mothers' Gardens* (London, 1983), p.250.
63 Wilson, *Joe Turner's Come and Gone*, p.71.
64 Interview with the author.
65 Wilson, *Joe Turner's Come and Gone*, p.72.
66 *Ibid.*, p.87.
67 *Ibid.*, pp.93–4.
68 DeVries, 'The Drama of August Wilson', p.54.
69 Walker, *In Search of Our Mothers' Gardens*, p.261.
70 DeVries, 'The Drama of August Wilson', p.52.
71 Interview with the author.
72 August Wilson, *Two Trains Running* (New York, 1993),p. 42
73 August Wilson, 'The Ground on Which I Stood', *American Theatre*, September 1996, p.14.
74 *Two Trains Running*, p.42.
75 *Ibid.*, p.85.
76 *Ibid.*, back cover.
77 *Ibid.*, pp.34–5.
78 *Ibid.*, p.110.
79 August Wilson, 'A Note from the Playwright', *Seven Guitars* (New York, 1997), n.p.
80 August Wilson, 'That's Why they Call it the Blues', *American Theatre*, April 1996, p.21.
81 *Ibid.*
82 *Ibid.*, p.18.

83 *Ibid.*, p.23.
84 Suzan-Lori Parks, *The America Play and Other Works* (New York, 1995), p.4.
85 *Ibid.*, p.5.
86 *Ibid.*, p.11.
87 *Ibid.*, p.17.
88 *Ibid.*, p.15.
89 *Ibid.*, p.19.
90 *Ibid.*, p.12.
91 *Ibid.*, p.20.
92 Suzan-Lori Parks, 'Alien Nation: An Interview with Michele Pearce', *American Theatre*, March–April 1994, p.26.
93 *The America Play*, p.10.
94 *Ibid.*
95 'Alien Nation', p.26.
96 *The America Play*, p.159.
97 Richard Stayton, 'An Interview with Anna Deavere Smith', *American Theatre*, July–August 1993, p.23.
98 Mari Evans (ed.), *Black Women Writers* (London, 1985), p.112.
99 Kathleen Belsko and Rachel Koenig, *Interviews with Contemporary Women Playwrights* (New York, 1987), pp.251, 253.
100 Adrienne Kennedy, *Cities in Bezigue: Two One-Act Plays* (New York, 1969), p.5.
101 William Couch Jr, *New Black Playwrights: An Anthology* (Baton Rouge, 1968), p.61.
102 Adrienne Kennedy, 'A Growth of Images', *The Drama Review*, (December, 1977), pp 44–7.
103 Ntozake Shange, *For Colored Girls Who Have Considered Suicide/When the Rainbow Is Enuf* (New York, 1977), p.xi.
104 Karen Malpede, *Women in Theatre: Compassion and Hope*, 2nd edn (New York, 1985), p.167.
105 Helen Krich Chinoy and Linda Walsh Jenkins (eds.), *Women in American Theatre* (New York, 1987), p.177.
106 Helen Keyssor, *Feminist Theatre* (London, 1984), p.2.
107 *Ibid.*, p.5.
108 Malpede, *Women in Theatre*, p.69.
109 *Ibid.*, p.185.
110 *Ibid.*, p.236.
111 See Sue-Ellen Case, *Feminism and Theatre* (London, 1988), p.128.
112 Belsko and Koenig, *Interviews with Contemporary Women Playwrights*, p.351.
113 Bonnie Marranca, *American Playwrights: A Critical Survey* (New York, 1981), p.163.
114 Belsko and Koenig, *Interviews with Contemporary Women Playwrights*, pp.347–8.
115 *Ibid.*, p.352.
116 *Ibid.*, p.158.
117 *Ibid.*, p.166.

118 Case, *Feminism and Theatre*, p.122.

119 *Ibid*, p.123.

120 *Ibid*.

121 Belsko and Koenig, *Interviews with Contemporary Women Playwrights*, p.334.

122 *Ibid*., pp.338–9.

123 *Ibid*., p.329.

124 *Ibid*., p.329.

125 *Ibid*., pp.334–5.

126 *Ibid*., p.339.

127 *Ibid*., p.215.

128 *Ibid*., pp.215–16.

129 Philip C. Kolin, 'Public Facts/Private Fictions in Emily Mann's Plays', in *Public Issues, Private Tensions: Contemporary American Drama*, ed. Matthew Charles Roudané (New York, 1993), p.238.

130 Phyllis Jane Rose, 'Dear Heidi: An Open Letter to Dr. Holland', *American Theatre*, October 1989, pp.114–16.

131 Misha Berson, ed., *Between Worlds: Contemporary American Plays* (New York, 1990), p.179.

132 *Ibid*.

133 *Ibid*.

134 *Ibid*., pp.178–9.

135 David Savron, *In Their Own Words: Contemporary American Playwrights* (New York, 1988), p.118.

136 David Henry Hwang, *Broken Promises: Four Plays by David Henry Hwang* (New York, 1983), p.xi.

137 *Ibid*., xii.

138 *Ibid*., p.xi–xii.

139 Savron, *In Their Own Words*, p.120.

140 *Ibid*., p.122.

141 David Henry Hwang, *M Butterfly* (New York, 1988), p.100.

142 Misha Berson, 'The Demon in David Hwang,' *American Theatre*, April 1998, p.18.

143 Berson, *Between Worlds*, p.30.

144 Hanay Geiogamah, *New Native American Drama: Three Plays by Hanay Geiogamah* (Normal, 1980), p.61.

145 *Ibid*., p.98.

146 *Ibid*., p.88.

147 *Ibid*., p.132.

148 Savron, *In Their Own Words*, p.265.

149 *Ibid*., p.268.

150 *Ibid*., p.270.

II BEYOND BROADWAY

1 Wallace Shawn, *Wallace Shawn: Plays* (London, 1997), p.xi.

2 *Ibid*., p.xviii.

3 Terrence McNally, 'Author's Note', *Love! Valour! Compassion!* (New York, 1995), pp.4–5.
4 Toby Silverman Zinman, 'The Muses of Terrence McNally: Music and Mortality are his Consuming Themes', *American Theatre*, March 1995, p.214.
5 Jackson Bryer, *The Playwright's Art* (New Brunswick, 1995), p.185.
6 Philip C. Kolin and Colby H. Kullman, *Speaking on Stage* (Tuscaloosa, 1996), p.342.
7 Bryer, *The Playwright's Art*, p.191.
8 Terrence McNally, *Lips Together, Teeth Apart* (New York, 1992), pp.44–5.
9 Kolin and Kullman, *Speaking on Stage*, pp.339–40.
10 Terrence McNally, *A Perfect Ganesh* (New York, 1994), p.23.
11 Kolin and Kullman, *Speaking on Stage*, p.341.
12 McNally, 'Author's Note', *Love! Valour! Compassion!*, p.6.
13 *Love! Valour! Compassion!*, p.86.
14 Terrence McNally, *Corpus Christi* (New York, 1999), p.10.
15 *Ibid.*, p.48.
16 *Ibid.*, p.56.
17 Toby Silverman Zinman, 'Inside Lanford Wilson', *American Theatre*, May 1992, p.18.
18 John Guare, *Gardenia* (New York, 1982), p.11.
19 *Ibid.*
20 *Ibid.*, p.15.
21 John Guare, *Six Degrees of Separation* (New York, 1990), p.81.
22 David Rabe, *Hurlyburly* (New York, 1985), p.95.
23 Toby Silverman Zinman, 'Rabe on Rabe', *American Theatre*, January 1991, p.17.
24 *Ibid.*, p.18.
25 *Ibid.*, p.16.
26 A. R. Gurney, *Nine Early Plays 1961–1973* (New York, 1995), p.27.
27 *Ibid.*, p.201.
28 A. R. Gurney, *The Wayside Motor Inn* (New York, 1978), p.6.
29 *Ibid.*
30 A. R. Gurney, *Four Plays* (New York, 1985), p.194.
31 A. R. Gurney, *The Perfect Party* (New York, 1986), p.9.
32 *Ibid.*, p.53.
33 A. R. Gurney, *Sweet Sue* (New York, 1987), p.6.
34 *Ibid.*
35 A. R. Gurney, *Overtime* (New York, 1996), p.32.
36 *Ibid.*
37 D. L. Kirkpatrick (ed.), *Contemporary Dramatists* (London, 1988), p.221.
38 Ros Wetzsteon, 'Wallace Shawn, Subversive Moralist', *American Theatre*, September 1997, p.13.
39 *Wallace Shawn: Plays*, p.xix.
40 *Ibid.*, pp.xix–xx.
41 *Ibid.*, p.129.

42 Wallace Shawn, 'On the Context of the Play', in *Aunt Dan and Lemon* (New York, 1986), p.72.

43 *Ibid.*, p.70.

44 *Wallace Shawn: Plays*, p.xx.

45 *Ibid.*, pp. xx–xxi.

46 *Ibid.*, p.172.

47 *Ibid.*, p.202.

48 Wetzsteon, 'Wallace Shawn, Subversive Moralist', p.15.

49 *Ibid.*

50 *Ibid.*, p.17.

51 Paula Vogel, *The Baltimore Waltz and Other Plays* (New York, 1996), p.12.

52 Tony Kushner, *Plays by Tony Kushner* (New York, 1992), p.80.

53 Robert Vorlicky (ed.), *Tony Kushner in Conversation* (Ann Arbor, 1998), p.58.

54 *Ibid.*, p.82.

Index